HISTORY
OF
SOUTH
CAROLINA

HISTORY
OF
SOUTH
CAROLINA

By REV. ROBERT LATHAN, D.D.
From the 1876 Yorkville Enquirer

Collected by S. Robert Lathan, Jr., M.D.

Published by
Wings Publishers
1700 Chattahoochee Avenue
Atlanta, Georgia 30318

Book design and composition by Melanie M. McMahon

Manufactured in the United States of America

10 9 8 7 6 5 4 3 2 1
First Edition

ISBN 1-930897-10-3

EPIGRAPH

A "History of South Carolina," by Rev. Robert Lathan (the historian of the A. R. P. church) was initially published serially in the *Yorkville Enquirer* in 1876. Rev. Lathan sent the collected newspaper columns as a manuscript to Harper Brothers in New York City. Their reply expressed "keen appreciation and high praise of what is indeed a most valuable contribution to the history of our state." They added that "if it were written by a New Englander it would have a ready sale, but you people down South do not buy books, so its publication would be at a loss to us."

FOREWORD

Over fifty years ago, I inherited two ledger books filled with pasted newspaper clippings. The articles were written by my great uncle Reverend Robert Lathan for the *Yorkville Enquirer,* Yorkville, South Carolina in 1876. I had heard that he had written the best history of South Carolina (including the Revolution) up to that time. However, the books remained unopened in my bookcase until recently. On perusal, I found that he was an eloquent and interesting writer.

Rev. Lathan was not only a minister but also a teacher, school administrator, theological professor and writer. He was regarded as the leading historian of the Associate Reformed Presbyterian Church. His most famous publication, *The History of the Associate Reformed Synod of the South,* in 1882, led to his being awarded the Doctor of Divinity degree from Westminster College in Pennsylvania. Known as a "scribbler," he also wrote historical sketches of the Hopewell and Union ARP Churches and contributed numerous articles to the *Yorkville Enquirer* newspaper and the *Associate Reformed Presbyterian* bulletin.

Rev. Lathan's lifetime love of books is legendary. The story is told that his wife Fannie was complaining to her mother after they had been married only a short time. Fannie allegedly reported that he spent all of his money on books and did not provide enough for groceries and other household staples. The mother-in-law decided upon a solution and said she would take it on herself to provide dinner for Robert and Fannie. Robert, who was as usual preoccupied with his books, was called to the dinner table by Mrs. Barron, with the words, "Robert, this is your first course." A small book had been placed at each place. Upon removal, each succeeding "course" consisted of larger volumes of books. No food was provided, as it was "not in the budget." However, we are told that as a result of this incident, a future household allowance was established.

In my love for South Carolina and its history, I have spent much of my free time searching and tracing family geneology. One of my excursions even included a full day tromp through the woods with bleach bottle in hand to uncover 200-year-old headstones in the Lathan family private cemetery in Fairfield County, SC. The relics and maps that have accumulated in my home somehow obscured a true historical keepsake gathering dust on my own bookshelf. As soon as I opened the ledgers of Rev. Lathan's most ambitious project and realized its historical value, I showed it to my brother-in-law John Rivers and it was decided to have this work published. The reader can see from the Epigraph that this was not the first attempt. Rev. Lathan had tried himself and been rejected by a northern publisher with the very disparaging quote concerning the reading habits of southerners.

It was his desire in 1876 to "turn the wheels of time back two hundred years that our senses might be ravished with the primitive grandeur of nature" and to evoke the "strange and indescribable feeling (that) pervades the soul when we stand upon the ground where once camped a British Army."

The reading of this history of South Carolina made me curious about the sources of his material for these articles as well as the origin of the ledgers themselves. Apparently the Reverend had a large personal library of over 3000 volumes. At his death these books were given to his son-in-law, Rev. T. B. Stewart and unfortunately lost to fire in 1906. In the Author's research he had also relied upon materials in the Erskine College Library that was destroyed by fire in 1892. What seems to remain of the original articles are the two very old ledger books with the actual newspaper clippings pasted side by side in extremely neat double columns, a very ambitious project in itself. The only found record of their devoted creator is the small note inside bequeathing them to me by my aunt Susie Lathan, Reverend Robert's niece. Through the efforts of many people searching their files, old boxes and recesses of their memories, the Reverend's "scribblings" and family history have again come to life to be appreciated for its eloquent historical record.

I especially would like to recognize the assistance of Dr. Lowry Ware of Due West, South Carolina for his helpful research suggestions. Recognition is also appropriate for several of my cousins who have through the years stimulated my interest in Lathan genealogy: Leila Stroud Welch, Birmingham, AL, Anna L. Stewart McCartney, Fresno, CA, L. Barron Mills, Asheboro, NC, George Henry Moore, Chester, SC, William C. Lathan, Triangle, VA, and Ann Davidson Marion, Chester, SC. The transfer of these important passages could not have happened without the extraordinary help of Luci Gross, the typist and Ginger Watkins, my publisher.

My special thank you to each of these individuals. Their combined contributions have provided the platform for new channels of distribution that disproves the 126 year old quote that "you people down South do not buy books, so its publication would be a loss to us." A loss then is now a great gain.

S. Robert Lathan, Jr., M.D.

SECTION THREE

EARLY SETTLEMENTS

Deg. West from London
P. of VIRGINIA
In Bath County Col. Barnwell Defeated the Indians A.D. 1712
In Granville County Col. Craven Routed the Indians A.D. 1716
PART OF NORTH
English Miles
Good Pasture Ground
NORTH CAROLINA
AMERICA
Charakeys
Charakeys 110 villages
Charakey's Mt.
Appalache Mountains
AZILIA
SOUTH
CAROLINA
Limit of King Charles y II Granted to y Present Proprietors of Carolina in 1663
P. of the GULF of MEXICO
FLORIDA
Fort St Augustin to Spain
Matances I.
Matances Inlet
The South Bounds of Carolina according to the last Charter
Long Sandy Bay
Colleton County
Granville County
Craven County
Clarendon County
Charles Town
The Improved Part of Carolina or The English Settlements
Port Royal
Port Royal Island
St Catherina Sound
Sapela Sound
Golden Island
C. Fear Divided N. and S. Carolina
Clarendon R.
The French Refugees Settlements
C. Cartaret
James T.
C. Charles
Bay of Chesapeck
C. Henry
Currituc
Sand Bank
Roenok
Albemar
Bath
Sound
C. Hatteras
Sholes of Hatteras
Drum Inlet
Cape Lookout
Sampe B.
THE WESTERN OCEAN
CAROLINA
By
H. Moll Geographer
The English Claim the Property of Carolina from Latt. 29 &c. Degrees as part of Cabots Discoveries who set out from Bristol in 1498. at the Charge of King Henry y 7th but they did not take Possession of that Country till King Charles the II's time in 1663 who Granted a Patent to divers Persons to plant all the Territories within the North Latt. of 31 to 36 Deg. and so West in a direct line to the South Sea.
1729 H. Moll

INTRODUCTORY

On the 12th of Oct. 1492, Christopher Columbus landed on one of the Bahama Islands. The Indians called it Guanahani. It is now known by the name of Watling. The three ships which constituted the fleet of Columbus, together with the ninety individuals who accompanied him in his expedition had been furnished by Spain. Hence Spain in part based her claim to the country which is now known all over the civilized world by the name of America. Whilst Columbus was at the court of Spain, he communicated with Henry the Seventh, of England. Before the messenger, his own brother Bartholomew, returned however, the Spanish government which at first acted very slowly had made provisions for the expedition to search for land on the western side of the Atlantic.

On the 5th day of March, 1467, Henry the Seventh, of England, granted a commission to John Cabot and his three sons - Lewis, Sebastian and Sanctius - to take possession in the name of the King of England, of any and all countries in the north, east, or west, not occupied by any Christian state. For some reason not now known, Cabot did not set sail until May, 1497. He and his son, Sebastian sailed from Bristol. The king furnished them one ship, and the merchants of Bristol furnished them four other small vessels. They touched upon the continent of America, some place near St. John's, New Foundland, and proceeded as far south as the latitude of Virginia, and returned home. Upon this, the English government laid claim to the continent of America. The expedition amounted to nothing, however; for Henry, on many accounts, was not inclined to accomplish the undertaking which he had begun with so much zeal. Both Spain and Portugal claimed the continent of America, although it was not yet, in fact, discovered. The controversy between these two contending powers was put into the hands of the Pope for arbitration. On the 7th of May, 1493, he decided that Spain was to have all countries which she had discovered or might in the future discover, west of a line drawn through the Azores from pole to pole; and Portugal, all east of said line. Henry, at that time, was negotiating a marriage between his son, Arthur, and Catherine, the daughter of Ferdinand, King of Spain, and had no time to plant colonies.

In the year 1498, Columbus landed on the northeastern coast of South America at some place not far from the mouth of the Orinoco. This was six years after his first voyage. Cuba, St. Domingo and Puerto Rico were in a short time settled by the Spaniards and served as a kind of nucleus from which they attempted to send out colonies. These colonies advanced in a north and northwesterly direction.

There was a tradition amongst the natives of Puerto Rico that, in one of the Bahama Islands, there was a certain fountain which possessed magic virtues. It was currently reported, and generally believed by both the natives of Puerto Rico and the Spaniards, that whoever would bathe in this fountain and drink of its waters would be instantly restored to all the vigor and bloom of youth, and life with all its joys would be perpetuated. In the year 1512, Juan Ponce de Leon, once governor of Puerto Rico, now an old man and veteran soldier, fitted out three ships and set out in quest of this fountain of youth. On the 18th of March 1512, the fleet of Juan Ponce de Leon set sail. It cruised about amongst the Bahamas in search of the fabled fountain of youth until, on Easter Sunday, a forest adorned with the richest flowers was discovered. To this newly discovered land, the Spaniards gave the name Florida, which it still retains. The fountain was not discovered, and Juan Ponce de Leon, after returning to Puerto Rico and being appointed governor of Florida, and having returned to it, was mortally wounded in a conflict with the natives. He was driven by them from the country, and in his flight he went to Cuba, were he died of his wounds.

About the year 1520, a company of seven rich planters and miners, residing on the island of St. Domingo, equipped two vessels and put them under the command of Lucas Velasquez de Aylon, Judge of Appeals. The object of this cruise was to gather up laborers to work their farms and mines. The vessels reached the shores of South Carolina, about thirty-five miles southwest from where the city of Charleston now stands. The spot where the shore was reached was at, or near, the mouth of the Combahee River. The natives called the country Chiquola.

Velasquez was at first an object of wonder to the natives. They were cautious; but soon their reserve gave way to acts of kindness and hospitality. Velasquez was, at heart, a monster. He enticed the unoffended natives to visit his ships and, at a time when a large number had gathered on deck, he hoisted his sails and set out for St. Domingo. On his way to St. Domingo, one of his vessels went down into the deep, taking with it all the Spaniards and captured Indians on board. Many on the other vessels, in which was Velasquez himself, died before they reached their place of destination. Notwithstanding the great loss with which Velasquez met in this expedition, it still was profitable to him. Animated by hopes of the greater gain, he invested his whole fortune in three ships, and calculated to amass a large estate by engaging extensively in the slave trade. In the year 1524 he again landed, or rather was driven to, the shore of Chiquola at the mouth of the Combahee River. The largest of his three vessels ran aground. The Indians, thirsting for vengeance, seized the occasion, rushed upon the Spaniards, buffeting the waves, and with a cruelty which is characteristic of untutored savages, put to death two hundred, Velasquez being of the number. Thus ended the expedition of Velasquez. It was not designed for anything else than to supply the slave market of St. Domingo with slaves.

The object of Velasquez was to decoy the unoffending natives of Chiquola around St. Helena Sound, on board his ships, and transport them to St. Domingo and there sell them. The expedition was begun in sin and ended in shame. Upon it, however, and previous discoveries made by Columbus and the grant of the Pope, Spain laid claim to all the new world. As yet, those individuals in her employ had only cruised amongst the islands.

France also laid claim to the continent. The thirst for gold then, as now, was great; and Spain, England and France were anxious to get possession of the land discovered by Columbus. In the year 1523, Francis the First sent out John Verazzano, a Florentine; but he did not touch upon the coast of South Carolina. He arrived on the coast of the new world at some place near the latitude of Wilmington, North Carolina. France based her claim to the territory now known as North Carolina and South Carolina, upon the fact that it was thus visited by Verazzano.

In 1527, Spain sent out an army under Narvaez to conquer the country. The conquest commenced in Florida, Narvaez failed. He was succeeded by Ferdinand de Soto. In order that he might succeed in the undertaking of conquering Florida, a country to which no definite bounds were fixed at that time, De Soto fitted out, at his own expense, seven ships and a thousand soldiers. On the 10th of June, 1539, he entered Tampa Bay. With four hundred foot soldiers and two hundred cavalry, he set out to conquer the country. His men were well armed and an ample supply of stores had been provided. Besides this, he drove before him 300 swine with which he designed stocking the country. Previous to this time, there were no swine on the continent of America. No sooner had De Soto landed, than he was attacked by a large body of the natives. No decisive victory was gained by either side, but the advantage was in favor of the natives. Finally he reached Mississippi. Here, after wandering about for some time, he sickened and died, and on the 10th of May, 1542 was, after having been placed in a hollow log as a coffin, sunk in the middle of this noble stream.

In this march, De Soto crossed through a part of the southwestern section of South Carolina. It has been thought that he commenced mining for gold in South Carolina, whilst conducting this most remarkable march. From 1539 to 1561, nothing was done by either England, France or Spain to settle the country. In fact, up to this period, no efforts had been made to settle the continent as far south as South Carolina. De Soto had run over the country from Tampa Bay on the western coast of Florida, to the Wachita in Arkansas. He crossed, in his march the territory now occupied by South Carolina, Georgia, Alabama and Mississippi; but he planted no colony.

In 1562, Cologni, Admiral of France, undertook to plant a colony in the new world. The object he had in view was to secure a place of refuge for the French Protestants, who at this time were persecuted and oppressed in their native country. In the latter part of 1561, Cologni obtained a commission from Charles the Ninth to establish a colony near Florida. The work of actually planting the colony was entrusted to a man by the name of John Rebault. A considerable number of the nobility joined the expedition, and on the 28th of February, 1562, Rebault and his squadron set out for Florida. In May, the St. John's River was discovered, to which Rebault gave the name May. He continued his course northward, and entered Port Royal Harbor. Here he erected a fort which, in honor of Charles the Ninth, was named Fort Charles. In July, Rebault set out to return to France, leaving twenty-six men to retain the country in possession until he would return with more settlers and supplies. With the country around Port Royal the colonists were charmed. They had never seen anything like it before. The woods were full of wild animals and the waters of the bay swarming with fish. The natives were kind and hospitable. They manifested their interest in the newly arrived strangers by beginning to construct an arbor from the branches of the trees, to protect them from the heat of the sun. Although these colonists came from France, and had obtained a commission from Charles the Ninth, to plant a colony in the New World, the founding of the colony was really a private enterprise. Charles was a Catholic by profession and a monster at heart; and in practice, Rebault was Protestant, and so were those connected with him. Cologni, the originator of the scheme, was a Protestant of the highest type. Charles was a Catholic - bigoted, cruel, and deceptious. The commission granted to Cologni was only, in reality, a permission, if not something worse, for some good men, who nevertheless were a trouble to Charles, to leave the country.

The fate of this Huguenot colony is full of interest. When Rebault arrived in France, he found the country in a state of great confusion. When he left the colony, a man by the name of Albert was placed in command of the twenty-six men left behind. Albert fortified the place where the settlement was made. This fortification was consumed by fire, but the natives generously rebuilt it. Rebault not returning, the supplies left for the support of the colony failed, and it would have perished of hunger had it not been for the kindness of the Indians. The circumstances of the colonists were very trying, but a greater calamity awaited them. For some trivial crime, Captain Albert hanged Guernache, the drummer. The other members of the colony did not approve of this summary proceeding of Captain Albert. The captain was not to be awed by their disapprobation. Whilst the colonists were greatly exasperated on account of the high-handed, harsh and arbitrary conduct of their captain, he banished Le Chere to a lone island, nine miles distant. This man was not very popular with his companions. No provisions were made for his sustenance upon the island. In fact, the avowed object of Captain Albert, in banishing him to the island, was to starve him to death. This, his companions would not bear. They rebelled and slew Captain Albert, and sent and brought Le Chere from his place of banishment.

In place of Captain Albert, Nicholas Barre was chosen. By this time, they had become so disheartened, since Rebault had not returned, that it was determined to return to their native country. To accomplish this, they set about to build a ship. This, circumstanced as they were, was no small undertaking; but in spite of all the difficulties to be encountered, the vessel was built. We may safely conclude that it was both small and of rude construction. Their clothes were taken off their backs and from these, together with their bedcovers, sails were made for the first ship ever built on the continent. Full of bright hopes of reaching their native land, they bid their Indian friends adieu.

For some time, the voyage promised fair to be prosperous. Winds and waves favored them. When, however, they had commenced to look with anxious eyes toward the end of their voyage, the winds lulled into a dead calm and the waves slumbered on the bosom of the deep. Their provisions scanty, we may conclude at first, began to fail with fearful rapidity. They ate their last grain of corn and then their shoes. The ship began to leak. It required all the strength of the men to free it from water. Death, in its most dreadful form, stared them fair in the face. Despair seized them, and they resolved to permit the water to sink their leaking vessel. All, except Le Chere became despondent, and ceased to make further efforts to save themselves. Le Chere begged them to hold on, that they could not be more than three days from land. This aroused them and, without a morsel of food to eat or a drop of water to drink, they laved the water out of the ship. When three days passed, no land was to be seen yet. Le Chere advised them that one of their number must die for the rest. A lot was cast to decide who should give his flesh for food and his blood for drink to save the lives of his companions. The lot fell upon Le Chere. Without a murmur, he submitted. His flesh was doled out to his companions. Upon it they subsisted until picked up by an English vessel and taken to England. Thus perished, we may say, the first colony that was planted in South Carolina. Its end was tragical, but its memory should be cherished. The intercourse between it and the natives was honorable to both. The colonists were just and honest in their treatment of the Indians; the Indians were kind and obliging. When the colonists set sail in their rude ship, the hearts of the Indians were filled with sadness, and tears of grief streamed down their cheeks.

DISCOVERY OF AMERICA

The discovery of the New World was not a mere accident. As long as the world lasts it will remain one of the grandest triumphs of science. Christopher Columbus was no ordinary man. Intellectually, he must have been a giant. His mind was well stored with useful knowledge, and he possessed some mental qualifications which do not fall to the lot of many men. He possessed those traits of mind with which Philips says Napoleon Bonaparte was eminently endowed. He was capable of meeting any emergency which might take place in the life of a man engaged in great undertakings.

Although the Cabots discovered the Continent of America before Columbus, still, we may safely say, had not Columbus discovered Watling Island, the Cabots would have never seen Prima Vista. In 1492, Columbus left Polos with three small ships and only ninety men; but on the 25th of September 1493, he again set sail from Cadiz, on a second voyage, with seventeen ships and fifteen hundred men. It was difficult to persuade men to join the first expedition and those that were secured belonged to what might have been the floating population. When preparations were making for the second expedition, it became manifest that a change had come over the minds of the multitude. Everybody was anxious to go to the New World, and many of the first families of Spain embarked with Columbus. On the 8th of December he landed on Hayti, where he had left thirty-nine men when he returned to Spain after his first voyage. The men were not to be found and the fort he had erected for their defense was totally destroyed. The natives reported that the men had become desperate in their conduct toward the aboriginal inhabitants. They plundered the surrounding country for supplies and mal-treated the women, and were guilty of so many and so great outrages against honesty and decency, that the natives rose in their fury and killed the garrison and destroyed the fort. Near a rock where was a spring of water and a favorable position for a fortification, but in a different locality than the first fort, Columbus built a town; the first built by Europeans in the New World. In honor of his benefactress, he named it Isabella. In May 1494, he discovered Jamaica.

Here again the cruel and voracious nature of the Spaniards showed itself. The men were full of plunder and licentiousness. A spirit of revenge was kindled in the hearts of the greatly wronged natives and, in order to prevent extermination, Columbus prepared for war. Early in 1495, he set out with an army of 200 men, twenty horses and an equal number of dogs. With the latter, the poor savages were chased and caught, and butchered by the men. The natives were subdued and quantities of gold were collected.

With this gold and many other strange and valuable things which had been found on the various islands which had been discovered or stolen from the peaceful inhabitants, Columbus, in 1496, returned to Spain. The sight of this gold was more than the avarice of Europe could bear. A spirit of maritime adventure was kindled in the minds of thousands. The reckless and profligate, the idle and licentious, as well as the avaricious were anxious to board a vessel and set sail. The gold taken by Columbus from the West Indies to Spain proved to be a magnet which attracted adventurers to Mexico and South America. The eyes of the inhabitants of Europe were turned expectantly toward the land of perennial flowers, fountains of youth, rivers sparkling with diamonds, and sands yellow with gold. Thus, whilst the discovery of America was the result of scientific knowledge, its settlement was due, in part, to the basest of all passions - the thirst for gold.

But there was another cause which tended to the settlement of the New World. Like the thirst for gold, an evil in itself, but so overruled that good came out of it. We refer to the character of the government of Europe. It may be said that with truth, that all the nations of Europe were at this time badly governed. In French history it is known as the period of the "Religious wars." These wars threw all Europe into a state of confusion. They were called religious wars because it was a struggle between Protestantism and papacy. These Protestants are known in history by the name of Huguenots.

Since these Huguenots occupy an important position not only in the history of South Carolina, but in the history of the United States, it is necessary that we have a correct idea of their character and early history. Three of the presidents of the Continental congress were of Huguenot origin. Henry Launens, Elias Bondenot, and John Jay were the men. In France, about the year 1560, the name Huguenot was, in derision given by the Catholics to the Protestants in and near the city of Tours. Why there were called Huguenots it would be difficult at this late period to say positively. At some time prior to 1560, there lived in or near Tours a man by the name of Hugo. He was a desperate character, the terror of the whole country, whilst living, and after his death the superstitious people believed that his cruel ghost still tormented them. As the spirit of Wayne, which was called "Mad Anthony," was a terror to the North American Indians, so the ghost of the reputed monster, Hugo, was an object of dread to the inhabitants of Tours. The Huguenots, it is thought, were so named from this man. Another way of accounting for the appellation is this: There was a gate of the city of Tours which bore the name Hugo. Near this gate, in sequestered places, the Protestants met in the night to worship God. By others the word Huguenot is thought to be a corruption of the German word "Eignote," which means confederates. It is highly probable, from all the circumstances, that the name is derived either from Hugo or his gate.

We may safely say that in no land have Protestants been so prosecuted as in France. The reformation commended in that ill-fated land in the city of Paris, with the conversion of one Lefevre, a professor in the university and a student, William Farel. From this period to the present moment a spirit of persecution has been ripe in France. At the time of reformation, and consequently at the period of the settlement of South Carolina under Charles the Ninth, the French people were brutally immoral. The dark deeds of Nero and Diocletian were eclipsed by the French persecutors. The mind shudders at the remembrance of St. Bartholomew's day. By a satanically revised and hellishly executed plan, not less than thirty thousand -

probably one hundred thousand citizens - men, women, and children, were brutally murdered. This was on the 24th of August, 1572. Not less barbarous were the persecutions which were conducted during the reign of Louis the Fourteenth, to which we will refer in the proper place. The persecutions drove some of the best men of the nation to seek homes in other lands. All that could came to America. Thus, it may be said that the United States became, in time, the home of every religious creed.

When Ribault returned to France, having left, as mentioned before, twenty-six men in charge of the fort, he found France distracted with civil commotion. Coligni was not able to assist the colony for two years. A treaty in the meantime, was entered into between the Huguenots and Catholics, which enabled Coligni, in 1564, to send another colony to the New World. Rene Laudonniere was chosen to conduct the expedition, and early in the year he set out with three ships, and on the 25th of June, a landing was effected on St. John's River. The Indians had not forgotten Ribault. They conducted him to a pillar that Ribault had erected to perpetuate his discovery. The honor of being the spot on which this pillar was erected is claimed by several islands - Paris, Lemon and Beaufort. On the first there are some remains of an ancient structure, which may be debris of Fort Charles. The Indians showed their love and respect for the memory of Ribault and his colony by crowning this pillar with flowers and heaping up baskets of provisions at its base. Laudonniere was sent out principally to supply the wants of the colony attempted to be planted by Ribault. Its tragical fate had, as yet, not reached France. From the Indians this was learned. Laudonniere, for some reason, determined to abandon the spot selected by Ribault, and commenced the work of the settlement at a point on the St. John's River within the present limits of the state of Florida. This, however, does not detract from the interest which we should have in this undertaking. As South Carolinians, our interest in the colony of Laudonniere is increased when we remember the great likeness existing between it and the colony planted by Charles the Second, of England, in 1670, and especially its likeness to those who cast their lots with the colony of Charles, in 1685. We should also feel an interest in this colony from the fact that the early boundaries of South Carolina included nearly all of the present state of Florida on the south, and extended as far north as the northern limits of the state of Tennessee. It included all the territory between twenty-nine degrees and thirty-six degrees thirty minutes, north latitude, from the Atlantic on the east, to the Pacific on the

west. Hence, Laudonniere planted his colony in what was once South Carolina.

Laudonniere had visited this country and seems to have given the utmost credence to the stories told about the Fountain of Youth. In fact he seems to have gone farther than to give assent to the ridiculous absurdity, for he says he has seen Indians who were more than two hundred years old, still in the bloom and vigor of manhood. This strange delusion of the old Huguenot is only explained by remembering that men suffer their hopes and fears to control their judgments, and often, to get the better of their senses. Hence, wise and more experienced men than Laudonniere have sometimes reported that they saw what they only wished to see, and that they heard what they only wanted to hear.

Among the first things done by Laudonniere, after selecting a place for settlement, was the erection of a place for fortification. A minute description of this fort has been preserved. It was a triangle, one side of which faced the river. On the south side was the magazine. It was simple in construction, being merely an embankment of sand held together by sods of grass and logs of wood. The side facing the river was lined with planks and otherwise strengthened by driving stakes in the ground. The embankment was made nine feet high. The work when completed was named "La Caroline," in honor of Charles the Ninth of France.

The Indians treated the newcomers with the same kindness which they exercised toward Ribault and his men. No doubt the colonists promised themselves a happy future. They were free from the troubles that had so long and grievously harassed them in their native land. Whatever may have been their dreams of future bliss and quiet, they found their new home anything else but pleasant, and a more tragical end awaits them than befell Ribault's colony at Fort Charles.

As might have been expected, many of the colonists were idle and dissolute. They, by their unrighteous acts, provoked the Indians to acts of hostility. Laudonniere lowered himself by his conduct to these benighted people. Soon the colonists commenced quarreling among themselves. They had breathed the air of civil war from their youths, and although they had left France and crossed the Atlantic and taken up their abode on the shores of the New World, they retained the same spirit of contention which they had before leaving their native land. A plan was concocted for degrading Laudonniere. Two soldiers - one by the name of La Roquette and the other by the name of La Genre - attempted first to poison Laudonniere. Failing in this, they attempted to kill him by exploding the powder in the pot. In this they failed also. In a short time, these desperadoes were joined by several others, evil disposed and insubordinate like themselves. Laudonniere was taken sick. These outlaws entered his chamber and, by violence, forced him to grant them permission to scour the seas.

Two ships belonging to the colony were taken possession of, and the pilot was forced to join them. They proceeded to attack the Spanish colonies planted in the West Indian Islands. They even captured the governor of Jamaica. But the governor managed to communicate with his friends, who came to his relief. One of the vessels escaped the Spanish, and by the guidance of the pilot was taken back to La Caroline, where the chiefs of the outrage were chastised. Ribault was sent out to relieve Laudonniere; but La Caroline was destined to be destroyed. It is more than probable that although Charles the Ninth granted the Huguenots permission to plant a colony, he planned, if not directly, indirectly, its destruction.

A bold, but exceedingly fanatical and desperately cruel man, Melendez, was sent out by Philip the Second of Spain, to watch the movements of Ribault. All the plans of the latter seem to have been well known to the former. Melendez plainly and boldly declared that the purpose for which he was sent out was to exterminate the Huguenot colony. Ribault determined to defend the colony as best he could. He pushed out to sea, taking on board his fleet and all the able-bodied men, leaving Laudonniere less than one hundred men, and the women and children and the sick and infirm. The two fleets came into sight, but before an engagement took place, and equinoctial storm scattered the fleet of Ribault, and drove it far from the colony. Melendez, when the storm ceased, took advantage of Ribault's misfortune and hastened to the fort. This he captured, and brutally put to death men, women, and children. Only a few escaped by taking shelter in the woods. Afterward, Ribault and those with him preserved from the storm, returned to the fort. They were shown the dead bodies of their companions hanging from the limbs of the trees, and then at a signal given by Melendez, they were made to share the same fate. It is said that Melendez skinned Ribault while still living, and having stuffed his skin, sent it to his sovereign, Philip the Second, and the Pope of Rome. Charles made no attempt to avenge the blood of his citizens. No doubt he was well pleased.

One De Gorgues did, however, visit merited punishment upon the Spaniards for this inhuman massacre. Having equipped a small fleet for the ostensible purpose of engaging in the slave trade, he set out in 1567 for Fort Caroline. He make known his real purpose to his men as soon as he was fairly out to sea. They readily entered into his plans. The garrison of Spaniards who were left in Fort Caroline were taken and put to death. When Melendez hanged the garrison he had placed above them this inscription: "I do this not to Frenchmen, but to heretics." De Gorgues took this down and inscribed upon it these words: "I do this not to Spaniards or Catholics; but to traitors, robbers, and murderers." For La Caroline perished to the Huguenots in 1565. This earth has no more tragical spot. St. Bartholomew's day was Fort Caroline re-enacted. Both are blots on the name of Charles and Melendez, which time never can erase.

COMING OF THE ENGLISH

De Gorgues made no attempt whatever to plant a colony in the New World. He came to avenge the blood of his injured countrymen. This done, he returned to France, not however, to be hailed as a deliverer, but to be hunted as an outlaw. He repaired to Portugal. From the sovereign of this country he received a commission and prepared to enter the Portuguese army. At that time Spain and Portugal were at war; but De Gorgues died of grief before entering the service of his adopted country. This was in 1567.

For a period of more than one hundred years, what is now known as South Carolina remained in the nominal possession of Spain. The Spanish called it Florida; the French named it New France; and the English, South Virginia. The forest remained untouched, and the wild beast still continued to sport through its valleys and over its hills. Settlements were made in Virginia, Massachusetts, New York, Connecticut, Maryland, Delaware, and in what is now North Carolina; but no permanent settlement was made in South Carolina previous to 1670.

In the year 1622, some individuals fled from the hostilities of the Indians in Virginia, and came down to some part of the country and acted as missionaries. Their labors in this capacity, according to an old author, were greatly blessed. The king of one of the tribes, or of the country it is said, was converted and baptized. The labors of these missionaries were, it would seem, confined to the Mallicans and Apalachites. As the latter tribe inhabited the head waters of the Altamaha and Savannah Rivers, we may conclude that the gospel was preached by these persons, whoever they were, in the states of Georgia and

South Carolina, soon after the settlement of Virginia. The same authority (Old Mixon) informs us that a man by the name of Brigstock found, in the year 1653, Englishmen amongst these tribes. He further informs us that this Brigstock was gladly welcomed and honorably entertained in English style by these missionaries. This fact is given by Old Mixon on the authority of Brigstock.

In 1660, a few persons from Virginia came to South Carolina, in the neighborhood of Hilton Head, but on account of the dreaded hostilities of the Indians, who still, and long afterward, retained a vivid recollection of Velasques and Melendez and on account of the still more dreaded barbarities of the Spaniards, they did not remain.

On the 24th of March, in the fifteenth year of the reign of Charles the Second, of England, this potentate granted to Edward, Earl of Clarendon; George, Duke of Albemarle; William, Earl of Craven; John, Lord Berkley; Anthony, Lord Ashley; Sir George Carterett, Knight and Baronet; Sir John Colleton, Knight and Baronet; and Sir William Berkley, Knight, all that part of America in north latitude between thirty-one degrees and thirty-six degrees from the Atlantic on the east, to the Pacific on the west. This was in the year 1663. Two years afterward, on the thirteenth of June, as a special favor to Edward, Earl of Clarendon, and his associates, the grant was extended to thirty minutes northward and two degrees southward. Whatever was the motive of the donor, this was a lordly gift. It embraces, we may say, the garden spot of America, and contains many times as much territory as the British dominions in Europe.

In 1667, a vessel was fitted out and put under the command of William Sayle, for the purpose of exploring the territory thus granted. Sayle was driven by a storm amongst the Bahamas. He discovered that the situation of one of these islands - Providence - was such that on being fortified, it would afford both a retreat and defense to any colony that might be planted in Carolina. Finally he reached the coast of South Carolina and attempted to land, but was beaten back by the natives. He was delighted with the appearance of the country and, on returning to England, gave a glowing description of the excellencies of it to the proprietors. In January 1670, the proprietors, having fitted out three vessels at their own expense and a "goodly number of men," placed the whole under the command of Col. William Sayle, for the purpose of taking actual possession of the territory embraced in the grant, and planting on it a colony. The proprietors formed a joint stock, and made liberal provisions for the undertaking. It is evident that they were in earnest. They did not contemplate a failure. The commission of Sayle was dated July 26th, 1669. On the 17th of March, 1670, the fleet arrived at Port Royal. The nearness of the point to the Spanish settlements to the south, and the well known hostility of that people to any attempt being made to plant a colony near them, induced Sayle and his men to leave Port Royal and seek some other locality less exposed to Spanish cruelty. In April, they landed on a high land on the west side of the Keawaw, as the Ashley River was then called. A settlement was commenced at this point in earnest. A fortification was built and a ditch dug around the settlement. This was a wise precaution, and in all probability saved this infant colony from experiencing the same suffering and meeting the same tragical fate which had befallen La Caroline. But a short time after the settlement had commenced, a Spanish vessel was sent out by the authorities at St. Augustine to exterminate this English colony, the vessel entered Stono inlet but, finding that they were too late - the English having fortified themselves - they concluded that it was best to leave the colony undisturbed and return to St. Augustine. This attempted invasion on the part of the Spaniards seems strange, when we remember that England and Spain were at peace.

The hardships which the new settlers were called to endure were too much for Governor Sayle. He sickened and died, leaving the government in the hands of Joseph West. The spot that contains the dust of the first governor of the state is unknown. No monument slab marks his final resting place. Where, or how, West succeeded Sayle it is impossible, at this late date, to say. All that we certainly know is that, on the 10th of April, 1671, the will of Sayle was, upon oath, proved by Paul Smith and Joseph Dalton before Joseph West as governor of the province of Carolina.

With the landing of Sayle commences the history of South Carolina. It cannot be otherwise than interesting to the inhabitants of the state of the present day to know something about this germ which has, amid a multitude of disasters, grown to be a great state, sending out colonists at various times to settle up the rich lands of the west and northwest.

Charles the Second of England granted permission to Edward, Earl of Clarendon, and his colleagues to plant a colony in South Carolina and that was all. The company supplied everything else. Their vessels were furnished, together with a considerable number of able men, how many we do not know; provisions for a year and a half, clothes, tools, ammunition, and everything else thought necessary by the proprietors alone. The sum invested in the undertaking amounted to about fifty thousand dollars. The avowed purpose which the proprietors had in view was to spread the gospel amongst the aborigines, but there are many unmistakable evidences that there was at least something necessary in their designs. They expected the money expended in planting the colony to be a first-class investment.

It would be interesting to know all of the hardships which this noble band of pioneers suffered, and all the triumphs they achieved; but although it is only a little more than two hundred years ago, much that transpired in the infancy of the colony is lost. Even the names of most of them are hopelessly forgotten. The spot on which they first settled has passed through various hands, and is now in part the wharf, railroad track, and grounds of the Charleston and Savannah railroad company.

From the first, the colony flourished and increased. The Constitution of the Colony breathed a spirit of "universal and absolute toleration," in things pertaining to religion. Provision was made in the charter granted by Charles for the establishing of churches by the Dissenters. The articles of the "Fundamental Constitution" also provided that an effort be made to Christianize the Indians. All the liberty of conscience was granted, by both the king and proprietors, which any reasonable individual could desire, unless it be objected that it was further provided, that "no person above the age of seventeen years, shall have any benefit or protection of the law, who is not a member of some church or profession, having his name recorded in some one religious record." This, it is admitted, is objectionable since it, for the sake of protection, forced persons to join some church whether they were converted or not. We must take into consideration all the circumstances of the case, before we condemn too harshly. In fact, the religious liberty granted to the Carolina colony is one of the most wonderful facts recorded in history. We see those same men who, for the native country, had enacted what they called the "Bill of Uniformity" and, in the enforcing of said bill, had silenced John Owen and sent Richard Baxter and John Bunyan to prison, permitting each individual in the colony to worship God in that way which, to himself, appeared most agreeable to the Divine will as revealed in the Bible.

In order to understand this thing, we must know something of the men to whom the grant was made, and we must also have a knowledge of the history of the times. For many years previous to the settlement of South Carolina, the natives of Europe had been in a disturbed state. France and England, the only two nations that made any serious efforts to plant colonies in the New World had, for a period of more than one hundred years, been lacerated by the bitter feuds which existed amongst themselves. In each of these kingdoms, citizens had been arrayed against citizens. The waters of the rivers had been tinged and the soil made rich with the blood of the slain. In each country, Protestants and Catholics had arrayed themselves against each other in deadly hostility. No less bitter had been the contest between the Protestants of different creeds. The system of persecution existed during the reign of Elizabeth, and was continued in the time of James the First. It culminated in the reigns of the two Charles of England, and Louis the Fourteenth of France. Victory sometimes perched upon the banners of one party and sometimes on the banner of another. Charles the First was beheaded, and Charles the Second was driven into exile. Cromwell established a Commonwealth which lasted whilst he lived and when he died his Commonwealth died. Charles the Second was brought from his exile and seated upon the throne of his fathers. The people were tired of war. To escape the vengeance of the restored sovereign, the judges who condemned Charles the First had fled to America. Other persons did the same thing; whilst some who were regarded as implicated in that deed remained in England and suffered the extreme penalty of the law. A few were, through the clemency of the king, pardoned. On the restoration of Charles the Second, May the 8th, 1660, England was in a lamentable condition. Bitter and unrelenting animosities existed in all parts of the kingdom. Tired of war, the people gladly welcomed Cromwell as a Protectorate. For the same reason, they hailed with joy the return of Charles the Second. On the 29th of May, 1660, the king who had been in exile for sixteen years entered London, conducted by General Monk, afterward known as one of the proprietors of South Carolina, with the title of Duke of Albermarle. The war was brought to a close. The sword had been replaced in its scabbard; but the spirit of persecution still hovered over the land. In derision, the Dissenters from the national church were called Roundheads, because they wore their hair closely clipped. The adherents to the crown were, in the same spirit, called Cavaliers on account of their levity of manners and looseness of morals. These were terms of reproach. The times were onerous. Prominent individuals shifted their support from one cause to another, as the tide of victory ebbed and flowed, for the different contending parties. Edward, Earl of Clarendon, the first named in the "Letters Patent" granted to the proprietors of South Carolina, once was a supporter of Cromwell. Now he was "the right trusty and well beloved cousin" of Charles the Second. Socially and morally, the atmosphere of England had, by so many and so long civil wars, become polluted. Good and pious men of all creeds were, at the heart, sick of the immorality of the times. They longed for some sequestered spot where, undisturbed, they could pursue the associations of life and worship God according to the dictates of their own consciences. In England, there were multitudes of individuals whose presence was a source of annoyance, fear, and dread to the crown. It was no doubt felt that whilst these persons remained in the kingdom the existence of the crown was precarious. Hence, it was thought wise to open up some channel by which these suspected persons might, of their own free will, leave the kingdom. Others, in one way and another, had experienced great pecuniary reverses, and lost their caste and were reduced to that state of recklessness which impelled them to go to any quarter of the globe, and with the adherents of any party or advocates of any creed with no other expectations than to repair their ruined fortunes and afterward return to their native land.

France, as well as England, contributed to the settlement of South Carolina. In the reign of Henry the Fourth, twenty-five years after the memorable St. Bartholomew massacre, an edict was passed at Nantes which guaranteed to the Huguenots the rights of citizens, and partially put a stop to the persecutions which had been waged against these people. It was, however, but a momentary lull in the storm. The Huguenots were slumbering on the edges of a yawning whirlpool, whose deceptive waters were only sleeping, that they might rage and foam with wild and cruel violence never before known.

In the year 1685 in the reign of Louis the Fourteenth, the edict of Nantes was revoked, and the worst passions of men turned loose, unbridled and unrestrained. The Huguenots were slaughtered by the thousands. The trials and difficulties through which they were called to pass beggar description. Those who could fled from their native lands - some to one place and some to another. A few, but a noble few, made their way to South Carolina, and joined the colony planted by the English. Ireland and Scotland also contributed to the early settlers. Not only Europe sent out colonists but, as will be noted more particularly in the proper place, emigrants came from Virginia and Pennsylvania. All, whether they came from Europe or the other American Colonies, came in search of a quiet home. Those who came from Europe had fled from persecution on account of their religion.

Those, or at least many of them, who came from the other American colonies had fled from the hostilities of the red men. In truth, may it be said, that as was true with regard to the other states, South Carolina was settled by the oppressed of Europe.

A knowledge of the political and ecclesiastical condition of England and France gives us an idea of the peculiar liberal features of the charter granted by Charles the Second. We can hardly suppose that he was moved wholly by motives of honesty in being so gracious. In fact, the peculiar features of the "Fundamental Constitution," as the laws of the colony were called, were due to the liberal mind of the celebrated philosopher, John Locke. Anthony Ashley Cooper was a great man, and perhaps more liberal in his views than any of the other proprietors; but even he was guided and directed by Locke, who was his secretary. When we take a survey of all the attending circumstances, we are prepared to conclude that the main reason why the charter granted by the king to the proprietors and the "Fundamental Constitution" of the proprietors was so liberal was simply necessity. In no other way could a colony be planted. This, no doubt, was due rather to the foresight of Locke and Ashley Cooper than to the wisdom of any other persons. It may be said that Locke and the earl did the work, and it reflects their views.

Under normal circumstances the laws of a nation reflect the character of the people. As we are enabled by the advertisements contained in a village newspaper, to judge of the character and occupation of the inhabitants, so we can form an approximately correct idea of the morality, civilization and social condition of a people by studying the laws by which they are governed.

The letters patent granted by Charles the Second were English in all their peculiar sentiments. The object, evidently, was to make the Carolina colony a part of the British empire. It was of liberal character, when we consider the time at which it was granted and the service from which it emanated. The eight proprietors were made, created and constituted the true and absolute lords and proprietors of all the territory and of all the premises. They were granted the power to have and to hold the same "in free common socage and not in capite or by knights' service." The Crown of England reserved to itself the faith and allegiance which was due to it. Among other reservations made by the king was that which required the proprietors to give to Charles the Second, his heirs and successors, one-fourth of all the gold and silver ore found within the territory granted; and the proprietors were further required to pay an annual rent of twenty marks. It was further granted, in the "letters of patent" that the proprietors could confer titles, and in one word, act through the palatine, as a king. In the "Fundamental Constitutions" which were drawn up by John Locke and signed by the Proprietors, March 1st, 1669, English sentiments, English customs, and English notions generally are manifest. It is not, however, English sentiments as they prevailed at the time of Charles the Second; but rather as they existed in the time of Alfred. Both the "letters patent" and "Fundamental Constitution" were a degree above the aristocratic notions which existed during the time of Alfred, and a degree below the prevailing notions of the times. We may say that while the government of the proprietors was kingly in all its leading features, still it had a tendency toward a democratic government. Provisions were made for a parliament, for a grand council, for palatines land graves, caciques and all the long list of titles and dignities which obtained in England, only the names being different. The territory was divided into counties, each county contained eight seniorities, eight baronies, and four precincts. The seniorities belonged to the proprietors, the baronies to the nobility of the province, and the precincts to the people. In each precinct there were six colonies. It was provided that in each county there should be a land grave and two caciques. A county contained 750 square miles, or 480,000 acres. Of this, the proprietors and provincial nobility received two-fifths and the remaining three-fifths fell to the share of the people. The parliament consisted of the proprietors or their deputies, the land graves and caciques, and one freeholder chosen from each precinct. The proprietors and hereditary nobility would, since each member was entitled to a vote, have the majority until more than eight counties were organized. Although there were two elements in the parliament - the aristocracy and the democracy - all were required to meet in the same room.

The grand council consisted of the governor and five deputies appointed by the proprietors and five other individuals chosen by the people. The powers of this council were very great. They could try almost any and every kind of case and mulct in heavy fines and inflict severe punishment.

The Fundamental Constitution drawn up by Locke was styled the "grand model." In truth, it is a wonderful document. It is worthy of the man. No doubt it is the result of the combined effort of Ashley Cooper and Locke. Its grand defect consisted in its impracticability. No man nor set of men could establish, in an unbroken forest, amongst untutored Indians that form of government set forth in the "grand model." There was wealth in the forest of Carolina; but the people were all poor - hence lords and earls, caciques and barons were out of place.

THE INDIANS

No history of South Carolina - in fact, no history of America - is complete which does not assign a place to the aboriginal inhabitants. They were called Indians because Columbus set out to reach the Indies by a westerly route. How this people got to America and from what country they came are questions that have never been satisfactorily answered; and from the peculiar circumstances of the case, nothing perhaps better than a reasonable conjecture will ever be arrived at. It has been, by some individuals, conjectured that the Indians, as they are called, came to this country from Asia. The point at which they crossed over is supposed to have been Behring Strait. This strait, which at present is less than forty miles wide, it is supposed may have at some time been much narrower; or the two continents may, it is conjectured, have once touched each other. Supposing this not to have been the case, it is argued that when the strait was frozen over, enough families or tribes may have crossed over the sea and thus reached the continent of America. Other individuals, on account of the great difference which appeared to exist between the people of Europe and the aborigines of America, have been led to conclude that the latter are a different species from the former. This theory, notwithstanding that it has been held by men of eminent scientific attainments, is attended with so many and so great difficulties that it hs been generally rejected as destitute of facts to establish it. The theory or conjecture that the Indians came to America from Asia by the way of Behring Strait, whilst it is not satisfactory, is attended with as few difficulties as any supposition, and may be accepted until something is discovered which will throw light upon this mysterious subject.

We are accustomed to speak of America, when discovered by Europeans, as a waste, untrodden only by the feet of wild beasts. This is not strictly correct. All of the America was inhabited, and some of it densely populated by partially civilized men. The natives of Mexico and Peru had magnificent cities and vast quantities of gold. When Columbus visited Hispaniola and Jamaica he found that the former had three millions of inhabitants and the latter 600,000. These, we are forced to add, were all cruelly exterminated.

In South Carolina, when settled by the English, there were, as near as can be ascertained, twenty-eight tribes. Some of these were small and insignificant, but others were large and powerful. Their territory was from the mountains to the seaboard. The two most powerful tribes were the Westoes and Savannahs. The Westoes occupied the territory between Charleston and Edisto River. The Savannahs were located in the middle country, on the Savannah River. On the northeast side of Savannah River, back of Port Royal Island, were the Yemassees. The Creeks had established themselves on Broad River, which was called by them and the Cherokees, the Cherokee River. The present counties of Anderson, Greenville, and parts of the adjoining counties as far as Broad River was the home of the Cherokees. The Congarees lived on the river which still bears their name. Newberry county was the hunting ground of the Saludas. The Catawbas roamed northward from Camden on both sides of the river, which retains their name. The Waterees located themselves below Camden. There were many other tribes - as the Chickasaws who, since they did not live wholly in the territory now occupied by South Carolina, are omitted. Some of these, as we will see in the sequel, were numerous and valiant, rendering in some instances signal service to the whites; and at other times spreading terror through the country.

Of the twenty-eight tribes which once inhabited the state, only about seventy individuals remain. These are in the eastern portion of York county, on the Catawba River. They remain as the debris of a once numerous and, we may be permitted to add, generous people.

In person, the Indian is described as being tall and slender, with high cheek bones and long, straight, black, coarse hair. Their hair, it is said by old historians, was as strong as that of a horse. The Indian was active, rather than strong; capable of enduring much fatigue, rather than of performing great labor. He was not brave in the modern sense of that word, but was possessed of fortitude to a degree unknown to most other people. He was cunning. He never attacked his foe in the open field, but concealed himself behind trees and rocks and, when a favorable opportunity was presented, poured death and destruction upon his enemies. He was sad and taciturn. Rarely did he speak and more rarely did he laugh, and never did he indulge in even moderate hilarity. His mode of life made him sober. His existence was a precarious one. He lived by hunting and fishing. The forests and rivers spontaneously produced his supplies. To capture his game with his rude weapons required great skill and a noiseless motion. A failure for a few days in the chase would subject him to much suffering, and perhaps death. Hence he was sedate and all his movements were made with great caution.

With regard to the religion of the Indians, very little is certainly known. That they had some kind of religion, there is unmistakable evidence. In some of their religious ceremonies there is, at least, a resemblance to the ceremonies of the ancient Jews. Hence some persons are of the opinion that the Indians are of Abrahamic origin. The god of the Indians who inhabited Manhattan Island was called Manitou; that of some of the tribes of South Carolina was called Toya. To this deity they celebrated feasts which, however solemn they might have been to the worshippers, appeared silly and ridiculous to Europeans. They had priests, but in what their duties consisted, we are not able to say. One duty of the priest seems to have been to cure the sick. Not, however, by the use of medicines, but by the means of magical incantations. The science of medicine had no existence among the Indians. They were subject to but very few diseases, to that class of ailments called nervous diseases they were total strangers. They were subject to fevers and liable to be wounded. They cured fevers by lying down in water until the fever cooled. The remedies which are published as Indian cures for diseases are all humbugs.

In his intercourse with others, the Indian was often cruel and unjust. If a member of one tribe injured a member of a different tribe, the injured regarded each individual of the tribe to which the trespasser belonged as guilty, and he would wreak his vengeance on the first one he met. This shows that his notions of justice were very vague and incorrect. He made the innocent suffer for the transgressor. Notwithstanding all this, there are many evidences of the humanity and generosity of those untutored sons of the forest. In no instance did they make an unprovoked attack upon any of the colonies planted in the New World. They sometimes attacked individuals that had not injured them, but it was from the mistaken notion that all white men were the same man. Melendez provoked the Indians by his cruelty and they never forgot it, and often on account of the injury done by Melendez, took vengeance upon the English. Often did the savages, as settlers called them, save the colonists from perishing. There is something painfully sad in the history of the Indian. He is gone. Nothing but his name remains. He has melted away before the march of the white man, as snow melts beneath a tropical sun. He fought bravely for the graves of his sires and the hunting grounds of his fathers, but undisciplined valor could not withstand the skill and bravery of the early settlers of America. We are glad to be able to say that, whilst the first settlers of South Carolina were not always just and humane in their dealings with the Indians, her record is stained with as little, if not less, Indian blood than any of the thirteen colonies.

Installment V

THE LORDS PROPRIETORS

Precisely two hundred and five years ago, South Carolina was first permanently settled by Europeans. For ages - how long no one can tell - it had been in the possession of a people whose origin is as mysterious as their end was tragical. Carolina then was one unbroken forest from the mountains to the seaboard. The grandeur of the scene ravished the sight of the colonists. The air was loaded with the odors of uncultivated flowers, and from every tree proceeded charming notes made by birds of the richest plumage. It was in reality a New World to the newly arrived immigrants. They had never seen anything like it before, and the accounts which they had heard concerning it, and which they had regarded as extravagant, fell far short of the reality. The forest was full of wild animals of different kinds, many of which have long since disappeared from the state. So numerous were the deer, that an eye-witness said "the whole country seems but one continuous park." Hunters often killed, in a single year, two hundred. Bears were in great numbers and the wolves made night hideous with their howlings. These are nearly all gone. They fled on the approach of civilization, and the forest in which they found a home melted before the axe of the European. When imagination paints the territory now occupied by the state of South Carolina as it was two hundred years ago, and we take a survey of it as it now is, a feeling of sadness creeps over the soul. We almost wish we could turn the wheels of time back two hundred years that our senses might be ravished with the primitive grandeur of nature. This we cannot do. The best that can be done at present is to gather up the fragments of the history of these early times and string them together as pearls.

It was the intention of the proprietors to settle a colony at Port Royal. They had attempted to plant colonies at Cape Fear and Albemarle, in the present state of North Carolina; and, not being as successful at these points as they desired, they were anxious to make an attempt in a more southern portion of the territory granted them by Charles the Second. To accomplish this desire, the proprietors made ample arrangements. Three vessels, and supplies for eighteen months, were provided. William Sayle was appointed governor; Joseph West, commander-in-chief of the fleet; Henry Bairne, commander of one of the vessels; and John River was placed in charge of the military stores. Sayle's commission bears the date of July 26, 1669. In January, 1670, the colonists set out for their point of destination and, on the 17th of March, the effected a landing. Here they remained for only a short time and went to a high point on the west bank of the Ashley River. This they called Albemarle Point. To Sayle was given not only a commission, but also instructions.

The intention of the proprietors juts out prominently in the instructions given to Governor Sayle and the other officers. For this reason they should be generally known. The proprietors were aware that it would be impossible to put the "Fundamental Constitutions" which they called the "grand model" into execution on the first arrival of immigrants. Hence, provision was made for a temporary deviation from its requirements. It was, however, enjoined upon Sayle that he "come" as nigh the grand model as practicable. Sayle was instructed to call the free people of the colony together, so soon as he arrived, and hold an election for five individuals who, together with the five deputies appointed by the proprietors and the governor, would constitute the council. Whether Sayle did this at Port Royal, or whether he waited until after the arrival at Ashley River, or whether he did it at all, does not appear from any record. We may reasonably suppose that he carried out his instructions and that the election was held at Port Royal, and that it was in accordance with the advice of this council that the settlement was made at Ashley River, rather than at Port Royal. The five members elected by the people were required to swear allegiance to the King of England, and subscribe fidelity and submission to the proprietors and the form of the government by them established. It was, however, granted to anyone who had conscientious scruples about swearing according to the prescribed form, "to subscribe to the same in a book provided for the purpose, and this subscribing shall be deemed the same with swearing." It was enjoined upon the governor and the council to select a proper location for a fort and place upon it, when erected, guns which would command all the streets of the town. This goes to indicate that no settlement was, in fact, commenced at Port Royal. From all the circumstances with which these immigrants were surrounded, we may conclude that among the first things they would undertake would be the building of a fort. This they did the moment they arrived at Ashley River, and it was well that they did.

The instructions given to Joseph West, the commander-in-chief of the fleet, are more in detail and even more interesting than those given to Governor

16

Sayle. In fact, the duties of Admiral West resembled those of an overseer of a large plantation. West was ordered to sail with all possible speed, with the fleet under his command, for Kinsaile, Ireland. The object of sending him to Ireland was to get twenty or twenty-five servants. Having accomplished the object of his visit to Ireland, or having discovered that the servants could not be procured, he was to sail directly for Barbadoes. No free man who had no servants on board was to be allowed to leave the vessel. If a free man died or left the ship at any point, his servants became the property of the proprietors.

The object of sending Admiral West to Barbadoes was to secure seed of various kinds for the colonists. This shows the wisdom of the proprietors and also the real interest they took in the colony. Seed grown in the Barbadoes, they no doubt thought, would be more likely to flourish in Carolina than that grown in England. Everything was to be paid for by the proprietors. This was the case with respect to the servants which West was ordered to procure from Ireland. From Barbadoes, West was ordered to furnish himself with a supply of cotton seed, indigo seed, and ginger roots, together with wines of various kinds, canes, and olives. The roots were to be placed in tubs, partly filled with earth, so that they would not perish before arriving at Port Royal. When he arrived at Port Royal, he was then to plant these roots and seeds in what we may call an experimental farm or nursery. On this farm the cotton seed, indigo seed, ginger roots, and cane roots were to be planted, and all the seed produced the first year to be saved for planting the next year. On this farm which seems to have been under the absolute control of Joseph West, he was ordered to erect for himself and thirty servants, good warm houses. So soon as the houses were built, West was to put the servants to clearing up the forest, so that it would be ready for cultivation the next spring, when it was thought the roots of the previous year would be ready for transplanting. Ginger was to be the main crop. More attention was to be paid to it than anything else.

Whether Admiral West went to Kinsaile, Ireland, or not, does not appear. It is certain that he arrived at Barbadoes in February, 1670, and in all probability brought with him the first cotton seed that was ever brought into the state of South Carolina. No doubt it was planted, and we may conclude that South Carolina commenced her existence with the cultivation of cotton on the west bank of Ashley River. Cotton was found growing in Mexico, Peru, Texas, and Louisiana when these regions were discovered, and Sir Walter Raleigh found cotton cultivated in Virginia and North Carolina. It is thought that the cotton found in Mexico, Peru, Texas, and Louisiana was what is now called the short staple; but what West brought with him was the long staple or the Sea-Island cotton. The botanical name of this variety indicates very clearly the region from which it came. It is known amongst botanists by the name Gossypium Barbadense; literally, cotton from or of Barbadoes. We may as well add that very little effort was made to cultivate cotton in the state of South Carolina, at least sea-island cotton, for a number of years. Prior to the Revolution of 1776, only small quantities of the variety called green seed was produced for home consumption. Very little was shipped.

In 1747, seven bales were shipped from the city of Charleston and when in 1784, seventy-one bales were shipped to England, the authorities seized them as stolen goods, alleging that all America could not produce so much cotton. The first successful effort to grow sea-island cotton in the state was made by William Elliott, in the year 1790, near Hilton Head in the neighborhood of the spot where Ribault attempted to plant a colony in 1562.

The proprietors instructed West to take with him from Barbados "half a dozen young sows and a boar" with which to stock the country. This is a fact of some interest. No doubt, in the swamps around the present city of Charleston these animals proved very prolific. Cattle and sheep were brought to the state from Virginia. The circumstances of bringing them were these: On the first of May, 1670, the proprietors sent out Captain Halstead with supplies to the colony planted at Ashley River, now called the Ashley River colony. So soon as the supplies were unloaded, he was instructed to load the ship with lumber and take it to the Barbadoes and exchange it for rum and sugar. These were to be taken to Virginia, and exchanged for cattle for the Ashley River colony.

When America was discovered by Europeans there were neither horses, hogs, cows, nor sheep in the country. We cannot refrain from remarking that the increase of these domestic animals is most wonderful. Previous to the war of 1776, the country was full of wild horses, wild cattle, and wild hogs. This is more wonderful when we remember that the country was also full of bears, wolves, and panthers. Guthrie, an old geographer, informs us that the beasts of prey were not so ravenous in America as the same kind of animals are in Africa and Asia. As the country became settled and the number of wild animals decreased and food for those which live on flesh became scarce, the wolves and panthers became more troublesome to the planters and made greater havoc on their domestic animals.

Capt. Halstead arrived at Ashley River in the month of August, 1671. He brought further orders to the colonists respecting their organization. The orders were addressed "to the governor and council of Ashley River." Before this, the proprietors had learned that the colony had given up the idea of settling at Port Royal and had already located themselves on the Ashley River, on a high point which they had named in honor of one of the proprietors, Albemarle Point.

It is evident that nothing but some very potent reason could have induced the colony to make this change. The harbor at Port Royal is all that they could have desired, and more over, as we have seen, they were instructed to plant the colony at Port Royal. The reason, no doubt, was that the Indians in the neighborhood of Port Royal were incensed against the whites, on account of the ill-treatment which, at various times and in different ways, they had received from the Spaniards. It is almost certain that the Spanish were dreaded by Governor Sayle and his men. It is true that a treaty had but very recently been made between England and Spain, which granted the Bahamas to England; but the Spaniards at St. Augustine cared very little for treaties as many of their subsequent acts plainly show. The exact number of the colony we do not know, but many things lead us to conclude that it was comparatively small. The Spanish had been settled at St. Augustine for a long time, and had grown comparatively strong. The colony under Sayle was by no means prepared to engage in a war with the Spaniards, and hence it was no doubt resolved to select another location less exposed to their hostile neighbors. The proprietors ordered Captain Halstead to leave with the colony at Ashley River, eight small guns, and their carriages. The military stores were under the control of John Rivers, subject, however, to the governor. Previous to the arrival of Halstead in August, 1671, it is probable that the colonists were in possession of no cannon. This, also, is another reason why Governor Sayle was unwilling to risk settling at Port Royal.

Installment VI

FOUNDING OF CHARLESTON

Captain Halstead brought instructions to the governor respecting the Colonial parliament. These instructions are addressed to Governor Sayle. This shows that the death of the governor was not, on the 1st of May, 1671, known to the proprietors; but, since the location of the colony was known, we may infer that Captain Bairne removed the colonists from Port Royal to Ashley River and, having landed them, returned to England. The governor was required, within thirty days after receiving the instruction, to summon the freeholders of the plantations and require them to elect twenty men who, together with the deputies of the proprietors, were for the present to be the parliament of the colony. These, or the majority of them, were to make such laws as might be necessary for the prosperity of the colony. The parliament was to meet every two years, on the first of November. The first thing the parliament was required to do on assembling was to choose five men whom they might think fittest to act in concert with the five deputies of the proprietors and who, with the five oldest of the nobility, were to constitute the grand council. On the 25th of August, 1671, Thomas Gray, Maurice Matthews, Henry Hughes, Christopher Portman, and Ralph Marshall were chosen. Joseph Dalton was chosen secretary of the Province and Thomas Thompson, marshal. The militia was put under the command of Captain Thomas Gray and Capt. John Godfrey.

They were now put into working order. Governor West was a man of energy. The work of laying out and fortifying the town, which, in honor of Charles the Second, had been named Charles Town, progressed rapidly. The works were finished in May, 1672, and Stephen Bull was put in command with the titles of master of ordinance and captain of the fort of "Charles Town." A constant watch was kept by the citizens. No night was permitted to pass without a patrolling party being sent out. The inhabitants of the town were required to do duty twice as often as those who were settled on farms in the country. The Grand Council, with Governor West for its chairman, met frequently - once every week and frequently oftener when necessity required it. The first meeting of which we have any notice took place three days after the organization, or on the 28th of August, 1671. The first matter that seems to have merited its attention was the form of oath to be administered to each member of the council. One of the clauses of the oath bound each member of the council to "doe equall right to the rich and poore." Each member of the council was required to swear as follows: You shall not give or be of councill for favor or affection, in any difference or quarrell depending before you; but in all things demeane and behave yourself as to equity and justice appertains."

The first item of business proper that came up before the council, was a petition from John Newton and Originall Jackson against Maurice Matthews, a member of the council, and others. The difficulty, if such it really was, seems to have been about seventeen pieces of cedar timber. It may be thought strange that men in an almost unbroken forest would have any sort of difficulty about a few sticks of "cedar timber," or would ever have thought of petitioning a dignified council about such a thing. It must be remembered that at that time cedar was regarded as the most valuable of timbers. It was highly prized for making boxes, chests, and drawers. It was then supposed that it was a perfect preventive against moths. The case of John Newton and Originall Jackson against Maurice Matthews and others was thus disposed of: "It is ordered that the petitioner doe appeare before the governor and council upon Saturday, the ninth day of September next, peremptorily, to prosecute the said complaint against the defendants." On the day appointed (September 9, 1671), the council met and made this decision: "Upon hearing the matter of the petition of John Newton and Originall Jackson against Mr. Maurice Matthews, Mr. Thomas Gray and Mr. William Owen - both parties having referred themselves to the determination of the governour and council - that the said John Newton and Originall Jackson shall have the sixteen pieces of cedar timber desired, and one piece of cedar timber more claymed by the said Mr. Maurice Matthews, Mr. Thomas Gray, and Mr. William Owen, &c."

These old documents possess an interest in themselves and they possess an interest on account of the time in which they originated. The English language, as will be readily perceived by the spelling of several words, has undergone great changes. When the petition of John Newton and Originall Jackson was read before the Grand Council, South Carolina was less than two years old. In November of the same year (1671) "Henry Hughes appeared before the Grand Council and made his complaint on the behalf of our Sovereign Lord, the King, against Thomas Screman, upon the --- of October, 1671, at Charles Town, this province, did feloniously take and carry away from the said Henry Hughes, one turkey cock of the price of tenn pence of lawful English money, contrary to the peace of the sovereign Lord, the King, his crowne." This was a complicated case. Thomas Screman, from the fact that the title "gent" is given him, was a man of some position among the colonists. Two other individuals, Thomas Oldys and Captain - Lieut. Robert Donne, were connected with Screman in this offense. Donne in some way assisted Screman to steal the turkey, and Oldys assisted him to conceal it. Since Donne was an officer and Screman a gentleman, it is probable that this turkey was "feloniously taken and carried away" in the same spirit that boys of good birth and irreproachable characters at home some-

times, while at college, make raids upon hen roosts. Be this as it may, the council thought it a grave offense. It was ordered that Screman be stripped to the waist, inflict upon him nine lashes with a whip prepared for the purpose. It was also ordered that in December, Captain Donne, in full uniform, appear at the head of the company, and that his sword be taken away from him by the marshal, and he be further required to give security for his good behavior in future, or otherwise to remain in the custody of the marshal. No doubt this was the first case of the kind that came before the council, and the punishment was well calculated to make it the last.

The Grand Council possessed almost unlimited powers, but at first it acted in such a way as to secure peace and prosperity. The people obeyed, with promptness, all its orders, and the result was that the colony was soon placed in a condition of comparative security. Those who in any way conducted themselves so as to be detrimental to the common good were punished severely. Idlers were regarded as nuisances. No individual was allowed any assistance from the public store who did not have two acres of corn or peas planted for every member of his family. The whole colony was a well organized military post. Every individual was required to be ready at a moment's warning to meet any foe that might assail the settlement. The gunsmith, Thomas Ashcraft, was required by the Grand council to keep the guns in complete repair. In fact, every man, woman, and child was required to do something to produce supplies for the colony.

We cannot better show the state of things in the colony during the first two years, than by quoting a part of an ordinance passed by the Grand Council at its meeting on Feb. 10th, 1672: "It is further advised, ordered, and ordayned by the Grand Council, that no person or persons whatsoever (except for the excepted) shall have any benefit of the Lords Proprietors' stores who shall not have two acres of land at least, well and sufficiently planted with corne, pease or both, for every person in his or her family and the same to be well cultivated till the gathering of the next crop.

* * *

And if any person or persons (except before excepted) during this crop doe or shall loyter or slothfully spend his, her or their time, or doe exercise or follow any worke, labour or imployment, not hereby allowed, or not especially directed by the Grand Council, such person or persons soe offending, upon notice thereof given, shall be disposed and committed to the care and charge of such industrious planter as the Grand Council shall judge convenient for the better raising of provisions and their present maintenance as aforesaid." Carpenters and smiths were allowed permission to labor at their trade. These are the classes of individuals meant by the words "except before excepted" in parenthesis.

We cannot but admire the wisdom which was thus displayed in providing for the general welfare of the colony. Had there been no controlling power exercised over the whole, the colony must have perished. Sickness, hunger and the Indians would have swept it away in a short time.

The name of Joseph West is inseparably connected with the first settlement of South Carolina. He was appointed, as we have seen, by the proprietors, commander of the fleet which was to transport the first settlers to the state; and on landing he was to have sole charge of the commissary department and the plantation on which the proprietors designed making experiments. On the death of Sayle, he became governor. How, or by what authority, it is not known. Probably Sayle and the council, before the death of Sayle, made arrangements to the effect that West was, in the event of Sayle's death, to become governor until further instructions were received from the proprietors. Sayle made his will on the 13th of September, 1671, and sometime between that date and the 10th of April, 1672, West became governor. Never was man better fitted for a position than Colonel Joseph West was for that of governor of an infant colony. He was energetic, prudent and foresighted.

On hearing of the death of Sayle, the proprietors appointed John Yeamans governor. This was on the 21st of August, 1671; but neither Yeamans, it would seem, nor the colonists heard of it until some time afterward. Sir John Yeamans was the son of Robert Yeamans, who lost his life and estate on account of his faithfulness to the royal family of England. At the period that the charter for planting a colony in Carolina was obtained, John Yeamans was residing in Barbadoes. He had gone thither to repair his ruined fortune. He was appointed governor of the Clarendon colony, with a grant of a large tract of land. The king also conferred upon him the title of baronet. He was made governor of Clarendon colony - which extended in the language of the time "from Cape Fear to the river Saint Matheo" - in the month of January, 1665, and landed in the autumn of the same year, with a colony from Barbadoes, on the southern bank of the Cape Fear River, in the present state of North Carolina. He remained as governor of that colony for four years, and then returned to Barbadoes. His management of the colony at Cape Fear was highly cred-

itable to himself and satisfactory to both the people under his care, and the proprietors. He ruled with the affection of a father, rather than with the authority of a governor. On learning that a colony was planted at Ashley River - influenced by the same desire which, at first, directed his course to Barbadoes - he set out for that point. He obtained land grants and brought with him, in 1671, from Barbadoes, a number of negroes to cut lumber and work his plantation. These were the first negroes ever brought to the state. On the 14th of December, 1671, he appeared before the Grand Council and declared that since he was the only landgrave in the province and, in accordance with the Fundamental Constitutions, and also in accordance with instructions contained in a letter from the lords proprietors to him, he was vice palatine and formally demanded the government of Ashley colony to be placed in his hands. The council, without a dissenting voice, resolved that Joseph West should remain governor of the province until further orders and instructions were received from the proprietors. Cut to the heart by this plain dealing of the Grand Council, Yeamans returned to Barbadoes, but shortly afterward he received a commission as governor of South Carolina, south and west of Cape Carteret, at present called Cape Fear. On the 19th of April, 1672, Yeamans was publicly proclaimed governor. He continued as governor until 1674, when he was removed and West again appointed.

INSTALLMENT VII

GOVERNOR WEST'S SECOND TERM

During the period of West's first term, several things worthy of being remembered took place. The colony received reinforcements from England, from Barbadoes and from New York. A town was laid out on Stono Creek, west of Charles Town, and near by it. The tract was to contain twenty-five acres, five of which was to be reserved for a church yard, and the remainder to be used for planting lots. In December, 1671, some additions to the colony arrived from New York, among the number Michael Smith, a man of some importance. On the 20th of the same month, the Grand Council appointed Stephen Bull and Thomas Gray to assist Smith in selecting a place for a settlement. The Wando River, by an order of the Grand Council, was examined with reference to its adaptedness for making settlements.

Soon after a settlement was made at Charles Town, a tribe of Indians, called the Kussoes, in conjunction with other tribes living southward from the town, became troublesome. From all that we can learn respecting them, they were greatly addicted to thieving. The fields, and no doubt the private stores, of the colonists were plundered by the untutored savages. It is also clear that their minds were inflamed by the Spaniards.

From the first, the Spanish colonies bitterly opposed the English colony in South Carolina. As we have seen, Sayle and his men had scarcely landed when a Spanish vessel from St. Augustine entered Stono inlet with hostile intentions. During the first term of West's administration, in the very infancy of the colony, they commenced intriguing with the Kussoes for the purpose of making the Indians enemies to the English. Not that the Spanish were moved with pity or compassion for the Indian; not that they were grieved at heart because the Indian was about to be driven from the hunting grounds of his fathers and the graves of his sires. Nothing of this kind moved the Spaniard at St. Augustine to form a secret confederation with the Indians for the destruction of the Ashley River colony.

No people ever treated another as the Spaniards treated the aboriginal inhabitants of the New World. Every cruelty that satanic hate could devise was, without restraint, inflicted upon them wherever they were met. Spain, wherever she attempted to plant a colony, literally tortured the Indians out of existence. It is not claimed that the Ashley River colony treated the Indians in every respect as a correct morality and an enlightened civilization enjoined, but it is evident from the time and all the attending circumstances that, in the first difficulty which occurred between the English colony at Ashley River and the Indians, the latter were to blame. No doubt there was a lively tradition of the cruelties practiced by Velasques at St. Helena one hundred and fifty years previous to that time. The Indian retained in his memory, during life, the recollection of either a favor granted or an injury done. Sons were taught to bear eternal hatred to the enemies of their fathers. The Indian could not distinguish between the guilty and the innocent. Injured by one pale-face, his wrath was immediately kindled against every white man. The French, under Ribault, treated the Indians kindly, and they never forgot it. We may safely say that the Indians never would have maltreated the white settlers had they not been first wronged by the immigrants. No doubt there were great differences in the moral character of the various Indian tribes; but, generally, they made greater mistakes in punishing wrongs received than in deciding as to what is right and what is wrong in the intercourse of one individual with another. The first salutation the Pilgrim fathers gave the Indians at Plymouth Rock was

a shower of musket balls; at Jamestown, in Virginia, they were cheated and swindled; in the Albemarle and Clarendon colonies in the present state of North Carolina, they were justly dealt with; by the Spanish in Hispanola, Peru, and Mexico they were butchered as only the vilest of beasts are.

The tale of these injuries, we may well suppose, had spread from the sunny plains of the south to the frozen regions of the north. Warriors would, no doubt, sit around the fire of their wigwams and tell their children of the evils the tribes had suffered at the hands of the white men. All the circumstances conspired to beget hatred in the bosom of the Indian for the white man. The fault of the Indian was that he did not discriminate between the innocent and the guilty. The fact that the Spanish had injured the Indians was no reason why they should wreak vengeance upon the English. Still, we find that soon after the arrival of the colony at Ashley River, the Kussoes manifested a hostile disposition. A constant guard had to be placed around every plantation from the very beginning. This, to a colony weak in numbers and dependent in part upon the product of their fields for bread, became burdensome; and even a guard did not prevent raids from marauding parties.

Daily the Indians became more insolent and hostile in their bearing and actions. They would agree to no fair terms upon which the colony and the tribe could live together, as neighbors in peace; but on the contrary threatened the lives of peaceable and, may we say, defenseless members of the colony. In view of all the circumstances it was deemed advisable by the governor and council to take some decisive measures by which the Kussoes and their confederates would be forced to live peaceably with the colony, and deport themselves consistently with uprightness and honesty.

On the 27th day of September, 1671, war was formally declared by the governor and council against the Kussoes and Southwest Indians. Commissions were granted to Captain Joseph Godfrey and Captain Thomas Gray. They were instructed to prosecute the war "effectually," and the dispatch with which the Kussoes and their "coadjutors" were subdued shows that these captains obeyed the orders of the council implicitly, and executed them promptly. So soon as the ordinance declaring war was passed, hostilities began in earnest. There was no delay. Stephen Bull, who held the office of master of ordinance in the colony, seized, by the order of the council, two Kussoes who were in town. The colonists were ordered to rendezvous and the march against the enemy commenced at once. There was no waiting to get up a suit of clothes or to cook up a month's ration;

but each man set out the moment he received the order, for the seat of war. With such dispatch and secrecy was the expedition conducted, that the Indians were not given any time to prepare for it. The campaign lasted only from the 27th of September to the 2nd of October - four or five days - but the victory was as complete as if it had been prolonged for as many months.

On the 2nd of October, an order was passed by the council that the prisoners should be held by the individuals who had taken them, and unless they were redeemed by the tribe, they should be sold and the proceeds of the sale divided among the members of the company by which they had been captured.

This looks like the war orders of the olden time - when the soldier got his monthly pay out of the sale of prisoners he took on the battlefield. What was done in the present instance, we do not certainly know. Some of the captives, no doubt, were ransomed by the remainder of the Kussoes, while others were sold into bondage and became laborers on the plantations of the immigrants.

From this first military campaign, we may form some idea of the condition of things in the colony. We may safely conclude that the people had great confidence in the prudence and good sense of the governor and council. The fact is, Colonel West, the governor, was the main spirit of the colony. For a period of twenty years he exercised great power and enjoyed great privileges, but neither were made conducive to his own benefit exclusive of the public good. When war was declared against the Kussoes, the colony must have been under good military discipline. Most of the immigrants had, in the language of a Latin poet, "learned the art of war in boyhood." They had been accustomed to strife in some form or other in their native land. However well the colony may have been previously organized, this campaign against the Kussoes influenced the council to take into serious consideration ways and means for better protecting the lives of the inhabitants of the colony, and preventing the property of the people from being stolen or injured by depredators.

Two days after the favorable termination of the campaign - on the 4th of October - it was ordered by the council that the powder belonging to the colony be distributed so as to be more safe and more accessible in case of an invasion. Six barrels were ordered to be stored on the proprietors plantation, under the charge of Godfrey; ten barrels in the house of Yeamans, and whatever was left to remain in the proprietors store house.

On the 26th of the same month an order was passed requiring every individual in the colony except the members and the officers of the Grand Council to appear in arms whenever and at whatever place they might be ordered to parade by their respective officers. Any person who failed to obey the orders of his captain was, unless he had a good and valid excuse, to be heavily fined or severely punished as the Grand Council might see fit. Every gun was to be put in thorough repair and that this might be done captains were granted authority to order peremptorily smiths, whether freemen or slaves, to repair the guns.

A list of those required to do patrol duty had been previously made out, but for some reason many individuals had become negligent in the discharge of this important duty. At this juncture of affairs it was thought proper to make out a new list. This duty was assigned to Thomas Thompson, marshal of the province. He was required to inform, either in person or by a note left at the house of the individual, the particular time that each person was to perform this duty of watching. It was provided that in case any individual was sick then the next man on the list was to take his place. The fine imposed for neglecting to patrol was five shillings, and in case the defaulter was poor he was to be severely punished. The marshal was allowed about seven dollars and a half per month for his services in this capacity. The pay was to continue so long as the marshal was employed as chief of patrol, and to be paid by the inhabitants "proportionately." With propriety might it be said that the Ashley River colony regarded eternal vigilance as the price of liberty.

The classical scholars cannot fail to see the striking resemblance of the colony during the period of Governor West's first term, to that planted in ancient Carthage by the Tyrian princess Dido. In the chaste and elegant language of Virgil, "necessity forced both to place a guard around their dominions." The inhabitants tilled the soil, built their houses, fished in the streams and took the oysters out of the coves, clad in all the panoply of a soldier. The men were, in the literal sense of the phrase, "citizen soldiers." The homes which now shelter us from the scorching suns of summer and the pelting storms of winter were purchased for us by our illustrious forefathers, with a treasure more precious than gold. It cost them anxious days and sleepless nights.

As is always the case under similar circumstances, there were no doubt some individuals destitute of moral character. An example of this class of persons we find in Dennis Mohoon, a servant of Richard Coale. Mahoon plotted with the Spanish to the detriment of the colony. On one occasion, having been detected in his plans to escape from the colony and seek protection from the crown of Spain, he was apprehended and brought before the council, but on confessing his guilt and declaring his sorrow and penitence, he was pardoned. From his conduct afterward, it was evident that his sorrow was only fear of punishment, for he was again detected in making arrangements to escape from the colony to the Spanish, and also in persuading John Rivers and John Cooke to go with him. The sentence of the council was that for this second offense, he should be stripped naked to the waist, and received thirty-nine lashes on the naked back.

In these days, when there is a store in every neighborhood of five miles square, it may be interesting to know who were the first merchants in the state and in what their stock consisted. Sometime after the settlement was commenced at Ashley River - the precise time is not known - John Foster and Thomas Gray formed a copartnership for the sale of general merchandise, to adopt the language of the present day. On the 13th of January, 1672, they dissolved the copartnership and divided the stock on hand. The stock in trade in this first store in South Carolina consisted of eight servants, of whom, on the division, John Foster received Thomas Witty, Wm. Davise, John Ratliffe, and James Powell, and Thomas Gray received Richard Poore, Richard Barginer, Edward Howell and Joam Burnett. The other part of the stock consisted of deer skins, a few yards of linen, hoes, shovels, axes, picks, saws, chisels, frows, hammers, wedges, beef, peas, oil, hens, hogs, turkeys, and one sheep. The most of the stock consisted in agricultural implements.

Installment VIII

ADMINISTRATION OF JOHN YEAMANS

On the 19th of April, 1672, Joseph West retired from the office of governor of the colony, settled at Ashley River, and Sir John Yeamans was publicly proclaimed. This was the beginning of a series of calamities, both to the immigrants and the proprietors.

Yeamans had won for himself at last the approbation of the proprietors in the manner in which he had conducted their affairs at Cape Fear. It is, however, doubtful whether or not he ever had anything in view except the reparation of his own ruined fortune. The proprietors from the beginning were favorably disposed toward Yeamans. He and they had many views, respecting men and things, which were common. The majority of the proprietors were cavaliers, and so was Yeamans.

Whatever may be said regarding Yeamans' gubernatorial career at Cape Fear, he signally failed at Ashley River. He commenced a course of conduct which showed that he had no desire to advance the welfare of the infant colony or to promote the interest of the proprietors. His acts resembled those of a selfish landholder. He who had ruled at Cape Fear with the affection of a father now grasped with the rapacity of a miser. No sooner was he proclaimed governor than the whole face of things was changed. On the 20th of April, the very day after he assumed office, the people were assembled and a new parliament chosen. Stephen Bull, Christopher Portman, Richard Conant, Ralph Marshall and John Robinson were chosen members of the Grand Council. The deputies of the proprietors were Colonel West, Captain Thomas Gray, Captain John Godfrey, Maurice Matthews and William Owens. The influence of West was not lost, notwithstanding the fact that he was removed as governor. He remained true as steel, both to the people and the proprietors.

Yeamans had a plantation in Barbadoes, and he had a definite knowledge of the wants of the community. He knew the kind of merchandise that was in the greatest demand there and which would command the greatest amount of money. All Yeamans seemed to have in view was the amassing of a fortune for himself. To effect this purpose, he commenced buying up the produce of the settlers and shipping it to the Barbadoes. The colony was thus, if not impoverished, retarded in its progress; and the proprietors, in their efforts to support the colony, were involved in a heavy debt. They became disheartened and concluded that in the future they would be more sparing in granting supplies. The colonists asked for a supply of stock. This was refused them by the proprietors on the ground that it was not the intention of the latter to establish a colony of graziers but of planters.

The official character of Yeamans has been supported by a certain class of old writers; but it is clear that they were favorable to him because of his political notions and ecclesiastical connections. Those who defend him said that he incurred the disapprobation of the proprietors by making too many and too large demands upon them for the welfare of the colony. This conclusion is not well supported. The inhabitants of the colony would scarcely have been dissatisfied with a governor who was thus zealously striving to advance so much, and there was no prospect that the demand upon them for supplies would come to an end. There is one fact which must settle this matter forever. It is this: Sir John Yeamans was poor when he was made governor of the colony, and when he died in August 1674 he was rich. He had no other means of making his fortune except his plantations and his traffic with the colonists.

23

During the infancy of the colony, manual labor was all, or nearly all, performed by white servants who had been brought from England, and by Indians who had been either bought from their enemies or captured in war, and sold into slavery to defray the expense of the war. It was customary for the immigrants to hire an Indian hunter. Such an individual could be procured for less than five dollars a year, and he would supply a family in meat of the choicest kind all the time.

GOVERNOR WEST AGAIN

In May, 1674, Joseph West was again commissioned governor and made a landgrave by the proprietors. Sir John Yeamans, on account of bad health, had, previous to this time, gone to Barbadoes where he died in August of the same year. On the departure of Yeamans the people selected West to be their governor, and the selection was confirmed by the proprietors.

When West commenced his second term of office, the colony was in a bad condition. Dissension had sprung up, and old animosities which had been lulled to sleep, were aroused in all their original strength. The very existence of the colony was threatened. Yeamans, by purchasing the products of the people and sending them to the Barbadoes, had reduced the colony to the greatest extremity. Famine began to stare them in the face. The cry for bread was heard in various quarters. Open rebellion was plotted. The facts concerning it are few, but the inferences are plain and easy.

The proprietors, with the exception of Ashley Cooper, were cavaliers; the people were mostly Dissenters. Ashley Cooper and John Locke, who were intimately connected from the beginning with the planting of the colony, were favorable to the Dissenters, whilst it was the evident intention of the other proprietors to establish in Carolina the Church of England. The members of the Church of England were favored. They were regarded as men of culture, whilst the Dissenters were regarded as an ignorant and quarrelsome set of people. No doubt, there was some truth in this. The probability is that, whilst the Dissenters had more mental power, the Cavaliers were a more refined class. They had no love for each other, and hence could not live long together in harmony.

RELIGIOUS LIBERTY

It is true that the first set of laws drawn up by the proprietors granted each individual the greatest liberty in religion. In these Fundamental Constitutions there is no denominationalism. It is evident that some peculiar and only temporary circumstance induced the proprietors to be so liberal. This liberality was due to Ashley Cooper and John Locke - mainly, however, to the latter. None of the proprietors were men eminent for piety; and although Ashley Cooper, was nominally a Dissenter, he was too much engaged in other schemes to devote much attention to the cultivation of his own heart. He was a man of talent, and we should respect his memory. He is the author of what is known in England and America as the Habeas Corpus Act. John Locke was a great man and, it would appear, a good Christian. He seems to have imbibed the spirit of his divine Master. He had less prejudice in his mind than was common among the men of his age. He said: "At the day of judgment I will not be asked whether I was a Lutheran or a Calvinist, but had I embraced the truth in the love of it."

In the fist set of Fundamental Constitutions, signed by the proprietors on the first day of March, 1669, three sections have special reference to religion. They are sections 100, 101, and 102. Other sections have reference to religion, but not so special as those referred to. We quote them accurately:

C. In the terms of communion of every church or profession, these following shall be then, without which no agreement or assembly of men, under pretence of religion, shall be accounted a church or profession within these rules.

1. There is a God.

2. That God is publicly to be worshipped.

3. That it is lawful, and the duty of every man, being thereunto called by those that govern, to bear witness to truth; and that every church or profession shall, in their terms of communion, set down the external way whereby they witness a truth as in the presence of God, whether it be by laying hands on or kissing the Bible, as in the Church of England, or by holding up the hand or in other sensible way.

C. — 1. No person above seventeen years of age shall have any benefit or protection of the law or be capable of any place of profit or honor, who is not a member of some church or profession, having his name recorded in some one, and but one religious record at once.

C. — 2. No person of any other church or profession shall disturb or molest any religious assembly.

Provision was also made that any individual might leave one church or denomination and join another; and also that slaves be permitted to connect themselves with any church they might see fit. All this was liberal - Christian, we might say - but it is clear, from the future conduct of the proprietors, that they did not mean all they said.

These Fundamental Constitutions were to "remain the sacred and unalterable form and rule of government of Carolina forever;" but the proprietors did themselves, on the first of March, 1670, change these Fundamental Constitutions. One of the changes introduced these words:

As the country becomes to be sufficiently planted and distributed into fit divisions, it shall belong to the Parliament to take care of the building of the churches and the public maintenance of the divines, to be employed in the exercise of religion according to the Church of England; which being the only true and orthodox, and the national religion of all the king's dominion, is so also of Carolina; and therefore it alone shall be allowed to receive a public maintenance by grant of Parliament.

In 1672 the proprietors drew up and signed what they styled the "agrarian laws." The evident tendency of the "agrarian laws," was to give the proprietors and colonial aristocracy the permanent control of the colony. In February, 1673, whilst West was temporary governor, the Fundamental Constitutions were proposed to the people for adoption, but by them rejected. Everything was calculated to stir up old and bitter feuds. Yeamans had bought up, at a mere nominal price, the produce of the inhabitants and sent it to Barbadoes, and the immigrants were too dependent on the proprietors. No doubt the large number of them were not disposed to do much for themselves. Some of them were gentlemen of ruined fortunes. The were not accustomed to labor. Others, no doubt, were idle and prodigal. The adherents of the Church of England were jealous of the Puritans; and the Puritans, on the other hand, had not much good feeling for the Cavaliers. Public sentiment in the little colony was in a state of general ferment. At such times a leader is rarely wanting. At this time he appeared in the person of John Culpepper - a name afterward prominently connected with an insurrection in North Carolina, which under his direction was successful in deposing all the officers in the Clarendon colony.

TROUBLES WITH THE SPANIARDS

Florence O'Sullivan had been placed on an island, (which, in honor of him, is called Sullivan's Island) in charge of a "big gun." He was charged to fire this gun on the approach of any "topsail" as a warning to the inhabitants of the town. O'Sullivan, during the confusion of the colony, had been forgotten, and was reduced to a point bordering on starvation. Incensed at such treatment, he quitted his post and joined the discontents of the town. This was not all; for at the time, the Spaniards at St. Augustine, having learned of the state of things in the colony, determined to take advantage of it for its destruction. For some reason there seems to have been a disposition on the part of the servants to run away from their masters at Ashley River, and go to the Spanish at St. Augustine. We cannot suppose that the Spanish were kinder masters than the English. No doubt, the reason was that the servants who were inclined to run away were Catholics, and they were ill at ease in a Protestant colony.

At the time of this disturbance, a noted scoundrel by the name of Brian Fitzpatrick, ran off to the Spaniards, and communicated to them the unsettled state of things at Ashley River. The Spanish sent out a party of men who encamped at St. Helena Island. Captain Godfrey was sent out with a body of fifty men. So soon as Godfrey approached the post of the Spaniards they fled.

In order to meet the necessities of the colony, one ship was sent to Virginia and another to Barbadoes to bring supplies. Before these returned, a ship sent out by the proprietors with supplies and a few immigrants arrived. This changed the appearance of things. Florence O'Sullivan was required to give security for his future good behavior.

This calamity taught the colonists a very important lesson. It taught them to depend on themselves. It was an evil in itself; but it resulted in good. The attentive observer of events cannot fail to discover the superintending providence of God in the most trivial occurrences.

In the neighborhood of Ashley River colony, there lived two powerful tribes of Indians - the Westoes and Saranas. The latter had their home near the Isindiga, now called the Savannah River. The former were the relentless and uncompromising enemies of the white man. Between these two formidable tribes a fierce war broke out about the time of the disturbances in the colony at Ashley River. So bitterly was it waged that both tribes were completely ruined. It is worth remarking in this connection that Providence seems to have paved the way for the settlement of South Carolina by reducing in one way and another the number of Indians.

Previous to the settlement of the state by the English, disaster had greatly reduced the number of some of the tribes, and the hostility of the tribes to each other kept their ranks thinned.

It should not be forgotten that Ashley Cooper, one of the original proprietors, by his agent, Dr.

Henry Woodward, purchased, in 1675, a large tract of country from the Indians. The deed of transfer specifies the country sold as that of the "Great and Lesser Castor, lying on the river Kyewaw," (now called Ashley) "the river of Stono, and the fresher of the river Edisto." The price paid was a "valuable parcel of cloth, hatchets, beads and other goods and manufactures." This deed was signed and sealed by the marks and seals of four chiefs, with the marks of eleven war captains, and, what is stranger still, by "fourteen women captains." If Pennsylvania can boast that William Penn purchased her territory from the Indians, South Carolina can boast that Lord Shaftesbury purchased at least part of the present state of South Carolina.

At a later date, the Indians ceded to the English all their lands as far as the Appalachian mountains. This last grant seems to be accompanied with no compensation.

The fact that Ashley Cooper, Earl of Shaftesbury, was the author of the Habeas Corpus act, and that he, at least in part, purchased the soil of South Carolina from the Indians, should cause his name to be held in grateful remembrance.

Installment IX

NEW CHARLES TOWN

The individual who has only a limited knowledge of human nature might be ready to conclude that all the circumstances connected with the settlement of South Carolina would have inspired the first European inhabitants that came to this country to live together in perfect harmony. This was far from the case; nor is it to be wondered at. As we have seen, the majority of the immigrants were dissenters from the Church of England; but the proprietors and the Grand Council were Cavaliers. There is not a shadow of doubt that the Cavaliers designed from the first to establish a kind of religious oligarchy. This, together with the recollection of the fiery struggle which had been passed through in old England, fed the bitter hate which still lived in the bosom of the dissenters. No doubt, both parties were greatly to be blamed. To allay the party feeling which existed amongst the settlers required all the skill, energy and prudence of Joseph West. Notwithstanding the great zeal manifested by the different religious sects, very little was done directly, by any of them for many years, to promote piety. A minister and church was an appendage of every New England settlement. A church was built and the people settled around it. Such was not the case in South Carolina. For a period of ten years, we have no certain account of the erection of any church, or even of any preaching, in the colony. Joseph West is characterized by all parties as a devoutly pious man, and we may reasonably conclude that, occupying the position and exercising the influence which he did in the colony, he would exert a happy restraint over the wayward, and encourage those religiously disposed.

However retarding these religious bickerings might have been to the growth and prosperity of the colony, they did not put a stop to its expansion. The locality chosen on the west side of Kyewaw River was found not suited to the purposes of the colony. The express object which was had in view in selecting it, was because it was so situated that no large vessel could approach it. The simple fact is, that the first settlers were afraid that they would be attacked by the Spanish. They were aware that the mercies of that people were cruel. Hence, they selected a "high ground" on Kyewaw River, thinking that at that point they would be comparatively safe. Port Royal was abandoned because it was a good harbor and near the Spanish. The "high ground" on Kyewaw was selected because it was farther away from the Spanish, and had no harbor. The proprietors enjoined it upon the immigrants to settle at a distance from the coast for the sake of health. The point of land between the Kyewaw and Walno Rivers - not the Ashley and Cooper - was soon discovered to be more favorable for a settlement than the first chosen. Individuals had settled on this place, which was called Oyster Point. The Grand Council, on the 13th of January, 1672, directed Captain Maurice Matthews and Captain Godfrey to make an examination of the Wando River with reference to its suitableness for a settlement. What the character of the report of these individuals was we can only conjecture. It may be well supposed that they were pleased with the situation. It was now found that the spot first selected, whilst it could not be approached by an invading fleet, was still greatly exposed to the Spanish and Indians. The peculiar situation of Oyster Point - being simply a tongue of land, bounded on both sides by river - rendered it much more desirable for a town constantly liable to be attacked by an enemy. It also possessed commercial advantages. This, however, was a matter of secondary consideration. The great object with the immigrants in selecting a site for a town, was its advantage in a military point of view. Any individual who will look at the map of the state of South Carolina will not be slow in concluding that, for all the purposes of the early settlers, there is no other location equal to Oyster Point. This tongue of land had been, at an early period in the history of the colony, taken up by Henry Hughes and John Coming.

The object of the survey made by Captain Godfrey and Captain Matthews does not, however, seem to have been made with special reference to a change of location, but only with the view of securing a safe locality on which other immigrants might settle. From the nature of the surrounding circumstances, all the settlements were made in what were, with propriety, called towns. Single individuals could not have protected themselves against the hostile Indians. That it was not contemplated in 1672 to make Oyster Point the chief town is evident, from the conduct of Hughes and Coming. On the 21st of February, 1672, they met the Grand Council, and Henry Hughes gave up one half of his land, "near a place upon Ashley River, known by the name of Oyster Point, to be employed in and toward the enlarging of a town and common of pasture there intended to be erected." Mr. John Coming and Affera, his wife, came likewise before the Grand Council, and freely gave up one half of their land near the said place, for the use aforesaid. In fact, the settlement of Oyster Point must have commenced very soon after the settlement on the west bank of the Kyewaw, which the immigrants named Ashley, in honor of the Earle of Shaftesbury.

As early as June 18th, 1672, we find the Grand Council devising ways and means for the defense of the province. One amongst many other orders issued by that body, is in these words: "All the inhabitants on the other part of the river, called Oyster Point, doe repaire to the plantation there now in possession of Hugh Carterette Cooper, and being soe embodyed, doe march forward to the plantation now in possession of Mr. Thomas Norris, or Mr. William Morrill, which may be thought most safe and useful for that design, under the command of Mr. Robert Donne, there to remayne and exercise such orders and rules as the Grand Council shall think fitt to be prosecuted for the better safety of that part of this settlement."

The town was, by order, or rather by the consent of the Grand Council, laid out by John Culpepper in 1672. The warrant issued by Governor Yeamans to Surveyor General Culpepper bears the date of July, 1672. The spot attracted a considerable number of inhabitants; but owing to the hostile disposition of the Indians and the fear of the Spanish invasion, the settlers generally preferred that section which was most densely populated.

In 1673 John Culpepper got into a difficulty with the authorities of the Ashley River colony and went to the Albemarle colony. There, in 1677, he got into a more serious difficulty, which has, with some good ground, been regarded as the beginning of forcible resistance to the British government in America. This was about one hundred years before the American Revolution, and more than fifty years before Carolina was divided into North and South Carolina. Culpepper's difficulty in Albemarle colony was simply this: The British government levied a special tax of two pence on every pound of tobacco sold in the colony, or not sent to England. The object, evidently, was to give England a monopoly of the tobacco trade. At the time, a man by the name of Miller filled the offices of governor, collector and secretary of the colony. He proceeded to collect the tax on tobacco, and made himself both odious and oppressive to the people. Culpepper resisted his acts. The governor was seized, and all the money found in his possession was taken from him and appropriated to the resistance of what the people thought high handed measures and to the defense of the colony. The fact that Albemarle colony now, since it did not have to pay a tax on tobacco, enjoyed a great advantage over the colonies in Virginia and Maryland, made the latter discontented.

A plan was set on foot to subdue Culpepper, and in order that he might receive justice, he went to England for the purpose of making an appeal to the ruling sovereign for a repeal of the tax and to beg for mercy for having resisted royal authority. He was arrested; but Shaftesbury managed to get the matter quashed, fearing lest it would ultimately come before the House of Commons and put an end to his ministry. Shaftesbury openly declared that the laws of England did not extend to the remote and insignificant province of Carolina, and that the difficulty was only a petty feud amongst the people of Albemarle and their rulers. It is hard to reconcile this declaration of Shaftesbury with the fact that Miller had collected, by authority, fourteen thousand dollars off of the people of Albemarle.

THE STREETS OF CHARLESTON

So soon as he was out of this difficulty, Culpepper came to Carolina and engaged in laying out the original streets of what is now the city of Charleston. This was in 1680; but in 1679, the people generally had become disposed to cross over the Ashley River and settle on Oyster Point. The proprietors were duly informed of this fact, and also of the advantage to be gained by making a change in the location of the colony. This met with hearty approbation of the proprietors. On the 17th of May, 1680, they wrote to the governor and Grand Council in the following words: "We again desire you to take notice that the Oyster Point is the place that we do appoint for the Porte Towne wch (which) you are to call Charles Towne,"

&c. The same instructions, in almost the identical words, had been sent to the governor and Grand Council by the Richmond frigate, on the 17th of December, 1679. We quote those of May, 1680, to show that the proprietors felt much interest in the contemplated change of location. No doubt, before the last instructions arrived, the change had been affected. All the public offices had been removed to Oyster Point, and at that point the Grand Council was summoned to convene. The town, in obedience to the instructions of the proprietors, was duly named Charles Town. For the first two years it was, in contradistinction from the place that had been left, called New Charles Town; but, gradually, Old Charles Town was abandoned and, until the close of the Revolutionary war, the name of Charles Town was retained.

The streets were ordered to be laid out east and west intersected by others at right angles. This, no doubt, was done at least as well as the nature of the location and the circumstances of the case would admit. The proprietors were particular to enjoin it upon the governor and Council to pay particular attention to the regularity and straightness of the streets. The houses were not built as to correspond with the surveyors' lines. The section of the city first laid out was that which presently lies between Broad and Water streets, from the Cooper River westward, to Meeting street. It is in this quarter we find Zig-zag alley.

There is good reason for concluding that the change from old Charles Town to New Charles Town was made in the spring of the year. Thirty houses were erected; but what the exact number of the colony was, it is impossible to say with certainty. In order to increase the growth of the town and give it an importance which it could not otherwise have, the proprietors ordered that all ships be loaded and unloaded at it. In laying out the town, a lot of five acres was to be laid out for each of the proprietors, wherever they might see fit, either in person or by their agents, to select it. Any individual who took up a lot was required to lay a foundation of a house upon it within one year and have a house erected upon the foundation within two years. Any person taking up a lot and failing to comply with this requirement forfeited all his claim to the lot; and the Grand Council could grant the lot to any one else, and he would be at liberty to build upon it. The object of this proviso, no doubt, was to preclude any speculation. Any person could take up as many lots as he desired, provided he would build upon each extra lot within twelve months, a house at least thirty feet long, sixteen feet wide, and two stories high, beside garrets.

Immigrants flocked in from all quarters. England, Ireland and the West Indies and the colonies in the northern part of North America each sent its quota, and the town grew rapidly. Land increased in value. Within two years after its settlement, a hundred houses were built. Land sold for five dollars per acre and rented for half as much per annum. Almost from its very foundation, the town began to assume a commercial aspect. In November, 1680, sixteen ships - some of them large for that period of the world - entered the harbor at one time.

Heretofore the colony had been without any church building or regular church organization. A five acre lot had been reserved, as we have seen, in one of the contemplated settlements, for a church; but we have no evidence that any church was erected upon it. In 1682, during the administration of Governor West, the first church in the state was begun. It was long called the English church. Its distinctive name was St. Phillips - Now St. Michael's. A law was passed by parliament forbidding drunkenness and idleness enjoining the observance of the Sabbath.

The saddest event of this period was the removal of Governor West from office. From the first he had been intimately identified with the colony in all its movements, and under his wise and prudent management, it had grown and flourished. Old Mixon says the reason that West was removed from office or governor was because he dealt in Indians and opposed the proprietary party. There seems to be some strange inconsistency about the charge, which it is not easy to reconcile. The immigrants were allowed, from the first, to hold negroes in slavery, and exercise over them absolute control. It could not be said that the proprietors were opposed to slavery. The main point of opposition to West was his religious creed and his political notions. The proprietors saw that West kept the Cavaliers in check. Joseph Morton succeeded West as governor. From a letter written to Andrew Percivall by the proprietors we learn that Joseph Morton and Landgrave Axtel, about this time were instrumental in "bringing five hundred people to the colony in less than a month's time." It is barely possible that this circumstance influenced the proprietors to degrade West and elevate Joseph Morton.

FRICTION BETWEEN THE PROPRIETORS AND THE PEOPLE

For various reasons the proprietors and the first inhabitants of South Carolina never acted in perfect harmony. The proprietors were unable to carry out their plans of government from the fact that, under the circumstances, these plans were impracticable in a forest. Another reason why the proprietors failed in their plans arose from the peculiar character of the immigrants. The result was that neither the conditions of the charter, nor the Fundamental Constitution, either as originally drawn up, nor as subsequently altered at various times and in different respects, never were complied with in the colony. The Atlantic rolled between the proprietors and the colony, and the latter seemed to have begun to breathe the air of freedom the moment they landed on the shore of Carolina. This was the case, also, in the two colonies which had been previously planted under the same charter in what is now the state of North Carolina. At this distant period where the scenes are all enacted, we can see the point to which things early commenced to drift. The proprietors were not always wise in their acts toward the colony; but generally they were liberal in supporting it. Up to the time of the founding of the present city of Charleston, the colony had cost the proprietors in one way and other, near if not altogether one hundred thousand dollars. As yet they had not received anything in return for all their trouble and expense in founding the colony, and the prospects were, unless soon changes were made, by no means encouraging for the future. They became disheartened and vexed. The Fundamental Constitutions which they had not hesitated to declare were "unalterable," they changed time and again; but to their chagrin the immigrants persistently refused to adopt them. Joseph West, whom the proprietors had declared to be the fittest man for the office of governor, was removed, and Joseph Morton was commissioned. No doubt the proprietors thought, or at least hoped, that this change of governors would produce a change in the general aspect of the colony. It did effect a change; but not for the good of the colony, and surely not for the proprietors. When West vacated the office of governor, and Morton commenced his gubernatorial career, the colony was in a very flourishing condition. Immigrants were coming in from all quarters. The capital was fast building up. The only drawback seems to have been the health of the locality. For a number of years, from June to October, it was very sickly and the people went elsewhere to reside during this season. This, no doubt, retarded its growth very materially.

On the 10th of May, 1682, the proprietors issued instructions to divide the province into three counties. This Morton did, and named the counties Colleton, Berkley and Craven. The county lines were vague and poorly defined. Colleton embraced Port Royal and the adjacent islands, together with the inland, for a distance of thirty miles from the coast. Berkley, in which was the capital, was limited by Stono Creek and the Sewee River. Craven county contained all northward towards Cape Fear. At this time, Craven county contained but few settlers. In the other two counties, there were between fifteen hundred and two thousand inhabitants, the most of whom were in Berkley. The proprietors ordered that an election should be held in London - now Wiltown - and Charles Town, for members who would compose the Colonial Parliament. Ten were to be chosen from Berkley and ten from Colleton.

In order that an individual could be chosen a member of the parliament, it was necessary that he be the owner of five hundred acres of land, in the county from which he was chosen. It seems that at the last election for members of the parliament, many individuals had sent their vote by others. This was justly regarded by the proprietors as a dangerous practice. Still, no provisions seem to have been made to establish election precincts. In a country full of hostile Indians, and with deficient means of travel, it was a very great undertaking to attempt to go a few miles from home. Every man's presence was required on his own farm. Previously the members of the parliament were chosen at Charles Town, and now, in the face of the instructions and wishes of the proprietors, they were chosen at Charles Town again. Whether the inhabitants of Colleton were dissatisfied with the manner in which the parliament was chosen or not, we are not certain; but the proprietors were incensed and ordered the parliament to be disbanded and no other parliament to be called until their instructions were complied with.

This last order was equally disobeyed. The parliament went to work and passed various laws. Among them was one which declared, in substance, that "all prosecutions for foreign debts were suspended." This filled the proprietors with indignation, and they railed out on their deputies, and wrote to Governor Morton, asking him "Are you to govern the people, or are the people to govern you?" The proprietors now found that Morton managed their affairs no better than West had done. The great trouble with them was that the individuals whom they appointed governors were, to a very great extent, unknown to them. Not only so, but people and governors were implicated in the same crimes - if crimes they were - and breathed the same spirit. The proprietors were not always consistent. They granted privileges, and then threatened to punish those who had the courage to enjoy them. They made laws which they said were "unalterable," and then in order to meet some new case which might spring upon them, they changed these laws. They granted permission to sell Indians at one time; and at another, they deposed West because he sold them. The proprietors were often fickle, and the people unyielding. The proprietors aimed at accomplishing one object, and the people another.

To meet the critical condition of things, the proprietors determined to appoint a man who was not in the colony, to the highest office of governor. Accordingly, in April, 1683, Richard Kyrle of Ireland was appointed to succeed Joseph Morton. Kyrle was a man of some fame and of considerable energy. It was thought that he would, by his energy and skill, place the colony in a more favorable condition toward the proprietors. In this expectation they were disappointed; for death terminated his life some time during the first summer after his arrival in the colony.

As an evidence of the eminent fitness of Joseph West for the office of governor, and of his great popularity in the colony, he was again, for the third time, chosen to that high and responsible office. He was not in the colony at that time, but in October, 1684, he was in due form chosen by the Grand Council, who immediately wrote to the proprietors informing them of their action. The proprietors, although they had only a short time before dismissed West, were gratified and sent him a commission.

During the absence of West, which continued for a few months only, Col. Robert Quarry acted as deputy. Quarry, although sometimes mentioned as one of the governors of the colony, in fact, was only a deputy. He never was chosen by the Grand Council or commissioned by the proprietors. At one time he was secretary of the province, and in virtue of this position he was honored with the office of temporary governor.

At this time, the sea was infested with a band of pirates, partially at least, under the protection of the English government. These pirates often came to Charles Town and received various favors from the people for which they received ample compensation. These pirates kept the Spaniards at St. Augustine in check. The proprietors, however, did not favor this friendly intercourse between the colony and the pirates. At least, they pretended not to favor it; but in this, as in may other things, they were not wholly consistent. The English government favored to some extent the pirates. To say the least of it, they winked at their raids in many instances.

The proprietors were thoroughly English in all of their sentiments. Col. Robert Quarry was bold and imprudent, showing favors to these robbers on the seas. So imprudent was his conduct that he was deprived of the office of secretary.

In September, 1684, Joseph West returned and assumed the duties of his office. A great change had taken place in the colony since he was succeeded by Morton in 1682. The proprietors had so changed the laws that it was almost impossible for the people to pay the "quit rent," which was about two cents per acre. At first, the land-holders had been allowed the privilege of paying this quit-rent either in money or in produce. Now the money was demanded and a failure to pay the money subjected them to a forfeiture of their lands. It is easy to see that this new law placed the poor colonists in a very critical condition. Many of them saw that in the midst of a boundless forest, where land was in great abundance and settlers few, they were, for the want of a few pence, about to be turned out of house and home. It was vain to entreat for mercy. The proprietors were irritable, and declared that they had a right to do with their land as they pleased. They claimed the right to sell the land for whatever they saw fit. This right they insisted upon.

The parliamentary difficulty was still unsettled. Maurice Matthews, Arthur Middleton and James Moore, then perhaps the most influential members from Berkley county, had been expelled from the parliament because they had engaged in sending Indian slaves from the colony. In the meantime the proprietors sent instructions for West in which all the former laws and regulations of the colony were abrogated. The proprietors evidently determined to make a complete transformation of the colony. West saw that the condition of things was hopeless. No room was left for him to exercise his own judgment in the government of the colony. He gave up the task as hopeless and retired.

Here the history of Joseph West ends. Whether he quitted the colony entirely or went, as some think, to his plantation on the Ashley River, is not certainly known. It is more than probable that he left the colony entirely, from the fact that his name never again appears in any of the records of the colony. It is barely possible that a man of West's wisdom, influence and popularity could have lived in the colony in perfect obscurity. His own public spirit would not have permitted this, and his fellow citizens would not have suffered it.

The character of Joseph West is worthy of imitation. The world has furnished few such officers. For a period of more than twenty years, in one capacity and another, he had been intimately connected with the colony. His first position was that of commander of the fleet which brought the settlers to Carolina. Then he had charge of the public stores. On the death of Sayle he was chosen governor. For his arduous labors it is clear he received poor compensation. His salary as governor was about four hundred and fifty dollars, and this was not fully paid. In 1677, the proprietors gave him up their plantation to liquidate his claim against the colony. George Chalmers, in his Political Annals of Carolina, says in speaking of this transaction, "This is the first factor who, at the end of ten years of prudent management, received the whole product of his traffic, as a reward of his services, without any impeachment." The graves of West and Sayle are unmarked. Monumental piles have been reared to perpetuate the memory of tyrants, but Joseph West's virtues will transmit his name to posterity so long as the English language is read or spoken.

Installment XI

FIGHTING THE SPANIARDS

No one can form even a tolerably correct idea of American history, without some knowledge of the history of Europe, and especially of England. Although only about fifteen years had transpired between the landing of the colony at Ashley River, and the departure of Joseph West from the colony, still great changes had taken place amongst the proprietors and in the English government. George Monk was dead; Ashley was committed to the Tower in 1681; in 1667 Clarendon was banished for life; John Locke was forced, in 1684, to leave England and take up his abode in Holland.

On the 6th of February, 1685, Charles the Second died, and on the same day his brother James ascended the throne with the title of James the Second. On his death bed Charles made a profession of the Roman Catholic faith, and made confession to Father Huddleston, a second rate priest. James the Second was a professed papist. This the Protestant part of the kingdom, and especially the dissenting Protestants, had been dreading for years. Things had been drifting in this direction for a long time, and many had left the kingdom and come to America that they might escape future trouble. Not only did individuals unknown to fame quit the land of their birth and seek a home in the wilds of America; but many persons of wealth and position bid an adieu to all that was dear, and fled to the New World that they might escape the cruelties of a papal monarchy.

Amongst those who came to South Carolina were Joseph Blake from England, and Lord Cardross from Scotland. Blake was a brother of the admiral. He sold out his estate in Somersetshire and came to South Carolina in 1683. From what we can learn concerning him, he was an old man, and also a man of exemplary life and of great influence. The reason he gave for leaving England was that the miseries which the Dissenters at that time suffered were nothing compared with what they would be called on to "endure under a Popish successor." The son of Joseph Blake was in after years, governor of South Carolina, and his daughter married Joseph Morton, another governor. Blake, by his presence in the colony, greatly encouraged the sober and law abiding portion of the people. About the same time, Lord Cardross obtained permission to transport to Carolina 10,000 immigrants. The proprietors so altered the Fundamental Constitutions as to be very favorable to these Scotch. Cardross had been most unrighteously treated. His property had been destroyed by the king's troops and his income taken from him and given to another.

In 1683, he, with a number of families, arrived in Carolina. A settlement was commenced at Port Royal. The town they founded was in honor of his wife, named Stuart's Town. How many families and what number of immigrants came with Cardross it is not easy to say. Some think that only ten families came; but there are reasons for believing that there were more than ten. Amongst the individuals who came was a Scotch clergyman, by the name of William Dunlop. The settlers at Charles Town viewed, with a jealous eye, the new comers. Cardross was summoned to appear before the Grand Council at Charles Town, to give an account of himself and colony. Irritated and disgusted at such demands he, as soon as his health would permit, returned to his native land, and took an active part in the Revolution of 1688. A part of his colony remained but in a few years it was broken up and amalgamated with that at Charles Town.

On the retirement of Joseph West, Joseph Morton became governor. His commission was only signed by the proprietors. In November, 1685, only a few months after receiving his commission, Morton convened the parliament and, agreeable to the instructions of the proprietors, called upon the members to subscribe to the Fundamental Constitutions of 1682. Of the twenty commoners, only nineteen were present. Only seven of this number would subscribe to the constitutions. This irritated the governor, and he ordered the twelve who refused to comply with the instructions of the proprietors, to leave the house forthwith. The reason that the twelve members gave for not subscribing to those of 1682 was that they had subscribed to those of 1669. These latter the proprietors declared were "unalterable." The eight deputies and seven commoners went to work and passed various laws. These acts are entitled as follows: "An act for the restraining and punishing of privateers; an act for the better security of the province, etc.; an act for the revival of several acts of parliament heretofore made, etc.; an act for the reviving and ascertaining the fees heretofore chargeable to the register of marriages, births and burials, etc. In the statutes at large of South Carolina, edited by Thomas Cooper, these acts are numbered 26, 27, 28, 29, and are signed by Joseph Morton, Robert Quarry, John Godfrey, Paul Grimball, Stephen Bull, Joseph Morton, Jr., John Farr and Will Dunlop.

About this time, a serious difficulty occurred between the settlements at Charles Town and Port Royal, and the Spanish at St. Augustine. In the country there were, at this time, two notorious Indians named Antonio and Wina who, besides acting as spies for the Spanish, greatly irritated the various tribes against the white settlers. In the year 1686, the Spanish at St. Augustine sent their vessels, with an armed force, to attack the settlers at Charles Town and Port Royal. The force landed on the Edisto, and first made an attack on the houses of Joseph Morton, governor, and Paul Grimball, the secretary of the province. Both these individuals were in Charles Town on the day that the attack was made. No sooner had the Spaniards landed, than they commenced plundering. They killed the brother-in-law of the governor, took away about thirty slaves, and nearly fifteen thousand dollars worth of other property. This secured, they set out to make an attack upon the feeble Scotch colony at Port Royal. Nearly all the men were sick, and those who were in good health were in no way prepared to defend themselves against the invaders. Some were killed; others were taken captive and inhumanely treated. Thus ended the colony planted by Lord Cardross.

As was natural, all party feelings were laid aside, and the repelling of the enemy was made a common cause. The provincial parliament was assembled, and on the 15th day of October, 1686 an act was passed "for the defense of the government and for the assessing of five hundred pounds, etc." This act is marked in the statutes at large of South Carolina, No. 30. The five hundred pounds were assessed, and the governor and four of the Grand Council were invested with supreme power. Two vessels were equipped and four hundred men armed and mustered into ranks, and every preparation made to invade the neighboring Spanish settlement. The five hundred pounds was to be equally distributed by assessment, amongst the freeholders of the province. Servants and seaman were not to be assessed; but every other resident in the colony was required to pay in proportion to the value of the property owned by him. Provision was made that those who were not prepared to pay money, might furnish corn, peas, beef, pork or tar. Merchantable sound corn was to be taken at about fifty cents per bushel; beef at four dollars per hundred; pork at five dollars per hundred, and tar at two dollars and forty cents per barrel.

For a time a grand military expedition was undertaken. All party feeling was buried, and all parties were anxious to annihilate the Spanish. The fleet set sail for St. Augustine. The campaign was destined soon to come to an end. On its way to St. Augustine, the fleet met James Colleton coming from Barbadoes to Charles Town. Colleton had, in August, been made a landgrave and governor of Carolina, and was now on his way to enter upon the duties of his office. So soon as he met the little armament, he ordered it to return, threatening to hang the whole of them if they disobeyed. Mortified and disgusted, the fleet returned. The proprietors commended the action of Colleton in thus abruptly terminating a military expedition which all parties in the colony thought just and honorable. The colonists claimed that the charter under which they were settled gave them the right to drive away and exterminate their persistent foes. The proprietors thought differently. England and Spain were at peace, but the Spanish colony at St. Augustine and the English colony were at open hostilities. The very existence of the latter was in jeopardy. Hence, it does seem, if war was ever justifiable, it would have been right for the colony at Charles Town to have invaded the Spanish possession at St. Augustine. At least so thought the majority of the colony. Bitter complaints were made against Colleton that he had tarnished the name of England, and brought disgrace upon the nation.

During this period the colony received many valuable accessions from France. The edict of Nantz was revoked, and many of the French Protestants were forced to leave their native land. These Protestants were called, in contempt, Huguenots. Several families of these came to South Carolina, and their descendants are today, and always have been amongst the most honorable portion of the inhabitants. They settled in Craven county, on the Santee. Notwithstanding the fact that there were so many discouragements and so little agreement among the proprietors and people, still the colony multiplied in numbers and increased in importance. In the province there must have been at this time, several thousand European inhabitants. As we will see in the sequel, their troubles increased each year. No doubt, both proprietors and people were, at times, in fault, but the weight of the blame rests upon the former.

INSTALLMENT XII

PERSECUTION OF THE FRENCH SETTLERS BY THE ENGLISH SETTLERS

In 1691, Colonel Philip Ludwell of Virginia succeeded Seth Sothell as governor of what was then called the Ashley River colony. On the death of Sir William Berkley, Philip Ludwell married his widow, and was in 1689 appointed by the proprietors to succeed Sothell as governor of the Albemarle colony. About this time, the province began to receive the titles North Carolina and South Carolina, but no fixed bounds were established for many years after.

In 1729, the province was ordered to be divided; but nothing was done respecting it until 1732. The dividing line was not run until the year 1735, and even then it was not executed with anything like correctness. It was not until 1762, one hundred years after the charter for settlement was granted, that by order of George the Third, king of England, the dividing line between the two sections of the province was established. This was found to be incorrectly located and it was not until 1801 that the line was permanently established. In 1736, the year after the province was divided, a silver medal was struck to commemorate the event. This medal was found in a cabinet of curiosities, in the city of Philadelphia, in the year 1845.

The first line of separation between North and South Carolina was very different from the present dividing one. The line in some places was much farther south than the present. York, Chester and part of Fairfield, together with several other counties, were regarded as being in North Carolina. The line was at one time regarded as being as far south as Rocky Mount, in Fairfield county. We have an old document in our possession, which bears the date April 24th, 1772, in which Rocky Mount is stated as being in North Carolina. The territory which fell to the state of South Carolina, by the correction of the dividing line, was called the "new acquisition." It will be seen that, up to 1729, the colonies of Carolina had a common interest. They had different governors, but the charter under which they were settled was the same.

So much has been said respecting the dividing line, in order to avoid confusion in point of time, we have anticipated events. Hereafter, we will drop, only when necessity requires it, the titles Ashley River colony and Albemarle, and adopt those of North Carolina and South Carolina.

From 1685 to 1695, the colony of South Carolina was in a most wretched condition. The English settlers were disposed to treat, in an unrighteous and persecuting manner, the French settlers. Persecuted at home on account of their religion, many men of wealth and influence had sold their possessions in France and removed to England, and from thence they came to America. The proprietors instructed the settlers of South Carolina to receive these immigrants kindly. This governor Ludwell did; but it is evident that the English settlers were disposed to be hostile in their treatment to all immigrants except those who came from England. This was demonstrated by their treatment of the Scotch settlers at Port Royal, under Lord Cardross. The French immigrants generally settled in what was called Craven county, on the Santee. They were men of more means than the English, and one reason why they were disliked, was simply because they commenced their settlement under more favorable circumstances. Some of the English were, no doubt, in fair circumstances, but the majority were poor. Envy moved them to hate the French because they were comparatively rich. Such is human nature. The rich look down with contempt or disdain upon the poor; and on the other hand the poor view the rich with an envious eye. The great reason of the bad feeling which the English bore toward the French, was that national animosity which the two people bore toward each other. No good feelings were cherished by the two nations. The arrival of a colony of Frenchmen, considerable in numbers, of itself awakened the hate which had been slumbering in the bosoms of the English on the banks of the Wando. They had no disposition to grant them equal rights with themselves. On the contrary, they determined to regard them only in the light of foreign citizens.

The proprietors were more liberal in their views than the people. Instructions were sent to the governor to allow the French colony six representatives in the Colonial Parliament. The English settlers declared that the proprietors, in granting this, had gone beyond the letter and spirit of the charter. Governor Ludwell, who was a kind and humane man, received the immigrants who came into the country, with marked civility. He did everything in his power to make South Carolina an asylum for those who had been forced to leave their native country on account of persecution. He exerted himself that they might not be disappointed in their expectations. They heard, in Europe, that America offered a home to the persecuted of every creed, and an asylum to the oppressed of every nation. Governor Ludwell did all, perhaps, that he could situated as he was, to make South Carolina what report said it was. The stubborn English cared little for what report said about America, or the world thought of their action. They determined that the French should have no power in the government of the colony. Hence, here in the wilds of the New World, they commenced putting in execution the English alien laws.

All this, at this day, seems strange; but human nature is a strange thing. The Puritans of New England, who had themselves fled from persecution, inaugurated a system of persecution. The "uniformity act" had driven them first to Holland, and then to America. One would be ready to conclude that men who would not submit to a "uniformity act" would be the last men to establish a "uniformity act." Such, however, was not the case. The Puritans banished Roger Williams from Massachusetts, for the same reason that the Puritans were banished from England. No doubt, many of the first settlers of South Carolina were mere adventurers; but the majority of them had come to America that they might escape the sufferings of a Popish succession as it was called. In their fear, they were correct. James the Second, with Lord Chancellor Jeffreys and Colonel Kirk as tools, brought a stain upon old England, which all time cannot wipe out. To avoid the terrible events which brought about the revolution of 1688, many had left England and come to South Carolina. The French on account of the revocation of the edict of Nantz, by Louis the Fourteenth, had come to the same place. The same cause had brought both people to the same place. Hence, we might have reasonably expected that they would have embraced each other as brothers, and lived together in perfect harmony. We might have expected that a similar history would have filled their hearts with sympathy for each other. Such, however, as we have seen, was not the case.

That which distressed the French colonists most was that in accordance with the English alien laws, they would not be able to dispose of their property when they died. They felt that they might labor during a long life and overcome any amount of obstacles and accumulate a competency for their children, but they had no surety that their natural heirs would ever be permitted to enjoy it.

The French brought their own clergymen with them from France. To these they were devoted. One of the strange and most unreasonable demands made by the English population was that the service should commence in the French churches at the same hour that it did in the English church. This betrayed a persecuting spirit in perfect harmony with the times; but an unreasonableness which is a disgrace to the human family. Both French and English were Protestants. In their creeds and mode of worship, there were some minor points of difference; but as far as men can agree, they were one in faith and one in practice. We are sorry that we are called to record these facts, but they are facts.

Although the attempt certainly was made to deprive the French settlers of Craven county from sending representatives to the Colonial Parliament, it was not effected, at least not permanently; for, in 1692, six members from Craven county came and took the oath of allegiance to William and Mary, the successors of James the Second. To relieve the French settlers with regard to their fears concerning the forfeiture of their estates, and also to correct the ill-defined notions of the English settlers, the proprietors wrote to the governor and their deputies in the province that the French settlers, in many instances had bought the lands on which they were settled from them, and consequently, in case it was forfeited, it would escheat to them, and the English settlers would in no way be the gainers. One of the grounds of complaint which the French had, was that the English declared that since the French parents were not married by the regularly ordained ministers, that is by ministers of the Church of England, their children in the eyes of the law were only bastards. This was, the proprietors declared, contrary to the spirit and even letter of the constitution which granted liberty of conscience, and it was even higher ground than had ever been taken by the English at home. "We have here" (in England) say they, "persons who have been married in Dutch and French churches by ministers that never were ordained, and yet we have never heard that the children begotten in such marriages are reputed unlawful or bastards."

In this connection, we must not omit to notice the glaring inconsistencies which were, at times, manifest in the actions of both proprietors and people. In may, 1691, during the administration of Sothell, the Colonial Parliament passed a law by which all French and Swiss immigrants were made free born. (2 Statutes at Large No. 65.) This law, because it was passed during the administration of Sothell, was by both the people and proprietors, repealed. It does seem that a spirit of contrariness often had full possession of both people and proprietors. There was no concert in their action. A bad state of feeling had been engendered, and it was determined by both parties to keep it up.

It would be a difficult matter to give a correct picture of Governor Ludwell. By all, he was regarded as a gentle and humane man; but there is not wanting evidence that he was, at least on certain occasions, a harsh man. When he first assumed the government, the assembly petitioned him to exercise clemency towards the offenders under the previous governor. An act of "free and general indemnity and oblivion and confirmation of all judicial proceedings in the late government." was asked by the Colonial Parliament. This Ludwell refused, in rather a harsh manner, to grant.

Governor Ludwell seems to have been a man whose greatest defect was a want of firmness. Sometimes he was on the side of the people and, at others, on the side of the proprietors. The proprietors were very careful to caution him, lest he should fall into the same errors with Colleton. No Jacobites, or Goose Creek men, were to be taken into his employ. He was to concert with the deputies of the proprietors, and not to expect to govern to the satisfaction of the people, who were to be convinced, by his actions, that the Grand Council had the power to pass all bills. He was also instructed to punish all offenders during the former administration; but in the event the number was too great, or if in any other way he was able to punish the whole, he was to grant a general pardon, except to a few of the more notorious, and to punish those so as to make them a public example. None of these items of instructions did he fully carry out. No doubt, he was by nature, unfit for the emergencies of this situation. He tried to please both proprietors and people, and really pleased neither. During the latter part of his administration a band of pirates came into Charles Town. These he apprehended and brought to trial. This greatly aroused the indignation of the people. The pirates were cleared, to the undoing of Governor Ludwell.

The people and the proprietors now began to wrangle. Right or wrong, the people were openly inclined, as heretofore, to shelter and protect the pirates. The proprietors seemed to be determined to punish them. The difficulty respecting the punishment of the pirates having commenced, other and no less conflicts between the proprietors and people soon followed. Governor Ludwell, no doubt from a want of decision of character, which was sometimes mistaken for mildness, seemed to take part with the people. He even went so far in favoring the people as to propose to the parliament a "new form of deed for holding lands." This the proprietors would not hear, since they claimed the sole right to dispose of the land. On account of this popular act, he was removed from office in 1693, and Thomas Smith was appointed to succeed him. Governor Ludwell went back to Virginia, glad, says an old historian, to get rid of his charge.

GOVERNOR SMITH

Thomas Smith, the successor of Philip Ludwell, was amongst the first settlers of South Carolina. He was a native of Devonshire, England. On account of the religious intolerance and persecution which existed in England at that time, he, with his brother James, came to South Carolina in the year 1671. They were amongst the first individuals who settled at Oyster Point, the present site of the City of Charleston. The lots owned by them were, on the laying out of the city at first, numbered 41 and 57. The were living where Charleston is now situated as early as 1672. James Smith left South Carolina and went to Boston. Thomas Smith was a man of property and highly respected by the people and proprietors. On the removal of Colleton, he was chosen governor, but Sothell coming into the colony previous to his being formally inducted into office, Sothell asserted his priority and was, as we have seen, to the injury of all parties, made governor. At different times the proprietors had made grants of land to Smith, and he had purchased a large amount besides. He also married the widow of John D'Arsens, to whom the proprietors had made a grant of twelve thousand acres of land. In 1691, he was made a landgrave, which by the regulations of the proprietors, entitled him to the enormous amount of forty-eight thousand acres of land. The whole summed up, must have made Thomas Smith the owner of not much less than one hundred thousand acres of land. He had held several offices in the colony before he was chosen governor. He had been a deputy of the proprietors, sheriff of Berkley county, and honored and respected generally. We may safely conclude that Thomas Smith was a good man. In 1693, after the departure of Ludwell, Smith entered upon the duties of his office as governor of South Carolina. His long and intimate connection with the colony led both proprietors and people to look upon his induction into office as the dawn of a new and prosperous era in the history of the colony.

The instructions which were given to Ludwell were repeated to Smith. The difficulties which had sprung up between the people and the proprietors still continued - not, however, so threatening in their aspect. From the outset, the Fundamental Constitutions, and generally the instructions given by the proprietors to the governors, were stubbornly, and sometimes violently, resisted by the people. The charter given by the king was not objected to and both proprietors and people appealed to it. The former claimed that the charter gave them all the powers and prerogatives that they had inserted in the Fundamental Constitutions, and in the instructions which, at various times, they had sent to the different governors of the province. This was denied by the people, and giving this interpretation to the charter, they persistently opposed everything that seemed to them to be an encroachment upon their chartered privileges. At different times concessions were made and liberties granted by the proprietors, but the people had become irritated, and either could not or would not see that the changes made in the Fundamental Constitutions were for their good. One of the instances in which the proprietors yielded to the clamors among the people for more liberty, is contained in the changes which they were "prevailed upon" to make in 1682, on the Fundamental Constitutions of 1669. The following is the fifty-first law of what, by the proprietors, was honored with the high sounding title of Fundamental Constitutions, and which they unhesitatingly said were to "remain the sacred and unalterable form and rule of government of Carolina forever": "The Grand Council shall prepare all matters to be proposed in Parliament, but what hath first passed the Grand Council; which after having been read there several days in the Parliament, shall by a majority of voice, be passed or rejected." The Grand Council was composed of the governor, five individuals chosen by the people and five deputies appointed by the proprietors. The deputies were generally men if illiberal views, and opposed and thwarted every effort of the governor in conducting the government of the colony on democratic principles. The powers granted them by the Fundamental Constitutions were very great. The Parliament could do but little more than approve of what was done by the Grand Council. Whether for the interest of the colony, or whether from necessity, we will not undertake to say, but in 1682 the fifty-first law of the Fundamental Constitutions was so altered as to grant the "juryes of the countyes" to propose laws to the Parliament. It was also granted by the same instructions of 1682 that in the event the Grand Council had made no arrangement for the proposing of a law likely to benefit the colony, any member of the Parliament might take cognizance of it and propose it to the house. This was a great concession on the part of the proprietors, but the people seem not to have seen it, or to have been too much irritated in feeling, to give the proprietors due credit for the privilege. This practice continued in the colony, and the Colonial Parliament began to resemble more closely that of England.

Notwithstanding the character of Thomas Smith, he found it no easy task to discharge the duties of governor of South Carolina. The difficulties and feuds existing between the English and French colonists had been partially adjusted by Sothell, but still the line of demarcation which separated the two nationalities was clearly visible. Sothell did many bad things, but he did some good things. Whilst he was governor of the colony, in May 1691, an act was "passed and ratified in open Parliament for the better encouragement of the settlement of South Carolina." In this act it was declared, "for the sake of the Protestant religion and for the advancement of the interest of the lords proprietors, and for the preservation of justice and equity, that all and every French Protestant or person born in Switzerland, at present in South Carolina, or who shall be in it in the year 1692, shall be adjudged free born to all intents and purposes as if born in the province." The English portion of the inhabitants complained loudly on account of these and other equally great privileges granted to the French and Swiss immigrants. By a special favor of the proprietors, the county of Craven, the section in which the Huguenots had settled, was entitled to six representative in the Colonial Parliament. Thus, sometimes this section was allowed to enjoy, and at other times it was not. This bad state of feeling, or perhaps we had better say this species of persecution, thwarted the efforts of Thomas Smith to promote the interest of the colony and unnerved his energies.

Smith was strictly charged to enforce, by law, the collection of the unpaid quitrents and to supervise the collector of these quitrents. This was an onerous task. The people had previously determined not to pay these quitrents, and every effort to collect them stirred up the embers of opposition which the popular breeze soon kindled into a flame. The proprietors threatened to dispossess the landholders in the event the quitrents were not paid. On the other hand, the people, led by James Moore, a bold spirit, defiantly replied their title was worthless, since the deeds which they had made out were only signed by a part of the proprietors. So far did the opposition to paying the quitrents go, that a number of individuals, rather than be, as they thought, trampled in the dust, left the colony, and others made preparation to leave. The governor himself concluded that harmony could not be established in the colony between the proprietors and people, and amongst the people themselves. In October, 1694, he wrote to the proprietors that he had concluded, with others, to leave Carolina and go to some other section of the New World. Before he had time to hear from the proprietors, he resigned his charge, and Joseph Blake was selected to act as temporary governor until another would be commissioned by the proprietors. Thomas Smith did not, as he intimated to the proprietors, leave the colony, but remained and became the founder of an honorable and useful family.

ORIGIN OF JURY DRAWING

It was during the administration of Smith, or possibly during that of Ludwell, that the mode of drawing jurors, so long practiced in the state, was inaugurated. It has without sufficient evidence been regarded as the result of the profound mediations of the immortal John Locke. It is not to be found in either the charter of King Charles, or in the Fundamental Constitutions of the proprietors. The process was simply this: The names of all the free men in the colony or precinct were written on slips of paper of the same size and appearance, and placed in a box prepared for the purpose. From this box a child, which could not read, drew the required number of persons. The idea seemed to have been suggested by the ancient statues and painting of the goddess of justice. Truth was painted naked, and justice blind. It matters not who originated the process of drawing jurors in South Carolina, it was an honor to the originator and a blessing to those who were permitted to practice it.

INTRODUCTION OF RICE

It has been customary to date the introduction of rice into South Carolina at the time of Smith's administration. The circumstances of the introduction of this staple commodity into the state may be briefly related thus: A ship, on her voyage from the island of Madagascar on the coast of Africa to England, touched near Charleston and anchored off Sullivan's Island. The captain of the vessel invited Thomas Smith to visit him, which he did. The captain gave Smith a bag of rice. This seed he distributed amongst some friends, Stephen Bull and Joseph Woodward being of the number. Smith planted the portion reserved by himself in his garden. It was found that the soil about Charleston was adapted to the culture of rice and it ultimately became an important article of food in the colony and a source of great wealth to the planters. The period at which this took place has, without sufficient reason, been regarded as the time that Smith was governor.

In 1691, during the administration of Seth Sothell, the parliament granted Peter Jacob Guerard what might, with propriety, be called a patent for a "Pendulum Engine, which doth much better, and in lesse time and labour, huske rice, than any other heretofore hath been in use within this province." (Statutes at Large, No. 72.) From the wording of this act, it is clear that rice was cultivated in the colony prior to 1691, and that other "engines" had been invented for husking it before the one brought to perfection by Peter Jacob Guerard. It may be that Thomas Smith introduced the cultivation of rice into South Carolina, but if he did - and it is not certain that he did - it was several years before he was governor. In a fragment of an early description of South Carolina, the following language is found: "A brigantine from the island of Madagascar, happened to put into that colony; they had a little seed rice left, not exceeding a peck, or quarter of a bushel, which the captain offered and gave to a gentleman by the name of Woodward; from a part of this he had a very good crop."

This extract makes it difficult to say whether rice was first introduced by Joseph Woodward or Thomas Smith. Some years after the first introduction, a gentlemen by the name of Du Bois, treasurer of the East India Company, sent a bag of rice to South Carolina. This gave rise, it is said, to the distinction which was made in the kinds of rice. One kind was called red rice, and the other white rice.

It is probable that the bag of rice sent by Du Bois arrived during Smith's administration and, as it is reasonable to suppose, was given to him since he was governor; and hence some were led to conclude that the cultivation of rice in the colony commenced at that period. With the introduction of rice is intimately connected the rapid introduction of slaves into the colony. Africans were first brought into the colony by John Yeamans from Barbadoes; but the number did not increase rapidly until rice began to be cultivated extensively. Rice was first planted on what we call upland; but it was soon discovered that low damp lands were better adapted to its growth. These places proved unhealthy to the English servants and Indian slaves, but not so to the Africans. It was not long until the negro population was, as it is yet, greater than the white. Sir William Berkley, governor of Virginia, sowed the first rice that was ever sown in North America. This was in the year 1677. He sowed one half bushel and made sixteen bushels.

For a number of years after the settlement, the staple productions of South Carolina were rice, indigo, tar, pitch, and turpentine. In time the indigo gave place to cotton. At one time an effort was made to introduce the cultivation of silk into the province. The eggs which were sent over from France to propagate the silk worms, were hatched whilst the vessel which was conveying them was still at sea, and the young silk worms died for want of food. This was as early as the year 1681, during the reign of Charles the Second of England. Afterward, silk was, to a limited extent, produced in South Carolina, and a royal belle of Europe once wore a silk dress which was the production of South Carolina.

Installment XIV

A PROPRIETOR AS GOVERNOR

It is difficult to tell whether Thomas Smith's career, as governor of South Carolina, was a success or a failure. In fact, it was neither. Although wedded to the people by all the ties of a long residence, and respected by them universally for great moral integrity, he did not succeed so well as some of the governors who had preceded him; but on the other hand, he did little if any injury. Smith either felt his incompetency for the task, or was unwilling to subject himself to the great inconveniences and countless annoyances to which a rigid and faithful discharge of his duty as governor would have subjected him. Shortly after entering upon the duties of his office, he wrote to the proprietors that in no way could a friendly state of feelings be established between the people and the proprietors, and between the people themselves, but by the proprietors sending over one of their own numbers to act as governor. The proprietors regarded this suggestion as worthy of consideration, the more so since Sir Nathaniel Johnson was of a similar opinion with Smith. The proprietors called a meeting and, after due deliberation of all the proprietors, it was determined to send Lord Ashley, the grandson of the Earl of Shaftesbury. This young nobleman was thought by the proprietors to be eminently qualified, but such was the condition of his father's estate that he regarded it as incumbent upon him not to undertake the work. In the next choice, John Archdale was selected.

The commission of Archdale bears the date July 18th, 1694. This was prior to Smith's letter, in which he declared his intention to quit the colony. It was later in the year 1694 - perhaps the last of October or first of November - that Smith, unceremoniously, and it would seem somewhat irregularly, ceased to act as governor. Archdale did not arrive in the province until the 17th of August, 1695. During the interval between the resignation and abandonment of the government by Smith and the arrival of Archdale, Joseph Blake acted as governor of South Carolina.

INFLUENCE OF JOSEPH BLAKE

Blake came into the colony in 1683. He was the brother of Robert Blake, the celebrated English admiral. He came from Bridgewater in Somersetshire, England. His father had at one period of his life been a merchant who, having amassed a fortune, retired from business and settled in Bridgewater. In his day we may safely say that no individual exercised greater influence over the colonists, morally, than Joseph Blake. He was a man of some property, all of which he sold, and brought the proceeds and invested it in Carolina. His daughter, Elizabeth, had married Joseph Morton. The Blakes, both in America and England, were Dissenters and staunch republicans. So soon as Joseph Blake joined the colony in South Carolina, the moral aspect of things began to change for the better. The irreligious and profane were, by his presence, checked and the pious encouraged.

The government of Joseph Blake was only a temporary arrangement to meet the exigencies of the case. He continued in office only from October or November of 1694, to August 1695, and never received commission, as governor, from the proprietors. It was understood, by both Blake and the people, that so soon as a successor to Smith arrived he would retire from office. This being the case, his administration of the public affairs of the colony was conducted with caution.

A law was passed by the assembly "for the raising of a public store of powder for the defense of the province." In this same act it was provided that about twenty large guns be mounted on carriages, "made of good sound cedar plank and timber," and be so arranged as to be always in readiness for the defense of Charles Town.

COMMENCEMENT OF THE DRINK ISSUE

Another law was passed for regulating public houses. By this act the owners of "taverns, tapphouses and punch-houses," were required to obtain license from Joseph Blake. The license for selling wines and all sorts of liquors, was five pounds - about twenty-five dollars; and for all other kinds of liquor, except wine, three pounds - about fifteen dollars. It was by the law "exacted that no person, whatsoever shall sell any wine, cider, beer, brandy, rum, punch or any strong drink whatsoever, under the quantity of one gallon, at one draught until he or they have first obtained a license from the right honorable Joseph Blake, landgrave and governor. Any person selling any of the aforesaid liquors under the quantity aforesaid, shall forfeit, for every time he shall sell any quantity less than one gallon, five pounds current silver of this province, to be levied by bill, plaint or information in any of the courts within this province." This act was to continue in force in the colony but, owing no doubt to the sudden and informal resignation of Governor Smith, the owners of public taverns had become very careless in observing it.

During the administration of Joseph Blake, things continued about as they had been for a number of years previous. A bad state of feeling continued to exist between the settlers from England and those from France. In this whole thing, from beginning to end, the English were greatly to blame. Governor Blake was, by the English portion of the colony, requested to withhold from the French settlers every privilege. It was asked that they might be both excluded from the privilege of being represented in the colonial assembly, and also denied the privilege of voting at the elections. This was a petition to degrade the French and deny them all the rights of freemen. Blake, either because he was aware that this petition was, both in letter and spirit, directly opposed to the wishes of the proprietors, or because he was unwilling to undertake so grave a work, situated as he was, did not grant the unreasonable request of the petitioners.

ARRIVAL OF ARCHDALE

On the 17th of August, 1695, John Archdale arrived in Charles Town. More than a year had transpired since his appointment to the high and responsible office of governor of the Province of South Carolina. He first came to Virginia and thence to Carolina. The instructions given him were full, and whatever defects there might, on trial, be found to exist in them, he was directed to consult the instructions sent to Philip Ludwell for guidance and direction in the management of the government. Before setting out from Virginia to enter upon the duties of the office to which he had been appointed, he asked the power to appoint new deputies and moderate the quitrents that were in arrearage, and institute a somewhat different mode of selling land from that which had been heretofore practiced in the colony. This request the proprietors generously granted him; and on arriving in the colony, he commenced to work in earnest for the establishing of peace and harmony amongst the people. Power was granted him to sell lands adjacent to town, at about ten cents an acre, and lands which were in the interior at half that price. All mines of precious stones were excepted. Of the proceeds of these, the proprietors were to remain in sole possession. Of the proceeds of all mines of baser metals, the proprietors were to have one-sixth, if given in its unwashed state, or one-tenth when refined.

When Archdale arrived in the colony, all parties were glad. Joy pervaded the hearts of the adherents of every political creed and of every religious faith. He made a congratulatory speech, and the people returned him heart-felt thanks. Among the first things that the people did after the first excitement passed away, was to petition the government to remit the quitrents which were onerous. They had been, perhaps, in most instances accumulating since the first settlement of the colony. The quitrents did not amount to much; but to most of the colonists a very little was more than rent was demanded in money.

MONEY FROM PIRATES

Most of the money which was in the colony was what was brought in by the pirates. This nefarious practice had been strenuously opposed by the proprietors, although winked at by the majority of the people. Laws had been enacted forbidding these robbers on the high seas from landing in Charles Town. By the sanction of these laws and the instructions of the proprietors, pirates had been apprehended and tried, but not condemned. We may safely conclude that for a number of years, money was exceedingly scarce in South Carolina, and that although two cents an acre of quitrent was a very trifling sum, still to those who had no money, it was more than they could pay.

The people asked that these quitrents be remitted; but Governor Archdale did not, at first, see fit to do so. This seems to have cooled down the ardor of both the governor and the people. The first parliament called by him, on his coming into the province, was dissolved after a stormy session of only a few weeks. Jonathan Armory, on behalf of himself and the people generally, petitioned the governor that another parliament of thirty members be chosen. A proclamation was forthwith issued for the selection of the members of this second parliament. The Huguenots were left out entirely. Twenty members were elected at Charles Town for Berkley county, and ten at the plantation of Captain Bristow, for Colleton county.

This treatment of the inhabitants of Craven county, who were amongst the best citizens of the province, was cruel. As we will learn in the sequel, Archdale was a man of great piety, and the wonder is that his moral nature did not prompt him to make provision for the people of Craven county, so far that they might be represented in the parliament of the colony. It may be that prudence dictated the course he pursued. Probably, he felt certain that the presence of representatives in the assembly from Craven county would only engender strife and confusion, and stir up bitter feelings. Be this as it may, when the assembly met in January, 1696, no Huguenots were in it.

QUITRENTS REMITTED

Soon after this assembly met, the remittance of the quitrents came up again. The people seem to have been determined that something should be done to lift this burden off them. On the 16th of March, 1696, a law was enacted which partially removed all grounds of complaint. In the preamble to the act, it is said that the lords proprietors, out of paternal care for the province, "have been graciously pleased to empower and commission the right, Honorable Archdale, Esq., general admiral and governor of this province, to do and act such things, with the advice and consent of three or more of their deputies, and by and with the delegates or representatives of the people, as to him and them shall seem not to conduce to the peace and welfare of the present inhabitants and to encourage others to inhabit and plant here." It was then enacted "that three years' arrears of rent shall be and is hereby remitted and forgiven to all persons which hold land by grant or patent from the lords proprietors or from any person by them empowered to grant or to sell land, * * * and that four years' rent may be and is hereby remitted and forgiven to all persons which have held lands by survey of the same." These amendments, together with others of a similar character, quieted the people at least with respect to the quitrents. At the same session that the above laws were passed, another enactment was ratified by the assembly, providing for the compensating to some extent, of the proprietors for the great expenditures which they had made for the good of the colony. In fact, if the several enactments ratified on the 16th of March, 1696, may be regarded as an index of the mind of the people, we may conclude that a very great reconciliation had taken place.

INJUSTICE TO THE INDIANS

Governor Archdale, more than some of the previous governors of the province, directed his attention to the various Indian tribes amongst which the settlers were located. The ostensible object which the proprietors had in view in planting the colony was to spread the gospel amongst the heathen. This was not the chief object, their declarations to the contrary, notwithstanding; or, if so, it was soon lost sight of,

almost entirely by both proprietors and people. Indians were reduced to slavery and put to work on the plantations of the settlers or sold to the settlements farther south. We dare not say the proprietors approved of this course in every instance; but on the contrary they were not as careful to prevent it as they were to prevent intercourse with pirates or to collect their quitrents. Captives taken in war were reduced to slavery, or otherwise ransomed by the tribe to which they belonged.

The people generally imposed upon Indians by encouraging broils and wars among the different tribes. This course was pursued for the two-fold reason that it served as a kind of protection to the colony, from the fact that so long as the Indians fought among themselves, they would leave the colonists undisturbed. This was not all. The captives taken by the successful party were brought into the colony and sold, often for toys and rum. These were either kept as laborers in the colony, or sent to Jamaica or Barbadoes and sold.

To Archdale such practices were revolting, and he set about in earnest to treat the Indians as human beings and to establish peace and friendship between them and the colony. His kind and humane treatment of the Indians was not without good results to the colony, and to settlers in various other sections of the country. The ideas of Archdale, respecting the mode of Christianizing the Indians was strange, not to say silly and unpracticable. He thought that the missionaries who were sent amongst them should, in his own language, "be well skill'd in chymistry, and some natural genius to seek the virtues of herbs, metts and minerals, etc." He seems to have thought that men who were chemist and botanist were the very kind of persons to make a favorable impression on the savages. He also advised that the children of the colonists and the Indian children be allowed to associate together. This would have been good advice if we had been assured that the white children would always have acted as teachers and the Indian children as learners; but the probability is that the opposite would have been the case. It requires no effort to descend into barbarism, but to rise from the savage state to that of Christian civilization, is in every country and at all times, rowing against the inclinations of human nature.

AMALGAMATION SANCTIONED

At a later period Lawson recommended intermarriage as the quickest and only sure way of Christianizing the savage Indians. It sounds strange to recommend a Christian woman to marry a savage man, or for a Christian man to marry a savage wife. We may say that the whole thing ended in a vague theory. No very great effort was ever made in any part of America, only by individuals, to convert the Indians.

As said once before, the first settlers of South Carolina shed as little Indian blood as any of her sister colonies; but why did they shed any at all? The first settlers brought rum with them, and they came prepared to make rum. One of the utensils they brought with them when they first came to the country was an "alembic" - a still. The Indians soon leaned to drink rum, and the rum made them perpetrate deeds of violence amongst themselves and among the settlers. During the administration of Sothell, both powder and rum were forbidden to be distributed amongst the Indians. The law was evaded then as now. A musket in the hands of the savage, whose brain was fevered by rum, was a dangerous weapon. During the administration of Archdale, an Indian was allowed a pound of powder and thirty bullets for every wolf, tiger or bear he might kill, and for every two cats. The settlers taught the Indians the use of firearms and to drink rum, the Indians taught the settlers to cultivate maize and make ash-cakes.

Installment XV
ESTIMATE OF ARCHDALE

John Archdale remained in South Carolina only a short time. His arrival in the colony was, as we have seen, on the 17th of August, 1695, and in the latter part of 1696 he returned to England. From the meagre material which has been left us, it is not easy to give a complete sketch of his life and labors. He was a Quaker by profession and, we have good reason to believe, a pious man. From his own account of his management of Carolina, he evidently was a vain man. He had a good opinion of himself and attached very great importance to his labors, and was by no means backward in expressing his opinions of himself to others. He was a weak man in this respect. He was easily puffed up by the flatteries of others. He left the colony fully convinced that he had settled all difficulties that existed on his arrival and had, by his wisdom, laid a foundation deep and broad for the future prosperity of the province. Such, too, was partially the opinion of the people. On the eve of his departure from the colony, the assembly addressed through him "to the right honorable the true and absolute lords proprietors" a paper which they are pleased to style, "The humble address and recognition of thanks by the commons, assembled at Charles Town." In this address the commons declare that by the prudent conduct and wise management of Governor Archdale, peace and prosperity seemed to be in store for the colony. This made a vivid and indelible impression on the mind of John Archdale and he felt fully convinced that all that could be desired was that his plan of government be carried out in the letter and spirit. John Archdale did many good things, but he did nothing to remove one of the main causes of contention in the colony at Charles Town. He so managed the affairs of the colony that "the conclusion of all matters," to use his own language, "ended amicably," so far as he and a part of the people were concerned; but for another part of the colony - the French Huguenots - he did nothing. The special favor for which the people were so grateful, and for which they returned thanks to the lords proprietors, was that "some arrears of rents" had been remitted. That indefinite pronominal adjective, "some" seems to indicate that the people were not even yet wholly satisfied with the rental system.

Archdale was granted extraordinary powers. He was made governor of Carolina, that is, of the whole province including what we now call North and South Carolina. He bought lands in Albemarle, in the present state of North Carolina, and some of his descendants are still in that state. In 1688, his daughter, Ann, married Emmanuel Lowe of Pasquotank county. A daughter of Ann Lowe married a man by the name of Pendleton. Mary Pendleton married Dempsey Conner. Frances Conner Blount, daughter of Dempsey Conner, was the second wife of William Hill, at one time secretary of state of North Carolina.

During the administration of Archdale, many very important events transpired. To say he had nothing to do with them would be to slander his memory; but to say that he was the only agent in bringing about these events would be doing great injustice to the memory of others. Some very important laws, which were highly beneficial to the colony, were passed. But it should be remembered that there were a number of men in the colony who thought for themselves, and were not afraid to propose anything that they thought would prove advantageous to the settlement.

It is admitted that these leaders of the people were sometimes carried headlong into measures by a blind and unreasonable prejudice. They had no love for the French, nor had they much sympathy for the Scotch. Their treatment of the first immigrants from Scotland and France was as wicked as it was unwise. Notwithstanding all this, there were men of skill and energy in the colony, and many of them had been taught lessons of great practical importance by Joseph West. The passage of many of the laws was as much the result of the mature judgment and experience of the people as the wisdom of Archdale. Giving the people what is due to them is by no means detracting from the fame of Archdale. During the time of Archdale's administration the colony received some valuable accessions. The Rev. William Hubbard wrote to Governor Archdale relative to the emigration of several families from Massachusetts to South Carolina. About the time that this correspondence between the Rev. Hubbard and Governor Archdale was in progress, a considerable number of families left Salem, Massachusetts, and came to Carolina. The particular spot to which they came, was some place in the neighborhood of Sewee Bay.

COMING OF THE PRESBYTERIANS

About the same time a very important company of emigrants came to the state from Dorchester, Massachusetts. These individuals were Puritans, originally from the southern part of England. In the year 1630, on account of the many trials to which they were subjected in consequence of their religious belief, they determined to come to the wilds of America. They came as a congregation to Massachusetts, bringing with them as their pastors the Rev. John Warham and the Rev. John Maverick. With New England colonies, the custom of bringing from England their pastor was very common. Impressed with this mode of evangelizing the world, the descendants of these same individuals, in the year 1695, about sixty-five years after the settlement had been made in Massachusetts, determined to send out a similar colony to South Carolina.

It seems that some persons from South Carolina had solicited such a thing. William Norman had gone from South Carolina to induce the Congregational churches of New England to establish such a colony in South Carolina.

The Puritans of New England were Congregationalists. In South Carolina there were Presbyterians, High Church men, and Low Church men, and Baptists.

It was customary to call all who were not High Church men Puritans. There were some individuals in South Carolina who, although Puritans or Dissenters were neither Presbyterian, Baptist nor Low Church men, but of the same persuasion of the New England Congregationalist. These individuals were desirous to have a church of their own established in the colony. William Normal was sent out to make known their desires, and on the 22nd of October, 1695, a confer-

ence of the ministers in the neighborhood was held at Dorchester, Massachusetts, and the Rev. Joseph Lord was, according to the Congregational mode, duly ordained and set apart for the work of accompanying as pastor a congregation to South Carolina.

Two small vessels were provided for their transportation. The members of this newly organized church embarked on the 5th of December, 1695, and set sail on the 14th of the same month. One vessel arrived on the 28th or 29th, whilst the other did not arrive until near the middle of January, 1696. They made their way as best they could up the Ashley River and finally found, as they thought, a favorable place for a settlement. This, in honor of the place whence they came, they called Dorchester. On perhaps the second, or it may have been the first, Sabbath after their landing, the Sacrament of the Lord's Supper was administered by Joseph Lord to this church. The place was under a large oak, which remained until within a few years to mark the precise spot.

SETTLEMENT OF DORCHESTER

At that time, Dorchester was twenty miles from any white settlement. The Westoes and Stonos were in the neighborhood. From various causes, these tribes had become bitterly opposed to the white men. Whilst this New England colony or church was building houses in which the families might settle, sentinels had to be posted in the surrounding forest to warn the laborers of the approach of hostile Indians. Notwithstanding the many difficulties which the colony had to encounter from the very beginning, and the many hardships it had to endure for a number of years, it succeeded. It was a real addition to the population of the state, and in after years the descendants added much to the first settlers of Georgia. It may be truthfully said concerning this Dorchester colony that it always furnished upright citizens - men who were ready to defend the rights of their country when these rights were threatened.

EARLIEST CHURCH ORGANIZATIONS

It has been said without good reason that this Dorchester church was the first church organized in the state of South Carolina, and that the communion which was administered to the members of it by their pastor, the Rev. Joseph Lord, was the first Sacrament of the Lord's supper which was ever administered in the state. This is, we think, hardly correct. There were several church organizations in the state before Feb.

2nd, 1696, the time that the Sacrament was first administered at Dorchester. There were at least seven churches in the state with pastors, ten years before this period. An English church in Charles Town was founded in 1683. The first pastor of this church was the Rev. Atkin Williamson, who had been in the colony for some time previous to the organizing of St. Philip's (Now St. Michael's). The house was built of cypress timber. There were three Geneva Presbyterian churches in the colony as early as 1689, or probably 1686 - one in Charles Town and one on the eastern branch of the Cooper River. The pastors of these churches were the Revs. Florent Philip Trouillart and Elias Prioleau, of the one in Charles Town and the Rev. De La Pierre of the one on Cooper River. There was also a Huguenot or Geneva Presbyterian church on the Santee, founded about the same time with the Rev. Pierre Robert for a pastor, and still another on Goose Creek, which was under the pastoral care of the Rev. Florent Philip Trouillart. This fact makes it probable that its organization was before 1696. There was also in the province what was called the Independent church or mixed Presbyterian. This was probably the first organized congregation in the colony. The Rev. Thomas Barret, who was, so far as is known, the first minister of the gospel in the colony, was in some way connected with this congregation. This church was organized not more than ten years after the arrival of the first settlers. The Baptists had a church organization in Charles Town as early as 1683. Some of the immigrants who came with Lord Cardross, and some of those who came with Joseph Blake, were Baptist. Blake himself was a Presbyterian, but his wife was a Baptist, and so was her mother, Lady Axtell.

From the close of Archdale's administration up to the time that the government passed out of the hands of the King of England, but few groups of settlers came into South Carolina. Many individuals and families came from time to time. When the colony was first settled in 1670, it is estimated that about one hundred and fifty individuals took up their abode on the banks of Ashley River. At the close of Archdale's administration, there were, according to the best authority, about seven thousand persons in the colony. When we take all things into consideration, this shows that the colony had increased very rapidly.

When Governor Archdale concluded that the affairs of the colony were properly arranged, he prepared to return to England. No difficulty occurred between him and the proprietors, but he did not wish to retain his position as governor. The difficulties and deprivations he found more than counter-balanced the honor. He appointed Thomas Harvey deputy governor of North Carolina, and Joseph Blake to the same office in South Carolina. The administration of Archdale may be justly considered as an important period in the history of the colony. Things now began to show in what direction they were drifting. The proprietors had made, through Archdale, very great concessions. They had yielded, in part, to the wishes of the people, and the people now saw clearly that the proprietors were not nearly so unfaltering in their purposes as they pretended to be at first.

GOVERNOR BLAKE

On the departure of John Archdale, Joseph Blake, as previously stated, commenced his gubernatorial career. The circumstances were auspicious of a tranquil and prosperous administration. The difficulties between the proprietors and people, some of which had been of long standing, were, if not settled to the satisfaction of all parties, so smoothed over and adjusted as to enable Blake to commence his administration without any particular prejudice against him from any quarter. There were no difficulties to be compromised or settled before he could commence a direct administration of the affairs of the colony.

There was another circumstance greatly in Governor Blake's favor. He was well and favorably known, through his father and uncle, to all the leading persons in the colony. He was not an upstart. Such being in part the surroundings of Joseph Blake, he was looked upon as the "fittest person," says Archdale, "to succeed to the government, and in which office he behaved himself to the satisfaction of the country, which he governed with equal prudence and moderation."

REVISION OF THE CONSTITUTION

When John Archdale returned to England, he reported to the other proprietors the condition of the colony. In this report he suggested certain changes which should be made in the "unalterable constitutions." A meeting of the lords proprietors was held and the matter was taken into serious consideration, and the original one hundred and twenty "laws of Carolina" or articles of the Fundamental Constitution, were reduced to forty-one. Much that was contained in the first set of Fundamental Constitutions relative to the system of nobility which the proprietors at first evidently contemplated establishing in Carolina, was left out of the last set, as they were called. No doubt, Archdale told the proprietors that it was impossible to establish in America such a government as was contemplated by the Fundamental Constitutions. The new laws which were called the "Last Fundamental Constitutions," were signed by John, Earl of Bath; Palantine, Anthony, Lord Ashley, the lord of Craven, the Lord Carteret, the Earl of Bath, Sir John Colleton, William Thornburgh, merchant, Thomas Amy, and William Thornburgh. These last Fundamental Constitutions were signed on the 11th of April, 1698. Major Daniel was entrusted with the duty of bringing these last constitutions to the colony and through the governor, Joseph Blake, presenting them to the Colonial Assembly for adoption. This was done; but the assembly, as stubborn as on former occasions, coldly saw fit to lay them on the table to be considered at some other time. The determination of the people was to adopt no laws or "Fundamental Constitutions" sent out by the proprietors. Very little more was every said about these constitutions of forty-one articles and nothing was done. They never were adopted.

MORE DISCONTENT

Notwithstanding the many favors granted by the proprietors during Archdale's administration and the many thanks returned by the people for the same, it soon became manifest that the people had not obtained all they desired. In February, 1699, "an humble address and remonstrance" was drawn up by "the House of Commons" and sent to the proprietors. In this "address" there is much flattery, some censure and no small amount of begging. The proprietors are lauded and extolled for the many favors that they had been pleased to grant the colony, and at the same time they are modestly censured because they had done, or suffered to be done, some things which were detrimental to the prosperity of the colony. They are most praised because they had sent out John Archdale as governor of the colony, and they are censured because the King of England was attempting to put in force the English navigation act and "the act for the restraining of privateers and pirates." They complained that the proprietors had, in many instances, made grants of "such great tracts of land" as to be prejudicial to the interest of the colony. In this same address many petitions are made. It was desired that no laws might be put in force except those which were passed by the consent of the Colonial Assembly, and that this assembly might have power to enact such laws as it might regard necessary for the good of the colony, and change any that were in force, prejudicial to the well being of the settlement. The proprietors replied to Governor Blake that they were astonished at him, since he was a proprietor, in suffering such a petition to be sent up. There were other petitions but none of so grave a character as that just mentioned. The proprietors were begged to entreat the King of England "to take off the duties on rice, tar, pitch and turpentine," and to grant the colonists such encouragement in the exporting of these articles as might tend to the development of the resources of the country.

TRANSFERRED TO THE CROWN

An effort had been making for some time to bring all the American colonies into closer connection with the government of England. The king's council complained to the proprietors of Carolina that the laws of England were either disobeyed or evaded by the colonists, in various particulars. To shield themselves from the blame, the proprietors censured the governors. It is evident that the proprietors were anxious to retain sole possession of the province. Any defect that might be in the management of the colony, or apparent conflict between its regulations and the laws of England, were charged to the account of the governors. Several of the proprietors had obtained a share of the vast territory embraced in the whole province of Carolina, for the trifling sum of less than fifteen hundred dollars - a paltry amount, when it is considered that it was paid for one-eighth of all the territory included between Florida and Virginia, and the Atlantic and Pacific. The territory was only settled in what is now called North and South Carolina. But there was a disposition to extend the settlement westward; and, in spite of mismanagement, the colony at Charles Town was growing. No doubt the King of England saw this, and grieved that so rich a treasure had been permitted to pass so easily, partially out of the hands of the royal family. The proprietors saw the prospects of the colony brightening, and were anxious to retain the possession of it as the king was to add it to the acquisitions of the British crown. The proprietors yielded to both the people of the province of Carolina and to the King of England. At the insistence of the crown, the proprietors were induced to appoint Nicholas Trott, attorney general of the province. One of the principal duties of Trott, in virtue of his office, was to examine all the laws of the colony, to ascertain if they were consistent with the laws of England. This may be regarded as an act done by the proprietors to secure the perpetuation of the government of the colony in their hands.

During the administration of Joseph Blake many legislative acts were made. From these we are enabled to form a tolerably correct idea of the real condition of the colony. The laws of the people may be regarded as a fair index of their social and moral character. Laws designed to punish crime show that there are lawless persons in the community, but they also show that there is a determination on the part of the rulers to cut the lawless, protect the weak and encourage justice and equity. Judging from the character of the laws enacted and re-enacted during the administration of Blake, we may safely conclude that the colony of South Carolina was at that time in a healthy moral condition - at least as much so as could be expected, when all the surrounding circumstances are taken into consideration.

Among the first enactments made, was one relative to false or defective measures or weights. This shows that the colonists were commencing to trade in earnest, and to merchandise in an upright way. David Maybank was appointed by the assembly, on the 5th day of December, 1696, surveyor of all weights and measures used in the colony. All persons engaged in buying and selling in the colony were required, within two months, to bring their weights and measures to the office of David Maybank, that they might be tested by the English standards. Those found correct were to be marked thus **** (four stars), and those incorrect were to be immediately burned, broken or destroyed. The law forbid, with heavy penalties annexed, any persons using two sets of measures or weights - one set to be used when any commodity was bought, and another set to be used when a sale was effected.

At the same time, a law was enacted designed to increase the number of inhabitants and favor those coming into the colony to settle. In this enactment of the assembly, it was provided that no persons coming into the colony could be sued or imprisoned for debt during the period of two years after their arrival. No doubt the assembly meant well; but such a law is and always must be, unrighteous. No court or legislative body has any right to interfere between creditor and debtor. If any compromises are to be made or favors shown, the persons themselves, and no one else, have the inalienable right to make the negotiations. This act for the relief of debtors was repealed by the King of England.

To prevent vessels coming into Charles Town from being injured from a want of knowledge of the harbor by the officers, pilots were appointed by the assembly to take charge of all vessels, and conduct them into the harbor safely. From this law we may learn that only very small vessels could enter. The pilots were not required to take charge of any vessel that drew more than nine feet of water. Up to this time the greater number of vessels entered the harbor through what they called the "North Channel," but measures were taken to learn the capacity of the "South Channel" and to encourage shipmasters to enter through it. These, together with may other laws, show that the settlers were beginning to see what was for their advantage.

RELIGIOUS PERSECUTION

The most important enactment of this period was "an act for the making aliens free in this part of the province, and for granting liberty of conscience to all Protestants." The preamble to the act is worthy of note. In the colony, at this period, there were persons from many nations of Europe. The preamble to this act referred to, gives us a brief history of the causes which had brought these men who "could not speak the English language," to the colony, and also of the manner in which they had conducted themselves, "Whereas, persecution for religion has forced some aliens to this colony." This was one reason why some were in the colony. Persecution on account of religion brought to the colony the main body of the first settlers on the Santee, on Goose Creek, on the eastern branch of Cooper River, on Sewee River, and on Sewee bay. There was another cause why so many aliens had come into the province. This is thus stated in the preamble: "The trade and fertility of this colony has encouraged others to resort to this colony." The fame of South Carolina had spread all over the world. It was regarded as the garden spot of the New World. The preamble also states the general character of the alien immigrants. "All have given good testimony of their humble duty and loyalty to his Majesty and the Crown of England, and of their fidelity to the true and absolute lords and proprietors of this province, and of their obedience to their laws, and their good affection to the inhabitants thereof, and by their industry, diligence and trade have very much enriched and advanced this colony and settlement."

In view of these facts all Protestant aliens were, by and act of the assembly, ratified on the 10th of March 1697, made free as those born in England, those who heretofore lived in a kind of dread lest their children would not inherit their property were put to rest on this subject. The children of aliens could inherit property the same as the children of English parents. All

Christians (Baptists excepted) which were then in the colony, or might in subsequent time come into the colony, were allowed to enjoy full, free and undisturbed liberty of conscience. The provisos were that the public peace be not disturbed, and that all aliens of age "do sincerely promise and swear that they will be faithful and bear true allegiance to his majesty, King William." This enactment was in perfect harmony with the charter granted by Charles the Second, and with the desires of the proprietors.

TERRIBLE SCOURGE OF SMALLPOX

The administration of Joseph Blake was peaceful and prosperous. It was not, however, without its share of calamities. In 1697 the smallpox raged with dreadful fatality in the colony. Near four hundred persons were carried off by this loathsome disease. A fire broke out in Charles Town in February, 1696, which destroyed a vast amount of property. About one hundred and forty thousand dollars worth of property was consumed and fifty families left without a shelter. The fire was preceded by a terrible hurricane which swept with unbridled fury over sea and land. Death and destruction marked its track. These visitations of Providence were closed by the appearance of yellow fever. It spread with fearful rapidity, and multitudes died. These calamities, together with the raids of the pirates upon the commerce of the colony, no doubt had much to do in allaying the spirit of civil strife. In the ravages of wind and wave, fire and disease, the people forgot their old and unfounded prejudice.

INSTALLMENT XVII
LOOKING OUT FOR GOLD

The charter granted by Charles the Second to the proprietors of Carolina required one fourth of all the gold and silver, which might at any time be found in the territory, to be given to the king, "his heirs and successors." At an early period in the history of the state - long before the granting of the charter - some attempts had been made to discover gold and silver mines. On the Savannah, some digging had been done; but little if any of these precious metals had been discovered. After the settlement of the state there was manifested some interest in the mineral resources of the country, but the various troubles through which the people had to pass, and the many difficulties by which they were surrounded, prevented them from devoting much attention to the subject. The people were generally so engaged that they had no time to make any extended research, yet the opinion prevailed that in some places in the territory there was gold. The Spaniards in their march through a corner of the state in 1538, reported that they saw gold, and it is thought that, notwithstanding the hurried character of their march, they actually dug for gold. It is probable they found little, if any, gold or silver in South Carolina. They may have been more successful in Georgia, and the territory west of the Savannah River.

PROSPECTING ON THE QUIET

During the administration of Joseph Blake, an effort was made, rather in a clandestine or secret way, to search for mines of the precious metals. Edward Loughton and David Maybank, carpenters who came into the colony about 1682, went over to England some time during the time that Joseph Blake was governor, and made an impression on the minds of their relations by the name of Green and Cutler. All the information Loughton and Maybank seem to have possessed respecting the existence of gold or silver mines in Carolina, they obtained from the Indian traders. Cutler and his wife came to Charles Town in January, 1698. They brought with them a stock of goods, and Mrs. Cutler opened a milliner's shop in the town. In this gold hunting enterprise, the Earl of Bridgewater, the Earl of Pembroke, Edward Randolph and the Chancellor of the Exchequer, and many other individuals of position in the English government, became intensely interested. A correspondence was begun between Randolph, who was in Charles Town at the time, and the Earl of Bridgewater. James Moore, who was afterward governor, took an active part in this enterprise. The facts in the case are few and of little importance but the circumstances connected with the undertaking are very significant.

THE KING WAS INTERESTED

Edward Randolph had been sent out early in the administration of Joseph Blake, by the English Board of Trade, for the purpose of supervising commerce of the English colonies in North America and the West Indies. He administered the oath of office to Joseph Blake, and remained for several years in South Carolina. He seems to have been especially anxious to promote the interest of the king. The correspondence between him and the Earl of Bridgewater, and also his conference with Cutler, were kept a profound secret, so far as the lords proprietors of the province were concerned. So soon as James Moore heard of the plans for searching for gold, he wrote to Thomas Cutler. In this transaction, Moore, as will be clearly seen in the sequel, betrayed the trust that was reposed in him by the proprietors, and showed that he was capable of double dealing. He was secretary of the province and deputy of Sir John Colleton. Yet he hesitated not to join heartily in a conference, the avowed object of which was to put the mineral resources of the territory, whatever they might be, under the control of the king. We have little doubt but the real object of the whole combination was to cheat and swindle both king and proprietors out of any gold and silver that might be discovered in the province. Clearly, it was the purpose of Green, Cutler, Moore and, in one word, of all the company to make the King of England pay all the expenses the company might be at in searching for gold. The king seems to have gone into the enterprise with considerable zeal. He advanced to some of the party two thousand dollars and promised another thousand. The facts which gave rise to the enterprise were obtained by Loughton and Maybank from Richard Tranter. James Moore also furnished some facts, but not of much importance. The gold region was, according to current reports, about one hundred and seventy miles distant from Charles Town in the regions of the Appalachian mountains. Moore, in his letter to Cutler, says that in the year 1691, he made a journey to these mountains and, whilst on the journey, he found gold ore at seven different places. These specimens he numbered and sent to England to be tested. Two of the specimens proved to be very rich, one indifferent, and the other four of no value.

Moore informed Cutler that he could, with the aid of the journal which he kept while on the journey referred to, find each of the localities from which the specimens were taken. Moore seems to have been very sanguine in his expectations. "I think" he says, "the workings of these mines will be of a vast advantage to the crown of England, and the occasion of enriching and strengthening this, his majesty's weak plantation." This is strange language for a deputy of one of the lords proprietors to use. It plainly shows that Moore had some sinister end in view. It is, as we shall see, in keeping with his future history.

TREASURES IN THE MOUNTAINS

Richard Tranter was a very extensive trader amongst the Indians. He could speak the language of several tribes, and acted as a kind of factor to the Indians. Another individual by the name of Jean Courture, who also had made himself thoroughly acquainted with the language of nine tribes of Indians, and had traveled beyond the Appalachian mountains more than three hundred miles, was engaged by Loughton and Tranter as an interpreter. Courture disclosed the fact that he had, in some rivulets beyond these mountains, picked up four pounds of gold. In the same locality he found a number of blue stones which he believed to be lapis lazuli. One of his expeditions gave him as "many pearls of good size as filled both his hands." Some traders, as he believed, seduced his Indian companions, and the one who carried his box of jewels ran away. On arriving at Charles Town, Courture was imprisoned by the governor, but released on his paying five hundred dollars. "The governor," Courture said, "endeavored by threats, to force him to reveal the locality where the gold was discovered; but not being able to extort from him the fact, he then imposed upon him a heavy fine."

So soon as the facts in reference to the search for gold, under the patronage of the King of England, was communicated to Courture, he entered into the scheme with all his heart. A company of explorers was formed. The names of the party, at least of the leading spirits - were Jean Courture, John Smith, David Maybank, Solomon Legare and Henry Netherton. The scheme thus concerted, did not on account of two circumstances, succeed. One Good, who was connected with the party, was drowned by falling into the Savannah amongst the rocks, and James Moore dealt unfair and made false promises.

TROTT GIVES TROUBLE

The peace and comfort of the last days of Blake's administration, were disturbed by Nicholas Trott. The precise time that Trott came into the colony, we are not able to say. On the 5th of February, 1697, the lords proprietors constituted him, during pleasure, attorney and advocate general of the province south of Cape Fear. His instructions are dated March the 8th, 1698. At the same time, instructions were sent to Joseph Blake, the governor, enjoining upon him to give Trott all countenance and encouragement. It would appear that Trott arrived at Charles Town in the spring of 1698. The history of Nicholas Trott is intimately connected with the history of South Carolina during this and the subsequent twenty years. He was a native of the city of London, and had at one period of his life been governor of the Bahama Islands. When sent to Charles Town he was, by the proprietors, clothed with very extensive and great powers. All the laws proposed by the assembly had to be examined by him before finally passed. He had authority to take entries of all ships either coming into Charles Town or going out. All legal matters of great importance were under his control. According to some historians, it would appear that Nicholas Trott was the first chief justice of the state of South Carolina. This is an error. Edward Bohun was, by the proprietors, constituted chief justice on the 22nd of May, 1698. Bohun did not live long. He and Samuel Marshall, the pastor of the Episcopal church in Charles Town, together with many of the provincial officers and one half of the members of the general assembly, were carried off in the fall of 1698 by yellow fever. When Trott became chief justice, it is not easy to say. It is probable that as soon as Bohun died, Trott was by the governor appointed to fill his place. Provision was made by the proprietors for filling the place of Chief Justice Bohun in the event he should die. It is probable that the attorney general was made Chief Justice at this time, and continued up to 1719.

QUARREL IN COUNCIL

Trott was, beyond all controversy, a man of great learning, no small share of ambition, and very little stability. He was on all sides of the questions of the day, and really on no side. He managed to gain the good esteem of the populace, and in the fall of 1690 he was chosen a member of the general assembly.

During the conference of some of the committee, a serious difficulty took place between Governor Blake and Trott. The governor, as he thought, was grossly insulted. The conference was broken up. The whole affair was brought before the assembly and Trott managed, by his shrewdness, to have a resolution passed by the assembly, "that any manager appointed by this house have freedom of speech." The governor had Trott suspended from exercising the functions of the office of attorney general, because he had in several instances acted with partiality. This was a serious state of things. In the midst of this commotion, Governor Blake died. Trott did not find it a difficult task to persuade the next assembly to remove his suspension and restore him to office.

INSTALLMENT XVIII

GOVERNOR MORTON

On the death of Joseph Blake, in 1700, Joseph Morton, the oldest landgrave, was, by a majority of the deputies of the proprietors, elected governor. The intentions of the Grand Council were thwarted, and Morton never entered upon the duties of the office. In the colony there was a man by the name of James Moore. This Moore was a restless character, hopelessly involved in debt. Without extraordinary endowments, he was ambitious, reckless and unscrupulous. Governed in his acts not by principle, but by policy, he was ready to do anything or espouse the cause of any party, provided there was a slight hope that such a course on his part would retrieve his ruined fortune or exalt him to position. Moore was one of those strangely constituted men who are never in their element unless opposing some measure or some person. Every time that Moore's name occurs in the previous history of the colony, it is connected with some opposition movement. He was not always on the wrong side; for he was, no doubt, one of those vacillating creatures that readily unites with any party, and as readily quits it.

The history of James Moore and Nicholas Trott is intimately associated with all the events of the colony, from the time of which we are speaking up to the time that it passed out of the hands of the proprietors into the hands of the crown of England; a period of nearly twenty years. Both were unprincipled and designing men, and were capable of instigating others to perpetrate base deeds.

USURPATION OF MOORE

When the majority of the deputies of the proprietors, in accordance with the constitutional regulations of the colony, chose Joseph Morton as governor, James Moore, also one of the deputies, opposed the choice, on the ground that Morton had been commissioned Judge of Admiralty by the King of England. All the previous history of Moore proves that this was a vile subterfuge. It was true that Morton was Judge of Admiralty, and had been advanced to this position of honor by the king; but this could not, in itself, disable him from exercising the office of governor of the colony. Neither the Charter nor the Fundamental Constitutions of the province made any provision for any such office as Morton held. The necessity of such an office was admitted by all. Admitting that it was unsafe in any individual in the colony to hold office at the same time under the proprietors and under the King of England - or rather to hold two offices at the same time - one under the proprietary government, and the other under the Crown of England; James Moore was the last man in the world that should have objected to such a thing. He had, but a short time before this, been negotiating with the King of England to work the mines of the province for the promotion of the interest of his majesty. So secret had this negotiation in reference to the working of the mines been conducted, that it is very probable that few, if any, of the colonists, except those immediately concerned in the scheme, knew anything about it. Had they known this fact, it is reasonable to suppose that they would have rebutted Moore's argument against Morton with his own conduct. The only reason why James Moore did not hold a commission from the King of England was that the English Board of Trade did not see fit to give him one.

The unblushing audacity of Moore prevailed and he, we may say, thrust himself upon the people as a governor. He commenced his administration with a kind of political fraud and deception, and its continuation was marked by a series of outrages seldom equaled in the annals of government. In fact, the commencement of James Moore's administration marks the beginning of the downfall of the proprietary government in South Carolina.

A few individuals, amongst whom was Nicholas Trott, constituted themselves into a kind of oligarchal rules and inflicted upon the people trouble of mind, suffering of body, and intolerable expense. Sometimes these self constituted managers of the affairs of the colony were agreed amongst themselves, and sometimes they were not. To these restless and evil-designing spirits, it was a matter of the utmost importance to have the members of the Grand Council, and also of the Assembly, either to think as they thought, or to be wholly under their control. In November, 1701, a new assembly was chosen. All kinds of frauds were practiced. Persons, in every sense disqualified by law to vote, were taken to the polls and voted. Strangers, aliens, negroes and mulattoes were not only permitted to vote, but solicited to do so. In this fraudulent way some "men of no sense and credit" were chosen members of the assembly. Those who opposed such a course were rudely treated by the frantic mob which espoused the side of the governor and his party. At this time Lord Granville was Palatine, and he sanctioned the course of Moore, first by confirming him in the office of governor, and then by treating with contempt any petition that was sent up by the people of the colony asking for relief from the high handed measures of the governor.

INVESTIGATION FRUSTRATED

Notwithstanding the fact that Moore had succeeded in having several individuals chosen members of the assembly, who were wholly under his control, still the majority of the assembly was true as steel. When the assembly convened, petitions were sent up from various quarters, but especially from Colleton county, asking an investigation of the official conduct of the sheriff, who had acted as manager at the precinct where the illegal votes were cast. To prevent an investigation, Moore by a wise stroke of policy, prorogued the assembly. Previous to this, Moore had attempted to have a bill passed by the assembly, which was designed to give him, individually, a monopoly of the Indian trade. The object of Moore, in securing the office of governor, was to repair his ruined fortune and to amass a large estate. This purpose he steadily kept in mind.

TROTT ANTAGONIZES MOORE

By some freak of fortune, Nicholas Trott opposed this bill of monopolizing the Indian trade, and it was defeated. The probability is that had Trott been a sharer in its gains he would not have opposed it; but since Governor Moore alone was to be benefited by the passage of the proposed bill, Trott opposed it, and mainly by his opposition it was defeated. During the session of 1701, but few laws were enacted, and none of very great importance to the prosperity of the colony. The time of the members was consumed in angry and excited debates. There was one law ratified on the 1st of March, 1701, which serves to confirm the truthfulness of one of the traditions of the country. It is well known to all the old inhabitants of the state that less than a century ago, the country was full of wild horses. Such was the case within the recollection of some persons still living. In Fairfield county there is a stream which is now known by the local name of Horse River. The original name of the stream was Horse-pen Branch. This name was given to the stream because the farmers constructed pens near it for the purpose of catching wild horses.

THE FIRST HORSES

Now, the question may be asked how did the wild horses get into the country? It is well known that when the colony was first planted at Charles Town, there were neither hogs, horses, nor cows in the territory. Horses were brought from the northern colonies; but especially from Virginia. Great numbers of these animals were, during the few last years of the seventeenth century, driven from Virginia to Charles Town. Some were sold to the planters; but the larger number of them were turned loose in the swamps. Here they were permitted to remain, summer and winter, and in these swamps they increased in numbers, and in a short time many of them became so wild as never to be recovered by their owners. As the low country became more densely populated and the swamps drained, the wild horses as well as other animals, made their way into the up-country. The northern colonies, and especially Virginia, made South Carolina a grazing ground. Any and every kind of horses were brought into the colony, and turned out to graze. This had a tendency to increase the number of horses, but to injure the quality. The planters paid little attention to breeding, either fine or serviceable horses, but depended upon what was called "woods colts."

To prevent stock being driven into the state, and "for the better encouragement of more serviceable horses to be bred amongst us," the assembly passed a law that twenty-five dollars should be paid for each horse brought by land into the colony.

It is probable that this had the effect to lessen the number of horses brought into the settlement about Charles Town; but it did not wholly prevent the practice.

We find that forty years after this, the practice of driving horses from Virginia to South Carolina still continued. Richard Kirkland came to Fairfield county about 1745. He came from Virginia, and settled on the Wateree, in the eastern part of Fairfield county. His descendants, at least many of them, still form a part of the population of the county. He was a man of considerable wealth for that time, and brought with him a large amount of stock, amongst which were fifty brood horses.

CHANGED LANDSCAPE OF THE UP-COUNTRY

Whilst this subject is under consideration, we cannot refrain from remarking that the general features of the up-country have been very greatly changed in the last one hundred and twenty-five years. At that time, according to reliable traditions, there were but few large trees in the forests, and the country was during the summer covered with clover and wild pease. Many of the branch bottoms and some of the ridges were covered with canes. Stock of all kinds became fat during the summer, and suffered but comparatively little during the winter. A large portion of Abbeville county was, when first settled, a cane-brake and all the Wateree section was covered with red clover; and in some sections it still remains in spite of the raids made upon the forest by the devotees of cotton. These facts, together with others of a similar kind, which might be presented, accounts for the practice of the Virginians driving their horses down into South Carolina; and also for the fact that there were many in the country shortly after its first settlement.

TRICKS OF THE GOVERNOR

We now return to the main subject. In April, 1702, Governor Moore again summoned the assembly. So soon as they met, the members concluded that it was to their interest to adjourn until the 5th of May. The reason assigned for this was that since most of the members were planters, and April was the month for planting the crops, it was important for them to be at home superintending their farms. On the 5th of May they met, and Governor Moore abused them for adjourning, charging them with selfishness. To retaliate, he prolonged the assembly till August. It is clear that bitter feelings existed. The assembly had lost all confidence in the governor, if indeed, it every had any; and the governor was bitterly enraged by the independent course of the assembly.

To increase the mutual distrust, it was currently reported that, at the suggestion of Robert Daniel, the governor had determined to declare martial law. This infuriated the assembly, and but for a shrewd device of the governor, something in keeping with their feelings might have been done. For several reasons Governor Moore determined to make an attack on St. Augustine. The real object of the governor was, in all probability, to capture Indians and reduce them to slaves and plunder the Spanish towns.

CAMPAIGN AGAINST THE SPANIARDS

No friendly feeling existed between the colonists and the Spanish; and no doubt Moore thought that by proposing to the assembly an expedition against St. Augustine, he could divert their minds from the frauds which had been practiced in the recent election. The expedition was proposed, and with closed doors the assembly began the discussion. All those in the colony who knew anything about the fortifications of St. Augustine were summoned before the assembly and asked to communicate all they knew. This was just on the eve of the breaking out of "Queen Anne's War" or the war of the Spanish succession. It seems that when Moore proposed the expedition against St. Augustine, nothing was known in America about this war between England and Spain, and that the assembly opposed the governor's scheme until it was ascertained that war was declared.

Governor Moore had at least a plausible pretext for undertaking this military expedition. The Spanish of St. Augustine had, at various times, made unprovoked attacks upon the settlers in South Carolina. In

1686 they came to Port Royal with three galleys and, in a most inhuman way, destroyed the infant colony planted at that point by Lord Cardross. From thence they proceeded to North Edisto, plundered and burnt everything before them, and carried away a number of prisoners, amongst whom were the brother and brother-in-law of Governor Morton. Their ravages upon the people were stopped by a storm. Two of their galleys were blown to the shore and rendered useless. On one of these vessels was the captive, Morton, in chains. So soon as the Spanish saw that the vessel could not be relieved, they set it on fire and left Morton bound. Both were consumed. This was barbarously cruel.

SPANIARDS COME AGAIN

In the early part of 1702, another design was formed against the colony in South Carolina by the Spaniards of St. Augustine. An army of nine hundred Appalachee Indians were raised by them and actually on its march before the settlers learned that the Spaniards had any intention of attacking the colony. The Creek Indians, who were on amicable terms with the whites of South Carolina, made the discovery and communicated the fact to the traders. These traders collected as speedily as they could, five hundred Creek Indians and set out to meet the invaders in the territory now belonging to the state of Georgia, on the Flint River. Late in the evening both armies met on the banks of the river and camped for the night, expecting to begin the attack early in the morning. It was a custom amongst the Indian tribes to commence battle early in the morning - long before sun rise. The traders and Creek Indians, aware of this fact, had recourse to a stratagem which succeeded in securing them a complete victory, and in driving the invaders back. Long before day, the traders and Creek Indians got up and kindled their camp fires and then retired into the surrounding forest. Their blankets and camp stuff were all arranged as if they were still reposing in camp. Soon the Appalachees, led on by the Spaniards, raised the war whoop, and rushed into the camp of the Creeks. They found nothing but empty blankets. The bewilderment was of short duration, for the ambushed traders and Creeks poured in a deadly volley of arrows and bullets, which soon put the enemy to flight. It is true that these invaders did not reach the settlement, but evidently the destruction of the South Carolina colony was its design.

SLAVES OF THE INDIANS

It is not certain what part Governor Moore took in the military expedition which resulted in the battle of Flint River. The probability is that he knew nothing about it until after it was ended. One of the charges brought against the governor, by a respectable number of the most worthy inhabitants of the colony, was his barbarous treatment of the Indians. Whether Governor Moore introduced into the colony the traffic of Indians or not, one thing is certain, he practiced it to an extent and in a manner unprecedented in the history, it would seem, of any of the colonies in America. Before his time, Indians captured in war were reduced to slavery, and in some instances they were sent off and sold into bondage. In some instances victorious tribes brought those whom they had captured from the enemies, and sold them to the colonists for a trifle. Governor Moore, however, instituted a new system of reducing the Indian tribes; or rather, he adopted a plan for securing slaves, different from any heretofore practiced in the colony. He sent out parties to capture Indians. The object was to secure slaves for his own use. The Indians from whom he was most solicitous to make captives and thus reduce them to bondage, were friends of the Spaniards and consequently, the enemies of the English. The Appalachees were the allies of the Spanish and the Creeks of the English. This being the case, the two tribes were hostile to each other. Governor Moore sent out a party of his minions under the direction of Anthony Dodsworth and Robert MacKoone, to capture, for the purpose of making slaves of them, as many Appalachees as they could. In this vile work, they were assisted by the Creeks.

This band of kidnappers had made their way on one of their scouting expeditions out of the present limits of the state, when they were apprised of the approach of nine hundred Appalachees under the direction of the Spaniards, to make an attack upon the colony at Charles Town. Such being the facts in the case, we are prepared to say that, bad as the Spaniard were, they sometimes were not wholly in the wrong. No one can censure the Spaniards for defending their allies.

This Indian traffic of Governor Moore is the worst feature of his history. No palliation can be offered for it. All the best men of the colony, at the time, declared it was "unjust and barbarous in itself, and will in all probability draw upon us an Indian war with all the dreadful consequences of it."

THE PRETEXT OF A WAR

The attempted invasion of the colony by the Spaniards and Appalachees, in the early part of 1702, cannot be offered as even a pretext for the expedition against St. Augustine in the latter part of the same year. Neither can it be said that it grew out of the fact that war had been declared by the English government against Spain. The fact is, it was an expedition planned by James Moore and undertaken by him for the sole purpose of plunder. Neither the advancement of the English government nor the prosperity of the colony in South Carolina were consulted. The Spanish of St. Augustine had never, it is true, respected any treaties of peace entered into between the home government and that of England; and, besides being the first to make an attack upon the colony at Charles Town, and had ever acted the part of depredators upon the colony and inflamers of the worst passions of the Indians against it; but the expedition planned and undertaken by Governor Moore against St. Augustine, was in no sense a strategical movement to avenge these wrongs. The impression was made upon the minds of the assembly that the object of the expedition was to maintain the security of the colony. It had been discovered that St. Augustine was in such a condition as to render it probable that it could be taken with comparative ease.

TRICKY AND UNSCRUPULOUS

The people were greatly incensed at Governor Moore on account of the manner in which the election of 1701 had been conducted. In order to becloud their minds and thus screen his fraudulent conduct from an investigation; and at the same time oppressed with debts, and withal of an avaricious disposition, his fertile brain devised an expedition against St. Augustine.

Although the matter was debated in low tones and with closed doors, it was not kept a secret from the Spaniards. They sent to Havana for aid, and in the meantime busily employed themselves in removing to the castle all that was valuable in the town. In this stronghold they stored away a sufficient amount of food for four months.

The assembly in order to meet the expenses of the war, levied a tax of two thousand pounds - about ten thousand dollars - on real and personal estates, and of and from the profits and the revenues of the inhabitants. The ships in the harbor were seized for the purpose of conveying the troops. Port Royal was fixed upon as the place of general rendezvous. An army of twelve thousand men was collected, one half of whom were Indians. At first Col. Robert Daniel was made commander-in-chief of the expedition; but for some reason this order was changed, and Governor Moore was assigned to this post of honor and Col. Daniel made second in command. Col. Daniel entered into the affair with all his soul and was a brave man and skillful officer.

In September, 1702, the troops assembled at Port Royal, and the final arrangements were made for the grand expedition. Col. Daniel, with a part of the troops, took the inland route, whilst Governor Moore, with the remainder, proceeded by sea. On his way, Daniel took the two Spanish villages, St. John's and St. Mary's. On arriving at St. Augustine, he boldly attacked the town and took it. This was comparatively an easy task, for the inhabitants immediately retired to the castle. Governor Moore had not yet arrived; but coming up the next day, commenced without delay, a vigorous siege of the castle. This fort was, at that time, perhaps one of the strongest fortifications in North America.

OLDEST AMERICAN TOWN

St. Augustine is the oldest town in North America, having been laid out by the Spaniards in the latter part of the year 1565. Consequently, at the time of the expedition, it had been built one hundred and thirty-seven years. The Spaniards had two objects in fortifying it with some care. The defending of St. Augustine was equivalent to maintaining their claim to Florida; and further, the town served as a kind of light-house to the fleets passing through the gulf of Mexico and along the coast of Florida. The castle was a square fort constructed of soft stone with four bastions. The curtain was about sixty yards in length; the parapet nine feet thick; the rampart twenty feet high, casemented underneath for lodgings and arched over. The town itself was not fortified. The castle was depended upon almost entirely in case of an attack. At the time of which we are speaking, St. Augustine was a kind of military post. In the town a number of regular troops were stationed by the Spanish government, and the citizens were all registered and enrolled as a kind of militia. They received soldiers' pay and depended entirely upon this pay for a support. Most of the inhabitants were mulattoes, and were a lazy, trifling set, who were ready at any time to engage in any plundering expedition that might be gotten up. They engaged in no kind of trade, nor even in agriculture; but whenever the pay granted them by the Spanish government was insufficient to meet their wants, they supplied the deficit by plundering their neighbors. This accounts for the fact that they had no regard for any treaties which might be entered into between the Spanish and any other government.

BEFORE ST. AUGUSTINE

So soon as Governor Moore landed his troops he commenced entrenching himself. The town was wholly in his hands; but from the fact that his artillery was light, he made but little progress in getting possession of the castle. After the siege had lasted about a month, Governor Moore discovered that, with his present ordinance, it would be impossible for him to get possession of the stronghold. With this conviction firmly established in his mind, he started an agent to Jamaica for bombs and heavier artillery than he had. This agent, for reasons not well known, did not go to Jamaica, but returned to Charles Town. It is very probable that the individual sent on the business did not enter fully into the spirit of the governor with respect to the expedition. Old Mixon says the reason the commander of the sloop, which was to bring the mortars and bombs from Jamaica, returned to Carolina, was "out of fear of treachery."

Growing impatient, Col. Daniel volunteered to go to Jamaica after the desired ordnance. During his absence, two small Spanish vessels appeared in sight, and Governor Moore became panic-stricken. One of the vessels had twenty-two guns and the other sixteen. The valiant Governor Moore never waited one moment to prepare for either further attack or defense. He immediately burnt his ships, and hastened with all possible speed, to return to Carolina. Sometime after, Col. Daniel returned from Jamaica with ordnance and shells, and found to his utter astonishment that the siege was raised and Governor Moore gone. Col. Daniel narrowly escaped being captured. Fortunately for him he fell in with Admiral Whetstone, by whom he was convoyed into Charles Town.

Thus ended the military part of the expedition against St. Augustine. The town was burned, but the inhabitants were not captured; and the reputation of Governor Moore, as a military man, was not established. He so conducted himself as to be charged by many as imbecile and cowardly. His retreat was so precipitate at first as to resemble a rout. The vessels which had conveyed the troops that were under the command of Col. Daniel were left at St. John's. So soon as the two Spanish ships appeared in sight, Governor Moore made for these with all possible speed, leaving all his artillery and stores to fall into the hands of the Spaniards. Arratomakaw, king of one of the Indian tribes, commanded the Indian forces. As soon as he arrived at one of the vessels, he determined to rest. Governor Moore was still uneasy, and urged Arratomakaw to hasten up his braves and make good his escape. The brave chief told him he might go if he saw fit; but as for himself, he was determined to remain at that point until his men had arrived.

EXPEDITION A FAILURE

Very little blood was shed in this expedition. Only two men were lost; but it cost the colony an enormous amount of money. No one except Governor Moore derived any advantage from the expedition against St. Augustine, and it cost the colony the enormous sum of thirty thousand dollars, and filled the minds of the people with bitter animosities.

The headquarters of Governor Moore whilst conducting the siege was the Roman Catholic church. This, as is always the case with such churches, was richly furnished. Hasty and precipitate as was the retreat of Moore, he did not neglect to strip the church of all its plate. In this consisted his gain. Arriving at Charles Town, he felt that he was at least a richer man than he was when he left. To some extent he felt that this plate compensated him for his inglorious campaign of a few months.

During the time Governor Moore had gone on his St. Augustine expedition, the assembly was prorogued. Soon after his return it was convened, and ways and means devised for paying the expenses of the expedition. Strange as it may seem, the people, either because they felt that their governor had disgraced them or because war actually existed between England and Spain, desired to engage in another expedition for the subjugation of St. Augustine, Pensacola, and other strongholds of the Spanish. A vessels was, by the assembly, offered to Col. Daniel that he might scour the coast of Florida. So zealous were the members of the assembly, that communication was held with Admiral Whetstone, informing him that the colony would furnish an English ship with provisions if it would engage in the same work. Col. Daniel, having been taught an important lesson by his past experience, did not accept the offer so generously made him by the assembly and the honor was conferred upon Captain William Rhett.

STRIFE BETWEEN GOVERNOR AND ASSEMBLY

During the time that the assembly, laboring under great excitement, was devising and planning these visionary schemes of again invading the Spanish dominions, committees of investigation and committees on account were busily at work. Day after day they worked, and still asked to be indulged.

At last a bill was proposed for raising twenty thousand dollars, in addition to the ten thousand already levied. This astonished the people. It was not until that moment that they learned the cost of war. About the same time a bill for regulating the elections in the colony was passed in the assembly and sent to the Grand Council for approval. The governor and his council treated this bill with the greatest possible contempt. It was not so much as read over. This insult was resented by many of the best members of the assembly leaving the house. The majority of the house were good men who studied the interests of the people, and had the prosperity of the colony at heart. A small minority were nothing but the tools of the governor. On the next day the members who had withdrawn returned and declared their willingness to sit in the assembly, provided the rest would unite with them in asserting their rights. One half of the members had protested against the proceedings of the governor, and others would have protested, but were prevented from doing so. No sooner had the members, who had left on the day previous, entered the house, than they were loaded with abuse. The governor joined with those members of the assembly who were said to be "of no credit and no sense," in scurrilously abusing the oldest and best men in the colony. The thing did not end in vile epithets and empty threats. The governor commenced to treat the multitude. Inflamed by liquor and encouraged by the governor, his tools commenced a work of infamy and shame which was kept up for several days. John Ashe, a member of the assembly, was beaten in the streets by a drunken crowd and forced to rush into the bed room of a friend. The house in which he took refuge was surrounded, and at last, under false pretenses, he was induced to come out, when he was seized and dragged on board of Captain William Rhett's ship and threatened to be hanged, sent to Jamaica, or sent off and placed on some uninhabited island and there left to perish. Col. George Dearsby drew his sword on Thomas Smith, who was an old settler, a landgrave, and had at one time been governor of the colony. Captain William Rhett beat Edmund Bellinger, a justice of the peace, over the head because he attempted to restore order in the town. Neither age nor sex was respected. Private houses were broken open and private apartments entered and deeds of horrid cruelty perpetuated. During all this time Governor Moore was either a silent spectator or drinking and carousing with the infuriated rabble. Petition after petition was sent him by the insulted and injured people, begging and entreating him, as governor, to put a stop to the riot. The only reply they got was, "that is the business of a justice of the peace."

THE FIRST POST OFFICE

James Moore became governor of South Carolina by the practice of fraud and deceit, and he so discharged the duties of that high office as to be neither honorable to himself nor profitable to the province. Although the official head of the colony, and the acknowledged leader of a clan, he is still by no means to be regarded as a true representative of the people; nor are his hasty and inconsiderate acts to be regarded as the acts of the people. He and his party although in the ascendancy were by no means in the majority. There are many evidences that in spite of the party which he represented, the colony still continued to advance in civilization and increase in numbers. The majority of the assembly were earnest in their efforts to promote peace, to advance the welfare and increase the comforts of those whom they represented. As an evidence of this, a post office was established in Charles Town, and Edward Bourne appointed postmaster. In 1698, a law was enacted that the masters of all ships coming into the province should deliver all letters which might have been entrusted to their care to Francis Fidling and to no one else. Whilst this enactment of 1698 must have conduced much to the convenience of the people, still, it was not contemplated by it to establish a post office; but was designed rather for the security of the province. Fidling was required to make a list of all the letters and packages which came into his hands, and to keep this list in some public place. On delivering a letter or package, he was required to write the name of the person to whom it was delivered, opposite the name of the individual to whom the letter or package was addressed. For the delivery of each letter or package, Fidling was to receive six and a quarter cents; and in each instance that he failed to discharge his duty faithfully, he was to forfeit ten dollars.

The act, ratified September 10, 1702, was to all intents and purposes an act to establish a good general post office. This is evident from the preamble which states that "Several (many) foreign letters are imported into this province; therefore, for the maintenance of mutual correspondence, and the prevention of many inconveniences that may happen by miscarriage of the same, and that an office may be managed so that safe dispatch may be had, which is most likely to be effected by erecting one general postoffice for that purpose." The date of the establishment of a post office in South Carolina is September the 10th, 1702. This was just a short time before the governor and his troops set out to capture St. Augustine.

SIR NATHANIEL JOHNSON, GOVERNOR

The gubernatorial career of James Moore was short. In 1703, he was succeeded by Sir Nathaniel Johnson. The commission of Johnson is dated the 18th of June, 1702. Owing to the troubled state of affairs both in Europe and America, the commission and instructions did not arrive in the province until after Moore returned from St. Augustine. As was the case with several other governors, Nathaniel Johnson's commission embraced both the Carolinas.

On the same day that Johnson was commissioned governor of North and South Carolina by the Palatine and other proprietors, James Moore was commissioned receiver general of South Carolina; Nicholas Trott attorney general; and Job Howes surveyor general. Thomas Broughton was also, at the same time, appointed deputy for Lord Carteret. During the administration of Moore, political strifes and ecclesiastical difficulties had been engendered, and now they assumed a tangible form and shape. Lord Granville was one of those deluded creatures who think that the religion of no one is worth anything which is not, in every respect, similar in all its forms and ceremonies to that practiced by themselves. In one word, Lord Granville was maliciously opposed to all dissenters. His opposition was measured by his ability. Nathaniel Johnson was easily swayed by Granville. Attorney General Trott was a man of deciding talent and very considerable learning; but withal, an unprincipled and designing politician. James Moore would enter into any scheme, provided there was a prospect of remuneration. With Lord Granville as Palatine, and Johnson, Trott and Moore as chief officials of the colony, a party was organized to which it would be difficult to give a proper name. It was neither political nor ecclesiastical; and yet it combined some of the features and assumed some of the prerogatives of both. The party which had been opposed to the course of Moore now despaired of redress.

MOORE TOO STRONG FOR INVESTIGATION

A petition was sent to the grand jury, by Edmund Bellinger, asking that the disorderly, unbecoming and unconstitutional conduct of the late governor be investigated; but to no purpose. The dominant party exercised too much power. The prosecuting officers were the most guilty persons. Deprived of what they regarded as their inalienable rights, one hundred and fifty of the best citizens of South Carolina drew up a fair and unbiased representation of the facts and circumstances connected with the late election riots in Charles Town. John Ashe, who had been one of the sufferers in the riot, was sent to England to make a statement of the facts in the case, and lay the representation before the proprietors. The complaints met with no encouragement from the proprietors. The governor and Grand Council had done nothing contrary to the notions of Granville.

Notwithstanding the fact that Granville's party was in power, it was still greatly in the minority. In Colleton county it scarcely had an existence. Such being the case, it was necessary for the governor, the attorney general and the receiver general to make a vigorous effort to carry the election in Craven and Berkley counties. The election for both these counties was held in Charles Town. As the day for the biennial election was approaching, every effort in the power of these individuals was exerted. When the day arrived, a scene more ignoble and more disgraceful than that which was enacted at the previous elections was exhibited. The laws of England were trampled in the ground, and all the customs and regulations of the colony were treated with the utmost contempt. In the language of the honest petitioners for right - "Jews, strangers, sailors, servants and negroes," were dragged to the polls and voted for the tools of the dominant party. Thus the enemies of the welfare of the counties, and the disregarders of justice and right, triumphed. Whilst such proceedings were undermining the abilities of the proprietors to hold possession of the territory it was the subject of mirth and drunken hilarity to the party in power.

EXPEDITION AGAINST APPALACHEES

The resources of the colony were completely exhausted by the St. Augustine expedition; still, for some reason, it was determined to send out another expedition - not against St. Augustine - but against the Appalachee Indians. These Indians were allies of the Spanish, by whom they had been partially converted to the Roman Catholic religion. The Pope of Rome, through his agents, had established missions in many of the Indian towns and villages in the territories now embraced in the states of Florida and Georgia. In these towns churches had been built and richly furnished. As a rule, the church formed a component part of the fortification of every town. What Governor Johnson had in view in sending out ex-Governor Moore against the poor mal-treated Appalachees, it is not easy to tell. It is barely possible that on account of the recent failure to capture St. Augustine, these savages had assumed a more threatening attitude. The probability is that Governor Johnson simply yielded to the entreaties of Moore. There is scarcely a doubt that Moore's object was to wipe out the stains of his St. Augustine expedition, and enrich himself by capturing Indians and reducing them to slavery and to plunder churches of their plate.

Late in the fall of 1703, an army of one thousand Indians and fifty volunteers from the colony was collected. Ex-Governor Moore was made the commander-in-chief, and John Bellinger and a man by the name of Fox, captains. Late in November or early December, the army commenced its march to the south-west, toward the territory occupied by the Appalachees. These Indians supplied the garrison at St. Augustine with provisions. Hence, Moore thought, no doubt, that by cutting off the Appalachees, he would inflict a heavy blow upon the Spanish, by whom he had been so recently caused to retreat. About sunrise, on the 14th of December, Moore arrived at Ayaville. So soon as Moore approached, the Indians poured upon him and his men a volley of arrows. Near by the town was a huge mud-walled house. To this house the invaders fled and held a consultation, when it was determined to take the town by first making an assault upon the church. Perhaps Moore and his military advisers thought that by attacking the church, they would awaken some superstitious notions in the minds of the savages. Be this as it may, a vigorous rush was made upon the church by the soldiers with axes. The door was soon broken down and the fort taken. The church was set on fire. The only white man in the fort was a Catholic friar. When the invaders entered the fort, he came out and begged for mercy. Moore lost two men, Francis Plowden and Thomas Dale. Twenty-five Indians were killed and eighty-four taken prisoners, including the women and children, who were considerably more than half.

The next morning after the battle of Ayaville, the commander of Fort St. Louis, with twenty-three Spaniards and four hundred Indians, boldly attacked Moore and his men. In this battle, also, the Carolinians were victorious. The commander of the fort and eight Spaniards were captured, and six killed. Of his Indian allies, he lost two hundred. The Carolinians lost Captain John Bellinger, who was shot down while bravely leading on his men, and Captain Fox, who died of wounds received on the previous day at Ayaville.

Two days after the affair at St. Louis, the chief of the Ibitachka tribe, who was stationed in a strong fort with one hundred and thirty men, surrendered, buying peace with the invaders by granting them all his church plate and ten horses loaded with provisions.

After this, Moore continued his attacks upon the Indian towns and forts. The inhabitants of five towns surrendered without conditions, and the inhabitants of one town fled. Four of the captured towns were reduced to ashes, and the whole Appalachian country overrun and subdued.

In March, 1704, James Moore returned in triumph to Charles Town, He published an account of his expedition in the Boston News. When he returned he had thirteen hundred free Indians and one hundred slaves, together with a vast amount of plate taken out of the Roman Catholic churches. The ignomy of St. Augustine was wiped out, and James Moore felt that he had added much to his pecuniary resources.

INSTALLMENT XXI

NATHANIEL JOHNSON

The administrations of Moore and his successor mark an important epoch in the history of South Carolina. The importance consists not in what was done, but in the direction in which the current of public sentiment began to flow. At this time, a political party was formed which culminated, in 1719, in the transfer of the province from the proprietors to the Crown of England.

Nathaniel Johnson was a man in many respects admirably adapted for the high position to which he was appointed; but unfortunately he was banded together with Moore, Trott, Howe and others high in office. These formed a kind of nucleus around which gathered a multitude of creatures who had neither the spirit to resist insult nor to maintain their rights. In every country there is a class of men who are easily bought. In the colony, at the time of which we are speaking, such a class of persons existed. These - Moore, Trott and Johnson - bought up and kept under their control, to the great detriment of the peace and tranquility of the colony. Their votes were bought with rum, and with the same price they were both hired and inflamed to make attacks upon peaceful citizens.

PROSPERITY IN SPITE OF CORRUPTION

One would be led to conclude that under such a government the colony would have ceased to flourish. Such, however, was not the case. Charles Town was put in a proper state to be defended against the invasions of the Spanish, both from Havana and St. Augustine. The liability to be attacked at any moment never permitted them to lose sight of the necessity of being well fortified. The assembly were ever careful to inquire into the military condition of the province, and generous in making appropriations for the defense. For the time, strong fortifications had been erected on Cooper River. Magazines had been built, and ammunition of various kinds stored away in them. When Governor Johnson assumed the duties of his office, there were about one hundred cannon, planted in different localities, for the defense of the city. Some of these were small; but when we remember the youthfulness of the colony, we are ready to conclude that the people displayed much energy in fortifying themselves. During the administration of Johnson, Fort Johnson was commenced and completed, which was, at that time, regarded as sufficient to command the harbor.

AIMED AT THE DISSENTERS

Among the first acts ratified whilst Nathaniel Johnson was governor was one which was designed to deprive the Dissenters of all power in the administration of the government of the colony, and place all power and all the offices of honor and trust in the hands of Episcopalians. It is entitled "An act for the establishment of religious worship in this province, according to the Church of England." The first section required that all the forms and ceremonies of the Church of England be strictly observed by all ministers in the province. This seems strange, when we remember that far the greater number of the inhabitants were Dissenters of various persuasions. It must not be forgotten that it was the purpose of the original proprietors of the province to establish in it the form of religious worship held and practiced by the Church of England; but through the influence, no doubt, of John Locke, the section was introduced which granted religions liberty to Dissenters. Honesty demands us to say that we do not think strange of the original proprietors cherishing such an intention. They had been educated in the Church of England and, if not consistent members of it, at least all of their prejudices were in its favor. It does not appear that the original proprietors were men of more than ordinary piety; but they were strongly inclined to favor the Church of England, whilst they acted leniently toward Dissenters.

Up to the time of Johnson, no effort was made to disturb the inhabitants of the colony in their religious belief. Infidels and papists were excluded; but Christians of all persuasions were permitted to worship God according to the dictates of their own conscience. It is true that in 1698, during the time of Governor Blake, an act was passed settling a maintenance upon a minister in the Church of England in Charles Town; but this was not designed, as we understand it, to establish a particular form of Christian religion in the province. The act of 1698 provided that seven hundred and fifty dollars (£150 sterling), to be settled upon Samuel Marshall and his successors forever. Samuel Marshall was a pious minister of the gospel, and was at that time pastor of the Episcopal church at Charles Town. Blake, who was either a Presbyterian or a Baptist, proposed the law, and it was through his influence and the influence of other Dissenters that it was passed by the assembly. It is evident, from this fact alone, that it was not designed by the assembly to establish the Church of England in the colony. The fact is, the Episcopalians were greatly in the minority and, as said before, no question was made in the colony respecting religious creeds or professions. Great harmony existed amongst all sects. It rather seems that the acts of 1698 had its origin in a generous and noble Christian spirit. The strong assisted the weak, the many stretched out a helping hand to the few. Samuel Marshall was a very pious man and greatly beloved by all parties. The character and instruction of this good man, no doubt, had much to do in the passage of the act to which we have referred.

EFFORT TO ESTABLISH CHURCH OF ENGLAND

From the first day that Granville became Palatine, he determined to establish the Church of England in the colony of South Carolina, and either banish or render powerless the Dissenters. The character of Granville was well known to the leaders of the dominant party in the colony and, for purposes purely mercenary, they favored his unholy scheme. Truth requires us to say that the Episcopalian church, as such, is not chargeable with the many laws which were passed during the administration of Nathaniel

Johnson in reference to religion. Neither was it done by any act of the Episcopalian members of the assembly that passed the act most destructive to the rights and liberties of the majority of the people. Several of the Episcopalian members voted against the act, and the Rev. Marston was called "the pest of the country" because he declared, in several sermons, that the assembly had usurped to themselves unrighteous powers. The Rev. Marston was the successor of Samuel Marshall as pastor of the Episcopal church in Charles Town. The passage of the act filled his soul with righteous indignation and, for his opposition to the course of the usurpers, he was made to answer. His salary was withheld, and he was otherwise made to suffer.

The acts passed are too long to quote. To give the reader an idea of their general character, we will transcribe some portions of them. Section II of the act ratified May 6, 1704, was as follows:

Whereas some persons scruple the receiving the sacrament of the Lord's Supper, for reasons they fear they are not rightly fitted and prepared to partake of that ordinance, who do, nevertheless, out of real choice, conform to the Church of England, as established by law, and do sincerely profess the same, and do not abstain from the sacrament of the Lord's Supper out of dislike to the manner and forms of the administration thereof, as used by the Church of England, and prescribed in the communion office in the book of common prayer of the said church; be it therefore enacted by the authority aforesaid, that every person that after chosen a member of the Commons House of Assembly in this province, in case that he hath not received the sacrament of the Lord's Supper, according to the right and usages of the Church of England, as is before prescribed by this act, then every such person, before he votes in the said Commons House of Assembly, or sits there during any debate in the said house after the speaker is chosen, shall, upon his oath, taken on the Holy Evangelist, declare that he is of the profession of the Church of England, as established by law, and that he doth conform to the same, and usually frequents the said church for the public worship of God.

The first section of this act made it incumbent upon each member to have taken the sacrament of the Lord's Supper, as prescribed by the Church of England, within the last twelve months previous to his taking his seat. Section II is a kind of proviso to meet the case of those Episcopalians who had conscientious scruples about their fitness to partake of this holy ordinance. Section IV of the same enactment absolutely forbids any one, except an Episcopalian, to take his seat as a member of the assembly, although

duly elected by the votes of his fellow citizens. The penalty for such presumption on the part of a Dissenter was, for the first offense, two hundred and fifty dollars, and fifty dollars a day for each repetition of the offense. This was tyranny in its worst form. There was something mean in it also. Half the fines were to be paid over to Granville, The Palatine, and the remaining proprietors; and the other half to be disposed of by an ordinance of the general assembly. It seems as if the proprietors were determined, in some way or other, to make money out of their poor, dissenting tenants.

To further show that the acts, having for their avowed object the establishment of the Church of England in South Carolina, was not an ecclesiastical movement, a bench of the high commissioners was created, who had granted them all the powers of the Bishop of London, under whose control the American churches were. These commissioners were granted power to cite any minister before them and proceed at once to try him; and if they saw fit, to silence him from preaching. This was assuming unheard of authority. The names of the commissioners were Nathaniel Johnson, Thomas Broughton, James Moore, Nicholas Trott, Robert Gibbes, Job Howes, Ralph Izard, James Risbee, George Logan, William Rhett, William Smith, John Stroud, Thomas Hubbard, Richard Beresford, Robert Seabrook, Hugh Hicks, John Ashley, John Godfrey, James Serurier, alias Smith, and Thomas Barton.

The character of most of these individuals is known. The names of some of them are covered with disgrace. The pastor of the church of Charles Town testified that most of them were irreligious men; and we know from the previous acts of some of them, that they had not the fear of God before their eyes. Moved by ignorance and prejudices, they determined to reduce to a state of vassalage the greater number of the inhabitants of the colony. The spirit of persecution is manifest in all their acts. This bench of lay commissioners met, and the Rev. Marston, rector of St. Phillip's, was forbidden to exercise the functions of his office any longer.

During this period, the dominant party was jubilant. Everything was working as they desired. A scheme far reaching and malicious, although clothed in the language of religion, had been devised and inserted in a body of laws, which would effectually stop the mouths of the people and vacate the pulpits of the province. A law had been ratified on the 6th day of May, 1703, excellent in words, but a goat in sheep's clothing. It was a trap set to catch Dissenters. It professed to be an act to suppress blasphemy, but was proposed with the mistaken notion, firmly fixed in the minds of the dominant party, that the Dissenters denied all the fundamental principles of religion, and were only a set of vile blasphemers. The act passed, establishing the Church of England as the church of the colony, drove all Dissenters from the assembly, and shut the door upon them so long as this law should continue. The law for suppressing blasphemy deprived every one who should, in haste, or from grievous provocation, speak a hasty word against this self constituted oligarchy, from exercising the most ordinary rights of a citizen. He was made incapable of receiving any legacy or gift; in one word, he was made a mere cipher. The trap was set, and the prospects, for a while, were favorable. But the vile schemes of a few for the ruin of many, were soon to come to an end.

HOME GOVERNMENT ADVISED
OF SITUATION

After the election frauds, Joseph Ashe was prevailed upon by several of the best, as well as the oldest, inhabitants of the country, to go to England and make a plain statement of the miserable condition of things in the colony. He met with no encouragement from John Somers (Lord Granville). Ashe came back to Virginia and commenced the publication of the facts in the case, but died before the work was completed.

The few sheets which were finished fell, by improper means, into the hands of the Grand Council, and Thomas Smith, one of the oldest in the colony, was persecuted because of the connection he held with Ashe and the other memorialists.

After the passage of the laws establishing the Church of England as the church of the colony, Joseph Boone, on behalf of himself and many of the inhabitants, as well as some London merchants, presented a petition to the proprietors, in which they set forth their grievances. John Somers treated the petition and petitioners with the utmost harshness. The Palatine refused, for some time, to call the proprietors together; and when he did call them, had no intention of showing the petitioners any favors or removing any grievances of which they complained. John Archdale, one of the proprietors, and at one time governor of Carolina, was, from principle, opposed to the acts which the assembly had passed. He and Somers quarreled, when Somers declared, in an angry tone: "I am for this bill, and this is the party that I will head and countenance."

When Boone requested that he might make his statement, Somers (Lord Granville) replied: "I will do as I see fit." The end was approaching. The people of England were incensed at the high-handed measure of appointing a lay commission, which to all intents and purposes, was a direct thrust at the Bishop of London. "The society for the propagation of the gospel," which had done much to support the gospel in the colony of Carolina, met and passed a resolution to send no more assistance to the colony in Carolina, until the clause of the act establishing a lay commission should be repealed.

APPEAL TO THE HOUSE OF LORDS

Boone, thwarted in his efforts to obtain redress for injuries received at the hands of the proprietors, placed his case in the hands of the House of Lords. These saw in the colonial laws respecting religion, much that was not granted by the original charter, and much that was subversive of the English Constitution. The petition was examined as carefully as the short time of the session would allow, and then presented to the Queen for her examination. In April, 1706, the whole matter was referred to the Board of Trade. The lawyers of the crown declared that the acts establishing Episcopacy in South Carolina ought to be repealed, and that the proprietors had forfeited their charter and recommended that it be annulled. All that saved the charter to the proprietors was the fact that they were peers of the realm. On the 10th of June, the Queen of England nullified the enactments of Johnson, Moore, Trott and a few others, who composed the oligarchy in South Carolina.

Installment XXII
TROUBLE BRINGS UNION

Calamities often befall nations, as well as individuals, in quick succession. The infant colony of South Carolina was no exception. Harassed by designing men in her midst, and surrounded by blood-thirsty neighbors, her very existence was almost in jeopardy. The usurpation of a few unscrupulous fanatics nearly drove many of the best citizens from the colony. They had heard of the mild and just government of William Penn and, being oppressed by a set of mongrel ecclesiastical tyrants, they formed the resolution to leave the home of their adoption, and cast their lots with the honest Quaker. But few actually left the colony; still many had been planning their departure. Two calamities befell the colony which, to some extent, caused the disturbances amongst the inhabitants to cease, and united the advocates of the various creeds in common cause.

In the summer of 1706, the yellow fever again made its appearance in Charles Town. This dreadful disease commenced its ravages at an early period amongst the settlers of the New World. In St. Domingo, in 1494 and 1498, it prevailed amongst the Spaniards. It made its appearance in Boston as early as 1693 and two years afterward in Philadelphia and Charles Town. Again it appeared with more virulence and with greater fatality in Charles Town, in July and August of 1706. In the city, for some time, five and six deaths from yellow fever occurred daily. Many of the prominent citizens were swept off. All that could do so left the city and retired to the country. The governor went to his plantation, which he called Silk Hope. Dissenters and High Churchmen alike fell before the plague. With death all around them, the inhabitants forgot their differences; or at least ceased, for a time, to cherish their hatred for one another.

QUEEN ANNE'S WAR

But at this juncture, another event occurred, which still further tended to cause them to lose sight of their party quarrels. England was at war with France and Spain. Both of these powers laid claim to the Continent of America. The claim of England rested upon a grant made by the Roman Pontiff to the English Monarch, and both France and Spain based their claim to the same territory on priority of discovery and occupancy. So soon as war was declared in England by Queen Anne against France and Spain, both these nations turned their attention to wresting the country from the hands of the English. It was thought that the colony in South Carolina would be easily captured. Impressed with this idea, an expedition was planned by the French fleet under the command of Le Feboure. The plan was concerted in Havana. The governor of St. Augustine agreed to render him his assistance in the enterprise. From Havana, Le Feboure sailed with a frigate and four sloops. He touched at St. Augustine to receive the promised aid. On arriving at St. Augustine, it was learned that the yellow fever was raging at Charles Town. This was thought to be favorable to the undertaking. It was confidently expected that they would find the inhabitants of Charles Town unprepared. This was the case. It is true that the city had been, comparatively speaking, well fortified. But many of the inhabitants were sick; others were waiting upon the sick and watching over the couches of dying friends; whilst not a few had fled from the plague into the country.

A circumstance trifling in itself, saved the city from being attacked whilst in this unprepared condition, and saved it, perhaps, from total destruction. The governor had sent out a Dutch privateer, formerly from New York, to cruise on the coast. The command of this vessel was given to Capt. Stool. It was known that a vessel was to pass from Havana to St. Augustine, bearing the money to pay off the garrison at the latter place. This vessel Capt. Stool was instructed to capture. Suddenly, Capt. Stool came up with the fleet under command of Le Feboure. Hotly pursued by the fleet, he made his escape by entering the harbor of Charles Town. This was on Saturday, August 24th. Scarcely had he entered the harbor when signals were given by those posted on Sullivan's Island, that five armed vessels were in sight. The signal was given by kindling five separate fires, in different places, on the island. The sun was only about two hours high, and it was feared that the invaders would immediately sail into the harbor and commence the attack. A dispatch was sent to the governor with all possible speed. Runners were sent in all directions, to gather up the scattered militia. The enemy came to the bar, but feared to cross, lest they might become entangled in its windings. Alarm guns were fired in the city and through the surrounding country during the night. The Sabbath and Monday were spent by the invaders in taking surroundings. During the Sabbath, General Broughton arrived in the city with two foot companies and Colonel Logan with one company of cavalry. On Monday Governor Johnson arrived from his plantation. He found the inhabitants in the greatest confusion and distress. His presence soon restored confidence in the people. The first thing he did was to declare martial law. He did everything calmly and deliberately. The Indian allies were sent for from the surrounding country, and preparation was made for defending the city. As the yellow fever was still raging in Charles Town, it was wisely determined not to lead the troops into the city. The governor established his headquarters about half a mile out of town. On Tuesday morning, Captains Linch, Hearne, Drake and Johnson, with their companies, took their places among the defenders of the country. The enemy began to make summary preparation for entering the town. Four of their ships and a galley, provided with boats for landing, crossed the south bar. The wind and tide were favorable, and they steered for the town. The fortifications were manned, and the governor and his men waited to receive them. When, however, the invaders saw the fortifications around the town, and the inhabitants ready to meet them, they changed their course and anchored near Sullivan's Island. The galley which accompanied the enemy attempted to cut off a sloop which had been sent to Wando to transport Capt. Fenwicke and his company. It failed, and the captain and his company arrived in safety and joined in the defense. Thus Tuesday was spent. On Wednesday, two other companies - the one under the command of Capt. Longbois and the other commanded by Capt. Seabrook - arrived to strengthen the defense.

ENEMY BACKS DOWN

The promptness with which the militia assembled from the various sections of the colony shows that the inhabitants, for the time, forgot their internal feuds and joined heart and hand in repelling the old and inveterate enemies of the settlement. Governor Johnson had been educated a soldier, and was a brave man and skillful officer. All parties had the utmost confidence in his strategical powers. Those who would not subscribe to his notions respecting church establishments willingly rendered obedience to him as a military commander. As soon as the governor discovered that the invaders were hesitating about making an attack, he called a council of war. By this council it was determined to equip all the ships in the harbor, and go out and boldly make an attack on the enemy's ships. These were put in condition for the attack with all possible dispatch and Colonel Rhett was placed in command. When the enemy discovered the preparations for a naval engagement, a flag of truce was sent in.

INGENIOUS DECEPTION

George Evans commanded Granville Bastion, which was located on the Cooper River, not a great distance from what was then called White Point - now known as the Battery. Evans received the bearer of the flag of truce. He was blindfolded and conducted into the fort. In the meantime the governor was apprised of his arrival. The troops were, by the governor's orders, immediately so arranged as to make the best possible impression on the mind of the truce-bearer, of the ability to defend the place. This done, the French officer who bore the flag of truce was led before the governor, who received him in military style at the head of his forces. He was then asked to deliver his message. The purport of this message was that Admiral Le Feboure demanded the unconditional surrender of the fortifications and men of the province; and that only one hour would be allowed him in which to give an answer.

Governor Johnson, with the spirit and promptness of a military genius, replied that he did not need a moment to give an answer. He informed the officer that he could depend on his men, and that he would die before he would surrender. This spirited answer having been given, the governor told the truce-bearer to go and attend to his own business.

FIGHTING ON JAMES ISLAND

No attack was made on the town by the enemy; but they commenced landing predatory parties at different points. One party landed on James Island. As the property of Captain Drake was situated in this quarter, he, with his company and some Indian allies, was sent by the governor to repel the invaders. The Indians could be restrained by no command; but rushed on furiously and in no order, and before Capt. Drake could place his men in position to make an attack upon the enemy, they fled to their boats. Another party landed on the opposite side of the river and burned two vessels and a store house. Several houses were also burnt on James Island. A party of one hundred and fifty of the enemy landed at Haddrell's Point and commenced killing the cattle and hogs and appropriating them to their own use. Captains Fenwicke and Canty, with one hundred select men, were ordered to cross the river in the night, for the purpose of checking their progress into the country, and also to watch their movements. They came upon them before the break of day. Their fires were burning all around them. A spirited attack was made upon the plunderers, which resulted in their complete discomfiture. Of the enemy's forces, twelve were wounded, thirty-three were taken prisoners, several were drowned in attempting to make their escape, whilst the rest were either killed or surrendered unconditionally. The Carolinians lost but one man.

SHIPS RAN AWAY

Thus far successful on land, the governor determined to make an attack upon the enemy on the water. Colonel Rhett, with the fleet which had been, but a few days before, hastily equipped, was ordered to push out boldly against the enemy's ships. With six small and insignificant vessels, he sailed down the river to the point where the enemy lay at anchor. So soon as the French fleet saw Rhett and his little armament approaching, they fled. The weather was unfavorable for pursuing his foe, and Rhett returned without an engagement. To all human appearances, it seemed that in a fit of despair the French had determined to give up farther prosecution of the attack upon Charles Town. Governor Johnson, to be sure that his conclusion was correct, sent out the Sea Flower, under the command of Capt. Watson, to search for the enemy. He found some men whom the French had left on the shore, but none of the enemy's ships were to be seen. Having taken on board the Sea Flower the men left by the French, he returned to Charles Town and reported that the enemy was not to be seen. The prisoners captured by him reported that they were certainly gone.

ENEMY COMPLETELY DEFEATED

Martial law was now suspended, and the people began to feel easy once more. That same evening (Friday), it was reported that an armed ship had entered Sewee Bay, and that a considerable number of armed men had landed. The governor at once determined to make an attack upon them, both by sea and land. Capt. Fenwicke, with one hundred and thirty men, was ordered to cross the river and attack those who had landed, whilst Colonel Rhett was to sail with the Dutch privateer and a Bermuda sloop against the ship anchored at Sewee Bay. Colonel Risbie, Captain Evans, the commander of Granville Bastion, and a number of volunteers, accompanied Colonel Rhett. Captain Fenwicke came up with those who had landed at Hobeaw, but a short distance from Charles Town. An engagement, which lasted but a short time, took place. The Carolinians were entirely successful. Thirty of the enemy were killed, and seventy taken prisoners. Colonel Rhett, about the same time, entered Sewee Bay, and the enemy's ship surrendered. Ninety prisoners were secured, together with a number of subaltern officers, and General Arbouset, of the land forces.

It seems that the plans of the enemy were either badly matured, or they were greatly frustrated in their execution. The fleet consisted of ten ships and eight hundred men, who were a mixture of whites, mulattoes, Indians, and Negroes. The ship which entered Sewee Bay was commanded by Capt. Pacquereau, and carried the land forces. In some way, it seems to have become separated from the rest, and to have known nothing of the fate of the other vessels near Charles Town.

The French lost nearly one half of their men, whilst the Carolinians lost only a few men. The whole expenses of the defense of the provinces were borne by Governor Johnson. As a reward for his services, it is a tradition that the proprietors granted him a large tract of land, which afterwards fell into the possession of the Manigaults.

Certain it is, that the invaders made a complete failure, and no doubt the success of the defense was due mainly to the military skill of Governor Johnson.

INSTALLMENT XXIII

ESTIMATE OF JOHNSON

The administration of Nathaniel Johnson extended from 1702 to 1709. It was a period of trouble and vexation. Governor Johnson was, in some respects, a strong man; and on others a weak man. An old writer speaks of him as having "transmuted the civil differences in the colony into a religious controversy." Governor Johnson's strong point was his skill in military affairs, and his weak point was his hatred to all Dissenters. He was evidently the tool of Lord Granville. The laws establishing the Church of England in the colony will stand as a blot on the names of Granville, Johnson and Trott. The thing itself was not so odious as the manner in which it was brought about and the intrigues by which it proposed to perpetuate it.

RELIGIOUS TOLERATION

The proprietors, beyond all doubt, contemplated from the beginning the establishment of the Church of England in the colony; but at the same time, the greatest liberties were granted by the charter to all denominations of Christians. None except Papists were excluded. This is not the place to criticize this restriction; but we may be permitted to remark, in passing, that no colony in America enjoyed greater peace and prosperity than the Catholic colony of Lord Baltimore, in Maryland.

It was only by taking advantage of the people that the objectionable laws were passed. So soon as the people became aware of what the governor and his council were determined on doing, and the parliament assembled in full numbers, all the church laws from 1697 were repealed. This was done before the action of the Queen was known.

Another law was enacted which, to all intents and purposes, established the Church of England as the church of the colony. The objectionable features of the previous enactments were, however, left out, and religious liberty was granted to all sects. This law continued in force until after the Revolution of 1776.

The population of the state in the latter part of 1708 was 9,580. Of this number, 1,360 were free white men, and 900 free white women. In the colony there were 120 white servants, one half of whom were males and the other half females. The excess of the male population over the female is accounted for by the fact that many single men came over from various portions of Europe. In the colony there were 2,900 Negro slaves, 1,800 of whom were male. There were also 1,200 Negro children in the colony. These also were slaves. Besides the whites and Negroes above enumerated, there were, at the time mentioned, 1,400 Indian slaves in the colony. Of the 9,580 inhabitants, 3,960 were free slaves or in a state of servitude. Near one-third of the whole population was in Charles Town.

The Negro slaves were Africans, stolen from their native land by the nations of Europe and brought to America. For a number of years the traffic in Negroes was carried on between the islands of Barbadoes and Jamaica and South Carolina. The first Negro slaves that were ever brought into the state were brought from Barbadoes, by Joseph Yeamans, shortly after the colony was planted. The first Negro slaves that were ever brought into the English colonies in America were brought in the month of August, 1620 - two hundred and fifty years ago. These were brought by the Dutch. The Indian slaves were captives reduced to bondage, or captives sold by their enemies.

The colony was weakened by the yellow fever and other causes during the five years preceding 1708, about two hundred adults; whilst the children had increased five hundred during the same period. In those five years, five hundred Negroes had been imported into the state.

The military strength of the province was nine hundred and fifty white men. They were organized into two regiments, consisting of eight companies in each regiment. The French, on Santee, had one company of forty-five men and a patrol of ten men. The governor's bodyguard consisted of forty men. By an action of the assembly, each captain was required to arm, with either gun or lance, and drill any able-bodied Negro slave for every white man in his company. This would make the military force of the state about two thousand.

EARLY COMMERCIAL DEVELOPMENTS

The commerce of the colony was carried on with the English colonies in the north, with the islands of the south, and with England. The principle exports were rice, pitch, tar, skins of various kinds, barrel staves and white oak timber. Some silk was also exported. Indian slaves were sent to Boston, Rhode Island, Pennsylvania, New York and Virginia, and sold. To Barbadoes, Jamaica, Antigua, and the Bahama Islands, staves, hoops, shingles, beef, pork, rice, tallow, butter, peas and leather were sent and exchanged for molasses, sugar, cotton, salt, Negro slaves and various other articles of use or ornament. Among the exports of the colony were candles made of myrtle berries, and a large amount of the imports consisted in wines, brandies and rum.

The commerce of the colony would have been much greater, had it not been on account of the heavy duties which were imposed. These duties had been greatly increased by the recent wars. By the expedition against St. Augustine and more recent invasions of Charles Town by the French and Spanish, the debt of the colony had been increased to near fifty thousand dollars. The income from imports and exports amounted to more than twenty thousand dollars. The annual expenses of the government were near the same amount. The annual expenses were distributed in the following way: For the ten Episcopal ministers settled in the province, five thousand dollars; for completing the fortifications already begun, and keeping others in repair, five thousand dollars; soldiers' pay, including military officers, three thousand dollars; military stores, one thousand five hundred dollars; governor's salary and other incidental expenses, three thousand two hundred and fifty dollars. The current expenses deducted from the income, left a sum amounting to something between four and five thousand dollars. This sum was set aside for the purpose of redeeming the bills of credit that had been emitted for the purpose of meeting the heavy debt which had been incurred by the government.

WHAT THEY DID FOR MONEY

At this time there was scarcely any English coin in circulation in the colony. At various times, bills of credit passed at their face value; but soon, on account of their great numbers, they depreciated very much. The gold and silver in circulation was German, Mexican, Peruvian, French and Spanish coin. No uniformity of value was attached to the bills of credit when exchanged for coin of these nations. To prevent this confusion, Queen Anne, in 1707, issued a proclamation, by which the value of the currency of the colony was fixed. One pound English money was, by this royal proclamation, made to be worth one and one-third pounds of the colonial currency. This is the origin of what was called "proclamation money."

Belonging to the colony, there were, in 1708, twelve ships, more than half of which had been built in Charles Town. Taking all things into consideration, we cannot but wonder at the rapid growth of the colony. It was not yet thirty years old, but it had assumed the importance of a little nation.

MANUFACTURE OF SILK

The mention of silk as amongst the exports of the colony leads us to inquire into the history of its introduction into the colony. In 1697, Charles the Second sent out the frigate Richmond with some French Protestants to the colony at Charles Town. The main object that was had in view, in transporting these French Protestants, was to secure their aid in the production of silk in the country. The vessel was too late setting out on its voyage, and the result was that the eggs of the silk worms which were placed on board all hatched; and, as no preparation had been made for such an event, the young worms died for want of food. At a later period, Nathaniel Johnson, amongst other citizens, was more successful. The plantation of Johnson, situated in the St. Thomas parish, was named "Silk Hope," from the fact that on it considerable attention was devoted to raising silk. By many of the planters, forty and fifty pounds of silk were annually made, and the annual income of Governor Johnson from silk alone was two thousand dollars. It cost very little to produce the silk. The forest abounded with mulberry trees, the leaves of which furnished the proper food for the worms; and little Negroes who were too small to work on the farm were employed to feed the worms. The silk was mixed with wool, and manufactured into what the manufacturers called "druggets." The production of silk was continued for a long time. The mothers from whom sprung some of the most illustrious families in the state, continued for a long time to spin their wool and silk, and wove it into dresses for their daughters. In Abbeville county, silk was produced by the descendants of the French, who first settled in that county as late as 1808. In 1753, the mother of General Charles Cotesworth Pinckney took with her to England a quantity of silk yarn, which she spun with her own hands in the neighborhood of Charles Town. From this yarn she made three dresses, one of which she gave to the Princess of Wales; another to Lord Chesterfield, and another to her daughter, Mrs. Horry.

EDUCATIONAL PROGRESS SLOW

As might have been expected, the educational advantages of the colony, for a long time, were very poor. Still we are not to conclude that the education of the children of the colony was entirely neglected. Although there is, so far as we have been able to discover, no account of any classical schools in the colony prior to the year 1700, still, we may, we think, safely infer that such was the case. In favor of this inference, we would state that many of the early colonists were men of learning, and it is scarcely conceivable that they would suffer their children to grow up in comparative ignorance. We are not, however, left to inferences. In 1671, Thomas Smith, who was made landgrave in 1691 and governor in 1693, came into the province. In 1672, one year after his arrival, his second son, George, was born. In 1700, when near thirty years old, he graduated in Edinburgh. The probability is that at least part of his education was obtained in Charles Town. Through the influence of Rev. Thomas Bray, the bishop of London's Commissary in Maryland, a library was established in Charles Town in 1696. By an act of the assembly in 1697, this library was placed under the care of the Episcopal minister of the town. The books were mostly religious. The missionaries, sent out by the society for the propagation of the gospel, were not only required to preach, but also to teach. They were both preachers and school-masters. Instructions were specially given them, both as to what and how the children were to be taught. It was a long time before young men, in any considerable numbers, received what is called a collegiate education. So soon as the production of rice and indigo became so great as to make the trade between England and the colony of South Carolina direct and to supply the planters the means, they sent their sons to England to be educated. This circumstance accounts for the fact that there was, previous to the Revolution of 1776, more of English manners and English customs in South Carolina than in any of the colonies.

DANCING MASTER RICHLY SUPPORTED

Prior to 1708, a French dancing master, true to the instincts of his nation, opened a music school in Craven county, on the Santee. There he taught Indians to play the flute and the hautboy. The savages were delighted, and supported their teacher with an extravagance which enabled him soon to amass a considerable fortune.

GOVERNOR TYNTE

The gubernatorial career of Nathaniel Johnson commenced in 1703, and terminated in 1709. He was succeeded by Col. Edward Tynte. It is difficult to say why this change was made. Johnson had not, so far as the records show, in the least offended the proprietors. No doubt it was the policy of the proprietors to make frequent changes in the chief officer of the colony. There is also another circumstance which, in all probability, had something to do in the removal of Johnson and the appointment of Tynte. Lord Granville died and William Craven became Palatine. Craven was decidedly a man of more liberal views than Granville. Craven had the prosperity of the colony at heart; whilst Granville seems to have made everything else of secondary importance to the establishing of High Churchism in the province. Probably it was the thought that it would have a tendency to obliterate all the bad feelings which had been engendered by the passage of laws respecting religion.

JOHNSON'S ACHIEVEMENTS

It is due to the memory of Nathaniel Johnson to say that, whilst he was not free from faults, he was both a good citizen and excellent governor. By birth he was an Englishman, and at one time was a member of the House of Commons. For a period of three years - from 1686 to 1689 - he was governor of the Leeward Islands. He was what we are accustomed to call an English gentleman; high-toned and dignified in his intercourse with his fellow men, but withal not remarkable for his talents. He had received a military education, and in this respect he proved a great blessing to the colony. It is due to his memory to say that he put the colony in a condition that it could be defended, and inspired the people with confidence in themselves. In common with many of his age, he did not have liberal notions respecting religion and, unfortunately, became connected with others less liberal than himself.

He came to the province in 1689, and at once engaged in developing the resources of the country. He engaged in the manufacture of silk, in the making of salt, and in raising grapes. His experiment with silk was, all things considered, a success; and it is said he made wine, perhaps prior to the time that he was governor, but in what quantity and of what quality, we have no means of ascertaining. Whether he succeeded in making salt or not, we do not know. All that we certainly know is that he engaged in making salt on Sewee Bay. To Nathaniel Johnson more, perhaps, than to any other man, were the early settlers of South Carolina indebted for their success in raising rice. He introduced several kinds of rice, and experimented with them in order to discover which kind was best adapted to the soil and climate.

Governor Johnson's defects were two. He was exclusive in his religious notions and, being educated an English gentleman, he had ideas which were ill adapted to a people who had chosen a forest for their home. Impelled by the first idea, we find him assisting in enacting a law which, to all intents and purposes, reduced dissenters to a state of vassalage. Influenced by the latter notion, he was often led to say to the people whom he governed, when they would demand a reason for his manner of procedure, that it was none of their business. As much as you say "you are tenants, and have no right to demand a reason for anything from a nobleman."

Having been removed from office, Governor Johnson returned to his plantation near Charleston, and died in 1713. His remains were interred on his premises. In after years a brick wall was built by Gabriel Manigault, to perpetuate his memory. The male line of Nathaniel Johnson has become extinct.

AN ERA OF PROSPERITY

Col. Edward Tynte commenced his gubernatorial career under more favorable circumstances than some of his predecessors. The calamities which had befallen the people had tended somewhat to make them forget their differences, and to feel the necessity of being united in sentiment. The proprietors had concluded that the southern portion of their possessions in America was by far the most desirable. Brief histories of the country had been published in London. In these histories, the authors lauded, in no moderate terms, the soil, climate and production of that portion of North America which is now called South Carolina. These glowing descriptions, in the main correct, were disseminated all over the United Kingdom and as far as the Rhine. The proprietors, at last, as we will see in the sequel, when it is too late, began to be more accommodating in their actions and more conciliatory in their notions. Hence, in February, 1710, they wrote to Tynte earnestly requesting him to do everything in his power to conciliate the minds of the inhabitants, so that every semblance of party might be extinguished. The reason they assign for thus instructing Governor Tynte they thus express: "We can by no ways doubt by their (the inhabitants) unanimous concurrence with our labors for their prosperity will eventually render Carolina the most flourishing colony in America."

Various causes had almost annihilated the settlements made in what is now North Carolina. The Indians in that section were more hostile than in South Carolina. Such being the case, the settlements in North Carolina commenced to decrease so soon as the settlement in South Carolina became permanent. During the time of Governor Tynte's administration a town was laid out southwest of Charleston, and in honor of the Duke of Beauford, was called Beauford.

FIRST FREE SCHOOLS

It is worthy of note that the first act passed by the assembly establishing free schools was enacted while Governor Tynte was governor. It bears the date April 8th, 1710. Sixteen persons were, by this act, named and appointed a body politic in deed and in fact, to be known by the name of the "commissioners for founding, erecting, governing, ordering and visiting a school for the use of the inhabitants of South Carolina." The act provides for a perpetual succession of commissioners. From the names of the individuals appointed commissioners of this provincial school, it may be safely inferred that there was nothing sectarian in its character. Some of the staunchest dissenters were members of this board. Evidently, Tynte had no disposition to carry out the ultra ecclesiastical notions inaugurated by his predecessors. Palatine Craven was a very different man from Granville, the former Palatine. Peace began to reign and prosperity to smile upon the colony. Queen Anne's war was still raging, but all was peace in South Carolina. Just as things commenced to assume a more prosperous aspect, Colonel Tynte died.

SALE OF THE GOVERNORSHIP

An election was held by the three deputies of the proprietors in the colony. Two candidates - Robert Gibbes and Thomas Broughton - proposed themselves for this high office. It is clear that the result of the election depended entirely upon the vote of Tuberville, the other deputy of the proprietors. It seems that on the morning of the election, Tuberville voted for Broughton, but on the evening of the same day, for some reason or other that we do not understand, the vote was cast again, when Tuberville voted for Gibbes. He was declared duly elected governor and entered upon the duties of his office.

On the day of the election, Tuberville died very suddenly, and it was discovered by the Broughton party that Gibbes had bribed Tuberville to vote for him. The vote he cast in the morning being his uncorrupted vote, and being for Broughton, it was now claimed that Broughton and not Gibbes had been elected governor. Each individual had his friends, and soon preparations were made for settling the dispute with the sword. Happily, some men of moderate views interfered, and it was agreed by all that Gibbes should act as governor until the will of the proprietors was learned. The proprietors decided that Gibbes had secured his election by bribery and therefore they ordered that no salary should be paid him. This was virtually to decide that Robert Gibbes never was, only by fraud, governor of South Carolina. Notwithstanding this fact, Robert Gibbes was, for a period of two years, in reality, governor of South Carolina, and his administration was marked with wisdom and prudence. For a long time he had been intimately connected with the colony. He had held various offices, the duties of which he had discharged acceptably to the people. Still, he was not a popular man in the colony. It seems strange that an old man should have suffered the fires of youthful ambition so far to inflame him as to induce him to seek the office of governor. He did it, however, and the result was, if not his own mortification and disgrace, partial triumph of his political opponents.

GOVERNOR CRAVEN

Although the proprietors did not approve the manner in which Gibbes secured for a time the office of governor and consequently did not continue him in office, still they did not grant it to his rival. They appointed Charles Craven, at that time secretary of the province, and the brother of the Palatine, governor.

At this time, notwithstanding all the unfortunate events of one character and another which had taken place, the colony was in a very prosperous condition. The commerce of South Carolina was now carried on with all parts of America with all the nations of Europe sustaining friendly relations with England; and a considerable amount of commerce was carried on with some parts of Africa. During the first year of Governor Craven's administration the imports brought into South Carolina were valued at more than one hundred and twenty-five thousand dollars. The exports for the same year consisted in part of 12,677 barrels of rice; 4,580 barrels of pitch; 2,037 barrels of tar; 29 quarter barrels of tallow; 1,969 barrels of beef; 1,241 barrels of pork; 1,965 sides of leather; five barrels of snakeroot; six hogsheads of sugar; besides quantities of soap, candles, oil, garlic, salt-fish and salt. What was the value of the exports we cannot tell; but it must have been considerable.

PUBLIC IMPROVEMENTS

Not only was the colony in a prosperous condition, in a pecuniary point of view, but the arts of civilization were cultivated to a laudable extent. Men of property had, in their wills, donated considerable sums of money for the erecting and supporting of seminaries of learning. Schools were established and teachers employed. The children and youth of the colony were taught all that is usually taught in the high schools of the present day, and besides, they were carefully instructed in the principles of Christian religion. At this period the colony presented a bright picture of a happy family. Under the fostering care of Palatine Craven, the dissenters were protected in their liberties. The Church of England had been established in the colony by law, and continued to be the church of the province for a period of more than sixty years, but the dissenters seem not to have objected to this so long as they were allowed to enjoy the privileges granted them in the charter granted the proprietors by Charles the Second.

INSTALLMENT XXV

CRAVEN MAKES ENCOURAGING PROMISES

When Charles Craven entered upon the duties of office of governor, he made, in April 1712, an address to the House of Commons, in which he declared that the highest aim of his ambition was to advance the prosperity of the colony. Placing the colony in a proper state of defense, and making it the most flourishing in America would, he said, be more pleasing to him than all the glory that might be attached to the fact of his being governor of the province. The assembly had the utmost confidence in the sincerity and honesty of the man, and consequently, the words which he uttered were believed not only by the assembly, but by the people. Charles Craven was not only a popular man, but he was a pure man. The inhabitants of the colony were aware of this fact. New energy was infused into the people and the arts of civilization began to grow and flourish under his benign influence.

THE FIRST STATE HOUSE

In June, the assembly voted seven thousand five hundred dollars for the purpose of "building a convenient state house for the holding the general assembly, courts of justice and other public uses." This sum, at present set apart by the legislature for building of a state house, would be niggardly small and indicate a miserably low state of civilization; but when we consider that the colony was only forty years old, and that it had been involved in heavy expenses by a rash invasion of St. Augustine under James Moore; that it had been invaded by the French and Spaniards and that it had suffered by floods and diseases and its progress had been impeded by civil bickerings and contentions, when we consider all these things, we are prepared to conclude that seven thousand five hundred dollars appropriation by the general assembly of South Carolina in 1712 was a large sum, and indicates the liberality and refinement of the people at that time. From the occurrence of the word "convenient" in the title of the bill, we may infer that previous to this time no suitable house was in existence.

GOVERNOR'S MANSION

At the same time that an appropriation was made for the purpose of building a state house, five thousand dollars were appropriated for purchasing a tract of land and erecting a house upon it for the use of the governor. In the preamble to this act, it is stated that the appropriation was made to obviate in future the necessity of the governor living at a great distance for Charles Town, and that the assembly might "give an instance of that very particular deference and respect, which is so justly due to the birth and merit of the Right Honorable Charles Craven, Esq., our present governor." This preamble very clearly indicates the good state of feeling which prevailed in the assembly and consequently in the colony. Three commissioners - Charles Hart, William Rhett and Hugh Grange - were appointed to purchase the land and build the house. They were charged not to purchase less than one hundred acres of land nor more than three hundred. It was to be within six miles of Charles Town. The house was to be a brick building, constructed in such a manner as to be convenient. Prior to this time, the governors had resided on their plantations, except when necessity demanded their presence in Charles Town.

INDUSTRIAL ENTERPRISES ENCOURAGED

During the same session of the assembly, laws were enacted establishing schools in Charles Town and in the province. Sums of money were appropriated to individuals who would erect saw mills, invent rice mills, or improve the mills already in use in the colony. Premiums were offered individuals for making potash, and liberal offers were made to induce settlers to come into the country. The contentions of past years died away, and the frauds ceased which had been practiced heretofore in the elections. Chief Justice Trott was engaged in arranging the statutes; and Col. William Rhett was appointed to several offices of importance. The business in which Trott was now engaged was more congenial to his nature and education than the broils in which he had been a conspicuous actor. Trott was a lawyer by profession, and evidently a man of decided talent and extensive erudition. William Rhett was a quarreling, carousing creature, who could live in peace with no one, but the vast amount of work which was now imposed upon him kept him at least quiet. Taking all things into consideration, perhaps the colony never had been in so flourishing a condition.

MORE TROUBLES WITH THE INDIANS

But in the history of nations as in the lives of individuals, two extremes are seldom far apart. The happy laugh is often quickly followed by the wail of sorrow. Adversity treads on the heels of prosperity. The Indians throughout the entire province, embracing both Carolinas, became less friendly until they broke out in terrible hostilities which, for a time, threatened the very existence of the colony. The cause of these Indian hostilities was the unscrupulous conduct of the traders. To say that the Indians were never in the wrong would not be true; but it is most certainly true that the whites were more frequently the aggressors. The traders, as a general rule, had no respect for the rights of the Indians. In fact, it was taken for granted by the Europeans generally, with the exception of William Penn, that the Indians had no rights. During the contentions in the colony regarding elections and ecclesiastical laws enacted by the civil authorities, the traders had perpetrated many outrages on the poor sons of the forest. To some extent these outrages were, if not sanctioned, at least winked at by the inhabitants generally. In the colony, at this time, there were fourteen or fifteen hundred Indian slaves, and Indian slaves formed a part of the exports of the colony. Great numbers of these poor untutored savages were in one way and another reduced to slavery or kidnapped and sent, some to the northern colonies and some to the Spanish dominions. There were two classes of Indians in the province. One class was regarded as the friends of the English, and the other class as the friends of the Spaniards. The Spaniards, on the one hand, incited their Indian allies to make invasions upon the territory of the English, and the English urged their Indian allies to maltreat the Spanish. The cruel practice of scalping, if not practiced by the whites, was indirectly encouraged.

GENERAL MASSACRE

The difficulties of the present period commenced in North Carolina, on the Neuse River. The cause of the outbreak was this: Some unscrupulous traders had defrauded the Indians. This incensed the Indians. About this time John Lawson, surveyor general of the province, laid out some lands which were claimed by the Tuscaroras. This invasion of their rights, added to the fraudulent acts of the traders, infuriated the savages, and they determined upon vengeance. Lawson was apprehended and, after a hasty trial, was condemned and put to death. Individually, Lawson was guilty of no fault and the Indians seem to have been conscious of the fact. They became alarmed lest the surrounding settlers would fly to arms and avenge the blood of Lawson. To avoid this, they concocted a plot to exterminate the whole settlement of whites. The 22nd of September, 1711, was set apart for the work of utterly destroying all the colonists south of Albemarle Sound. They divided themselves into small parties and commenced the work of death. The thing was kept a profound secret. They went from house to house, putting to death, without regard to age or sex, all the inmates. One neighbor did not know what was going on in the house of his nearest neighbor. One hundred and thirty of the North Carolinians fell on that bloody day.

PUNITIVE EXPEDITION

Those who survived this horrid massacre, greatly alarmed, sent with all possible speed for succor, to South Carolina. So soon as the messenger arrived, great solemnity pervaded the minds of both the assembly and the people of South Carolina. The 19th day of November was set apart by the assembly as a day of humiliation and prayer. This, so far as we know, was the first day of the kind that was observed in the colony. An army, or rather a few hundred men, were hastily raised and placed under the command of Col. John Barnwell. This little army, of which Col. John Barnwell was commander-in-chief, consisted of six hundred men, most of whom were Indians. The Cherokees were commanded by Captains Harford and Luston; the Creeks, by Captain Hastings; the Catawbas, by Captain Canty; and the Yemassees, by Captain Pierce.

INDIANS PUNISHED

It is at present scarcely possible to imagine, much less describe, the difficulties with which these men had to contend in their march from Charles Town to the Neuse River. The distance several hundred miles, the country one unbroken forest. Numerous small streams and several large rivers, together with a multitude of dismal swamps, lay between them and the place of their destination. No wagons could be conveyed, and consequently no supplies could accompany the army. The men supported themselves on this march by hunting. Notwithstanding all the difficulties with which Colonel Barnwell had to contend, he crossed the Neuse on the 28th of January 1712. He at once commenced operations. Fifty of the hostile Indians were killed and two hundred and fifty taken prisoners. Col. Barnwell marched directly against their stronghold. This was a wooden structure erected on the Neuse River. The garrison consisted of six hundred Tuscaroras. This fort, Col. Barnwell could have easily taken by storm, but he proposed terms of capitulation, which were accepted by the Indians. The treaty concluded, the allies were disbanded. They immediately set out for home. Col. Barnwell sent to Charles Town for a sloop to convey his wounded and disabled men home. Barnwell himself was wounded. This was in July.

TROUBLE COMMENCED AGAIN

No sooner were the Indians apprised of the fact that Barnwell's forces were disbanded, than they violated the treaty so recently made and commenced hostilities again. Aid was again sent for to Charles Town. Col. Barnwell, not having recovered from his wounds and being also sick, the command was entrusted to James Moore, son of the former governor. An army of eight hundred Indians and forty whites was raised. They assembled on the banks of the Congaree, and Governor Craven went up to inspect them. Whatever may have been the difficulties attending Barnwell's march, that of Moore was attended with greater difficulties. It was in the dead of winter. The army assembled on the Congaree in the month of December 1712. After a march which beggars description, Col. Moore arrived at the Taw River. There he found the enemy fortified and well armed. Unawed by these circumstances, he boldly laid siege to their fortifications. The siege lasted but a few hours. An engagement took place which resulted in the complete discomfiture of the Tuscaroras and their confederates. Two hundred were killed and eight hundred taken prisoners. The prisoners were claimed as spoils and were brought to Charles Town and sold into slavery.

BARNWELL CENSURED AND MOORE REWARDED

Colonel Barnwell was greatly censured by the North Carolinians. He was blamed because he made any treaty with the garrison. The censures were not altogether just. Col. Barnwell was out of supplies, and no doubt he did what would have appeared to any other man as best under the circumstances. His allies, after being disbanded, plundered some of the Tuscarora towns and carried off some of the inhabitants and sold them as slaves. Barnwell was charged with this. But every one who knows anything of Indian character is aware that it is impossible to restrain them when they are victorious. No doubt, the reason the Tuscaroras proved faithless to the treaty concluded with Barnwell was the fact that after it was made, their towns had been plundered and their citizens carried off by the Indian allies of Barnwell. Col. James Moore received the approbation of all parties and was voted by the assembly five hundred dollars extra pay.

Installment XXVI

WAR WITH THE YEMASSEES

History teaches, and experience confirms its testimony, that troubles rarely came alone and single handed. The cares of today are but the prelude of the calamities of tomorrow. The war with the Tuscaroras in North Carolina, in which South Carolinians were so actively engaged, and by whose aid it was so successfully, to the province, conducted and concluded, was followed by another war of far greater magnitude against the Yemassees. The war against the Tuscaroras was ended in 1713, and that against the Yemassees commenced in 1715.

So great was the magnitude of this war, and so wide-spread was it in its operations, that the very existence of the colonies planted in Carolina was threatened. The bloody stick was sent throughout the various tribes in the adjacent territory, and a grand uprising was planned. All this was done with their usual secrecy. Intercourse with the members of the various tribes and the settlers continued as heretofore. Nothing was suspected until the war whoop was raised and the carnage commenced.

The Yemassees, who seem to have been the prime movers in this war, lived in the region back of Port

Royal, on the north-east side of the Savannah River. At one time they lived in Florida and were the confederates of the Spaniards; but some of their chiefs having been executed by this nation, they deserted the Spaniards and came and settled in South Carolina. Their principal town was Pocotaligo.

During the whole of Queen Anne's war the Yemassees were the faithful allies of the colonists. They, at that time, cherished an inveterate hatred for the Spaniards. Several traders connected with the colony had settled amongst the tribes, and on several occasions the Yemassees had rendered valuable aid to the settlers in and around Charles Town. This hostility to the Spaniards prompted them to ravage the Spanish territory and to keep up almost a constant war with the Indian allies of that nation. So closely did they watch the inhabitants of St. Augustine that it was dangerous for them to leave the garrison. The woods were scoured, and every Spaniard that was seen was captured and brought away as a prisoner. These prisoners the Yemassees treated in the most inhuman way. Sometimes the cruel savages satiated their brutal hatred by cutting the poor prisoners into pieces, joint by joint, with their knives and tomahawks. Sometimes the prisoner was buried in the ground, all except his head, and then they shot at the head as a target. That method of putting a prisoner to death was always chosen which was thought to be the most painful. To prevent this cruel treatment, the Indians were given, by the colony, twenty dollars for every live Spaniard they would bring to Charles Town. The prisoners brought were sent by the government to St. Augustine, and the expenses charged to the Spanish government.

The Yemassees, cherishing so much hatred toward the Spaniards, and being on friendly terms with the English settlers, no fears were entertained of any hostilities. The cause of dissatisfaction among the Indians seems to have been the manner in which they were treated by the traders. The truth is, the traders were unprincipled men, who made no scruples to cheat and defraud the poor savages out of everything they possessed. There is another thing that should not be lost sight of. Near two thousand Indians had been, in one way and another, reduced to bondage; besides vast numbers had been sent off to other colonies and sold. This fact stirred the spirit of revenge in the bosoms of the sons of the forest. The Indians must have seen that their tribes were fast melting away, before their English neighbors. All these things, together with the intrigues of the Spaniards, aroused the Indians, from the mountains to the sea-board, to wreak their vengeance upon the settlers of South Carolina.

Although by nature cruel and unforgiving, the Indian is not reckless. Rarely does he enter upon any enterprise until it has been deliberated upon. For a period of more than a year previous to the Yemassee outbreak, the traders settled amongst them discovered that the bitter hate which they once bore toward the Spaniards had been changed to friendly intercourse. The chiefs frequently visited St. Augustine and returned loaded with presents. Amongst the Yemassees there resided a Highland Scotchman by the name of John Fraser. This man was respected by the Indians for his honesty, and the savages had no disposition to conceal anything from him. Frequently, after their return from southern expeditions, they would enumerate the presents they had received from the governor of St. Augustine. One had received a hat, another a suit of clothes trimmed with silver lace, and another a hatchet. Among other things they had received were guns and implements of war. As an evidence of the friendly feeling existing between them and the governor of St. Augustine, they related that they had dined with him and washed his face. This custom among the Indians, of washing the face, was a kind of pledge of friendship. Still, the English settlers were not alarmed.

It was a general custom amongst the traders to make a friend of the leading man or chief amongst the Indians. John Fraser found such a friend in a leading Indian of the Yemassee tribe, by the name of Sanute. Between these two individuals a great intimacy existed. Sanute, together with his warriors, was accustomed to make expeditions into Florida. These expeditions lasted for more than a year. At this time, during one of Sanute's southern strolls, John Fraser married. So soon as Sanute returned, he came to the house of his friend. No sooner had he entered, than he called for a basin of water. This being brought, he took some aromatic herbs, which he said he had received from St. Augustine, and began to bruise them in the water. This accomplished, he asked for the privilege of washing the face of Mrs. Fraser. After performing this ceremony, Sanute placed his hands upon his breast and declared that all that was in his bosom should be revealed to her. No doubt this strange conduct excited some misgivings in the breast of Fraser. Mrs. Fraser ceremoniously thanked the chief for his kindness and proffered friendship, and gave him presents. He departed, and in about ten days before the savage war whoop was raised, he returned. True to his promise, he revealed the fact that a grand confederacy had been formed for the utter extermination of the English settlers. The bloody stick, he said, had been sent to the various tribes in the adjacent region and, so soon as it returned, the work would begin. The

English, he said, were heretics; the governor at Charles Town was no longer their king; and that the governor of St. Augustine was their king. Sanute revealed the fact that the design of exterminating the English had been formed more than a year before hostilities actually commenced. The Spanish had selected a warrior named Ishiagaska, to visit the Creeks and inflame them against the English. Fraser was urged to make all haste to leave the region in which he was and make sure of his escape to Charles Town. Sanute promised to assist him in making good his escape by lending him his canoe. Fraser hesitated, but his wife became dreadfully alarmed, and he put his wife and child, together with most of his effects, into the canoe and set out for Charles Town.

For some reason Fraser failed to communicate the facts which he had learned from Sanute to any one else of the settlers. This, as the sequel will show, was a most unfortunate neglect. It may be that Fraser did not lay much stress upon the information received and that he set out to Charles Town only at the urgent request of his wife. The report of Fraser was, perhaps, the first intimation that Governor Craven and the citizens of Charles Town had of the intended hostilities of the Indians. Notwithstanding this fact, the settlers of the regions adjacent to Pocotaligo had, for a long time, seen may things amongst the tribes which were mysterious. So soon as the governor heard of the hostile design of the Indians, he sent Capt. Nairn and John Cochran, in company with several other individuals well known to the Indians, to make inquiries respecting the difficulties. The Indians were discovered to be very gloomy. Capt. Nairn told them if they had been injured in any particular way, that he came for the purpose of making amends for any injustice which they had suffered. They replied that no one had injured them, and intimated that the cause of their gloominess was the fact that on the next morning at an early hour, they designed on setting out on a great hunting expedition.

On the night of the 14th of April, 1715, as a manifestation of friendship, the chief warriors gave the English a supper. The night was spent as such occasions are usually spent. The supper over, the warriors retired to their tents and Capt. Nairn and his party retired to sleep. At the break of day on the morning of the 15th of April, 1715, the war whoop was raised. The council room in which the English, the Yemassee king, and war-chiefs had spent the night was surrounded. Capt. Nairn, Thomas Ruffly and John Wright were instantly murdered. John Cochran, together with his wife and four children, were taken prisoners but afterwards they were put to death. An

athletic man by the name of Seaman Burroughs beat his way through the savages and, although severely wounded in the cheek, he, together with a little boy, swam the river and ran with all possible speed and warned the settlers in the vicinity of Port Royal of what was going on and what they might expect. Around Pocotaligo, ninety individuals fell before the infuriated savages. Hideous were the yells of the monsters as they rushed from house to house killing all before them. The scene was rendered more hideous by the screams of the women and children.

It soon became evident that all the tribes, from Florida to Cape Fear, were combined together. Desperate was the condition of the inhabitants. The only place of safety in the province was Charles Town. The Indians divided into two parties. One party directed its course toward the settlement in the neighborhood of Port Royal; the other toward St. Bartholomews. A merchant ship lay at anchor in the Port Royal River. The people, having been warned by Burroughs of the hostilities of the Indians, at once took refuge on this ship. The Rev. Guy and about three hundred of the people of St. Helena were thus providentially saved. A few families who, from the great dispatch with which the Indians acted, not having warning of their approach, fell prey to their cruel hate. The inhabitants of Bartholomews fared worse.

The Indians proceeded as far as Stono. About one hundred of the inhabitants fell victims to their cruelties. The missionary of the parish, the Rev. Osborn, and a few of the inhabitants, made good their escape to Charles Town. In their march, the Indians burned and destroyed everything within their reach. The property of the country was left to their mercy. From all sections, the inhabitants, in a state bordering on desperation, rushed to Charles Town. Between eight and ten thousand Indians were in arms, and on the muster roll of the colony there were only twelve hundred men.

Governor Craven acted with the promptness which the occasion demanded. Trusting in the fortifications around Charles Town as sufficient with a few men to protect the women and children of the province, he determined to advance boldly into the country and attack the invading foe. Charles Town was placed under martial law, and the assembly passed a law authorizing the governor to seize the arms, ammunition and provisions wherever they could be found; to impress vessels and to arm the trusty Negroes. Agents were sent to Virginia and England to solicit aid. Robert Daniel was appointed deputy governor, and Governor Craven, like a true hero, prepared to lead, in person, the colonial forces against the foe.

So soon as Governor Craven learned, perhaps from John Fraser, of the intended attack of the Indians, he collected a company of two hundred and forty horsemen, from Colleton county, and followed after Capt. Nairn for the purpose of learning the precise state of the difficulties. At the same time he ordered Colonel Mackay to raise all the forces he could and proceed by water to Pocotaligo. The governor, having arrived within sixteen miles of the Indian chief's town, encamped for the night near the Combahee River. At break of day on the next morning he was suddenly attacked by five hundred Yemassees. The colonial forces were promptly placed in order, and after a spirited engagement of forty-five minutes the enemy was routed. The loss to the colony by this engagement was one sentinel, by the name of John Snow, killed, and a few men wounded. The Indians lost several of their war chiefs, and a large number of their warriors were killed and wounded.

Colonel Mackay, in pursuit of his orders, gathered what forces he could and embarked by water and, on landing, marched to the Indian Yemassee town; and though he was disappointed in meeting the governor there, yet he surprised and attacked the enemy and routed them out of their town, where he got vast quantities of provisions that they had stored up, and what plunder they had taken from the English.

"Colonel Mackay kept possession of the town, and soon after, hearing that the enemy had got into another fort, where were upward of two hundred men, he detached, out of his camp, about one hundred and forty men to attack it, and engaged them. At which time a young stripling, named Palmer, with about sixteen men, who had been out upon a scout, came to Colonel Mackay's assistance, who at once, with his men, scaled their walls and attacked them in their trenches, killing several; but meeting with so warm a reception from the enemy that he was necessitated to make a retreat. Yet, on a second entry with his men, he so manfully engaged the enemy as to make them on their flight, when he slew many of them." - Boston News, of June 13th, 1715.

This prompt action on the part of the governor and Colonel Mackay checked the progress of the enemy in this quarter, but a body of four hundred of the enemy came from the north in the direction of Goose Creek. They came to the plantation of John Hearne, near the Santee. Here their wants were supplied, but they barbarously murdered Hearne. Captain Thomas Barker, hearing of their approach, collected a company of near one hundred cavalry and marched to meet this party. Trusting to an Indian as a guide, whom he regarded as faithful, he was led into the very midst of the enemy. In a thicket, with which the country at that time abounded, the Indians lay concealed. At a moment when Captain Barker was expecting no danger, the Indians sprung from their hiding places and poured in deadly fire. Capt. Barker was killed and his men were thrown into disorder and fled. This untoward event threw the whole of the Goose Creek section into a panic. A rush was made for Charles Town. A fortification, in which was seventy white men and forty Negroes, frightened by the great number of the Indians, surrendered only to be inhumanely butchered.

On the 13th of June, the savages, thus far triumphant, were met by Capt. Chicken and the Goose Creek militia, and were defeated and driven from this section of the colony. The Indians soon found that although their numbers were much greater, they were no match for the English. By the prompt and united action of the people, they were driven beyond the Savannah River and ultimately fled to Florida.

This Yemassee war cost the colony four hundred men and not much less than one hundred thousand dollars in the destruction of property. The whole burden of the war fell upon the colony. Governor Spotwood, of Virginia, furnished one hundred soldiers at twenty dollars per month, but there is no evidence that any engagement took place after their arrival.

PERIOD OF DISTRESS

The various calamitous events which had, during the first fifteen years of the eighteenth century, transpired in the South Carolina colony, reduced the settlers to great straits. The most distant settlers from Charles Town had been, by the attacks of the Yemassees, almost exterminated. Vast numbers of people had been driven from their homes, and their property totally destroyed. Gloom settled upon the countenances of all. The Yemassees had been conquered, and the capability of the few settlers to contend, successfully, with the combined tribes of the savages fairly demonstrated; but this victory had cost the province an enormous sum of money and near one-fourth of the population. Many children had been made orphans by the scalping knife of the savages.

In the midst of the gloomy circumstances, it became evident to all that the proprietors, or someone else, must render the colonists aid or the colony must prove a failure. The debt of the province had been increasing for a number of years until it amounted, at the close of the Yemassee war, to not much less than half a million dollars. At various times the assembly had issued bills of credit. These at first were taken at par; but soon they began to depreciate in value. To increase the exigencies of the colonists, they and the proprietors were not on good terms. After the Yemassee war, bills of credit to the amount of nearly four hundred thousand dollars had been put into circulation by the assembly. These bills were made receivable dollar for dollar, for all debts. Circumstances combined to cause these bills to depreciate in value so that they were not worth more than one-eighth of their face value. This loss fell upon the London merchants and moneyed men of Charles Town. The merchants of England became alarmed, lest they would lose all that was due them.

Such was the financial condition of the colony. There were other difficulties. When in 1713, Anthony Craven, the palatine, and brother of Charles Craven, the governor, died, permission was granted Charles Craven to leave the colony and return to England. At the same time they signified their desire that Robert Johnson, the son of the former governor, be his successor. The colony being involved in difficulties with the Indians, Charles Craven, like a true-hearted patriot, would not quit the province until these difficulties were adjusted.

On the 25th of April, 1716, the Yemassees being subdued, he left Robert Daniel, deputy governor. During the administration of Daniel, the law respecting the mode of conducting the elections was very materially changed. Previous to this time, the members of the lower house were all chosen at Charles Town. This was attended by many disadvantages, and was a source of annoyance to the people. As we have seen, the elections were fraudulently conducted. Chief Justice Trott and Collector Rhett were ever ready to resort to unfair measures in order to secure the election of a party man. The law was at this time so changed that the thirty-six members of the lower house should be elected in the different parishes at the parish churches. This change gave general satisfaction.

ADVENT OF ROBERT JOHNSON

On the 30th of April, 1717, the proprietors commissioned Robert Johnson as governor of South Carolina. So soon as he arrived, he called the attention of the assembly to the condition of their currency. He insisted that the honor of the province demanded that the bills in circulation be redeemed. The colony was in a bad condition for undertaking such a huge work. Both the agricultural and commercial operations of the colony had been greatly injured by recent events. The farmers had been called from their fields to fight the Tuscaroras and Yemassees, and the pirates were then making sad havoc of their commerce. Notwithstanding all these things, the assembly passed an act by which the paper money of the colony was to be redeemed in three years. To accomplish this, a tax was levied upon land and Negroes. This law gave general satisfaction.

No one was disposed to disturb the general quiet except Trott and Rhett. These two individuals were brothers-in-law and were, in some respects, very similar in traits of character. Both men were of talent. Trott especially was endowed with great mental powers, which were developed by close study. Notwithstanding all this, he was a man in whom no dependence could be placed. One great defect in his character was that he was given to fawn upon the great. Another weakness in his nature was an avaricious love of money. At this time, Trott and Rhett opposed the change in the election laws. They saw it would deprive them of much of their influence which they were accustomed to exercise on election days. In spite of these two individuals, the law went into operation, and was working to the satisfaction of all others, and for the general good of the province.

ORDER TO DISSOLVE ASSEMBLY

Just when, however, the assembly were busily engaged in devising ways and means for sinking the public debt, Governor Johnson received an order from the proprietors to dissolve the assembly, and cause another to be elected according to the ancient mode. In this order to Governor Johnson, the proprietors expressed their dissatisfaction of the new election law, and virtually declared it null and void, because it had not been submitted to them, in London, for their approval. No doubt the proprietors were induced to take this insane course through the influence of Trott; for although he fawned upon the proprietors, he, by his talent and learning, controlled them very much as he pleased. Governor Johnson and the deputies of the proprietors, with the exception of Chief Justice Trott, thought it best not to carry out this order of the proprietors; but to permit the assembly to go on until they had accomplished the business in which they were engaged.

The proprietors also ordered a repeal of the law which laid an import duty on Negroes, liquor and other articles brought into the colony. This part of the law, because it was "an order of the King in Council," the governor and the deputies asked the assembly to repeal, since it was the wish of the king.

Governor Johnson and the deputies of the proprietors used every effort to keep the instructions and orders of the proprietors secret from the assembly. They were unsuccessful. So soon as the facts became known, the assembly flew into a violent rage. It was boldly asserted that the proprietors had encroached upon the chartered rights of the province. Immediately preceding this juncture of affairs, the lawyers of the province had brought before the assembly a complaint of thirty charges against Chief Justice Trott. Amongst the complaints brought against him, he was charged with devising a multitude of ways by which his fees were increased. He was also charged with giving advice to parties having cases pending in his court. Everything now tended to alienate the minds of the people of the colony from the proprietors. It was known that the lawyers of the crown of England had declared that the proprietors had forfeited their charter, and the people of the colony now became anxious that the change be made.

During the reign of Queen Anne, application had been made by the colony to the proprietors for aid and, they not being disposed to render the desired assistance, application was made to the crown. The queen manifested a willingness to assist the colony, but declared that she could not consistently do so, since the colony was under a proprietary form of government. The people of the colony complained that they were under a form of government that could not render them assistance when in great need; and yet it stood in the way of their receiving aid from the crown of England. Many of the grievances of which the people complained, were of such a character that they could be removed only by the authorities in England.

Chief Justice Trott held his office during good behavior, and could be tried only before the proprietors. The assembly drew up a representation of the mal-administration of Trott and desired the governor and his council to join with them in petitioning the proprietors, if they did not see fit to remove the chief justice, at least to limit his jurisdiction. That they might better succeed in this undertaking, it was thought proper to send the memorial by Francis Yonge, surveyor general of South Carolina.

Yonge arrived in London in May, 1719, and presented the memorial on the 4th of June. In this memorial, in which the governor and most of his council joined with the assembly, the general condition and necessities of the colony were plainly and earnestly brought to the attention of the proprietors. Several requests were made. They were asked to make a donation of six thousand acres of land, for the purpose of erecting three garrisons. One on the Savannah River at a point called Savannah town; another at Congaree; and the third at the Apalachocoles. The proprietors were also asked to make some provisions for the custom house offices at Port Royal, since the town at that point had commenced to increase and was favorably situated for carrying on the commerce of the colony. In this memorial presented by Francis Yonge, complaint was made respecting the unbounded powers of Chief Justice Trott, and the former arbitrary action of the proprietors in repealing certain laws passed by the Colonial Assembly. With this memorial, Governor Johnson sent the charges brought against Trott. Several other documents were sent to the proprietors, all of which were designed to give them a clear and correct idea of the real condition of things in the colony.

After a delay of three months, Yonge was sent back to the colony with sealed packages, containing the decision of the proprietors. During the time that Yonge was consulting with the proprietors, Trott was corresponding with them, and his power over the proprietors was much greater than that of Yonge or anyone else.

This letter brought by Yonge from the proprietors to Governor Johnson revealed the minds of the proprietors very clearly. Governor Johnson was gently censured for not carrying out, to the very letter, his previous instructions respecting the dissolving of the present assembly and causing another to be chosen according to the mode originally in existence in the colony. He was now instructed to put his former instructions into execution. They peremptorily refused to make a grant of land for garrisons or any other purpose. They increased their power in the colonial parliament by appointing twelve individuals as their deputies. Heretofore there had been but eight; seven deputies, who represented the seven proprietors, and the governor, who represented the oldest proprietor, or palatine. Trott's power, instead of being lessened, was increased; and he, instead of being censured for malfeasance in office, was thanked.

This reply of the proprietors to the memorial sent up by the assembly stirred up a spirit of revenge in every bosom except that of Trott. Evidently, the proprietors designed punishing the colonists for what they regarded as insolent conduct. Three of the four deputies of the proprietors who signed the memorial were left out of the new appointment. The fourth, Francis Yonge, who would have been left off but for the fact that he was an intimate friend of Lord Carteret, the Palatine. The names of those left off were Thomas Broughton, Alexander Skene and James Kinlaugh.

PEOPLE GREW REBELLIOUS

Governor Johnson, although a warm friend of the proprietors, was not pleased with the manner in which they had acted. Possibly, the fact that his brother-in-law - Broughton - was degraded, had something to do in arousing his disapprobation. He now saw that Trott was to virtually govern the colony while he held the office of governor. This being the case, the governor, in a kind of pet, determined to follow out the instructions of the proprietors to the letter, let the consequences be what they might. He called the twelve newly appointed deputies together and issued a proclamation dissolving the assembly, and ordered another assembly to be chosen at Charles Town according to the original mode. The excitement was intense. Many individuals boldly asserted that the proprietors had forfeited their charter. They were denounced as tyrants. Several of the newly appointed deputies refused to qualify; whilst others who did qualify, were known to be friends of the people and opposed the arbitrary proceedings of the proprietors.

Trott and Rhett, who expected since the election was changed back to Charles Town, to be able play the games in which they once proved themselves adept, found themselves egregiously mistaken. They could influence no one, and failed to elect a single man. The inhabitants of the colony were, with a few exceptions, firmly united in their opposition to the arbitrary and despotic measures of the proprietors. For them they cherished no love, and being aware of their weakness, they had no fear for their authority. They saw it demonstrated that the interest of the colony and that of the proprietors conflicted. It had now become evident that, if things remained as they now were, that the reduction of the people of the colony to mere serfs of the soil was only a matter of time.

Installment XXVIII

The manifest intention of the inhabitants of South Carolina, during the period at which we have arrived, was to throw off the yoke of the proprietary government of England. They were, in a certain sense, English subjects; not directly, but through the proprietors. They enjoyed some peculiar privileges; but, on the other hand, they were deprived of many advantages. The proprietary government was nothing but a kind of a tenantry. Under it the people never could have accomplished anything, either for themselves or for the world, so far as advancing the arts of civilization is concerned. Still, had the proprietors been wise and prudent, they might have retained their government over South Carolina for a long time. The people had no disposition to rebel. They were goaded to it. Nicholas Trott contributed more than any other man to bring about the revolution of 1719. The proprietors were extremely fond of Trott and he possessed the power of deluding the proprietors. They granted him an amount of power, in managing the affairs of South Carolina, in which it was said, at the time, no other man in the world possessed; and Trott was disposed to exercise all the authority granted him.

The time when the South Carolinians began to think of throwing off the proprietary yoke was very favorable for such an undertaking. The English people generally were anxious that all the proprietary governments be abolished, the merchants of the kingdom were desirous that the change be made, and George the First was a stranger to the individuals who at first obtained the charter for settling South Carolina. Still, there was no disposition on the part of the Crown of England to act hastily in this matter. The parliament of England at this time was the most scrupulously honest legislative body in the world. It determined to act in this matter only when dire necessity required it. Clearly had it been proven to the parliament that, through the influence of their secretary and a few others, the proprietors had forfeited their charter; but, since some of their number did not approve of their unconstitutional acts, the charter was not taken from them.

As said before, Governor Johnson, on receiving his instructions from the proprietors, which were conveyed to him from the proprietors by Francis Yonge, who had taken over the memorial of the colonists to England, he prepared to carry them out to the very letter. The newly appointed council, consisting of Nicholas Trott, William Bull, Samuel Wragg, Charles Hart, Benjamin de la Consilliere, Peter St. Julien, William Gibbon, Hugh Butler, Jacob Satur, Francis Yonge, and Jonathan Skrine, were called together and, as many of them as would, were qualified. The old assembly was dissolved and a new one elected. As might have been expected, it was even less favorable to the proprietors than the one dissolved.

In the interval between the regular time for the assembling of the Colonial Legislature and the election, Governor Johnson received intimation that the Spaniards were planning an attack upon the colony. He called his council and as many of the newly elected members of the assembly as were convenient together and made known to them the condition in which the province was situated. The fortifications around Charles Town were in no condition to resist an invading foe. Having been hastily erected and constructed out of improper materials, the winds and rains had greatly injured them. The governor intimated that since there were no funds on hand for accomplishing the work of repairs, and as the time for the convening of the assembly had not arrived, it would be necessary to raise, by private subscription, a sum sufficient to put the province in a defensible condition. Generously he headed the list with a subscription of about two thousand five hundred dollars. This was generous, manly and patriotic; but the die was cast. The members of the assembly who were present affirmed that the revenues arising from certain imports were sufficient for meeting the expense of repairing the forts. The governor told them the proprietors had repealed the law. The members of the assembly replied that there was an order requiring every man who refused to pay their imports to be sued, and as for the repeal of the proprietors, it was their intention to pay no attention to it. Chief Justice Trott, a member of the council, declared that if an action was brought into his courts against any individual for the purpose of forcing him to pay the duty, he would give judgment in favor of the defendant. No subscription was raised. The council and what few members of the assembly were present, stood face to face, in determined opposition to each other's views. The consultation effected nothing but to widen the breach between the people and the proprietary party. Rather than succumb to the governor and his council, the assembly men preferred to leave the province in an unprotected state to be invaded by their old and uncompromising enemies.

Governor Johnson, moved, no doubt by praiseworthy motives, and having the prosperity of the colony at heart, since he could effect nothing through his council and the members of the assembly, ordered the military officers of the colony to call out their men and appoint a place of general rendezvous. This order the military captains and men willingly obeyed, but with far different intentions from those contemplated by the governor. On assembling, articles of confederation drawn up by the leading spirits of the popular party were presented to the men and signed by nearly every man in the province except council men.

The leading spirit of this confederation was Alexander Skrine, one of the rejected members of the council. Indignant on account of the treatment which he had received at the hands of the proprietors, he was determined to push the opposition to the proprietors to the utmost limit. He was eminently qualified,

besides, for heading a Democratic party. He had for many years been secretary of the Island of Barbadoes, and understood the manner in which to conduct the popular assemblies.

The governor knew nothing of what was going on. His plantation was four miles from Charles Town. Here he was all this time, no doubt, fretting about the past and planning for the future. On the night of the 27th of November, 1719, a committee was appointed to wait upon him and inform him of the present condition of things and make certain propositions to him.

On the next day, November 28th, a letter, signed by A. Skrine, George Logan, and William Slakeway, was prepared and sent to the governor. In this letter, the signers, on behalf of the inhabitants, expressed their love and esteem for the governor, and asked him to assume the office of governor of the colony in the name of George the First until they would hear from his majesty. The letter was conveyed to the governor at his plantation, but the committee left Charles Town before the governor arrived. It seems that the committee, on due reflection, hesitated about holding an interview with the governor. Why they hesitated, we are left to conjecture. This fact was almost the only circumstance which gave the governor any hopes of regaining his authority over the people.

Trott now counseled mild measures. He saw that there was no place for force. Governor Johnson, aware of Trott's influence with the proprietors, readily fell in with the views of the chief justice, and let things drift. Meetings were common amongst the people, and various consultations were held and inflammatory speeches made, until the meeting of the newly elected assembly, about the 10th of December. The movement had, by this time, become emphatically Democratic. The assembly could act boldly, for the people were ready to sustain them in their acts. The governor, as usual, sent them his message informing them that he and his council, which formed the upper house, were ready to join with them in their transaction of business. The assembly replied to this message by going in a body to the governor and, through Arthur Middleton as spokesman, declared to the governor that they recognized him as their governor since he had been acknowledged by the king; but as for the newly appointed council, they regarded them as an illegally appointed set of officers and would have nothing to do with them. Governor Johnson was now placed in a fearful dilemma. If he acted in concert with the council, the assembly would have nothing to do with him and, if he acted in concert with the assembly, he would virtually discard the proprietors.

The assembly soon discovered that they occupied

an awkward position. They had been elected by writs issued by individuals, whom they publicly declared exercised no legal authority in the colony. To relieve themselves from this inconsistency, they changed their name and declared that they were not a legislative body, in the usual sense of that word, but a convention of the people. They proceeded to undo what the proprietors had done, and even to declare that no one who had held office under the proprietors should be recognized any longer as a officer in the colony. The illegality of the council was argued because there was more than one deputy for each proprietor, and one of these was a foreigner, having never become a naturalized citizen of England. It was also claimed that even in accordance with the late instructions of the proprietors, the assembly was not dissolved. The instructions required six of the twelve deputies to act in order to form a quorum. In this case a less number had signed the order, and one of those was a foreigner. These conclusions served as a stimulus to the hesitating amongst the people, and a support to those who were in doubt respecting the course adopted by the popular leaders.

A resolution was passed in which it was, in no ambiguous language, declared that the proprietors had forfeited their charter. An address was prepared, asking Governor Johnson to take the government of the colony into his hands in the name of the king. Johnson hesitated, but sent a message to the assembly in which he said that he and his council desired a conference with the convention. The convention (for this was the name by which the assembly called itself) refused to receive any message, or to transact any business whatever, with the governor in conjunction with his council. Governor Johnson then, in his own name, invited the convention to hold a conference with him. To this the convention assented. On presenting themselves to the governor, his excellency delivered a long speech, in which he used a variety of arguments to arrest the revolutionary spirit of the convention and people. He demanded that the convention should say expressly whether or not they designed freeing themselves from the government of the proprietors. He also demanded, since they said that the proprietors had violated the colonial charter, that they specify in what particulars and when it had been violated. The governor argued that in the event it was discovered that the proprietors had forfeited their charter and it was declared by the British authorities to be null and void, that all the previous acts of the proprietors would be abrogated. That the titles which they had made the settlers of the colony to the land which had been sold by the proprietors, would be rendered worthless.

To the long, and we may say learned, address of Governor Johnson, the convention replied that he was honored, loved and esteemed by both the convention and by the whole people of the colony and that no man was "fitter to govern so loyal and obedient a people to his sacred majesty, King George." The reason for their present course of action, they declared, is well-known to the world. Nothing, say they, but the absolute necessity of self-preservation could have reduced them to adopt their present course of action. This reply of the convention to Governor Johnson was closed with an earnest repetition of the invitation to him to become their governor in the name of King George the First.

The governor again replied, but refused to accept the offer of the convention. The conference between Governor Johnson and the convention now ceased. Still, the governor did not cease to struggle for his lost power and lost honor. He, with the ostensible purpose of putting the forces in a condition to meet an attack of the Spaniard, which might take place at any time, ordered all the military companies to get ready for a general review on Monday, the 21st of December. Capt. Paris was instructed to carry out this order. This, no doubt, was a trick of the governor's, for previously he had ordered the convention to be dissolved; but the order was wrested from the hands of the marshal and torn to pieces. The governor thought, no doubt, that through the aid of the militia, he could drive the convention into submission. In this he was mistaken, for, before the day for the review arrived, he learned to his astonishment that the people had chosen that day as the most fit to proclaim a Royal governor. He, on receiving this information, countermanded the order for the muster but the people were not to be thwarted in their undertaking. Capt. Paris and the governor, on Saturday, talked over the matter, and Paris promised not to have a drum beat in Charles Town on the following Monday. When Monday came, Governor Johnson came from his plantation to town. On entering the town, his ears were greeted with martial music and the beating of drums, and flags were seen flying from the forts and from the masts of the ships lying in the harbor. The people were drawn up in the market and every preparation was making to proclaim a governor in the name of the king. Governor Johnson raged. He threatened, he entreated, he begged. He demanded of Capt. Paris why all this parade was going on contrary to his order. Paris replied, "In obedience to the convention." Deserted by Trott and Rhett, the governor, attended by one member of his council and a man by the name of Lloyd, paced the streets. Almost frantic with rage, he ordered Capt. Paris, in the name of the king, to disperse the men. Paris ordered his men to level their muskets upon the governor and told him if he advanced it would be at the risk of his life. Governor Johnson, notwithstanding his great popularity, was powerless. James Moore was, with great solemnity, proclaimed governor in the name of George the First of England.

Installment XXIX

So soon as a governor was proclaimed, the convention at once changed its name and called itself by the original name, Assembly. With a zeal characteristic of the men, they went to work. Hovendine Walker was chosen president of the assembly and, in conformity with the mode practiced in the other colonies of the king, twelve individuals were chosen as a council. They were now in perfect working order, and they went to work. Laws were enacted, new officers were appointed and old ones thrust out. Chief Justice Trott was deposed and Richard Allein appointed in his stead. All the old officers of the colony, with the exception of Francis Yonge, the surveyor general, and William Rhett, the receiver of the province, were turned out. There was no inconsistency in retaining Yonge, for he was thoroughly in favor of the popular party; but the retention of Rhett was an act of policy of very doubtful propriety, as we will see in the sequel.

The people of the colony had, by their acts, placed themselves in a somewhat peculiar condition. Many of them had come to America that, in its wilds, they might be free. This was the case with by far the greater number of the settlers. That they had received many favors from the proprietors, no one dare deny. Had it not been for the liberality of the original proprietors, the colony never could have had an existence. For a period of nearly fifty years they had, at various times, had assistance. But, during this period, great changes had taken place both in the character of the people and of the proprietors. A new king, who knew not Locke, nor Clarendon, nor Monk, was seated on the throne of England. By a number of successions, a new class of proprietors had become possessors of Carolina, and they knew neither Sayle or West. The colonists themselves had commenced, notwithstanding all the disadvantages under which they labored, to increase in wealth and advance in the arts of civilization. No longer could they be treated as mere serfs of the soil. They determined to rebel. Before the world they stand as rebels against the unjust usurpations of a lazy and avaricious company of men styling themselves "lords proprietors of South Carolina." It was the determination of the people that this first revolution in South Carolina should be in conformity to law and justice. That this might appear to the world, they published the following declaration:

"Whereas the proprietors of this province have, of late, assumed to themselves an arbitrary and illegal power, of repealing such laws as the general assembly of this settlement have thought fit to make for the preservation and defense thereof, and acting in many other things contrary to the laws of England, and the charter to them as free men granted; whereby we are deprived of those measures we have taken for the defense of the settlement being the southwest frontier of the majesty's territories in America, and thereby left naked to the attacks of our inveterate enemies and next door neighbors, the Spaniards, from whom, through the divine providence, we have had a miraculous deliverance, and daily expect to be invaded by them according to the repeated advices we have from time to time received from several places; and whereas, pursuant to the instructions and authorities to us given, and trust in us reposed by the inhabitants of this settlement, and in execution of the resolutions by us made we did, in due form, apply ourselves in a whole body, by an address to the Honorable Robert Johnson, appointed governor of this province by the lords proprietors, and desired him in the name of the inhabitants of this province, to take upon him the government of the same, and in behalf of his majesty, the king of Great Britain, France and Ireland, until his majesty's pleasure had been made known, which the said governor refusing to do, exclusive of the pretended power of the lord proprietors over the settlement, has put us under the necessity of applying to some other person to take upon him as governor, the administration of all the affairs, civil and military, within the settlement, in the name and for the service of his most sacred majesty, as well as making treaties, alliances and leagues with any nation of Indians, until his majesty's pleasure herein be further known; and whereas, James Moore, a person well affected to this present majesty, and also zealous for the interest of the settlement, now in a sinking condition, has been prevailed with, pursuant to such application to take upon him, in the king's name, and for the king's service and safety of the settlement, the above mentioned charge and trust: We, therefore, whose names are hereunto subscribed, the representatives and delegates of his majesty's liege people and free born subjects of the said settlement, now met in convention at Charles Town, in their names and in behalf of his sacred majesty George, by the grace of God, King of Great Britain, France and Ireland, in consideration of his former and many great services, having great confidence in his firm loyalty to our most gracious King George, as well as his conduct, courage and other great abilities, do hereby declare the said James Moore his majesty's governor of this settlement, invested in all the powers and authorities belonging and appertaining to any of his majesty's governors in America, till his majesty's pleasure herein shall be further known. And we do hereby, for ourselves, in the name and on the behalf of the inhabitants of the said settlement, as their representatives and delegates, promise and oblige ourselves most solemnly to obey and maintain, assist and support the said James Moore in the administration of all affairs, civil and military, within this settlement as well as in the execution of all of his functions aforesaid, as governor for his majesty, King George: And further, we do expect and command that all officers, both civil and military, within the settlement, do pay him all duty and obedience, as his majesty's governor, as they shall answer to the contrary at their utmost peril. Given under our hands at the convention, this 21st day of December, 1719."

Governor Johnson now saw that his power over the people was gone. The people were determined. Nothing but an express order from the king could reduce them to subjection to the proprietary government. He wrote to the proprietors and to the commissioners for trade and plantations, giving them an exact and truthful account of the wretched state of things in the colony. He stated that some of the more important causes which had brought about the rebellion. These were the heavy debts contracted by the recent wars in which the colony had been engaged, and the encroachments of the French upon the territory originally granted to the proprietors together with constant exposure of the people to the attacks of the Spanish and Indians.

The colony being in a state of jeopardy, the proprietors paid no attention to their importunate beseechings for assistance; but seemed to thwart every effort put forth by the colony to aid itself. This they did by repealing certain laws and refusing to sell land to emigrants. At this time there were "several hundred" Irish emigrants in the colony, to whom the proprietors would not sell "one yard of land." This excited the fears of those settlers who had accumulated some property, and they stimulated others to join with them in securing the immediate protection of the British government.

Governor Johnson was a warm friend of the proprietors, but it is evident that he was extremely anxious to retain his position as governor. He so acted that in the event the province was transferred to the English crown, he would still be retained as governor. In fact, he asked in his letter to the proprietors, "that their lordships would interest themselves so far, as that if his majesty thought fit to take the government in his own hands, he might be honored with his majesty's immediate commission, or otherwise that he might be restored to his government as formerly." From this it was clear that Governor Johnson was zealously intent upon offending neither party, so that whichever party in the event might be successful, he still would be governor.

By the proprietors he was charged with favoring the popular party. This, however, was not true. Further than that, he made it apparent that he was anxious to be governor whoever might be owners of the soil.

About the same time Governor Johnson wrote William Rhett, surveyor of customs, not to grant clearance to any vessels that might come into the harbor. This would have been a death blow on the popular part, had Rhett seen fit to obey the orders of the governor; but Rhett now showed his proper character. He and the governor were personal enemies, and Rhett, moved by personal hatred, disobeyed the governor and joined in with the popular party. As a matter of policy the assembly retained him in office, and besides, appointed him lieutenant general of the militia.

Rhett still kept up a correspondence with the proprietors, in which he told them that he thought his course was the best for them. In one word Rhett was a friend of the proprietors when with friends of the proprietors, and a friend of the popular party when with friends of that party. He was all things to all men that he might hold lucrative offices.

Turned out of office, Nicholas Trott prepared to embark for England. Before leaving, he wrote to Governor Johnson and told him that if he would go before the authorities in England and make such a showing of his case that he would have him reinstated as governor. This Johnson refused to do. From this time Trott treated Johnson with neglect, and in some way or other influenced the proprietors to do the same.

The assembly sent Colonel Barnwell to England as their agent, to make a statement of the condition of things in the province. In the meantime it became known that the Spaniards were fitting out a fleet in Havana for the purpose of making an attack on the island of Providence and South Carolina. Governor Johnson, whose perseverance knew no limits once more, determined to make an effort to secure his lost authority. He wrote to the assembly telling them that the hostile Spaniards were coming to desolate the colony, and that he was convinced that the troops would fight better under him as a commander than under James Moore. He offered the services of himself and council to advise with the assembly for the general safety. This was shrewd, but he mistook the character of the men he was addressing. The assembly never answered his letter. They treated it with icy neglect.

Hovendine Walker took umbrage at some of the proceedings of the assembly and went to his plantation, and Chief Justice Richard Allein was made president of the assembly. A tax was levied on land and Negroes to meet the current expense of the government and to put the fortifications in proper repair. Governor Johnson and his party refused to pay the tax, but the assembly was not to be trifled with in this way. The property of those who refused to pay the tax was seized and sold, and the tax was paid out of the proceeds of the sale. This was the case with all who refused except the governor. The whole country was in arms, and Rhett was busy with his regiments getting ready for a fight with the Spaniards. This, however, did not take place, for after the whole country had been under arms for two weeks, it was learned that the Spaniards had made an attack on Providence, but had been beaten by Governor Rodgers, and their fleet, having been overtaken in a storm, was nearly destroyed.

After the excitement occasioned by the expected attack of the Spaniards had subsided, Capt. Hildesley, commander of the warship Flambrough, came to Charles Town. Both parties were anxious to secure the cooperation of the captain. Governor Johnson and his party was successful. The neglected governor, in a fit of desperation, now determined to make a dying effort. With the assistance of the Phoenix, commanded by Capt. Pierce, and the Flambrough, he determined to frighten the citizens of Charles Town into subjection. But the governor found that those whom he could not persuade, could not be easily frightened. They laughed at his empty parade. From the ramparts of the town, seventy canon frowned down on his vessels, and the scheme, which was conceived in a fit of rashness, ended in bitter humiliation to its devisor. To add fuel to the popular excitement, it was now learned that the proprietors contemplated selling or had actually sold their charter to a company of Quakers. This produced bitter opposition to the proprietors. Since the proprietors had commenced to barter their charter no one could tell where the thing would end.

The colony was in a very disturbed condition. The majority of the people were in favor of the revolution-ary movement; but Governor Johnson had his friends. With the aid of these he continued to throw every obstacle he could in the way of the new government. In accordance with the instructions of Governor Johnson and his council, Charles Hart, the secretary of the colony, secreted the public records; and the clergy who seem to have favored the governor, refused to marry those who desired to enter into matrimonial relations without license procured from Governor Johnson. Captains Hildesley and Pierce still continued to encourage Governor Johnson to make an effort to regain his former position. Some time in the early part of 1721 he called together a few men, and from the rear of the town made an advance upon the fort with the intention of surprising. Unfortunately for Johnson, his movement was discovered by Governor Moore. Two guns from the fort were fired over the heads of Johnson and his men. This frightened them and brought them to their senses. They saw now that they were wholly at the mercy of the revolutionary party. After promising not to disturb the peace of the community again, Johnson and his party were permitted to enter the town. Here ended the career of Governor Johnson. For some reason or other, the proprietors paid no attention to his letter, and by all parties he was suffered to sink into obscurity. It is just to say that Robert Johnson did not merit the treatment he received at the hands of the proprietors. His ruin may be traced to Rhett and Trott.

When Col. Barnwell arrived in England for the purpose of making arrangements for the transfer of the government of the colony of South Carolina from the proprietors to the English crown, King George was in Hanover, his native land. The matter, however, was taken into consideration by the lords of the regency, and after due deliberation it was declared that the proprietors had forfeited their charter and the attorney general of the kingdom was ordered to make the fact known in a legal way. In September, 1720, Francis Nicholson was commissioned provisional governor of South Carolina. With the appointment of General Francis Nicholson as governor commenced the royal government of South Carolina. It must be remembered, however, that at the time the proprietors only surrendered the government. They still remained possessed of the soil. This, as we will see, was, in 1729, sold to the king. At least seven-eighths of the whole state was sold for only a little more than one hundred thousand dollars.

Seventeen hundred and nineteen marks an important epoch in the history of South Carolina. It was the first revolution in the state, followed by another in 1775, very similar in many of its important features. From the settlement of the state to the first revolution was a little less than fifty years; from the first revolution to the second, was a little more than fifty years.

Installment XXX

EFFECT OF THE REVOLUTION

The transition from one form of government to another is ever attended with inconveniences. A revolution, whatever may be its final results, is, at the time of its consummation, attended with sacrifices. Most of the great revolutions which have taken place have been perfected with blood. A revolutionary period is commonly a period of blood. Such, however, was not the case in South Carolina during the revolution. No blood was shed. Still, it had been attended with bitter feelings and harsh and provoking words. So intense had been the interest of the people in the movement that everything else was partially neglected. Agriculture and commerce were in a languishing condition. Science and religion flourish only in times of peace.

The transition from the proprietary to the royal government was not so abrupt as most other revolutions. It was not a revolution from a republic to a monarchy; for the proprietary government of South Carolina, as it existed from the settlement of the colony until 1719, was neither a monarchy nor yet a republic; but a kind of mongrel aristocracy. A few nobles, often with little sense and less prudence, ruled. These nobles were themselves the subjects of England. Perhaps no better description could be given of the proprietary government than to call it a kind of feudal system. The inhabitants of the colony were of British descent and British in all of their notions of government. They loved the English laws and they loved the English manners and customs. Hence there was nothing abrupt in the change from the proprietary to the royal government. They were bound to England by the strongest ties. It was the native land of large numbers of them, and the native land of the fathers of by far the largest portion of the remainder. They called England home. Even that portion of the inhabitants who had come from other countries preferred the government of England to that of the weak and inefficient government of the proprietors. Such being the true condition of things in the colony of South Carolina at the time of the first revolution, the transition was easy and attended with but few of those evils that follow in the wake of revolutions generally.

NICHOLSON A GOOD GOVERNOR

The king was fortunate in the appointment of a governor. Francis Nicholson was eminently qualified for such a position at such a time. By education a soldier, and possessed of fine administrative powers, the only blemish that attached to his character that he was irreligious and profane. As we will learn from his subsequent history in connection with the colony of South Carolina, he presented one of those anomalous instances of an individual, impious himself, but not approving of impiety in others.

So soon as Governor Nicholson arrived, which was about the middle of the year 1721, the waves of popular tumult ceased to roll. He was met by the advocates of both the royal and proprietary government with open hands and open hearts. Joy pervaded every bosom. Governor Johnson, we are almost prepared to say, gladly yielded up all pretensions to power, and united with the people in their demonstrations of joy. We are not to conclude that Robert Johnson was a man blown about by every popular breeze. He remained true to the proprietors until the change of government was legally effected and then yielded. To have done otherwise would have been treason. The determination seems to have been formed by every individual to bury the past. No references were made to the past difficulties; but all vied with each other in promoting the peace and prosperity of the settlement.

At this period but a very small portion of what is now the state of South Carolina was settled by Europeans. No one except some traders ever ventured more than fifty miles from the sea. All of the middle and upper sections of the state were in the undisturbed possession of the Indians. At Dorchester and Wilton a few families had settled and constructed something that at least bore the name and to some extent served the purpose of fortifications against the attacks of their Indian neighbors. The great majority of the inhabitants were settled in and around Charles Town. During and after the Yemassee war, many of the frontier settlers removed to Charles Town for protection. This, together with immigrants who, from time to time joined the colony, tended to spread the town beyond the fortifications. Still, Charles Town, in 1719, was but a small place.

RESTORATION OF GOOD FEELING

The first thing that Governor Nicholson did on assuming the government was to order an election to be held for members of the assembly. The election passed off to the satisfaction of all parties, and the assembly, on convening, chose James Moore, their governor, speaker. Governor Nicholson confirmed their choice. Among the first things done by the assembly was to pass an act recognizing King George I, as the lawful and undoubted sovereign of Great Britain, France and Ireland, and especially of South Carolina. The wisdom and goodness of the king was acknowledged for appointing General Francis Nicholson governor of the colony.

So far as it could, the assembly, with the assent of the governor and his council, blotted out everything that tended in any way to foster bitter feeling between the late parties. This effort to reconcile the late adherents of James Moore and those who espoused the cause of Robert Johnson, was entirely successful.

Governor Nicholson now directed his attention to strengthening the colony against its enemies. Previous to his departure from England, a treaty of peace between England and Spain had been signed, in which it was agreed that the Spanish colony in Florida should not molest the English colony in South Carolina, neither should the English colony in South Carolina molest the Spanish colony in Florida. This was a favorable circumstance. By the terms of this treaty the Indians residing within the territory claimed by the two colonies were to be restrained from depredations on the settlers. Gov. Nicholson had the foresight to discover that the good will of the neighborhood tribes of Indians was necessary to the peace and prosperity of the infant colony. On learning that the Indians had, in most instances, been provoked to acts of cruelty and blood by the rapacious and unjust acts of the whites, he called a convention of the neighboring chiefs. The Cherokees were invited to come and enter into an alliance with the colonies. This invitation was joyfully accepted by the Indians, and representatives from thirty-seven of their towns were sent to consult with Governor Nicholson.

PROGRESS IN CIVILIZATION

At this convention a multitude of little things in themselves, but of vast importance to the comfort and security of the colony, were arranged. A uniformity of weights and measures was established. The various minor tribes were united into one, and one chief placed over all. The honor of the chief warrior was conferred upon Wrosetasalaw. To him was granted the power to punish those who might be guilty of trespassing upon the rights secured by the treaty both to the Indians and whites. Between the Creeks, one of the most powerful tribes, and the whites, the Savannah River was to be the boundary. A resident agent was appointed for the tribe, whose business it was to regulate all dealings with the Indians.

This convention was of vast importance to the colony. It secured, at least for a time, the good will of the Indians, and gave to the inhabitants, already so long harassed with war and civil strife, time and opportunity to devote their attention to the arts of civilization.

In 1721, when Francis Nicholson became governor, the white population of South Carolina was about 10,000 and the Negroes about twice that number. Schools had been established and churches built; but neither the cause of education nor of religion was in a flourishing condition. The government had, from the beginning, been too unstable for the welfare of either religion or education. The Yemassees had reduced several country churches to ashes, and in some communities, not far from Charles Town, no public religious teaching had been enjoyed for a number of years. Governor Nicholson and a number of good men of the colony directed their attention to this matter.

NICHOLSON ENCOURAGES RELIGION

As said before, Governor Nicholson made no pretensions to religion. On the contrary, he is represented as being an exceedingly profane man. Still, in a very laudable manner, he gave both his approbation and pecuniary support to the spread of the gospel. The Georgetown community had been so much neglected that the people retained scarcely a resemblance of religion amongst them. To reclaim these people, Governor Nicholson proposed to build a church in their midst by private subscription. This subscription he headed with a liberality worthy of the object in view and the position which he held. The parish of St. George was taken out of St. Andrews, and a church built partly by public donation and partly by private contributions. Application was made by the governor to the society in England for the propagation of the gospel in foreign parts, for an annual allowance to clergymen above what was paid them by the colony. In connection with churches, the necessity for schools was taken into consideration. It was argued that the school house and the church were mutually dependent upon each other, and civilized society absolutely dependent upon both. Impressed strongly with the idea, school houses were built and teachers employed. In these schools, not only the elements of education were taught, but the principals of Christian religion were explained. Every school house was, as it should be, a nursery in which plants were reared both for the church and for the state. A spirit of liberality possessed the men of the day, worthy of emulation of the men of the present time. Whitmarsh, Ludlam and Beresford left their estates, or the most of them, which in aggregate amounted to more than $67,000, for the purpose of establishing free schools of high order.

CHARLATANS IN THOSE DAYS

During the administration of Nicholson, a romantic but melancholy event transpired. In the colony there was a family of French descent by the name of Dutarque. This family was descended from a family which came into the colony after the revocation of the edict of Nantz. The family consisted of four sons and an equal number of daughters. The family was in moderate circumstances, but regarded by their acquaintances as respectable. An individual said to have been a Moravian preacher, (but, no doubt, if we have his correct character, either an impostor or a fanatic) came into the neighborhood in which the Dutarque family resided. He made their house his home. By argument and by the aid of certain books, he filled the mind of the Dutarque family with wild and extravagant notions about religion. They imbibed a contempt for the religion of their neighbors and went so far, as it would seem, to conclude that they were right, and every one else wrong; that their religion was the true religion and the religion of all others false. They went so far as to pretend that they received revelations from heaven. A certain individual by the name of Peter Rombert had married one of the daughters. Rombert pretended to have been divinely set apart to fill the sacred office of a prophet. He pretended that he had been informed by God that the world was soon to be visited by some dire calamity which would sweep off of the face of the earth all the human race, except one family. From this favored family the earth would again be peopled by faithful seed. Strange as it may seem, some persons believed what this wild enthusiast preached. That man who is bold enough to claim to the world that he has been to heaven, will find some individual who will follow him even to the stake. Rombert declared that he had been instructed by revelation to put away his wife and take her younger sister to be his wife. The father, at first, was amazed by such a revelation; but Rombert affirmed that the thing proceeded from heaven, and God would give a sign confirmatory of the fact.

Whatever may have been the sign, it is said that it was given and Rombert took his new wife. Thus, Rombert and Judith Dutarque lived in adultery and incest. This was in open violation of the law concerning bastardy, enacted Sept. 17th, 1703. By the provisions of that law, it was incumbent upon Capt. Simmons, the trial justice in the neighborhood, to summon Peter Rombert and Judith Dutarque before him. A difficulty had occurred with the family in consequence of their refusal, under plea of revelation, to obey the militia law of the country. They said that God had warned them to bear no arms, and under this delusion they refused to obey the civil and military officers. The constable to whom the warrant respecting the incestuous life of Rombert and Judith was given, being aware of the condition of things, and anticipating a difficulty, took several of his neighbors with him. So soon as the constables came in sight, the family consulted Rombert, the prophet, as to what they must do. He ordered them to arm themselves and defend their lives and property against the ungodly invaders of their right. This order was promptly obeyed, and the constable and his party were obliged to return without effecting their object. No one, however, was killed.

Captain Simmons concluded that no such conduct as this ought to be tolerated. He summoned a posse of men and went to protect the constable in the discharge of his duty. When Simmons and his party approached the house, the Dutarques shut themselves up in the house and commenced a brisk fire on the party. Simmons was shot down dead at the first fire, and several of those who accompanied him wounded. The fire was returned by the Simmons party and a woman within the house killed. The house was then broken open and the rest taken prisoners.

THE STERN HAND OF THE LAW

In September, 1724, all the party except Judith were tried. All except two of the sons, David and John, who were minors, were put to death. This was a sad affair. Seven individuals lost their lives. Four were executed, one killed, and two murdered. No doubt the Dutarque family were the subjects of a gross delusion, but it is highly probable that Captain Simmons acted rashly and precipitously. Who the individual styling himself a Moravian preacher was, we do not know; but it would be an exceedingly unjust conclusion to suppose that this fanatical deportment of the Dutarque family was a natural result of embracing the Moravian creed. Peter Rombert, the prophet of the family, was, in all probability, an accomplished impostor. Like many another villain, he attempted to cover his lecherous conduct beneath the cloak of religion. We can easily conceive a happy family brought to ruin by suffering themselves to be duped by an impostor. Such events are sad, but by no means of seldom occurrence.

Installment XXXI

It is thought that about one hundred and fifty persons constituted the colony that, in 1670, made a settlement on the right bank of the Ashley River. The exact number is not known, but there are reasons for concluding that it was somewhere in the neighborhood of the number stated above. These were all white and the majority of them were dissenters. That is, they were either individuals who were opposed to the Church of England, and were members of some other denomination of Christians, or they were members of the Church of England, but opposed to some of the practices of that church.

Slaves were brought into the colony by John Yeamans, but a very short time after its settlement. By these, and the Indians who were reduced to bondage, most of the manual labor in the colony was performed. In 1701, the whole population, including the whites, the Negroes, and the Indian slaves, amounted to 7,000. In 1724, the period at which we have arrived, the whole number of the inhabitants was thirty-two thousand. Of this number, eighteen thousand were slaves, the most of whom were Negroes.

It was now fifty-four years since the landing of Sayle and his little band, and when we take all things into consideration the increase was very great. On several occasions the number of inhabitants had been thinned by the wars with the Indians and Spaniards; and, at other times, disease, in its worst form, had preyed upon the settlers. Smallpox and yellow fever had visited the province. In fact, shortly after the settlement was made, it seems to have been very sickly. Besides these things, during the latter part of the proprietary government, the encouragement to immigrants was not very great. When we consider all these things the increase from one hundred and fifty inhabitants to Thirty-two thousand in a period of fifty-four years is, we think, very remarkable.

The mode of life of the first settlers was exceedingly simple and frugal. The majority of them were English, but other nations of Europe were represented. Some of the settlers were possessed of considerable fortunes, but by far the greater portion of them were from the humble walks in life. There was an abundant evidence that the settlers generally were intelligent, high-minded and patriotic, and a very respectable number of them were men of culture and refinement. The enactments made by the Colonial assembly, even in the very infancy of the colony, are an honor to any nation. They give unmistakable evidences of both moral and intellectual stamina. The early laws of South Carolina are unsurpassed by those of any of the colonies in America. Like the manners and customs of the people, they are English in all their leading features. The people were frugal. They indulged in but few luxuries. Each farm produced an abundance of supplies to meet the necessities of its owner and some to sell. The rivers and bays were filled with fish and the forest abounded with game of great variety. It was customary for the planters to hire, for a mere trifle, an Indian hunter. This Indian was able to keep the family of his employer in an abundance of animal food.

The principal cereals cultivated were maize, or Indian corn, peas, and rice. The two former, the settlers found to be the principal farinaceous food of the Indians. Both of these the first settlers found to be more healthy and better adapted to the wants of laboring men than rice, and hence their cultivation was at first more extensive than was that of rice or any other crop.

For a long time after the first settling of the state, the plow was but little used. This arose from two circumstances. At first no domestic animals, such as horses, mules and oxen, were possessed by the settlers; and most of the settlers, coming from old countries, from which all stumps, roots and stones had been removed from the fields, they entertained the notion that the plow could not be used in this country until the soil was reduced to a similar condition. The manner of cultivating the maize was learned from the Indians. Ridges about five feet apart were made with the hoe, and the maize planted on the top of the ridge. During the growth of maize it was worked exclusively with the hoe. The grass was cut out and the soil drawn up in a kind of hill around the root of the stalk, After the maize had attained a considerable height, peas were planted at each stalk of maize. Spanish potatoes were also cultivated. Rice was sown in the wet places that were unsuited to the cultivation of maize. The luxuries in which the people indulged occasionally were coffee, sugar, tea and rice. Sayle, and his little party who settled on the Ashley River, brought a still, but there is no evidence, so far as we have discovered, that it was used. Orchards and vineyards were planted and, at a very early period, the inhabitants learned to convert the fruit into alcoholic beverages.

The commerce of the colony was, at this time, as previously, carried on with the West Indies and the northern colonies. Lumber and naval stores were sent to the West Indies for which molasses, sugar, coffee, rum and cotton were received in exchange. Nearly all the money that was in the colony came from this quarter. Rice, tar, pitch and hides were sent to the English colonies in the north and exchanged for flour, fruit, beer, cider and salt fish.

As early as the year 1710 a considerable variety of fruits had been introduced into this country. Grapes had been brought from Madeira and other grape growing countries. Figs, apples, pears, peaches, oranges, and quinces had been introduced, and many of the trees were bearing. Of many of these there were several varieties, especially of the peach. At first peach trees were planted with a view to feeding hogs on the fruit.

Up to this period, no peach brandy seems to have been made in the colony. The peach is, we believe, generally regarded as a native of Persia. This seems to be indicated by its botanical name, "Persica." Yet, it would appear from some old accounts of the first settlement of South Carolina that the peach was found here when the settlers first came and that the Indians made a delicious cordial out of the fruit.

The woods of South Carolina, one hundred and fifty years ago, were full of wild animal, many of which have entirely disappeared. Besides the few wild animals which still remain, there were then elk, buffalo, bears, tigers, and wild cats. Buffaloes were abundant in some sections of the state. These animals, like many others, had their particular territory which they frequented. This territory was almost always watered by some stream of water. From the fact that the animals were found in abundance in the neighborhood of that stream, it was given the name of the animal. Thus we have, in various sections of the state, streams bearing the name Turkey Creek. We have in York county a Wolf Creek and a Buffalo Creek. In Chester county a Bull Run; in Fairfield a Coon branch, and in the state there are several small streams which once bore the name Wild Cat.

Although when the government of the state passed from under the control of the proprietors into the hands of the King of England, the state had been settled for more than fifty years, it was still almost a virgin forest, grand with its native beauties. But little of the soil had been cultivated. Only a small portion of the territory embraced in the original grant had been seen by any European.

Several causes prevented the early emigrants from extending their settlements to any great distance beyond Charles Town. The Spanish on the south and the Indians in all directions prevented this. Sometimes the Spanish were at peace and sometimes at war with

England; but at almost every period previous to 1724, they were the bitter enemies of the colonists planted on the soil that now bears the name South Carolina.

The French were now making rapid encroachments upon the territorial grant of the state. In 1712, Louis the Fourteenth granted Crozat a large tract of country at the mouth of the Mississippi. This was a part of the territory granted by Charles the Second of England to the original proprietors. From this point, the French colony planted in what is now the state of Louisiana gradually extended to the settlement of Charles Town. By them a fort called Alabama was erected on the Mobile River. Their object in building this fort was to put themselves in easy communication with the Indian tribes of the country. In this lay the danger of the colony of South Carolina. The Indians were incited to hostilities.

In 1725, King George granted Governor Nicholson permission to return to England, and the government devolved upon the president of the council, Arthur Middleton. Nicholson had been generous, liberal and patriotic, and consequently very popular. The income from his office had been freely expended in promoting the public good. Arthur Middleton had been active in bringing about the change from the proprietary to the royal government. He was firm and unwavering in his attachment to the king; but not disposed to make great personal sacrifices for the good of the colonies. His aspirations were not for popularity; but rather for individual wealth. He does not seem to have had much ambition for popular honors, but to have been anxious to secure the position of an English Lord with ample wealth.

Soon after his administration began, a difficulty occurred between him and the Spanish authorities respecting the boundary line between Florida and South Carolina. The Carolinians had built a fort on the Altamaha for the purpose of preventing the Negroes of the colony from escaping to Florida, and also for the purpose of preventing the Indians who were allied with the Spanish from depredations upon the property of the settlers. In this fort a few soldiers were kept.

The Spanish governor of St. Augustine complained to the Spanish king of this encroachment. The complaint was brought by the Spanish ambassador at London before the British government. It was agreed, in order not to disturb the peaceable relations then existing between England and Spain, that the governor of South Carolina and the Spanish governor of Florida should meet and settle the dispute in a friendly manner. The meeting took place at Charles Town. Francisco Menandez and Joseph de Rabiero represented the Spanish government. In the conference which took place, Governor Middleton showed the Spanish representatives that the fort erected at the Altamaha was within the territory originally granted to the colony and that the claims of the Spaniards were without foundation. This was the case. The Spanish had no well-founded claim to the territory on which that fort was erected.

The fort may have been erected, in part at least, with a different intention from what was mentioned; but the soil upon which it was erected was, beyond controversy, the property of South Carolina. No doubt one object which was contemplated in erecting the fort was to decoy the Indians, who were friends to the Spanish, from their allegiance. The Spanish government asserted that such was the case, and no doubt there was some truth in it. Middleton complained that the Spanish authorities of St. Augustine encouraged the Negroes of South Carolina to run away from their masters. This was not denied, but justified on the ground that it was in accordance with the wishes and instructions of the court of Madrid. It was declared that the object which was designed to be accomplished by decoying these slaves away from their masters was to convert them to the Catholic religion. Middleton asserted that to act thus was neither consistent, just, nor honorable. For twenty years the practice of the Spanish authorities in St. Augustine had been to decoy all the slaves they could from the colony in South Carolina. When these slaves were demanded, the Spanish government engaged to pay for them, but only in a few cases was this done.

The conference broke up without effecting anything but bad feeling. The Yemassees, the friends of the Spanish and bitter enemies of the English colony at Charles Town, again commenced to plunder the country and scalp the inhabitants. Incensed by the outrages, Colonel Palmer determined to retaliate. He, with a body of three hundred men, invaded Florida. Everything in his course was destroyed. The country was ruined. Nothing escaped except what was protected by the Fort of St. Augustine. The crops were totally destroyed and the domestic animals were driven off, the houses burned. Some of the Indians were killed on the spot, whilst others were taken captive and treated as captives at that time were usually treated. This taught the Spaniards an important lesson. They now learned that the colonists at Charles Town not only could defend themselves, but utterly annihilate the colonies in Florida, if they saw fit.

NOTABLE PERIOD OF DROUGHT

The summer of 1728 was, in South Carolina, excessively hot and dry. The crops were cut off and so great was the evaporation that many of the small upland streams and ponds were dried up. Wild animals were reduced to the greatest straits and many of them perished for want of water. This drought was followed in August by a terrific storm. The streets of Charles Town were covered with water driven in from the river. Houses and trees were blown down. Twenty-three ships lying in the harbor were dashed with violence on shore and totally destroyed. Only two large vessels - the Fox and the Garland - outrode the storm. These were warships stationed at the entrance of the harbor for the protection of the town. For security from the flood, the inhabitants of the town were forced to take refuge in the upper stories of their houses. It may not be uninteresting to remark that this was the third hurricane that had visited the country since the settlement by the English. The first was in 1700, the second in 1713. These, as we will see, were followed by others at irregular periods.

YELLOW FEVER SCOURGE

The storm of 1728 was followed by the yellow fever. This was the third time that this dreadful disease made its appearance. So fatal was it at this time that it was often difficult for friends to obtain assistance in burying their dead. The people in the country became alarmed and no person from the plantations was permitted to visit the town, lest the disease might be contracted and carried into the country. The town was dependent upon the plantations in its vicinity for supplies. None being brought in, the town was threatened with famine.

SALE OF THE SOIL TO THE KING

In the year 1728, the proprietors, with the exception of Lord Carteret, sold their interest in the soil to the king of Great Britain. The purchase of the seven-eighths of this extensive territory was made for the insignificant sum of eighty-seven thousand five hundred dollars. The payment was to be made in 1729. In 1719 the government of the state was surrendered to the King of England. Now the soil was bought and the province became directly under the control of the crown of England. All things considered, this was a good thing. Under the proprietary government it is very probable that the colony would have struggled for a few years and then died. By the act of the British parliament, power was granted the king of England to appoint a governor for each of the Carolinas. In 1729 the province was divided into North and South Carolina, but the division was not effected until 1732. The line was not run until 1736, and then with no degree of accuracy.

SITUATION BEGINS TO BRIGHTEN

So soon as the province was placed wholly in the hands of the king, everything began to assume a new and favorable aspect. Among the first undertakings of the royal government was an attempt to conciliate the Indian tribes and form, with them, alliances of friendship. To effect this object, Alexander Cummings was sent out with full power to treat with the various tribes living in the region now occupied by the northwestern counties of the state. In 1730, Cummings penetrated the forest as far as Keowee town. Here, in April, the chiefs met and, in a friendly manner, entered into negotiations for the general welfare of themselves, their people and the English settlers.

Six of the chiefs accompanied Cummings to Charles Town, where they were joined by another and all seven set sail for England and, in the month of June, arrived safely in England. They landed at Dover; thence they went to London, and were ushered into the presence of the King of England. Speeches were made by the Indians and by King George, and finally a treaty was drawn up and signed by Alured Popple, secretary of the lords commission of trade and plantations for and in behalf of the English crown, and by the marks of the six chiefs for and in behalf of the Cherokees. These six chiefs had gone to England as deputies to Moytoy, the chief warrior of the Cherokees; and of course, their action was regarded as binding. In 1731, these Indian deputies returned to America. They accompanied Robert Johnson, who was appointed by the king, governor of South Carolina.

GOVERNOR JOHNSON COMES BACK

This was the same Robert Johnson who was governor of South Carolina when the proprietary government, in 1717, was superseded by the royal. The appointing of Johnson governor showed that he had not, in the least, forfeited the confidence of either the people or the king. He had struggled hard to retain the proprietary form of government, but had failed. He did his duty. He was faithful to his employers, the proprietors of the province, and now, in 1731, he is again honored with the office of governor. The choice was certainly a wise one. Robert Johnson was thoroughly acquainted with the colony. He knew the men.

THE NEW GOVERNMENT

Thomas Broughton was appointed lieutenant governor, and Robert Wright, chief justice. William Bull, James Kinloch, Alexander Skene, John Fenwick, Arthur Middleton, Joseph Wragg, Francis Yonge, Jno. Hamerton and Thomas Waring, were the remaining members of the council. From the commencement of his administration, Johnson manifested great interest in the Royal government, and also in the people of the colony. He recommended the assembly to pass a vote of thanks to his majesty, the King of England, for his great kindness manifested toward the colony, in purchasing seven-eighths of the soil of the province. He urged that the laws for the suppression of vice be enforced, and that the children and youth of the settlement be carefully educated, as the best possible means for the promotion of virtue. Towards the settlers, who were at this time poor, and many of them sad from the sore bereavements which they had suffered, the English government was kind, gentle and encouraging. The quitrents which were bought at the time the soil was purchased were, by an act of royal bounty, remitted. The king sent seventy pieces of cannon to the colony, and instructed Governor Johnson to build a fort at Port Royal and another at Altamaha. A company of foot soldiers was granted the colony for its protection by land, and ships of war were stationed in the harbors and along the coast, for the protection of the commerce of the colony. These and similar acts of kindness and generosity stimulated the people to struggle against the difficulties of the wilderness with energy and hope.

COMMERCIAL IMPORTANCE RECOGNIZED

The colony began to assume an importance which attracted the attention of the large mercantile cities of England. The merchants of London, Bristol and Liverpool, established branch-houses of their business in Charles Town. Large numbers of Negroes were brought from Africa by these European merchants and sold to the settlers in South Carolina.

In return, rice, silk, timber, furs and leather were sold by the settlers to these merchants. The exports of the colony now began to be so extensive as to secure to the people credit in England. During the year 1731, nearly forty-two thousand barrels of rice were sent by the colony to England and to the other colonies in America; and fifteen hundred Negroes were brought into the state.

It would seem that the year 1731 marks a very important period in the history of South Carolina. Prior to this period, the inhabitants enjoyed very few comforts. The homes in which the people lived were miserable wooden huts. In Charles Town, there were, in 1731, between five and six thousand dwelling houses, most of which were wooden structures.

The county possessed fewer artificial comforts than the town. The farmers at that early day were notoriously slovenly. All that the majority aimed at was to procure a sufficient amount of the absolute necessities of life. This could be accomplished almost without an effort. The restrictions which heretofore had been laid on commerce, and the inefficiency of the proprietary government, had conspired to make the farmers careless and indifferent.

So soon as the province became a part and parcel of the British dominions, a marked change took place. The farmers became energetic, and in the year 1731, two hundred and seven ships were employed in exporting the surplus productions of the colony.

NEW TOWNS LAID OUT

The king instructed Governor Johnson to extend the settlement of the territory in various directions. For the purpose of effecting this object, he was ordered to lay out eleven towns. It was ordered that the district connected with each of these towns should contain a tract of 20,000 acres of land. These towns were to be located on the Altamaha, Savannah, Santee, Ponpon, Wateree, Black, Waccamaw and PeeDee Rivers. On each of the three first named there were to be two towns, and one on each of the others. Each man, woman and child of every family which would settle on these tracts of land was to receive fifty acres, which was to be increased as the necessities of the family might demand.

MANY CAME AS SERVANTS

At that time it was very common for individuals to come into the country in the capacity of servants. These individuals had engaged to labor in the capacity of servants only for a certain number of years. The king made provision for this class of persons. So soon as their term of service expired they were to receive fifty acres of land, free from all rents for two years. Women as well as men were entitled to this bounty. This was a wise provision. Many persons of good character came

at different times into the country in the capacity of servants. By the wise provision of the king these individuals were, so soon as their term of service expired, enabled to assume, with credit to themselves, and profit to the country, the position of citizens. From this class of persons, some of the most worthy citizens of the state, in after years, sprang. Whether or not all the towns that Governor Johnson was instructed to lay out were actually located, we are not able to say positively. Perhaps they were not; but one thing is certain, about this time the population of the state first began to spread over the territory.

Purrysburg, on the banks of the Savannah, was settled by a Swiss colony. This town was about thirty miles from the sea and seven miles above tide water. This settlement was begun under the auspices of John Peter Purry, of Neufchatel; James Richards of Geneva; Abraham Meuron and Henry Raymond, both of Sulpy. In order to aid Purry in accomplishing his undertaking, the assembly granted him $2,000 and sustenance for the 300 persons for the period of one year. Provision was made that the immigrants be Swiss Protestants of good moral character.

The country had now been settled sixty years. Still the people enjoyed but few of the blessing of civilization. We have already seen that the dwelling houses of the majority of the country people were rude in appearance, and afforded but little comfort to those inhabiting them. There were even at this early period in the country a few stately mansions, but these were exceptions. A few rich men came to South Carolina and from the infancy of the colony lived in English style. What we now called outhouses were, of course, even more neglected than the dwellings.

CATTLE LEFT TO THE WEATHER

In 1731, there were but few barns in the state. The domestic animals were rarely, even in winter, put in stables. They were turned into pens, nearby the dwelling house, more for the purpose of keeping them tame than with the view of protecting them from the inclemency of the weather. Horses, cows, hogs, and sheep had increased most wonderfully. At this time it was no uncommon thing for a farmer to own several hundred head of cattle. These were no expense whatever, except the time that was spent in watching them and preventing them from going wild. They were fed neither in summer nor winter. In summer they grew very fat; but in the winter they became exceedingly poor, and vast numbers of them died. It is said that during the winter of 1730-31, not less than 10,000 head of cattle died from hunger and cold. Up to this period the farmers laid up no food for their domestic animals and it is said that there was not a cow shelter in the country. Very little use was made of the domestic animals by the early settlers. Milk and butter were scarce, notwithstanding the fact that one individual would often own two hundred cows and calves. The cows and calves were allowed to run together in the forest, and the owner of this vast herd rarely had either milk or butter on his table. Butter sold for $1.50 per pound, and sometimes for twice that amount, in Charles Town. The first individuals who settled in the state were, it would seem from their conduct, extremely ignorant with respect to agriculture, and very little progress was made either in the science or art of agriculture by their descendants for more than half a century. They learned to cultivate maize from the Indians, and rice from the Negroes that were brought into the colony from Africa.

SKILLED LABOR HIGH

In 1731, there were very few mechanics in this state. The wages of a good carpenter at that time was about $7.50 and diet per day. Blacksmiths ranked about the same. Such a condition of things could not last long. In a country which afforded freedom to all, such wages would entice the struggling multitudes of Europe. The first settlers of the state did not, however, think of settling up the state with the laboring classes of Europe. They looked to Africa for laborers. Hence the Negro population increased more rapidly than the white. When the white population numbered only a little more than 10,000 the Negro population was 40,000. The price of a Negro slave on an average was about $150. This sum was paid with ox hides and deer skins, or with a few barrels of rice or of tar. Such a system was calculated to make the white people lazy.

INSTALLMENT XXXIII

EARLY ISOLATION

The colony of South Carolina occupied, for a period of more than sixty years, an isolated position. On all sides, it was a frontier settlement. By land it was exposed to the scalping parties of the Yemassees; and by sea it was exposed to the plundering pirates. These latter were, at first, favorably treated by the settlers; but he who forms a league with rogues must either turn rogue himself or be deserted and plundered by his confederates. Such was the case with the first settlers of South Carolina. They formed with the pirates a kind of tacit arrangement that these plunders of the sea might enter the port of Charles Town and go out again undisturbed. The colonists sorely needed money, and the pirates brought Spanish coin into the country and spent it freely. The early settlers of the colony never asked how or from whom this money was obtained. So far, they winked at the conduct of these robbers on the high seas. Farther than this, they did not go. When, however, the colonists were disposed to obey the enactments relating to pirates, the pirates turned their vengeance upon the commerce of the colony.

The Yemassees, and tribes in alliance with the Spanish in Florida, often sent out marauding parties. These kept the inhabitants of the country in a state of continual dread, and often drove them, panic stricken, to Charles Town.

SETTLEMENT OF GEORGIA

Beyond the Savannah, no settlement was attempted. By the terms of the treaty made by Nicholson with the Indians, this river was made the dividing line between the tribes and the English settlement. All the territory west and south of this river was a waste, inhabited only by wild beasts and savages. Both the English and Spanish claimed the soil. Neither, however, had made any attempt to settle it. This territory now forms the state of Georgia. Sir Walter Raleigh, in 1587 - more than eighty years before the settlement was begun at Charles Town - landed at the mouth of the Savannah, but made no settlement.

In 1732 some benevolent persons in England determined to open up a home in the New World for the poor and oppressed of Europe. Chief amongst these individuals was James Oglethorpe. A variety of propitious events had conspired to elevate Oglethorpe to a high position of influence in the English government. He was born some time in December, 1688, in Sully county, England. At an early age, he exhibited a military turn of mind and, in 1714, was commissioned an officer in the king's guards. The Duke of Marlborough was impressed with his personal beauty and dignity, and recommended him to Prince Eugent. In the campaign of 1716-17 against the Turks, he distinguished himself and, on returning to England, was, in 1722, elected a member of parliament from the borough of Hazlemere. This position he held for a period of more than thirty years. During this time he devised a scheme for ameliorating the condition of London debtors. Having succeeded in this, he next turned his attention to the poor and indigent of Europe. Such is the origin of the settling of the state of Georgia. A company was formed and funds raised by private subscriptions for the purpose of erecting a home in the New World for the poor, especially of England and Ireland. Application was made to the king by whom a charter was granted on the 9th of June, 1732. The main object contemplated by this undertaking was to furnish a home for the poor; but it was also designed to make the new colony a kind of protection to South Carolina.

Twenty-one persons were appointed trustees of the undertaking and the money was deposited in the Bank of England. Every precaution was taken to secure a proper investment of the funds. In July the trustees had their first meeting, and Lord Percival was chosen president. On the 28th of November, 116 emigrants set sail from Gravesend, and on the 24th of January, 1733, they arrived at Charles Town.

It had been determined by the trustees at their first meeting to form the settlement on the territory embraced between the rivers Savannah and Altamaha. Hence, so soon as they arrived in Charles Town, preparations were made for reaching this point.

SOUTH CAROLINA HELPS

The new comers were gladly welcomed by Governor Johnson and the people of Charles Town. The people of South Carolina showed their generosity by sending the newly arrived colonists provisions and also cows and hogs with which to stock the contemplated settlement. William Bull, afterward - in 1737 - governor of South Carolina, volunteered to accompany the colony to its point of destination. General Oglethorpe was with the lately arrived settlers. Governor Johnson sent the boats belonging to the colony to accompany them on their journey. On the 12th of February, 1733, they arrived at Yamacraw bluff and laid the foundation of the present city of Savannah. In honor of George the Second, the king of England, by whose liberality the scheme had been greatly advanced, the trustees had named the settlement Georgia; whilst the town built was, from the river on which it was located, named Savannah.

This settlement was of vast importance to the English colony in South Carolina. It extended the borders of civilization, increased the number of Europeans in the country, and placed a settlement between Charles Town and the Indian tribes. Oglethorpe, being experienced in military affairs, set about to put the new settlement in a proper shape for defense. A fort was built and cannon placed on the breastworks. The Indians in the immediate vicinity were the Lower and Upper Creeks. To these, the territory west of the Savannah River had been granted by Governor Nicholson, of South Carolina. The Upper Creeks numbered about 25,000. The Lower Creeks had been greatly reduced in number by war and disease.

TREATY WITH THE INDIANS

To conciliate the Indians, Oglethorpe called together a council of their chiefs. In the execution of this he was aided by an Indian woman named Mary, who had married a white trader. This woman was intelligent and exercised very considerable influence amongst her people. By Oglethorpe she was loaded with presents, and her services secured at an annual salary of $500.

Fifty of the chiefs came to the council called by Oglethorpe. A treaty of peace was made between Oglethorpe and Tomochichi, the chief of the Creek warriors. Having arranged the settlement, General Oglethorpe returned to England, taking with him Tomochichi and his queen. On arriving in England they were, with great pomp, introduced into the presence of George the Second, King of England. The Indian chief was struck with astonishment at the greatness and grandeur of the English, and on the other hand everything was done by the English people to make a favorable impression on the mind of the chief. The princes and noblemen flocked from all quarters to gaze upon the savages of the New World. The people gathered around them for the purpose of seeing and men high in state invited them to take of royal banquets. The king bestowed upon them eighty dollars a week during the four months they remained in England, and when they departed for America, loaded them with presents.

Thus, by acts of kindness and deeds of generosity, the Indians residing between the Savannah and the Altamaha were induced to surrender a portion of their dominions to the English.

This Georgia colony, although separate and distinct from the South Carolina colony, still sustained to it an important relation. The general object of both was the same. Both were in search of land of freedom. America was then regarded as a home for the oppressed of every creed. The poor who were oppressed with want saw a prospect for bettering the condition of themselves and their children. But the two colonies had another grand feature in common. They were Protestants and spoke the same language. Hence the planting of the colony by Oglethorpe in Georgia was but extending the borders of South Carolina.

LAND THIEVES

About this time a difficulty appeared among the settlers respecting the manner in which lands were taken up. Grasping individuals ran out large tracts of land to the great detriment of the colony. This was especially the case in the region bordering Port Royal. Some individuals, with the expectation of making themselves the owners of vast tracts of land, had unjustly laid claims to tracts of land which had been laid out as baronies under the proprietary government. All these empty titles had been abolished by the royal government. Still some individuals endeavored to enforce their claims to large tracts of land to the great detriment of the colonies. All the best lands on the water-courses in the direction of Port Royal had been marked out for no other purpose, it would seem, than to secure the foundation for certain individuals, in time, to become mighty landlords.

St. John, the surveyor general for the province, so far favored these individuals as to mark out for them lands contrary both to the laws of the colony and the general welfare of the country. It was a matter of vital importance to the existence of the settlement that the number of inhabitants be increased. This could not be done if a few individuals were permitted to lay claim to all rich lands, and force the multitude to either settle on the poor and unproductive lands or settle on the rich lands in the capacity of tenants. This was in part what brought them to the New World. They had been mere serfs in Europe. They came to America that they might have a home of their own.

ASSEMBLY TAKES A HAND

It was determined that such a system of oppression should not have an existence in South Carolina. Job Rothmaller and Thomas Cooper, two individuals who had laid claim to larger bodies of valuable land were, by order of the assembly, taken into custody. The assembly was incited to take this action by a petition sent up by thirty-nine citizens of Granville county. Cooper appealed to Chief Justice Wright, by whom he was released. The assembly declared that the writ of habeas corpus did not apply to persons committed by the assembly, and resolved that "no writ of habeas corpus lies in favor of any person committed by the house, and that the messenger attending, do yield no obedience to such, and that the Chief justice be made acquainted with these resolutions." The chief justice complained that the resolutions of the assembly had a tendency to subvert the principles of the government. His views were neither favored by the governor or his counsel, who concluded that the lower house possessed the same power in this particular as was possessed by the house of commons in England. The chief justice was not without strong friends. They were, however, individuals who were influenced by selfish ends prejudicial to the general welfare. The assembly were not to be balked in their course. A resolution was passed that Chief Justice Wright had conducted himself in a manner unworthy of the high and responsible office which he held and that it would be for the benefit of the province to suspend him from office. The conduct of the surveyor general was censured. He, in order to make his office more profitable, had encouraged unscrupulous individuals in locating lands. The result was that St. John was forbidden to survey any land unless he had first received a warrant from the governor.

GROWTH OF POPULATION

For many reasons, the increase of population in South Carolina was not so rapid as was desirable, nor so great as might have reasonably been expected. In 1724, the population was 32,000, of which number 14,000 were whites. In 1734, the population was only 30,000, of which 8,000 were whites and 22,000 slaves. The whites had, in ten years, decreased 6,000 and slaves increased 4,000. If the census returns of 1734 are correct, it would be difficult to account for the decrease. The province was visited in 1728 by yellow fever, which greatly reduced the number of the inhabitants, and from a petition sent up by the people to the King of England, we are informed that many colonists had gone with their effects to North Carolina.

About the time of which we are speaking, it was, it seems, a daily occurrence for individuals to leave South Carolina and go to North Carolina. The reason of this was the fact that up to the time of the settlement of Georgia, South Carolina was a frontier settlement, and exposed as we have already seen, to the Spaniards of St. Augustine, and various surrounding Indian tribes.

MENACE OF THE FRENCH

There was another fact which had a tendency, for a time, to retard the growth of the population of South Carolina. The French, in 1712, made a settlement at the mouth of the Mississippi. Louis the Fourteenth granted a large tract of country to Crozat. This, as will be remembered, was within the limits of the territory granted by Charles the Second to the original proprietors and by their successors ceded to the crown of England in 1729. The simple fact that a French colony had been planted at the mouth of the Mississippi was, of itself, a matter of little consequence. The distance from South Carolina was so very great and land so very abundant that no very great inconvenience could have resulted from the settlement of a colony of French at this point. It will, however, be remembered that France, from an early period, laid claim to the whole of the North American continent and she thought upon as good grounds as those by which it was claimed by England. Louis had no good design in granting a tract of land to Crozat. This colony was not content to remain in the neighborhood of the spot on which it was first located; but gradually extended itself eastward. Forts were built in the territory now occupied by the present state of Alabama. In these forts, soldiers were stationed and, from these strongholds, emissaries were sent out amongst the various Indian tribes for the especial purpose of alienating their affections toward the English. This fact, as much as anything else, retarded the increase of population in South Carolina and, no doubt, tended to cause it to decrease.

GEORGIA AS A BUMPER STATE

The settlement of Georgia changed the aspect of things in South Carolina. Immigrants now began to flock in from all quarters of Europe. The eleven townships which had been, by the order of the assembly, laid out were gradually receiving settlers. Germany, Ireland, Scotland, Switzerland, and even France as well as England, contributed to fill the country with inhabitants. In twenty years after the settlement of Georgia, the white population of Georgia amounted to 30,000 and the slaves to 70,000. The Georgia colony contributed both directly and indirectly to the growth of South Carolina.

The form of government established by the trustees in Georgia was by no means adapted to the circumstances of the people. The people were restricted in their agriculture labors to the production of wines and silks; the first settlers, being poor people collected from the cities of Europe, were totally unfit for making a settlement in a forest. The result was that many of them became dissatisfied and crossed the Savannah and became citizens of South Carolina. In order to obtain settlers of the proper character for that colony, the trustees of Georgia had recourse to the highlands of Scotland and the rural districts of Germany. From Inverness, in Scotland, 130 Highlanders were received, and from Germany, 170. These new comers settled in different sections and proved valuable accessions to the inhabitants of Georgia.

The Purrysburg colony soon became dissatisfied. At first the members of this Swiss colony were delighted at the prospect of being, in a short time, the owners of large land estates; but the climate proved unfavorable. Many of them sickened and died. The survivors murmured and repined, and Purry was censured for inducing them to leave the mountains and glens of their native lands.

INFLUX FROM EUROPE

The condition of things in many of the governments of Europe contributed to increase the number of inhabitants of South Carolina. Religious persecution drove some of the best men, with their families, from their native land to the New World. With great propriety it may be said that God opened up America that the oppressed of every creed, might find a home in its wilds - that the downtrodden might be free. It is worthy of note that North America offered its extensive forests as an asylum to the persecuted Protestants of Europe.

About the year 1731, the Scotch-Irish began to pour into South Carolina in large numbers. The history of these immigrants is intensely interesting, and is intimately interwoven with the history of South Carolina. Scotch-Irish is used in contra-distinction to Catholic Irish. The Scotch-Irish were all Protestants, whilst the Irish were the downtrodden subjects of the Pope of Rome.

STORY OF THE COVENANTERS

But Scotch-Irish had another signification. It is used to designate an individual whose ancestors originally came from Scotland and settled in Ireland. Still, again, Scotch-Irish means a class of persons who, at a very early period, were called Covenanters. The history of these Scotch-Irish or Covenanters is the most thrilling chapter in the history of the world. Their name is derived from a particular act performed by them. In 1537, on the 3rd of December, a number of the Protestant nobles met at Edinburgh and signed a paper which from its nature was called a covenant. In this document they solemnly covenanted "that we, by God's grace shall, with all diligence, continually apply our whole power substance and our very lives to maintain, set forward and establish the word of God and his congregation; and shall labor at our possibility to have faithful ministers, purely and truly to minister Christ's evangel and sacrament to his people." The object of this document was simply a voluntary pledge on the part of the signers to be for God in opposition to all popish errors. They pledged their lives and their sacred honor in this holy cause. On the 31st of May, 1559, this covenant, or rather another covenant similar in import, was again signed. From the time of the signing of the first covenant, these people were persecuted as none others ever had been. The trials and difficulties to which they were exposed beggared description. Old men, leaning on their staffs, were tied to the stake and burned to death, whilst young men were confined in dark dungeons to draw out a miserable existence. No people ever more dearly loved liberty. They detested both civil and ecclesiastical tyranny. Patrick Henry reiterated their sentiments when he said, "Give me liberty or give me death."

Again, in 1638, the Covenanters assembled at their capital and proceeded to the Greyfriars church. It was the 28th of February, a day ever memorable in Scotch history. At daybreak the commissioners met and read the covenant over. People at an early hour began to assemble. The capacious house was soon filled; then the graveyard. Henderson led the vast multitude to the throne of grace. The covenant was produced and unrolled and read by Johnson. This done, the silence of death followed. All present felt that upon the transactions of that hour depended the prosperity of the church of God for years in the future. At last the awful silence was broken by the Earl of Sutherland, tottering beneath the weight of years, making his way through the dense crowd, and with trembling hands subscribing his name to the document. The spell was not broken. Name after name was added until finally, that more room might be secured, the covenant was taken out and spread upon one of the tombstones in the graveyard. Here the scene became intensely affecting. Multitudes wept aloud while others added, after their names, "till death", and others opened the veins in their arms and with the warm blood thus obtained, subscribed their names pledging themselves to God.

In after times, sorely were the signers of this covenant persecuted by the minions of Rome. Their children and grandchildren shared the same fate; but still they were noble, generous and brave. Many of them in the reign of Charles the Second, fled to Ireland and settled in the county of Down. Here they remained for a period of about sixty years, and then being oppressed by landlords they turned their eyes toward America. In 1733, a company of these Scotch-Irish or Covenanters came to Charles Town, South Carolina. A petition was sent to the counsel by James Pringle and other Protestant Irish asking that their passage be paid. The council agreed that their passage would be paid and supplies furnished them, provided they would settle a township as had been done by the Swiss at Purrysburg. On their arrival, a quantity of corn, peas, beef and salt was furnished them, and they made their way up the Black River and settled in Black River township. Another supply of provisions was, by the counsel, furnished these settlers, when those previously granted were exhausted. They, on their arrival, found but two settlers in this section of the state - one by the name of Finley and the other by the name of Rutledge. These two individuals had come from Charles Town up Black River for the purpose of raising rice; but failing, returned.

COMING OF THE IRISH

The first Irish settlers came up Black River and landed at Potato Ferry. Lands were laid out to them on the Santee. The name - Williamsburg - in honor of William III, Prince of Orange, was given to the settlement. It grew but slowly at first. The climate and the great labor of clearing up the forest and preparing it for cultivation proved more than many of the settlers could bear. Their number was greatly reduced by death; but from time to time others came and joined them, and the merchants sold them slaves, by whom they were relieved of much toil. The settlement began to grow, both in numbers and in wealth. No section of the state can show a brighter record than that of Williamsburg. Those Scotch-Irish acted out what Patrick Henry said. During the Revolutionary war, there was not one Tory among their descendants, and but one Royalist. No people are more ready to take up arms, where liberty is at stake, than the Scotch-Irish. Find them where you may, you will find men of great moral courage and physical endurance.

STORY OF TRIALS AND SUFFERINGS

These trials which these early settlers were called to pass through we may learn in part from the history of the Witherspoon family written by Robert Witherspoon who, in company with his father, emigrated from the county Down, Ireland, in 1734. As was common at that time, a part of the family preceded the rest in order to make preparations for them. The preparation often amounted to no more than constructing a pole hut and covering it with dirt. "We went on shipboard," says Robert Witherspoon, "the 14th of September, and lay windbound in the lough at Belfast fourteen days. The second day of our sail, my grandmother died and was interred in the raging ocean, which was an afflictive sight to her offspring. We were sorely tossed at sea with storms, which caused our ship to spring a leak. Our pumps were kept incessantly at work day and night; for many days our mariners seemed many times at their wits end. But it pleased God to bring us all safe to land, which was about the first day of December. We landed in Charles Town about three weeks before Christmas. We found the inhabitants very kind. We stayed in town until after Christmas, and were put on board an open boat with tools and a year's provisions, and one still-mill. They allowed each hand upward of sixteen one axe, one broad hoe and one narrow hoe. Our provisions were Indian corn, rice, wheat and flour, beef, pork, rum and salt. We were much distressed in this part of our passage. As it was the dead of winter we were exposed to the inclemency of the weather day and night; and (which added to the grief of all pious persons on board) the atheistical and blasphemous mouths of our patrons and the other hands. They brought us up as far as Potato Ferry and turned us on shore, where we lay in Samuel Commander's barn for some time; and the boat wrought her way up to the King's Tree, with the goods and provisions, which I believe is the first boat that ever came up so high before. While we lay at Mr. Commander's, our men came up in order to get good houses to take their families to. They brought some few horses with them. What help they could get from the few inhabitants in order to carry children and other necessaries up, they availed themselves. As the woods were full of water and the most severe frost, it was very severe on women and children.

"We set out in the morning and some got no further that day than Mr. McDonald's and some as far as Mr. Plowden's; some to James Armstrong's and some to Uncle William James's. Their little cabins were as full that night as they could hold, and the next day every one made the best they could to their own place, which was the first day of February, 1735. My father had brought on shipboard four children, viz: David, Robert, John and Sarah. Sarah died in Charles Town and was the first buried at the Scotch Meeting House graveyard. When we came to the Bluff, my mother and us children were still of the expectation that we were coming to an agreeable place. But when we arrived and saw nothing but a wilderness and instead of a fine timbered house, nothing but a mean dirt one, our spirits sank. And what added to our trouble, our pilot we had with us from Uncle William James's, left us when we came in sight of the place. My father gave us all the comfort he could by telling us we would get all these trees cut down, and in a short time there would be plenty of inhabitants so that we could see from house to house. While we were at this, our fire we brought from Bog Swamp went out. Father heard up the river swamp was the King's Tree, although there was no path, neither did he know the distance, yet he followed up the swamp until he came to the branch and by that found Rodger Gordon's. We watched him as far as the trees would let us see, and returned to our dolorous hut, expecting never to see him nor any human person any more. But after some time he returned and brought fire. We were some comforted; but evening coming on, the wolves began to howl on all sides. We then feared being devoured by wild beasts, having neither gun nor dog, nor any door to our house. Howbeit, we set to and gathered fuel and made on a good fire and so passed the first night. The next day being a clear, warm morning we began to stir about; but about midday, there arose a cloud southwest, attended with a high wind, thunder and lightning. The rain penetrated through the green poles and brought down the sand that covered them over, which seemed to threaten to bury us alive. The lightning and claps were very awful and lasted a good space of time. I do not remember to have seen a much severer gust than that was. I believe we all sincerely wished ourselves again at Belfast. But this fright was soon over and the evening cleared up comfortable and warm. The boat that brought up the goods arrived at the King's Tree. People were much oppressed in bringing their things as there was no horse there. They were obliged to toil hard and had no other way but to convey their beds, clothing, provisions, chests, tools, pots, etc., on their backs. At that time there were very few or no roads, and every family had to travel the best they could, which was here double distance to some, for they had to follow swamps and branches for their guides for some time. After a season, some men got such a knowledge of the woods as to blaze paths so that people soon found out to follow blazes from place to place. As the winter season was far advanced, the time to prepare for planting was very short. Yet people were very strong and healthy. All that could do anything wrought diligently and continued clearing and planting as long as the season would admit, so that they made provision for the ensuing year.

"As they had but few beasts, a little served them and as the range was good, they had no need of feeding creatures for some years. I remember that among the first things that my father brought from the boat was his gun, which was one of Queen Anne's muskets. He had her loaded with swan shot. One morning when we were at breakfast, there was traveling 'possum on his way passing by the door. My mother screamed out saying, "There is a great bear." Mother and us children hid ourselves behind some barrels and the chest at the other end of our hut, whilst father got his gun and steadied her past the fork that held up that end of the house and shot him about the hinder parts, which caused poor 'possum to grin and open his mouth in a frightful manner. Father was in a haste to give him to a second bout; but the shot, being mislaid in the hurry could not be found. We were penned up for some time. Father at length went out and killed it with a pole.

"Another source of alarm was the Indians. When they came to hunt in the spring, they were in great numbers, and in all places, like the Egyptian locusts; but they were not hurtful.

"We had a great deal of trouble and hardships in our first settling; but the few inhabitants continued to stay in health and strength. Yet we were oppressed with fears on diverse accounts, especially of being massacred by the Indians, of being bit by snakes, of being torn by wild beasts, or of being lost and perishing in the woods. Of this last calamity there were three instances."

Such were the sufferings endured by the early settlers of that section of the state, which is called Williamsburgh, as narrated by one who experienced them.

Installment XXXV

Early in 1735, Robert Johnson died. The last law to which he assented is dated April 28, 1735. He was succeeded by Thomas Broughton. Robert Johnson was governor of South Carolina in 1719, when the government of the state passed out of the hands of the proprietors and became a royal province. In 1730, he succeeded Arthur Middleton as the third royal governor. Robert Johnson was more than popular - he was universally beloved. To perpetuate his memory, a monument was erected at the public expense. From the inscription over this monument, we learn the following facts. He died on the 3rd of May, 1735, aged fifty-three years. He was the first captain, general, governor and commander-in-chief, and vice-admiral of the province of South Carolina after the purchase of it by the King of England. The marble upon which these facts are recorded was given, we learn from the same source, by the general assembly as a "mark of peculiar esteem and gratitude." He was buried near St. Philips church, of which he was a member.

His successor, Thomas Broughton, had long been connected with the colony. In 1710, we find him contending, as one of the deputies of the proprietors, with Robert Gibbes for the office of governor. Again, we find him speaker of the lower house of the assembly, under Nicholson and Middleton; and now in 1735, governor of South Carolina. Thomas Broughton is quaintly described as a "plain honest man, but little distinguished, either for his knowledge or valor." He continued in office until 1737.

At this time that portion of the state south of a line drawn east and west across the state, as high up as King's Tree, was partially settled. In some sections of this territory, there were only a few settlers, and in other sections there were only a few traders. In 1704, a trader by the name of Henry Sterling established a kind of trading post on Lyon Creek, in the present county of Orangeburg.

During the administration of Broughton, as previously, multitudes continued to pour into the country from Germany, Ireland, Scotland and England. All of them were Protestants and most of them poor. One of the first acts that was passed by the assembly after Broughton became governor was "An act to provide a full supply for subsisting poor Protestants coming from Europe and settling in South Carolina." Previously to this the sum of 5,000 pounds - about $25,000 - had been annually appropriated by the assembly for this purpose; but so great was the tide of immigration and so needy were the immigrants, that this sum was found insufficient. It was proposed that some of the immigrants be bound out to masters for a term of years, but this proposition was not acceded to, and a tax was imposed for the purpose of relieving the poor.

Charles Town, about this time, presented a very strange spectacle. Husbands were seen carrying all sorts of household stuff on their backs, whilst their wives and children were following at their heels, each loaded with something. The old settlers were kind, but so great were the numbers of newcomers that all could not be comfortably provided for. Some of these immigrants were the sons and daughters of wealthy families, whilst many of them were from the humbler walks of life. The tyranny of the governments of Europe in conjunction with the oppression of landlords, drove to South Carolina some of the best families of the Old World.

These immigrants had at first many things in common. Prominent among these was the fact that they were, whatever might be their nationality, all Protestants. At first the majority of the settlers were dissenters. These dissenters embraced, Baptists, Presbyterians, Huguenots and other individuals who, although members of the Church of England, were not in full sympathy with it. The Huguenots, who were what are known in church history as Geneva Presbyterians, gradually became almost as a whole, a part and parcel of the Church of England. They were kindly treated and gently dealt with by "the Society for the Propagation of the Gospel in Foreign Ports." By this society, ministers who spoke the French language were furnished to Huguenots. This had a powerful effect upon the minds of these French immigrants. Almost imperceptibly the majority of them soon became warmly attached to the Church of England. In 1698 an effort was made to establish Episcopacy as the form of religion of the province. This law was modified in 1704, and Episcopacy became the established religion up to the time of the Revolution in 1776. This enabled Episcopacy to grow and flourish as no other form of religion could. For this particular denomination, churches were built and ministers supported out of the public treasury. Dissenters not only had to build their own houses of worship and support their own pastors; but also to contribute their part to the support of the established church. At the time that Broughton was governor of South Carolina the province was, when we take everything into consideration, well supplied with churches and ministers of the gospel. With regard to the ministers it may be said that they were men of learning and excellent natural endowments.

At a very early period, the settlers of South Carolina directed their attention to the propagation of the gospel and the establishing of high schools. A public library was established in Charles Town within thirty-five years after the settlement of the colony; and in 1710 and 1712 free schools were established by legislative enactment. In 1723 the Rev. Thomas Morrit proposed to the assembly a plan for establishing a college.

The early settlers of South Carolina read the Bible with great regularity, and the effect was seen in all their acts, both public and private. People that study the Bible and make themselves thoroughly acquainted with its history and its laws will always be a strong minded people; and those who make its precepts a rule of conduct will always be a moral people. During the administration of Governor Broughton, the Carolinians and Georgians became very near being involved in a serious difficulty. After Oglethorpe had put the Georgia colony in a state of defense, he returned to England in order to adjust a difficulty with the Spanish government in Florida. During his absence, the Carolina traders discovered that Augusta, on account of its fortifications, was a favorable trading post. In order to reach this point with a supply of goods suitable for Indian traffic, it was determined to boat the goods up the Savannah River. It was one of the fixed regulations of the Georgia settlement that rum should be excluded from the colony. The restriction was made not so much, it would seem, on modern temperance principles as from the fact that rum was thought to be deleterious to the health. The settlers were not forbidden the use of wine. In fact, they were required to make wine. One of the principal articles which the traders sold to the Indians, or rather bartered with them, was rum. A company of traders got their cargo of rum and other commodities ready and commenced to make their way up the river. When opposite Savannah, the officers of the town ordered the boat to be stopped. The goods were all opened and the barrels of rum knocked to pieces. This incensed not only the traders but the people of the province generally. The result was that a deputation consisting of two individuals - one from each house of the legislature - was sent to inquire into the matter. The Georgia authorities were not slow to discover that they had acted rashly, and promptly restored the articles of traffic, set the traders whom they had imprisoned at liberty and made ample apology. It was then agreed between the two colonies that the Savannah River should be used in common by the two colonies, and that South Carolina traders were at liberty to trade where they saw fit. The Carolinians agreed on their part not to engage in the sale of rum or any strong liquors to the white settlers of Georgia.

It now became evident that the Georgia colony must prove a failure if the plan of government adopted by the trustees continued in force. The location was unhealthy, especially to Europeans. So many restrictions were made by the laws that the people became discouraged, and many of them crossed over the Savannah River and settled in South Carolina. By law, the Georgians were forbidden to own slaves. The South Carolinians were not. A petition was addressed to the trustees praying that this provision might be abrogated, and the citizens be allowed to purchase slaves. The Scotch Highlanders who had settled at New Inverness protested against the introduction of slavery into the colony. Their protest was founded upon conscientious scruples mainly; but they regarded the introduction of slavery as dangerous to their settlement, since it would expose them to constant attacks of the Spaniards.

The relations existing between the courts of Europe to the time of the Revolution of 1776 materially affected the American colonies. On the 19th of

Oct., 1739, war was proclaimed by the British parliament against Spain. Previous to this, however, the two nations had been at variance, and more than once been on the verge of open hostilities. It was the practice of the European nations that had planted colonies in America to make these colonies a kind of battleground. Whenever any difficulty occurred between the courts of Europe, each at once set about to destroy the other's colonies. Not only so, but France, England and Spain each claiming the sole right to all of North America, made it a point to do all it could to get full possession of the country, and to prevent either of the other two from establishing colonies in the country. The contest in the north was between England and the French; in the south it was mainly between England and Spain. Previous to the declarations of war, Spain had been making preparations for it by sending reinforcements to St. Augustine. Treaty after treaty had been made respecting the possessions of the two nations in America, and boundary lines had been pointed out; but neither respected the treaties or feared to cross the boundary line. English vessels claimed the right to cut log wood on some of the West Indies Isles and to navigate the Gulf of Mexico. The right was practically admitted by Spain for some time; but about the time of which we are speaking, every vessel that was found in these waters was captured. The merchants began to complain and the matter was referred to Sir Robert Walpole, the English minister. Walpole was beguiled with fair promises but the practice continued.

In 1737, Thomas Broughton was succeeded by William Bull. Samuel Horsley had been appointed as a successor to Broughton, but he died before he left England. So soon as Bull assumed the duties of his office, he immediately informed the British government of the true state of things. Since, from circumstances and situation, the same fate awaited both South Carolina and Georgia, he also opened a correspondence with the trustees of Georgia. The trustees at once made application to the king for Assistance, in view of the threatened invasion of their colony. A regiment of six hundred men was raised, and James Oglethorpe made military governor of the two colonies of South Carolina and Georgia with the rank of major general. Two ships - the Hector and Blandford - were ordered to convoy the transports which were to convey Oglethorpe and his regiment to America. Forty individuals accompanied the expedition, who might be ready to take the places of those who might sicken, die or be killed in the expedition. So soon as Oglethorpe landed, he commenced the work of fortifying the posts on the coast of Georgia and some of the most important islands.

In order to be successful, it was necessary that the friendship of the neighboring Indians be secured. The Creek nation was warmly attached to Oglethorpe, but during his absence in England the Spaniards had been tampering with them. Some of their more prominent leaders had been invited to visit the governor of St. Augustine. That they might be induced to accept the invitations, large presents were promised them. On arriving at St. Augustine, these chiefs were told that Oglethorpe was sick on board of a vessel then lying in the harbor, and was very desirous to see them. The wily Indians discovered the plot and would neither go on board the vessel nor accept the proffered gifts. This was a trick of the Spaniards to cut off the Creek chiefs, that they might the more easily in some way or other overcome the whole nation. On returning home, these chiefs found an invitation awaiting them to meet Oglethorpe at his headquarters. This invitation was accepted, and a thousand warriors were at once promised Oglethorpe whenever he would call for them.

The British soldiers soon became disheartened. The difficulties with which they were called to contend were much greater than those to which they had been accustomed. Two of the companies belonging to the regiment had been formerly stationed at Gibraltar. Some of the men could speak Spanish, and one of them was a Catholic and at heart favorable to the government at St. Augustine.

These companies were stationed on Cumberland Island within speaking distance of the Spanish outposts. This Catholic soldier was corrupted and induced to engage in a secret plot to kill Oglethorpe and then escape to St. Augustine. The plot was a bold one and as fearlessly attempted to be executed. A band of armed soldiers came to the general and made a most unreasonable demand. This he peremptorily refused. With a shout the whole band rushed upon him, one shooting him from a distance of only a few feet. Fortunately Oglethorpe sustained no further injury than the singeing of his clothes and the burning of his face. Another soldier aimed at him, but, his musket failing to fire, he drew his sword and was about to plunge it into him, when an officer came to the assistance of Oglethorpe and killed the mutineer at once. The others of the band attempted to escape but were captured and put in chains.

UPRISING OF SLAVES

The headquarters of General Oglethorpe were at Fredrica, at the mouth of the Altamaha. Both the Ashley River colony and that planted west of the

Savannah depended upon him for protection against Spanish invaders. Had they succeeded in assassinating him by the hands of one of his own regiment, it would have proved at least a temporary shock to both the English colonies, and infused spirit and energy into their common enemies. Failing in the scheme of murdering Oglethorpe, the authorities of St. Augustine, whose minds were accustomed to devise murderous plots, had recourse to another infamous intrigue, and even more dangerous. In the province of South Carolina there were at this time, (1739) between forty and fifty thousand Negro slaves, whilst the whites were less than one-third that number. The Negroes, many of them, had been but lately brought from Africa. The climate agreed with them in a remarkable degree, and all of them were strong and capable of great physical endurance.

It was with difficulty that in times of peace these slaves were kept in bondage, and almost impossible in times of war. The Spanish governor had previously issued a proclamation of freedom to the Negroes of Carolina. This proclamation was kept a profound secret by the whites; but in spite of every precaution to keep it a secret many of the Negroes had learned the fact and availed themselves of the offer made by the Spaniards. Of those Negroes who had fled from their masters in Carolina, the governor of Florida had formed a regiment. This regiment had officers from among themselves and enjoyed all the privileges of the other Spanish troops. The slaves of Carolina were all aware of this fact and this made them long for freedom. It was also a common practice for the Spanish authorities to send enlisting officers clandestinely into Carolina for the purpose of raising recruits from amongst the Negro slaves.

The Spanish proclamation of freedom to the slaves was made in November, 1733, and from that time to 1739, the people lived in a constant dread of an insurrection. Negroes would take their masters' horses and boats and make good their escape to Florida where they were safe. From the dread of a Negro insurrection and the liability to be attacked by scouting parties of Indians, the whites were accustomed to go armed at all times, even to church. This was required of them by law. Several individuals lost their lives in attempting to prevent their slaves from flying to the Spaniards.

In September, 1739, at Stono, less than twenty miles from Charles Town, a terrible insurrection took place. The prime instigator of this bloody scene was a Catholic priest. A small company of Negroes, probably from the immediate neighborhood, first "murdered two young men in a warehouse and then plundered the house of guns and ammunition." Here, they elected one of their number, bearing the name of Cato, their captain. A flag was hoisted, and with beating drums they proceeded to execute their barbarous plans. Inflamed by rum, and flushed with the success which attended their first onset they marked their path with fire and blood. Every Negro in their march was forced to join them and every white - whether it was man, woman or child - was butchered. The house of one Godfrey was entered, plundered and then burned, whilst he himself, with his wife and children, were killed. Then they proceeded to Jacksonburgh. On their march, they were met by Governor Bull, who escaped from them by leaving the road. It was on the Sabbath. The Presbyterian community of Wilton, in large numbers, had turned out armed with their guns to hear the Rev. Archibald Stobo preach. The alarm soon reached the church, and the women were left in the house of worship, whilst the men rushed at once to meet the insurrectionists. The militia of the country were soon in arms and, under command of Captain Bee, set out in pursuit of the banditti. Their track was easily followed. It was marked by desolation. From the point where they started, they had marched about twelve miles. Not a house was left standing, and twenty-three whites had been murdered. When the militia came up with them they had stopped in an open field and were singing and dancing merrily. Many of them were drunk. In this condition they were attacked from different points by the militia. Several were killed on the spot, among whom was Cato, the leader. The rest, who were not too drunk, took to the woods. Some were caught and killed. Others ran back to their former masters, hoping thus to escape; but all except those who had been forced to join the party were executed.

Thus ended this horrible affair. Different conclusions may be drawn from it. Some may be led to lay the blame of the whole matter at the door of the fanatics of the Pope of Rome, whilst others may be ready to conclude that it was but a legitimate result of slavery. That Cato and his followers were to some extent incited to form themselves into a band of insurrectionists by evil-designed adherents of the Church of Rome, there seems to be no good reason to doubt. The authorities at Savannah captured an individual, whom they took to be a priest, and whom they suspected to have been employed to set on foot a general insurrection of the slaves in Carolina. The governor of South Carolina was, by letter, informed that such an individual had been taken into custody; but we suppose, (although it is not said so) that the information was not received until the plot had been partly put into execution. At the time of which we are speaking the government of Spain was violently opposed to the institution of slavery. Whenever a demand was made for a slave that had fled from South Carolina and taken refuge in the Spanish colony of Florida, the reply by the authorities of that colony was that it was contrary to the principles of his Catholic majesty to hold any human being in bondage, and that rather than remand the runaway slaves to their masters, they would be paid for. This promise was only fulfilled in exceptional cases. Runaway Negroes were formed into companies by the Spanish, no doubt for the purpose of annoying the English settlers in the country, and with the hope that with the assistance of these slaves, the English might be driven from the shores of North America, and that the whole country might be brought under the sway of Spain.

That this insurrection was the legitimate result of the institution of slavery we will neither affirm nor deny; but that the inhabitants of South Carolina were to blame for the existence of the institution in their midst we care not admit. The institution was to a very great extent forced upon the first settlers by the merchants of Europe and the northern colonies.

RESPONSIBILITY FOR SLAVERY

As the institution has been abolished in the state forever, and is now to all intents and purposes a matter of history, it is fair that it be known how and when slavery was brought into the state. In August of 1620, a Dutch man-of-war landed twenty Negroes in Virginia and sold them. In 1671, fifty-one years afterwards, Sir John Yeamans brought a number of Negroes from his plantations in Barbadoes to South Carolina. Sir John Yeamans was the son of Robert Yeamans who lost his estate by his adherence to the interests of the king. Sir John succeeded Joseph West as governor of South Carolina. By the proprietors he was highly honored and was really appointed by them governor of the province in 1665. This was five years before the settlement was made at Charles Town. The original proprietors of South Carolina were men of wealth and influence in England. Some of them at least were the dear friends of Charles the Second, the ruling sovereign at the time of the settlement of South Carolina. What they did was done, not only for their interest, but with the approbation of the English government. That Sir John Yeamans brought his slaves from Barbadoes to South Carolina with the knowledge and approbation of the proprietors and consequently of the English government, is absolutely certain. We may safely conclude that at first the institution of slavery did not meet with a hearty approval by all of the settlers. We have seen that the Highlanders from Scotland, who settled in Georgia, protested against the introduction of slavery into that colony; and since there were Scotch in South Carolina from an early period, we may infer that they held the same views on this subject with their countrymen in Georgia. We may conclude that slavery was not only introduced into South Carolina, indirectly by the English government, but that the institution was, by the direct acts of that government perpetuated. All laws passed by the Colonial legislature had to be approved by the proprietors before they became of any permanent force. Not only so, but no law could, by the terms of the charter, be passed which, in any sense, was at variance with the laws of England. Now there were a multitude of laws enacted respecting slaves. At a very early period some of these laws were passed and approved by the original proprietors. Laws respecting the regulating of slaves continued up to the time of the Revolution of 1776. Not one word was said, either during the proprietary government or during the royal government, in opposition to the institution. Not one effort was made to abolish it. Such is briefly the history of the introduction of slavery into the state of South Carolina. Negroes were brought from Barbadoes, from Africa and from the other English colonies, by the merchants and bartered for tar, pitch, lumber, peltry, rice and the other commodities of the country. Vast multitudes were brought into the country and they increased rapidly. After the first few years the number of slaves was double the number of whites and frequently their number was three times that of the whites.

Before dismissing this subject, we cannot refrain from mentioning a strange notion which seems to have been somewhat prevalent amongst the early colonists. We refer to the question of the propriety of making an effort to convert their slaves to Christianity. It may be possible that some persons will be slow to believe that a people who had come to the western world for the avowed purpose of disseminating the gospel amongst the savage Indians would have hesitated for one moment with respect to the propriety of making an attempt to Christianize the no less savage Africans. Here we may say that much that was proposed to be done towards Christianizing the Indians never was undertaken. The guilt of killing Indians and of enslaving them lies at the door of all the English colonies except the one planted by William Penn. The first salutation the wild savages of Massachusetts received from the Puritans was a "shower of bullets."

The fact is, from the day that Columbus landed on Watling Island, Europeans commenced to treat the savages of the western world as wild beasts. Every nation of Europe had a hand in exterminating the Indians, and either directly or indirectly in kidnapping Africans and selling them into slavery.

The society for propagating the gospel sent, in 1702, the Rev. Samuel Thomas as a missionary to South Carolina. He was instructed "to attempt the conversion of the Yemassees." From attempting this work he was prevented by Governor Nathaniel Johnson. The reasons assigned for not attempting this work were political and selfish. The Yemassees once had been in alliance with the Spaniards, but had revolted from them and entered into an alliance with the English. The Spanish had endeavored to convert the Yemassees to the Catholic religion, but they rejected it with scorn; and because of the attempt to convert them they revolted from their Spanish friends. Nathaniel Johnson was of the opinion that any effort, on the part of the Carolinians, to Christianize these savages would likely result in making the Indians the foes of the colony. Rather than run the risk of sacrificing their friendship they were left undisturbed in their barbarism.

SLAVES KEPT IN IGNORANCE OF CHRISTIANITY

Little effort was made to Christianize the Africans from the fact that it was thought that it would be unlawful to hold them in bondage after their conversion. In other words, many of the colonists had conscientious scruples about holding a civilized and Christian man in bondage, whilst their scruples did not exist with regard to enslaving a savage. This was a common notion of the time. Acting upon this principle, the sovereigns of Europe bestowed the American continent upon their friends. The Indians were killed or driven away from their homes and their hunting grounds taken possession of without giving to them any compensation whatever. Might made right. The reasoning was short. "The Indians," said they, "are savages; we are Christians; therefore this good land belongs to us, and we have a right to kill the savages." This was the logic used by every colony planted in America, except William Penn's Quaker colony of Pennsylvania. For two reasons then, the first settlers of South Carolina made no special effort to convert their Negro slaves to Christianity. The first was the one just mentioned, and the other was the notion that so soon as the Negro slaves were made Christians they would become rebellious. It is a historical fact, well attested, that from a very early period the people lived in dread of insurrection amongst the slaves. As early as 1790, slaves were not allowed to leave their master's premises without a permit from the master, and slaves were forbidden to have in their possession any guns or even clubs. Every master or mistress was required by law to have the houses of their salves "searched once a month, for clubs, guns, swords and mischievous weapons." This shows the state of things as they existed in 1790. The political economist and the theologian are left to draw the inferences; our business is simply to record the facts as they transpired.

The early slave laws of South Carolina have been stigmatized as barbarous and cruel. We have no disposition to call this declaration into question. They are on record and speak for themselves; but the origin of the laws should be taken into consideration. They were British, not American laws. About the same time that the legislature of South Carolina was, by the authority of the English parliament, passing laws forbidding slaves to have in their houses "clubs or guns," lest an insurrection might be successful in securing freedom to the slaves, Cotton Mather was fulminating anathemas against witchcraft, and the descendants of the pious Puritans were hanging witches. There are many things in the colonial history of our country of which we ought not only to be ashamed, but for which we should be sorry. But, after all, these things were British, rather than American in their origin and nature.

Installment XXXVII

On the 19th of October, 1737, war against Spain was publicly proclaimed in London. For this event, the English people, with a few honorable exceptions, had been clamoring. The streets were crowded with idle vagabonds, following the heralds, shouting for joy. The bells were rung and great were the demonstrations of delight. Walpore, now unpopular, but with more prudence and foresight than the multitude of the nation, ominously whispered to himself, "they may ring the bells now; but soon they will be ringing their hands." This war with Spain is a blurred page in England's history. It was unjust - it was unrighteous. It was a war for trade. England, Spain, and France each had its own colonies in the New World. Every foot of the continent and most of the islands had been claimed by one or the other of these nations. Bounds - vague and ill-defined, it is admitted, but still bounds - had been fixed as lines of demarcation, separating the possessions of one from the possessions of the other two. Each claimed the profit from the trade arising in its own colonies. The English forbid her colonies from sending their rice, tobacco, indigo and peltries to any but English ports, and in anything but English ships. This was the plan adopted by the government in order that it might be remunerated for the expense of the purchase and maintenance of the colony. In fact, when the Crown of England purchased the Carolina colony from the original proprietors, it bought the soil and the inhabitants then settled upon it. England, although she, in her tyranny, claimed the sole right to traffic with her colonies and allowed them to traffic only with or for her, she utterly refused to grant this right to Spain. She at least winked at her merchants smuggling goods in the Spanish towns in America. This was not all. At that time, no trade was so profitable as the traffic in slaves. England desired the privilege not only of furnishing her own colonies with Negroes stolen from Africa; but she coveted the privilege of furnishing the Spanish colonies also with these miserable and unfortunate creatures. This privilege she would enjoy even if it would cost her blood and treasure.

A company of reckless adventurers was formed, whose stock consisted in the main of certificates of indebtedness. To explain this more definitely, we may say that the company was thus formed, and its capital stock increased. Persons holding claims against the English government either sold these claims to the South Sea company, or deposited them as so much stock. The government paid the claims held by this company by granting a right to trade in the Gulf of Mexico and in the Pacific ocean, otherwise called the South Sea. In other words, the company was granted the privilege of destroying the Spanish commerce in America if it could. It was a success. Vagabonds, encouraged and protected by the flag of England, fitted out vessels and soon the coast of Africa was lined for thirty degrees, or more than two thousand miles, with English slave vessels. Not only the South Sea company, but other companies, and even private individuals, encouraged by royal favor, protected by British legislation, and, more than this, forced by English common law, engaged in kidnapping the ebony sons and daughters of Africa.

The colonial commerce of Spain was spoiled. It dwindled from fifteen thousand tons to two thousand. Spain began to retaliate by seizing smugglers and plundering vessels. An attempt was made to settle, by negotiation, the difficulties between the nations. The English people were incensed that such a course should be resorted to. The nation was clamorous for war. It was decided that Spain should be paid three hundred and forty thousand dollars for damages done her commerce; but that she shall pay the South Sea company four hundred and seventy five thousand dollars damages done it by seizing its vessels.

With this, the English nation claimed that it had nothing to do; but she did claim for her merchants the right to maraud and smuggle when and where they pleased. To obtain this right, the nation voted for war to the hilt. It was confidently expected that all the Spanish dominions in America would, by easy transition, pass over into the hands of the English. Idlers imagined that they would grow speedily rich, and prodigals hoped to find in the balmy regions of the Spanish America everything that could be desired by their wasteful spirits.

With this war, any further than it affected the English and especially that of South Carolina, we have nothing to do. Hostilities commenced on the 21st of November, 1739, by an attack on Porto Bello by Edward Vernon. It was a success. The next day he was in full possession of both the town and castle, besides $100 of booty. It was a victory sad in its results to the English colonies. Vernon returned to Jamaica, and England determined to send the largest fleet that had ever sailed on the Gulf of Mexico. A call was made for each of the colonies to furnish men. No one of the colonies failed to respond promptly. The men were furnished and some of the colonies voted a supply of money.

General Oglethorpe was placed in command of the South Carolina and Georgia forces. His daring idea was to capture St. Augustine and maintain the boundaries of the English colony as far south as the St. John's River. The English nation had commenced offensive operations, and her two colonies, South Carolina and Georgia, had caught the spirit. Oglethorpe had received orders to act on the offensive in Florida. To effect this purpose he was assisted by a regiment raised partly in North Carolina and partly in Virginia.

In April, 1740, the legislature of South Carolina made a provision for raising one hundred and twenty five thousand dollars for assisting Oglethorpe in this expedition. The troops furnished were not in readiness until May. The regiment was put under command of Colonel Alexander Vanderdussen. A naval force of four ships of twenty guns each and two smaller vessels was commanded by Vincent Price. The Indian allies sent in their warriors. The other forces were Georgians. The mouth of the St. John's River was appointed, by Oglethorpe, as the place of rendezvous.

Hostilities were begun on the 10th of May, by Oglethorpe's making an attack upon Diego, a place of little importance, about twenty-five or thirty miles from St. Augustine. Oglethorpe had under his command at this time only 400 men. Diego, after a feeble resistance, surrendered. Lieutenant Dunbar, with a garrison of sixty men, was left in charge of the fort, and Oglethorpe went to the place appointed for general rendezvous. There he was joined by Colonel Vanderdussen and the regiment from South Carolina, and a company of Highlanders under the command of Captain McIntosh. In about a week the forces set out for St. Augustine.

In the meantime, the Spanish were reinforced. Six armed vessels and two provision ships had entered the harbor of St. Augustine. Oglethorpe's forces now consisted of but two thousand men. The intention was to take St. Augustine by surprise. In this they totally failed. The Spaniards were fully aware of their approach. All the cattle from the surrounding country were driven into the town, and the forces, together with supplies for their maintenance, were placed in the castle. The Spanish garrison consisted of seven hundred regulars, two companies of horses and four companies of Negroes, together with the Indians and militia of the surrounding country. All things considered, the Spaniards were in a much better condition to capture Oglethorpe than Oglethorpe was to capture them. Within two miles of St. Augustine was Fort Moosa. As the English forces approached, the Spanish garrison retired to St. Augustine. Oglethorpe, on his arrival, destroyed Fort Moosa with fire. The walls were broken in several places and then, no doubt with bright hopes of soon being in complete and absolute possession of St. Augustine, he set about making preparations for the attack. The town was ordered to surrender. The commanding officer sent back for a reply that he would be very glad to shake hands with General Oglethorpe in the castle of St. Augustine.

Oglethorpe, on his approach, discovered that it would cost him dearly to make a direct attack on the castle. This place was not only well manned, but at the time was probably one of the strongest fortifications in America. It was determined to besiege the place and thus starve out the garrison. This was impossible, for the Spanish ships brought in both fresh supplies of provisions and reinforcements. Whilst conducting the siege, Colonel Palmer, with ninety-five Highlanders and forty-two Indians, was placed at Fort Moosa with orders to capture all supplies on their way from the country to the Spanish garrison at St. Augustine. Palmer was charged particularly to be constantly on the lookout. Colonel Vanderdussen, with the South Carolina regiment, was sent to Point Quartel, about a mile from the castle. On this neck, Vanderdussen was

ordered to erect a battery. General Oglethorpe, with his Indian regiment and English allies, went to the Island Anastatia. The Spanish forces on this island fled to the castle of St. Augustine, on the approach of Oglethorpe. The mouth of the harbor was guarded by the ships under the command of Captain Price, one vessel being ordered to guard the pass of Matanzas.

The besiegers being placed in position, the batteries from the different forts began to open upon the castle. Bombs were thrown into the town. The enemy returned fire promptly. Because of the greatness of distance and the lightness of the guns on both sides, but little damage was done. Captain Warren of the Navy proposed to make a night attack on the enemy's ships. He proposed to lead the attack but he found that the bar was too great to admit large vessels across it, and to engage in such an undertaking with only small vessels was regarded as extremely hazardous.

The Spaniards now discovered that Oglethorpe and his army were in a difficulty. An attack was made on Colonel Palmer and, finding him off his guard, he and his men were cut to pieces. The few that escaped made their way to Point Quartel. The South Carolina regiment under Vanderdussen got up and returned to Charles Town. Oglethorpe rebuked some Indians because they presented to him the scalps of some enemies slain, and this offended the whole and they left. The commander of the fleet, fearing storms, left and thus ended the expedition.

Oglethorpe was censured by the Carolinians, but without just grounds. No doubt he made too long a delay at Diego; but under the circumstances it was impossible for him or any other man to have taken the strong fortifications of St. Augustine. Forced by the circumstances, General Oglethorpe returned to Fredrica and, in spite of every attempt of the Spaniards, continued daily by the aid of his Georgia colony to retain the territory as far South as the St. John's River.

This expedition cost South Carolina a large sum of money, and a considerable number of men. Only two were killed by the enemy, but many sickened and died. England gained nothing by the expedition; but indirectly the colony gained much. The manner in which England acted toward Spain suggested to the colony the idea of freedom. Even at this early period, we may discover the tendency to throw off the yoke of England and be free and independent. To the colony, England was kind, but at the same time she acted arbitrarily. Multitudes of raw Africans were brought into the colony, contrary to the wish of the settlers. These Negroes, the colonists were by law forced to buy and keep in slavery, in opposition to the conscientious scruples of at least a large number of the people. The colony was called upon to espouse the quarrels of the English people with their European neighbors, and required to assist in fighting their battles, and contribute to the support of their armies. England herself had little regard for the rights of her neighbors. All these things pointed to the revolution of 1776.

Installment XXXVIII

Man is a social being. No individual of all the numerous posterity of Adam lives independent. He is linked to the whole by countless ties. Invisible it may be, but still strong and indissoluble. The countless hordes of human beings that swarm upon the face of the habitable earth are made up of two nations; these nations are made up of families; and these families are composed of single individuals. Often it is that the history of a single person contains all that is important in the history of a nation during the period of his earthly existence. More frequently it is the case that a single act of one individual gives direction to the acts of succeeding generations. A single stone completes the arch. This stone, however small or insignificant of itself, adds beauty and strength to the whole fabric. So it is with human acts. One single deed has often saved a nation, whilst a slight neglect has changed the course of events and caused victory to perch upon the standard of the discomfited. James Oglethorpe saved South Carolina, if not from extermination, at least from invasion and temporary destruction. He did this, not directly but indirectly. He saved Georgia and, by saving Georgia, saved South Carolina.

After this unsuccessful invasion of St. Augustine, Oglethorpe returned to Fredrica, near the mouth of the Altamaha. He was grieved and distressed. The Carolinians abused and vilified him. They had lost all confidence in him as a military chief, and were not backward to express their opinion concerning him. This wounded his generous heart; but the havoc which the Spaniards had made upon the brave Highlanders, under Col. Palmer, grieved his noble spirit.

Exhausted by toil and broken down by incessant watching, he returned to Fredrica. Not to rest, however. This the Spaniards would not permit. An expedition was planned in Cuba. A large naval land force was raised, part in Cuba and part in Florida. The intention was first to subjugate Georgia and then South Carolina. From Havana two thousand soldiers, under command of Don Antonio de Dondondo, embarked and arrived in May at St. Augustine. Here, further preparations were made for the expedition. The movements of the Spaniards were discovered by

Oglethorpe whilst they were still at St. Augustine. The fact was communicated to the governor of South Carolina. Oglethorpe could not be mistaken with respect to either the intended invasion or its main object. The Spanish fleet had been seen by Capt. Hamer, whilst cruising between Florida and Havana. The information sent to the governor of South Carolina was true, beyond a doubt. The Carolina authorities treated the intelligence with indifference and positively refused to send Oglethorpe any assistance. The object of contention equally concerned Carolina and Georgia. It was avowed a struggle for the extension of boundaries, but in reality a struggle for empire.

The territory claimed by Spain extended farther north than the English were willing to admit. On the contrary, the English claimed farther south than the Spanish would allow. Each was in fact attempting to root the other out of the country. The destruction of Georgia would have been followed by the extermination of Carolina. Hence the saving of Georgia was the saving of Carolina.

Notwithstanding the many adverse circumstances by which Oglethorpe was surrounded, he determined to defend the country, even if it cost him his life. The Highlanders, whose countrymen had been cut to pieces at Fort Moosa, heartily encouraged his resolution. They were burning for revenge. Forts were built at different places on the banks of the Altamaha, on the islands contiguous to its mouth, and Fredrica was put in readiness for an attack. On the 16th of July, a fleet of thirty-six vessels and carrying more than three thousand men, entered the harbor of St. Simon, about eight miles below Fredrica. The troops landed on the west side of the island of St. Simon, only a short distance from the town which bore the same name. Here they commenced to erect fortifications. A battery of twenty guns was soon in working order. Oglethorpe, who was at this time on St. Simon's Island, commenced firing upon the invaders as they entered the harbor, but the enemy, having learned that the water was of sufficient depth, rushed past him until they got out of reach of his guns. Amongst the land forces of the Spaniards was a regiment of Negroes, elegantly uniformed and commanded by officers of their own race. This regiment was equipped and brought along more for the purpose of producing discontentment amongst the Carolina slaves, and thus instigating insurrection, than for the purpose of fighting.

General Oglethorpe had only eight hundred men on St. Simon's Island. He was anxiously expecting reinforcements from South Carolina. The Carolinians had determined that since they had no confidence in

Oglethorpe, they would put Charles Town in a state of defense and let Oglethorpe make the best he could in repelling the Spaniards from Georgia.

Finding that it would be impossible to accomplish anything by remaining on St. Simon's Island, Oglethorpe spiked his guns, destroyed his military and other stores, and went to his headquarters at Fredrica. On the 18th of July, the town was attacked by the advance party of the enemy, but failed to accomplish anything; besides many of these were killed. The commander of the Spanish forces sent three hundred men to support his advance guard, but these were entrapped and about two hundred of them taken prisoners. This encouraged both Oglethorpe and his men. The old Roman generals were accustomed to say that the results of the first skirmish indicated the final results of the campaign.

Oglethorpe perceived that his safety depended upon constant watching. The Indian allies, who had been sent for as soon as intimations of the invasion had been received, responded promptly. These Indians were sent out in scouting parties for the purpose of retarding the progress of the Spaniards as much as possible. For such a work, no class of men were better adapted than the aborigines of America. Accustomed from youth to scour the woods in search of game, they were by their mode of life trained to watch an invading foe. In this work of scouting they were assisted by the Highland regiment. These Highlanders were no less brave than the Indians and but little less savage; and, besides, their hatred for the Spanish was unconquerable.

Repeated attempts were made by the invaders to reach Fredrica. Every effort was in vain. The fierce savages and the Highlanders, thirsting for revenge, lay concealed in the thickets and in the swamps and from these dark hiding places poured destruction and death into the advancing columns of the invading foe. So great was the hindrance produced by these scouts, that the Spanish soldiers said "the devil himself could not reach Fredrica, so long as the Highlanders and Indians lay concealed in the surrounding thickets."

Don Manuel de Monteano, the commander-in-chief of the invaders, after having lost a number of his officers, besides several hundred men killed and more taken prisoners, determined to change his mode of attack. During the flowing of the tide some vessels were sent up the river, whilst the main body of his army was kept under cover of his cannon. However Oglethorpe conducted himself during the expedition against St. Augustine, he now showed himself an able general. Necessity may have stimulated his brain and

self preservation prompted to vigorous action. Be that as it may, he showed himself equal to the emergency. The Spanish commander did not entrap him. A body of Indians were sent secretly up the river to watch the vessels and prevent the men from landing. It was not their object to land. It was simply a ruse de guerre - a trick of war.

Oglethorpe now determined to attack the Spanish camp during the night. A prisoner whom the Spaniards had captured, managed to effect his escape and made good his return to Fredrica. From this individual it was ascertained that there was a serious difficulty existing between the Spanish troops. On account of this difficulty, those troops from Havana camped in one place and those from Florida in another place. This fact suggested to Oglethorpe the propriety of a night attack upon one of the camps. For the execution of this plan, three hundred men were chosen, together with the Highland regiment. With a perfect knowledge of the country, the party succeeded without being discovered in arriving within two miles of the enemies' camp. Here they halted and Oglethorpe and a few men went forward to reconnoiter. In this party of men was a Frenchman whose treacherous soul led him to fire off his gun and dash, with all possible speed, to the Spanish camp. This frustrated the present plan, but it did not frustrate General Oglethorpe. He saw at once that it would, since the Frenchman had gone to the Spanish camp, be extremely hazardous to proceed farther with this night attack.

He immediately set out for his camp at Fredrica, and set to work to counteract any and every thing the deserting Frenchman might do or say. He wrote a note to the Frenchman, in which he addressed him as if he were a spy whom he had sent into the enemy's camp for the purpose of learning their movements and secretly directing their actions. Among other instructions given this deserter in the letter, he was charged to persuade the Spaniards to make an immediate attack on Fredrica. He was instructed to tell them that it was in a defenseless condition and the garrison was weak, and that success would be sure in the event it was at once assailed. In the event he should fail in this, he was to make a strenuous effort to detain the Spanish forces for at least three days at Fort Simon; for within that time, he (Oglethorpe) would be reinforced by a land force of two thousand men and a fleet of six British ships. The deserter was further charged to keep it a profound secret that General Vernon was soon to make an attack upon St. Augustine. A Spanish prisoner was hired, by

Oglethorpe, to take this letter and give it to the deserter. The work was readily undertaken, since the prisoner gained his freedom by it.

Instead, however, of giving the letter to the French deserter, it was placed in the hands of Monteano, the commander-in-chief of the Spanish army. This was just what Oglethorpe especially desired. The Frenchman who had deserted from Oglethorpe was put in irons on the spot. A consultation was held over the mysterious letter. Some thought it was a letter written by Oglethorpe to a genuine spy and its meaning was what its words literally imparted. Others thought it a sham, intended simply to deceive the Spanish commander. What the final conclusion would have been it is hard to say, but whilst the consultation was going on, three small ships, which the governor of South Carolina had sent out, appeared in sight. This settled the question. The three ships were taken for a part of the six British ships mentioned in the letter, and the whole Spanish camp was soon in a panic. Their fort was set on fire and in the greatest confusion all embarked - leaving their cannon, ammunition and supplies all behind. The wind was unfavorable for the three South Carolina ships, and the Spanish army sped past them and hastened to St. Augustine.

Finding that they had been outwitted and gained no advantage whatever, the Spanish threatened another invasion; but the threat was never put into execution. Oglethorpe showed himself, in every respect, more than a match for the Spanish. Taught by their failure in this expedition a lesson which they never forgot, the Spanish in Florida, and the English in South Carolina, lived without any further hostilities. In 1763, Spain ceded Florida to England and then the bone of contention was removed.

Truth requires us to say that, in this matter, South Carolina acted badly. Nothing was done, although Oglethorpe was importunate until, in the language of the statute itself, "a considerable body of Spanish troops had actually landed in the colony of Georgia." This statute is dated July the 10th, 1742. No doubt our fathers were ashamed of their conduct, and made honorable amends for the indifference with which they had treated their younger sister when in distress. At least from that day to this, Georgia and South Carolina have lived side by side in harmony; rejoicing with each other in their prosperity and sympathizing with each other when in trouble.

It is a pity that the history of a nation is so often nothing but a narration of its wars with its neighbors; of its rebellions and civil strifes. In the history of the human race, war holds the most prominent place, but by no means the most important place. The carnage of a battlefield is an awful sight, but a sight which human eyes desire to see. The shouts of victory often drown the cries and shrieks of the widow and the orphan. The conqueror excites the admiration of the humble peasant, and the tale of his blood-bought victories kindles the ambition of the humble sons of toil. The fame of the military hero is borne by every breeze to the remotest nooks of the globe. School boys with sparkling eyes tell of his reckless daring, and blushing maids sing his praises. Great as may be the worth of him who leads battling armies to victory, infinitely greater is he who subdues the forest or converts the swamps into a cornfield. He who constructs a fort from whose walls death and destruction are hurled into the columns of his country's foes, deserves to be held in remembrance by all who love liberty and hate oppression. We should not, however, let the glitter of the warrior consign to oblivion him who, in his rude workshop or on his humble farm, does something which ameliorates the condition of society.

The first settlers of South Carolina, although often engaged in war, were not savages. They did not come to America that they might satiate a thirst for blood. It is true that, for a number of years, every man was a soldier. This was the case until after the Revolutionary war. The mechanic went to his shop, the farmer to his field, and the worshippers to the house of God; each armed and equipped as a soldier. The circumstances by which they were surrounded demanded that each man be a soldier. Spaniards, Indians, French and pirates watched them as the eagle watches its prey. It would not be too much to say that for more than 200 years, a people had been undergoing a process of training which terminated in the establishing of American liberty. It may be that neither the first settlers of Carolina nor their descendants for several generations did all they could to beat the sword into a plowshare and the spear into a pruning hook. Still they desired peace, and never ceased to cultivate the arts of peace. Whilst they were erecting forts, they were at the same time decorating the city and subduing the forest. They found the Indians in the country cultivating only maize or Indian corn. Taught by these children of the forest, they also engaged in its cultivation. Only a short time after the first settlement was made, rice was planted, and so great was its increase that the hunger-ridden nations of Europe soon looked to South Carolina for food. In less than 100 years, although almost continually engaged in war, the products of South Carolina had so increased that several hundred vessels were required to export them to the markets of Europe. Rice, Indian corn, barley, peas, potatoes, live stock, beef, pork and bacon, together with vast quantities of lumber, tar, pitch and turpentine were annually exported. Charles Town was a busy place.

The effort was made, at an early period, to introduce the cultivation of silk into the colony. The first effort was unsuccessful. The eggs, from which it was designed to propagate the worms, hatched whilst the vessel which brought them from Europe was still at sea and, no provision having been made for their maintenance, they all died. The enterprise was not abandoned. In different sections of the state, some attention was paid to the culture of silk. Governor Nathaniel Johnson devoted his attention to this subject as early as the beginning of the eighteenth century. In 1755, the mother of Charles Cotesworth and Thomas Pinckney took with her to England a sufficient amount of silk to make three dresses, one of which was presented to the Princess Dowager of Wales, another to Lord Chesterfield and the third remained in the family. Not many years since, it was still in the city of Charleston and may be there still. Mrs. Pinckney, although the wife of the chief justice of the state, possessed of considerable wealth and the descendant of an honorable family, still she prepared this silk with her own hands. In 1742, eighteen and one-half pounds of raw silk were exported from South Carolina to England. The Swiss at Purrysburg, and the French in what is now Abbeville county, continued to devote some attention to the culture of silk for a number of years. The descendants of the French colony that settled on the Long Canes, in Abbeville county, continued to cultivate silk for domestic purposes as late as 1830. It is worthy of note that European judges pronounced the silk made in South Carolina excellent. "It was remarkable for its beauty, firmness and strength." The fact that the forests of South Carolina were covered with the mulberry tree, the leaves of which constitute the principal food of the silk worm, suggested to the early settlers the idea that the country might be well adapted to the culture of silk. The first experiment was made within less than ten years after the settlement of the state.

Prior to the introduction of cotton, indigo was one of the staple productions of South Carolina. So favorable were the soil and climate to the production of this dye, and so great was the income accruing from its production, that it became a matter of English legislation. Indigo is a native of Hindostan, but it was, for a long time prior to its introduction into the South Carolina colony, cultivated extensively in that portion of the West Indies subject to France. Wild indigo, a plant which very much resembles indigo proper, and possessing the same properties but in less degree, grows in all parts of the state. It is found in almost every field. As the mulberry growing in the forest suggested to the first inhabitants the probable fitness of the country to engage in the culture of silk, so the wild indigo growing in the fields suggested to them that indigo might be cultivated with profit in the same territory. Nothing, however, seems to have been done in this matter until the year 1741. George Lucas, at that time, was the governor of the island of Antigua. At the same time, he owned and had cultivated a plantation a short distance west of Charleston on the Wappoo. Here his family resided. His daughter, Eliza, a young woman of energy and also a great lover of nature, devoted her spare moments from the wheel and cards to the cultivation of useful and beautiful plants. Her father gave her every encouragement and, at different times, sent her various tropical plants and roots with which to experiment. Sometime during the winter of 1740-41, he sent her some indigo seed. Some of these seed she planted with her own hands in the month of March, 1741. They came up, but the young plants were killed by frost. She planted again in April. These also came up, but were cut down by a worm. She did not, as some other girls and most modern boys would have done, become discouraged; but tried again and was successful. The plant grew and matured to the satisfaction of the cultivator and her father. Governor Lucas now determined to make a business of the cultivation of indigo. More seed were purchased and a practical indigo maker procured from the island of Montserrat, and sent to Carolina to superintend the culture and manufacture of George Lucas' farm on the Wappoo. The name of this superintendent was Cromwell.

He engaged in the work at first with apparent good will. Vats were constructed and everything put in preparation for the work of making merchantable indigo. Cromwell fearing, no doubt, that if this experiment proved a success it would be injurious to the French colonies in the West Indies, declared that indigo could not be grown in Carolina. To dishearten Eliza Lucas, who still continued to watch the experiment with intent interest, he put too much lime in the vats and thus destroyed the indigo. Eliza Lucas discovered the trickery and dismissed him, and with the assistance of a Frenchman by the name of Deveaux, she went to work and discovered the whole process of making indigo. Other individuals in the neighborhood now began to cultivate small quantities of indigo for their use.

Not long after this, Eliza Lucas married Charles Pinckney, commonly known as Chief Justice Pinckney. In 1746 she became the mother of Charles Cotesworth Pinckney, the man who said, "Millions for defense - not a cent for tribute" and in 1750 of Thomas Pinckney. Two noble sons of a noble mother. After her marriage her father gave the indigo farm, which she had watched with anxiety, to her husband. All the growing crop was permitted to go to seed. At the proper time the seed was gathered. Some was distributed amongst the neighbors and the rest planted. Every one became interested in the production of indigo. It was not long after its introduction into the colony by Eliza Lucas until it became one of the principal articles of export. "It proved," says an old writer, "more profitable to the Carolinians than gold mines did to some of the other European colonies in America." Indigo continued to be cultivated with profit both to the colony and the mother country. In 1747 the merchants of England, who traded in Carolina, petitioned parliament that a bounty might be allowed on Carolina indigo. This petition was favorably received and an act passed in 1748 allowing a bounty of six pence - about twenty cents - on every pound of indigo produced on any of the British plantations in America. It now began to be cultivated in every settlement and its cultivation continued until several years after the Revolutionary war. It was rooted out by cotton.

It is probable that indigo would have been able to withstand its rival cotton, had it not been for the ingenuity of Miller and Whitney. These men devised a saw gin which enabled the cotton planter more expeditiously to separate the lint and seed. It is probable that even Whitney's gin, as originally constructed, would not have been sufficient to cause cotton to supersede indigo had it not been for the ingenuity of a woman. Miller and Whitney's gin, when first constructed, had no brush wheel. Mrs. General Green, while watching the gin in operation, saw this defect and removed the lint by the gentle motion of her fan which she held in her hand. This suggested the brush wheel. It was made and, as a woman had introduced indigo into the state, so a woman, by a stroke with her fan, did that which drove it out. It was a proverb once often repeated in the state, that on an indigo farm everything looked as if in a starving condition. The same may be said with respect to cotton, which as a money crop has taken the place of indigo.

In summing up the details of events which transpired during Governor Bull's administration we must not forget to mention the great fire which occurred in Charles Town in 1740. On the 18th of November, the wind blowing a stiff gale from the northwest, at two o'clock in the afternoon, a fire broke out on Broad street, near its western extremity. With fearful rapidity the flames were hurried in a southeasterly direction from one building to another. Soon it seemed as if the whole city was in flames. The air was full of blazing fagots, carried by the maddened wind. The inhabitants were panic struck. The screams of women and children rose above the cracking flames and falling houses. Property was abandoned to be devoured by the fire. The houses were all wood and the stores were filled with tar, pitch, deer skins and powder, all of which added fury to the flames. No effort was made by the citizens either to stop the progress of the fire or to save their property. An effort was made by the sailors, but for six hours the work of destruction continued until the flames were arrested by the Cooper River. At eight o'clock in the morning the wind calmed and the fire ceased to make farther progress. Its work of destruction was done. Three hundred of the best houses in the city, together with vast quantities of merchandise, were reduced to ashes. Only a few lives were lost, but hundreds were without a shelter. Over the scene of desolation a wail of anguish went up. Those who escaped the devouring flames kindly welcomed the unfortunate to their homes and shared with them their comforts. The British government in the exercise of its love and pity, generously contributed one hundred thousand dollars for the relief of the distressed.

INSTALLMENT XL

In the year 1743, James Glen succeeded William Bull as governor of the English colony of South Carolina. Glen continued in office for a period of thirteen years, or to the year 1756. During the administration of Glen, the whole middle and up-country, with the exception of a few remote sections, was at least partially settled. Two classes of persons first pushed their way into the regions remote from Charles Town. These were traders and wild adventurers. Of the latter class, there is evidence that some individuals, at a very early period, abandoned the comforts of civilization and took up their abode with the wild savages of the New World. It is difficult to say by what spirit these adventurers were moved, or what object they had in view, unless it be that to some minds there is something fascinating in savage life. The traders had much to induce them to push their way far into the interior. The Indians, although poor, were in possession of some things which were valuable to civilized people, and these things could be bought for a mere trifle. A few trinkets, which were of no intrinsic worth to the Indians, and of but little relative value to the trader, would purchase from a savage the hard earnings of the chase during a whole year. The consciences of the traders were not generally very tender. They seldom scrupled at swindling the poor Indian out of all the meager comforts which he possessed. Sometimes a cheated Indian would become incensed and pour out his fury upon the first pale face that he met, on account of some misdemeanor which had been done him by a trader. Really the traders did little to initiate the Europeans into the good graces of the savages. Few of the traders settled down and became good citizens. Most of them became amalgamated with the Indians, and the half bloods were even more dangerous than the native savages. Most of the half bloods, the descendants of European traders and Indian mothers, were, during the Revolutionary war, either plundering Tories or thieving loyalist.

It is somewhat a remarkable fact that the whole of the middle and upper sections of the state of South Carolina were settled about the same time. For the first half century, settlers kept almost within sight of the sea coast and the Savannah River. The first permanent settlement which was made at any considerable distance from Charles Town was that made by the Scotch-Irish colony in 1733 in the present county of Williamsburgh. This is not to be wondered at. The immigrants came not to a well cultivated country with fields waving with generous harvest; but to a dense forest inhabited by ferocious wild beast and by human beings little less ferocious. The first settlers had to build forts as well as fell the trees of the forest. The French on the north and west, and the Spanish on the south, watched the movements of the first settlers of South Carolina. By these two nations - not in concert, but each for itself - every obstacle was thrown in the way to prevent the spreading of the colony. No small portion of the first seventy-five years of the colony's existence was spent in war. Add to this the fact that the colony was, during this period, visited by fire and flood, and the wonder is that it was not annihilated.

Many circumstances contributed to entice settlers to South Carolina. The government, after it passed out of the hands of the proprietors into the hands of the Crown of England, was more favorable, in many particulars, than that of any of the colonies in America. In no region in America was a home offered to a poor man on easier terms than in South Carolina. Land was cheap and taxes light, whilst ample provisions were made by the crown to secure the comfort and prosperity of immigrants. Notwithstanding all the hardships to be undergone and deprivations to be endured, poor men, if they were sober and industrious, soon accumulated so much property as to put them beyond the reach of want. Many in a short time grew comparatively rich. About the time that James Glen became governor, many circumstances tended to the rapid settling of the territory now embraced in the state.

When Glen became governor, he called together the chiefs of the Indian tribes in the northwest section of the state. He met them in their own territory and, after a friendly salutation and the delivery of speeches which, at this day, sound like flattery, a treaty was entered into by which a large portion of the upper part of the state was ceded to the English. The Indians in that section were, by this treaty, made friends and there was comparatively little danger in making settlements among them. The misfortunes of the people of Europe, and the faults of the European government, furnished settlers for this region of the country. The pretender, Charles Edward Stuart, was defeated and his followers reduced to the utmost extremity by the battle of Culloden. Multitudes of brave Scotchmen who had, whether right or wrong it matters not, still unfortunately espoused the cause of the pretender, were made prisoners. The English government had more prisoners than it knew what to do with. To put all to death was too cruel; to pardon all would rob the government of all its vindicative power. To meet the case, nineteen out of every twenty were pardoned and furnished transportation to America. Many of these hardy Caledonians came to South Carolina.

Another circumstance, whilst it materially retarded the growth of the northern colonies, added settlers to South Carolina. In 1744 the French and Indian war broke out. This war grew out of the claims which both the English and French laid to the continent of North America. It was waged mostly on the northern frontiers. Whilst all was peace in South Carolina it was nothing but war and carnage in the more northern colonies. Eight thousand young men fell upon the battlefield. Many towns were burned, vast tracts of territory were laid waste, and the inhabitants sought homes in other sections of the country. South Carolina received its full share.

In 1755, Gen. Braddock suffered himself to fall into an ambuscade in which he was mortally wounded, and sixty-four of his officers killed. This left Pennsylvania and Virginia exposed to the French and

Indians. Multitudes driven from their homes in these states came and settled in all of the upper counties of South Carolina.

It will, no doubt, be interesting to give a brief history of the settlement of the several counties of the state. It must be remembered, however, that the division of the state into counties did not take place until after the Revolutionary war.

After the territory embraced in the present counties of Charleston, Colleton and Beaufort, that embraced by Barnwell and Orangeburg was the first to induce a settlement. As early as 1704, a man by the name of Henry Stirling made a settlement in the present county of Orangeburg, on Lyons Creek. It was not, however, until 1755 - two years after the settlement of Williamsburgh - that a permanent settlement was made in this section of the state. From 1704, the time of Henry Stirling's settlement, to 1735 only a few individuals located in this region. In 1735 a number of Germans made a permanent settlement. They were a people of good moral character. By them the settlement was called Orangeburg. Barnwell is so named in honor of the Barnwell family of Beaufort. Horry and Williamsburgh were both settled about the same time and both by Irish. In Horry, many of the French Huguenots found a home. Georgetown was settled early in the beginning of the eighteenth century by Baptist, Presbyterian and Episcopalians, mostly of English origin; but it was not until 1737 that the settlement became permanent.

Following the tide of emigration from the seacoast northward, the next settlement was made in the present county of Richland, in the year 1740, at a point a few miles northwest of the present city of Columbia.

When the county was first settled, stockraisers constructed what they called "cowpens." These were rude fabrics, generally reared on some stream or at the confluence of two streams. The object designed was to have some place where their stock, consisting mostly of horses and cows, might be collected, sorted and branded. In some cases there was no house, nor even a pen. The name cowpen was given to a certain locality. The owner of the stock, on arriving at the place, uttered a call, which was recognized by the stock and to it they rushed.

At the mouth of Cane Creek, Benjamin Singleton, and afterward, Porcher, established cowpens. Settlements were soon made in the neighborhood by German immigrants. This was in the region of the Cherokee Indians; and for protection, the settlers constructed two forts - Fort Granby on the Congaree and Fort Kinnerly on the Saluda.

The remaining counties of the state were mostly first settled by immigrants from the northern colonies. Fairfield was settled in the year 1745 on Broad River by two brothers, John and Ephraim Lyles. The old homestead is, we believe, still in possession of some of their descendants, who bear the same name. The Lyles were Virginians by birth. They were natives of New Brunswick, Virginia, but had emigrated to North Carolina; thence to South Carolina. Soon after their settlement, Ephraim was killed by the Cherokee Indians. At the same time, the Indians killed a Negro belonging to Ephraim Lyles, but Mrs. Lyles and eight children were not disturbed. Previous to this, Thomas Nightingale, the maternal grandfather of Rev. R. P. Johnson, the present pastor of the Episcopal church of Yorkville, established a cowpen on little Cedar Creek, about six or seven miles below Winnsboro. About the same time, a cowpen was established near Winn's bridge by a man named Howell. The Scotch-Irish, both before and after the Revolutionary war, settled in great numbers in and around Winnsboro.

Chesterfield and Lancaster counties were settled in 1745 by Virginians and Pennsylvanians. Kershaw was settled in 1750 by a colony of Irish Quakers; Chester in 1750 by Pennsylvanians and Virginians; Darlington and Edgefield in 1750 by Virginians - mostly the latter. Lexington county was settled in 1750 by Germans. The first township laid out in this county was called Saxegotha. Marion and Marlborough were both settled by Virginians, the former in 1750, the latter in 1755. The first settler in the present county of Newberry was John Duncan, a Scotchman; but an immigrant to South Carolina from Virginia. The counties of Laurens and Union were both settled in 1755 by immigrants to South Carolina from Virginia. Samuel and James Bradley made, in 1750, the first permanent settlement in what is now Sumter county. Spartanburg county was settled in 1750 by a few individuals from Virginia, Pennsylvania and North Carolina. The territories embraced in the counties of Anderson, Pickens and Oconee was not settled until 1755, after Braddock's defeat, when a number of persons, exposed to the ravages of the Indians, came from Maryland, Pennsylvania and Virginia and located in that mountainous region. Abbeville, York and Greenville were the three last counties in which permanent settlements were made. In 1756, Patrick Calhoun, with four other families, made a settlement in Abbeville county on Long Cane Creek. They were preceded by two other families - one by the name of Edwards and the other by the name of Gowdy. York was first settled in 1760, and Greenville in 1766, by Virginians and Pennsylvanians.

When the upper and middle sections of the state began to receive settlers, the territory was soon at least partially filled with inhabitants. The Irish came in by hundreds. Ireland and Scotland furnished the up-country with the largest amount of immigrants. Germany and France furnished several colonies, whilst the English immigrants remained mostly in the low country. The Huguenots followed the Santee.

Installment XLI

THE CHEROKEE WAR

James Glen was succeeded as governor of South Carolina by William Henry Lyttleton. One short sentence will give an accurate description of Lyttleton. He was a vapid coxcomb. He belonged to that class of men who, with but a small amount of sense and incapable of turning to any wise account either their own experience or that of others, still think that they are competent to govern the world.

Evidently, Governor Lyttleton was anxious to secure the approbation of the board of trade. The good of the colony was consulted no farther than it would concentrate the power of England over the American people, and advance to positions of honor and offices of profit, a few favorites.

After the treaty which Glen made with the Cherokee Indians, peace and harmony subsisted between the Cherokees and the English colony of South Carolina. Not only were the Cherokees friends to the South Carolinians, but they were friends to the English colonies generally. During the period of the French and Indian war, which was so destructive to the northern frontiers, South Carolina enjoyed a comparative peace. The Cherokees sent their brave young warriors to assist in repelling the assaults of the French and Indians in the north. South Carolina became an asylum to which many, exposed to the cruelties of savage warfare in Maryland, Pennsylvania and Virginia, fled. The fields of South Carolina began to bring forth in abundance and the exports of the colony increased rapidly. A stream of immigration poured in from all the countries of Europe. All lived together in the enjoyment of peace and plenty.

An unhappy end was brought to this prosperous and peaceful state of things by the foolish resentment of Governor Lyttleton. We will not say that he had sinister motives in view, but we are forced to conclude that he was either a knave or a fool. He acted as if he were ignorant of the fact that the Cherokees were the friends of the English. As he could not, however, have been ignorant of this fact, his acts towards them were in open violation of previous treaties and showed that his heart was as cruel as his judgment was weak.

He was not the only individual who acted cruelly and in bad faith towards the Cherokees. In 1757, a number of the Cherokee braves volunteered to assist in protecting the English frontier settlers south of the Potomac. After they had done their part faithfully and rendered material assistance to the English colonies, they were totally neglected; and but for the prudent forethought and consummate wisdom of Washington, would have been left to starve or to be cut to pieces on their return home by the common enemies of both the English and the Cherokee.

The proud savage of the New World was no doubt cruel; but the colonies were not always generous. The party of the Cherokees which had left their homes and joined the Ohio expedition found that they were treated with neglect. Cut to the heart, they determined to return to their homes. No provision was made for them. They were in a starving condition. As they passed through Virginia on their way home, they supplied their wants from the country through which they passed. In the expedition they had lost their horses. The horses of the Virginians were unceremoniously taken to supply their present wants. The Indians did not have very correct ideas with regard to property. This was especially the case with regard to animals. Possession of an animal amounted to ownership. The Virginians, in an ill-fated moment, urged on by hasty resentment, set upon these tired and famishing bands of the common allies of the English, and in three encounters killed fourteen and took several prisoners. The remnant of the party returned to their homes in the vicinity of Fort Prince George, on the head waters of the Savannah.

The tale of their suffering was soon spread abroad. The shrieks and cries of those who had been robbed of their relations echoed from mountain top to mountain top and through the winding valleys of the Toogaloo. "The blood of your murdered kinsmen calls for vengeance," was proclaimed by proud chiefs, and the young braves were sent out to retaliate. The war belt was sent from town to town. The region of country which had enjoyed almost uninterrupted peace now became the theatre of hostilities. The French learned the existing state of things, and persuaded the Cherokees that the intention of the English was to kill all the Indian men and make slaves of the women and children.

The aged chiefs, who had long known the English, and from the Cherokees had received many and valuable favors, were opposed to war. Even the young warriors would have laid down the tomahawk when they had avenged the blood of their murdered kinsmen, had they been dealt with prudently.

Fort Loudon, on the Tennessee, was garrisoned with two hundred men under the command of Captains Demere and Stuart. Some soldiers, having gone out into the woods to hunt for game, were attacked by the Indians and several killed.

Captain Cotymore was in command of Fort Prince George. He communicated with Governor Lyttleton at Charles Town. The hazardous condition of the northern frontier of the province was made known. Governor Lyttleton, either fearing a confederation of the Creeks and Cherokees, or anxious to make a gorgeous display of his military talents, summoned the militia of the country to arms. The neighboring colonies were solicited to send him aid. The banks of the Congaree were appointed as a place of general rendezvous. The signal guns were fired and the colony began to prepare for war. Soon the Cherokees learned that Governor Lyttleton contemplated invading their territory. In order that the disastrous consequences of war might be avoided, a delegation of thirty chiefs set out from their mountain homes to entreat for pardon. The Cherokee nation, with only a few exceptions, were still the warm and trusty friends of the English. When these chiefs, of whom Oconostata was the principal, arrived at Charleston, Governor Lyttleton received them with no small amount of empty parade. He recounted, in a threatening tone, the injuries which the Cherokees had done to the frontier settlers. When Oconostata attempted to reply, the governor assumed a dictatorial attitude and told the chief that he would "hear no talk from him." The chiefs were told to march with his army and by so doing, not a hair of their heads would be hurt.

Fourteen hundred militia assembled at the Congaree. Here Lyttleton showed his littleness of soul. Twenty-eight of the chiefs were put under guard, two having previously fled. The proud chiefs now showed, by their grim and sullen countenances, that they felt that they had been dealt with contrary to promise. On arriving in the neighborhood of their principal town, twenty-eight chiefs were confined in a miserable hut, scarcely sufficiently large to contain, with any degree of comfort, one-fourth of their number. Lyttleton, as if about to make a treaty of peace with some of the enlightened nations of Europe, sent for the old chief Attakullakulla. From this old and trusty friend of the colony, Governor Lyttleton demanded that the twenty-four individuals who had been guilty of perpetrating the wrongs complained of should be delivered up to him that he might put them to death, or else he would hold the chiefs in his possession as hostages.

The old Indians knew nothing of the customs respecting hostages. Although as chief he knew that such was the nature of the government of the tribes, that one individual had no control over another. In despair of effecting anything toward peace, he retired, determined to wait the result as a brave old man. Scarcely had he gone, until Gov. Lyttleton recalled him and succeeded in having a treaty signed in which was embodied a number of articles of which the chiefs either did not understand or were forced to sign from the necessitous condition in which they were at the time. In the meantime, some of the perpetrators of the violent deed complained of, were delivered up to Lyttleton. By him an equal number of hostages were released.

It was now certain that the smallpox was raging among the Indians. Lyttleton's army became panic-stricken, and a disorderly rush was made by each one, separately and alone, for his home. The governor ordered his hostages to be kept in close confinement in Fort Prince George and with his prisoners, he set out to follow his army to Charles Town until they died. Not a drop of blood was shed during the expedition and no good was accomplished, but much harm; yet it cost the province more than one hundred thousand dollars.

When Lyttleton arrived at Charles Town, he was received by his party as a mighty conqueror. Scarcely had he arrived in the city, when it was learned that hostilities had broken out again in the neighborhood of Forth Prince George. Fourteen individuals were killed within the range of the guns of the fort. For Cotymore, the commander of the fort, the Indians had contracted an irreconcilable hatred. They surrounded the fort, determined if possible to release their twenty-six chiefs imprisoned within its walls under the refined name of hostages. Unable to effect their purpose by assault, they determined to have recourse to stratagem. Oconostata placed a body of Indians in a dense thicket near the fort, and sent a friendly Indian woman to the fort requesting Cotymore to meet him at a certain point on some important business. Without reflecting, Cotymore with two lieutenants, Bell and Foster, went to the spot. Oconostata was present with a bridle in his hand. He told Cotymore that he had determined to go to Charles Town that he might solicit Governor Lyttleton to release the prisoners and that he had desired a guard. He was then, he said, on hunt of a horse to ride. Cotymore at once promised the chief the desired guard. In the midst of the conversation,

Oconostata slung the bridle around his head three times. This was the signal to his ambushed colleagues. Out of the thicket they rushed and fired upon the unsuspecting captain and his two lieutenants. Cotymore fell mortally wounded, and Bell and Foster, dangerously. The men in the fort, seeing what was going on, attempted to put in irons the prisoners in the fort. The Indians resisted, severely wounding three of the garrison. Enraged by this resistance, the men in the fort put all the prisoners to death on the spot.

Every move either by the English or by the Indians only made matters worse. The inhuman butchery of the hostages, as they were called, in Fort Prince George aroused the Cherokees as they never had been aroused before. The cry for revenge pierced the darkness of the night. The wild natives laid aside all restraint. The houses of the frontier settlers were visited by hideously painted savages, and children were mercilessly put to death and scalped without distinction. The smallpox was raging in the low country, and but few of the militia could be induced to leave their afflicted families to render aid to their distressed countrymen. Never was there such a time in South Carolina before. The whole country, from Ninety-Six in the present county of Abbeville, to Fort Loudon on the Tennessee, was exposed to the tomahawk and scalping knife. Dogs grew fat on the carcasses of human beings. Tender babies were snatched from their mother's bosom, and their brains dashed out against trees. The savage war song, and the shrieks and cries of helpless women and children were heard above the howling of the wolves.

In order to relieve the afflicted colony, a dispatch was sent to General Amhurst, the commander of the British forces in America. Amhurst detached Colonel Montgomery, with six companies of Highlanders and six companies of the seventy-second regiment. In April 1760, Montgomery arrived in Carolina. he was joined by a company of volunteers from the low country. Previous, however, to the arrival of Montgomery, Lyttleton was appointed governor of Jamaica, and William Bull succeeded him as governor of South Carolina. Bull applied to Virginia and North Carolina for assistance, and seven companies were sent to assist in keeping the Indians from penetrating into the interior further than Ninety-Six.

After his arrival in the province, Colonel Montgomery encamped at Monck's Corner. All things being arranged for the campaign, he set out with all possible dispatch for the Cherokee country. His time was limited, and he was forced to act promptly. On entering the Indian settlement, he literally laid it waste with fire and sword. New Keowee, Estatoe, Quacorelchie, Toxawaw, Sugaw Town and Aconnee, were reduced to ashes. The Indian women and children, together with a few men, were made captives; but the multitude of the warriors fled on the approach of Montgomery.

Thinking that the Indians were not yet sufficiently humbled, Colonel Montgomery pushed into the middle settlements, the abode of the over-hill Cherokees. The march lay through a pathless forest. Rugged mountains and streams with precipitous banks impeded his progress.

When within five miles of Etchoe, a town of over-hill Cherokees, Montgomery was attacked by the Indians. The battle ground was chosen with consummate skill. It was a deep valley, densely covered with underwood. In this the savages were concealed. Captain Morrison led the van-guard. No sooner had he entered the brake, than the savages sprung from their ambuscade and poured in a destructive fire upon him and his men. Morrison fell dead, many of his men were wounded. The main body of Montgomery's men came up and the fight became general. The forest echoed and re-echoed with the Indian war whoop. The fight lasted about an hour and terminated to the advantage of the British; but it was a dear bought victory. Montgomery lost twenty men killed and seventy-six men wounded. The savages were routed, but not subdued. In the recent fight they lost in killed only forty; and Montgomery, in order to save his wounded, was obliged to make a hasty retreat to Fort Prince George. All the way from Etchoe to the fort, the savages kept annoying him. On arriving at Fort Prince George, he announced that he was under orders to set out immediately for New York. This announcement filled the frontier settlers with grief. To quiet their fears and afford them some protection, he left four hundred men, and in August set out to join General Amhurst.

The departure of Montgomery left Fort Loudon in a most critical condition. From its location, it was cut off from the civilized world and exposed to continued assaults by the savages. In the fort there were two hundred men, but the Indians kept it so long blockaded that the officers were reduced to the alternative either to surrender or submit to starve to death. It was decided that Captain James Stuart should go to Chota, the town of which Oconostata was chief, and make the best terms for surrender that he could. It was agreed, that after delivering up the guns and ammunitions of the fort, except what each soldier might need. the garrison was to march out with a kind of military honors and be escorted either to Fort Prince George or to some point in Virginia. The sick and disabled were to be taken care of by the Indians in the neighborhood, for which they were to be paid.

Having surrendered everything except ten bags of powder, and ball in proportion, which were buried in the ground. the garrison marched out and proceeded on the first day fifteen miles on their way to Fort Prince George. During the night the Indian escort left them. Early on the next morning a band of savages was discovered near their camp. Captains Demere and Stuart had scarcely time to arouse their men before the Indians poured in a deadly fire - killing Captain Demere and twenty-six of the men. The rest were all surrendered and hurried back to Fort Loudon. Stuart was the friend of Attakullakulla. This old chief bought his friend Stuart and released him from captivity. The other prisoners suffered unutterable hardships and were afterwards at a great cost redeemed.

The condition of things were now gloomier than they had ever been before. The Cherokee towns had been burned and multitudes of their old men and women and helpless children had been starved to death; but they were still masters of the field.

In the early part of 1761, Lieutenant Colonel James Grant was sent by General Amhurst to South Carolina to reduce to subjection or annihilate the Cherokees. His force consisted of a regiment and two companies. Another regiment commanded by Col. Henry Middleton was furnished by South Carolina. The other officers of this regiment were Francis Marion, Isaac Huger, William Moulton, Owen Roberts, Andrew Pickens, William Mason, Adam McDonal and James McDonal. These men had made names for themselves during the Revolutionary struggle. Several individuals of the Indian tribes also joined the expedition.

With all possible speed, Grant hastened to the Cherokee country. Salona, the young warrior of Statoe, was shouting amongst his fellows: "I am for war, whoever will not follow me is no better than a woman."

On arriving near the same spot where the engagement between Montgomery and the Indians occurred in the year before, the advance party under Capt. Quantine Kennedy met the Indians. A terrible conflict took place. For three hours the Indians fought with desperate courage. At last the undisciplined sons of the forest gave way. Grant pursued them with fire and sword. The towns were reduced to ashes, the corn fields were destroyed, the hogs were killed and men,

women and children were put to the sword. The strength of the Cherokees was broken. The name of Grant was a terror. Afterward, when they would drive their cattle out of their fields they would shout "Grant, Grant." Colonel Grant returned to Fort Prince George. The Indians had gone beyond the mountains.

Whilst at Fort Prince George, Attakullakulla came to his camp and begged for peace. He was sent to Charles Town and a treaty was made and signed by Governor Bull.

Thus ended the Cherokee war. Both parties had suffered much and neither had gained anything. The Cherokees simply made a virtue of necessity. They remained the bitter and uncompromising enemies of the Carolinians. During the Revolutionary war, they joined the British and gave the settlers of Watauga and Nollickucky no little trouble.

A century has passed away since our fathers declared themselves free and independent. When we contemplate that act, and the struggle which followed in all its results, it seems more like a highly wrought romance than the sober details of facts. The oldest of the thirteen colonies which entered into that struggle was a little more than one hundred and fifty years old; and the youngest was less than fifty. The nation whose yoke they threw off was powerful in all the munitions of war. For more than a thousand years she had been growing in wealth and power. She was the proud mistress of the sea, and her land forces had done themselves honor on more than a hundred battlefields. The thirteen colonies were weak. They had no ships, no arms, no powder, no standing armies, and, besides, the whole population amounted to less than three million.

For a people thus situated to think of opposing the armed forces of England, seems like unparalleled recklessness. The history of the world presents no similar case. When we consider the fact that these thirteen colonies not only dared to oppose the armed forces of England, but forced that gallant old nation to acknowledge their independence, we are struck with amazement. When the British soldiers laid down their arms at Yorktown, and the struggle was virtually at an end, General Washington told his men not to huzza. "Posterity," said he "will huzza for you." This was prophetic. So long as noble deeds are regarded as worthy of admiration, men of every nation will delight to honor that handful of men which wrung from the British government an acknowledgment of their rights and liberty. Not only so; but the government which they established, after the conflict was over and the victory won, was such as the world had never seen. The good of all governments of antiquity was adopted and the evil rejected. Even today, abused and corrupted as is the government which our fathers left us, it is still the best government on earth.

The part which South Carolina took in the Revolutionary struggle was honorable. No state in the Union can boast of a fairer fame than South Carolina. She stands second not even to Massachusetts, "the cradle of liberty." South Carolina's Revolutionary statesmen were wise and prudent; her soldiers were bold and daring. The descendants of South Carolina's statesmen and soldiers have no need to be ashamed of the record of their ancestors.

It is impossible to treat the causes which led to the Revolutionary war as simply connected with one state. The causes of that event were common to all the colonies. What affected one affected all. The proximate cause was an insignificant tax upon tea, glass and paints. The avowed object for which the British parliament proposed to raise this tax was to assist in liquidating the debts of the English government. Some of this debt had been incurred by the wars which had been fought on American soil and in defense of the American colonies. Not only so, but the British government had incurred much expense in founding and fostering some of the colonies. It might appear at first sight that the colonies acted rashly in not submitting to the tax. It must be remembered that it was not the amount of the tax that they resisted, so much as the principle. They claimed that taxation and representation are inseparably connected. They felt that, as Englishmen, they had a right to resist all taxation except such as was imposed by their own proper representatives. It is true that, on several occasions, England had sent over armed forces, in appearance for the defense of the colonies, but really for the establishing of her own claims to North America. Both Spain and France claimed the territory which was now occupied by the United States and, on moral principles, the claim of either was as good as that of England. In fact, then, whatever expense England had been at in planting the colonies and defending them against the French, the Spaniards and the Indians, was only so much done to extend her own dominions. It was not only unwise in England to impose any tax upon her colonies, but it was unjust.

The wonder is that the colonies were wise enough to see the injustice of the attempt or bold enough to resist it. This can only be understood by a careful consideration of the characters of the individuals who formed the bulk of the first settlers of North America. They were bold adventurers, but not in the ordinary sense. The majority of them were subjects of the British government. They were Protestants as distinguished from Papists, and Dissenters as distinguished from the established church. They left their native land, not from choice, but from necessity. They came to the wilds of America, not that they might amass a fortune, but that they might live in peace and worship God according to the dictates of their own consciences. Massachusetts could boast of her Puritans, and South Carolina of her Huguenots and Scotch-Irish. All of these had ceased to love kings before they came to America. Many of those who had assisted in beheading one king, and in banishing another from his throne, had sought a home - an asylum - in the forests of America. Even the judges who had presided at the trial of Charles I, and sentenced him to the block, fled to America.

Nothing but oppression could have driven any people to have taken up their abode in the bleak and barren region near Plymouth Rock, or in the swamps of South Carolina and Georgia. To reconcile their children to their lot, and cheer them under the many hardships which they were called upon to endure, parents told them of the many afflictions which they had borne in their native land. Generation after generation had passed away, and England to many had ceased to be regarded as their mother country. They had never seen its gorgeous cities, but they had heard the tale of the woes which their fathers had suffered from England's oppression. Not only did England drive away some of her citizens, but she sent away some that she might get rid of troublesome inhabitants. The providence of God, in bringing about the Revolution of 1776, is clearly seen after the event is passed.

From the days of Elizabeth, the acts of the sovereigns of England tended to make America free and independent. Walter Raleigh was treated in such a way as to stir up the righteous indignation of any people. Truthfully was it said by Colonel Barre that "the tyranny of England planted the American colonies and they grew in spite of England's neglect."

The men who first came to North America were, at least may of them, men of sound judgments and extensive learning. The early state papers show this clearly. The early enactments of the provincial legislature or parliaments of South Carolina, as it was called, would do honor to any people or any age. The children of these first settlers were educated at a vast expense. Some of the Revolutionary documents have never been surpassed for beauty of diction or vigor of thought. We are not to suppose because our Revolutionary fathers were reared in a forest, surrounded by wild savages, that they were ignorant and illiterate. Such was not the case. They were able to see at a glance the injustice of English enactments.

Various circumstances led the colonies to conclude they could successfully resist the arms of Great Britain. England had advised the colonies to unite for the purpose of common resistance. The skill of American officers, as compared with that of British, had been put to the test. Washington had saved the fragments of a fine army, which had been led into a slaughter pen by a pompous British general. In 1755, twenty years before the Revolution, Col. Washington was a more experienced officer than General Braddock. Francis Marion and Henry Middleton had fought side by side with soldiers of the standing army of England. They saw that they feared the foe as little, could load and fire as often, and their aim was as unerring as that of England's boasted troops. All these things tended to inspire confidence in American officers and American privates.

The part which South Carolina took at the commencement of the Revolutionary war is highly honorable. When a vessel laden with tea entered the harbor at Boston, a company of men, disguised as Indians, boarded the vessel and threw the tea overboard. The British government treated this act as treasonable and blockaded the harbor. Boston was, if left alone and unaided by the other colonies, in a hopeless condition. No sooner had South Carolina heard what was done than she approved of the course of her sister colony and espoused her cause. This act appears the more striking when we remember that the relations between the South Carolina colony and England were perhaps more intimate than that of any other colony. There were many things to induce the people of South Carolina to remain at peace with the British government, and there were many things to dissuade the colony from entering into a war. In South Carolina the Negro population was at least twice that of the white. The institution of slavery had been thrust upon the people, contrary to their wish, by England; and in spite of all their remonstrances the slave trade had, by the same authority, been kept up. These slaves, it was thought, would make an effort to secure their freedom in the event a war broke out between the colonies and the mother country. The Cherokee Indians had been routed, but not subdued. Besides all this, the colony was in a very flourishing condition. Notwithstanding all the disadvantages to be encountered, the colony boldly determined to defend the right, let the consequences be what they might.

During the Revolutionary war, especially the latter part of it, the sufferings of the people of South Carolina were, as we will see, great; but they bore it without a murmur. Their heroism was of the highest order. If the battle of Lexington was the beginning of hostilities, and the surrender of Cornwallis at Yorktown the end of the war, the battle of King's Mountain was the turning point of the contest.

SECTION TWO

REVOLUTIONARY WAR

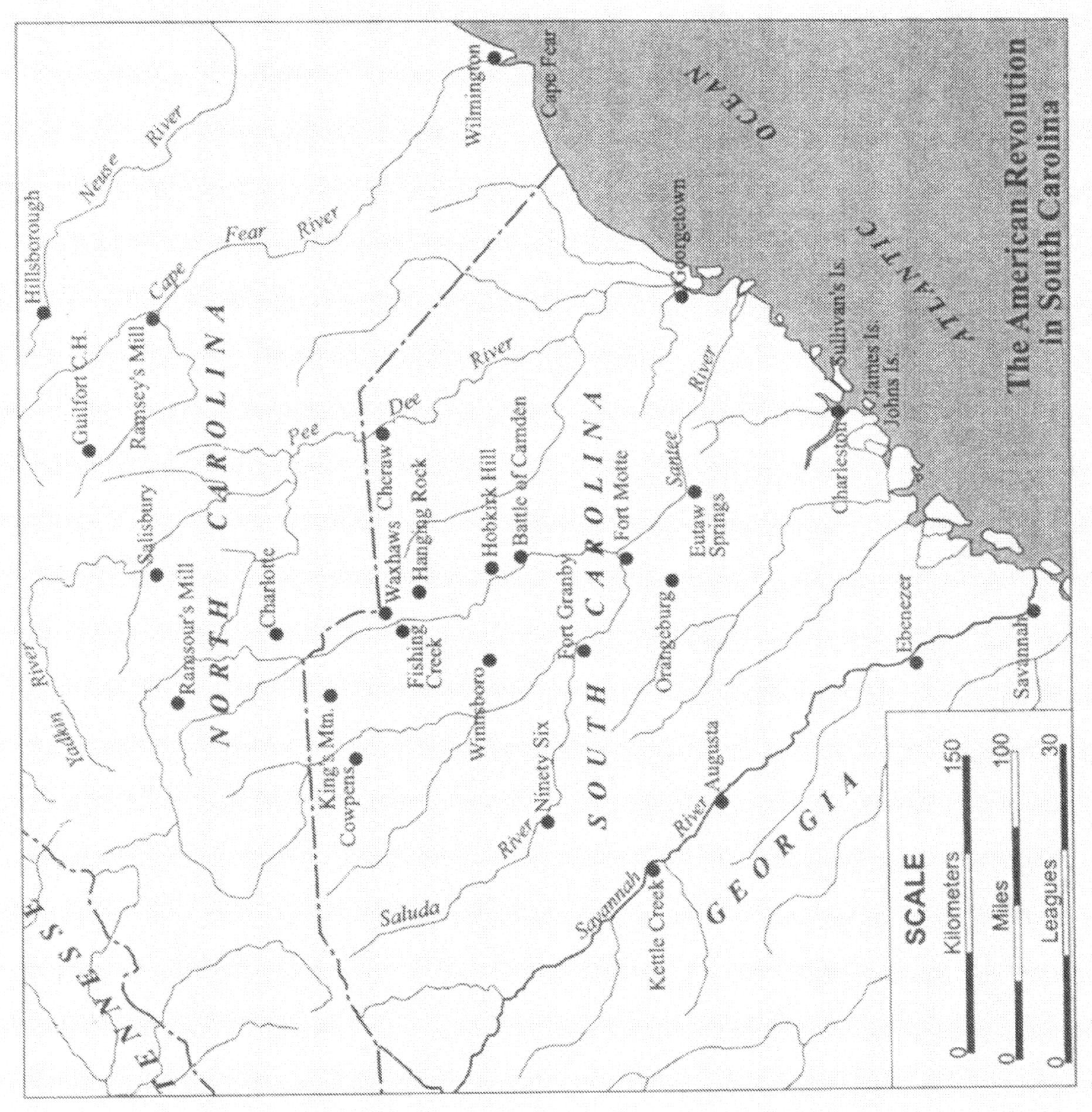

The American Revolution
in South Carolina
1779–1781
TENNESSEE
NORTH CAROLINA
SOUTH CAROLINA
GEORGIA
ATLANTIC OCEAN
Hillsborough
Guilfort C.H.
Ramsey's Mill
Salisbury
Charlotte
Ransour's Mill
King's Mtn.
Cowpens
Fishing Creek
Winnsboro
Ninety Six
Waxhaws
Cheraw
Hanging Rock
Hobkirk Hill
Battle of Camden
Fort Granby
Fort Motte
Orangeburg
Eutaw Springs
Augusta
Ebenezer
Savannah
Kettle Creek
Charleston
Sullivan's Is.
James Is.
Johns Is.
Georgetown
Wilmington
Cape Fear
Neuse River
Yadkin River
Cape Fear River
Pee Dee River
Santee River
Saluda River
Savannah River
SCALE
Kilometers
150
Miles
100
Leagues
30

CAUSES OF THE REVOLUTION

Whatever honor may be attached to those infant colonies which deliberately threw off the British yoke and declared themselves free and independent, no small share of that honor is due to South Carolina. In the preliminary events which culminated in an open rupture with the mother country, she led the way. It was, as we will see in the sequel, the misfortune of her leading men often to be far ahead of the age in which they lived. Really, the government of South Carolina was never anything but a republic. The Fundamental Constitutions drawn up by the philosopher, Locke, and adopted by the original proprietors, never were put in force over the people for whom they were designed as a power of government. The proprietors were forced to change and remodel those constitutions, as much from the character of the people as from the nature of the country.

South Carolina was, in 1670, an unbroken forest; and those who came from Europe to make their home in that unbroken forest longed for freedom, and freedom they would have. From the very first they quarreled with the proprietors, and in a short time the proprietors cast them off with the angry declaration that they did not intend to feed the colonists when there was no longer any reasonable expectation of being compensated. Thus they were turned out into the wilds of the New World to work for themselves or starve. With an energy which put failure out of the question, they went to work. They depended upon themselves. Necessity forced them to think and plan for their physical existence and for their social and political equality with the nations of the earth. Thus, whilst the early settlers of South Carolina cut down the forest and drained the swamps and planted and cultivated Indian corn, they sowed broadcast the seeds of genuine republicanism. In 1729, by a bold effort, they freed themselves from the yoke of the original proprietors and placed themselves under the protection and government of England, but with greater privileges and more liberty than British subjects in England.

From the first day that the colonists set their feet on the banks of the Kiawah, they were jealous of their rights, and every event in their history had a direct tendency to make them watch their chartered rights with sleepless vigilance. In 1762, Governor Thomas Boone sent a message to the general assembly in which he stated certain objections to the election law of 1721 and recommended that the enactment of "a new law was absolutely necessary." Boone acknowledged that zeal to promote the "prerogatives of the crown" had induced him to make this recommendation. When the message of the governor was received it was immediately placed in the hands of a committee. On the 23rd of March, just four days after the date of the message, the committee made its report, and on the next day the report was considered and the following reply sent to Governor Boone:

May it please your Excellency, this House having fully considered the election act now in force, and not knowing or not having heard of any bad consequences from the method thereby directed, for issuing, and executing writs of election, are of opinion that it is not necessary, at this time, to alter that law in any respect.

In September of the same year, Christopher Gadsden was duly elected a member of the assembly from St. Paul's Parish. Governor Boone not only refused to administer the oath of office in the case of Gadsden, but also dissolved the assembly. He was determined to force the representatives of the people into measures; but he had men to deal with who could neither be wheedled nor bullied into measures. Governor Boone's avowed reason for not admitting Gadsden as a member of the assembly was because the church wardens, who, under the law, were the managers of the election, had not been sworn. It was proved that this was not the case, and the assembly determined to admit Gadsden to his seat in spite of governor Boone's objection. This gave Boone a pretext for dissolving the assembly. Shortly afterward, another assembly was chosen and Christopher Gadsden was again elected. This greatly irritated Boone, and the new assembly was not slow in manifesting its disapprobation of the governor's course with regard to the previous assembly. A series of resolutions were passed, the purport of which was that the assembly itself and not the governor is the judge of the legality of the election of its own members; that the course of the governor respecting Christopher Gadsden was a violation of the privileges of the assembly of the province; that the previous conduct of Governor Boone was unconstitutional, and had a direct tendency to subvert and destroy the most essential and invaluable rights of the people of the province and reduce the power and authority of the assembly to an abject dependency on the whims of the governor. It was also resolved by this assembly that since the governor had refused to apologize for his recent conduct, that the assembly would have nothing more to do with him. This surely was a bold step and was indicative of what followed.

The quarrel between Governor Boone and the assembly of South Carolina continued up to the time of the passage of the notorious Stamp act by the English parliament. The leading men were thoroughly aroused to oppose anything that had the semblance of an enactment upon their liberties. The leaders in the movement in opposition to Governor Boone were Charles Pinckney, Henry Laurens, Peter Manigault, Isaac Mazyck, John Rutledge, James Moultrie, Christopher Gadsden, Thomas Lynch, William Roper, William Scott, E. Simmons, R. Lowndes, James Parsons, David Oliphant, Thomas Bee, Benjamin Smith and Thomas Wright. The controversy between the assembly and Governor Boone was thoroughly discussed, both in public and private, by these men, and the result was a hatred for oppression, and an intense love of liberty was disseminated throughout the whole of the lower section of the province. When, in 1764, the British parliament passed the stamp act, to take effect after the 1st of November, 1765, the people were as a whole prepared to resist it.

When the stamps arrived in Charleston, no one could be found who was willing to incur the odium and risk the danger of accepting the office of receiver. Hence the stamps were conveyed to Fort Johnson. The people were divided into their opinion as to the proper course to be pursued. Henry Laurens was opposed to violent measures; but public sentiment was against him. A party of one hundred and fifty men were armed and set out to surprise the fort in which was stored away the stamps. It so happened that, although Fort Johnson was a strong fortification, the garrison was weak. The party found but little difficulty in surprising the fort and getting possession of the stamps. The heavy guns of the fort were loaded, a flag raised and every preparation made for a conflict with the vessel which had brought over the stamps. It was, however, agreed that the stamps would not be destroyed, provided the captain of the vessel would convey them away and not land them elsewhere in America. This was agreed to. The captain took the stamps and the men returned to the city. Again the people were triumphant. They had driven Boone from South Carolina and now they had sent the stamps from America. Nothing was talked of in the province but liberty. Christopher Gadsden was accustomed to meet the multitude under a large live oak near the residence and discuss the great political questions of the day. Gadsden saw a grand republic - far grander than that of Greece or Rome - springing into existence in South Carolina. Under this live oak Christopher Gadsden, long before any of his compatriots in any quarter of North America, spoke of American Independence. American liberty was conceived in the brain of Christopher Gadsden.

In 1769, the people of Charleston entered into what was called a "non-importation" agreement. In this it was determined not to import any goods from England, and thus get rid of the tax which was imposed upon certain articles.

In 1774, the Continental Congress adopted what was called the American Association. This was compiled by the people of South Carolina generally. The tea brought into the colony was stored away in warehouses and there it rotted; not a single pound of it was ever sold. On the 11th of January, 1775, a Provincial Congress chosen by the people met at Charleston. Charles Cotesworth Pinckney was chosen president. Things now began to assume a warlike appearance. Volunteer companies were formed and drilled, and everything indicated war. On the 19th of April, 1775 - the very day the battle of Lexington was fought - the Swallow, a packet ship, arrived in Charleston. She had dispatches for the governors of the southern colonies. Henry Middleton, John Rutledge, Christopher Gadsden, Thos. Lynch and Edward Rutledge, by order of the council of safety, seized the mail. The private letters were returned to the post office, but the dispatches to the governors were opened. From these dispatches it was learned that England had determined to force her colonies into subjection. These dispatches were sent to the Continental Congress and from them that body first learned the real intention of Great Britain.

So soon as the people of South Carolina heard of the battle of Lexington, they regarded every tie which bound them to England as severed and began to make preparation for both defensive and offensive war. All the arms and ammunition within their reach were seized and a vessel was sent out to capture the Brig Betsy, which was known from the intercepted dispatches to be on her way with a large quantity of powder for John Stuart, the Indian agent. The brig was found at anchor off the bar of St. Augustine, and completely surprised. Ninety-one barrels of powder, amounting to about ten thousand pounds, were obtained and safely delivered to the council of safety. Part of this powder was used at the battle of Bunker Hill.

We have thus hastily run over the events leading to the Revolution of South Carolina. Briefly as they have been treated, they still show that South Carolina was one of the principal actors in the beginning of that wonderful undertaking, the American Revolution. In future, we will confine ourselves to the particular battles fought during that eventful period in South Carolina, North Carolina and Georgia, together with a brief sketch of the principal heroes in the various conflicts.

BATTLE OF SULLIVAN'S ISLAND

We have already seen that through the prompt and energetic action of the authorities of South Carolina in seizing the mail brought from London to Charleston, the true position of England toward her North American colonies was first discovered. This bold and, in one sense, treasonable act was performed on the 17th day of April, 1775, by William Henry Drayton, John Neufville and Thomas Corbett. It was now manifest that non-importation acts which had, on two former occasions, proved successful in causing Great Britain to redress the grievances she had, by her parliamentary acts, inflicted upon her colonies would, in this case, fail to effect the desired results. The people of South Carolina became more thoroughly aroused. There were in the state multitudes of individuals who afterward were designated by the infamous titles of Tories; and then some who, from conscientious scruples, dared not oppose by word or act, the British government; and there was another class composed of traders, mostly Scotch and half-breed Indians, the offspring of Indian mothers and Indian traders. This class sympathized with the British government. The great majority of the men and women of influence and moral worth, in every section of the state, were Whigs.

From 1764, the time that the stamp act was passed by the British parliament, up to the time that the British mail bag was wrested from the postmaster in Charleston by William Henry Drayton and his colleagues, the movements of the mother country had been closely watched. The British parliament made, during this period, various efforts to encroach upon the chartered rights of the colonies, but the vigilance of the leading statesman of South Carolina never suffered the people to be entangled in a snare.

On the 11th of January, 1775, the provincial congress of South Carolina met in Charleston. It consisted of one hundred and eighty-four members, chosen from all sections of the province. The Constitutional Assembly consisted of only forty-nine members. Hence the Provincial Congress was nearly four times as large as the Constitutional Assembly. During the sitting of the Provincial Congress, Lord William Campbell, the newly appointed Royal governor, arrived in Charleston. He was received by the people with the manifestations of joy which it was customary to show on the arrival of a new governor. An address was prepared and presented to Governor Campbell by the Provincial Assembly. In this address the representatives of the people declared that they had been moved to do what they had done, not from a love of innovation or a desire to alter the constitution of the government; nor even had a lust for independence driven them to take the step, but they had been impelled by the law of self preservation. Governor Campbell refused to recognize the Provincial Assembly as a legally constituted body and would not treat with them.

For several months after Governor Campbell's arrival, nothing occurred between him and the people to disturb the progress of preparation for war which the people were making. Either from policy or believing that the thing would ultimately amount to nothing, Governor Campbell commissioned the officers of the volunteer companies which were raised for the purpose of resisting the encroachments of the British parliament. At the same time, Governor Campbell was secretly stirring up the people in the back country to resist the acts of the Provincial Congress. His success in distracting the minds of the people amounted to very little except in that portion of the state between the Saluda and Broad Rivers. This opposition did more good than evil. It showed the friends of the Provincial Assembly their real strength, and the royalists their real weakness. Zeal and energy were infused into the minds of the former while the latter became disheartened.

The friends of the Provincial Assembly were not ignorant of the secret intrigues of Governor Campbell. Adam McDonald, a staunch Whig and member of the committee on safety, prevailed upon some one to introduce him to Governor Campbell, under the name of Dick Williams, a messenger from the back country and a royalist. To this feigned Dick Williams, the governor made very important disclosures. He informed Dick that he had but recently received information from England that a large number of troops would soon be in the country and that the colonies would be forced to submit to British legislation. The duped governor was not long in finding out his mistake. He was soon waited upon by a number of gentlemen and among them was the veritable Dick Williams. His correspondence with England was demanded. He refused; but became alarmed for his personal safety and went on board the Tamar. This was in September, 1775, and the last time that a royal governor set his foot on South Carolina soil.

To instruct as well as encourage the people of the back country, the Rev. William Tennant and William Henry Drayton were sent out in 1775. They left Charleston on the second of August and passed up through the center of the state. On the Sabbath Mr. Tennant would first preach the gospel to the people and then deliver a political speech. Having arrived at King's Mountain, they then visited the western part of the state, and returned to Charleston after an absence of about two months. Thus it may be said that every effort was made to inform the ignorant and to correct the errors of those who had been misinformed. Every event which, for several years, had transpired had a direct tendency to alienate the minds of the masses of the people of South Carolina from Great Britain and cause them to bestir themselves to prepare for an open and avowed rupture with the English government. The city of Charleston was put in a state of defense and the forts which commanded the entrance to the city were seized.

No hostile blow had as yet been struck in South Carolina, but evidently the moment was fast hastening. Military companies were seen parading in every section of the state, and although the people were sensible of their own weakness and the strength and resources of England; still they determined to have their rights, let it cost what it might. On the departure of Governor Campbell, John Rutledge was made president of the Council of Safety, with the general instruction which was, on important occasion, given to the trustworthy amongst the old Romans. "See that the Republic suffers no injury" was the instructions he received and promptly did he meet the emergency of the case.

During the year 1775, the British government was active in making preparations for reducing the thirteen colonies into subjection. Two days before Christmas, Sir Peter Parker sailed from Portsmouth, England. His fleet consisted of eight armed ships, carrying, in all, about three hundred guns. Accompanying the fleet was a large land force, designed to act in conjunction with the fleet. Sir Peter met with delays on the coast of Ireland, and the weather was bad, so that he did not reach Cape Fear in North Carolina until the first of May. At Cape Fear the fleet met with General Clinton. The season was fast advancing and the troops were becoming sick. Clinton and Parker concluded that nothing could be effected in that region. All that they could learn respecting General Howe's situation was through the American newspapers, which was, to them at least, very unsatisfactory. After a month's delay at Cape Fear, it was determined to make an attack upon Charleston, South Carolina. This city lay in the field of operation assigned to Cornwallis and Sir Peter Parker.

Unfortunately for the British and fortunately for the Americans, the whole plans of the British government were discovered in time to give the Americans an opportunity to prepare to oppose them. A boat bearing dispatches from Lord Dartmouth to Governor Eden, of Maryland, was captured by James Barron. These dispatches revealed the whole plans of the enemy. Brigadier General John Armstrong had been sent early in the year 1775 to Charleston; and after the evacuation of Boston, General Washington sent out Major General Charles Lee to watch the movements of Sir Henry Clinton. On the 4th of June, Lee arrived in Charleston. On the same day, Sir Peter Parker's fleet made its appearance off the bar.

So soon as Major General Charles Lee arrived in Charleston, Governor Rutledge formally placed all the forces under his command. An order was issued for the militia of the country to hasten to the defense of the city. This order was promptly obeyed. The forces now at his command amounted to near six thousand. They were disposed of in the following manner. The first regiment of South Carolina regulars were placed at Fort Johnston, on James Island; Colonel William Moultrie was placed in command of the recently constructed fort on Sullivan's Island; Col. Thomas, with a body of riflemen, was placed on the east end of Sullivan's Island. General Lee, with a strong force, took position on Haddrell's Point, now Mt. Pleasant. Governor Rutledge retained the command in the city.

The British land forces, under the command of Clinton, were put off on Long Island. This island is separated from Sullivan's Island by the Beach Inlet. They were told that it was possible at some times to wade across this inlet. Clinton, with his forces being landed, commenced to fortify themselves, and Sir Peter Parker commenced to make preparations to cross the bar. It was known that this could not be effected by the large ships in their present condition. The large ships were lightened as much as possible by taking off some of their guns, and still the crossing of the bar was attended with considerable delay.

The arrangement of the troops was made mainly by Governor Rutledge and the South Carolina authorities. General Armstrong was a man of but very moderate abilities, and Major General Charles Lee was a strange man. He was a man of whom the most contradictory opinions might be formed. He was brave but not cool; he was patriotic but selfish. A Welchman by birth, but no land could claim him as a citizen. He neither feared God nor regarded man and was passionately fond of war because it enabled him to satiate his wicked passions. From the moment that he arrived in Charleston until the hour the attack was made upon Fort Sullivan, he was as restless as a caged hyena. He cursed Fort Sullivan as a mere slaughter pen and was constantly insisting upon Governor Rutledge to withdraw the troops from it. Rutledge wrote to Moultrie that he would sooner cut off his right hand than make such an order. Lee attempted to construct a bridge of boats, by which the troops in Fort Sullivan might retreat; and not having a sufficient number of boats, he attempted to complete the bridge with barrels. This bridge was a failure. He told Moultrie that a couple of British frigates would knock his pen about his ears in thirty minutes. "Very well," replied Moultrie, "we will then fight them behind the rubbish."

Fort Sullivan was wisely regarded by Rutledge as the key to Charleston. The British admiral also was aware of its importance. It was located on the southwestern end of Sullivan's Island, and derived its name from that of the island. "It was constructed of palmetto logs laid in sections and filled with sand. The merions were sixteen feet thick, and sufficiently high to cover the men from the fire of the enemy." Although the men had been working on it night and day since the approach of the enemy was discovered, that portion which was nearest to Charleston was still in an unfinished state. Lee, in a fit of rage, withdrew from the fort one-half of the powder and one-half of the force. He determined that Moultrie and his Charleston troops might suffer all the losses and enjoy all the glory of defending Fort Sullivan. The whole number of men left to defend this important point was only four hundred and thirty-five - all South Carolinians. They were the Second South Carolina regiment of infantry, consisting of four hundred and thirteen men and twenty-two of the Fourth South Carolina regiment of artillery. In this act, General Lee showed more temper than good sense.

It was the intention of the British commanders to attack Fort Sullivan simultaneously by water and land. Clinton was to cross over Beach Inlet and drive Thomas from his fortification and proceed to attack Fort Sullivan by land, whilst Parker was to attack it by water.

From the 4th of June, to the 28th, preparations were vigorously made by both parties. The British were preparing for the attack and the Americans for the defense. On the morning of the 28th of June, 1776, the British fleet began to take position. It consisted of the Bristol and Experiment, each fifty gun ships; the Active, Solebay, Acteon, Sphynx and Syren, each of twenty-eight guns; the Friendship of twenty-two guns; and another of twenty guns, together with an armed schooner and the Thunder-bomb-ketch. In all, about three hundred guns of large caliber. The Active, Bristol, Experiment and Solebay ran up nearest the fort; the Sphynx, Syren, Thunderbomb and Friendship arranged themselves a little in the rear of the others and more distant from the city. All things being ready at half past ten in the morning, Sir Peter Parker gave the signal to commence the attack. As the several vessels had been getting into position, the guns of the fort had been fired upon them, the vessels returning a broadside. About eleven o'clock the action became general. The inhabitants of the city were watching the battle from the tops of houses and other elevated places. The fire from the fort was slow, but well directed.

Early in the engagement, Sir Peter sent the Syren, Acteon and Sphynx to attack the extreme western side of the fort. This was the part of the fort which was unfinished; and had these vessels been able to execute their orders, the result of the battle might have been different. As the vessels advanced to take a position, so that they could entilade the garrison, they became entangled in a shoal, called the Middle Ground. The Acteon stuck fast, the Sphynx lost her bowsprit and, although she got away, she was no longer fit for action. The Syren, more fortunate than the other two, escaped with little damages.

During the action which lasted more than ten hours, the garrison had only lost ten men killed and twenty wounded. In the fort there was a morass which extinguished the fuses of the bomb and rendered them harmless. The loss of the British was fearfully great. The commodore's ship - the Bristol - was twice swept of every man on its deck, and the tradition is that Sir Peter Parker had his silk pantaloons shot off him. The loss in killed and wounded on the Bristol was one hundred and eleven; on the Experiment seventy-nine. The whole loss of the British in killed and wounded was two hundred and twenty-five. Among the wounded was Captain Morris, of the Bristol, who afterwards died of his wounds; captain of the Experiment lost an arm. Lord William Campbell, late governor of South Carolina, served as a volunteer on the Bristol and was wounded in the beginning of the action. The forces stationed on Long Island, under the command of Clinton, effected nothing. Colonel Thomas, with his riflemen, kept them back.

At one time the powder in the fort was exhausted and, the firing having ceased, the British thought the garrison was about to surrender. Governor Rutledge sent a fresh supply of powder from the city, and Francis Marion obtained another supply from the schooner Defence. At sunset the firing began to slacken and ceased entirely before ten o'clock. At eleven the shattered fleet, except the Acteon, which was still stranded, withdrew to Five Fathom Hole. Soon, the next morning, the garrison opened a fire upon the Acteon, which at first was returned. Sir Peter Parker, seeing the condition of the Acteon, sent word to the crew to set her on fire and leave her. This was done, but, before she blew up, a small party of Carolinians, under Captain Jacob Milligan, boarded her, took her flag, which the crew left, her bell, and three boat loads of supplies. Then, having fired her guns, which were left loaded, upon the Bristol, they left. In a few minutes after the departure of Captain Milligan and his party, the Acteon blew up.

Clinton again attempted to cross Beach Inlet, but Captain Thomas again drove him back. The fleet proceeded to Long Island to recruit. On the 13th of July, with a ruined fleet and a heart filled with sorrow, the whole British force left South Carolina for New York. Moultrie's slaughter pen had blasted the hopes of Parker, Cornwallis, Clinton and Vaughn. Fort Sullivan was afterward, in honor of its brave defender, named Moultrie.

Among those who covered themselves with glory was Sergeant William Jasper and Sergeant McDonald. When the flag staff was shot down, Jasper leaped over the beach, secured the flag, and then, amid a shower of iron hail, mounted the ramparts and planted it on the walls of the fort. Poor McDonald was mortally wounded. When dying he said: "I die, my comrades; but do not let the cause of liberty die with me."

Governor Rutledge presented Jasper with his own sword and offered him a commission in the army. The sword he accepted, but declined the commission because he could not read.

Mrs. Barnard Elliott presented Moultrie's regiment with a pair of colors. Moultrie, for his men, pledged that they should never be dishonored. This pledge cost Jasper, Bush, Hume and Gray their lives at Savannah.

Installment III

REGULATORS AND SCOVILLITES

The successful defense of Fort Moultrie against the British under Parker and Clinton had a most decided effect upon all parties. The Tories and loyalists began to fear for their sovereign's power in America, and the Whigs came to the conclusion that it was possible for them to throw off the British yoke and be free.

For a period of about three years after the battle of Fort Moultrie, the state of South Carolina, although she was one of the thirteen colonies which had solemnly pledged their lives, their fortunes and their sacred honor to resist to death the unjust acts of the British government, enjoyed comparative ease. Her sons flocked by the hundreds to the northern colonies to aid in vanquishing the common foe. The distinction north and south did not then exist. Massachusetts loved South Carolina and South Carolina cherished no less love for Massachusetts. From June 28th, 1776, to January 1779, the war was carried on principally in the states north of the Potomac. It was not, however, during these three years, a period of perfect tranquillity.

For more than ten years prior to the commencement of hostilities between the colonies and Great Britain, there had existed in South Carolina two parties, which cherished toward each other bitter hatred. These parties were at different times known by different names; but the same individuals composed them.

When the up-country was settling up, a vast multitude of strangers were brought into contact with one another, and still they were totally different from each other in their manners and customs, and especially in their notions of civil government. Some were intensely loyal, while others were as intensely republican. There was also not a few who came to the up-country for no other purpose than that they might live free from all the restraints of law and good order. They were a thieving set of fellows, and contemplated amassing fortunes by stealing horses and Negroes. The order-loving portion of the inhabitants were kept in a state of constant dread by these desperadoes.

Prior to 1769, there was no general court, except in Charleston. There were magistrates' courts, the jurisdiction of which extended to all sums below twenty pounds. To catch and convey to Charleston one of these horse thieves for trial was no small job. The probability was that, after being captured, he would be rescued by his partners in crime; or, if brought to trial, he would be saved from suffering the penalties of the law by the false swearing of his fellows.

As early as 1752, the inhabitants of the PeeDee and Lynch's Creek region presented a petition praying that Craven county might be divided and that for the portion situated in the east, twelve justices be appointed, without fee or reward, "to hear and determine all cases, as well civil as criminal." These petitioners of the PeeDee region were laboring under a great burden in that they were surrounded by a set of horse-thieves and cut-throats. The western section of the state, that portion between the Broad and Saluda Rivers, was full of these desperadoes. This was chosen by them as a kind of headquarters, whence they sallied out in all directions to the great annoyance of peaceable citizens.

Thomas Woodward, who lived in the region that is now embraced in Fairfield county, together with Barnaby Pope and Joseph Kirkland, got up an organization which was called the "Regulation" and the members of which were called "Regulators." The Regulators went to work with zeal to remedy the evils under which the country groaned. It was evidently their intention, at first, to do good by punishing outlaws; but sometimes they permitted their judgment to be controlled by their individual feelings. Horse-thieves and other violators of the rights of others were hunted up and, according to the statutes of the Regulators, were given thirty-nine lashes on the naked back. In many instances, notorious characters were dealt with more severely, and some were shot when attempting to escape.

The horse-thieves were more numerous than the Regulators at first supposed them to be. The line of demarcation between the Regulators and the horse-thieves, and horse-thief sympathizers, soon became clear and distinct. The people began to arm themselves and a civil war seemed to be not far distant. To prevent this, Gov. Montague appointed one Scovill to act as a kind of arbitrator, with unlimited powers, of the difficulties existing amongst the citizens. Scovill was a most consummate villain. He espoused the cause of the horse-thieves with whom he was no doubt in league, and prepared for the conflict. The horse-thieves and ruffians flocked to his standard. The Regulators armed themselves and determined to resist the government as administered by Scovill.

The two parties confronted each other on the plantation of John Musgrove, afterward a Tory colonel. It was on the Saluda River in what is now Newberry county. Scovill summoned the Regulators to surrender. This they did not do and yet there was no one killed, although some shots were exchanged. It appears that some of the more prudent of both parties interfered and put a stop to the strife. The parties separated without a battle, but still their love for each other was not increased nor their hatred diminished.

Tradition has preserved a most laughable circumstance which took place whilst the two parties were drawn up in battle array. Amongst the Regulators was one who had but recently joined the party. He was a great braggart. He was absolutely hungry for a fight. Whilst the Regulators and Scovillites were confronting each other, some firing was done. This was more than the new-made Regulator could stand. He showed that if he was hungry for a fight he was no glutton. He took to his heels and ran like a quarter-horse. It happened that he had in his coat pocket a lead inkstand. In his flight, he jumped a large gully and his coat tail flew up, and the pocket with the inkstand struck him on the back of the head. He fell on his face, crying at the top of his voice, "I'm shot! I'm shot! I'm a dead man! Gentleman, don't kill me!"

In 1769, courts were established at Ninety-Six, Orangeburg, and Camden. This was all the relief the Regulators desired. Multitudes of the horse-thieves were gathered up and brought to trial. Tradition says that Scovill was tried at Ninety-Six for stealing chickens. The evidence adduced to prove the charge was that on a certain night, Colonel Scovill did steal from some one thirty-eight chickens. Colonel Scovill most solemnly declared this was a most infamous falsehood. "There were only, " he said, "Six and thirty, for I ate the gizzards." As a matter of course, we suppose, he was acquitted of the charge of having stolen thirty-eight chickens, but found guilty of having stolen thirty-six. Ridiculous as this may seem, it is said on good authority to be a fact; and if so, gives us a correct idea of the kind of man that Governor Montague selected to settle a difficulty between honest men and thieves.

The Regulators, on the breaking out of war between the colonies and England, were generally Whigs, whilst the Scovillites were Tories or loyalist. The two parties still continued; but under their new names, Whig and Tory.

It must be confessed that the Whigs often acted imprudently and sometimes very rashly. In the western section of the state, there were many men of influence who refused, they said, from conscientious scruples, to take any part with the Whigs in throwing off the yoke of Great Britain. Amongst these we might mention the three Cunninghams, Patrick, Robert and William (generally known as "Bloody Bill"), Brown, Fletchall and some others. Whether gentler measures would have won these men over or not, it would have been wiser, and with all due respect to the gallant old Whigs of 1776, it would have been more honorable to have first tried gentler measures and then acted as the circumstances of the case might demand. It is not claimed for the Whigs of 1776 that they were infallible. On the contrary, it is admitted they were but men, liable to do wrong. In their zeal for the American cause, the Whig leaders attempted by abuse to dragoon the loyalists to side with them. That which was at first a speck on the face of the heavens, soon enveloped everything. Difference of opinion was merged into determined opposition in every respect.

Robert Cunningham and his brother Patrick were men of very considerable influence in their region of the country. They were of Scotch descent and were loyalists. Robert was the first judge appointed for Ninety-Six district and before him the notorious Scovill was tried. Patrick was deputy surveyor-general of the province of South Carolina. Lord William Campbell, then governor of the province, opened up a secret correspondence with these up-country loyalists. They were told to make all possible preparations for resistance, but to be quiet until a blow was struck by the British government. It is, however, no easy matter to keep men of violent passions within the bounds of moderation. It is no less difficult to restrain violent partisans from acts and words that are calculated to develop slight dislikes into open and avowed hatred. Thus one word led to another and one violent act was but the forerunner of another act more violent. Finally the different parties assembled under leaders of their own choice or self-constituted leaders, armed themselves, and prepared for civil war.

Late in August of 1775, the Rev. William Tennant and William Henry Drayton visited the Ninety-Six region. They made an honest attempt to conciliate the people. Both these men were enthusiastic on the subject of American rights, and although they were honest in their efforts to advance a righteous cause, they were not always prudent in dealing with those who could not or at least would not see things as they saw them. Vague and false rumors were put in circulation by both parties. It was reported that the royalists were preparing to seize the agents of the Council of Safety; whilst it was as firmly asserted that it was the purpose of the Whig party to force, by an appeal to arms, the royalists to sign the articles of association. The royalists assembled in camp on the Enoree. Drayton called out the militia and prepared to march against them and drive them from the country. His proclamation is dated September the 13th, 1775. Moses Kirkland, who had been appointed a captain by the Whigs, but who had turned a traitor, fled to Charleston and went on board the Tamar. On the 16th of September, a treaty was entered into between the hostile parties, signed on the part of the Whigs by William Henry Drayton, and on the part of the royalists by Colonel Thomas Fletchall, Captain John Ford, Captain Thomas Greer, Captain Evan McLaurin and Captain Benjamin Wofford. In this treaty it was agreed that all parties should go home and live in peace. Robert Cunningham claimed that he was not bound by the articles of this treaty and still continued to stir up the people in opposition to the Whig party. He was arrested and taken to Charleston and confined. This aroused Patrick Cunningham, and he made a desperate effort to rescue his brother before he would reach the city. In this he failed; but he succeeded in capturing a quantity of powder which the authorities of South Carolina were sending as a kind of conciliatory present to the Cherokee Indians. Both Whigs and royalists were now furious. Major Andrew Williamson, who commanded the militia in the Ninety-Six district, was ordered to call out his men and proceed at once to capture the powder. The royalists were as keen for battle as the Whig militia and far more numerous. Williamson and his men were forced to take refuge in a stockade. For three days they were closely besieged and made to suffer. The condition of things was for some days critical. At last a treaty was again entered into between the contending parties. It was agreed that hostilities should cease on both sides.

These treaties were only temporary in their results. The Ninety-Six district was thoroughly aroused - neighbor against neighbor - and in some instances, brother against brother. To keep the royalists in awe, Colonels Richardson and Thomas were sent into this region.

The royalists were aided and abetted by Governor Campbell and did the country a great injury by stirring up the Cherokee Indians to hostilities. These deluded savages were persuaded by John Stuart and his brother Henry, together with several other persons, to take up arms against the Whigs. The plans of Stuart and his colleagues were defeated; but still the Indians commenced to massacre the whites almost simultaneously with the battle of Fort Moultrie. These Indian wars grew out of old contests between the Regulators and the Scovillites.

THE WAR WITH THE CHEROKEES AND TORIES

From what has been already said, it is evident that a very undesirable state of things existed in the up-country of South Carolina, at the commencement of the Revolutionary war. It has been recorded as a historic fact that the Whigs of South Carolina and Georgia had more difficulties to overcome than the Whigs in any of the thirteen colonies. There were, in the region between the Broad and Saluda Rivers, more Tories and loyalists than in any other region of the country embraced in the thirteen colonies, in proportion to the number of the inhabitants. It was more honorable to be a patriot in South Carolina than it was in Massachusetts. The two colonies were situated totally different in their relations to the mother country. Self interest moved Massachusetts to rebel; but self-interest prompted South Carolina to cling to England. In 1719 she had voluntarily given up the proprietary charter and placed herself under the government of England. In this relation she was happy and prosperous. A South Carolina Whig was a Whig from pure principle. If he had been asked why he threw off his allegiance to the crown of England, he would have exclaimed with emphasis - Liberty.

A well concerted plan had been arranged by which to attack the patriots of South Carolina and Georgia, both on the sea-board and in the interior, at the same time. The loyalists, Tories and Indians were to make an attack upon the Whigs living in the interior, whilst the British fleet was to besiege and capture the seaport towns. John Stuart was the principal agent in devising and in attempting to carry out this plan. The colleagues of Stuart were the loyal Governors Wright of Georgia; Campbell of South Carolina; Martin of North Carolina; Dunmore of Virginia; and Tonyn of Florida.

When we consider all the circumstances, we will be enabled to see that the plot was well conceived, and the men chosen to put in execution eminently fitted. John Stuart was a Scotchman. According to some authorities, he was born in Charleston, South Carolina. This we are disposed to think is incorrect. It is probable that John Stuart came to Georgia with Oglethorpe. It will be remembered that amongst the first settlers of Georgia was a company of Highlanders under the father of General Lachlin McIntosh. John Stuart and his brother were, in all probability, in the Highland colony that settled on the Altamaha. Stuart was a man of talent, and besides there was something in the dress and general appearance of the Highlanders which made them great favorites with the Indians.

We have already met John Stuart in 1761, a prisoner in Fort Loudon. After his release by an old chief, Allakullakulla, he became very popular in the colony, and was appointed Indian agent in the south. His territory embraced all of North America south of Pennsylvania. He had, by virtue of his office, a seat in the King's council of the provinces of Virginia, North Carolina, South Carolina, Georgia and Florida. His residence was in Charleston, South Carolina, in the house now owned by William Carson. He married a Miss Fembrick, and thus was brought into close relationship with the oldest and most honorable inhabitants of Charleston.

In order that the work of crushing the rebellion in the colonies might be successful, Stuart concerted with Dr. John Connolly, who resided at Pittsburgh, Pennsylvania. Connolly was commissioned by Governor Dunmore, of Virginia, to raise a regiment in Canada and the adjoining region and, with the aid of the Indians, overrun and destroy the country. Had the plans of Stuart and Connolly succeeded, it is doubtful what would have been the results to the cause of the patriots. Allen Cameron, John Smythe and Connolly set out for Ohio. In the neighborhood of Hagerstown, Maryland, they were taken up as suspicious characters and taken to Fredericktown. Here they were examined. Connolly's papers were found in the tree of his saddle. The whole plan was revealed and Connolly was sent first to Philadelphia and then to Baltimore and kept a prisoner until the end of the war. In Charleston, Stuart became an object of suspicion and, that he might act free and without trammel, he went to Florida.

In an interview with Colonel Habersham of Georgia, Stuart intimated his intention of uniting the various Indian tribes against the enemies of the King. This declaration admitted of but one interpretation. The King had no enemies at that time in America but the Whigs. This was a most unfortunate disclosure for the cause of Stuart, but fortunate for the people of South Carolina and Georgia. Habersham communicated what he had learned from Stuart to the Council of Safety at Charleston, and Stuart, becoming alarmed, fixed his quarters at St. Augustine out of the reach of the patriots of South Carolina and Georgia.

Arrangements had been made by the English government to supply the Indians with arms and ammunition. Part of the powder was to be shipped to St. Augustine and part to Savannah. All this powder was captured by the patriots and used in defense of the country against those who sent it. Part was used at Fort Moultrie and part was sent to General Washington and by him used at Boston.

We cannot refrain from remarking that it seems that a divine providence favored the plans of the patriots, and disconcerted the best laid schemes of their enemies. Had Stuart, Connolly and Dunmore succeeded in carrying out their plan, the cause of the patriots would have been crushed in the bud. Had they concerted no plans, no powder would have been shipped to St. Augustine and Savannah, and Moultrie might have failed at Sullivan's Island, and Washington at Boston, for the want of powder. Providentially, we will say, the plans of Stuart were frustrated. Humanly speaking, they were wise in their vastness, and minute and particular in their details. They were, however, not so far frustrated as to prevent all attempts to put them into execution. The Indian tribes from Florida to Canada, had been tampered with and preparations had been made to violate all treaties they had entered into with the whites. All the western sections of both Virginia and North Carolina, as well as the northwestern portion of South Carolina, were in the greatest alarm. They had unmistakable evidence that, unless checked, the wild savages would visit the inhabitants with the tomahawk and the scalping knife.

These fears were not imaginary. But two days after the British fleet commenced to bombard Fort Sullivan, the Cherokees raised the war whoop and commenced the work of carnage in the north-western portion of the state. Scovillites, loyalists, and plundering Tories united with the infuriated savages in their attack upon the Whigs of that region. White men painted like savage Indians, and clad in the habiliments of these wild children of the forest, entered their ranks that, under the appearance of savages, they might perpetrate deeds at which even savages blush. The Whigs had but few arms and but little ammunition. For safety they fled to the forts. The crops were committed to the mercy of wild beasts. Desolation hovered over the land and hunger, lank and lean, stared the inhabitants in the face. "Unless," said one who wrote from the scene of these massacres at the time, "we get some relief, famine will overspread our bountiful country."

To oppose the progress of the Indians and Tories, Col. Andrew Williamson was sent to the scene of their operation. His own home was in this region and consequently the love of his own fireplace inspired him with energy. He found the people panic struck. Each one was disposed to secure a place of safety for his own family, before he engaged in pursuing the maddened foe. More than two weeks were required to raise an army of five hundred men.

On the 14th of July, a party of ninety Indians and one hundred white men made an attack upon Major Downs, in Fort Lindlay. Downs defeated them, taking thirteen prisoners, ten of whom proved to be white men painted so as to resemble Indians. The loyalists had expected the Indians to spare the families of those white men who were not in sympathy with the patriots. In this they were mistaken. The savages used the tomahawk and scalping knives on Whigs and loyalists indiscriminately and the property of both was recklessly destroyed by the savages. This cooled the ardor of the loyalists and aroused the slumbering energies of the patriots. Another thing greatly changed the state of things in the Ninety-Six region.

About the 22nd of July, the news of the successful defense of Charleston, on the 28th of June, reached the up-country. The Tories and loyalists were not prepared for such news. They confidently expected to hear of Charleston being in the hands of the British, so soon as the fleet under Parker arrived. The result of this news was great depression to the loyalists and prompted resistance on the part of the Whigs. The loyalists, under Cameron, began to desert and straggle, and the patriots to rush by the hundreds to the camp of Williamson. When the news reached Colonel Williamson's camp on Baker's Creek that the formidable British fleet, under Sir Peter Parker, had been driven away from the coast of South Carolina by Colonel Moultrie's battery on Sullivan's Island, Colonel Williamson had only seven hundred men. It was but a few days until he had eleven hundred effective men and was in full pursuit of the Cherokees and Tories. Their camp was on Oconee Creek. To this point, Williamson, with more than eleven hundred infantry and three hundred cavalry, set out. His men were in good spirits and, although but poorly equipped, they were anxious for the contest. Some were burning with revenge and longing for an opportunity to chastise those who had scalped their children, wives and neighbors, and put the torch to their dwellings. Others were anxious to strike a blow in defense of American liberty.

The savages were aware of the approach of the patriots and laid in ambuscade for them. When Williamson and his men least expected it, they were attacked in front, and on the flanks, by a concealed foe. The war whoop was heard all around them. Williamson's horse was shot, and the whole army in an instant was thrown into the utmost confusion. Francis Salvador, a brave and accomplished Jew, fell at the first fire and was instantly scalped by the savages. For a time, a shameful rout seemed to threaten the forces of the patriots. In the midst of this disorder, Colonel LeRoy Hammond of Edgefield, with twenty men, charged upon the savages as they lay behind a fence. On the approach of the bayonets of Col. Hammond and his twenty determined followers, the Indians fled.

The main body, under Williamson, rallied and rushed to the conflict. Williamson determined to make a clean work as he advanced. Every Indian wigwam and town was burned down and every cornfield was destroyed. Neither man, woman, nor child was spared. It is no figure to say it was a bloody war. The Whigs flocked to his standard, and he crossed the mountains and swept with the besom of destruction everything in his way.

On the 13th day of September, Williamson, with his army numbering more than two thousand, fell into another ambuscade. In the mountainous region, near the site of the present town of Franklin, North Carolina, the Indians had posted themselves. On the rugged crags which fringe a narrow pass, the twelve hundred Indians and Tories had placed themselves. From behind rocks and trees, they poured in a destructive fire upon the Whigs. Experience had taught Williamson's men an important lesson. They were not as before thrown into confusion; but, in detachments, filed off and flanked the foe. Again the Indians fled and Williamson and his men continued to burn.

About the same time, Colonel McBury and Major Jack of Georgia entered the Indian settlements on the Tugaloo, and on the north their settlements were entered by Col. Christie of Virginia and General Rutherford of North Carolina. Thus, by the concerted action of the states of Virginia, North Carolina, South Carolina and Georgia, the Indians were ruined. There is nothing in the annals of American war that equals Williamson's march through the Indian country.

Of the remaining Indians, those that could left the country and went to Florida and were fed during the war in part, at least, by the English government; and those that could not leave the country, remained and suffered, in many instances, all the horrors of starvation. This campaign of 1776 annihilated the power of the Cherokees and their confederates and almost exterminated the tribe.

Installment V

THE INVASION OF FLORIDA

During the Revolutionary war, or at least during the early part of it, Florida was a place of general rendezvous for the British Tories, loyalists and Indians. Hon. John Stuart, early in the struggle, fixed his headquarters there and, in conjunction with the loyalists of South Carolina and Georgia, he laid plans by which he might serve his royal master.

Shortly after the battle of Fort Moultrie, an expedition was planned for the purpose of thwarting the designs of these faithful subjects of the English government and bitter and treacherous foes of the patriots. The expedition was to proceed against St. Augustine. Major-General Charles Lee, who was then in command of the southern department, approved of the plan, and sent out a body of troops under Brigadier-General Howe.

In the month of August, 1776, Howe reached Sanbury. The weather was hot, and the preparations for the expedition had been poorly made. Howe had no cannon and was in every other respect ill-prepared to proceed further. The troops began to sicken and Lee was forced to abandon the undertaking. The failure of this contemplated expedition infused spirit into the Tories, Indians and loyalists. In turn, they determined to make an expedition against the Whigs. Richard Winn, in honor of whom the county seat of Fairfield county is named, Winnsborough, had been placed in command of Fort McIntosh. This fort was built on the north side of the Saltilla River. It was simply a stockade, one hundred feet square, with a block house in the center.

On the 7th of February, a large body of Tories and Indians made an attack upon Winn. For two days he was successful in maintaining his ground; but on the third day, Major-General Provost, coming up with a large force and renewing the attack with energy, Winn was compelled to surrender. Two of the officers were retained as hostages and sent to St. Augustine. The rest of the garrison were paroled.

The surrender of Fort McIntosh, like the failure of the recent expedition against St. Augustine, inspired the enemies of the patriots with confidence in themselves. Preparations were made to invade Georgia from the south and west. The Tories of the Ninety-Six region began to collect in bands and cross the Savannah River. The aiders and abettors of the English government in Florida and the Indians of the west began now to menace Savannah. The Whigs of South Carolina saw that, in the event that Georgia fell into the hands of the enemy, South Carolina would then become a frontier state.

Robert Howe was made a Major General by the Continental Congress, and placed in command of the southern army. It was evident that, unless prompt measures were resorted to, Georgia, and possibly South Carolina, would, in a short time, be in the hands of the enemy. Large bodies of loyalists, British and Indians were collecting on the St. Mary's, St. John's, and at various other points, and reinforcements of British troops were daily expected.

Howe, notwithstanding the previous failure, determined to make another attempt to invade Florida. The exigencies of the times, it was thought by Howe and his military advisors, demanded that this be done. Savannah was made Howe's headquarters. He had only five hundred and fifty regulars who were fit for service. At Savannah, he was joined by the regiments of Colonels Pinckney, Williamson and Bull. Governor Houstoun of Georgia furnished three hundred and fifty militia.

Although miserably prepared for such an expedition, Howe was certain that he would succeed. Many circumstances conspired together to cause him to cherish such a hope. The expedition met with the approbation of all the Whigs, both in Georgia and South Carolina. Hence, Howe felt that whilst he was not fully prepared, so far as men and army supplies were concerned, still he had the sympathy of all the Whigs.

In addition to this, Lieutenant Colonel Samuel Elbert, who had been stationed at Fort Howe, had, but a short time before, made an attack upon a body of the enemy at Fort Oglethorpe. Although Elbert had but three hundred men, and a small detachment of artillery, still the garrison abandoned the fort and took refuge in their boats. Amongst other valuables captured by Elbert was three hundred uniform suits, which had been sent from Charleston to Savannah for Colonel Pinckney's regiment. These uniforms had been sent out in the sloop Hatter, and whilst on the way were captured by the enemy.

Encouraged by these circumstances, Howe pushed on to Fort Tonyn, on the St. Mary's. On the approach of Howe, the enemy fled after having rendered the fort useless. Howe ordered all the troops to rendezvous at Fort Tonyn. On his arrival at Fort Tonyn, he learned that twelve hundred men and two galleys, having on board a number of field pieces, had been sent from St. Augustine to St. John's, to operate in conjunction with the troops at that point. It was also learned from a deserter that the effective forces of the enemy was about fifteen hundred. In order that the arrival of the forces from St. Augustine might be anticipated, great promptness was absolutely required. Howe called a council of war, consisting of the three colonels from South Carolina, Governor Houstoun and Commodore Bowen, who was in command of a few galleys. Whatever were Howe's hopes previous to this time, they were now suddenly blasted.

Governor Houstoun absolutely refused to be commanded by Howe or any one else; the same position was taken by Colonel Williamson, and Bowen refused to be commanded by a land officer. The success of the enterprise depended upon union of sentiment with regard to who should be commander-in-chief. Houstoun, Williamson and Bowen determined to do as they pleased.

The army, numbering about two thousand men, lay around Fort Tonyn for some time. Provisions were scarce, the men were exposed, and the country was unhealthy. Sickness set in and the soldiers died at a fearful rate. Howe saw that it was, under the circumstances, impossible to advance; hence it was determined by the officers to retreat. Pinckney, with what remained of his regiment, returned by water to Charleston. Howe had under his command, when he first set out on the expedition, about eleven hundred men. Sickness and death had reduced the numbers to three hundred and fifty. With these he marched to Savannah. Thus ended the second expedition against Florida. It was a complete failure. More than half the army was lost and not a gun fired.

On whom the blame should be placed for its failure, it is hard to say. At the time, General Howe was severely censured by certain individuals. Chief among these was Christopher Gadsden. In a letter written by Gadsden, the failure of the enterprise was ascribed to Howe. Howe demanded of Gadsden that he would retract or apologize. Gadsden refused to do either, but declared that his mind had undergone no change. Howe sent a challenge to Gadsden which was accepted. Bernard Elliott acted as second to Gadsden, and Charles Cotesworth Pinckney acted the same part for Howe. On the 13th of August, 1778, they met near Camden and fought with pistols. The only damage sustained by either party was a scratch upon Gadsden's ear. Gadsden did not aim at Howe at all; but fired his pistol in a different direction. From all the facts in the case it is almost certain that Houstoun and Williamson were the cause of the failure of this second attempted expedition against St. Augustine.

The subsequent course of Williamson would seem to favor this conclusion. Christopher Gadsden was an impetuous man. A true patriot as he was, he no doubt censured Howe without a cause. His after course justifies this conclusion. When required to retract or apologize he would do neither; but still he would not shoot at Howe. Not only so, but after the duel was over and Howe was satisfied, he and Gadsden were good friends.

So far as the actual result was concerned it matters not who was censurable; the expedition was an absolute and disastrous failure. Emboldened by the failure of Howe, a party of British regulars and loyalists made a raid into Georgia. The garrison at Sunbury was commanded by Lieutenant John McIntosh. The enemy advanced toward the fort in two divisions; one commanded by Colonel Fuser and the other by Mark Prevost. Fuser sent a message to McIntosh demanding the surrender of the fort. McIntosh's laconic reply was, "Come and take it." Fuser was nonplussed by this bold reply, and concluded that it was best to let the fort alone. Fuser had in his command six hundred regulars, and could have taken the fort without much difficulty, but the defiant reply of McIntosh chilled the ardor of his spirit. The division under Prevost, now strengthened by a band of Tories, commanded by McGrith, commenced to skirmish with the Whigs. Having abandoned the idea of capturing the fort at Sunbury, they proceeded until met by Col. Elbert, with two hundred men. Baffled in their purposes, they wheeled about and laid the country waste through which they passed. Nothing escaped them. Dwelling houses, barns, and churches were burned to ashes.

Up to this period, the war had been carried on mainly in the northern and middle states. More than three years had elapsed since the first blow had been struck for independence. Battle after battle had been fought, and the rebellion was more formidable now than ever before. It was now determined by the British to change the field of operations. The failure of the Whigs to invade Florida encouraged the British to hope that they might be more successful in the south than they had been in the north. Savannah, the capital of Georgia, was regarded the weakest point; or it may be they had not forgotten their defeat at Fort Moultrie, and hence determined to make an attack upon Savannah. Near the end of November, 1778, Sir Henry Clinton sent out Colonel Campbell with more than two thousand troops, consisting of the 71st regiment, four battalions of Provincial troops; two battalions of Hessians, and a detachment of artillery. Sir Peter Parker accompanied these land forces with a part of the British fleet. Orders were sent to General Prevost to march, with all his available force, from Florida to Savannah. When the news arrived in Savannah of the approach of the British from the North under Campbell and Parker, and of the British Tories and Indians from Florida under Prevost, Howe was encamped at Sunbury. He had only about seven hundred men with which to meet the formidable army of the invaders. Immediately, he went to Savannah and made all the preparations the limited time would permit. On the 23rd of December the fleet arrived at Tybee Island. On the 29th, the troops were landed three miles below the city. Howe had less than nine hundred men, whilst the British numbered more than two thousand.

By some means, Howe was mistaken with regard to the actual strength of the enemy. By some mistake he supposed that his own force, which numbered less than a thousand men, was equal to that of the enemy, or so nearly so that he could defend the town. The town was almost without fortifications; hence one party possessed as much advantage as the other. When Howe learned more accurately the number of the enemy, he called a council of war. The British were at this moment forming for the attack. It was resolved by the council that they would first fight and then retreat if necessary.

In the disposition of his forces, Howe made some blunders; or rather he omitted to station troops at important points. From the point at which the British landed, there was a causeway with a ditch on each side. This causeway led through a swamp near half a mile, and terminated on firm ground. Opposite to the point at which the British landed is an eminence called Brewton's Hill. The gallant Colonel Elbert suggested to Howe the propriety of stationing a strong force on this eminence, and offered to defend it with his regiment. Howe thought the position one of little

importance believing that the British would advance directly against the town. At the end of the causeway, Howe drew up his centre. Colonel Huger was placed on his right and Colonel Elbert on his left. In front of Huger was a swamp and on his flank was a swamp covered with trees. At this point, Colonel Walton was stationed with one hundred Georgians. Colonel Elbert's force extended down the river. Captain Smith was sent, with a few men, to defend Brewton's Hill. Howe commanded the centre himself. About three o'clock the British took possession of Brewton's Hill and then formed, and advanced to within seven or eight hundred yards of the Whig lines. Here they halted and seemed to be making preparations for attacking the centre and left wing of the Americans. This, however, was only a feint. Through the swamp, on Howe's right, there was an obscure path. The British learned this fact from an old Negro by the name of Quamino Dolly. Sir James Baird, with a considerable force, was ordered to pass through the swamp, and thus gain the Americans' rear. Quamino Dolly acted as a guide, and the rear was gained. Sir James Baird attacked Walton, both on the rear and on the flank, and Colonel Campbell attacked Howe's forces in front. In a moment the American forces were thrown into confusion, and Howe ordered a retreat. The troops had to pass over Musgrove's swamp on a causeway. To keep this way opened, Colonel Roberts had hastened with the artillery. The enemy were there in force as soon as Roberts. The centre and right crossed, after suffering severely; but when the left under Colonel Elbert came up, they found the way blocked. An attempt was made to escape through a rice-field, but the creek was so deep that none escaped except those who could swim. Numbers of the soldiers were drowned, and some taken prisoners. The American loss was in killed, wounded, and prisoners, five hundred and thirty-eight; the British only twenty-six. This was a sad affair. The British had now, to all appearance, a firm foothold in the south. It was enough to dishearten the brave patriots; but it did not.

INSTALLMENT VI

INSTALLMENT VI

THE WAR IN GEORGIA

The fall of Savannah was followed by the surrender of Sunbury. In order to join Colonel Campbell, General Prevost left St. Augustine about the time that Campbell sailed from Sandy Hook. His army consisted of about two thousand men, together with a small artillery force. It was a mixed multitude of British regulars, savage Indians and Tories, who had fled from South Carolina and Georgia. On the sixth of

January, Prevost reached Sunbury. Major Lane was in command of the American forces at that point. His force was not one-tenth of that of the enemy. Still, when Prevost demanded an unconditional surrender, Lane, without hesitation, refused to comply. Prevost placed his forces in order and commenced to open upon the fort with his cannon. Lane saw at once that it was utterly impossible, with two hundred men, most of whom were militia, to withstand the force of the enemy. After he had lost in killed one captain and three privates, and seven wounded, Lane agreed to surrender. Everything fell into the hands of the enemy. Two American galleys lay in the river. These the crews took to Assabaw Island and there burned them, and tried to escape in a sloop to Charleston, but were captured and brought back to Savannah.

To all human appearances Georgia was ruined. The whole territory of the state was completely in the power of the British. Flushed with victory and, no doubt, confident of final success, the officers of the royal army proceeded without delay to establish civil government in Georgia. Cruelty was mingled with lenity. The prisoners held by the enemy were crowded in the ships where they died; some of disease, more of neglect and hunger.

Commodore Hyde Parker acted the part of a vile monster. Wives and daughters, whilst pleading for mercy in behalf of their husbands and fathers, were vilely insulted and the dead were thrown into the swamps to be devoured by dogs and buzzards. Colonel Campbell was more lenient, and his policy was more injurious to the cause of the Americans and more favorable to that of his royal master. Loyalists flocked by the hundreds to the British standard, and the ardor of some, who before had been regarded as staunch Whigs, began to cool. This was, in fact, "the time that tried men's souls." Many of those brave men who had fought under Moultrie at Sullivan's Island had left their homes in Florida; others were prisoners, and the remnant of that noble little band were hotly pursued by a foe exulting on account of their misfortunes.

Campbell was commanded by Prevost to march in the direction of Augusta, that he might be joined by the Tories of South Carolina. Military posts were established in the interior, and agents were sent into the Ninety-Six region to urge the loyalists to arm themselves and assist in crushing out the rebellion. This was joyful news to the loyalists. They had been quiet for a long time only from necessity and policy.

General Robert Howe was ruined. He was unable to do anything to impede the progress of the enemy, or to awe and keep the Tories in subjection. General Elbert, together with Colonels Twiggs and Few, attempted to thwart the plans of Colonel Campbell, but, in spite of all their efforts, Campbell reached Augusta on the twenty-ninth of January. Here he found the noted loyalists, Bowen and Lieutenant Colonel McGrith of the British army. Brown was placed in charge of the garrison stationed at Augusta. The Tories, both from North and South Carolina, had been collecting in great numbers under Colonel Boyd. A body of eight hundred Tories, under Boyd, collected in the western part of South Carolina, marched along the frontier of the state, plundering and destroying everything within their reach and barbarously murdering every one who dared to object to their depredations.

Georgia, and in fact the western section of the up-country of South Carolina, was beneath the heel of the invading foe. Many of the Whigs of Georgia crossed over the Savannah and found temporary relief in South Carolina. The British and Tories burned their houses and destroyed their property. Many, unable to get away, took the oaths of allegiance to the king.

We are not to conclude that the cause of liberty was abandoned by all the people of Georgia and the adjacent region of South Carolina. There were several partisan leaders who watched the movements of the enemy, and were only waiting for a favorable opportunity to pounce down upon him. Colonels Elbert, Dooly, Clark and Pickens, were in the field. They were determined to dispute every step of the enemy's progress and make his recent victories as worthless as possible.

Major Hamilton, a vigilant soldier under Colonel McGrith, had made his headquarters at Carr's Fort. This position he had chosen as convenient, both for himself and the surrounding country, for the purpose of administering the oath of allegiance. Pickens and Dooly united their forces and determined to besiege Hamilton. They succeeded in cutting off the supply of water from the garrison, and everything was favorable for a speedy surrender, but about ten o'clock on the night of the 10th of February, 1779, Pickens received a dispatch from his brother, stating that the Tory, Colonel Boyd, was on his way toward the Savannah River.

Pickens thought it important to meet Boyd as soon as possible. Fort Carr was full of women and children, who had fled thither for safety. Pickens, not wishing to jeopardize the lives of these, raised the siege and proceeded to meet Boyd. They crossed the Savannah near where Broad River empties into it, opposite the present county of Abbeville. Boyd, hearing of the approach of Pickens and Dooly, hastened up his march and, crossing the river on rafts, continued his march in the direction of Augusta. He was pursued by Captain Anderson, who overtook him in a canebrake. Boyd lost about one hundred men, whilst the Americans, under Captain Anderson, lost only thirty.

This was very encouraging to the Whigs, and frightened Boyd and his Tory band. He now quickened his gait and on the morning of the thirteenth of February crossed Broad River in what is now Oglethorpe county, Georgia. Pickens, Clark and Dooly were in his wake, but he seemed to have been ignorant of the fact. The American force numbered only three hundred. On the 14th of February, Boyd, glad that he was out of reach, as he thought, of the troublesome Whigs, halted on Kettle Creek. The horses were turned out to graze, and a number of the fine beeves, which he and his men had stolen, were driven up and slaughtered. The men were busily engaged in preparing a bountiful meal. In this condition the Whigs fell upon them. Pickens commanded the centre, Dooly the right wing, and Clark the left wing. On the approach of the Whigs, Boyd's pickets fired and fled to the camp. In a moment all was in a great state of confusion. Boyd and his men began to retreat, or rather to run in disorder. The battle lasted about two hours. Boyd was mortally wounded, and seventy-five of his followers lay dead on the ground, and about the same number were taken prisoners. The rest fled in every direction. The Americans lost, in killed and wounded, thirty-two. The Tory prisoners were taken to South Carolina, and there tried for high treason and condemned; but only five, who were regarded as the most desperate of the gang, were executed. This was the beginning of a series of evils which ended in the total ruin of the Tories and their cause. It made them timid. They saw that there were men who would dare to fight and capture them, and then condemn and hang them for high treason, notwithstanding the presence of the British troops in the state.

Things began now to assume a different aspect. The Tories were dispirited and the Whigs were encouraged. From the beginning of the Revolutionary war there was no concert among the Tories in action, and no ability to endure reverses. The contrary was true respecting the Whigs.

It was the intention of the British, when Colonel Campbell was first sent to Savannah, to proceed northward in the conquest of the country. It was known that so soon as it was thought practicable, the state of South Carolina would be invaded. General Lincoln had been placed in command of the Southern army. His headquarters were at Purysburg.

Troops had been collecting in the region of South Carolina, near Augusta. Generals Ashe and Rutherford were in South Carolina at this time. The former was with Lincoln at Purysburg with fifteen hundred men, and the latter was stationed at Black Swamp, a few miles above Ebenezer Creek. Rutherford was in command of seven hundred men. General Williamson was encamped with about twelve hundred men on the South Carolina side of the Savannah, nearly opposite Augusta. Lincoln was anxious to strike the enemy whilst his troops were fired with zeal, on account of his discomfiture of the Tories under Boyd. To effect this design, he ordered General Ashe, with his North Carolina militia and what troops remained of the Georgia Continentals, to march from Purysburg and reinforce General Williamson. It so happened that General Ashe arrived at General Williamson's camp on the evening of the 13th of February. The battle of Kettle Creek took place the next day. The arrival of Ashe and the news of the defeat of Boyd induced Colonel Campbell to break up his camp at Augusta. He was evidently alarmed. The evidence of this was the fact that he left a large amount of his provisions, ammunition and some of his arms. About fifty miles below Augusta he halted and it seemed as if it was his intention to make a stand. This, however, he did not do, but continued his march to Savannah.

On the 16th of February, General Lincoln sent an order to General Ashe to pursue Colonel Campbell as far as Brier Creek. On the 25th, General Ashe crossed the river, and two days after reached Brier Creek. He found that Colonel Campbell had destroyed the bridge over this stream. General Rutherford was encamped about five miles above, on the opposite side of the Savannah. Colonel Marbury, with a few Georgia cavalry, was posted a few miles up Brier Creek. Ashe's forces amounted to less than two thousand men. Having given direction for the forming of his camp, Ashe crossed the Savannah River, for the purpose of consulting General Lincoln. On the 5th of March he returned and was disappointed to find the bridge over Brier Creek not repaired. Hands were set to work with all possible speed, but it was too late.

A dispatch from General Williamson announced the fact that General Prevost had crossed Brier Creek and had already gained the rear of General Ashe. Prevost had made a circuitous route and, unobserved, gained his object. In a deplorably unprepared condition, the American forces were attacked and routed. The North Carolina troops fled at the first fire. The whole army soon became panic struck and fled in every direction. Some rushed to the Savannah River, over which some swam, others crossed on rafts, and many were drowned. The gallant General Elbert and many of his men were taken prisoners. The British lost only sixteen men. Nearly all the artillery, provision, ammunition and baggage of the Americans, together with five hundred stand of arms, fell into the hands of the British, or were lost.

The real loss to the cause of the Americans cannot be estimated. Both Carolinas were now opened up to the inroads of Indians from the west, and Indians and Tories from Florida. In this unfortunate affair there were a number of men from York county. Only a few of them escaped.

At the time General Ashe was severely censured, and even court-martialed, on account of his conduct at Brier Creek. He was acquitted of the charge of cowardice and inability, but censured for a want of vigilance.

Things were now in a worse condition than when Savannah fell.

INSTALLMENT VII

BIOGRAPHY OF GENERAL ROBERT HOWE

Our plan allows us the amplest latitude. Whatever will throw light upon the history of South Carolina, we claim as legitimately within the scope of our undertaking. With this understanding, it is our intention, from time to time, to give a brief biographical sketch of those heroes who struggled for American independence.

Of the private life of him whose name heads this sketch, comparatively nothing can be said. General Robert Howe was born in Brunswick, North Carolina. It would be interesting to give a sketch of his early history; but this we cannot do. Like many other great men, he sprang into public life, not by degrees, but at a leap. Sometimes men control the circumstances by which they are surrounded, and become great in spite of their surroundings. During the Revolutionary period of American history, the circumstances made the men. Merchants, mechanics, farmers, lawyers, physicians and literary amateurs, were called from their various avocations and placed in command of armies. It was an age of heroes. For a long time, the political storm had been gathering. Boys drank in the spirit of resistance with their mother's milk. Robert Howe was a patriot by all the instincts of his nature, and by the force of education.

In 1773, we find him in the house of commons of his native state. The Virginia legislature had passed certain resolutions with reference to the encroachments of England upon the liberties of the American colonies. The legislature of North Carolina approved these resolutions, and appointed a committee of correspondence. Robert Howe was a member of this committee.

In 1775, the Provincial congress of North Carolina ordered two regiments of five hundred men to be raised. James Moore was appointed colonel of the first regiment, and Robert Howe, colonel of the second.

At this time, John Murray, more commonly known as Lord Dunmore, the last royal governor of Virginia, was laying waste the lower section of the state of which he was governor. He had proclaimed martial law, and issued a proclamation in which he declared the state free. In his army he had a mixed multitude of British regulars, vile and abandoned Tories, and Negroes who had been stolen or enticed from their masters, under the pretense of freeing them, but really that they might be put into forts and made to do the dirty work of Dunmore and his abettors.

Dunmore scoured the country in search of Mrs. General Washington. He stole Holt's printing press, and carried away captive two of his printers. Finally, he made his headquarters at Norfolk, and placed a garrison of Negroes, Tories, and British regulars at what was called "The Great Bridge" on Elizabeth River. Colonel Woodford was sent against this motley band. With a body of Minute Men, he met them and, by the aid of brave and skillful subaltern officers, and brave and obedient men, the plunderers were routed. The battle of "The Great Bridge" was fought before daylight on the 9th of December, 1775. Five days afterward, Robert Howe, with his North Carolina regiment, joined Colonel Woodford and took command of all the troops.

Dunmore, after the affair at "The Great Bridge," abandoned his fortifications at Norfolk and, with his white troops, took refuge on his ships. The poor, deluded Negroes were turned off and left in a most deplorable condition. Some wandered back to their old homes, and many starved.

The supply of provisions on board Dunmore's ships was very limited. In fact, he was forced to send parties on shore to provide supplies for each day. Colonel Howe watched his movements closely. These foraging parties were cut off, and besides, a constant fire was poured into the ships from the upper stories of the houses. Dunmore and his band of outlaws were soon threatened with famine. Just when Dunmore was in the greatest distress, a British frigate entered the harbor. This timely circumstance revived the drooping spirits of Dunmore. The captain of the frigate was sent by Dunmore to Colonel Howe, with an imperious command that he instantly cease firing upon the ship, and furnish those on board with a supply of provisions. The haughty governor threatened, in the event his demands were not granted, that he would bombard the town. Howe boldly returned for a reply that he would neither cease firing on the ships, nor furnish the men on board the vessel with supplies. Dunmore prepared to put his threat into execution. On the last day of 1775 an order was sent to remove the women and children and, before daylight of the New Year, two vessels - the Dunmore and Liverpool - commenced to bombard Norfolk. A party, at the same time, were sent on shore to set the town on fire.

The population of Norfolk, at that time, was about 6,000. During the two years previous to the bombardment by Dunmore, it had grown up very rapidly. Most of the houses were wooden buildings, and many of them were filled with pitch and turpentine. The wind was favorable for the incendiaries. Soon the flames spread in all directions, and the bombardment was kept up by the ships. The city was reduced to ashes, and the inhabitants turned adrift in mid-winter. Dunmore accomplished nothing more than the destruction of the town. This was very great, amounting to near two millions dollars. The suffering of the inhabitants from the loss of their dwellings, in the dead of winter, cannot be estimated; but the loss of life by the bombardment was only a few citizens who were killed in the streets. No soldiers were killed. Dunmore was repulsed and his troops prevented from landing.

In 1776, Robert Howe was made a brigadier general and sent south. After General Charles Lee was ordered north, Robert Howe succeeded him as commander of the southern army. We have already traced the vicissitudes of fortune through which he passed up to the time of the fall of Savannah. After the affair at Savannah, he left the south and became connected with the army of the north. He was with General Wayne at Stony Point on the 16th of July, 1776. General Washington planned the battle of Stony Point, but it was executed by General Anthony Wayne.

Stony Point and Verplanck's Point on the Hudson River had been taken only a short time before, by Sir Henry Clinton, in person. These two forts secured communications between the different sections of the colonies. Their loss was a source of grief to General Washington. At once he began making preparations to recapture them, and General Wayne was consulted with reference to the undertaking. Wayne's reply was, "General, I'll storm hell if you'll only plan it." Washington knew that Wayne meant what he said.

In the neighborhood of Stony Point there resided a Whig by the name of Lamb. Captain Lamb owned a Negro who, in honor of one of Rome's great men, was named Pompey. Soon after the British got possession of Stony Point, Pompey visited the garrison, carrying strawberries, blackberries, and other early fruit to sell to the soldiers stationed at that point. His visits were daily and very acceptable to the garrison. He completely won the confidence of both men and officers. Pompey, like his master, was a good Whig. He gave a faithful report of all that he saw and heard in the fort, to his master, by whom it was communicated to the commander of the American forces. A few days before the attack was made by Wayne, Pompey reported to Colonel Johnston, the commander of Stony Point, that his master would not let him any longer bring fruit to the garrison in daylight, since he was busy with his crop. The garrison could not think of doing without blackberries. Arrangements were made by which the countersign was to be given to Pompey every night.

On the 15th of July, Wayne had all the dogs in the community killed so that, by their barking, his advance might not be made known. Abut one o'clock on the morning of the 16th, the army, under Wayne and Howe, commenced to advance with the utmost silence. Pompey, with a budget of berries, accompanied by two strong men, were sent ahead. They came to the first sentinel, who received the countersign from Pompey. On that night it was, "The fort is ours!" Without suspecting anything, the two men seized the sentinel and gagged him. The same thing was done to the other sentinels.

In this way the Americans were not discovered until they were within pistol shot of the pickets. The pickets fired, but the intrepid Americans rushed forward, with empty guns and fixed bayonets. The drums in the fort began to beat and the shout "To arms, to arms!" was raised by the officers. The Americans rushed forward, shouting at the top of their voices, "The fort is ours! The fort is ours!" In a few minutes such was the case, for at two o'clock Wayne sent the same words, as a report of the battle, to General Washington.

An attempt was made at once to take the British works on Verplanck's Point. General Robert Howe was sent to make an attack upon Fort La Fayette, but in some way or other, misunderstood the orders of General Washington and failed to accomplish the undertaking.

During the Revolutionary war, two rebellions or mutinies occurred in the American camp. The first in January, 1781, and the other in June, 1783. General

Robert Howe was sent by General Washington to quell both of these rebellions, which he did with dispatch and to the satisfaction of the commander-in-chief and the country generally.

It only remains to notice what may, with some propriety, be called the interposition of divine providence respecting Howe and some others. We met Robert Howe and Anthony Wayne at the storming of Stony Point. On a former occasion we met Robert Howe and Christopher Gadsden on the field of honor, as they termed it. In plain English, we met them fighting a duel. The history of two other individuals is intimately interwoven with that of Robert Howe and Anthony Wayne. These two individuals are Benedict Arnold, the traitor, and Major John Andre, the spy. Arnold had no love for Howe, and Andre was accustomed to regard with sneering contempt, both Howe and Wayne. The history of Arnold and Andre is inseparably connected. The mention of the name of one suggests that of the other. The name of Arnold is covered with disgrace, and Andre, with all his virtues, was not incapable of a little and mean thing.

Late in the summer of 1780, General Washington sent Wayne to make an attack upon a British post, a short distance below Fort Lee on the Hudson. The main object was to drive off a large number of cattle on Bergen's Neck, within reach of the British at Paulus Hook. Wayne made the attack upon the British post at Bull's Ferry, and sent Major Lee to drive off the cattle. Lee succeeded in driving away the cattle, but Wayne failed to take the post at Bull's Ferry and lost more than sixty men. This tickled Andre very much and, as he was a poet, or at least he thought he was, he made it the subject of a long epic called the "Cow Chase." It is divided into three cantos, and consists, in all, of seventy stanzas. The commanders are called by all sorts of ridiculous names, and all sorts of witty things, and sometimes obscene things are said concerning them. This epic, as he himself calls it, was published in "Rivington's Royal Gazette," on Saturday, the 23rd of September, 1780. It was on this day that John Paulding, Isaac Van Wart, and David Williams arrested Andre. The last stanza of the poem reads as follows:

"And now I've closed my epic strain,
  I tremble as I show it,
Lest this same warrior-drover, Wayne,
  Should ever catch the poet."

It will be remembered that Andre was tried at Tappan, on the 29th of September, 1780. Robert Howe was a member of the court and General Wayne,

the "warrior-drover" mentioned in the last stanza of the poem, had command of the troops at Tappan. Wayne did catch the poet.

After the duel of Howe and Gadsden, Major Andre made sport of it. Howe, Gadsden, Charles Cotesworth Pinckney and Bernard Elliott are, in the poem, held up to ridicule. Howe was president of the court-martial that tried Arnold and censured him; he was a member of the court that sentenced Andre to be hanged. Wayne was there as commander of the post. The presence of these two men must have called up strange reflections in the mind of the unfortunate Andre. The patriots, under Wayne and Lee, are stigmatized by Andre in his "cow-chase" as "dung-born tribes." On the original manuscript was written by Andre himself, the following stanza:

"When the epic strain was sung,
  The poet by the neck was hung,
  And to his cost he finds too late,
  The 'dung-born tribe' decides his fate."

In a military point of view, General Robert Howe was deficient in the ability to plan any great undertaking. His failure at Savannah resulted from want of forethought. Colonel Campbell discovered, in a few hours, a secret passage through the swamp by which General Howe's rear might be gained. Howe, although he had been in the neighborhood for days, failed to discover this passage. As an officer, General Howe's talents were only moderate; but his patriotism was such as to establish him in the favor of his countrymen. From the beginning his attachment to the cause of the colonies was unflinching. He was brave and patriotic, but incapable of planning and executing a great military expedition.

Installment VIII

THE ATTACK ON CHARLESTON

The discomfiture of General Ashe at Brier Creek exposed South Carolina to the British both by land and by sea. As already stated, it was the intention of the foe to lead his armies from the south to the north, and thus crush the rebellion. The reputation and influence of General Howe was demolished by his defeat at Savannah, and General Ashe quit the service after his surprise at Brier Creek. By the want of generalship in these two commanders, the country was placed in a perilous condition. By the surprise of Ashe, the army was reduced more than fifteen hundred men. Only a few of these, comparatively, were killed; but those not killed or wounded fled their homes. The militia of the country was terribly demoralized. General Prevost showed very great skill in his management of the whole affair and, had he followed up his victory, he might have literally ruined the country. General Benjamin Lincoln of Hingham, Massachusetts, was in command of the southern army. He was a man of great moral worth and considerable military reputation, but with little military talent. He had been appointed commander of the south in September, 1778, and arrived in South Carolina on December. His headquarters were at first at Purysburg. The cherished object of his heart was to rescue Georgia from the hands of the enemy. For this purpose he sent Ashe over the Savannah River and down its western bank as far as Brier Creek. Notwithstanding the reverses which his army had met, General Lincoln still contemplated driving the British from Georgia.

In view of the peculiar circumstances of the state of South Carolina, John Rutledge was again chosen governor. To him and his council were granted extraordinary powers. It became evident that a vigorous effort must be put forth, or the state would soon be in the hands of the enemy. The general assembly enacted more stringent laws concerning the discipline of the militia.

A knowledge of the position of the troops of both armies is necessary, in order that we may understand the critical condition of things in the state. About the time that Savannah fell into the hands of the British, Major Gardiner was sent to Port Royal Island. This point was about sixty miles from Charleston. This movement indicated very clearly what the intentions of General Prevost were. He designed, so soon as opportunity offered itself, making an attack upon Charleston. Gardiner had about two hundred men in his command and three field pieces. To dislodge Major Gardiner, Colonel Moultrie, the hero of Sullivan's Island, was sent with about two hundred Charleston militia and two field pieces. Gardiner was boldly attacked, on the morning of the 3rd of February and driven across the Savannah into Georgia. The scarcity of ammunition prevented Moultrie from annihilating Gardiner and his whole command. As it was, Gardiner lost most of his officers. Having driven Major Gardiner out of the state, Colonel Moultrie joined General Lincoln at Purysburg. On the twenty-third of April, General Lincoln, with four thousand men, moved toward Augusta. Colonel Moultrie, with one thousand men, was left for the defense of Purysburg. Governor Rutledge, by the advice of his council, had established a military post at Orangeburg. Here he was enrolling

and disciplining the militia of the middle and upper sections of the state.

At the time that General Lincoln moved toward Augusta, the legislature of Georgia was in session at that place. It was important, General Lincoln thought, that the body be so protected as to be able to deliberate with reference to the state of the country. General Prevost felt that it would be to the interest of his majesty's cause in America to thwart Lincoln and the Georgia legislature in their plans. This Prevost could have easily done, had he boldly attacked Lincoln. Prevost was more than a match for Lincoln, and the troops of the former were regulars, whilst those of the latter were militia, who, in all probability, would have thrown down their arms and fled so soon as the enemy came fairly in sight.

Heretofore General Prevost had displayed very considerable military talent, but from this time he began to fail. Instead of boldly attacking General Lincoln, he crossed the Savannah River opposite Purysburg. Whether this movement was designed by Prevost as a feint, in order to draw Lincoln away from his undertaking, or whether it was designed to attempt an attack upon Charleston, in its exposed condition, it is, at this period, hard to tell. One thing is very manifest. General Lincoln and General Prevost were unable to decipher each other's plans.

General Lincoln, with the main body of the American Army, marched down the Savannah River, on the Georgia side, in the direction of Savannah. General Lincoln's object was to drive the British from Georgia. Whatever may have been General Prevost's object, he drove Moultrie from Purysburg. Colonel Moultrie was obliged to retreat or be cut to pieces.

He had only one thousand men, and this number constantly decreasing, whilst General Prevost had two thousand regulars, besides a large number of loyalists and Indians. All that Colonel Moultrie could do was to keep out of Prevost's way. At Tulifinny bridge, he made a stand and a skirmish ensued. Little was accomplished. At Coosawhatchie bridge, Lieutenant Colonel Laurens, with eighteen Continental soldiers and some militia, came in contact with some of Prevost's forces. The enemy had the advantage in position, and Laurens was obliged to fall back on Moultrie.

It now became evident to Colonel Moultrie and Governor Rutledge that General Prevost's point of destination was the capital of South Carolina. To this point both Moultrie and Rutledge hastened with all possible speed. Dispatches were daily sent to Gen. Lincoln informing him of the progress of Prevost, and urging him to come at once to the rescue. For some unaccountable reason, General Lincoln continued his march toward Savannah, but sent three hundred light infantry, under Colonel Harris, to Moultrie's assistance.

Such was the condition of Charleston that Prevost could have taken it on the first assault, had he marched directly on to the city. On the land side it was not fortified, and the only impediment to be overcome was Moultrie and his few men. When Moultrie was on his way to Charleston, near half his men left and returned home. This dispirited those who remained. Unfortunately for Prevost, and fortunately for the capital of South Carolina, he made a halt of forty-eight hours at Pocotaligo. The reason assigned for this delay was some conflicting reports which he is said to have heard. What these reports were, we do not know.

The people of Charleston were aware of the threatened attack, and in the absence of the governor, Lieutenant Governor Bee and the council exerted all their powers to put the city in a state of defense. The forces under Moultrie, Rutledge and Harris arrived in the city on the ninth and tenth days of May. Prevost encamped on the south bank of the Ashley River, on the night of the ninth of May. The ferries on the Ashley had been fortified to retard or prevent his further progress.

The forces in the city numbered about three thousand, one hundred and eighty. Prevost's force was three thousand, three hundred and sixty. Prevost had a large amount of troops and they were better provided for and in every way superior to those under the American commanders, if we except the fact that they Americans were fighting for liberty, whilst the troops under Prevost were fighting for conquest. Instead of appointing one commander, both Moultrie and Rutledge claimed the right to command his own troops. Colonel Moultrie took command of the Continental forces in the city; whilst Governor Rutledge claimed the right to command, in person, the militia. It seems harsh to censure those brave men who bore so much that they might be free and bequeath freedom to their children; but we must remember that they were but men, and not only liable to err, but actually did err sometimes. So soon as the forces arrived in the city, every one that could handle a pick or use a spade was put to work. Everybody went to work. Men and women, boys and girls, worked night and day.

On the morning of the eleventh of May, General Prevost, with nine hundred British regulars, crossed Ashley River and marched within cannon shot of the American works. During the afternoon of the same day, Count Pulaski, the brave Pole, who had espoused the cause of the Americans, came from Mount Pleasant with a body of infantry and cavalry. Scarcely had Pulaski's troops crossed the Cooper River and entered the city, when it was announced that the vanguard of the British army was crossing the Ashley ferry. With weary horses, Pulaski dashed out to oppose the approach of the British. The onset was furious, and the brave count came near losing his life. After having lost most of his infantry and Colonel Kowatch, the second officer in command, Pulaski retreated back to the American lines, under cover of the cannon of the fortifications. Prevost left his heavy baggage, and the main body of his army, on the south side of the Ashley River.

Immediately on crossing the river, Prevost summoned the city to surrender. The civil authorities replied favorably. They signified their willingness to surrender the city on condition that it and the state should remain neutral during the war, and that the termination of the contest between Great Britain and the colonies should determine the final condition of South Carolina. This condition of surrender was rejected by Provost, and the next day he advanced within a mile of the American works. Here a brisk fire of the cannon was opened upon him. Again he demanded the surrender of the city. The same terms of surrender as those offered before were again made and rejected, Prevost insisting that the garrison should surrender as prisoners of war. Twelve hours were spent in passing flags between the two armies. Still the work on the American fortifications went on. It was certainly expected by Moultrie that so soon as the correspondence should close, that the works would be stormed.

The evil of two commanders was in a most afflicting manner demonstrated to the Americans. Governor Rutledge discovered a breach in some part of the fortifications of the city and, without informing Colonel Moultrie, sent out Major Benjamin Huger and a party of men, in the night, to repair it. They were discovered by Moultrie's men and mistaken for a party of the enemy and fired upon. Major Huger and twelve of his men were killed. This was on the night after negotiations respecting the surrender had ceased. Fearing an attack at any moment by the enemy, the Americans kept up the fire, commenced by mistaking Huger's party for the British, until morning. Every one felt certain that when morning came the British would storm the American works, but when morning came the British were gone. In the night they had re-crossed the Ashley River and were preparing to go back to Savannah.

The cause of Prevost's precipitate retreat was the fact that he had intercepted a letter from General

Lincoln to Colonel Moultrie, dated the 10th of May. At that time Lincoln was only fifty miles distant, and he begged Moultrie to hold out until he would arrive with the main body of the American army. Prevost intercepted this letter some time during the night of the 12th. Wisely, he concluded that it would be perilous for him to suffer himself to be fired upon both from the front and rear at the same time. No doubt Prevost was glad to make his escape, and the garrison and people of Charleston were glad that he was gone. Pulaski, with his cavalry, pursued him; but he and his troops were over the Ashley River before Pulaski reached it.

With regard to this whole affair, there is something very unmilitary. It seems strange that the privy council of the state would have made so disgraceful a proposition as to surrender the city and state without making an effort first to defend it. It is said that it was ruse, designed to gain time for the arrival of General Lincoln. Supposing this was the case, what would the privy council, of which Governor Rutledge was chief, have done had Prevost accepted of the proposition? Truth and honesty would have forced them to surrender. Three members of the council were violently opposed to it. Their names were Gadsden, Ferguson and Edwards. Colonel Moultrie and John Laurens were also opposed to it. A threat was made that in the event the proposition was carried into effect, it would cost the council their lives.

The strangest thing of all is the rejection of the proposition by General Prevost. Had he accepted the offer made by the privy council, he would have ruined the state. Prevost acted with no promptness. His delay at Pccotaligo and his delay in exchanging flags, after he had crossed the Ashley River, and finally his rejecting the terms of surrender proposed by the authorities of Charleston, show that he was only a second-rate general.

<h2 style="text-align:center">Installment IX</h2>

SURPRISE OF CAPTAIN MATTHEWS

In our last we left Prevost, on the morning of the 14th of May, 1779, retreating from Charleston, on his way back to Savannah. General Lincoln, with the main forces of the Americans, had arrived at Dorchester, about the time that Prevost had precipitately raised the siege of the city. In order that Prevost might avoid an attack by Lincoln in front, and by the forces of Moultrie in the rear, he filed to the left on crossing the Ashley River, and passed over to James Island. Here he remained, undisturbed, for a few days and then crossed over the Stono River, or inlet, to John's Island, and waited for supplies which he was expecting to be sent him from New York.

General Lincoln, having given his troops a few days' rest at Dorchester, and having collected all his forces, moved down towards the position of the British on John's Island. The two armies were now about thirty miles from the capital of the state, watching each other's movements. So soon as the British left their lines before the city, Peter Timothy ascended the steeple of St. Michael's church and watched all their motions. Prevost's intention was to return to Savannah, not by mainland, but by passing successively from one island to another, and thus evade an attack. General Lincoln's object was to throw every obstacle in his power in the way of Prevost, and if possible prevent him from reaching Savannah.

The coast of South Carolina, especially in this region which stretches between Charleston and Savannah, Ga., is dotted with an almost countless number of islands. These are surrounded by inlets which are affected by the flow and ebb of the tide. Such were the circumstances by which General Lincoln was surrounded, that it was difficult for him to do anything that would impede the movement of the enemy. Prevost was not well provided with boats to convey his men and military appendages over the inlets which surrounded the islands. Lincoln's condition was even worse than that of Prevost. He had no boats and no means of procuring any. The first encounter which occurred between the British and Americans, after Prevost left Charleston, occurred on the night of the 19th of May. When Prevost crossed over on the main land on James Island, the Americans had a small detachment of less than one hundred men on John's Island. The two islands are separated by Stono River, and the camps of the belligerents were nearly opposite each other, and so near as to be seen.

The American forces consisted of two companies of militia; one from Beaufort, commanded by Captain Robert Barnwell, and the other commanded by Captain John Raven Matthews of John's Island. Captain Matthews held the oldest commission and took command of the whole force. It is evident that Captain Matthews, with his small force of about seventy-five men, could not withstand Prevost who had fully two thousand men under his command. Captain Matthews unfortunately was both imprudent and self-willed. Contrary to the judgment and entreaties of those who understood the critical condition in which the small force on John's Island was placed, he persisted in drawing out his men in open day and mustering them in full view of the British. Their numbers were counted and a surprise planned. The personal friends of Captain Matthews entreated him not to expose his troops, and also begged him to double the number of his sentinels, that he might be prepared for a night attack. In his self-will, Captain Matthews pursued his own course. Thomas Legare was so much discouraged by the headstrong manner in which things were conducted, that he asked and obtained leave to join the guard stationed at Champlin's Point. Strange as it may seem, Captain Matthews had only two sentinels on duty, although he was in sight of the enemy. Possibly he thought the British contemplated making another attempt to capture the capital of the state, and cared nothing about him and his small force; or it may be that he thought they could not cross the inlet which separates the two islands. Whatever may have been his conjectures as to the future movements of the British, he was in a critical condition and either did not know it or, knowing it, did not care.

The condition of things by which Captain Matthews was surrounded was very peculiar, and at least afford some palliation for the surprise with which he met. The British, in strong force, were on James Island, and an intriguing loyalist was on John's Island. Thomas Fenwick, noted as a loyalist and friend of the British, and afterwards as the spy of General Green, came into the camp of Captain Matthews on the evening of the 19th of May. He enjoyed the hospitality of the officers and engaged with them in conversation. Having learned all that he desired respecting the position of the forces under the command of Captain Matthews, he communicated the same to the British commander on James Island. At midnight a detachment of the British, in two divisions, crossed from James Island to John's. One division marched to Fenwick's house, the other to Matthew's landing. They were now in position to surround the camp of the Americans. Every preparation being made, Fenwick gave the signal, and both divisions of the British commenced to march simultaneously on the American camp. Fenwick, although he had but a few hours before supped in the American camp with the officers, acted as guide in leading the British against his personal friends and neighbors. The first sentinel was taken by surprise, and the countersign extorted from him. Before the second and only remaining sentinel could give the alarm, he was bayoneted. The sentinels thus removed, the British were not long in surrounding the camp of Captain Matthews. Every man was made prisoner.

The camp of the Beaufort company under the command of Captain Robert Barnwell was then surrounded and a demand made for its immediate surrender. "What are the conditions of surrender?" asked Captain Barnwell. "No quarters to rebels," was the answer. Barnwell then turned to his men and said, "Defend yourselves to the last." In a moment every gun was cocked and leveled on the enemy. The British fell back a few paces. A sergeant of the royal army then announced to the Americans that if they would surrender they should have honorable quarters. "By what authority," inquired Captain Barnwell, "do you make this promise? What is your rank?" It was replied, "I am but a sergeant in his majesty's service, but my word is as good as that of any officer in the army." This assurance having been given of their safety, Captain Barnwell and his men surrendered. No sooner had they laid down their arms than they were set upon by the British with bayonets, and nearly all either killed or severely wounded. Captain Barnwell received seventeen bayonet wounds, and was left on the ground, supposed to be dead. He, however, afterwards recovered.

Connected with this affair of Captain Matthews with the British at John's Island, there are several little interests which are not wholly without interest. The name of the second sentinel with whom the British came in contact, in their approach to the camp of Captain Matthews, was Jas. Black. He was a brave man and did his duty to his country faithfully. He was a ship carpenter by trade and resided in Beaufort. One of the many wounds which he received was a bayonet stab in the fleshy part of the back, the point of the bayonet going towards the backbone. The wounds of the brave man were afterwards dressed and he was sent to Charleston. In order to keep the wound open, the surgeon, or whoever it was that dressed it, inserted a piece of gentian root, several inches long, in the cavity made by the bayonet. This was not discovered for some time, and the gentian root, becoming saturated with blood, increased in size and tore the wound asunder, causing great inflammation and pain. The gentian root was taken out, but the inflammation had reached the spinal-marrow and James Black died.

Robert Barnwell was, as we have already stated, stabbed with seventeen bayonet wounds and supposed to be dead. He was taken up and removed to the house of Robert Gibbs and kindly nursed by Mrs. Gibbs.

This suggests another noble deed that occurred in the Gibbs family. During the stay of the British on John's Island, the family of Robert Gibbs, one dark night, were forced to leave the house and seek a place of refuge. In their hurry to depart they forgot an infant, a distant relation of the family, in the house. No one would volunteer to go back for the child. The servants refused. Moved by a kind and pitying heart, Mary Ann Gibbs, a child of only thirteen, faced the darkness of the night and went back, more than a mile, after the child. After being several times refused by the occupants of the house, she succeeded, at last, in obtaining permission to enter the room in which the child had been left. There she found the little fellow sleeping soundly, unconscious of the booming of cannon and the clashing of arms. She took him up in her arms and hastened to join the other members of the family. This child, thus rescued by Mary Ann Gibbs, was the gallant Lieutenant Colonel Fenwick, of the War of 1812.

Installment X

THE FIGHT AT STONO

While the British were engaged in crossing from James Island to John's Island, General Lincoln thought it a favorable opportunity to attack their forces in detachment. On the 4th of June, he moved down in the neighborhood of Stono. It was his intention to at once attack the van of the British army; but after a close examination of the ground and the position of the enemy's troops, he thought it best to decline the assault at that time.

About two weeks after General Lincoln had taken his position near Stono, General Prevost detached Lieutenant Colonel Prevost and sent him, with a portion of the British army, to Savannah. A bridge, connecting John's Island with the main land, had been built out of boats. These had been taken away for the purpose of transporting the troops, under the command of Colonel Prevost, to Savannah. Lieutenant Colonel Maitland, a gallant officer, was placed in command of the British post at Stono, on the main land. His forces consisted of English, Hessians, and a regiment of North Carolina loyalists. In all, they amounted to five hundred, men. In some respects, the British under Colonel Maitland were favorably situated; in other respects they were not. Since the bridge of boats had been removed, communication with the main body of the army, which was yet on James Island, was difficult. As they had been there for some time, they were fortified and both their wings rested on swamps which, although not unpassable, could only be crossed with difficulty.

In this position, General Lincoln determined to attack Colonel Maitland. General Moultrie was ordered to set out from Charleston, with a body of six hundred troops under his command, and take possession of James Island. From thence he was to pass over to John's Island. The object of this movement, on the part of General Moultrie, was to divert the attention of General Prevost from General Lincoln, and prevent reinforcements from being sent to Colonel Maitland. The order of battle and plan of attack were well conceived and did General Lincoln great credit. In fact, he gave more evidence of military talent on this occasion than he ever did before or after. The Highlanders were regarded as the best troops in the British army. General Lincoln knew that these were placed on the enemy's right. Opposed to these, General Lincoln placed his Continental troops, commanded by General Jethro Summer. The Hessians were posted on Colonel Maitland's left. Opposite to these, General Lincoln place Brigadier General Butler, with the North Carolina militia. The loyal North Carolina regiment, commanded by Lieutenant Colonel Hamilton, composed the British centre. General Lincoln's flanks were covered by two bodies of light troops, Colonel Malmedy commanding the one, and Lieutenant Colonel Henderson the other. General Lincoln's reserve consisted of the cavalry and some Virginia militia, commanded by General Mason.

It was planned that the assault should be made on the morning of the 20th of June. On the 19th, General Lincoln put his army in motion, and on the 20th, in accordance with the previous arrangements with General Moultrie, he held his troops, disposed as we have stated, to the attack. Colonel Maitland's pickets were driven in, and of two companies of Highlanders that came to their assistance, only nine escaped being cut to pieces. This encouraged the American troops, and it was determined to rush forward upon the enemy with fixed bayonets. The American troops advanced steadily to within sixty yards of the enemy's works, when a heavy fire was opened by the entrenched foe. Here the American troops, contrary to orders, halted and began to return the fire. For half an hour the firing was sharp and the enemy's left was driven back. Colonel Maitland, in an instant, threw his Highlanders to his left, and supplied their vacancy with his reserve. The Hessians, which had been posted on the left, and who had given back, were again rallied and brought into line. General Lincoln was enraged that his troops had not carried out his orders to charge bayonet, but had commenced to fire as soon as they were fired upon. That his original plan might be carried out, he ordered the troops to cease firing. This order was obeyed. Again he ordered them to charge bayonet, but again the troops began to fire. Just at this juncture, General Prevost was crossing over the ferry on the Stono for the purpose of assisting Colonel Maitland. General Lincoln now ordered a retreat. This produced some confusion, and Colonel Maitland rushed out with all his available force to the pursuit, but the American cavalry dashed in upon him and enabled the forces under General Lincoln to get away in tolerable order.

In the arrangement of his troops, General Lincoln gave evidence of his military talent; but in the mode of attack his judgment was at fault. Along the whole British front there was an abattis. Besides this, they were entrenched, and their field pieces properly located. Instead of making the attack on the front, General Lincoln should have directed his fire upon the British flanks. It was also a grand mistake in placing the issue of the undertaking on bayonet. It was in an open field, and in every charge his men were exposed to a murderous fire. Situated as he was, General Lincoln might have known that success, by his mode of attack, would have been equivalent to ruin. Lincoln had more than twice as many men as Maitland and his troops fought well.

Despite the blunder in the mode of attack, General Lincoln would have succeeded had General Moultrie been on James Island in time to discharge the duty assigned him in the general plan. Many a brave man would have fallen in charging Colonel Maitland's works; but they would have been charged and taken, had General Prevost been prevented from sending reinforcements from John's Island. General Moultrie arrived, but after the battle was over.

Charity recommends that we be sparing in our censures of such men as General Moultrie. Callous, indeed, must be the heart that does not swell with generous emotions on the mere mention of his name. With all his greatness, General Moultrie had one fault. He was not a punctual man. This prevented his arriving on James' Island at the time. He was ordered by General Lincoln to take a galley, and as many small boats as would be sufficient to transport six hundred militia from Charleston to James' Island, and to set out at a particular hour. The hour was particularly specified, in order that he might pass through Wappoo Cut, at high water, the only time he could pass. At the hour appointed for his departure, there were a number of friends at his house. With them he remained, dispensing the hospitality of this table, until it was too late. When his transport entered Wappoo Cut, the tide was down and he ran aground.

The American loss in the battle of Stono was about one hundred and fifty in killed and wounded.

The British loss never was accurately ascertained. We may safely say it was equal to that of the Americans. Neither party gained a victory. Still, the advantage was in favor, rather, of the Americans than of the British. The former were not discouraged, and the latter were rendered uneasy.

STORMING OF SAVANNAH

After the battle of Stono, the British army returned to Savannah, and General Lincoln took up his headquarters at Sheldon. Such was the condition of things by which General Lincoln was surrounded, that he could not even thwart the progress of the enemy. Aware of his exposed condition, Prevost led his troops from island to island and thus conveyed them to the point of destination. The American general had no boats and no means of procuring any. General Lincoln was beset with another sore evil, one which pressed all the American generals during the Revolutionary war.

As soon as the battle of Stono was over and the British set out for their headquarters, the American militia set out for their homes. General Lincoln was thus left with only his Continentals, or regular soldiers. With these, destitute as he was of the accoutrements of war, he was able to do nothing more than prevent the enemy from undertaking any great thing.

The planters of the southern section of the state, in the track of Prevost, suffered greatly. In his march against Charleston, Prevost passed through the richest section of the state at that time. The houses of the planters were first plundered, and many of them burned. The slaves, made wild by the sudden transition from slavery to unbridled license, invaded the homes of their former masters like so many hungry wolves. Men and women were stripped of their clothing and jewelry, and every manner of insult heaped upon their persons. Whigs and loyalists fared alike. These deluded Negroes acted as guides to the British in gathering up the plate and jewels which the planters had hidden away in unfrequented places. Plate and various articles of jewelry were collected by bands of prowling Negroes, led by British instigators, and brought back to the camp of Prevost and packed away in rice barrels and sent off to be sold. At this time, although it was only a little more than one hundred years from the time the first settlement had been made in the state, many of the planters were immensely rich and lived in lordly style. Their furniture was of the most costly kind. This, together with their china and glassware, was taken and sent to some point where it could be sold. Nothing escaped these plundering bands. The churches were robbed and graves opened, and dead bodies stripped of whatever a thirst for plunder might crave. Unfortunately for these poor deluded Negroes, they received no compensation for all this wicked work. So soon as they had completed the job for which they had been engaged, the cruel British placed on board their ships about four thousand of these miserable wretches and sent them to be sold in the same marts in which was sold the plate and furniture they had so valiantly assisted in carrying away from their masters. The British had no need for the poor Negro, only so far as he could be used to thwart the efforts of his master who was struggling to throw off the yoke of British tyranny.

On the retreat of Prevost to Savannah, those Negroes, who had not been sent off to be sold, were driven from the camp of the British general. Disease, in its most frightful and deadly forms, broke out amongst them. Like so many starving wolves, they hovered around the camp of their new made friends. Multitudes of them died and their emaciated bodies were devoured by wild beasts and vultures, and their bones left to bleach upon the islands. They had been told that a return to their former homes would be visited by certain death. Anxiously, they watched the British boats as they wended their way among the islands. A guard was placed on the boats to prevent them going on board and then, when some of them attempted to escape with the British by taking hold of the sides of the vessel and floating with it, their fingers were chopped off by the soldiers who were assigned to this cruel work.

The battle of Stono was fought on the 20th of June. The hot season had set in, and both armies were forced to remain quiet for a time. Only active operations ceased. The leaders of both armies were planning great undertakings. Sir Henry Clinton, having failed to accomplish anything by his campaigns in the north, turned his eyes with hope for better success toward the south. The object of the commander-in-chief of the British forces in American seems to have been to destroy the resources of Virginia and South Carolina, and thus force North Carolina, for want of supplies, to submit. To put this well concerted plan into action, Brigadier General Matthews, with two thousand soldiers, was sent to Virginia. On the 9th of May, 1779, the British squadron anchored in Hampton Roads. The American military posts and magazines fell into the hands of the British and the whole country sustained great loss. General Washington, although sorely pressed for men, dispatched to the southern department two regiments of

cavalry and some new recruits of infantry.

Evidently, the cause of the patriots was in a critical condition. It is true that the British had, as yet, accomplished nothing but the destruction of property, and there was scarcely a field officer in the British army who did not look upon the subjection of the American people as an utter impossibility. These facts the patriots did not know, and day by day the resources of the country were wasting away, and the sufferings of the people increasing. It was thought that a blow must be struck that would drive the British from Georgia and, consequently, from South Carolina. During the hot season, while General Lincoln's army was in camp, a scheme was matured for effecting this desirable end. General Lincoln and Governor Rutledge felt satisfied that with the assistance of the French forces, under the command of Count d'Estaing, the British forces under General Prevost could be either captured or driven from the south.

The scheme was submitted to Plombard, the French consul in Charleston. Plombard approved of the plan and, in concert with General Lincoln and Governor Rutledge, dispatches were sent to Count d'Estaing, urging him to form a junction with the American army under General Lincoln. Count d'Estaing was, at this time, in the West Indies, where he had conquered a number of the British possessions and out-generaled Admiral Byron, of the British fleet. Flushed, no doubt, with his recent victories over the British, and desiring to make some preparation for his previous failure in behalf of the American colonies, the Count gladly complied with the request.

Expecting, with the aid of General Lincoln's army, to annihilate Prevost's forces, Count d'Estaing set sail from Cape Francois, with twenty ships of the line and eleven frigates, on board of which were ten regiments of soldiers, amounting to six thousand men. His point of destination, as previously agreed upon by him and Lincoln, was Tybee. Two ships of the line and three frigates commanded by Major General Fontanges were sent to Charleston to apprise General Lincoln and Governor Rutledge of his approach. General Lincoln set out at once for Savannah. He crossed the Savannah River at Zubly's ferry on the 9th of September. Governor Rutledge collected all the small boats that could be procured, and sent them to Savannah to assist d'Estaing in landing his troops. On the 13th of September, the French troops, to the number of three thousand, landed at Beaulien. On the 15th, Count Pulaski and his legion joined the French, and on the 16th General Lincoln, and the troops under his command, arrived, and the two allied armies were joined in front of the city of Savannah. The enterprise, so far, was, in the main, well conducted. Four British ships fell into the hands of the French fleet on its approach to the coast of Georgia. The British regarded themselves, at that time, mistress of the sea, and feared little from the naval forces of the French.

Prevost, on the approach of the French and American forces, began to make preparations, in earnest, to defend his post.

D'Estaing's fleet appeared off the coast of Georgia on the 3rd of September, like an eagle from the sky. The four British ships already mentioned were taken by surprise, and the whole region round about Savannah thrown into confusion. The Tories and the loyalists began to tremble. Prevost was a brave man and a skillful officer. He began to make every preparation in his power to defend the city. Every man who could be spared from other service was put to work on the fortifications. Besides, three hundred Negroes were decoyed from the plantations adjacent to the city. General Prevost called in his troops from the various posts in the neighborhood.

On the 4th of September, the French fleet disappeared, and the garrison and inhabitants of the city began to breathe more freely. Even General Prevost cherished, with delight, the hope that d'Estaing and his fleet were gone. Preparations still went on, with energy, for an attack. On Tybee Island was a British garrison, commanded by Captain Moncrief, and manned by one hundred and fifty soldiers. The fortification was strengthened. On the 6th, the French fleet again appeared in greater force than before, and on the 9th it anchored off Tybee Island and proceeded to land some troops on the south side of the island. Captain Moncrief, seeing that he could effect nothing by resistance, spiked his cannon and, having embarked his troops on boats, fled to Savannah.

General Prevost was now convinced that the object which d'Estaing had in view was the capture of Savannah. During the time that the armies of the allied powers were forming a junction, various skirmishes took place; but nothing of any great importance was effected by either party. At this time the city was prepared for neither a storm nor a siege. Many of the best troops of the British had not yet reached the city, and Lieutenant Colonel Maitland, without whom it could not, perhaps, have been defended, was at Beaufort. Had d'Estaing made an attack upon the city as soon as he landed, it is highly probable that a few hours would have been sufficient to have reduced it. General McIntosh urged that the attack be made at once, but d'Estaing was in this instance, as in many others, self-willed.

On the 16th of September, the forces under General Lincoln and Count d'Estaing sat down about three miles from the city, on the west. By this time General Prevost had constructed thirteen redoubts, fifteen batteries and a strong abattis in front of the whole. Still, he was not prepared for an engagement. Colonel Maitland had not yet arrived, but it had been ascertained that he was hastening, by forced marches, with eight hundred men to his assistance.

On the 16th of September, the very day that the French forces under d'Estaing and the American forces under Lincoln formed a conjunction, but before the arrival of General Lincoln, for some unaccountable reason, d'Estaing summoned General Prevost in the name of Louis XVI, to surrender. This was an insult, offered either through ignorance, hate, or design, to the American general and the forces under his command. General Lincoln was in a position that he could not venture to be a stickler respecting nice distinction, and perhaps took no notice of the thing at the time. Prevost promptly refused to surrender, because the summons was not specific and definite in stating the conditions of surrender, and asked that twenty-four hours might be given him to consider the matter. The truce was as hastily granted by d'Estaing, as the summons for surrender had been rashly made a short time before. Prevost determined not to surrender if he could possibly avoid it. Delays and the granting of a truce had caused him to fail in capturing Charleston a short time before, and he determined to make the French and Americans experience a similar failure before Savannah, if possible. All he wanted was time. Within twenty-four hours the gallant Maitland and his eight hundred veterans would be in the city, and then he felt he would be comparatively safe. In the meantime, entrenching tools were put in every man's hands and they were granted no rest, night nor day. The Negroes were forced, by the lash, to work as they had never worked before.

During the truce, Maitland arrived. D'Estaing no doubt thought it was impossible for Maitland to reach the city. In this he was sadly mistaken. When Maitland discovered that the French were in possession of the only regular channel which was navigable, he determined to reach the city in some other way. On arriving at Dawfuskie, he was piloted by a Negro fisherman through a creek which was, at that time, navigable. A dense fog prevailed, and Maitland and his forces escaped the notice of the French. He entered the city before the expiration of the truce. A shout of joy was raised and a feeling of confidence pervaded every breast. Lieutenant Colonel Maitland entered Savannah on the afternoon of the 17th, and soon after, General

Prevost sent Count d'Estaing a note informing him "that he should defend himself to the last extremity."

The Count now, no doubt, discovered that he had made a fatal mistake. Although he was eager to come to the assistance of General Lincoln, he seemed to have acted precipitately and strangely inconsistent from the moment he landed his forces. His intention, when he set out from Cape Francois, was to remain at Savannah only ten days. He had been informed by the French consul, by Governor Rutledge, and by General Lincoln of the condition of the British forces. From this information he thought that Savannah could be reduced in ten days. His information was true, and his deduction correct. The city could have been captured in less than ten hours, if the attack had been made as soon as the French forces landed.

When General Prevost refused to surrender, it was perceived that the city could not be taken by assault. Preparation was now being made by the allied powers for taking the place by siege. D'Estaing was restless. He feared a storm might dash his ships to pieces, and he feared Admiral Byron might follow him from the West Indies and surround him and capture him and all his fleet. The stores and heavy ordinance were brought up from the point at which the French had landed. The small vessels belonging to the French fleet moved up the Savannah and forced the British ships to seek refuge under cover of the guns of the batteries. On the morning of the 23rd of September, the besieging armies broke ground. Night and day they worked with an energy seldom surpassed, and rarely equaled. In less than two weeks, fifty-three heavy guns and fourteen mortars were mounted and ready for use. Prevost kept his forces within his lines, husbanding all his strength for the final conflict. Only two attacks were made upon the besiegers. The one on the 24th of September, led by Major Graham, and the other on the 27th of September, led by Major McArthur. These sorties amounted to very little. A few men were killed on both sides, but the work of the besiegers went on vigorously.

The work of the besiegers being complete, and the batteries all manned, the bombardment commenced with terrific fury on the morning of the 4th of October. The Truite, a French frigate, commenced firing at the same time. For five days and nights, the firing was kept up without intermission. The houses in the city were shattered to pieces by the guns of the besiegers. Men, women and children were killed in the streets. For safety, the citizens took refuge in damp, unhealthy cellars. Still the besiegers kept approaching the works of the British. The garrison became alarmed, for although their works, as yet,

were not much injured. It was evident to all that the garrison must soon be crushed by the combined efforts of the allied powers. General Prevost had hoped that Admiral Byron would come to his assistance, but now this only hope of safety had died. A grand victory and glorious triumph was within the grasp of the French count and American general.

At this critical moment d'Estaing became restless and impatient. A council of war was called and the engineers declared that ten days more would be required to reach the British lines. D'Estaing declared that an assault must be made upon the city at once or he would leave. Without the aid of the French forces, General Lincoln could do nothing. Rather than raise the siege, it was agreed to make an attempt upon the British works by assault. The morning of the 9th of October was the time to make the attack.

On the night of the 8th of October, a sergeant in one of the Charleston companies deserted and communicated to General Prevost an outline of the contemplated attack. The British, warned by this deserter, were on the lookout for the foe. The morning of the 9th was densely foggy. Three thousand five hundred French, six hundred North Carolina regulars, and three hundred Charleston militia, moved forward to the assault. The stormers advanced in three columns. Count d'Estaing, assisted by General Lincoln, led the first column against the Spring Hill redoubt, which was north of the city. The other main column was led by Count Dillon, and was directed to move along the edge of a swamp and attack the British lines on the east, near the river. The third column was led by General Isaac Huger. This column was ordered to attack the British in the front and thus divert their attention from the two columns. Under cover of a heavy fire from all the batteries, the three columns advanced to the several points assigned them.

A few words are sufficient to give a correct account of the assault. The allied powers were defeated with a loss, in killed and wounded, of fully one thousand, whilst the British loss, in killed and wounded, was only one hundred and twenty. The assaulting columns were not discovered until they had approached within musket shot of the British works. A dense fog concealed them from view. When day dawned, shower after shower of musket balls was poured into their ranks, and the batteries opened a cross fire which mowed the men down by hundreds. Early in the action, d'Estaing was wounded in an arm and thigh, and carried from the field of carnage to the camp. Lieutenant Colonel Laurens led the light troops on the left wing of the French. Aided by General McIntosh, Laurens led the American forces over the abattis, across the ditch, and planted the flags of America and France upon the parapet of the Spring Hill redoubt. Here the Crescent and Lilly would have floated in triumph, had it not been for the gallant Maitland. He sent Colonel Glazier with a body of fresh troops, who rushed upon the brave Americans and, with the bayonet, pushed many a gallant soldier into the ditch below. The flag of France and the colors given by Mrs. Elliott to Col. Moultrie's regiment were torn down.

For near an hour the brave assailants struggled to capture the British works, and were as gallantly met by the garrison. When further attempt was seen to be vain, a general retreat was ordered.

This was a sad affair. Many a brave man fell into the ditches or was pushed, by British bayonets, through the abattis. Here Sergeant Jasper fell, and the glorious Pole, Count Pulaski, lost his life. We cannot refrain from censuring Count d'Estaing. Only a few months before, he had showed himself a brave and skillful officer. At the siege of Savannah he was brave, but not wise. Justice demands that we say that d'Estaing was urged by the other French officers to act as he did.

Installment XII

THE FALL OF CHARLESTON

After the attempted but unsuccessful storming of Savannah, on the 9th of October, 1779, the French and American armies continued, in appearance, to prosecute the siege. It was only a feint. Both armies were making preparation for raising the siege. On the night of the 18th of October, the American forces, under General Lincoln, retired to Zully's Ferry, and the French forces, under Count d'Estaing, to Caustin's Bluff. From this point the French proceeded to Tybee, where they had left their ships. Here the French arrived on the 20th of October, whence the French count left the continent. General Lincoln marched from Zully's Ferry to Charleston.

No doubt both General Lincoln and his troops were cast down and sad. The two armies parted, say the American historians, with the kindest feeling towards each other; but the British historians give a very different account of their separation. The British historians say that no good feeling existed between the French and American armies before the attempt to take Savannah by storm and after this unfortunate affair, it was with great difficulty that an open rupture was prevented. Each party reproached the other for bad management and cowardly conduct. Gladly the two armies formed a junction and as gladly they separated. All the circumstances of the case seem to favor the British account rather than the American.

The fall of Savannah into the hands of the British, late in 1778, and now the unsuccessful attempt to drive the British out of it in 1779, were sore calamities; but they were only precursors of a more calamitous event.

Strange as it may seem, the British, although meeting with but little successful opposition, still they made but little headway in reducing the country to subjection. They were nominally in possession of all of Georgia, and much of the lower section of South Carolina. Actually, they were in possession of only Savannah.

So soon as it was learned that d'Estaing had left the American continent, Sir Henry Clinton set out in earnest to effect the long cherished plan of reducing South Carolina to subjection. On the 26th of December, 1779, Sir Henry Clinton, with Admiral Marion Arbuthnot, set sail from Sandy Hook. On board the fleet was a land force of five thousand troops. Every preparation had been made for the expedition. The equipment was perfect; but no human foresight can provide against all casualties. The voyage was not only tedious, but attendant with sore disasters. Several of the transports and provision ships were damaged by the sea; a few were taken by the Americans, and all were, more or less, injured. An ordnance ship with all her stores sank, and nearly all the cavalry and draught horses were drowned. After a long and tempestuous voyage, the armament reached North Edisto sound on the 10th of February.

The following day was spent in landing the troops on John's Island. The British army, led by the commander-in-chief in person, was now within thirty miles of Charleston. Had he marched immediately against the city, it must have fallen into his hands at once. General Lincoln had less than two thousand Continental troops, and the militia would have been panic stricken on the appearance of so formidable a force as that under the command of Sir Henry Clinton. Had an immediate attack been made by Clinton, the probability is that General Lincoln would have retreated and left the city of Charleston to the mercy of the enemy. Sir Henry Clinton, notwithstanding the great superiority of his forces over those of General Lincoln, determined to take the city by siege. Lincoln, on the other hand, went to work in conjunction with the civil and municipal authorities to put the place in a condition to stand a regular investment.

The course pursued by the British general showed that he feared the ghost of Fort Sullivan. Twice the forces of his Britannic Majesty had been repulsed and driven away, humbled if not disgraced, from Charleston. Now the commander-in-chief of the British forces in America determined to proceed deliberately and cautiously. With as much military ceremony as if he were about to besiege an old European city, whose frowning battlements looked down in contempt upon an approaching enemy, the British general began the work of besieging a city only one hundred years old, and defended by only a few undisciplined militia and a general bred a farmer.

Charleston, at this time, was in a very unfit condition to resist the attack of the enemy. The financial condition of the state of South Carolina was absolutely desperate. The price of a pair of shoes was near a thousand dollars, and everything else in proportion. The smallpox broke out in the city and served as an excuse to deter the country militia from joining the forces in the city. Most of them were conscious that they would flee at the first onset, and the idea of having no outlet begat within their minds feeling of despair. The truth is, the militia were hopelessly demoralized. They dreaded the idea of being cooped up in a beleaguered city.

When Sir Henry Clinton arrived, the legislature was in session. Governor John Rutledge was granted dictatorial powers. He was invested with the power to do anything that would prevent the republic from suffering harm. Absolute power was granted him, except that no man could be put to death until after trial by jury.

Governor Rutledge, together with all the friends of the Republican party in the city, advocated defending the place to the last extremity. General Lincoln's intention when Sir Henry Clinton's forces arrived was to evacuate Charleston and retire to the up-country, and then, at some fit time, having collected a sufficient force, return and drive the British out. This would have been the proper course, but General Lincoln was forced to yield to the wishes of the citizens. He was, no doubt, deceived by being told that reinforcements would flock to him from all quarters of the state. Not only so, but he had sent dispatches to Havana soliciting aid from the Spanish governor. Expecting that some event would occur, which would enable him to defend the city, he went to work to strengthen the fortifications. A ditch was cut across Charleston neck, from the Ashley to the Cooper River. This was protected by two rows of abattis. The works which had been constructed on the approach of Prevost were strengthened. Men and boys, and even women, went to work on the fortifications. Three hundred Negroes were brought in from the plantations in the neighborhood by Governor Rutledge and put to work. Night and day the axe and spade were plied.

General Charles Cotesworth Pinckney, with a small garrison, was stationed at Fort Moultrie. Captain Daniel Horry was sent to Ashley Ferry, to keep a look-out for the approach of the enemy. General Moultrie was ordered south to collect a militia force, direct the general movements of the American cavalry and, in any way that he could, harass the foe. The works in front and around the city from Hadrell's to Hospital Point were repaired, strengthened and manned as well as circumstances would allow. Whipper, with a small force which congress had sent south, was ordered to take his stand in the harbor, and prevent the fleet of Admiral Arbuthnot from crossing the bar. Such, briefly, was the disposition made of the American forces.

Determined to hasten slowly, Sir Henry Clinton established a military depot at Wappoo, on James' Island, and repaired Fort Johnson. After near two months' delay in preparing for the siege, his forces moved forward on the 28th of March, crossed the Stono, and on the same day crossed the Ashley at the point where the first settlement in the state was made. Here, to make assurance doubly sure, entrenchments were thrown up confronting those of the Americans on the opposite shore. From the time that Sir Henry Clinton landed on John's Island up to this time, the only opposition he met with was a single skirmish party led by Colonel Washington.

Arbuthnot and Clinton acted in concert, and this will explain, to some extent, the delay that Clinton made on James Island. Arbuthnot found it difficult to get his large vessels over the bar. The guns had to be removed and various contrivances resorted to in order to effect his purpose. On the 20th, Arbuthnot crossed the bar with his small ships and transports, and drove Commodore Whipper from Five Fathom Hole, near the city.

The British land forces, having crossed the Ashley River, filed to the right and marched down the Neck to a point within eleven hundred yards of the American works. Here, on Sabbath morning, the first of April, they broke ground. As Clinton marched down the Neck, the van of his column was attacked by a corps of light infantry led by Colonel John Laurens. In this skirmish the British lost, in killed and wounded, about thirty. One of the aids-de-camp of Clinton, the Earle of Caithness, was wounded. On the 5th of April, General Clinton made another advance and, having erected a battery and mounted twelve cannons, demanded a surrender of the town and all the forces in it.

Just about this time, General Woodford, with seven hundred Virginians, entered the city and reported that considerable numbers were hastening to the succor of his beleaguered city. This, together with the entreaties of the citizens, who, as yet, knew nothing of the horrors of war, induced General Lincoln to reject the summons to surrender. Two days after, the batteries of Clinton were opened upon the city and the American works, and for thirteen days a terrific cannonade was kept up by both parties.

On the 9th of April, Admiral Arbuthnot ran by Fort Moultrie and took shelter under the guns of Fort Johnson. As the British fleet passed Fort Moultrie, General Pinckney opened a terrific fire upon it. Twenty-seven seamen were killed, a transport ran aground, and was burned by her crew. General Pinckney hoped that Commodore Whipper would keep the British back, whilst he would be allowed to pour in upon it an enfilading fire from Fort Moultrie. Whipper ran his squadron up the Cooper River and sunk his vessels, together with some merchant ships, between Shutes and Folly Islands and the city. The object had in view in sinking these vessels at this point, was to prevent the British fleet from running up Cooper River and raking the town.

So soon as the British fleet crossed the bar and passed Fort Moultrie it was evident that unless succor was soon received the city must fall. About the time that the guns from the British batteries commenced firing, Governor Rutledge left the city for the purpose of arousing the country militia and sending them to the defense of the city. The civil affairs of the city were left in the hands of the Lieutenant Governor Christopher Gadsden. Governor Rutledge passed up the country between the Cooper and Santee rivers. He begged, he entreated, and threatened, but collected few men. The only quarter of the city which was open was on the Cooper River. To keep communication with the country open, General Lincoln sent General Isaac Huger, with three hundred cavalry to Biggin's Bridge, in the neighborhood of Monck's Corner.

Sir Henry Clinton, anxious to cut off all communication between the country and city, sent out a body of fifteen hundred chosen troops under Colonels Webster, Tarleton and Ferguson, to scour the country in search of Huger and his cavalry. On the night of the 14th of April Colonel Tarleton, with his legion of cavalry, and Colonel Ferguson, with his riflemen, led by a Negro through by-paths, completely surprised Huger's men. The Americans made but little resistance. The men fled to the swamp, and thus most of them escaped; but all the baggage of all kinds, together with most of the horses, fell into the hands of the British.

After the British fleet had stationed itself in a position not to be molested by Fort Moultrie, the greater part of the garrison was ordered to the city. Lieutenant Colonel Scott was left in command of it, with a few men. On the 7th of May, Colonel Scott, having been summoned by the British fleet, was forced to surrender. The British flag was soon seen over its walls.

When Sir Henry Clinton first landed on James' Island, he sent for reinforcements to Georgia and ordered three thousand more troops from New York. The troops under command of the gallant Earl Cornwallis, arrived four days after the overthrow of Huger's troops at Biggen's Bridge. Cornwallis was stationed at Hadrell's Point. All communication between the country and city was now cut off, and the investiture of the city complete. The third parallel of the enemy's works was finished, and the city was subjected to a terrific cannonade, both from the land batteries of Clinton, and the fleet of Arbuthnot. Night and day the firing was kept up. The defenses of the city gave way before the heavy guns of the enemy, and the houses of the city were set on fire by the carcasses thrown into the city. Men, women, and children were killed in the streets. No place was safe, and hunger began to stare at the besieged in the face. All hope failed the garrison, and the citizens were in a state of alarm bordering on despair. General Lincoln was urged by the citizens to surrender on the best terms he could obtain.

On the 9th of May, pressed on all sides, General Lincoln surrendered to Sir Henry Clinton and Admiral Arbuthnot. Everything passed into the hands of the enemy. This, as we shall see in the sequel, was the saddest blow the state of South Carolina had experienced. Men made of different material would have folded their arms in despair and given up the cause of freedom as lost. The American garrison lost in killed, ninety-two; in wounded, one hundred and forty-eight. The British lost in killed seventy-six; in wounded, one hundred and eighty-nine.

Installment XIII

THE BATTLE OF WAXHAW

So soon as Charleston fell into the hands of the British, the commander-in-chief of his majesty's forces in America determined to push his conquest until all the territory south of the Potomac would be prostrate at the feet of the British lion. Never, since the beginning of the war, had the prospects for the British been so bright and the affairs of the colonies in so discouraging a condition. The first object of Sir Henry Clinton was to send a strong force into different sections of the state of South Carolina, and gather up recruits for his regiments from the Tories and loyalists of the interior of the state, and protect the state against "cruelty and oppression," as he called the rule of the Whigs. This accomplished, the troops were to march into North Carolina, subdue it, and then into Virginia, when the rebellion of the colonies would be crushed out. So soon as the civil government of South Carolina was put into working condition, Clinton contemplated returning to the north and leaving Cornwallis in command of the southern division of the British forces. This was a wise arrangement. The plans of Clinton were well conceived, but he greatly mistook the character of the people he had to deal with. There was no better officer in the British army than Lord Cornwallis.

Whilst Clinton was busily engaged in the work of reconstructing the city of Charleston, that portion of the British army designed for the interior of the state moved off in three divisions under Lord Cornwallis. At Dorchester, one division, under the command of Lieutenant Colonel Balfour, moved off for Ninety-Six; and another, under command of Lieutenant Colonel Brown, set out for Augusta; and the third division, under Lord Cornwallis himself, marched for Camden.

When it was learned that Charleston had fallen into the hands of the British, Colonel Buford, with a force of about four hundred continental soldiers, some cavalry, and two field pieces, retired to Camden. This really was the only armed force of any importance in the state of South Carolina at that time. This captured, and the work of subjugating the state was complete. At least so thought the British.

Cornwallis' point of destination was North Carolina. Brown and Balfour were ordered to fortify Augusta to Ninety-Six. On his way to North Carolina, Cornwallis determined to capture or cut off Buford's command. When, however, Buford heard of Cornwallis' approach, he moved off leisurely from Camden in the direction of Charlotte, North Carolina. Cornwallis, hearing of this, detached Colonel Bannister Tarleton with about seven hundred men, consisting of cavalry and light infantry, for the purpose of overtaking Buford. No man was better fitted for such an enterprise than Tarleton - brave to a fault and full of energy; impetuous as a tornado; but at the same time with a mind cool and calculating. No man was ever more to be feared than Colonel Tarleton. He was charged with cruelty, and no doubt he was cruel, but all war is cruel. Tarleton always made a victory complete. To out-general him, as

Morgan did at Cowpens, was no small honor to any man; to out-fight him or Patrick Ferguson was as much praise as could be bestowed upon any officer.

Impatient of delay, Tarleton left his light infantry behind and pushed on with one hundred and seventy dragoons. On the twenty-ninth of May, he came up with Colonel Abraham Buford about nine miles north of Lancaster village, in Lancaster county. The American forces were encamped on Waxhaw Creek, near Waxhaw Presbyterian church. Before Buford was aware of the approach of the enemy, he was surrounded by Tarleton's cavalry.

Of this affair there are two versions. One is that Buford offered to surrender on the terms granted to Lincoln's army in Charleston. This Tarleton rejected. The other, and more probable, version is that Tarleton summoned Buford to surrender on the same terms granted to the American army at Charleston. This Colonel Buford rejected in the following words: "Sir; I reject your proposal, and shall defend myself to the last extremity." Tarleton, during the time that flags were passing back and forth, was, it is said, making preparation for battle. This was contrary to the usages of war.

So soon as Colonel Buford rejected Tarleton's proposal, the cavalry of the latter dashed in upon the Americans and cut them to pieces in a moment. Buford's men were in no position. They had received no orders and did not know what to do. Some commenced to fire upon the enemy, whilst others threw down their arms and begged for quarters. Of the Americans, one hundred and thirteen men were killed on the ground; one hundred and fifty were so mutilated with the sabres of the British dragoons that they were unable to be removed, and fifty-three were made prisoners. The British loss was five killed and fifteen wounded. Colonel Buford with his cavalry and near one hundred of the infantry escaped. Buford's whole command was totally ruined.

There is something mysterious about the whole affair. Colonel Buford must have acted with no decision, and it would appear that Tarleton acted with an amount of cruelty rarely heard of. No doubt both commanders were censurable. Colonel Buford was surprised and so agitated that he did not know what to do, and Tarleton, for various reasons, was anxious to make his victory a complete one. The simple fact that, whilst some of the Americans were calling for quarters, others were firing upon the enemy, was cause sufficient why no quarters should be granted.

Tarleton says that after the Americans had surrendered, they continued to take up their arms and continued to fire. There is some mistake about this.

The small loss on the British side shows that very little firing was done by the Americans.

It would seem that, although, as was acknowledged at the time, Buford's command was well officered, the officers became panic stricken and could do nothing. Everything Colonel Buford did was wrong. He did nothing to defend himself and he did nothing to injure the enemy. He neither prepared for fight nor flight. He had more than twice as many men as Tarleton, and Tarleton's light infantry were so far behind and so much exhausted by forced marches, that they could not have reinforced him until Buford could have reached Charlotte, North Carolina, where he would have met Colonel Porterfield and been safe.

No doubt there was a fearful amount of cruelty in Tarleton's nature, but we must not censure our enemies without a cause. After the lapse of a century, we can look back calmly at men and events, and we can say that both Tarleton and Cornwallis were brave men and skillful officers. Cornwallis was a gentleman, and he lauded and extolled Tarleton for his management of the affairs at Waxhaw. It reflects no dishonor upon the patriots to tell the honest truth about the men with whom they had to contend. On the other hand, no higher encomium can be passed upon the Whigs of America than to say that they won their liberty in spite of as brave men and as skillful officers as England ever sent to the field of battle.

Both Cornwallis and Tarleton were cruel, and the latter was often barbarous; but as we shall often meet these officers, we should at least endeavor to discover the incentive to this cruelty. Especially was their cruel acts perpetrated in the upper section of South Carolina and the lower and western sections of North Carolina. Both these regions of country were settled by the same kind of people. They were Whigs by every instinct of their nature. The men were Whigs and the women were Whigs. To be free was a part of their religion. Their history was known to every well-informed Englishman. They were Scotch-Irish. When Colonel Tarleton entered the Waxhaw country he saw signs of this fact. The thrift of the people and the defiant looks of the mothers and children revealed the facts. The Bibles in their houses with the Scotch versions of the Psalms, excited in his mind strange and conflicting emotions. He was afraid and he was enraged. He felt that he must massacre or be massacred. He was right. Had his command fallen into the hands of Colonel Buford and then into the hands of the Scotch-Irish of Waxhaw, he would never have seen the face of King George again. Even Tarleton's cruelty aroused the spirits of the Scotch-Irish of the up-country and made Tarleton's quarters a synonym

for no quarters. No doubt Colonel Tarleton thought by his cruelty he would crush the spirit of the Scotch-Irish; but he only aroused them to vengeance. The surest way to arouse a Scotch-Irishman, to put forth all the energies of his soul, is to contrary him. Torture only evolves the powers of his endurance. Treat him kindly, and he is as gentle as a lamb; impose upon him and he will nurse his wrath until it gains a momentum which bids defiance to all obstacles. Tarleton's cruelty at Waxhaw was the beginning of a death struggle for liberty. The Scotch-Irish never forgot the massacre of Buford's command and their great-grandchildren to this day feel their blood boil when Tarleton and Waxhaw are mentioned.

Installment XIV
BATTLE OF RAMSOUR'S MILL

After the discomfiture of Buford at Waxhaw, Tarleton repaired to Camden. The facts in the case were soon communicated to Sir Henry Clinton, the commander-in-chief of the British forces in America. Over the affair at Waxhaw, the British were jubilant. After the fall of Charleston they thought the state of South Carolina was subdued. Now they were sure of it. On the third of June, Sir Henry Clinton wrote that there were very few people in South Carolina who had not returned to their former allegiance to the British government. On the fifth of June, Sir Henry, full of bright hopes and cheered by the prospects that the thirteen colonies would be in a short time made as formerly a part and parcel of the British government, set out with the main body of his army for New York.

The British army in the south was left in command of Lord Cornwallis. Before leaving for New York, Sir Henry Clinton issued a proclamation, in which the paroles of citizens were nullified and all were required to take up arms for the purpose of crushing out, as speedily as possible, the rebellion. No neutrality was allowed. Whoever was not for the British government was to be regarded as against it. Citizens were required to enter the British army and assist in subduing their fellow citizens. This, when viewed in one aspect, was a wise step; but when viewed in another aspect, was very unwise. Sir Henry Clinton no doubt thought the people of South Carolina were in sympathy with the government of England. At least, he thought from all external signs of the times that the great majority of the people of South Carolina had despaired of the success of the colonies. His past experience ought to have taught him differently. The people were not subdued. They were only quiet. Those who had rebelled against the government of England were still, in heart, rebels. Necessity was forcing them to remain in a neutral state. Besides, multitudes of individuals had left the state and were, in connection with the citizens of other states, preparing for renewing the conflict. Pickens, Sumter, McCall, Hammonds, Hampton, Liddle and Rutledge, together with multitudes of other South Carolinians of little less note, and sought voluntary exile for a time. The same course had been pursued by Hawley, Clark and Dooley of Georgia. Like Alfred, one of England's early monarchs, these men had secreted themselves amongst the "back water" men, and were waiting, like Alfred, for a proper occasion to pounce down upon the invaders of their country.

Both Clinton and Cornwallis were mistaken. South Carolina was not subdued. Her patriots only made a virtue of necessity and kept quiet. The massacre of Buford's command drove the inhabitants of the Waxhaw settlement in various directions. Most of them sought shelter and protection amongst the Whigs of North Carolina, in the regions adjacent to Charlotte. The widowed mother of Andrew Jackson, with her two sons, found a home in the house of Widow Wilson, in Sugar Creek congregation. In this Whig region the tale of their suffering was told. The massacre of Buford's command was narrated and the "hornets' nest" region was thoroughly aroused. Generals Rutherford and Davie called out the militia and the Rev. Dr. McWhorter poured his patriotic soul into a speech to them. Everybody was full of patriotic sentiments and anxiously desired to a fit time to strike a blow, to defend the rights of their country, and avenge the blood of their massacred countrymen. Gen. Davie, having been wounded in the thigh at the battle of Stono, on the 20th of June, 1779, had now sufficiently recovered to take the field. With a part of his cavalry he undertook to reconnoiter the country between Charlotte and Camden. The militia were dismissed with instructions to put their arms in proper repair and be ready to meet Gen. Rutherford at a moments warning.

North and South Carolina were originally one, and under the royal government of England; and today they remain twin sisters. The region about Charlotte and the upper section of the state of South Carolina, was settled by people from the same country, by a people entertaining the same political notions and the same religious creed, and worshipping God in the same way. For more than two hundred years they have preserved their type, clear and well marked. The struggles and triumphs of South Carolina were the struggles of and triumphs of North Carolina. When Charleston surrendered, both wept. When Buford's command was butchered, both were incensed. When Ferguson fell and his command annihilated at King's Mountain, representative of both states were there and the joy was mutual.

The object of the British officers was to station garrisons in various sections of the state of South Carolina, gather up and embody the loyalists and as soon as the crops of wheat were harvested in North Carolina, march into that state and put its inhabitants under the yoke. Cornwallis was anxious to form a junction with the loyal Scotch in the region of Fayetteville. Here the romantic Flora McDonald had landed in 1775 and espoused with all her soul the cause of George the Third. Unfortunate woman, she in turn hazarded her life both for the house of Stuart and the house of Hanover; and in her own language, was "no great gainer by it."

When Sir Henry Clinton set out for New York, Lord Cornwallis returned to Charleston, leaving Lord Rawdon in command at Camden. Knowing that the Waxhaw country was a pest of determined Whigs, and also a fertile region of country, Lord Rawdon established a garrison on Waxhaw Creek about thirty miles south of Charlotte. The militia of the counties of Mecklenburg and Rowan were called out by Gen. Rutherford. Rawdon made an encampment at Hanging Rock. Rutherford had about eight hundred militia in camp, about eighteen miles northwest of Charlotte. On hearing of Rawdon's advance to Hanging Rock, Rutherford advanced ten miles, to Mallard Creek. The cavalry, numbering only sixty-five, under command of Gen. Davie, were formed into two companies and placed under the command of Captains Simmons and Martin. A battalion of five hundred light infantry was placed under the command of William P. Davidson. Such were the preparations made by the North Carolina Whigs to thwart the efforts of the British.

Before setting out for Charleston, Lord Cornwallis had sent a man by the name of John Moore into the region of country now occupied by the town of Lincolnton, North Carolina. This John Moore was a loyalist, and had been in the British army for some time. His parents resided some six or seven miles from Lincolnton. On the seventh of June, John Moore reached the neighborhood. He wore a sword and a ragged suit of regimentals. The particular account of the actual state of things in the south was brought to this region by John Moore. This candidate for military honors, announced himself as a lieutenant colonel of Colonel Hamilton's regiment of North Carolina loyalists. He called upon the loyalists in the community to meet him in the woods, on Indian Creek, on the 10th of the month. When the day arrived, about forty men were on the ground. Moore proceeded in a set speech to communicate the general instructions of Lord Cornwallis to the loyal citizens; the purport of which was that the loyalists were to lie quiet until after harvest, but in the meantime to get ready for operating with the British when called upon.

Just as this meeting was to break up, a runner arrived communicating the intelligence that Joseph McDowell, who was out scouring the country in search of the leaders of the loyalists, was only eight miles distant and had only twenty men in his command. Lieutenant Colonel Moore felt confident that with forty men, he could capture McDowell with only twenty. It was necessary to make some arrangements for the enterprise and the next morning all were to assemble for the onset. The next day came, but McDowell was gone. He was pursued as far as the mountains between Burke and Lincoln, but not overtaken.

On the 13th, a general rendezvous was ordered by Col. Moore at Ramsour's Mills. Two hundred loyalists met Moore on the 13th, and on the 14th the number was greatly increased. Nicholas Welch, a major in Col. Hamilton's loyal regiment was among the number. He was a native of the community, and instead of being clad in rags like Moore, he wore a splendid suit and was able to display a large amount of gold guineas. It was Welch's time to make a speech. He told the people of the success of the British arms and of the melting away of the American forces. Captivated by Welch's fine regimentals, or thirsting for his gold guineas, the loyalists were inspired with great confidence in the man and his cause. Poor Moore and his ragged uniform sunk into contempt. The camp of these loyalists or Tories was discovered by Col. Hugh Brevard and Major Joseph McDowell. These brave Whigs hung around their camp, and excited within them anything else but feelings of confidence. Welch attempted to capture Brevard and McDowell, but was unsuccessful.

So soon as Gen. Rutherford learned that Lord Rawdon had returned to Camden, he determined to make an attack upon this Tory camp at Ramsour's Mills. On Sabbath, the 18th of June, he set out from his camp, which at that time was south of Charlotte, for the Tuckasege ford on the Catawba. Whilst encamped at Mallard Creek, General Rutherford, not knowing as yet what course Lord Rawdon would pursue, ordered Col. Locke, Major Wilson and Captains Falls and Brandon, together with the other military officers in the region, to raise men and disperse the Tories. Rutherford's object in this was to retain his own force to oppose Rawdon. On the same day that Gen. Rutherford set out in the direction of Ramsour's Mill, he sent a dispatch to Col. Locke and his men to meet him near Tuckasege ford, on the evening of the 19th or the morning of the 20th. The early part of the 19th was wet and unfit for moving. About twelve o'clock, the rain ceased and the sun shone out. The guns of the soldiers, having become wet, were fired off. This caused a general rush of the Whigs of the neighborhood to Rutherford's camp. On the evening of the same day the Catawba was crossed at Tuckasege ford, and that night the men under Rutherford encamped about sixteen miles from Ramsour's Mill.

No plan of operation was concerted between Rutherford and Locke. The latter, in good faith and with proper spirit, in concert with other kindred spirits, set about making preparations in earnest to disperse the Tories. On the morning of the 19th, the forces under McDowell, Wilson, Falls, Brandon and Locke encamped on Mountain Creek, on the west side of Catawba, about sixteen miles from Ramsour's Mill and thirty-five from the camp of Rutherford. The whole force amounted to about four hundred men. Here a council of officers was held, and their future movements freely discussed. Some suggested that they should re-cross the Catawba and wait for reinforcements; others proposed that the whole force should march at once and form a junction with Gen. Rutherford. Both these propositions, for various reasons, were objected to. Some, in the overflowing of their patriotism, insinuated that both propositions indicated a fear of the Tories. This settled the question at once. It was determined to boldly attack the Tories as soon as possible. Col. Johnson was sent to inform Gen. Rutherford of their conclusion and to ask his co-operation. Johnson arrived at Rutherford's camp at ten o'clock on the night of the 19th. Gen. Rutherford, thinking that his message had reached the camp of Locke shortly after the departure of Col. Johnson, remained in camp anxiously awaiting the arrival of Locke's forces.

Late in the afternoon, Locke, McDowell, Wilson, Falls and others, set out with the four hundred men under them for the Tory camp at Ramsour's Mill. At the west end of the mountain the troops were halted for an hour and the officers consulted respecting the mode of attack. Every officer was left to his own discretion and to act as circumstances might demand. The only thing definitely arranged was that the companies under McDowell, Brandon and Falls should act as cavalry and march in front. At daylight they were within a mile of the enemy's camp. The camp was favorably situated for those occupying it. It was on the hill three hundred yards from Ramsour's Mill and about half a mile from Lincolnton. The Tories had a picket guard of twelve men stationed in the road which passed over the hill. The horsemen under McDowell, Brandon, Wilson and Falls were arranged by twos. So soon as the Tory pickets discovered the cavalry, they fired and fled to their camp. They were pursued to the lines and then the Tories poured in a galling fire, which drove the cavalry of the patriots back. The cavalry passed through the infantry under Locke and afterwards formed and renewed the attack. As might have been expected, the mode of attack was very disorderly. The Whigs moved forward boldly, but in great disorder. In a short time the Tories, driven from the hill, retired behind the ridge. Here their fire became more destructive and the patriots took shelter behind the bushes. Captain Harden, at this juncture of affairs, led a small band of Whigs into the fight. Protecting his men behind a fence, he poured in a destructive fire upon the right flank of the enemy. The Whigs made an oblique movement which put them in possession of a more favorable position. The conflict now became a hand-to-hand fight. The parties struck each other with the butts of their guns. The Tories, finding that they were pressed at all points, left the ridge and crossed over the creek on the other side of the mill. When they were seen thus posting themselves, Major Wilson and Captain Alexander were sent to urge General Rutherford to hasten to the assistance of the patriots. They met Rutherford about six miles from the battleground. Major Davie and his cavalry rushed at full speed to the scene of the action. Col. Davidson's command followed with all possible speed. These parties had not gone but a couple of miles until they were informed that the Tories had retreated and the battle was over.

The loss on each side was about equal. It was hard to tell a Tory from a Whig since both were dressed in citizen's clothes. The Whigs wore as a mark of distinction a piece of white paper in the front of their hats, whilst the Tories wore a branch of pine in the same place. When the fight became hand-to-hand, the Tories took the pine branch out of their hats and threw it away. The Tories sent in a flag asking a truce to bury the dead, but at the same time Moore and Welch marched the Tory troops away; or to speak more correctly, they ordered every man to run away or get away as best he could. Moore, with a squad of thirty men, reached Camden where he was abused and degraded by the commander of the British forces. After the battle was over about seventy men were found dead on the ground, about one half of which were Whigs. About one hundred on each side were wounded, and about fifty Tories were taken prisoners. Captains Dobson, Smith, Falls, Bowman and Armstrong were killed, and Captains Houston and McKissick wounded. The Tories lost, in officers, Captains Cumberland, Murray and Warlick, killed; and Captain Carpenter wounded.

The patriots were victorious; but it was a sad victory. The next day the dead were buried and a long and loud wail was uttered by the relatives of the slain, many of whom had fallen by the hands of their neighbors and kindred. It, however, taught the Tories a salutary lesson, and proved to the British that the country was not subdued.

BATTLE OF WILLIAMSON'S, OR CAPTAIN HUCK'S DEFEAT

So soon as the facts concerning the fall of Charleston reached the up-country, the Tories laid aside all disguise and began boldly to plunder in bands. To inspire these loyalists with greater courage and to incite them to acts of greater daring, the British stationed numbers of soldiers in different sections of the state. We have seen that the Whigs of that part of North Carolina bordering on South Carolina were thoroughly aroused. On the 20th of June, 1780, Col. Locke engaged Moore and Welch at Ramsour's Mill and discomfited them.

Tarleton's cruelty at Waxhaw kindled into a flame the patriotism of all the region round about Charlotte, North Carolina. It had the same effect upon the Scotch-Irish of Fairfield, Chester and York counties, South Carolina. Few if any of the Scotch-Irish of the territory embraced in these counties were paroled as prisoners, and none of them took British protection. Many of them left their homes and sought refuge with kindred spirits in less exposed regions. At different points the Tories had begun to collect as early as the latter part of May. They were a set of plundering thieves, utterly unfit to add strength or give dignity to any government; but fully competent to give great annoyance to all good citizens.

On the 24th of May, 1780, Capt. John McLure, with a few of his Whig neighbors, attacked Houseman, a Tory captain, at Beckhamville, Chester county, and routed him and his band. Two days after, Capts. Bratton and McLure attacked a similar band at Mobley's Meeting House, on Little River, Fairfield county. These bold attacks on the Tories aroused the British and they determined to avenge the blood of their Tory friends.

At this time Col. Turnbull was in command of a British post at Rocky Mount. To chastise the patriots for past acts of daring, and to keep them in awe in the future, Col. Turnbull sent out Captain Huck with two hundred British regulars, one hundred dragoons, one hundred mounted infantry and about five hundred Tories - in all near one thousand men. Capt. Huck's headquarters was for some time in the neighborhood of what is now Alexander Williford's Mill, on Fishing Creek in Chester county.

Capt. Christian Huck was a Tory, a lawyer and, by birth, a native of Philadelphia. The most remarkable feature in his character was that he was a most blasphemously profane swearer.

From this encampment on Fishing Creek, Huck sent out plundering and burning parties daily in all directions. In Huck's command was a man by the name of Ferguson, a colonel of the Tory militia. Most of the plundering was assigned to this officer. The houses of the Whigs for miles all around were plundered, and not a few of the houses of those who were regarded as prominent Whigs were burned; and Ferguson and his men went so far as even to shoot down, in cold blood, unoffending citizens. On Sabbath morning, the 11th of June, Capt. Huck sent a party of men to Fishing Creek Church, of which the Rev. John Simpson was pastor. Huck had two grudges against the Rev. Simpson and his congregation. The one was because Mr. Simpson had been prominent in planning the attack by McLure upon Houseman at Beckhamville. For the encouragement he gave Capt. John McLure, Huck and Ferguson determined that Mr. Simpson should be punished severely. The other grudge that these officers had against the Rev. Simpson and his congregation was that they were Presbyterians and continued to sing in worship to God the same version of the Psalms used by the Scotch. So great was the hatred of these men to the Scotch translation of the Psalms, that they went through the country and consigned to the flames every Bible which contained the Scotch metrical version of the Psalms. The object of the visit of the British to Fishing Creek Church on the 11th of June was to burn the church, pastor and people all together. On arriving at the church, they found no one there. Either there was to be no preaching there that day, or the congregation, for prudential reasons, had assembled at some other point. The disappointment of the plunderers was great, but they determined not to be outdone. The house of the pastor was but a short distance from the church. On they went to his house. He was not at home; he had gone on Friday to join Sumter at Clem's branch. So soon as Mrs. Simpson saw them coming she took her four children and, as well as she could, concealed herself and her children in the orchard. The British entered the house, first plundering it of everything they wanted, and took out the beds and ripped them open, throwing away the feathers and taking the ticks. This done, the dwelling house and pastor's study was set on fire, and away they went. On the same Sabbath morning they found a pious young man, by the name of William Strong, quietly reading his Bible. He, Ferguson, either in person or by his direction, shot. The mother of Capt. John McLure, a widow, lived in the same community. Her house these Tories also burned. Some time before this, perhaps about the first of June, a party having been sent out on one of these plundering expeditions had burned one of Col. William Hill's iron works on Allison Creek, York county, S.C. On their way to accomplish this deed, they burned the barn of Mr. Simril and perpetrated other foul and wicked deeds. The country for many miles all around Union church was constantly full of these plunderers.

At this time, Gen. Sumter was at Clem's branch, in the upper corner of Lancaster county. His place of rendezvous became known to the refugees from the upper section of South Carolina. To him they flocked, and it was not long until the nucleus of a little army was formed.

On the west side of the Catawba, the patriots were not idle. Edward Lacey, John McLure, William Bratton, John Mills, and many others were busily engaged in gathering up the patriots of York and Chester counties. The patriots readily joined these men and it was only a short time until four hundred men were ready for service. These were at this time nearly all the fighting men in the two counties. It was now determined to drive Huck and Ferguson from the county. About the time that Lacey, Bratton and McLure determined to drive Huck's forces from the Fishing Creek region, Cols. Hill and Neil were sent over the Catawba, to beat up recruits for Sumter's army, then forming on Clem's branch. When Hill and Neil heard that Bratton, Lacey and McLure had determined to attack Huck and Ferguson, they at once concluded to join in with these patriots. Hill and Neil had one hundred and thirty-three men. A junction was formed and the united forces amounted to more than five hundred men. It was determined to attack Huck and Ferguson during the night of the 11th of July at White's, now Williford's Mill. It was concerted that Captain McLure and a party under him should be sent out during the day to reconnoiter and that the whole force should be in the neighborhood before dark. About sundown, all arrived within a few hundred yards of the mill and, having tied their horses in the woods, without any commander, arranged themselves into platoons of six and commenced to march for Huck's camp. Just at this moment the first platoon, in which was Lacey, was met by McLure and his reconnoitering party, who told them that Huck had decamped during the day, and had gone to what is now Brattonville, ten miles south of Yorkville. A consultation was held by the leading spirits, and it was determined to follow Huck and Ferguson and attack them that night as they were distant only about fifteen miles. The word was given, "March, to your horses." Some of those who had not learned that the enemy was gone, supposing that the command "march, to your horses" meant retreat, rushed with all possible speed to their horses, and so great was the effect upon the minds of one hundred and fifty that, having mounted their horses, they never stopped till they reached Charlotte, North Carolina. So soon as the facts in the case were learned, everything became quiet and another consultation was held. It was again determined to make an attack upon the British and Tories before morning. They had only three hundred and fifty men. They set out on Huck's trail and had no difficulty in following it. Col. Lacey's father lived only a few miles from Bratton's, where it was thought the enemy was encamped. As was not uncommon in the Revolutionary war, old Lacey was an uncompromising loyalist, and so was his son, Reuben; but his son Edward was as uncompromising a Whig. Edward Lacey knew that his father, if he learned that the Whigs were about to attack the British, would be sure to go to the British camp and announce the fact. To prevent this, Edward Lacey sent a detail of four men to guard his father until morning and, as he knew his father to be both a shrewd and determined man, he gave them permission to tie him. The guard, finding that the old man could be controlled in no other way, did actually tie him and thus prevented him from frustrating the plans of his son and the other patriots.

Having arrived in the neighborhood of Bratton's, Col. Edward Lacey and Capt. John Mills, the grandfather of Thomas S. Mills of Chesterville, were sent out to learn the exact position of the enemy's camp. They learned that Reuben Lacey, the brother of Col. Edward Lacey, had gone the evening before to the British camp. Edward knew that his brother was an early riser and that he would be certain to return home in the morning before daylight. The two scouts, Mills and Lacey, place themselves near by the road which they knew Reuben Lacey would be obliged to travel in returning home. Here they waited quietly for

his return. Edward Lacey was right in his conjecture. Before day, Reuben came along. He was blind of one eye and, what was somewhat remarkable, he rode a horse that was blind of one eye, and he had a dog that was blind of one eye. This dog followed him everywhere he went. So soon as blind Reuben, on his blind horse, followed by his blind dog, came nearly opposite the place occupied by Edward Lacey and John Mills, he was accosted by Mills, in a feigned voice, with the demand "Who comes there?"

"A friend."

"A friend of whom?"

"Of the British."

"So are we; where is the camp?"

"At Williamson's, two miles ahead."

"Where are the sentinels posted?"

"One is north of Williamson's on the road, at the branch, another is half way between Bratton's and Williamson's; one about one hundred yards south of Williamson's house; and another is east of Williamson's, toward the creek."

This was all that the scouts desired to know. They bid blind Reuben Lacey good morning and hastened to communicate the important information to their comrades. The plan of attack was soon determined on. The whole force was divided into two divisions; one to be led by Bratton and Neil and the other to be led by Edward Lacey. Bratton and Neil were to lead their men up the road which passed by Williamson's house, whilst Lacey was to lead his men down the same road. The divisions were to meet at Williamson's. James Moore, understanding the locality, acted as guide for Lacey. At the branch, the sentinel was found posted, but was asleep. Samuel Williamson, the son of James Williamson, at whose house Huck and Ferguson were encamped, shot the sentinel down. This was the first man killed in the fight, and it occurred on the morning of the 12th of July, 1780. The British and Tories under Huck and Ferguson had, on the evening before, come to the house of Col. William Bratton and ordered Mrs. Martha Bratton to prepare supper for them. Mrs. Bratton's first thought was to prepare them a sumptuous repast, but to poison the food and thus exterminate all who might partake of her dainties. She had the poison in her house; but when the time came to make use of it, she refrained from the desperate act; lest she might do more harm than good.

Whilst supper was preparing, Huck nursed John Bratton, the father of a large family, many of whom are residents of York county. Huck asked Mrs. Bratton where her husband was. She replied, "In Sumter's army." Huck told her if she would send for him and induce him to join the British, he should have a commission in the regular army. This offer Mrs. Bratton treated with indignity, telling him she would rather her husband would fight the British and Tories than to fight with or for them. Huck became enraged and dashed the child from his knees, and, an ill-bred soldier, seized a sickle which was near by, and with it was about to cut the throat of the brave woman. He was only prevented from perpetrating this savage deed by the officer second in command to Huck. After supper, their camp was formed at Williamson's, less than half a mile from Bratton's. The road ran by Williamson's house on the east. The house and yard were fenced up. The British and Tories were inside of this enclosure. Just as day began to dawn, the patriots began the attack on the north and east of the house. They were only about seventy-five yards from where the British and Tories were lying, sound asleep in their tents. It was a complete surprise. They suspected no harm. When the firing first commenced, Huck woke up, but thought it was only some straggling patriots who had stolen in upon his camp and that the whole thing would be over as soon as the British regulars poured in one volley. With this impression on his mind, he turned over to finish his morning nap. Still the firing continued. In haste he arose from his bed, put on his shoes and pants, and ran out without a coat and commenced to ride back and forward along his line. Thomas Carroll, who lived and died on Toole's fork, near the present residence of Dr. Calvin P. Sandifer, seeing him and regarding him as of more than ordinary importance, rested his gun in the fork of a plum tree, saying to his companions near by: "I am going to try that fellow on horseback in his shirt sleeves, and if I kill him you will know it, for I have two balls in my gun." He fired, the man fell, and, after the battle was over, Huck was found dead with two bullet holes in his head, one only a short distance above the other.

Before Huck rose from his bed, Ferguson had attempted to drive the patriots away by the bayonet, but he failed. They fought behind the fence, which surrounded the house, and were not exposed. Ferguson and his British regulars were forced to give way before the murderous fire of the patriots. So soon as it was learned by the British and Tories that Huck had fallen, they became confused. The patriots were not long in making this discovery and the command was given: "Boys, take the fence and every man his own commander!" No sooner was the order given than it was executed. Over the fence the Whigs leaped and were, in a moment, right among the British and Tories. The cry for quarters soon became universal.

Even Ferguson raised his voice and pleaded for mercy. This could not be granted, because it was known that either by him or by his orders, William Strong was shot in his own house on the 11th of June. Ferguson was killed on the spot. The British and Tory force was scattered to the winds. Near forty were left on the battle ground, amongst which number was the profane Huck and the cruel Ferguson. About fifty were wounded; at least fifty were found wounded on the battle field and others, wounded, fled but afterwards perished in the woods. How many were taken prisoners is not known; but the officer second in command was amongst the number and his life was spared on account of the entreaties of Mrs. Bratton, whose life he had saved on the previous evening. The conflict lasted about one hour; and strange to say, only one Whig, whose name was Campbell, was killed.

On the evening of the battle, whilst at Bratton's house, Capt. Huck sent James McRanell, Thomas Clendenin, Robert Bratton, Charles Curry and John Moore - all old men - to a crib there to be guarded during the night. When the battle began, the old men rose upon their guard and when John Moore, Jr. went during the fight to release the old men, he found them guarding the guard which had been placed over them.

The wounded British and Tories were sent to the houses of the loyal families in the neighborhood and waited upon by Dr. Turner, who resided in the community.

The sword of Huck fell to the lot of Thomas Carroll. No doubt he received this as a reward for having killed the vile swearer. In his old age, Thomas Carroll became very much doted. One of the strange acts of his old age was, even when he was near ninety-five years old, to buckle on the sword of Huck and, by the assistance of his sons, John and Joseph, mount a fine black horse, which he owned, and flourish his sword as if he was a military captain in the bloom of youth.

Immediately before the battle commenced, Col. Bratton, knowing his house was on the battle ground and that his family would be exposed to the fire from the Whigs as well as the British, desired to go and inform his wife that she might protect herself and family. Col. Lacey, who was a most impetuous creature and, at the same time, a powerful man physically, swore that if he dared to do such a thing, it might frustrate all the plans of the Whigs, and he would run his sword through him if he attempted such a thing.

Bratton did not go to inform his wife of her danger; but when the firing commenced, Mrs. Bratton placed her little son in the chimney as a place of safety. A ball struck the opposite jamb and bounded back. This the little fellow secured as a keepsake.

The house in which Col. Bratton was living is still standing. It is said the timbers still contain bullets that were shot at the time of the battle. It is still owned by a descendant of Col. William Bratton.

The battles of Ramsour's Mill and Williamson's were productive of great good to the cause of the Whigs. They stopped, at least for a time, the plundering of the Tories and taught the patriots that they might dare to meet British regulars.

It would be interesting to see a full list of the names of those who were at the battle of Williamson's and Huck's defeat. This might once have been secured. It is now too late. We give below the names of the actors on that memorable morning, that we have been able to gather up. As there was really no commanding officer, but each man was his own commander, and as numbers of individuals distinguished themselves during the war and were promoted, we give simply the names without any title:

John McLure, James McLure, William Bratton, Hugh Bratton, Thomas Bratton, Thomas Carroll, John Moffett, John Nixon, James Moore, James Hemphill, James Mitchell, John McConnell, John Chambers, Jas. Wallace, William Guy, Andrew Love, Chas. Curry, John Kidd, Alexander Moore, Wm. Moore, John Moore, and his four sons, John, Samuel, William and Nathan, Robert Howie, David Leech, John Carson, William Hanna, James Hanna, William Davidson, Edward Lacey, John Mills, William Burris, Richard Wynn, John Miller, John Swann, James Ross, William Ross, Charles Miles, Robert Ashe, James McElwee, John Smith, Peter Wylie, Robert Brown, Thomas Rainey, Samuel Rainey, Benjamin Rainey, Francis Wylie, Joseph Gaston, Samuel Kelsey, James Adair, Wm. Adair, John McCaw, Wm. Lewis, John Martin, John Dennis, Thomas Boggs, David Sadler, G. Jameison, John Barry, William Carson, John Wallace, Henry Ray, James Gill, Thomas Gill, Arthur Gill, John Carroll, John Williamson, Adam Williamson, Samuel Williamson, George Williamson and James Williamson, all sons of Jas. Williamson, at whose house the British and Tories were encamped.

Installment XVI

GENERAL PREPARATIONS - ROCKY MOUNT

In order that we may have a clear and distinct knowledge of the subsequent movements of the contending powers, it is necessary that we have a correct and exact knowledge of the disposition of the British forces in South Carolina. When on the 5th of June, 1780, Sir Henry Clinton set out for New York, the command of the southern division of the British army in American was entrusted to Lieutenant General Earl Cornwallis. No better selection could have been made. Cornwallis was a soldier by choice and a soldier by profession. Brave, energetic and skillful, he entered upon the discharge of his duty as a soldier. In this particular instance, however, not because he thought it was right in the English government to subjugate the North American colonies, but because, as a soldier, he felt that it was his duty to obey. The subaltern officers designed to assist in executing the task assigned to him were, generally, skillful leaders and some of them were dashing heroes.

To keep South Carolina and Georgia in subjection, and when the proper time arrived to subdue North Carolina, Sir Henry Clinton left Cornwallis six thousand and five hundred effective troops. These troops were British regulars, hired Hessians and loyalists from the colonies. This force, to all human appearances, was more than sufficient. Both Georgia and South Carolina were lying prostrate, at least in appearance, at the feet of the British lion. Still it was the design of the British commander to augment his force by enrolling the loyalists scattered over the state.

So soon as the force was sufficiently strong, and the season of the year and the supplies of the country would warrant it, the commander contemplated marching into North Carolina and, having reduced that state, then to continue his progress northward until a junction was formed with the northern division of his Majesty's forces. In vision, both Clinton and Cornwallis saw the American forces melting away and the British flag waving in triumph from Boston to Savannah. It was a dream and, like most dreams, never realized.

To keep Georgia and South Carolina in subjection and be convenient at the proper time to advance northward, the following disposition was made of the British forces in the south: Savannah, the capital of Georgia, was garrisoned by a corps of Hessians and loyalists, under the command of Col. Alured Clark; Augusta was entrusted to Col. Thomas Brown, a Tory. His forces consisted mostly of loyalists from the adjacent regions of South Carolina and Georgia. Lord Rawdon, with the twenty-third and thirty-third regiments of infantry, a legion of volunteers from Ireland, Brown and Hamilton's corps of loyalists, and a detachment of artillery, was stationed at Camden. Major McArthur, with the seventy-first regiment of regulars, was stationed at Cheraw; Lieutenant Colonel Balfour was placed in command of a garrison at

Ninety-Six, and Lieutenant Colonel Turnbull was stationed at Rocky Mount, on the Catawba. Brigadier General Patterson, with three regiments of British regulars, two battalions of Hessians, a detachment of artillery, and whatever number loyalists he could gather up, was stationed at Charleston. At several other points, as necessity seemed to require, small detachments were stationed.

Taking everything in consideration, one would surmise that there was not even a possibility for South Carolina to make even an attempt to release themselves from the heel of the invader. As we have already seen, when Buford's command, on the 29th of May, 1780, was cut to pieces by Tarleton, the patriots had no armed forces left in the state. Instead of giving up in despair, those who could do so left the state and began to prepare for renewing the conflict.

It has been customary to say that the approach of General Gates, at the head of a considerable number of Continental troops, infused life into the people of the two Carolinas. This is not true. Sumter, Marion, Pickens, Clarke, Rutherford, Locke, Davie, Davidson, and a multitude of others, were preparing to meet the British.

The progress of the enemy through the country was announced, by refugees from Georgia and South Carolina, to the Whigs in western North Carolina and southwestern Virginia. Campbell, Shelby, Sevier, McDowell, and other patriotic spirits, determined to aid their kindred and their friends. The Whigs of the whole of upper South Carolina, northern Georgia, and southwestern North Carolina, were concerting measures to drive the king's troops and the king's friends from the shores of North Carolina.

After the defeat of Huck at Williamson's on the 12th of July, 1780, those of the British and loyalists who escaped made their way to Rocky Mount. The Whigs dispersed; some going home, and others joining Sumter at Clem's Branch. As is generally the case, victory had infused life and energy into the minds of the Whigs in all the region around Williamson's. Sumter's army at Clem's Branch began to increase rapidly. The Whigs of Fairfield, Chester, York and Lancaster counties were not long in discovering that Clem's Branch was a safe retreat and that Thomas Sumter was competent to lead a partisan corps to victory.

What was joy to the Whigs, was sorrow to the British and Tories. Fear and trembling seized the whole fraternity, from Cornwallis down to the meanest thieving Tory. After the fall of Charleston and the establishment of a chain of garrisons in the up-country, they had not even contemplated that the Whigs would make an effort to resist the king's troops; much less did they contemplate that the king's troops would be defeated, routed and cut to pieces by a band of unofficered and undisciplined farmers.

Sumter knew that the only way that the troops which were gathered around him, at Clem's Branch, could be retained and be of advantage to the country, was to keep them busy. It would have been impossible to have made Clem's Branch a drill camp. The men who had collected at that point would have rebelled against any such a course. Sumter was aware of this. He knew that the men were burning with hatred toward the invaders of their country and were anxious to be led into battle. They needed training; but they must not be trained in the camp, but on the battle field. After the fight at Williamson's, he began to look around for some enterprise in which he might engage the people who had flocked to his camp. The British post at Rocky Mount was selected as the place upon which to make an attack.

Rocky Mount is in the extreme southwestern corner of Chester county, between big Rocky Creek and the Catawba River. Lieutenant Colonel Turnbull was in command of the post. The garrison consisted of something more than three hundred soldiers - all loyalists. One hundred and fifty were New York loyalists and about the same number of South Carolina Tories. The place itself consisted of a rocky eminence; hence the name, Rocky Mount. The artificial fortifications consisted of two log houses, with loop-holes, which were surrounded with a ditch and abattis, the latter of which was some distance from the house.

The region around Rocky Mount was settled by Scotch-Irish Presbyterians - Covenanters. They were all Whigs. Not one of them took British protection. They never intended to submit to British rule. The Rev. William Martin was, at that time, pastor of the Catholic church. In every way that he could he stirred the people up to resist the encroachments of the British and the Tories. In the pulpit and out of it, he was the bold advocate for American independence. To keep these Scotch-Irish quiet was one object the British had in view in stationing a garrison at Rocky Mount. The truth is, the British hated them, and the British officers frankly acknowledged they feared them. They were troublesome. No defeat could discourage them; no victory could so elate them as to throw them off their guard.

East of Rocky Mount, in Lancaster county, is Hanging Rock. Here a British garrison also was stationed under the command of Col. Cardon. It was concerted by Sumter and Davie of North Carolina that a simultaneous attack should be made upon Rocky

Mount and Hanging Rock. The object was to prevent troops from being sent from one point to the other. The distance between the two garrisons was about fifteen miles.

To carry out this plan, Sumter moved down to Davie's camp on Waxhaw Creek. On the morning of the thirtieth of July, Sumter and Davie set out with their respective troops. Sumter crossed the Catawba River at what was then Blair's ford. He was accompanied by Cols. Neil, Lacey and Irvine, and Captain John McLure. Davie passed down the east side of the Catawba.

Early on the morning of the 31st, Sumter reached Rocky Mount. A Tory had apprised Turnbull of Sumter's approach, and preparations had been made to give Sumter and his men a warm reception. Sumter had no cannon. The Whigs poured volley after volley into the fortifications, and the British were soon forced to take refuge in the log houses. Here the enemy was safe and no victory could be gained unless they could be driven from the houses or the houses be destroyed. The houses were situated at the bottom of a slope. The idea occurred to Sumter that the houses might be burned. Accordingly, an old wagon was loaded with dry brush and straw, gathered from the abattis, and rolled down against the houses, having first been set on fire. This failed.

Sumter then, with his impetuosity, called out for two men to volunteer to set the houses on fire. Col. William Hill, the grandfather of Gen. D. H. Hill, and James Johnson stepped out and offered their services. An armful of rich pine was provided and the heroes set out to accomplish the task. If they were so fortunate as to succeed, Col. Turnbull would be made a prisoner; and if they failed he would be permitted to live to fight some other day. They had to face the loop holes of the houses. In front of them was a large rock. Protected by this, they boldly proceeded to accomplish their dangerous undertaking. Crouching on all fours, keeping the rock between them and the house, they boldly advanced. Johnson carried the armful of pine and Hill watched the enemy. When they arrived at the proper distance, in the face of a terrific fire, Johnson rushed forward and threw the burning faggots on top of the houses. The flames began to roll toward the heavens. Hill and Johnson rushed back to their fellows. Their clothes were literally riddled with bullets and the locks of their hair shot away.

Turnbull hung out a flag indicating his readiness to surrender. Sumter ordered his men to cease firing. Just at this moment, when both parties thought Rocky Mount and Turnbull would soon be in the hands of the patriots, it began to rain and extinguish the flames.

Sumter, now seeing that nothing could be done, led his men away and, having crossed the Catawba at Lansford, went back to Clem's Branch.

At this time, there were a number of Whig prisoners in the houses. Amongst these prisoners was the brave old covenanter preacher, William Martin. The Whig women of the neighborhood came to the spot so soon as the firing was heard. They came not to idly look on, but to act as angels of mercy to the wounded, and to fight if there should be need for it. No accurate count of Sumter's loss was kept. Amongst those who fell was Col. Neil. The British lost twenty in killed and wounded.

Neither Sumter nor his men were discouraged. They did all that men, situated as they were, could have done. The raw militia stood the fire of the enemy like veterans.

At ten o'clock on the same day, Major Davie, with forty riflemen and about the same number of cavalrymen, attacked a party of the British at a house in the immediate vicinity of Hanging Rock. Davie captured sixty horses and one hundred muskets and, without the loss of a man, reached his camp.

BATTLE OF HANGING ROCK

The upper counties of South Carolina are classic ground. As time rolls on, the thrilling events which transpired in this region during the Revolutionary struggle gathers around them a kind of enchantment. A Saratoga and Yorktown may be more imposing and their memories may be more deeply cherished, because more generally known; but the fields upon which the greatest daring was exhibited, and the most brilliant deeds accomplished during the war for independence, was in North and South Carolina. Brave men, and no less brave women, entered into the contest; not because they loved war, but because they hated oppression and loved liberty, without which, they rightly thought, there could be no peace. When the British had completed their chain of military posts, reaching from the Savannah River to the Atlantic ocean, they thought their work was done. Nothing more, it was thought, remained for the troops of George the Third to do, but the reorganization of the civil affairs of the state.

From the lipid waters of the Watauga and the Nollichucky, to the swamps of Georgia, brave and daring men were assembling and talking over the state of affairs. By multitudes of those who had been driven from their homes by the invading foe to seek a place of refuge in the vastnesses of the mountains, was uttered in sullen mutterings and knit brows - "give me liberty or give me death."

Major William Richardson Davie formed a camp on the north side of Waxhaw Creek. To this brave North Carolinian, Colonel Higgins, with the Mecklenburg militia, Col. Crawford with some South Carolina troops and thirty-five Catawba Indians under their chief, New River, repaired. Between the two Carolinas there was the kindest feeling and the greatest concert of action. They had only one object in view, and that was to establish the independence of the colonies.

In the southern part of Lancaster county, near the dividing line between Kershaw and Lancaster, on the road leading from Lancaster village to Camden, is a remarkable rock. From the peculiar shape, it is called "Hanging Rock," and it gives its name to the creek on the east bank of which it stands. Hanging Rock is about twelve miles, in a direct line, east of Rocky Mount and about the same distance a little east of south from Lancaster village, and between twenty and twenty-five miles northwest of Camden. In shape and substance this rock, as well as multitudes of others in the same community, is an object of wonder. Huge boulders are piled on top of each other, presenting to the beholder a most fantastic appearance. In substance these rocks are small, irregular, hexagonal flint stones, mixed with brilliant matter, black and smooth. The whole is cemented together, forming a beautiful and wonderful conglomeration. The one which bears the name of Hanging Rock is twenty-five feet in diameter and near one hundred feet high. On the west side it is hollowed out, presenting an appearance not unlike that of the rind of one-quarter of an orange.

Near this remarkable rock - on the west bank of Hanging Rock Creek - Major Carden was place in command of the British garrison. Here, on the sixth of August, 1780, the patriots under Sumter gained a victory over the British forces. Before, however, we undertake to give a sketch of the battle of Hanging Rock, let us go back for a short time and view the events which occurred in the vicinity.

On the thirty-first of July, Sumter attacked the British post at Rocky Mount and failed because he had no cannon with which to demolish the log houses into which the British retreated. On the same day, Major Davie made a feint upon a detachment of the British post at Hanging Rock. The results of this brilliant affair we gave in the sketch of Rocky Mount. It is, however, worthy of a more minute description.

From the camp of Davie, on Waxhaw Creek, Sumter and Davie set out on the night of the twenty-ninth of July. Sumter's point of destination was Rocky Mount; that of Davie, Hanging Rock. The two commands marched together until they came to the forks of the road, when the troops under Sumter took the road leading to Landsford. About sunrise, the forces crossed the Catawba. Davie led his force, consisting of about eighty men, down the east side of the Catawba and, in due time, they arrived in the neighborhood of Hanging Rock.

Whilst reconnoitering, he learned that three companies of mounted infantry, belonging to Bryan's command, were at a house in the immediate neighborhood. These light infantry, having been sent out on a plundering expedition, were returning to Major Carden's camp. For some reason they had made a halt at this private house. Davie at once determined to direct his attention to them, rather than to the main post. The house was at the bend of a lane, one end of which led to a woods and the other end to the main camp of the British. The troops were so disposed that a portion of the cavalry was between those at the house and Carden's camp. Davie ordered the militia, who were all dressed in citizen's clothes, to enter the lane from the woods and charge down upon the detachment of the British. The sentinels of the enemy mistook the Whig militia for royalists and suffered them to pass unchallenged. The militia, having entered the lane, dismounted and poured in a deadly fire upon the detachment. Most of them were loyalists, and they became panic stricken at the first fire. Without making the least resistance, they made a dash for their camp. They were met by Davie's cavalry and cut to pieces.

Almost in a moment, and totally unexpected, they were surrounded by Davie's men. There was no time to take prisoners, for the whole affair took place in full view of the British camp. Having secured sixty-four horses and one hundred muskets, and leaving most of the British detachment dead on the ground, Davie, without the loss of a single man, set out at full speed for his camp. There were few more brilliant exploits than this performed during the war. The whole British camp was called out to pursue Davie, but it proved vain, as he reached his camp in safety.

It would be doing an injustice to the memory of Major Davie, not to mention another attack which he had made upon the British in the same region. About five miles from Hanging Rock is a place called the Flat Rock. It takes its name from a flat rock which covers nearly twenty acres of ground. A space covering four acres is naked, nearly flat, with pits a few inches in depth sunk in the surface. These pits are said to have been dug at an early period by the Indians for the purpose of holding water. Whilst

Major Davie was scouring the country between Waxhaw Creek and Hanging Rock, he learned that a wagon train, loaded with supplies for the garrison at Hanging Rock, was passing between the latter place and Camden. The supplies consisted of rum, provisions and clothing. The guard consisted of an escort of cavalry and volunteer loyalists. Davie determined to attack this supply train. On the twentieth of July, at Flat Rock, he came up with it and captured the whole party. After securing the prisoners and destroying the wagons and rum and provisions, he mounted the prisoners on captured horses and set out at dark for his camp. Captain Petit, with the guides and a detachment of cavalry, led the advance; William Polk, with a detachment of cavalry, took charge of the prisoners. His place was in the centre. The rear guard was under the command of Davie himself. Thus far, the whole affair had been a complete success. About midnight, just as the rear guard had entered a long lane, the van discovered some British concealed behind the lane fence, in a corn field. Major Davie had calculated that he would be pursued by the British and an attempt made to rescue the prisoners. He regarded this lane as a favorable locality for such an enterprise, and had strictly charged Capt. Petit to advance into the lane and examine it before the main body came up. This, from some oversight, Petit failed to do. So soon as the British were discovered they were challenged, but gave no answer On being challenged a second time, they answered with a volley of small arms. The whole Whig force was in the lane. The fire of the enemy commenced on the right and extended in a running fire, down to the rear. Davie, who perceived at once the condition of things, rushed to the front and endeavored to push the men through the lane as quickly as possible; but the advance party, under Petit, not knowing that the enemy were in their rear, turned back and could not be induced to advance. This caused the whole force to pass the ambushed enemy again. All that Davie could do was to retreat until he got out of the enemy's fire, and then file off and pass their patrols. This he did very successfully, under the circumstances. The loss of the Whigs was not great. The fire of the ambushed forces was, through mistake, directed against the British prisoners. These being mounted, two on a single horse, suffered fearfully. Lieutenant Elliott was killed and Capt. Petit and two men wounded. Davie and his party reached their camp next morning without any other loss.

After the fighting at Hanging Rock, the forces under Sumter and Davie were not discouraged. On the contrary, although no decisive victory had been gained at either place, both men and officers were anxious to meet the British and loyalists again. On consultation it was determined that the respective forces, under Sumter and Davie, should meet at Landsford on the Catawba on the fifth of August. The Mecklenburg militia, under Col. Irwin, and Major Davie's corps, with some volunteers, all amounting to five hundred, including officers and men, met, according to arrangement, Colonels Sumter, Lacey and Hill, at Landsford with three hundred men. Here a consultation was held, with reference to what British post would be next attacked. The consultation was very unmilitary in one particular. Usually only the officers consult when and how the enemy shall be attacked; but in this consultation they claimed all the importance that usually attaches only to the officers. Both officers and men concluded that, all things considered, Hanging Rock presented the most favorable point for an attack by a force such as was assembled. No doubt the facts pertaining to Hanging Rock post were better understood by Davie than any other officer present. He and his corps had been in its vicinity often and, on two occasions, to the great detriment of the loyalists.

The post at Hanging Rock was garrisoned by Col. Bryan's North Carolina loyalists, part of Col. Brown's Georgia and South Carolina loyalists, the infantry of Col. Tarleton's legion, and the Prince of Wales' American regiment. The whole amounted to about eight hundred men, mostly loyalists, and under the command of Major Carden.

The disposition of the British forces was judiciously made. Hanging Rock Creek was in the rear; on the right flank was the British regulars; on the left flank was the North Carolina Tory regiment. The centre was held by a part of Tarleton's legion and Hamilton's regiment of loyalists. The centre was separated from the left flank by a skirt of woods. Such was the position held by the troops in the centre, that it could not be assailed without exposing those who attacked it to a destructive fire. The troops in the centre were provided with a three-pounder and were protected by a deep ravine. Capt. McCullock commanded the centre.

About dark on the evening of the fifth of August, Sumter, Davie, Lacey, Irwin, Hill and the troops under them set out from the neighborhood of Lansford for Hanging Rock. At the dawn of day they arrived within two miles of the British camp. Here a halt was called, and the plan of attack settled. Sumter proposed that the troops march in three divisions and advance on horseback, directly against the centre of the British, and dismount when in sight of the enemy. This mode of attack was agreeable to all the officers except Davie, who advised that the horses be left at the place where they then were. His objection to advancing on horseback was the confusion which nearly always occurs when troops dismount in view of the enemy. Sumter's opinion prevailed and the disposition of the troops was quickly made. The command of the whole, by universal consent, was entrusted to Sumter. Davie commanded the division on the right, which was composed of his own corps and a small number of volunteers under Major Bryan. The column on the left which was composed of South Carolina refugees, mostly from Chester and York counties, was commanded by Hill. The centre, composed entirely of Mecklenburg militia, was led by Irwin.

In order to avoid the enemy's pickets, the three columns filed to the left of the road, with the intention to return to it before approaching the camp of the enemy. The guides went too far and when the approach to the enemy was made, it was found that the three divisions were all opposite Bryan's Tory regiment which constituted the left flank of the British. At seven o'clock in the morning the three divisions dismounted and rushed upon the Tories. Irwin made the first attack, which was soon followed by Hill and Davie. The Tories fled for protection to the centre of the camp. This post was held by Capt. McCullock, with one hundred and sixty of Tarleton's legion of infantry and some of Hamilton's North Carolina Tory regiment. The Whigs followed the discomfited Tories under Bryan, to within range of the centre of the British camp. Here they were unexpectedly met by a terrific fire from the British legion. The Whigs passed on. Twice they were charged with fixed bayonets by the British regulars. A desperate effort was made to retain the position and save the three-pounder. Nothing could withstand the impetuosity of the Americans. Although the British centre fought behind a fence and was protected by a ravine, it was forced to give way. When Bryan's Tory regiment fled, Brown's regiment was also struck with consternation. When, however, Brown's men saw the determination with which the British regulars fought, a detachment of them went to the assistance of McCullock. The Americans were not prepared for this and, before they were aware, a heavy fire was poured in upon the militia now off their guard on account of apparent victory. It was not long before these undisciplined Whigs rallied and, getting behind trees and bushes, made desperate havoc with their trusty rifles in the ranks of the enemy. In a few moments, every British officer was shot down and the Prince of Wales' American regiment nearly annihilated. Major Davie, seeing the condition of things, rushed out from the right flank of the American forces and shouted out: "Britons ground your arms! You have but one officer left; to the ground, if you lives are worth preserving." The order was quickly obeyed.

Right at this juncture of affairs, when a complete victory seemed to be within the grasp of the patriots, the whole thing was spoiled. The British commander, with great coolness, now led part of his remaining troops into his former position and formed them in a hollow square in open ground. Opposite to this and near the woods, the other part, consisting mostly of Hamilton's regiment of Tories, commenced forming. After the rout and surrender of a portion of the British, a very large number of the Whigs, thinking the victory complete, rushed to plundering the British camp. Not a few found the rum and were drunk in a short time. Sumter made a desperate effort to restore order and make another dash upon the enemy, but only two hundred men could be got together. Major Davie, with his corps, made an attack upon Hamilton's regiment, which was dispersed on the first attempt. Davie was prevented, however, from accomplishing anything of consequence from the fact that he was fired upon by two pieces of artillery. Fortune also seems to have favored the British Captains Stewart and McDonald with forty mounted infantry, returned from Rocky Mount just as the contest was in a critical condition. These officers, when they came in sight of the American forces, extended their files so as to make the most formidable appearance possible. This added to the confusion of the Americans and a retreat became absolutely necessary.

An hour was spent in plundering the British camp and making litters for the wounded. The two armies, both in great disorder, were in full view of each other. The British shouted three cheers for King George, and the Americans answered it with three cheers for George Washington. Loaded with plunder and many of them full of rum, the militia were arranged for retreat. All were tired; some were wounded and were being carried on litters, whilst many were straggling. Major Davie, with his corps, covered the retreat. Exposed as were the Americans on their retreat, they were not troubled by Major Carden. He was satisfied to let well enough alone. The American loss in killed and wounded never was correctly known. The British say that about one hundred dead and wounded Americans were left on the field. Captain John McLure was among the mortally wounded. He died a short time afterward at Charlotte, North Carolina. Colonel Hill and Major Wynn were also wounded. The British loss was much greater than that of the

Americans. Sixty of Tarleton's legion were killed and wounded. Capt. McCullock, who commanded the legion, and two other officers were killed.

Under the circumstances, the Americans had the decided advantage in the battle of Hanging Rock. Nearly all the men except Davie's corps were raw militia and totally ungovernable when the action commenced. Had his soldiers not got to plundering and drinking, Sumter would have demolished Carden's command.

INSTALLMENT XVIII

THE BATTLE OF CAMDEN

In order that we may as far as possible keep up the chain of events, it will be necessary that we go back and take a cursory view of the general affairs of the American forces during the early part of 1780. General Washington saw so soon as Sir Henry Clinton directed his attention toward Savannah and Charleston that it was the intention of the British general to make the south the seat of war.

Heretofore this section had suffered comparatively nothing by war. The seat of hostilities had been in the north. The Americans had in one sense been unsuccessful; in another sense they had been very successful. They had gained no decisive victories and, in several instances, had suffered very great reverses. Still the Americans in the north were successful. They had baffled the efforts of the British. The country was no nearer being subjugated than it was after the battle of Lexington. Sir Henry Clinton determined to subject, at the same time, the extremes of the colonies to the horrors of war. His object was to subdue the southern states in detail. Success crowned his first effort, but in the end fortune deserted him.

To assist General Lincoln in his efforts to beat back the invading foe, General Washington was not prepared to do much. The American army of the north was weak and the British had a well appointed force in that region, which required constant watching. Notwithstanding the straitened circumstances of the commander-in-chief of the American forces, he determined to send Gen. Lincoln all the assistance in his power. For the purpose of reinforcing the southern army, the Maryland and Delaware troops, amounting to fourteen hundred effective men under the command of Baron DeKalb, were selected.

On the fourteenth of April, 1780, DeKalb left Morristown, New Jersey, for the south. He passed through Petersburg, Virginia, early in June. Then he passed through Hillsborough, North Carolina, and encamped on Deep River on the sixth of July. Two months previous to this, Charleston, South Carolina had fallen into the hands of the British and Gen. Benjamin Lincoln, the commander of the southern army, was a prisoner on parole. Baron DeKalb was consequently the commander of the southern army.

The Colonial Congress, always patriotic, generally in great straits, and sometimes not very wise or just in its decisions, determined to place some man of greater fame than DeKalb at the head of the southern army. General Horatio Gates, the illegitimate son of Horace Walpole, Lord Oxford of England, was at this time at the zenith of his glory. At Saratoga the army under his command gained a victory over General Burgoyne. The honor of that victory was not due to General Gates, but to Generals Schuyler, Arnold and Morgan.

On the thirteenth of June, General Gates was appointed by congress to the command of the southern army. DeKalb was then between Petersburg, Virginia and Deep River in North Carolina. Gen. Gates was at his home in Virginia, near Shepherdstown, when he received the appointment. General Gates was a man of good mind, a fine classical scholar, and bred a soldier; but withal a vain man who would not scruple to do a dishonorable act, provided his own position would be advanced or his power increased. His heart was set upon the position held by Washington and he had used means to have Washington removed and himself placed in his place. General Gates was one of those men who could bear neither success nor defeat.

Thirteen days after his appointment to the command of the southern army he set out with a heart full of joy. In vision, many Saratogas loomed up before him. Charles Lee, who was strongly eccentric, remarked to Gates on his setting out for the south: "Take care that you do not exchange northern laurels for southern willows." The words were, as we will see, prophetic.

On the twenty-fifth of July, Gates, with his secretary, William Clajon, reached DeKalb's camp on Deep River. The army which he was appointed to command and the circumstances by which he was surrounded was calculated to chill his ardor; but his hopes were as great as his ambition. It was now midsummer. The troops were poorly provided for and the country greatly depressed. General Caswell was in the field with a considerable force of North Carolina militia. The first step taken by General Gates was to form a junction of his troops with those of General Caswell. Retaining DeKalb in command of his own division, the troops crossed Deep River at Buffalo ford, on the afternoon of the twenty-seventh of July, just two days after he had taken command of the southern army. This shows that he was not disposed to idle his time in loitering about camp. During the evening of the twenty-seventh, a consultation was held with regard to the future movements of the army. DeKalb and Colonel Otho H. Williams, acting adjutant-general, advised that the army be led to Charlotte and that the heavy baggage and women be left at Salisbury. It was also recommended by DeKalb and Williams that a hospital and magazine be established at Salisbury. From Charlotte, it was proposed to lead the army toward Camden, South Carolina, through the Waxhaw settlement. The reason assigned for this course was that the army would be led through a rich country, inhabited by Whigs, and, in the event a retreat should be necessary, they would have something to fall back on at Salisbury.

In the counsel of DeKalb and Williams, there was a vast amount of good sense, but Gen. Gates would do his own way. He was encamped on the road leading to Camden, and to no other place would he go but to Camden. He was anxious to meet the foe as soon as possible. The shortest route to Camden, no matter what might be its disadvantages, was the route he would go and no other. On the morning of the twenty-eighth, he was joined by Colonel Porterfield and one hundred Virginians. At once, the army, with General Gates at its head, set out for Camden.

The sufferings of the army under General Gates, in its march toward Camden, can be better imagined than described. The country was poor and but sparsely populated. The army was poorly provided with supplies and the country afforded neither bread nor meat. The weather was intensely hot and the men sick. The bad food and green corn and peaches the solders were forced to eat, in order to support life, brought on disease and aggravated it when contracted. Gen. Gates, in spite of all impediments, pushed on slowly but surely.

On the fourth of August, whilst encamped on Little Lynch's Creek, he issued a proclamation, in which he announced to the people of South Carolina that he had been enabled by the patriotic exertions of the citizens of the United States, to come to their assistance with a numerous, well-appointed, and formidable army. In one word, he was able and he was determined to compel their late triumphant and insulting foe to retreat from his strong posts with precipitation and dismay. His proclamation was, when compared with his future conduct, mere braggadocio. In the same proclamation, pardon was offered to all except those who, in the hour of devastation, had exercised acts of barbarity and depredation on the persons and property of their fellow citizens.

On the sixth of August - the day that Sumter gained a partial victory over Colonel Carden at Hanging Rock, and only a few miles from that place on Lynch's Creek, General Gates was joined by General Caswell with his North Carolina militia.

Lord Cornwallis was in Charleston, adjusting the civil affairs of the state and maturing his plans for his future operations. So soon as he learned that General Gates was approaching with a considerable army, he left Charleston, on the thirteenth of August, for the British camp at Camden. Previous to his arrival, Lord Rawdon was in command of the post. This officer, on the near approach of General Gates, had called in his outposts. The principal points, at which detachments were stationed, were Cheraw, Hanging Rock, Rocky Mount, and Rugeley's Mill. Lord Rawdon, thinking it would be to his disadvantage to suffer Gates to attack him at Camden, marched out with nearly all his available force and took position at a strong post on Lynch's Creek. The two armies lay for four days facing each other with nothing between them but Lynch's Creek. Here, Gates began to blunder. Rawdon's post was strong and Gates hesitated to attack him, but he could have flanked Rawdon with the greatest ease and captured all his heavy baggage and put himself in a position to attack the British in detail. Lord Rawdon was aware of this and sent an order to Col. Cruger to send, from Ninety-Six, four companies of light infantry. Carden was ordered to Camden and Turnbull was directed to join Ferguson on Little River.

It is evident that Lord Rawdon had become greatly alarmed. The battles fought by Sumter, Davie and others at Flat Rock, Rocky Mount and Hanging Rock, as well as the great name of Gates, had filled the minds of both British and loyalists.

On the day that the battle of Hanging Rock was fought, Colonel Tarleton, with thirty dragoons and forty mounted militia, which he had picked up in Charleston, crossed the Santee at Lannieu's ferry. For some time, Tarleton had been prostrated with a fever. He was sick in Charleston and his legion was being cut to pieces by Sumter's and Davie's men. Tarleton, with his small force, scoured the region bordering on the Santee, striking terror as he was wont, into the inhabitants. After having committed various depredations, he set out for Camden.

Deceiving the inhabitants of the Black River region by pretending that he was an American officer on his way to join Gates, he secured a man by the name of Bradley, a member of the general assembly of South Carolina, as a guide. Bradley, with a few friends, conducted Tarleton safely until the neighborhood of the British camp was reached. At this point, Tarleton secured Bradley and his friends as prisoners and conducted them to Camden.

Tarleton joined Rawdon at Lynch's Creek on the 12th of August. On the same day, General Gates gave signs that he was about to move his camp to Rugeley's Mill. Rawdon gave orders to evacuate that point at once. He and the troops which were stationed at Rugeley's Mill and Lynch's Creek moved back to Logtown, near Camden. On the next day, Cornwallis arrived at Camden. He began to prepare for active operations at once. The troops were reviewed. The force from Ninety-Six arrived on the same day that Cornwallis did, but many of the British were sick. It was hazardous in Cornwallis to fight; it was more so to suffer himself to be attacked by Gates.

On the same day that Cornwallis arrived at Camden, General Gates moved the American army to Rugeley's Mill, about fourteen miles from Camden. By a strange coincidence, both generals began to make preparations to do the same. Gates contemplated surprising Cornwallis, and Cornwallis contemplated surprising Gates.

General Sumter, who was on the lookout for small parties of the British, learned that a large wagon train was approaching Camden from Ninety-Six. These wagons, under a small escort, were conveying supplies to the main army. Sumter advised General Gates of the fact. Gates detailed one hundred infantry, a company of artillery of the Maryland line, and three hundred North Carolina militia to assist Sumter in capturing this provision train. On the fifteenth of August, Sumter captured a small redoubt in Fairfield county and, intercepting the wagon train, secured forty-four wagons, loaded with various army supplies and several wagons loaded with sick and worn out soldiers. This was a brilliant affair, but in the end amounted to nothing, as we will, at the proper place, see.

At Rugeley's Mill, Gates posted the Maryland brigades, the Delaware regiment, the cannon, the cavalry, the baggage, and the militia on the north side of Granny's Quarter Creek. Colonel Armstrong's corps and Colonel Porterfield's command were posted on the south side, on the road leading to Camden.

On the fourteenth, seven hundred Virginia militia under Gen. Stevens joined Gates at Rugeley's. On the fifteenth, Cornwallis issued orders for the troops to be ready to march at a moments warning. In the afternoon of the same day, Col. Tarleton was sent out for the purpose of gaining intelligence respecting the American army. Abut ten miles from Camden, on the road to Rugeley's Mill, three American soldiers were captured. From these, Tarleton secured all the information he desired. From them, he learned that General Gates intended setting out for Camden that night. Tarleton hastened back to Camden with his prisoners. Cornwallis examined them carefully, and was convinced that Gates contemplated making an attack upon him as soon as he reached his camp. Orders were given at once for the troops to parade. At 10 o'clock the march to meet Gates commenced. Major McArthur, with a small force, was left in charge of the town. The British army set out from Camden in the following order: The first division was commanded by Lieutenant Colonel Webster. His advance guard was composed of his own cavalry and some mounted infantry, supported by four companies of light infantry and the twenty-third and thirty-third regiments of regulars. The centre was commanded by Lord Rawdon. This force was composed of Hamilton and Bryan's corps of loyalists and some volunteers from Ireland. The seventy-first regiment formed the reserve. Each division had four pieces of artillery and the reserve two. The army of the British was arranged with the expectation that at some place on the march from Camden to Rugeley's Mill, the American army would be met.

On the fifteenth, General Gates issued an order that the sick, extra military stores, the heavy baggage, and such quartermaster stores as were not immediately wanted, be sent under a guard to Waxhaw. This was another blunder in General Gates. By this move, in the event a retreat would be necessary, he had no place to fall back upon. Had this, however, been the only blunder, it would not have amounted to much. The order was made for the troops to march precisely at 10 o'clock - the very time that the British were to march.

Cornwallis must have gained a very correct and accurate account of Gen. Gates' intentions. Midway between Camden and Rugeley's Mill, is Saunders' Creek. On the north side of this creek is a favorable position to engage in battle. The keen eye of Tarleton had not failed to discover this spot. Cornwallis was anxious to gain this place and he succeeded in doing so.

Precisely at 10 o'clock on the evening of the fifteenth of August, 1780, the American forces commenced their march toward Camden in the following order: Armand's corps, commanded by Col. Armand, formed the advance. This was an awful blunder in Gen. Gates. Col. Armand was a Frenchman and most of his officers were foreigners and, worse than all, the majority of his men were deserters and by no means to be depended upon in an emergency. However brave Col. Armand may have been, he could not, in the strict sense of the word, have been called patriotic.

Notwithstanding these facts, Gates put Armand's corps of deserters in the advance. On the right of Armand's corps, Col. Porterfield's light infantry were ordered to march, in Indian file, two hundred yards from the road. Col. Armstrong's light infantry were to march on the left of Armand's corps, in the same order as that pointed out to Col. Porterfield. The centre was composed for the first and second Maryland Brigades, together with the North Carolina and Virginia divisions. The volunteers formed the rear guard and the baggage was guarded by the cavalry. The most profound silence was to be kept during the march and any soldier firing a gun was to be put to death on the spot.

At midnight the British troops crossed Saunders' Creek. A few minutes past 2 o'clock, on the morning of the sixteenth of August, the van guards of the two armies met. This was unexpected to the American general. He fully believed that Cornwallis, on hearing of his approach to Camden, would retreat with precipitation and dismay. The van guards of both armies began to fire. Armand's corps cowardly wheeled back and, in great disorder, fled, producing confusion in the main divisions of the army. Armstrong and Porterfield gallantly rushed forward to the contest and brought the van guard of the British to a halt. The firing continued for about fifteen minutes when both parties ceased firing and, with intense anxiety, began to make preparations for a general battle so soon as day would dawn.

Cornwallis found that his position was most favorable. A swamp was on both sides of him and he could not be flanked. So soon as General Gates learned that the British army was in his front, ready to give him battle, he called his general officers together. It was now evident to all that Gen. Gates had made a miscalculation. He thought his great name would frighten the British. When the officers assembled, profound silence prevailed. No one dared, for a long time, to make even a suggestion, knowing that in all probability General Gates would do his own way, in any event. Gen. Stevens, of Virginia, at last dared to break the silence by remarking that "it was now too late to retreat." Gen. Gates, conscious, no doubt, that he had committed a huge blunder in leaving Rugeley's Mill so precipitately, replied: "Then we must fight! Gentlemen, please take your posts."

As day began to dawn, the two military commanders began to arrange their forces for the conflict. The British general placed the twenty-third and thirty-third regiments in the front line of the army on the right. This advance was commanded by Lieutenant Colonel Webster. His right rested on the swamp and his left extended to the road. The left front division, composed of Hamilton's and Bryan's loyalists, some Irish volunteers, and a legion of infantry, was commanded by Lord Rawdon. The left flank of Rawdon rested upon a swamp. The artillery was placed near the road. The cavalry were ordered, on account of the thickness of the wood, to remain in column, and be ready, when an opportunity presented itself, to dash in upon the Americans. The British force, including officers and men, numbered two thousand and two hundred.

Immediately after it was determined on the part of the American general to fight, he made the following disposition of his forces: The right wing, composed of three regiments of the Maryland line, was commanded by General Gist. The Virginia militia, commanded by Gen. Stevens, with some light infantry and Porterfield's corps, formed the left wing. The North Carolina militia, commanded by Gen. Caswell, formed the centre. Col. Armand supported the left wing with his cavalry. The artillery was placed mainly on the left of the right wing near the road. The exact number of men under the command of Gates, it is perhaps impossible to ascertain with certainty. The British authorities say that he had two thousand continentals and four thousand militia and state troops. This, no doubt, was the number on his muster roll; but there must have been at least two thousand absent.

When the light of day approached, Gen. Gates found some fault with the position held by Generals Caswell and Stevens. This he attempted to remedy by making a change in their positions. The British officers perceived this and reported it to Cornwallis. No sooner did Cornwallis learn this fact than he ordered Webster and Rawdon to make the attack at once. The fight became general in a few moments, all along the line. At the first onset the American artillery opened on the advancing columns of the British. Col. Williams and Gen. Stevens pressed upon the British right. Col. Webster, seeing this, brought his forces to bear upon Williams and Stevens and soon the Virginia militia gave way, and fled in confusion. The North Carolina militia soon became panic struck on seeing the Virginians flee and they fled too. The right of the Americans was gallantly defended by Gist and DeKalb.

The Continental troops and Dixon's regiment of North Carolina militia were left alone to meet the foe. The Maryland and Delaware troops fought with desperate courage. Notwithstanding the fact that the British were now flushed with victory and pressed forward with that impulse, the troops under DeKalb and

Gist stood firm. Colonels Hoard and Williams charged the enemy and broke their line.

The result of the battle was uncertain, Tarleton and Webster had been ordered to pursue the fugitives and drive them from the field. DeKalb, ignorant of the real state of things, in order to follow up the advantage gained by Williams and Howard, made a vigorous charge with his whole force. Cornwallis, seeing the condition of affairs, ordered his whole force to concentrate against DeKalb and Gist. Webster gained their flank and the brave DeKalb fell, pierced with eleven balls He was ignorant to this moment of the confusion of the American army. In wild confusion the militia fled, casting from them everything that would in the least impede their progress. Gen. Gates followed the militia as far as Rugeley's Mill vainly attempting to stop them. He then hastened to Charlotte.

Cornwallis gained a complete victory. The British lost in killed, wounded, and missing, including officers, three hundred and twenty-four. The loss of the Americans was seventy-five officers and two thousand men in killed, wounded, and prisoners, eight pieces of cannon and all their stores. The road from Camden to Charlotte was strewn with guns and military trappings. Gates had exchanged his northern laurels for southern willows.

GENERAL SUMTER AT FISHING CREEK

On the approach of General Gates, the Whigs of every section of South Carolina began to throw off the cloak of disguise. As DeKalb passed through Virginia and North Carolina, the Whigs of these states were filled with joy and the loyalists began to fear and tremble.

Sumter had for sometime been scouring the country between Camden and Ninety-Six and Marion was watching the region between Camden and the Atlantic, making the swamps between the Santee and the PeeDee hiding places for himself and his men.

Both Sumter and Marion at this time were colonels of the South Carolina line. Both were very brave men and, although very different from each other in personal appearance and temperament, were admirably adapted for the kind of warfare in which they had engaged. They were near the same age, but in physical strength, Sumter was superior to Marion. Appropriately, Sumter was called "the game cock," and Marion "the swamp fox." Sumter was as impetuous as a storm and not over scrupulous. Marion was cautious. The former never thought about danger, the latter neither sought it nor avoided it. Both had the same object in view - the ruin of the British and Tories and the freedom of their country; but as warriors they chose different modes to secure the same thing. Both Sumter and Marion were of Huguenot extraction.

We have already met Sumter at Rocky Mount and Hanging Rock, and in future we will frequently meet both him and Marion, together with Andrew Pickens, James Lyles, and a host of others, who took the field as partisan leaders.

When General Gates encamped at Rugeley's Mill, the camp of Sumter was not far distant. Neither Sumter nor his men could be still. He was constantly on the look out for something to do. Learning that the troops were passing from Ninety-Six to Camden for the purpose of reinforcing Cornwallis, and that a large wagon train of supplies was also on its way from Ninety-Six to Camden, he concluded that with a few more men than he had and some pieces of cannon, he could, without any loss, capture the supplies. He made known his intentions and wants to Gen. Gates at Rugeley's Mill, on the fourteenth of August. Gen. Gates, since he had on that day been joined by Gen. Stevens with seven hundred Virginians, immediately detached four hundred men and three-pounders, under the command of Colonel Woolford, for the purpose of reinforcing Sumter.

The camp of Sumter at this time was on Waxhaw Creek in Lancaster county. Sumter and Woolford were ordered to unite their forces and carry out the intentions of Sumter. Early on the morning of the fifteenth of August, the forces of Woolford having joined Sumter, all the crossings of the Wateree River, for some distance above Camden and for five miles below it, were seized by Sumter.

During the previous night, the British had, for some reason, removed all the guards except from what was then called Wateree ferry, opposite Camden. At this point, a guard was stationed on both sides of the river. On the west side was a small fortification called Fort Cary. It was commanded by Col. Cary. A party of Sumter's men surprised the guard, killing seven and taking thirty prisoners, among whom was Col. Cary himself.

Up to this time, Sumter had not lost a single man. The British from the east side of the river fired upon the Americans across the river, but did no damage. The wagon train, in quest of which Sumter had set out, was in the immediate neighborhood of Fort Cary. In a short time, without any loss, Sumter was in possession of thirty-eight wagons loaded with army supplies, together with their escort. In a short time afterwards six more wagons and seventy prisoners were captured. In all, he captured forty-four wagons loaded with army stores of various kinds and three hundred prisoners and did not lose a single man.

After the battle of Hanging Rock, Davie's division, which formed a part of Sumter's command, was ordered to escort the wounded to Charlotte. So soon as Davie had performed this duty, he hastened back to join Gates at Rugeley's Mill. He arrived after Gates had set out for Camden, but by marching all night he met the fleeing troops of Gates about four miles from the scene of the conflict. Here he learned from Gen. Huger of the defeat of the American army. Davie at once concluded that Sumter was ignorant of the fact and would be cut off did he not get out of the reach of the enemy at once. Captain Martin, with two dragoons, was sent at once by Davie to inform him of the sad results of the battle and to advise him to hasten to Charlotte, North Carolina, when they could again form a junction.

On the night of the sixteenth, Capt. Martin reached Sumter's camp and found that the latter was totally ignorant of what had taken place. He was encamped with forty-four wagons and three hundred prisoners, many of whom were sick. He at once broke up his camp and set out up the river, expecting to cross at the Nation ford or some other place in that neighborhood.

Unfortunately for the brave Sumter and his heroic band, the British commander did not become so elated on account of his victory over the hero or Saratoga, as to forget them. Both Cornwallis and Tarleton were capable of making the most out of a victory. On the evening of the sixteenth of August, when Gates' discomfited army was fleeing in wild confusion, Cornwallis sent a messenger to Lieutenant Colonel Turnbull, who, with Patrick Ferguson, was stationed on Little River, in Fairfield county, to take the New York volunteers and Ferguson's detachment and go at once in pursuit of Sumter.

On the morning of the seventeenth of August, Col. Tarleton, with three hundred and fifty men and one cannon, was sent by Cornwallis in pursuit of Sumter, with directions to act as circumstances might indicate. From Rugeley's Mill he directed his course through the woods towards Rocky Mount, intending to cross the river at that point, if all things were favorable. On his way he picked up twenty American soldiers, who were escaping from the battle of the day before. In the afternoon, Tarleton learned that Sumter was retreating up the river. At dark he reached the ferry opposite Rocky Mount. Sumter's camp fires were distinctly to be seen. Tarleton ordered the boats to be secured and forbid any fires to be kindled by his soldiers during the night. At daybreak the British sentinels reported that they saw the Americans decamping. That the truth of this statement might be verified, Tarleton sent a small party, under command of Capt. Campbell, across the river. Campbell was instructed to hold out a white handkerchief if Sumter was actually retreating up the river. In the meantime Tarleton ordered his men to get ready to cross the river.

So soon as Campbell and his party arrived at Rocky Mount, they took a prisoner and learned that Sumter was on his way toward the Nation ford. The white handkerchief was hung out and soon the British infantry, with the three-pounder, were in the boats and the cavalry were swimming across the river. The first thing that Tarleton did, after crossing the river, was to send out a squad of men to search for Turnbull and Ferguson. Hearing nothing of them, the men returned.

Sumter had in his command about eight hundred men, one hundred of whom were Continentals. His movements were greatly retarded by the spoils captured on the fifteenth at Fort Cary. Tarleton had only three hundred and fifty men and his men and horses had been doing hard service for several days and were in a poor condition to execute anything brilliant. Both armies moved up the Catawba River. Sumter, in perfect ignorance of the presence of a foe, was retreating towards Charlotte, North Carolina. There he expected to form a junction with Davie.

Tarleton was in hot pursuit, watching for some favorable moment to dash in upon the unsuspecting Sumter. At 12 o'clock, Tarleton crossed Fishing Creek. Here he found the greater part of both his men and horses so exhausted by the intense heat of the day, that it was necessary to select those able to undergo farther service. One hundred of the dragoons and sixty infantry were selected to continue the pursuit. The remainder of the troops, with the three-pounder, were posted advantageously so that, having refreshed themselves, they might be ready in case of necessity to cover the retreat of the detachment.

The one hundred dragoons and sixty foot soldiers moved forward with great caution. It was a miserable force to make an attack upon Sumter. Had he only known that he was pursued by such a band, he could have easily annihilated it in a very few moments. For five miles after crossing Fishing Creek, Tarleton saw nothing to indicate the presence of his foe, but his freshly made tracks. Two of Sumter's videttes, who were concealed in the woods, fired upon the van of Tarleton's cavalry and killed one of the legion. His comrades rushed in fury upon the two Americans and cut them to pieces with their swords. The presence of these videttes indicated the nearness of the American army. A sergeant and four men were sent to the top of a hill near by. They were seen to lie down upon their horses and motion to Tarleton to come forward. Tarleton spurred his jaded horse and rode to the top of the hill.

On the opposite hill he saw the American camp. On the east was the Catawba; on the west, Fishing Creek; in front and near was a ravine. The camp was on the crest of a narrow ridge. Here Sumter had encamped on the night after the attempt to take the British post at Rocky Mount. It was a strong position, and had Sumter only known that Tarleton was in the region with only one hundred and sixty men he would, no doubt, have put an end to that Briton's career. It was ordered otherwise. Sumter was worn out with watching and his men were hungry and tired. Major Crawford of Lancaster was officer of the day and he, rather than Sumter, is to blame for the careless manner in which the camp was guarded.

When the videttes fired upon Tarleton's advance guard and killed one of his legion, Sumter sent out patrols to learn the cause of firing. The patrols returned and reported that it was only the soldiers killing beeves. Sumter had also sent out a squad of men to patrol the road to Rocky Mount. These men, tired and hungry and, besides, like militia, generally disobedient to orders, had returned without examining the roads for any considerable distance.

When Tarleton discovered Sumter's camp, the guns were stacked and everything presented a fit opportunity for a brilliant achievement. The officers, on account of the heat, had taken off their superfluous clothing. Sumter was asleep. Some of the men were slaughtering beeves, others were cooking, others were grazing their horses; some were sleeping on the ground, and a very considerable number were in the river bathing. Here, worn out with the toils and hardships of war, lay scattered on this ridge near the Catawba River, in the south-east corner of Chester county, in fatal security, the Whigs of Chester, Lancaster, York and Fairfield. Many of the men were in their own neighborhood. Here they had spent childhood's happy days, and here, as a bird caught in a net, they were entrapped and slain or made prisoners.

In a moment, Tarleton ordered the attack. His troops were formed into one line and, with a shout, dashed in upon the American camp. All was confusion. The men were cut off from their arms and thus deprived of all means of resistance. Behind the wagons and at several other points in the American camp, a slight resistance was made. So sudden, however, and so unexpected was the attack, and so spiritedly was it conducted, that the officers had no time to form their men. Sumter, it does not appear, gave any orders at all. He was aroused from sleep by Capt. John Steel and, in a half-dressed condition, mounted his horse and made for the Nation ford. The men followed the example of their commander. Some took to the river and attempted to swim across, while others made for the woods.

The Rev. John Simpson, pastor at that time of Fishing Creek church, was mending his bridle. He had leaned his gun up against a tree, and his mare was grazing around him. When he heard the shouts of the British and saw the confusion and slaughter in the American camp, he threw down the unmended bridle and mounted his mare, bare-back, and gave her a slap on the side of the jaw. The noble beast dashed off in the direction indicated by the slap on the jaw. A brush-fence, enclosing a turnip patch, seemed to obstruct his progress, but a word of encouragement from the kind master enabled the faithful, but jaded, animal to leap into the turnip patch and then leap out on the opposite side, bearing her master safe to the road. Here two of Tarleton's men, armed with muskets, confronted the escaping preacher. He was ordered to surrender but another slap on the cheek of the mare changed her direction. Into the woods she darted at full speed and bore her master beyond the reach of the British.

In all directions, and in every imaginable plight, the Americans fled. Some were barefooted and some had no clothing on except their hunting shirts, and not a few were absolutely naked. Of the naked some were supplied by the Whig ladies in the region with their husbands' clothes, and not a few went to their homes or joined their commander dressed in women's clothes. It is said that Sumter left camp bareheaded but was supplied with a hat by James Harbinson. Another account says that Sumter lost his hat in swimming the river and a Tory picked up the hat and plume, floating on the river, and brought it to Tarleton, from which circumstance Tarleton concluded that Sumter was actually among the number of the killed.

The surprise was complete. Only Capt. Moffett's company attempted to make any resistance, and this only for a short time. Tarleton increased the number of his force by promptly releasing the three hundred prisoners. These were, of course, delighted and signified their joy by frantically tossing their hats in the air.

Tarleton was unable to pursue the fugitives for any considerable distance. His men were worn out and his horses were jaded. The rout was complete.

Sumter's army was scattered to the winds. The wagons and supplies taken at Fort Cary, together with three hundred prisoners, all fell into the hands of the British. One hundred and fifty officers and men were either killed or wounded. Ten Continental officers and one hundred Continental soldiers, together with many militia officers and more than two hundred militia privates, were made prisoners. The two three-pounders sent by Gates to Sumter, two ammunition wagons, one thousand stand of arms, and nearly all the horses, fell into the hands of the British.

Tarleton's loss was comparatively nothing. Capt. Charles Campbell, who commanded the infantry, was killed just as the affair was drawing to a close. Fifteen non-commissioned officers and privates were killed and wounded. This, together with twenty horses killed, constituted the whole of the British loss.

The surprise of Sumter, following in quick succession the discomfiture of Gates, left the country in a most perilous condition. No wonder the British general concluded the rebellion was crushed.

It is but reasonable that the inquiry be made why Sumter was surprised. Who was to blame for this sad affair? The blame rests equally upon Sumter and his men, and if any one individual was more censurable than the rest, that individual was James Crawford of Lancaster. One of the characteristics of Sumter was that he rather courted than shunned danger. Many of his men were militia and could not, because they would not, be induced to observe strict military regulation. They followed Sumter not because they were compelled to do so, but simply because they were anxious to fight the British. Sumter should not have spent the night of the seventeenth at Rocky Mount. Had he marched all night, he would have been out of the reach of Tarleton. Had, however, the patrols at Fishing Creek done their duty, Sumter could have easily demolished Tarleton. James Crawford, it is said, granted most of the young men permission to go to the river to bathe. He should have place them on duty to guard the camp.

The prisoners and baggage being secured, Tarleton set out for the camp of Cornwallis. After three days' toilsome marching, he entered the camp of Cornwallis amid the acclamations and shouts of the British soldiers.

Sumter went to Charlotte. His routed men who escaped being captured, went either to their homes and from thence to Charlotte or followed Sumter directly to Charlotte.

CORNWALLIS' ADVANCE TO CHARLOTTE

The utter overthrow of Gen. Gates and dispersion of his army at Camden, followed by the surprise of Gen. Sumter at Fishing Creek, placed South Carolina in a condition which beggars description. Had the region of country now embraced in the counties of Rowan and Mecklenburg, North Carolina, and Lancaster, Chester, York and Fairfield, been settled by any other class of people, Cornwallis could have marched from Camden to New York and the stars and stripes would never have floated over a few people.

The part which the inhabitants of the region mentioned acted has never been fully understood, or at least it has never been clearly stated. American liberty was born in the south. The first man that ever advocated absolute independence was William Johnson, a blacksmith, of Charleston, South Carolina, and the first blood that was shed to water the tree of liberty was shed at Alamance, North Carolina. William Johnson and Christopher Gadsden advocated, in Charleston, American independence as early as 1766 and the inhabitants of North Carolina fought and bled and died for American liberty in 1771.

The region of country between the Yadkin River, North Carolina, and Broad River, South Carolina was settled by the same kind of people. Their religious creed was the same and in political sentiment they were a unit. By their enemies they were stigmatized as "pugnacious and pertinacious." For centuries they had been regarded as troublers of kings. Slow to be moved, patient under suffering, but when once aroused they were as furious as an enraged lion and as impetuous as a tornado in its maddened course. Their religious creed may be summed up in one short sentence: "Whatever the Bible teaches is right and whatever it forbids is wrong." Physically, morally and mentally they were a strong people. On all questions they claimed the right of thinking for themselves. In every house there was a family altar, upon which the head of the family offered up the morning and evening sacrifice. Such, briefly, was the kind of people that Cornwallis found when he arrived in the upper region of South Carolina. With them, Sumter fought at Rocky Mount and Hanging Rock, and with them he lay near the mouth of Fishing Creek, on the 8th of August, 1780.

After the defeat of Gates and surprise of Sumter, Cornwallis began to make preparations for the subjugation of North Carolina. The original intention of the British was to enter North Carolina further east than

Charlotte. In the region of Fayetteville there was a Scotch settlement which was loyal. The design of the British commander was to enter the Scotch settlement and afford these loyal Scotch protection from the assaults of their Whig neighbors. The success with which the British arms had thus met induced Lord Cornwallis to change his plans and move directly into North Carolina. The want of supplies and the condition of his army prevented the British commander from commencing his march immediately after the success with which he had met at Camden and Fishing Creek. The prisoners taken at these places had to be disposed of and various posts had to be fortified.

The British had gained a series of victories, but they were not bloodless victories. The ranks of the army had been greatly thinned. Many British soldiers had slept the sleep that knows no waking and a much greater number were wounded and worn out with hard fighting and harder marching. The weather was intensely hot, and Cornwallis could not advance until his army was reinforced. To effect this, Major Patrick Ferguson was sent to the western section of the state to enlist the loyalists of that section. Runners were sent into various sections of both the Carolinas to urge the well affected to the British government to join the British army. Detachments were sent out in every direction to plunder the country, to capture the scattered Whigs, and to cut off or capture all supplies designed for the Americans.

After the battle of Camden, or rather during the battle, Gen. Gates, panic stricken, set out for Charlotte. Incited either by fear or cruelty he rode so rapidly as to kill three horses. Late in the night he arrived at Charlotte and took up lodging at the house of the Widow Mason. Here, having taken a seat on the piazza, he called for a pipe, smoked, and reflected upon the terrible misfortune which had befallen him. From Charlotte, he set out for Salisbury; thence he went to Hillsboro and on the twentieth of August, four days after the battle of Camden, he wrote to the President of Congress thus: "In the deepest distress and anxiety of mind, I am obliged to acquaint your excellency with the defeat of the troops under my command."

Gen. Sumter, after the surprise at Fishing Creek, made his way to his old camp on Clem's branch, ten miles east of the Nation ford. Col. Lacey, who was with him, was sent back into the counties of York and Chester to gather up those who had made good their escape from Tarleton, at Fishing Creek, and to secure recruits for his regiment from the Scotch-Irish of that region. Lacey was successful and soon joined Sumter with a respectable regiment of mounted infantry.

Major Davie, with a small force, was with Sumter. Colonel James Williams, about the same time, with a body of North Carolinians, encamped in the same region. The Whigs had met with sore reverses, but were not discouraged. They determined to throw every obstacle in their power in the way of Cornwallis.

On the eighth of September, Lord Cornwallis, having made, as he thought, all necessary arrangements, set out for Charlotte. Cornwallis thought that so soon as the results of the late engagements were fully known throughout North and South Carolina, that the loyalists would be made bold and patriots awed into subjection. In this he was mistaken. From the Savannah River to the Atlantic ocean, and from Charleston to the mountains, and even beyond the mountains, small but active and determined partisan corps were in the field annoying the British posts whenever a favorable opportunity was presented. Tarleton, whose military judgment was scarcely inferior to that of Cornwallis, was not in favor of advancing into North Carolina by the way of Charlotte. The place was known all over England. Every officer in the British army had heard of the "pugnacious and pertinacious" disposition of the people.

Cornwallis had made every provision that he could for the undertaking. The several British posts in the state were put in proper condition. Gen. Patterson, on account of bad health, being advised to leave Charleston, the command of that post was assigned to Col. Balfour. Brown was left in command of Augusta; Cruger of Ninety-Six; and Turnbull of Camden. Redoubts were constructed to defend magazines and keep open free communication between the up-country and Charleston. Evidently, when the time arrived to act, the undertaking assumed dignified proportions. From Camden to Charlotte was only a short distance and the only foes who stood in his way had been twice routed. The territory between Camden and Charlotte had been so often traversed by both armies that it was well nigh a desert.

In order that the army might suffer as little as possible during the march from the want of supplies, Col. Tarleton was ordered by Lord Cornwallis to lead his command over the Catawba River, at the ferry opposite Camden, and to march up the west bank of the river as far as Landsford and then to cross. Cornwallis himself with the 7th, 23rd, 93rd, and 71st regiments of infantry, the volunteers of Ireland, Bryan's and Hamilton's regiments of loyalists, four pieces of cannon, fifty wagons and a detachment of cavalry, marched up the eastern bank of the Catawba River. The particular route followed by these British chieftains possesses much interest to the student of history. The difficulty of tracing it, with absolute accuracy, makes it still more interesting. From Camden, Cornwallis directed his course to Hanging Rock. At Pleasant Hill, a short distance from Hanging Rock, he took to the left, passing between where Lancaster village is now situated and the Catawba River. One mile and a half above Landsford was the mill of John Blair, the uncle of Gen. James Blair. Cornwallis took possession of this mill.

Tarleton followed the trail of Sumter as far as Fishing Creek and then followed the road leading to Union church as far as Williford's Mill - then White's. At Williford's Mill, he took the road leading to Landsford. On the march, Tarleton took sick and the command of his corps devolved upon Major Hanger. On the 22nd of September, Cornwallis ordered Tarleton to cross the river at Blair's ford, near Blair's Mill. The sick and a small guard were left at Blair's Mill, the remaining force moved forward for Charlotte. The route chosen was up what is called the Sugar, more properly "Sugar Creek" road.

The distance from Landsford to Charlotte in a direct line is about forty miles. The distance was comparatively short but it was attended with serious difficulties. Majors Davie and Davidson were in the field collecting supplies for the remnant of Gates' army and in preventing the British scouts and vanguards from depredating upon the inhabitants of the country. Many of the people fled as the British advanced and not a few took British protection.

Men who heretofore had been regarded as staunch patriots, on the approach of the British, so far deserted the cause of their country as to accept protection from Lord Cornwallis. Of this unhappy number was Cols. Ephraim and Thomas Polk. Fear, momentary fear, and the desire to save their property from destruction, impelled these men to desert the cause of their country. Afterward, when the cause of their fears was removed and their property saved from destruction, they renounced their allegiance to the British crown. We are sorry that we are called upon to record this dark spot in the history of men of high position in society and exercising great influence over their neighbors. Those were times that tried men's souls. The Polks were rich. They owned a large landed estate near Pineville, on the Charlotte, Columbia and Augusta railroad. The house of Thomas Polk was only a short distance from Pineville on the east side of the railroad. With Davie and his men the thing was different. They regarded property as valueless without liberty.

On the 21st of September, the day before Tarleton crossed the Catawba, Davie learned that some Tories and British were at Capt. Walkup's (also written Wahab) plantation, in the north-eastern corner of Lancaster county. The camp of Davie at this time was in the Providence country. Early on the morning of the 21st of September, he completely surprised the Tory party, killing and wounding sixty of the men and capturing ninety horses and one hundred and twenty stand of arms. This was a brilliant affair. Davie lost only one man and marched sixty miles in a day and night.

So soon as the captured horses and arms were secured, Davie beat a retreat. Capt. Walkup, who belonged to Davie's corps, stopped a few moments to speak to his wife and children, who ran out of the house so soon as the firing ceased. When the British and Tories who had fled on the approach of Davie, saw that Davie and his men were gone, they rushed back to the house. Capt. Walkup barely made his escape. On looking back, he saw his house in flames and his wife and little children turned adrift without a shelter.

When the British set out from Landsford for Charlotte, Sumter, who was in camp in the Providence country, set out for Salisbury, leaving Davie, who had lately been promoted to colonel with a few volunteers, under Major Graham, to watch the movements of the British. Davie and Graham hung around the British army and captured several prisoners.

On the 26th of September, the British army reached Charlotte. At that time Charlotte contained less than twenty houses. It could boast, however, of a court house, constructed of stone. This edifice stood at the intersection of two streets. On the right of the street, leading in the direction of the approaching enemy, was a plat of land thickly set with undergrowth. On the left of the same street was a field. The gardens and other enclosures of the village extended as far as the plat of undergrowth. Davie and his men determined to give his lordship a warm reception. The cavalry were dismounted and placed in front of the court house behind a stone wall, breast high. The infantry and Graham's volunteers were posted eighty yards in advance under cover of the village enclosures. Tarleton was still sick and unable to lead his legion; but Major Hanger, at the head of the legion, soon made his appearance in the plat of undergrowth.

On the part of the British, every movement was made with great circumspection. Hanger formed his men in regular order of battle and made every preparation as if an ambuscade had been laid for him by all the Whigs on the American continent. No sooner had the British reached the suburbs of the village than the militia began to shoot at them with their squirrel guns.

Hanger, having arranged his men for action, gave the signal to charge. The British column moved slowly and cautiously towards the Americans. As they advanced the Whigs received them coolly. Hanger made a rush towards the court house where he was received by Davie with a volley of musketry. Hanger turned back and formed again in the undergrowth. The Whig infantry on the right of the street fought like veterans, but were forced to give back when Col. Davie recalled those on the left. The British infantry continued to advance and the fight was renewed on the flanks. The American centre held their fire in reserve for the British cavalry, which had gone back to form at the plat of undergrowth near the village. When they made a second charge they were a second time driven back in confusion. The infantry of the enemy continued to advance steadily and succeeded in gaining Col. Davie's right flank. Col. Davie drew off his men from the court house to the east side of the village. At this time, Cornwallis rode up and abused the cavalry for bad conduct.

A third charge was ordered down the street. Soon they were met by Davie's men, now mounted, and a third time forced to retire. Davie, seeing that the contest was unequal, retired in good order, along the Salisbury road. Cornwallis tried to cut off Davie whilst retreating, but no sooner had the supporting company of Davie fired into his pursuers than they retired and returned to the main body. The Whig loss was Col. Locke and five privates killed; Major Graham and twelve privates wounded. The British loss was, in killed, twelve non-commissioned officers and privates. Major Hanger, Captains McDonald and Campbell, together with a very considerable of non-commissioned officers and privates were wounded.

Davie and his men literally crowned themselves with glory. Lord Cornwallis was utterly astounded. He did not expect a kind reception by the citizens of Charlotte, but he did expect to march into Charlotte in triumph. He had heard much about the fighting propensities of the Whigs of Rowan and Mecklenburg; but he never dreamed that a few backwoods militia would dare to face a well ordered British force. The British officers saw at once that they had arrived at the wrong place to live in peace and quiet.

TARLETON SENT IN PURSUIT OF THE KING'S MOUNTAIN MEN

Lord Cornwallis expected to have an easy time of it so soon as he reached Charlotte. Here he expected to rest his army, recruit his forces, replenish his supplies and ultimately march with flying colors through the state of North Carolina. Apparently his plans were wise and he undertook, with energy, to put them into execution. On all sides he was beset with difficulties.

The region of country now embraced by the counties of Mecklenburg, Rowan and Union, together with portions of adjoining counties, were full of as true Whigs as ever drew the breath of life. Over the entire region extending from the Haw River on the east to the Broad River on the west, and from Statesville, North Carolina on the north, to Winnsboro, South Carolina on the south, there were settlements made by Scotch-Irish immigrants. Some of these had come into the region from Bucks, Lancaster and Chester counties, Pennsylvania, and some of them had come directly from the Emerald Isle. Like the Huguenots, the Scotch-Irish never had a colony entirely under their control; but as early as 1730 they were almost the exclusive occupants of Cumberland valley. Harassed by the Indians, they wended their way south and as early as 1750 they were controllers of the region of the country embraced in Fairfield, Chester, Lancaster and York, South Carolina and of a considerable tract of country embraced in the state of North Carolina.

Charlotte was a kind of nucleus around which the various Scotch-Irish settlements clustered. To this point the Whigs of Fairfield, Chester, Lancaster and York fled for safety on the approach of the British, and here they assembled that they might organize for the purpose of resisting the invading foe.

When Cornwallis entered Charlotte he was in the midst of the most uncompromising enemies the British government had in all America. Here he met, at every turn, men and women who had imbibed the spirit of John Knox - men who not only dared to think for themselves on all subjects, both political and religious, but men and women who never feared to act with an invincible energy. Fathers had told their children about the trials and difficulties of the progenitors on the other side of the Atlantic. Mothers had sung the songs of the martyrs to their babes in the cradle. In their dreams at night, the children had been wafted to the land where the martyrs had lain weltering in blood. Young men and maidens had drunk in the spirit of the martyrs, and tears of indignation and sorrow alternately streamed down their cheeks. When the British encamped at Charlotte, the Whigs thought of "Wellwood's dark muirlands," and their blood boiled with indignation.

No man was more disappointed than was Cornwallis when he arrived at Charlotte. Foes beset him in the town and in the country, by night and by day. His videttes were shot down and it was only at the risk of his life that a single individual could go out of the British camp or enter it. Foraging parties had to be protected by large bodies of soldiers. The communication with Blair's Mill and Camden were almost cut off by individuals who lay concealed in the thickets, ready to shoot down all who might pass between these points and Charlotte. The mills of which Cornwallis had taken possession and by which he expected to be supplied with meal and flour for his army, had to be guarded with strong forces and still they were not safe from the attacks of the Whigs. The country afforded but a scanty supply for the army and the British concluded that the region of country around Charlotte, which is now regarded as one of the best agricultural sections in America, was little better than a wilderness.

Lieutenant Tarleton says: "The plantations in the neighborhood were small and uncultivated; the roads narrow and crossed in every direction; and the whole face of the country covered with close and thick woods." It was true that at that time most of the plantations in the Scotch-Irish settlements were small; but a Scotch-Irishman's religion forbids laziness.

The reason that the British army could not find an abundance of supplies in the Scotch-Irish settlement of Charlotte was not because the farms were not well cultivated, but because it was dangerous to enter a corn crib or a wheat house. At Col. Polk's mill two miles from Charlotte, the British found twenty-eight thousand pounds of flour and a large quantity of wheat; but they got possession of it after a severe skirmish. Seven miles from town, on the Beattie's ford road, it was ascertained that a large amount of grain and forage might be obtained. To secure these supplies a foraging party protected by a body of armed men was sent out. The point of destination was a plantation owned by a man by the name of McIntyre. As the British advanced they passed by a field in which a boy was plowing. He at once threw the harness off his horse and, mounting the animal, proceeded by by-paths to give the alarm to the neighborhood that the plunderers were coming. The women, children and servants mounted horses and fled before the British. The men left their work and, arming themselves, fled to the woods.

When the foraging party arrived at the house of McIntyre, the family had been gone only a few moments. Everything was left to be disposed of as the British saw fit. The wagons were driven up and the work of loading them with whatever was thought useful commenced. A party of the soldiers commenced to kill the pigs and calves which were in the yard; others undertook to catch the domestic fowls. Whilst chasing the chickens through the yard, a soldier by accident overturned a bee-hive which stood against the garden fence. The bees, enraged by this ruthless invasion of their rights, issued forth in countless multitudes and stung the soldiers of his majesty. The commanding officer at this time, was standing in the door of the house, with one hand on each of the posts of the doorway. He was pleased at seeing so many good things, but when the soldiers began to run about dodging from the bees and slapping at them in all directions, he laughed heartily at the sport. Just at this moment twelve Whigs, armed with rifles and pistols, had crept up on the plunderers and saw and heard all that was going on. One of the party, no longer able to bear the outrage, leveled his rifle on the captain in the door. With the keen crack of the gun, the merry captain tumbled, a lifeless corpse into the yard. Eleven other shots were fired by the concealed Whigs and nine men and two horses were stretched dead upon the ground.

The British cavalry began the pursuit, but soon the Whigs changed their position and poured in another volley. Again they changed their position and fired at intervals. The British put their dogs on the trail of the Whigs, and one of these creatures came up with a Whig just after he had discharged his rifle. The man drew his pistol and shot the dog down. The other dogs came up but when they saw their companion lying dead they set up a howl and returned to the wagons.

The British by this time had become frightened and, suspecting an ambuscade, began to retreat at once. The Whigs hung around them, shooting down the horses, until the road became blockaded with dead horses. No doubt this circumstance was in Tarleton's mind when he mentioned the narrowness of the roads about Charlotte.

Such was the condition of Cornwallis whilst at Charlotte, that he could neither receive nor send messages from any point. Not only so, but he did not know what to believe as true and what to regard as false. The Whigs were all around him, and he had scarcely force enough to enable him to remain in Charlotte safely. His supplies were wasting away and it was with great difficulty that he received anything from the surrounding country. The country abounded with cows - mostly milk cows - but very few sheep. The cows were poor and the British army killed on an average one hundred each day during their stay at Charlotte. On one day they killed thirty-seven cows with calf.

Surrounded by these difficulties, Cornwallis thought it was best to advance toward Virginia. Gen. Jethro Sumner, with a party of Whigs, was encamped at Alexander's Mill on a branch of Rocky River. To dislodge Sumner, Cornwallis was making preparations when he heard of the battle of King's Mountain. That memorable event took place on the seventh of October, 1780; but so closely was Cornwallis hemmed in, and so strictly were the roads and woods watched for messengers, that it was not until the mountain men were gone that he learned certainly of the battle.

So soon was it rumored that Ferguson had been defeated at King's Mountain, Cornwallis sent out Lieut. Col. Tarleton to assist Ferguson in the event that the rumor was false, and should it turn out that Ferguson was actually killed and his army annihilated, to prevent the victorious Americans from descending into South Carolina. The Whigs in the region of Charlotte were fully apprised of the fact, and despatches were sent to congress from Rocky River, beyond Charlotte, on the tenth of October; but Lord Cornwallis up to this time was in doubt respecting the battle. For an account of the battle of King's Mountain see Enquirer of January 6 and 13th, 1876.

On the tenth of October, Tarleton set out to learn the destiny of Ferguson. His force consisted of his own command, which was made up of a legion of cavalry and a number of light infantry. On this occasion, as often before, a three-pounder was added. The force was, at the same time, infantry and cavalry; with a small detachment of artillery. On the tenth of October, Tarleton, with his force, set out in the direction of the mountain region west of the Catawba. At Smith's ford, below the junction of Little Catawba with the main river, he learned with absolute certainty "the melancholy fate of Major Ferguson." The sad news was at once forwarded to Charleston. Already Tarleton saw that the tide of fortune had changed. At Wright's Ferry (then Bigger's) he crossed the Catawba and pressed forward, on what we now call the Charlotte road, in the direction of Yorkville. On the eleventh, he arrived in the neighborhood of Robert Cairnes' mill on Turkey Creek in York county. Col. Lacey and Hill were encamped at the same time with Sumter's army on Bullock's Creek. The British and American forces were only a few miles apart. During the absence of Tarleton, Cornwallis having learned the particulars of the battle of King's Mountain, determined to fall back. In other words, he found out that the Whigs would not suffer him to advance. On the fourteenth, his lordship broke up camp and left Charlotte. On the sixteenth, Tarleton was ordered to join Cornwallis at the Nation ford.

No American can be absolutely indifferent to the events which transpired during the Revolutionary war. Wherever the British went, events took place which are interesting to every American; but they are deeply interesting to those resting in the region in which these events transpired.

During the Revolutionary war there was no such place as Yorkville. The ground was then covered with native forest. The cross street near the court house was a stand for deer hunters. A man by the name of Henderson regarded it as a favorable place to kill a deer. Much of the ground upon which Yorkville now stands was a kind of swamp. Where the house of W.I. Clawson, Esq., is situated, was a huckleberry pond, and where the Enquirer office stands a maple swamp. No road ran through the town. The Charlotte Road inclined to the right at Dobson's two miles from town, and passed through the plantation of Thomas W. Clawson. A road leading from Crowder's Creek settlement passed through the eastern edge of where the town stands. The traces of it can be seen between the present Charlotte and Lincoln roads on the plantation of George H. O'Leary. It ran near by the gate of Richard J. Withers, through the lot of W.B. Steele and near the residence of J.A. Ratchford, two miles from town. We have in our possession a petition directed to William Wynn, the king's commissioner at Rocky mount, Tryon county, North Carolina, asking his excellency to grant permission to open a road from Matthew Biggers, on Catawba to Talbot's Ferry on Broad River. This document is dated April the 21st, 1772. On the 9th of August of the same year, the petition was granted by William Wynn. Evidently the part of this road which was east of the present town of Yorkville was what is now called the Charlotte Road. Talbot's Ferry was twenty miles above Fishdam Ferry. Whether the road was opened at this time or not, we are unable to say positively. We think, however, it was not, for on the 28th of March, 1778, the general assembly of South Carolina passed a law establishing a ferry on Matthew Bigger's land on the Catawba and opening a road from the ferry to Talbots Ferry on Broad River. This is the same for the opening of which a petition was sent, six years before, to William Wynn.

The Nation ford ran about two miles south of the site of Yorkville. It passed by the residence of A.J. Devinney and J.T. Lowry, out into what is now called the Pinckney road at Coker's old field.

The only house within the present corporate limits of Yorkville at the time of the Revolutionary war, stood near the King's Mountain road on the northwestern corner of the lot on which stands the King's Mountain Military school. A large hickory marks the place. The first settler was a man by the name of Matthew Dickson. On the lot now occupied by Edgar P. Williams, Matthew Dickson kept a store, in which he and a relative sold whiskey, treacle (molasses), salt, delf and other useful articles. Matthew Dickson came to the region with the Crowder's Creek Scotch-Irish emigrants, perhaps before Braddock's defeat. He married a Miss Carson, a relative of the Carsons in the neighborhood of Pisgah church in the lower edge of Gaston county, North Carolina. The marriage of Matthew Dickson and Miss Carson took place in Gettysburg.

When Tarleton and his men passed from Biggers Ferry to Cairnes' (then Ross') Mill, they went near by the house of Matthew Dickson, who was with Sumter's army. Mrs. Dickson was at home. They had several Negroes. Two of the Negro men left their families and followed the British. Mrs. Dickson, when she heard that Tarleton was at Nation ford, set out to recover the Negro men. She rode one horse and led another, causing a Negro woman to do the same. The led horses were for the Negro men to ride back on. When she arrived at the British camp, she made known the object of her visit. Tarleton told her that her Negroes were in camp, but remarked, "you have four fine horses. I think the best thing you can do is to return; for if you remain here long you will have to walk home." The good woman, anxious to save her horses, took his advice and returned, leaving the Negro men with the British. When she returned home she found her husband at home, and on consultation it was determined by them to abandon their present abode and go to Salisbury. Both of them thought that the region in which they lived would be for a long time the seat of war. From Salisbury, Matthew Dickson and family went beyond Broad River, South Carolina, and settled on Six-and-Twenty Creek in Pendleton district, about six miles from old Pendleton Court House. One reason he gave for not coming back from Salisbury to his lands in York, was that having heard that the town lands joined his, he thought it would be impossible to raise his boys right so near a little village.

Matthew Dickson owned the lands west of the Lincoln road as far as the present corporate limits of the town. On the south they were bounded by a line running a short distance south of the old male academy; on the north they extended as far as the Murphy branch. Matthew Dickson having abandoned these lands, they were taken up by Judge William Smith and from him passed through several hands into the possession of the present owners. Many of the descendants of Matthew Dickson are living in Anderson county.

It is worthy of note that the Ross on Turkey Creek, at whose place Tarleton lay in camp for several days, was the grandfather of Dr. F.M. Ross of Yorkville. Col. Ross was a gallant officer and fought bravely at Brier Creek, at which place he was killed by the Indians.

INCIDENTS

During the Revolutionary war there were in America three classes of citizens. One class was called Whigs or patriots. This class fought against Great Britain for freedom. The second class was called loyalists, and was opposed to the war on principle. They thought the rebellion was uncalled for and from pure motives they did not take part with the patriots. The other class was called Tories. This class was made up of a set of despicable vagabonds, who had no higher aims than plunder. In the lower sections of South Carolina, there were a great many loyalists from the fact that South Carolina had been a kind of pet with the English government, and many of the citizens had been treated very kindly and that placed them under lasting obligations to the British crown.

In the up-country - especially in the territory embraced by the counties of Lancaster, York, Chester and part of Fairfield, there were few loyalists, but a very considerable number of plundering Tories. These Tories were accustomed to make extensive journeys for the sake of plunder. For the sake of protection they had congregated into settlements of their own.

There was a considerable squad of them in the neighborhood of Mobley's Meeting House, on Little River, in Fairfield county. There was another squad near the present site of Chester village; another a short distance southeast of Yorkville, on Fishing Creek; and another near King's Mountain battle ground.

It was often hard times with these Tories. Frequently, they were forced to leave one neighborhood and fly to another for safety. In each of the communities mentioned there were leading men among the Tories. To the houses of these leaders the men of less note were accustomed to resort.

These Tories were regarded by the Whigs as friends of the British and such was the case generally; but, with most of them, friendship and the love of country were nothing and plunder everything. They were notorious horse thieves. They would form into bands and camp out and, in small parties, would scour the country in search of horses. Robbing parties would come from Newberry and, in conjunction with those settled on the east side of Broad River, steal and carry off every horse they could put their hands upon.

On one occasion, a noted Tory by the name of Peter Murphy, came from Newberry and camped near the spot where a man by the name of Hemphill now lives, on the road leading from John Mackrol's to the "old Glover place" in Fairfield county. This Peter Murphy had made very extensive horse stealing expeditions. He had extended his journeys as far as Jackson Creek. A band of Whigs collected and pursued him and, after a long pursuit, they came up with him at what is called the "county branch" on the road leading from Chester to Winnsboro on the plantation owned by William Douglass. Here he was shot by a McCreight, the great-grandfather of the McCreights about Winnsboro. From the "county branch" Peter Murphy was taken about three-quarters of a mile to the Tory camp. Here the party was met by the wife or concubine of Peter Murphy. She was desperately enraged and swore vengeance against all concerned in Peter's death. The grave of Peter Murphy is on the right hand side of the road, a short distance above where John Glover's overseer's house once stood, and about three miles southeast of Blackstock's Depot, on the railroad leading from Charlotte to Augusta.

Some time in September, 1780, a party of these Tories were passing through York county and stopped at the house of a man by the name of Stallions. This man, Stallions, lived on the plantation now owned by Mrs. Isabella Steele of Yorkville. The plantation is known as the "McCaw Fishing Creek Place." A brother of Stallion's lived on the plantation owned by B.T. Wheeler about fifty yards north of the bridge on the road leading from Wheeler's Saw Mill to J.T. Lowry's plantation. Both the Stallions were Tories. The Stallions that lived on the plantation now owned by Mrs. Steele married a sister of Col. Love, the great-grandfather of Dr. R.L. Love of McConnellsville. Notwithstanding this fact, both Col. Love and his sister, Mrs. Stallions, were true Whigs. By some means Col. Brandon of North Carolina and Col. Love, who lived within a short distance of where A.J. Devinney now lives, learned that a band of Tories were at Stallions'. Brandon and Love gathered up a few men and surrounded the house of Stallions. The Tories were desperately frightened and kept themselves as close as possible. Several shots were fired into the house, but no one was killed. At last Mrs. Stallions, seeing that the Tories would be taken and perhaps all shot, her husband amongst the rest, partially opened the door for the purpose of surrendering the house into the hands of the Whigs and begging her brother, Col. Love to spare the life of her husband. Mrs. Stallions had a man's hat on her head, and just as soon

as the head was seen a ball pierced it - she fell dead. What makes the thing more sad is, that it was generally thought that the shot which killed Mrs. Stallions was fired by Col. Love, her brother. So soon as Mrs. Stallions fell, Stallions leaped into the yard, and in a frantic state of mind cried out to Col. Love - "You have killed my wife! You have killed your sister!" Sorrow and anguish filled the hearts of the Whigs and they retired. Stallions was permitted to remain at home undisturbed.

At the house of the other Stallions on another occasion, a party of Tories was attacked by the notorious Jack McCain and two were killed. Jack McCain was a true Whig and one of the most shrewd and most successful foragers among the patriots of that day. He was adept at capturing horses from both the British and Tories. Unfortunately, what he learned during the war, he was inclined to practice in time of peace.

Some time in the month of June, 1780, a party of British and Tories - mostly the latter - were sent out by the British commander at Rocky Mount, to burn Hill's Iron Works on Allison Creek, in York county. It is probable that Capt. Christian Huck, who fell at Williamson's on the 12th of July, 1780, led this party. These iron works were justly regarded by the British as of great value to the patriots. When they were burned, the Whigs in all the upper section of South Carolina and the adjoining counties of North Carolina, regarded it as a sore calamity. Some idea of the value set upon these works can be obtained from following the anecdote: Some time whilst the struggle for independence was going on, the good people of a portion of Rutherford county, North Carolina, set apart a day for public prayer. A Scotch-Irishman, by the name of John Miller; an elder in the Presbyterian church, was called upon to lead in prayer. With reverence and in his native tongue, the venerable man proceeded as follows:

"Good Lord, our God, thou art in Heaven. We have great reasons to thank thee for the many favors we have received at thy hands; for the many battles we have won. There is the great and glorious battle of King's Mountain, where we kilt the great Gineral Ferguson, and took his whole army; and the great battles of Ramsour's Mill and Williamson's; and the ever memorable battle of the Coopens, where the proud Gineral Tarleton run down the road helter-skelter; and good Lord if you had na suffered the cruel Tories to burn Belly Hell's iron works, we would na have asked any mair favors at thy hands."

The party entrusted with the destruction set out from Williford's Mill on Fishing Creek and proceeded up the Catawba as far as the place now known as India

Hook. Here they commenced the work of destruction. On the plantation now owned by William N. Simril, there lived at that time a man by the name of James Simril. In the orchard of William N. Simril stood the barn of James Simril. This, together with four horses, was burned by the Tories. This accomplished, the party set out for the iron works.

On their way, they forced a man by the name of Henderson (the same man that was accustomed to kill deer at the Adickes corner in Yorkville) to show them a ford on the creek below the works. The people had been, for some time, expecting that an attempt would be made to destroy the works and had taken most of the cannon balls and thrown them into a hole in the creek not far below the works. These balls are in the creek yet. After Henderson had piloted the party across the creek, and given them all the information they desired, they stripped him and whipped him severely and then went off and left him tied to a tree.

William and Robert Hill, sons of Col. William Hill, part owners of the iron works, determined that they would resist the attempt of the British to burn their father's property. Although but boys they prepared a swivel which carried a pound ball and mounted it on top of a stump on the high hill north of Allison Creek. When these brave boys learned that the British were approaching, which fact was announced to the whole neighborhood by the burning of Simril's barn, they took their stand behind their swivel and waited for the advancing foe. They thought that the Tory party would advance to the iron works from the direction of Allison Creek Church. In this direction they had pointed their loaded swivel and in this direction they looked for the Tories. Before they were aware, the party noiselessly advanced up the creek and they were surrounded. They were made prisoners for the time and their swivel was taken by the Tories and thrown into the hole in the creek. Some time after the war ended, some one was fishing in the creek. His hook became entangled and whilst freeing the hook, he found the swivel. Some twenty-five years since, this swivel was over charged and bursted. Fragments of it still remain at Mr. Alexander A. Barron's, near Clay Hill.

On the road leading from Dallas to Rock Hill, about ten miles from the latter place, between Rocky Allison Creek and the residence of Mrs. Gillespie, lived Col. Samuel Watson, the grandfather of Rev. Samuel L. Watson, the present pastor of Bethel congregation. The house was for that time a substantial building, being constructed of brick and stone with, as was the case with most the houses of that time, a cellar beneath. From all accounts, Col. Watson was a man of stirling integrity and a true Whig. In consideration of this uprightness he was made by common consent of his Whig neighbors, a kind of a commissary, and his house was a depository for any supplies that the Whig organization might have on hand. Salt was very scarce in the country and any quantities of this article that might be captured from the British were sent to Col. Watson to be distributed. A peck was by some arrangement allowed at one time to each woman whose husband or sons might be in the army. Women were accustomed to mount their horses and ride from the lower edge of Chester county to Col. Watson's, after their share of salt.

After the defeat of Huck at Williamson's, the mother of Capt. John McClure, in company with some of her neighbors, set out for Col. Watson's. Mrs. McClure was at the time between seventy and eighty years of age. When the party of women came to the grave of Huck, Mrs. McClure said to Mary Johnston, the grandmother of James Johnston of Blackstock, Chester county, South Carolina: "Mary, as old as I am, I feel like getting down and dancing on that grave; but that would be wrong. God is just and will avenge his own cause."

As Tarleton and his men passed through the country in search of the heroes of King's Mountain, they visited the house of Col. Watson, killed all the geese, and one of the officers having scratched with his sword his name on one of the stones of the chimney, remarked that after the war was over and the Whigs were conquered, he intended to come to America and live in that house. The Whigs were not conquered and the officer never returned. The bricks which composed part of Col. Watson's house were taken away and rebuilt, and form the walls of the lower story of the house of Mr. Lee Williams, known all over York county as the Red House, six miles from Yorkville, on the Charlotte Road.

Installment XXIII

THE RETREAT FROM CHARLOTTE

The battle of King's Mountain was the turning point in the Revolutionary war. We do not mean that up to that time the British had always been successful and after that the Americans were victorious in every engagement. Before the battle of King's Mountain, the British had been steadily gaining ground; not so much by gaining signal victories as by wearing out the Americans and exhausting their resources. The American army, ever in a crippled condition, was gradually but surely becoming weaker with each successive year. The people generally had become depressed in spirit. The treasury of the country, never full, was now empty; the credit of the country, never great, was almost worthless. Congress was expected to do much for the relief of the suffering army, but it could do absolutely nothing. Georgia and South Carolina were, to all human appearances, hopelessly conquered. Gates was ruined and Cornwallis was on his way to flank Washington.

Because no titled officer led - veteran hosts against Ferguson at King's Mountain, the affair has been treated by historians as a mere skirmish. It was no child's play. It saved Washington and it saved America from British tyranny. Had the heroes of King's Mountain failed, as did Gates at Camden, and Cornwallis been permitted to pass Charlotte, the American rebellion would have resulted as have most of the Irish rebellions. It would have riveted the chains of British domination upon the Whigs of America and the Stars and Stripes would today have only a legendary existence. Whether South Carolina and North Carolina enjoyed the blessings of American liberty or not, they did more to secure it than any two states in the Union. This is said dispassionately, with the full conviction of its absolute truth. The history of other sections of the Union has been written and re-written. The lives of those who acted nobly on other battlefields constitute the nursery tales of the region in which they were born, whilst the names of Campbell, Shelby, Chronicle, Sevier, Williams, Lacey, Hill, Roebuck and Hambright are scarcely known in American history. The place that marks the resting place of Williams is unknown, and a miserable undressed stone marks the place where sleeps the dust of William Chronicle, John Mattocks, William Robb and John Boyd. Multitudes of those who fell at King's Mountain are unknown to history. Their very names are forgotten. Their noble deeds still remain.

Cornwallis had actually commenced his march from Charlotte towards Virginia. When the news, vague and unsatisfactory as it was, reached Charlotte, that the Whigs were preparing to attack Ferguson, Cornwallis delayed his onward movement until he would receive satisfactory intelligence from Ferguson. The unwelcome news was brought that Ferguson had been actually attacked and completely defeated. To learn the true state of the case, Tarleton, with a very considerable force, was sent out on the 10th of October. On the same day at Smith's Ford, on the Catawba, Tarleton received certain intelligence of Ferguson's fate. Not long after, the facts were communicated to Cornwallis.

It was a sad blow to the British and Cornwallis felt it. He saw at once that it was impossible to advance.

Rumor declared that the same undisciplined yeomanry who had out-generaled and out fought the brave Ferguson were hastening to make an attack upon Cornwallis at Charlotte. Fear invaded the British camp, and on the night of the 14th of October, Cornwallis began to retreat. Instead of conquering North Carolina, he now began to fear lest North Carolina would capture him. The country was full of Whigs. The fighting men of Fairfield, Lancaster, Chester and York, except those in camp with Hill and Lacey on Bullock's Creek, York county, were scattered over Mecklenburg and Rowan counties, North Carolina. These men were ready to join any expedition under any chieftain, who would lead them against the enemy.

When Cornwallis set out from Charlotte he had no particular point in view. The place where he would be safe from the attacks of the invincible Scotch-Irish was the best spot on earth. He was forced to direct his movements in conformity with the circumstances by which he was surrounded. No doubt, Camden was the point of destination in his mind when he quitted Charlotte, but he found the way thither blocked by the Whigs who had collected in considerable force at New Providence and Waxhaw.

The night on which Cornwallis left Charlotte, he met with many inconveniences and considerable loss. For more than ten days, it had been wet and was still raining. The roads were bad and the creeks and rivers were swollen. Cornwallis employed a wealthy Scotchman by the name of William McCafferty to act as a guide to the retreating army. The Scotchman was not well informed with respect to the roads and made great blunders.

The Whigs followed in the wake of the retreating foe, and before the morning of the 15th, relieved the British of much of their baggage. Twenty wagons, loaded with army supplies and a printing press, fell into the hands of the Whigs. All the baggage belonging to Tarleton's troops fell into the hands of the Americans. This was bad enough, but it was not the worst thing connected with that night's retreat. Many a Briton and Tory was made to bite the ground. No straggler from the main body was safe.

Cornwallis, sick and discouraged, made his way as far as Spratt's, near the Nation Ford. Here he remained as best he could awaiting the arrival of Tarleton. On the 16th, Tarleton arrived on the western bank of the Catawba and, finding the river swollen, he asked a hardy son of Green Erin to pilot him across the river. The Irishman promptly remarked to Tarleton that the people "plooted into the river ony where." Tarleton led his men in and soon found it was plooting sure enough, for all the horses were swimming. The Irishman received, for his prompt advice, a cursing in plain English. The river crossed, Tarleton joined Cornwallis. He found his lordship sick, and the British troop in a miserable condition. Their supplies had been taken from them, and they were afraid to venture into the country to secure the actual necessities of life. What corn could be secured from the surrounding country, they grated into meal.

During the sickness of Cornwallis, the command of the British forces devolved upon Lord Rawdon. In order to save the troops from starving, this officer ordered the forces to move beyond Sugar Creek. So soon as the royal forces commenced moving, the Mecklenburg militia began to assail them. The Hornet's Nest club watched every movement of the royal troops. Even the gallant Tarleton could not drive away the invincible Whigs. The British sentries were shot down at their posts and foraging parties were cut off. With his majesty's forces it was a critical time. The Scotch-Irish blood was warm and fear had seized upon the British.

The question sprung up in the minds of both officers and men: "Where shall we be safe?" Tarleton was sent out by Lord Rawdon in search of a safe retreat. To go back to Camden would be to expose all the British forces in the Ninety-Six region to the fury of the Whigs. To go to Ninety-Six would similarly expose all the eastern section of South Carolina. Some place must be sought, central between Camden and Ninety-Six. Multitudes of trembling loyalists and Tories were anxious for Cornwallis to fix his headquarters near their dwelling, that they might be shielded from Whig vengeance by the presence of the royal army.

So soon as Cornwallis was able to be moved the whole British army crossed Catawba River at Land's Ford. Passing through the country in a southwestern direction, he crossed Tinker's Creek, a few miles above its junction with Fishing Creek. Then, changing his course from a southwestern to a northwestern, he passed between Tinker's Creek and Fishing Creek, as far as White's Mill. Here he made another change in his course. From White's Mill (now Williford's) he set out in a south-western direction and continued his march as far as the site of the present town of Chester. Here he made another change in his direction and, steering a course a little east of south, he passed down the road leading from Chester to Winnsboro, past Purity, Pleasant Grove, and Hopewell churches. After a circuitous march of two weeks, the army of the British, still commanded by Lord Rawdon, arrived on the 29th of October, 1780, at Winnsboro.

The distance from Land's Ford to Winnsboro, in a direct line, is about thirty miles; yet it took the army of Cornwallis two weeks to accomplish it. Under the circumstances, it was performed as expeditious as possible. The roads were in a desperate condition and the army had to subsist by plundering the country. It was a retreat of a discomfited army through a country inhabited by uncompromising foes. It is true, the British had some friends in the region traversed, but they could not be depended on in the hour of danger. All the friends the British had in the region of country between Land's Ford and Winnsboro were a set of unprincipled horse thieves, some of whom, after the war, expiated their crimes on the gallows. At the time of Cornwallis' retreat from Charlotte to Winnsboro, these Tories were trembling like aspen leaves.

On the approach of the British, the Whig men, what few of them were at home, took to the woods or joined the nearest Whig organization. The women hid in the thickets what little provisions they had in their possession. Tarleton, in search of a fit place for winter quarters, scoured the country between Broad River and Catawba. The loyalists and Tories in the British army were sent out to search the country for supplies. Had it not been for these, the native Britons would have been forced to look starvation fair in the face. The British soldiers were ignorant of the country and they had been shot at so often, by unseen foes, that they were afraid to leave the main column. The loyalists and Tories had a good knowledge of the country and besides were less timorous than the foreign soldiers. By these loyalists the forest, fields, houses and thickets were searched for food. By these plundering loyalists, bacon was found where it had been hid by the Whig women in thorn thickets and meal and flour and rum was found stored away in secret places. The British officers declared they had never beheld so fine a country. A land where bacon grew on thorn bushes.

Tarleton's keen eye was not long in discovering the bounds of the Scotch-Irish settlements. When he passed the line, both he and the whole army breathed freer. The country assumed a different aspect and he named it Fairfield, a name which the county, of which Winnsboro is the capital, retains to this day.

The reason given by Tarleton for selecting Winnsboro as the site for winter quarters are briefly given by himself: "Its spacious plantations yielded a tolerable post; its centrical situation between the Broad River and the Wateree, afforded a protection to Ninety-Six and Camden; and its vicinity to the Dutch Forks, a rich country in the rear, promised abundant supplies of flour, forage and cattle." There was another reason, which pride, no doubt, suggested to Col. Tarleton not to make known. The region of country around Winnsboro was settled by true Whigs; but in the country around there were dens of Tories and beyond Broad River there was a nest of Tories.

When the British army passed up the country, the Tories became bold. Their boldness was increased by the success of the British arms at Camden and Fishing Creek. The Whig men had left their homes and were in Sumter's army. Not only so, but many of the women had taken their children and were following Sumter and his men that they might be safe from the Tories at home. The British officers knew all this and Winnsboro afforded a favorable place for the British army to spend the winter of 1780-81, because it was a considerable distance from any rendezvous of the Whigs.

Communication was soon opened with Camden and Ninety-Six. The sick and wounded were sent to Camden and a supply of army stores sent for. At Winnsboro, for the present, we leave Cornwallis.

Installment XXIV

CAPTURE OF PATRICK MOORE AND THE BATTLE OF CEDAR SPRINGS

After the fall of Charleston, the main army of the British marched through the state, by the way of Camden and thence to Charlotte, North Carolina. If we will lay a map of the state of South Carolina before us, we will see that the route of Cornwallis was near the centre of the state. His path led through a rich country, comparatively well cultivated and settled by as determined Whigs as were in America. In his march he passed through or near the counties of Williamsburg, Sumter, Kershaw, Lancaster, Fairfield, Chester, and York.

No other route could have been chosen by the British which would have led them through as many and as strong Whig settlements. The Revolutionary record of Williamsburg is the brightest in America. Every other section of the thirteen colonies had a few Tories and loyalists; but Williamsburg had only a single individual who was the friend of King George.

As might have been expected, the march of Cornwallis through the state greatly encouraged the Tories and loyalists in all sections of the country. From the Savannah to the Potomac, joy and gladness pervaded the breasts of this class of citizens. The Whigs were made to suffer, but it can hardly be said that they were dispirited. It was a dark day but the Whigs did not cease to hope. In fact, misfortune only nerved them to prompt and energetic action. Old men whose heads were blossoming for the grave, forgetting the ravages which time had made upon their constitutions, shouldered their rifles, and with the elastic step of youth, hastened to meet the foe. Beardless boys followed their fathers to the camp; and mothers and maidens took hold of the handles of the plow. Whilst the men and boys fought, the women tilled the fields and reaped the harvests.

From the 12th of May, 1780, to the 7th of October, of the same year, the Whigs of Georgia, upper South Carolina and western North Carolina, had been watching the British with the anxiety which a crouched lion watches his prey. After the fall of Charleston, the Whigs of Georgia and western South Carolina sought refuge - some in what was then known as Mecklenburg and Rowan counties, North Carolina, and others found a safe retreat in the valley of Nollichucky, in the homes of Colonels William Campbell, John Sevier, and Isaac Shelby. These noble men opened up their homes for the reception of those Whigs who had been made homeless by the foe and with these Whig neighbors, they longed for a fit opportunity to avenge the wrongs of their countrymen.

So soon as Colonel (afterwards general) Charles McDowell of Burke county, North Carolina, heard of the fall of Charleston and the contemplated advance of the British, he determined to raise a force and throw himself in front of the advancing foe. To effect this, he sent a requisition to Col. Isaac Shelby, of what was then known as Sullivan county, North Carolina (now Tennessee), for all the men he could raise. Shelby was in Kentucky surveying lands for Henderson & Co. When he heard of the fate of the army under Gen. Lincoln and the fall of Charleston, he determined to lay his compass and chain aside and again gird on his sword, never again to take it off until his country was free. In July, he returned to his home, and found the requisition made by McDowell. He went to work with all the energies of his great soul and in a short time raised a body of three hundred mounted riflemen in Sullivan county.

On the 19th of March - two months prior to the fall of Charleston - the citizens of Washington county, North Carolina, had met and raised a force of one hundred men to be sent to Gen. Rutherford, to assist South Carolina. These troops, owing to the fact that Gen. Rutherford was hurried off sooner than he was expected, did not leave Washington county. In the summer they, with probably some others, under the command of Lieutenant Colonel John Sevier and the three hundred mounted riflemen from Sullivan county under Col. Isaac Shelby, joined Col. McDowell near the Cherokee Ford on Broad River.

Patrick Ferguson, a major in the British regular army and brigadier general of the loyal militia, had been ordered by Cornwallis into the Ninety-Six district, for the purpose of arousing the loyalists and Tories to action. Patrick Ferguson was by birth a Scotchman and son of the distinguished jurist, James Ferguson and nephew of Lord Elibank - Patrick Mury. During the siege of Charleston and at the battle of Brandywine, Patrick Ferguson had distinguished himself. He was a skillful and energetic officer and a braver man never lived.

After Georgia in 1779 fell into the hands of the enemy, Col. Elijah Clarke, with about one hundred Whigs, fled from Georgia to the settlements beyond the mountains. Here among the inhabitants of the Watauga and Holston, Clarke and his confederates found warm friends. The glowing narrations of these refugee Whigs from Georgia, kindled into a flame the patriotism of the men who had engaged in the sanguinary battle with Indians, on the 10th of October, 1774, at the mouth of the Kenhawa.

With these daring spirits and his own followers from Georgia, Colonel Clarke returned to the scene of his former conflicts with the British. The enemy's posts were annoyed, their sentinels shot down, and their officers picked off. Hence, although the British through Georgia and South Carolina conquered territory, the officers commanding the posts of Augusta and Ninety-Six complained to the commander-in-chief that "a body of rebels have assembled against the peace of this province." To annihilate Clarke and his men, and others operating in a similar way, Patrick Ferguson was sent out.

When Shelby and Sevier joined McDowell at the Cherokee Ford, in July, 1780, Col. Clarke was with McDowell. Some twenty miles from McDowell's camp, at Cherokee Ford, Gen. Andrew Williamson had, during the Cherokee wars, built a fort on the waters of Pacolet River. From all accounts, this fort was advantageously situated and strongly built. It was surrounded by a strong abattis and could be entered only by a small gate.

When Lord Cornwallis sent his emissaries into North Carolina to warn the loyalists to be ready for action on his arrival, a certain Patrick Moore, of what is now Lincoln county, North Carolina, greatly interested himself in behalf of the British government. When Cornwallis reached Camden, Patrick Moore, thinking that the time for him to take the field had arrived, raised the royal standard. Multitudes of disaffected Americans in his neighborhood flocked to his standard. He invited all the loyalists in the region of country between the Catawba River and the mountains to join them. With bright anticipations this Patrick Moore and his followers set out for the fort on Pacolet. On his march from Lincoln county to the fort, Moore met with no interruption. Here he thought, no doubt, he was safe and in a favorable situation to render acceptable service to George the Third.

Col. McDowell determined that Patrick Moore should not remain in this stronghold. So soon as he was joined by Shelby and Sevier, he detached these two officers and Col. Clarke with six hundred men, according to the American account; but according to the British with "two or three hundred banditti without cannon." The British account we are disposed to think is correct, except that they were not "banditti." They were gentlemen then and afterwards through life, but the inveterate haters of tyrants. At sunset, Shelby, Clarke and Sevier set out, with the detachments under them for Patrick Moore's headquarters. As day began to dawn on the next morning, they had the fort surrounded. Shelby, who was first in command, sent William Coke to demand a surrender of the fort. Moore replied that he would defend the fort to the last extremity. The lines of the assailants were drawn in to within musket shot and preparation made for an immediate attack. To save the effusion of blood, Moore was again summoned to surrender. To this he replied that he would surrender on the condition that the garrison be paroled not to serve again during the war. This was granted. Ninety-three loyalists and one British sergeant were paroled. In the fort was found two hundred and fifty stand of arms, all heavily loaded. It was clear that Patrick Moore was neither a good officer nor a brave man. The British charged Moore with cowardice. Both the men and officers were anxious to defend the fort, but Moore, after agreeing to defend it, went out and brought in the American officers and put them in possession of the gate.

About the time that Patrick Moore surrendered, Major Patrick Ferguson arrived in the Ninety-Six district. His command consisted of one hundred choice regulars. The loyalists to the number of more than a thousand soon joined him. His camp soon became the rendezvous of all the desperadoes of the region. His name attracted swarms of Tories. Although his command at first consisted of only one hundred British regulars, he soon found himself at the head of an army of more than two thousand men. The greater part of these were natives, but they were decidedly better soldiers than his regulars. Ferguson was ordered to take possession of all the strong places in the district, enroll and discipline the militia and, in one word, do everything in his power to strengthen the royal cause and crush the spirits of the Whigs. To effect this object, public meetings were called and the men and officers of Gibb's, Flummer's, Cunningham's, Clairy's, King's and Kirkland's battalions of militia passed resolutions that every loyalist must be ready at a moment's warning, to rush to the contest. Those who lagged behind were to be regarded as the common enemies of the loyal cause, and were threatened with the confiscation of their property. Those who failed to join their regiments promptly when called upon, were ordered to be forced into the British regular army. Everything appeared bright on the side of the British. The Whigs were silent from prudence and the Tories and loyalists were as much elated as if they had not a foe in the land. The rapidity with which Ferguson's army was increased, the zeal of the loyalists and Tories in the countries, together with the acknowledged ability of Ferguson himself, as an officer, was sufficient to dispirit the Whigs.

Such, however, was not the case. Col. McDowell had his eye upon Ferguson. He knew the record of the men in his command. Many of them had met painted savages at the mouth of the Kenhawa; they had seen the British at Brier Creek, Kettle Creek, Augusta, and Savannah. Many of them had been made homeless by fires kindled by an invading foe. With implicit confidence in Cols. Shelby and Clarke, Col. McDowell detached them, with about six hundred mounted riflemen, to watch the movements of Ferguson. The instructions given these officers were to hang around the camp of Ferguson and cut off his foraging parties. Ferguson was, in the meantime, watching for an opportunity to cut off Shelby and Clarke and these men were no less anxious to dash in upon foraging parties of Ferguson.

Although Shelby and Clarke were sent by McDowell for the same general purpose with the understanding that they would act in concert, each seems to have acted separately and alone; but still in such a way as to be a mutual aid, the one to the other. This occasioned some confusion in the narration of the deeds accomplished by the party. What was actually accomplished by Clarke and the men in his command is sometimes spoken of as being the joint work of both Shelby and Clarke with their united commands.

On Col. Clarke's march from Georgia, to join McDowell at Cherokee Ford, he detached Samuel Alexander, with a squad of men, to scour the Ninety-Six region and learn the strength and operations of the British. Alexander joined his command and probably very soon after Shelby and Clarke left McDowell's camp, at Cherokee Ford. The report of Alexander was in substance, that Major Ferguson with a detachment of men variously reported from two to five hundred was out, in what is now Spartanburg county, on a recruiting expedition. The object of the British officer was to increase the number of his cavalry from the people of the country. To effect his purpose many individuals who had been paroled and promised the privilege of remaining peaceably at home, were impressed.

On receiving this information, Col. Clarke proposed to his men, all of whom or at least the majority of whom, were Georgians, that they set out at once in search of this recruiting party. This was on the afternoon of the 30th of July, 1780. Clarke's command, which was about one hundred strong - all mounted - readily agreed to the proposition of their commander. All hands went to work and preparations were soon made for the expedition. Guns were put in shooting order and those that could, replenished their haversacks with food. About sunset they were joined by Hammond, McCall and Lidde, each with a few men amounting in all to about eighty. The whole force now numbered one hundred and sixty-eight. The troops were mustered and the line of march was taken up through the woods and over more foot paths. Nothing was heard of the enemy during the night. Some time during the next day, it was learned that a scouting party of Tories was plundering through the county, at some distance from the main command under Ferguson. Their horses were spurred on, with the hope that this scouting Tory party might be surprised and cut off. The camp was reached, but they failed to surprise the Tories.

At a distance of some three miles, Clarke and his men rode round the Tory camp, taking the road leading from Bobo's Mill, in the direction of Berwick's iron works. At the iron works they were joined by eighteen recruits. At the house of Captain Dillard, who was with them, they halted, and Mrs. Dillard entertained the party as well as she was able with potatoes and milk. From this point it was concluded that the party would change their direction and cross over to the road leading from Ninety-Six to Green or Cedar Springs. Having marched through the woods for eighteen miles, they halted at Cedar Spring. Videttes were stationed, with orders to make no noise should any discoveries be made; but to dash into camp and make an announcement of their discoveries. The men dismounted, but the horses were not unsaddled and every man was ordered to keep his bridle reigns in his hand.

Shortly after Clarke and his men left the house of Captain Dillard, Colonel Ferguson and Major Dunlap, with a party of soldiers, arrived. They asked Mrs. Dillard if Clarke and his men had been at her house during the day. She replied that they had, but had been gone for a considerable length of time. She was then asked to what point they had gone. She replied that she did not know. This, as we will shortly see, was not strictly true. Col. Ferguson ordered Mrs. Dillard to prepare supper for himself and Major Dunlap immediately. Making a virtue of necessity she set out to work to execute the task. Whilst preparing supper for these two officers, it was necessary that she pass frequently by the place where they were sitting. In passing back and forth, she heard them concerting measures for the immediate pursuit of Clarke.

The bacon found in the house, or at least a part of it, was taken and given to the soldiers. Supper for the officers was soon prepared. After it was eaten, the plan was for Major Dunlap to take six cavalry and one hundred and fifty mounted riflemen and pursue Clarke. By some means the British had learned the plans of Clarke and the locality where he and his men would probably camp. Mrs. Dillard knew that Clarke had gone in the direction of Cedar Springs, and she heard one of the British officers inform the others that Cedar Springs was the point to which the Americans had gone. So soon as Mrs. Dillard had placed the supper on the table, she slipped out of the house and hastening to the stable, she bridled a colt and mounting it, without saddle or blanket proceeded with all possible speed to Cedar Springs. Here she arrived about half an hour before daylight. The vidette took her at once into the presence of Col. Clarke. She was at once recognized and proceeded to warn Clarke and his men of their danger. She told them they must at once get ready to fight or fly. At the same moment another Whig lady, Mrs. Thomas, apprised the Americans of the approach of the British.

The command was given to mount. In a moment every man was in his saddle and ready to meet the advancing force. Before it was light enough to distinguish friend from foe, Dunlap with his Tory band came charging into the American camp. He received a warm reception and instead of surprising the Americans he himself was surprised. The contest lasted only for a little more than a quarter of an hour, when the British beat a retreat. The Americans followed the flying foe, for more than a mile, when Dunlap was met by Ferguson with a strong reinforcement. The Americans returned to the scene of conflict, picked up their wounded, and retreated by the way of Berwick's iron works, toward North Carolina. The British under Ferguson, pursued as far as the iron works and then gave up the chase. At the iron works two of the wounded American soldiers were left. These fell into the hands of Ferguson, but he treated them kindly and permitted them to remain.

As the men fought hand to hand, most of the wounds were inflicted with swords. Col. Clarke was slightly wounded on the neck. The battle of Cedar Springs was fought on the morning of the first of August, and except the snack of milk and potatoes received at the house of Captain Dillard the men had eaten nothing since the evening of the 30th of July. The horses had neither been unsaddled nor fed.

BATTLE OF MUSGROVE'S MILL

Soon after the battle of Cedar Springs, a junction was formed by Col. Bratton of York; Col. Williams of Laurens; Col. Shelby of Tennessee (then North Carolina or Virginia); Col. Clarke of Georgia, together with Hammond, McCall and Liddle of the Ninety-Six brigade. Each of these officers had a few men who followed him as their commander. Shelby and Clarke had the largest force and each of them had only about one hundred men. The force under Williams was the next largest and the commands of Hammond, Bratton, McCall and Liddle consisted of a few of their neighbors, who were banded together for the purpose of offense and defense. Clarke was evidently the leading spirit. Not that he was the best officer or bravest man; but since the fall of Georgia, he and the men in his command had suffered greatly and were thirsting for vengeance. Col. Clarke's house was first plundered and then burned, and his family ordered to leave the state. Many of his men had shared a similar fate. The cruel treatment which they had received at the hands of the victorious foe had goaded them to desperation. Clarke was burning with rage and he longed for an opportunity to chastise the enemies of his country. He was constantly on the lookout for small parties of British and Tories.

The junction of these troops from regions far distant from each other, was formed near the headwaters of Broad River in Cleveland county, North Carolina. Gen. McDowell, with a small force, was encamped on Broad River, near the Cherokee Ford. McDowell was the highest officer in command in that region of country and his camp was, by common consent, regarded as a place of general rendezvous. Prudence dictated to McDowell to move his camp as frequently as possible. His safety and the safety of the region demanded this.

The American forces, having been successful in the enterprises against the Tories under Patrick Moore, and the British and Tories under Dunlap at

Cedar Springs, determined to continue what had been so favorably begun. Their intention of making another raid into the country then occupied by the enemy was communicated to General McDowell, then in camp near Smith's Ford, on Broad River. This officer approved of the plan and promised cooperation.

In order that the movements of the enemy might be ascertained, two individuals were sent out to make a tour of observation through the territory now embraced by the counties of South Carolina, west of Broad River and north of Hamburg. These individuals soon discovered that a party of two hundred Tories were encamped on the Enoree River, at Musgrove's Mills. It was determined to set out as soon as possible and attack them. Gen. McDowell was consulted and gave his hearty approval of the projected movement.

Musgrove's Mills are in the northeast corner of Laurens county on the Enoree River. These mills have, since 1780, passed through several hands and been known by various names. At present they are known as Yarborough's Mills.

The Tories were encamped on the south side of the Enoree. Opposite them was a rocky ford and regarded as very bad. This gave the Tories grounds to conclude that they could not be approached by an enemy from the mountain region. On the 16th of August, the day that Gates was defeated near Camden, the partisan leaders of the Americans were informed of the Tory encampment. On the afternoon of the 18th, they set out and a short time before night crossed Broad River at Smith's Ford. Here they halted, fed their horses and refreshed themselves.

On the night of the 16th, Col. Bratton, with the troops under his immediate command, set out to visit his own neighborhood, intending to join the party before they would reach the Tory camp. Either because he found something to do in the vicinity of his own home or, which is more probable, because the troops under Clarke, Shelby and Williams marched directly on to Musgrove's Mills, Bratton did not rejoin them until the battle was over. About sun down Shelby, Clarke and Williams, with their respective commands, set out for the Tories on the Enoree. The distance was about forty miles. Gen. McDowell accompanied them for a short distance and then returned to his camp near Smith's Ford.

Between the camp of McDowell and the Tory camp on the Enoree, Ferguson, with his whole force, had stationed himself. It was absolutely necessary for these partisan leaders to keep clear of Ferguson.

At sun down, on the evening of the 18th of August, 1780, a day made memorable by the surprise of the brave Sumter at Fishing Creek, the detachment of about six hundred horsemen set out through the woods to make a march of forty miles in the night. In order to evade Ferguson, they took a road which led them by the Briton's camp in safety. The party had good guides by whose assistance they reached the neighborhood of Musgrove's Mills just at the dawn of day.

The party had hoped to be able to surprise the Tories, but on approaching the neighborhood of the camp, they were met by a strong patrol force of the enemy. A skirmish of short duration took place, when the enemy retreated across the river. Whilst the skirmishing was going on, a Whig from the neighborhood came to Col. Shelby and informed him that the Tories had been strongly reinforced on the previous evening. The reinforcements consisted of six hundred regular troops, and the Queen's American regiment from New York, commanded by Col. Innis. The whole was designed as a reinforcement for Col. Ferguson. The force, amounting to about one thousand men, was under the command of Col. Innis and Major Frazer.

The Whig leaders held a hasty consultation and concluded that they would fight, notwithstanding the apparent disadvantage under which they were placed. It was agreed by Cols. Williams, Shelby and Clarke that they should share the command equally. These things being agreed upon, the next thing was to prepare for action. On a small creek, which rises in Spartanburg county and empties into Enoree River, in Union county, a short distance below the Spartanburg line, Shelby, Williams and Clarke drew up their men in a semi-circle. Col. Shelby commanded the right; Col. Williams the centre; and Col. Clarke the left. The place chosen for the action was a wood and served the double purpose of both concealing and protecting the men. The men were dismounted and the horses sent to the rear. The troops were ordered to form a breastwork of logs and brush. They were tired and hungry, and in good condition to make a stand.

After men have been marched for a day and night on short rations, they will fight hard. They come to the conclusion that the place they are in is as good as any other and, rather than be driven from it, they will die. Such was the condition of the American forces that met Colonel Innis at Musgrove's Mills. They had ridden all night on a short supper and had no breakfast. Hunger and fatigue aroused their patriotism.

Captain Inman of Georgia, with sixteen men, was sent forward to draw Col. Innis in to the ambuscade. Inman advanced upon the main body of the British and Tories and commenced to fire. The British in turn advanced and Inman fell back into the midst of his concealed friends. The enemy advanced in three columns; the regulars in the centre and the militia on the wings. With trailed arms and deployed columns the whole force of the enemy pursued Capt. Inman until they arrived within forty yards of the Americans concealed behind their temporary breastworks. The signal to fire was given, according to agreement, by Col. Shelby firing. In a moment a destructive fire was poured into the ranks of the advancing foe in front and on both wings. For a moment the advancing columns recoiled, but the regulars soon rallied and advanced. Another volley was poured into their ranks. The regulars fell back in confusion and the firing became brisk on both sides. So soon as the Tories saw the British regulars falling back in confusion, they gave way and fled. The American troops were ordered to get their horses and pursue the retreating foe.

On the battle field lay all the British officers either killed or wounded. Sixty-three privates and one Tory captain - Hawsey - lay dead on the ground and one hundred and sixty prisoners had been secured.

Whilst the American forces which had become disordered in pursuing the flying foe was forming and waiting for their horses, a consultation was held as to what course would be pursued. On the suggestion of Col. Williams, it was determined to advance upon the British and Tory post at Ninety-Six. These partisan leaders were not long in coming to conclusions. In this instance they thought that there would be less danger in making an attack immediately upon Ninety-Six, than in passing Ferguson's quarters on their way back to McDowell's camp on Broad River. They had gained a glorious victory, with the loss of only six or seven men.

The saddest thing about their loss was the fact that Capt. Inman, who suggested the stratagem of a skirmish with the enemy, whilst the Americans were forming, was killed. Much of the success which attended the patriots on this occasion was due to the skill with which Captain Inman managed the skirmishing and drew Innis across the river into the midst of the main body of the Americans. At the moment that victory was declared for the Americans, the brave Inman fell a lifeless corpse. The whole British and Tory army was scattered to the winds. Major Frazer, the second in command, was killed and Col. Innis wounded.

The Americans were flushed with victory. They forgot their hunger and fatigue and were anxious to push on to Ninety-Six which was about thirty miles distant. This was a wise conclusion and the undertaking was worthy of the men. In war, however, as in every other department of human life, well laid plans and wise conclusions are frustrated in the moment when they are near consummation. The men were mounted and waiting the command to march. At this moment, a courier arrived on the ground from Gen. McDowell. He bore a letter from Governor Caswell to General McDowell. It was dated August 16th, on the battlefield where Gates and Cornwallis met in horrid conflict. In a very brief sentence, it communicated the sad news that the army, under the hero of Saratoga, was completely routed and advised McDowell to get out of the reach of the enemy as soon as possible. McDowell had sent the letter without note or comment to Shelby, Williams and Clarke, that they might govern themselves as circumstances would indicate. Shelby recognized the handwriting of Governor Caswell. All were convinced that the letter was no trick of war. Another consultation was held. The attack on Ninety-Six was abandoned and it was determined, without a moment's delay, to make a push to keep out of the reach of Col. Ferguson.

Tired and hungry as were both men and horses, they determined to make their escape. They well knew that Col. Ferguson would be apprised of Gen. Gates' defeat; they knew that he was an enterprising officer and would be at their heels in a short time. The prisoners were distributed among the companies, giving one prisoner to every three men. This prisoner, the three men carried alternately, behind them on their horses. With all possible speed they set out for the mountain region of North Carolina. At Greenville, Col. Shelby left the party and retired beyond the mountains. Clarke and Williams changed their course in the direction of Charlotte, North Carolina. The march was kept up without intermission all day and all night and the next day until late in the afternoon, when they halted for a short time and fed their weary horses. It was well that they kept moving for Col. Ferguson had sent De Peyster in pursuit of them. This officer, with a strong force of mounted men, followed the Americans for two days, but becoming fatigued with the heat, gave up the chase.

At Charlotte a short stand was made and some men collected from the scattered forces of Gates. The prisoners were sent under charge of Capt. Samuel Hammond to Hillsboro, and delivered to Gen. Gates.

Col. Clarke returned to the western frontier of South Carolina. Col. Williams followed the prisoners to Hillsboro, North Carolina and was made a brigadier general by Governor Rutledge of South Carolina. At the same time, Governor Rutledge gave a major's commission to Capt. Samuel Hammond.

The battles of Williamson's, Cedar Springs and Musgrove's Mills, although in modern times they would be regarded as only small skirmishes, were in

Revolutionary times grand affairs. They were bright spots in the horizon which betokened the coming of a better day.

One of the prisoners captured at Musgrove's Mills was a man by the name of Saul Hinson. This Hinson had joined the patriots party and fought in Col. William's command at the battle of Stono in the summer of 1779. Saul Hinson, who was usually called Sauly, like many others had become discouraged and joined the Tories. He was a miserable little creature in body and could be recognized in any company. As Col. Williams was riding around the prisoners his eye caught Saul Hinson among the crowd. The colonel, with a smile of satisfaction, said to him "Ah! My little Sauly, have we caught you?" "Yes, and no great catch either," was the reply. At this Williams and all laughed heartily.

While the battle was raging, two American soldiers caught hold of the bridle reins of the horse on which the Tory, Colonel Clarey, was riding. The colonel's situation was very critical. To make any attempt to either resist or escape would have been followed with instant death. With a composure of mind which would have done credit to a Caesar, he sternly looked his captors in the face and abused them for two fools who did not have sense enough to know their officer. The men let loose their hold on the bridle reins, and the Tory colonel made good his escape.

ORIGIN OF GENERAL FRANCIS MARION'S PARTISAN CORPS

It is a fact much to be regretted that so little effort was made at the proper time to hand down to posterity a more complete biography of those Revolutionary heroes whose deed will live and brighten whilst men continue to love freedom. The names of Sumter and Marion are interwoven with the nursery tales of South Carolina and intimately blended with the history of the thirteen colonies in their struggle for freedom; but the most interesting portion of the lives of these heroes has been swept by the waves of time into the gulf of oblivion. Of their boyhood we know comparatively nothing. There was a time when the history of both these men could have been traced from the cradle to the grave. That period has passed and we must be content with their history commencing with their military exploits.

Gen. Francis Marion was of French extraction. His grandfather - Gabriel Marion - fled to South Carolina when, after the revocation of the edict of Nantes, a spirit of malice and hate kindled the fires of persecution which desolated the homes of the Huguenots. Like most of the Huguenots who fled to South Carolina during a bloody period, the grandfather was a gentleman by birth and education. He, with his young wife, whose maiden name was Louisa D'Aubrey, settled on the Cooper River. Here they bought a plantation and by industry and economy accumulated enough of material wealth to make them comfortable and respected. The oldest son of this worthy couple was honored with his father's name. He settled at Winyaw and became the father of one daughter and five sons, of whom Francis was the youngest.

The year 1732, the same that gave birth to Gen. George Washington, gave birth to General Francis Marion. The facilities for obtaining a thorough education were then poor, compared with what they are now; hence the education of Marion was limited. We are not to conclude that it was entirely neglected. At that time books were not so abundant as they are now; but what few books were owned by the first settlers of this country, were generally standard works and were better used than books are at the present day. They were studied rather than read.

In early youth, Marion was desirous to lead the life of a sailor. His mother, however, either from a maternal affection which would not suffer her to be separated from her son by broad oceans, or because she saw that her son was not fitted for such a life, set herself in opposition to this inclination. In spite of the remonstrance of his mother, young Marion at the age of sixteen, embarked on a schooner bound for the West Indies. The vessel foundered at sea and Marion narrowly escaped a watery grave. The crew consisting of six persons left the sinking ship and entrusted themselves to a small boat. On board this boat there was neither food nor water. On the flesh of a single dog, which had accompanied them, they subsisted a whole week. On the sixth day the captain and mate became delirious, leaped overboard, and were drowned. On the seventh day Marion and three others, nearly dead and suffering excruciating tortures, reached land. Marion returning home was content to follow his mother's advice rather than his own inclination. He now engaged, with energy, in the useful and honorable occupation of tilling the soil.

In 1758, when he was twenty-six years old, his father died. After this event he quitted the old homestead and settled on the Santee, about four miles from Eutaw. The next year marks the date of his military career. The Cherokee Indians, as we have already seen, were at this period giving the people of South Carolina a great deal of trouble. The brother of

Francis Marion raised, in 1759, a company of cavalry. Francis was a member of this company. In 1761, Francis Marion served as a lieutenant in Capt. William Moultrie's company in the war with the Cherokees and other tribes of Indians. The Indians being subdued and peace being restored to the country, Marion was, in 1775, chosen a member of the Colonial Congress of South Carolina.

From Boston to Charleston, the country was greatly agitated. The people talked about nothing but British oppression and liberty. In May, 1775, the news of the battle of Lexington reached South Carolina. Francis Marion was among the first to espouse his country's cause and to offer his services in defense of her rights. It was determined to raise three regiments - two of infantry and one of cavalry - for the common defense of the country. Christopher Gadsden was chosen colonel of the first infantry regiment and William Moultrie, of the second. Francis Marion was a captain under Colonel Moultrie.

Previous to the attack of the British upon Sullivan's Island, Marion had risen to the rank of major. After this battle, Col. Moultrie was promoted for his gallant defense of the fort, to brigadier general, and Marion rose to the rank of lieutenant colonel. From this period until the siege of Charleston in 1780, Moultrie and Marion were constantly together. They enjoyed each other's triumphs and shared each other's misfortunes.

In March, 1780, Col. Marion, with a company of friends, was invited to dine at the house of Alexander McQueen of Charleston. They were all true Whigs and their host determined that they should be entertained in a manner becoming their merit. Wine and intoxicating drinks were furnished in princely abundance and all were pressed to drink. The company were assembled in the second story. In accordance with a custom prevalent at that time, the door was locked that no one might retire until all were drunk and unable to leave. Marion had no inclination to enter into these Bacchanalian revels, and his companions were determined that he should lead in the banquet as well as on the battlefield. He attempted to make his escape through the door but was prevented by all present. At last, seeing that it was either leave or get drunk, he resolved to leave.

To effect his purpose, he leaped from the window into the street. Of two evils, he chose the one which he regarded the less. In the fall he broke his ankle bone. This rendered him for the time unfit for service and he was taken to the country that he might remain in quiet until his broken bone was healed. During this time, Charleston was besieged and captured and the whole of Gen. Lincoln's army fell into the hands of the British.

Marion suffered greatly from this broken ankle, but it proved a blessing in disguise, both to him and his country. So soon as he was able to ride, he mounted his horse and, attended by a servant, set out in the direction of Virginia. His object was to find some field on which he could serve his country. On entering North Carolina, he fell in with his old friend, Peter Horry. The latter was sad. He had concluded that the happy days of the Whigs were all gone. Marion thought differently. As Marion and Horry made their way slowly northward, they were joined by kindred spirits from various parts of South Carolina. Among this number was a gentleman by the name of White and Capt. Donom, the grandfather of our townsman, I.D. Witherspoon, Esq.

The glad news was soon received that an army was advancing to relieve the southern portion of the Confederacy from the power of the British. On the banks of the Roanoke their party met a well appointed army under the command of Baron DeKalb. Marion and his party were kindly received by the brave German and permitted to share his hospitality.

When this army, designed for the relief of the south, moved forward under the command of the ill-starred Gates, Marion moved with it. Previous to the engagement between Gates and Cornwallis at Gum Swamp, on the 16th of August, Gates sent Marion and about thirty men in the rear of Cornwallis. He was ordered to destroy all the bridges and ferries, in order to prevent Cornwallis from retreating. Gates contemplated nothing short of completely demolishing the British earl, and giving the flesh of his men to be food for the vultures and the bones to bleach upon the banks of the Wateree. He was, as we have already seen, sadly mistaken and he, rather than Cornwallis, lost an army. Marion, like a good soldier, obeyed orders strictly and was not long in clearing the rivers between Camden and the sea-coast of bridges and ferries. When the news of Gates' defeat reached this noble little band, they formed a circle and pledged themselves to be true to their country to the last. With her they determined to live and with her to die. Such, briefly, is the origin of Marion's corps. It was a nucleus around which brave men flocked and suffered and fled and died, for liberty.

MARION AND HIS MEN

When, on the twenty-fifth of July, 1780, General Gates joined the army under DeKalb on Deep River and took command of the forces sent by congress to assist the south, Francis Marion was in camp. For a short time he had been enjoying the hospitality of DeKalb, and profiting by the conversations of that brave man and experienced soldier. Marion had with him about twenty followers; some men and some boys; some white and some black. The dress of all was most unsightly. Their coats were nearly worn out and the men themselves were weather beaten. All - Marion as well as the rest - wore a little home made leather cap, which made them look most ludicrous. When they rode into DeKalb's camp, the Continental soldiers raised a shout. The ragged garments, little leather cap and unpromising appearance of the men filled the camp with merriment.

When Gates took command of the army, Marion was introduced to him, but that proud officer seems to have discovered nothing in Marion worthy of his notice. Governor Rutledge of South Carolina was also in Gates' camp and recommended Marion, but Gates was above being advised either with respect to men or measures. To get rid of Marion and his ragged men, Gates sent them, after commencing his march to the rear of Cornwallis, to burn the boats on the Santee. The diversion which Marion and his men caused was becoming troublesome to the officers and Marion and his men, although they loved their country, still were glad to be separated from companions who made no other use of them than to make sport of them. As an offset to this disagreeable state of things by which Marion and his few men were surrounded, he received an invitation from the Whigs of Williamsburg county to come and assist them in repelling the inroads of the enemy. The inhabitants of the region bordering on Kingstree knew more about Marion than General Gates did and they were anxious that he should be their leader. Gates and his army were on the march in the direction of Camden, when Marion received this invitation. Governor Rutledge of South Carolina was with the army of Gates. So soon as Rutledge heard of the request sent up by the Whigs of Williamsburg, he commissioned Marion as a brigadier general.

Let us go back and inquire what it was that prompted these men to send for Marion. In 1732, the year that Marion was born, the region of country that now bears the name of Williamsburg was settled by a colony of Scotch-Irish. These people left their native land that they might get rid of the onerous burdens laid upon them by the unrighteous exactions of cruel landlords and the proud and dictatorial clergy of the established church. The Huguenots, to which race Marion belonged, were driven to America by the cruel

and relentless persecutors, who lived in the days of Louis the Fourteenth. We may readily conclude that the Huguenot settlers on the Santee sympathized with the Scotch-Irish settlers on Black River. They lived in harmony as neighbors and together they rushed to the front in 1775, to drive the British from the state. Side by side they had fought the wild Indians; side by side they had fought under Moultrie in Fort Sullivan and at Savannah; and with General Lincoln, many of both the Huguenots and Scotch-Irish surrendered. The reason why the people of Williamsburg invited Francis Marion to take command of them, was they knew him and had confidence in him, both as a soldier and a patriot. That which prompted them to organized at this period was this:

When Charleston was surrendered, many of the Williamsburg militia were made prisoners. These prisoners were paroled and permitted to return to their homes. Maj. John James, the son of William James, one of the first settlers of the township, had been sent back by Governor Rutledge from Charleston to Williamsburg, to train the militia. When Gen. Lincoln surrendered, Maj. John James was at his home in the neighborhood of Indiantown Church. Maj. James and all those citizens of Williamsburg who were not in Charleston at the time of the surrender were, by a proclamation issued by the British commander, required to take up arms in the support of the English government. This was simply requiring them to turn out and fight their countrymen. This proclamation thoroughly aroused the settlers in the vicinity of Kingstree and Indiantown Church.

At that time a British officer by the name of Ardesoif was in command of Georgetown. The people of Williamsburg township met and appointed Maj. John James to visit Ardesoif and learn from him what was the true import of this royal proclamation. James, ever ready to serve his country, mounted his horse and rode down to Georgetown. Suspecting that the interview between himself and Ardesoif might not be of the most pleasant character, he took the precaution to hitch his horse near the door. On entering the office of the British commander, he, in true Irish style, announced his business and asked in a manly tone of voice on what terms he and others similarly situated with himself must submit. Ardesoif haughtily replied, "On no other terms than unconditional surrender." "But," remarked Maj. James, "will we not be allowed to remain at home in peace and quiet?" "No," replied Ardesoif, "you have rebelled against your king and you ought to be hung like dogs; but his majesty is merciful and he proposes to pardon all your past offenses, on the condition that you take up arms and fight for his cause." Both James and Ardesoif were by this time thoroughly enraged. Both rose to their feet. Ardesoif's hand was on his sword. James was unarmed, but he took hold of the chair on which he had been sitting, and with it between him and Ardesoif, he gently gave back in the direction of the door, near which his horse stood hitched. Ardesoif cautiously followed. On reaching the door James, with a defiant look, said: "Sir, the gentlemen whom I represent will never submit to any such conditions." Ardesoif swore like a fiend and threatened vengeance upon him and the rebels whom he represented.

So soon as James declared that neither he nor his friends would submit to unconditional surrender, he leaped out of the door, mounted his horse, and dashed away to Indiantown Church. His course was approved by his neighbors, and three cavalry companies were raised to defend the country against the British. The captains of these three companies were John James, Henry Mouzon and John Macaulay. In this community there was, at the time, a company commanded by William McCottry. These companies were organized perhaps in July.

So soon as the British learned that the people of Williamsburg were still in a state of rebellion, Lieutenant Banastre Tarleton was sent from Charleston to kill in the bud, the patriotism of the Scotch-Irish of Williamsburg. On the 6th of August, Tarleton crossed the Santee at Lenud's Ferry and pushed on, crossed Black River a short distance below Kingstree. Maj. James was on Lynche's creek. He sent McCottry to Kingstree, but Tarleton was gone before McCottry's arrival. It seems that a rumor was afloat in the country that Col. Washington, with a large cavalry force, would soon be in the Williamsburg region. Tarleton took advantage of this rumor and passed himself off as Col. Washington and completely deceived the people.

From Kingstree he set out in American uniform for Camden to join the army at that point. James Bradley, one of the first settlers of the country and at that time a venerable old man, was fooled by Tarelton's American uniform. Tarleton told the patriarch that he was Col. Washington and that he was seeking an opportunity to attack the British. Mr. Bradley, who was a man of influence and had a perfect knowledge of everything connected with the immediate country, told, in the simplicity of his heart and innocence of his soul, everything he knew. Tarleton, pretending to be Col. Washington, prevailed upon the old man to act as his guide across the swamps of Black River. When Tarleton had accomplished all he desired, he threw off his disguise and avowed himself as Tarleton.

No man can approve of such an act. It was mean and inhuman. James Bradley was put in irons and taken to Camden. For some diabolical purpose he was, frequently during his long confinement at Camden, taken out to witness the barbarous execution of his countrymen and often was the threat made that his time would be next. To the honor of the old man, he ever replied: "I am ready at any time to die for my country." In May, 1781, James Bradley was released; but he bore the marks of the irons upon his legs to his grave.

On his march from Kingstree to Camden, Tarleton burnt and destroyed everything in his way. All the houses on the plantation of Capt. Henry Mouzon, together with their contents, were burnt to ashes. The house of James Bradley was also burnt as well as the houses of William and Edward Plowden.

These acts of cruelty prompted the three companies organized in July and McCottry's company to send for Francis Marion. The largest of these four companies was McCottry's and it contained only seventy-five men, when organized before the fall of Charleston. These four companies, together with some twenty-five or thirty men and boys with Marion when he was commissioned brigadier general, constituted what was known as "Marion's Brigade." We must not confound Marion's brigade with Marion's regiment. The latter consisted of nine hundred companies and ceased to exist on the fall of Charleston.

After parting with Gates' army at some point between Deep River and Camden, General Marion hastened to the region between Camden and Charleston. With that zeal and energy for which he was noted during all his life, he began the work of destroying the boats upon the rivers. The object of this destruction, as stated before, was to prevent Cornwallis from retreating to Charleston. Gates calculated on nothing less than the complete extermination of all the British troops in the region of Camden.

So soon as it was learned that Marion was on the Santee, the Whigs flocked to him. The four Williamsburg companies were all mounted and sent under command of Col. Peter Horry into the region of country around Georgetown. General Marion, with a few men, directed his course towards the upper Santee.

On the 17th of August, he heard of Gates' defeat at Gum Swamp on the day before. The news of this defeat was carefully concealed by Marion from his men, lest it might make the already sad, sadder. That night his scouts brought him information that a large British force, with a considerable number of prisoners, were in the neighborhood of Nelson's Ferry. This was just what Marion desired. He wanted to do something to revive the spirits of his men. The fact of Gates' defeat, he knew they would soon learn, and under no more favorable circumstances could this fact be learned than when releasing those who had been captured by the enemy. No doubt Marion had another object in view. Most naturally would he conclude that the prisoners, when released, would join his little band and render good service to their country. In this fond hope, as we will see, he was disappointed.

No sooner had he learned that a British force was in striking distance, than he set about making preparations for attacking it. Nelson's Ferry is on the Santee near the corner of Orangeburg, Sumter, and Charleston counties. It is about thirty-five miles from Kingstree; about the same distance from Sumterville and fifty or sixty miles from Charleston.

About sun down, on the evening of the 19th of August, the British guard in charge of one hundred and fifty prisoners who had been captured in the late battle near Camden, crossed the Santee at Nelson's Ferry. They halted for the purpose of spending the night at what was called the "Blue House." The party had no idea that they were in any danger and the early part of the night was spent in singing comic songs and drinking apple brandy. Late in the night, overcome with fatigue and full of apple brandy, the British sunk into silence. Only a small detachment was left to watch the American prisoners.

Marion and his men, pretending to be a party of loyalists on their way to join the British, crossed the river between midnight and day. Col. Hugh Horry, with sixteen brave and daring men, was detached and sent to occupy the road in front of the British. The plan was to begin the attack just at the dawn of day - Horry in front and Marion in the rear. The surprise was not complete but the victory was. On approaching the "Blue House," the sentinels in front of the house fired upon the Americans and ran into the house. Both Marion and Horry pursued them and in a moment the whole party was surrounded. The British and Tories, panic stricken, ran in every direction. Nineteen British regulars and two Tories were taken prisoners; three were killed. One captain and also a subaltern were also captured. The spoils were a wagon loaded with supplies, and one hundred and fifty prisoners released. Marion's loss was comparatively nothing - one man killed and Capt. Benson wounded slightly on the head.

The recaptured prisoners were mostly Continentals of the Maryland line. These were part of the men who, only a few weeks before, had made all sorts of sport of Marion and his ragged men. Marion offered to take these liberated prisoners into his brigade, but strange and ungrateful as it may appear, only two, possibly three, could be induced to join the ranks of the man who had liberated them. They were completely demoralized. They said their country's cause was hopeless and they were unwilling again to risk their lives in freedom's cause.

Installment XXVIII

BATTLE OF FISHDAM FORD

When, in September 1780, the British commenced to advance into North Carolina, Colonel (afterwards general) Sumter, with the remnant of his troops which had escaped Tarleton at Fishing Creek on the 18th of August, was encamped on Clem's Branch. On the approach of the British, Sumter found it necessary to move his camp. He was not able to resist the onward movement of the enemy and wisdom dictated to get out of his way as soon as possible.

Before the movement from Clem's Branch commenced, Colonel James Williams, with a small force which he had collected in North Carolina, joined Sumter. Williams, it is said, had but a short time previous, received a brigadier general's commission from Governor Rutledge of South Carolina. Williams claimed the right to command the whole force, but the men under Sumter refused to submit to him. The whole force, notwithstanding the bad state of feeling which existed among them on account of the claim set up by Williams, marched together and crossed the Catawba at Wright's Ferry. Rawdon and Tarleton were pressing them closely. So near were the two armies together, that the Americans had scarcely effected the crossing of the river when the British appeared on the other side and commenced firing. To settle the dispute between Sumter and Williams, a convention of officers, with Col. William Hill as chairman, was called.

The convention decided to send Richard Winn, Henry Hampton, John Thomas and John Middleton, as commissioners to Governor Rutledge, who was at that time some where in the neighborhood of Salisbury, North Carolina. These commissioners were instructed to lay the facts before Governor Rutledge and report his decision. In the meantime, Sumter was to retire from the army and the command of all the troops, except those brought by Williams from North Carolina, devolved upon Hill and Lacey.

What decision Governor Rutledge made, if any at all, never, so far as we know, was made public. The battle of King's Mountain occurred soon after and Williams was mortally wounded. At King's Mountain

193

we hear nothing of any claim set up by Williams as an officer of higher rank than Campbell or any one else. On the contrary, if any one was first in command at King's Mountain, that one was, by the consent of all, William Campbell of Virginia.

After the battle of King's Mountain, the troops from western North Carolina and Virginia returned beyond the mountains. Hill and Lacey led the remainder of the army down to what was then Wright's (now Wm. Burris') Mill on Turkey Creek. Here the patriots lay encamped, when Tarleton, who had been sent by Cornwallis to look after Ferguson, lay encamped for two days on the hill west of Ross' (now Robert Carnes') Mill. On the 16th of October, Tarleton was ordered to join Cornwallis at the National Ford on Catawba.

Sometime about the first of November or last of October, 1780, Sumter joined Hill and Lacey, then encamped at what is now Burris Mill. The brave and patriotic Williams was dead and all cause of dispute among both officers and men was removed. Sumter, by general consent, took the command and led the troops against the British and Tories on the west side of Broad River. In order to keep open communication between Camden and Ninety-Six, the British had erected small stockade forts at several points in the counties of Union and Spartanburg. These posts, Sumter and his men annoyed greatly. They gave the British and Tories no rest. The heroic Elijah Clark, John Twiggs and Andrew Pickens, with small parties of Georgians, were in the same region operating in a way similar to that pursued by Sumter. On meeting Clark and Twiggs, it was determined to unite the South Carolina forces, under Sumter, with the Georgians, under Clark and Twiggs and make an attack upon Ninety-Six.

Each of the three officers agreed to furnish a certain number of men. Sumter found that before he could meet his engagement with Clark and Twiggs, he must raise at least one hundred and fifty men. On consultation with the officers of his command, it was determined to send a number of individuals on a recruiting expedition into what is now the counties of York and Chester. The inhabitants of this region of country were known to be true patriots, who neither asked for British protection nor accepted it when offered them. As the settlers were all, or nearly all, Scotch-Irish descent, four native born Irishmen and Edward Lacey were sent out to beat up the needed recruits. The names of the four Scotch-Irish recruiting officers were Billy Wylie, grandfather of Dr. A.P. Wylie of Chester; Jimmy Johnson, the grandfather of James E. Johnson of Blackstock, Chester county, S.C.;

Patrick McGriff and James Martin. The selection was made with great wisdom. Billy Wylie was a man of great good sense, joined with a droll manner; Jimmy Johnson was a witty Irishman who took everything easy; Patrick McGriff was brave to a fault; and James Martin was prudent. Edward Lacey was one of those impetuous creatures who never do anything by halves. Whatever he undertook, he did with all his might; daringly reckless but admirably suited for the kind of warfare in which he was engaged. On the 6th of November, 1780, these five recruiting officers set out to raise one hundred and fifty men. They were given three days to accomplish the work. The arrangement was that, in the mean time, Sumter would act as if he were about to advance in the direction of Camden, but would in fact camp at Fishdam Ford on Broad River.

At this time, Cornwallis with the main body of the British army in the south, lay at Winnsboro. On hearing of the operations of Sumter, he determined to send out a detachment to cut him off. The individual chosen to put this determination into execution was Major Wemyss. The troops put under his command for the capture of Sumter, were the 63rd regiment of foot soldiers and forty of Tarleton's cavalry. All were mounted, and on the evening of the 8th of November, 1780, the detachment set out for Sumter's camp on Broad River. The intention of Wemyss was to make the attack upon Sumter at dawn of day on the 9th, but having procured good guides and his horses being fresh, he arrived at Fishdam Ford about one o'clock.

Late in the afternoon of the same day on which Wemyss left Winnsboro, the recruiting officers sent out by Sumter returned according to previous appointment. As the new recruits were on their way to camp, it was ascertained that there was a barrel of whisky a few miles west of the present site of Chester. Men and officers all agreed that they were entitled to their share of this whisky. Their course was soon turned in that direction and on arriving the barrel was, without any great deal of ceremony, rolled out; and to expedite matters, it was raised up on one end and the head knocked out of the other end. Every man was instructed to help himself liberally as he saw fit. A halt of only some thirty minutes was made, but many of the men were full. The order was given to mount. This was promptly obeyed and men and officers dashed off at a brisk canter for Fishdam Ford. A few miles before reaching the camp, a squad of British scouts was discovered. No one knew how many British there were or anything about them. So far as either the men or officers knew, the whole of the British brigade might be in the neighborhood. It made no difference whether there were many or few. The men, and officers too, no doubt, all felt the effects of the whisky they had recently drank, and no sooner were the British scouts seen, than a deafening shout was raised, and away all dashed in the utmost confusion. The British took to flight at once and no doubt thought they were ruined. Farm horses were urged by their spirited riders over the Sandy River hills at such a fearful gait that it was not long till they were completely exhausted. The British scouts got out of sight and the new recruits reached Sumter's camp without a scratch and flushed with victory.

By some means, Sumter had received intimation that he would probably be attacked on the night of the 8th. Colonel Thomas Taylor, who after the fall of Charleston had joined Sumter at Clem's Branch, was connected with Sumter's army. To Taylor's vigilance is mainly due the repulse of Wemyss. Sumter had no inclination to lay plans by which he might entrap his enemy. He was a brave man and dashing soldier, but not remarkable for strategy. So soon as it became probable that Sumter's camp would be attacked, Col. Taylor began to make preparations for its defense. The horses were all saddled and tied some distance in rear of the camp. An order was made to have the guns all freshly primed. Taylor was placed in command in an advanced guard of twenty-eight men. At a short distance from the camp of Sumter was a small field. On the border of this field, Taylor had large fires kept burning from an early hour in the evening. Behind the fence and at gun shot distance from the fence, the vigilant Taylor placed his picket of twenty-eight men. Sumter lay near the river with his horses bridled and saddled, ready for whatever might be required in the event the British made an attack. All was silence. Sumter's men were waiting with sleepless anxiety. About midnight the sound of horses feet in the distance were heard. Taylor's pickets were wide awake. Their commander ordered them not to fire until the signal was given. When Major Wemyss came in sight of the camp fires, he saw that his plans of operation could not be carried out. He expected to come upon Sumter off his guard, as Tarleton had come upon him at Fishing Creek two months before. But for the sleepless vigilance of Thomas Taylor, this no doubt would have been the case.

So soon as Wemyss discovered that the Americans were apprised of his approach, he determined to make the attack at once, and not wait as had been previously arranged, until daylight. He feared that by postponing the attack, Sumter would cross the river during the night and by morning be out of his reach. At one o'clock Major Wemyss, at the head of his detachment, charged the pickets under Taylor. An order had been given not to fire until the enemy came in full view. The moment the British came within gunshot distance, the order was given to fire. The keen crack of five rifles was heard echoing among the Sandy River hills. The aim had been unerring. One ball entered the arm and another the knee of Wemyss. The British were thrown into confusion and dashed in among the blazing fires of Taylor's pickets. This brought them into full view and volley after volley was poured in by the pickets concealed behind the fence. The British could only discover the hiding place of the Americans by the flash of their guns. They fired in the direction of the blaze but only killed one man. Wemyss, having counted certainly on victory, had not communicated his plans to any of his subalterns. When he fell, the command of the detachment devolved upon a lieutenant, who ordered a precipitate retreat and hastened with the party back to Winnsboro as fast as possible. The British left on the field twenty-three men killed and wounded; two officers wounded - Major Wemyss and Lieutenant Hoverden. The Americans lost but one man. Wemyss was not found until the next morning. He was greatly exhausted from the loss of blood. In his pocket was found a list of the patriots he had hanged and the houses he had burned. Notwithstanding his notoriously brutal conduct on a multitude of occasions, his bleeding wounds were bound up and, at his own request, the document which contained an enumeration of his infamous deeds was destroyed.

About the time that the British, after having been disordered by the fire of the Americans, were preparing for a second charge, an accident took place which contributed to the advantage of the patriots. By some accident a cart load of cartridges became ignited. The burning cartridges kept up a continual cracking which the British mistook for platoons of Americans. They could hear nothing but a continual roar, and could see nothing but a continual blaze. The cart load of ignited cartridges frightened some of the new recruits among the Americans. These fled to the river and concealed themselves beneath its banks. Making a similar mistake with the British, they concluded the battle was still raging when it was only the exploding of burning cartridges.

This little fight threw the British camp in Winnsboro all in confusion. Cornwallis wrote immediately to Tarleton, who was in the low country looking after Marion, to return. In his letter which is dated Winnsboro, November 9th, 1780, he begs Tarleton "to return immediately." Evidently he began to fear not only for the post at Ninety-Six but for the no less important at Winnsboro. He began to feel that his own carcass was in danger.

THE BATTLE OF BLACKSTOCK

Immediately after the battle of Fishdam Ford, Sumter crossed Broad River and was joined by the partisan forces in that region. As already stated, plans had been concerted and preparations made for attacking Ninety-Six, the principal British post in the upper portion of South Carolina west of Broad River. So soon as the British troops which had been sent against Sumter at Fishdam Ford returned to Winnsboro, Cornwallis sent a dispatch to Tarleton, who was at that time in the region between the Santee and the Black rivers, begging him to return immediately. In his dispatch to Tarleton, Cornwallis says: "I am under the greatest anxiety for Ninety-Six and trust you will lose no time in returning to me." The overthrow of Wemyss and his detachment filled the mind of Earl Cornwallis with fears, lest Ninety-Six and all the posts west of Broad River would fall into the hands of Sumter and his partisans.

Cornwallis had really been driven back from Charlotte and now he began to fear that in the fortunes of war, he might be forced to retire from Winnsboro to some more safe position. Tarleton promptly obeyed the orders of his commander. Agreeable to instructions, he left a number of horses at Camden for the purpose of mounting some infantry. The loyalists in the Santee river being greatly dispirited, he encouraged them; and having concerted some plans with the commander at Camden by which intelligence of any threatened danger to the line of posts between Ninety-Six and Camden might be made known, with the utmost dispatch he crossed the Wateree River. Here he was met by a courier from Earl Cornwallis, instructing him to take the most direct route to Ninety-Six. Passing through the southern portion of Fairfield county, he crossed Broad River near the point where Alston Station, on the Greenville and Columbia Railroad, is located.

When Sumter crossed Broad River, perhaps on the ninth of November - he, in connection with the partisan leaders, Clarke, Thomas, Brannon, Bratton, Taylor, Chandler, Twiggs, McCall, and Hammond, concerted plans for making an attack upon Ninety-Six. In the region between Broad River and Ninety-Six, the British had supplies collected at three points - at Summer's Mill, at Captain Faust's and at Williams', fifteen miles from Ninety-Six. At each of these points, a few British troops were stationed and to them the loyalists in great numbers flocked. It was concluded by Sumter and the other partisan leaders just to take these posts and then concentrate all their forces and make the contemplated attack upon the strong post of Ninety-Six.

On crossing Broad River at Fishdam Ford, Sumter directed his course down the river. Col. Taylor of South Carolina and Colonel Chandler of Georgia, with a small detachment, were sent out to break up the British post at Summer's, bring away the supplies and gain what intelligence they could of the movements of the enemy. Lieutenant Colonel Williamson of Georgia, and Maj. Hammond of South Carolina, with a detachment similar to that under Taylor and Chandler, were sent for a like purpose, against the post at Faust's. Whilst these detachments were attempting to accomplish the object for which they had been sent out, Sumter received information that Tarleton had returned from the low country. This fact necessarily caused Sumter to change his plans. He determined to retreat, but leisurely, that the two detachments might be enabled to join him.

Evidently the advance of Sumter towards Ninety-Six had greatly alarmed the British. When Cornwallis instructed Tarleton to cross the Wateree River and take the most direct route to Ninety-Six, he sent a strong detachment, consisting of the first battalion of the seventy-first regiment, under Major McArthur, and a portion of the sixty-third regiment, under Lieutenant Money, to join Tarleton so soon as he would arrive at Broad River. No doubt the troops stationed at Summer's Mill, at Captain Faust's, at Williams' and at Ninety-Six, had been informed of the intended attack upon the part of the Whigs. From Faust's and perhaps from Summer's Mill, the garrison had been removed.

Before Tarleton reached Broad River, he learned that the Americans were on the opposite bank. That the patriots might be deceived, Tarleton ordered his troops to conceal their uniforms in order to deceive Sumter. The American militia dreaded Tarleton and his legion more than any command in the British army. He was brave and daring and at the same time wickedly cruel. The green uniform in which the legion was clad made the hearts of the undisciplined Whigs tremble, whilst they dreaded the red coats but little. There was a mutual dread existing between Tarleton and the Whig militia. At Waxhaw he had acted so cruelly as to make his very name feared, hated, and detested by every Whig. On the other hand, Tarleton knew that he was a doomed man and feared to fall into the hands of the Whigs, for he was persuaded that his life would be sacrificed at once.

Having reached Broad River with the green uniform of his legion concealed, he ordered Major McArthur to fire two pieces of cannon at the Americans on the west bank of the river. As the Whigs had no cannon they were forced to give way. This was on the afternoon of the 17th of November. By 10 o'clock in the night all the British forces had crossed the river and encamped three miles from its bank. Here Tarleton and his forces lay during the eighteenth, waiting to gain information respecting Sumter.

During the first part of the night of the eighteenth, Tarleton received information that Sumter was moving towards Williams'. At daybreak on the morning of the nineteenth, Tarleton and his forces set out to get in the rear of Sumter. Their course lay in the direction of Indian Creek, in Newberry county. Sumter was retreating slowly that his two detachments might be able to join him. Tarleton did not know this. No doubt the design Tarleton had in view was to get between Sumter and the mountains and thus place him between his own forces and the garrison at Ninety-Six. Had he succeeded in this design, it is difficult to see how Sumter could have escaped a calamity worse than that which had befallen him at Fishing Creek, a few months before.

On the night of the nineteenth, Tarleton camped in the vicinity of Enoree, near the mouth of Duncan's Creek. Sumter and his forces, with the exception of the detachment sent under Colonels Taylor and Chandler, were not far distant; Williamson and Hammond, with their detachments, had returned and joined Sumter on the nineteenth. Whilst Tarleton lay encamped near the Enoree on the night of the nineteenth, one of his soldiers deserted and, entering Sumter's camp about midnight, communicated to the Americans the fact that they were hotly pursued by Tarleton. The British were confident that they would surprise and cut off Sumter and his whole corps during the next day.

The next morning Sumter set out leisurely on his retreat before Tarleton, because of the continued absence of Taylor and Chandler. At dawn of day on the twentieth, Tarleton pushed forward and by 10 o'clock he learned that Sumter was only a short distance ahead of him. On arriving at the Enoree, he learned that Sumter had crossed about two hours before. The American partisan had left a small detachment for the purpose of assisting Taylor and Chandler, should they come up. The advanced guard of the British cavalry made a charge upon the detachment left by Sumter at the ford of the Enoree. In this skirmish the British were partially successful. The Americans were forced to retire and join the main force.

When about half a mile from Blackstock's house, Sumter determined to halt and wait for the detachment under Taylor and Chandler. During the halt, the horses were fed and the men refreshed themselves. The halt was only for a few minutes. The retreat had scarcely been resumed when Taylor and Chandler came up and, at the same moment, the American videttes fired into the advance guard of the British. Taylor and Chandler had succeeded in capturing a considerable quantity of flour and other supplies from the enemy. These they were so fortunate as to secure from the scouting parties of Tarleton's army. Sumter now saw that he must prepare for battle. This he was anxious to avoid, but further retreat under the circumstances was of doubtful propriety. The Tyger was in his front and Tarleton in his rear. Weighing all the circumstances, he determined to risk an engagement and, in the event he was not successful, to cross the Tyger during the night and continue his retreat. No time was to be lost. Tarleton with one hundred and ninety cavalry and eighty mounted infantry was in sight. The place where Sumter's forces were was favorable to the employment of a partisan force.

It is in the extreme south-western corner of Union county on the south bank of the Tyger River, about one mile from the line between the counties of Union and Spartanburg and five or six miles from the line between Laurens and Union counties. At that time a man by the name of Blackstock lived at the place. Hence the name of the ford on the river and the name of the battle ground.

The two forces were now in full view of each other. Tarleton had his men marshaled for a charge and Sumter had his arranged for a retreat. With all possible speed, the Carolina "Game Cock" set about to put his forces in position to receive the charge of the enemy. In this important work he was greatly assisted by Major James Jackson of Georgia.

In front of Blackstock's house and between the two forces ran a small stream, a branch of Tyger River. The course of this branch was a semi-circle, the concavity being towards the British. The banks of this small stream were covered with thick undergrowth. North of this branch was a hill, rising abruptly from a branch. On this hill was Blackstock's house. A lane made of logs notched into each other led up to the house. Near the house was a large log tobacco house and a hog pen constructed of logs. The tobacco house, hog pen and dwelling house, Sumter filled with troops. Men were also stationed behind the lane fence. The opening between the logs of the houses and fence enabled Sumter's men to shoot the enemy as they came up, whilst the logs protected them from the balls of the British soldiers. One wing of the American force was secured by the Tyger River, and the other was protected by the tobacco barn. The road leading to Blackstock's Ford, on the Tyger, passed through the centre of the American forces.

When Tarleton saw that Sumter was prepared to give him battle, he ordered the detachment of the sixty-third regiment and part of the cavalry to dismount, in order to rest their horses. It was Tarleton's intention to wait until the remainder of his troops would come up.

It is in place to remark that the fighting commenced at one o'clock when the advance guard of the British crossed the Enoree. At four o'clock, Tarleton left his main forces and hastened forward with this detachment of cavalry and light infantry. His object was to prevent Sumter from crossing the Tyger before dark or to attack him whilst crossing. A short time before five, the near approach of Tarleton brought Sumter to a halt.

When Sumter discovered that Tarleton had divided his forces, he determined not to wait to be attacked, but to make the attack himself. This was a wise move. The order was given for the troops behind the hill to advance against the enemy. This they did, pouring in a destructive fire upon the enemy. The British received the fire in a manner becoming tried veterans and rushed forward upon the Americans with fixed bayonets. As they rushed up the lane, the Whigs from behind the fence poured in a second volley, which literally blockaded the road with dead men and horses. Those not shot down fled.

Between the enemy and the river was a thick wood. Sumter ordered Colonels Clarke and Chandler of Georgia and Major Hammond of South Carolina to take one hundred choice men and through this wood gain the enemy's rear. In the charge which the British made up the lane, Major Money and Lieutenants Gibson and Cope fell. Tarleton saw that something must be done or his forces would be cut to pieces in a short time. With that impetuosity for which he was noted, he charged with the main body of his cavalry, with the determination to drive the Americans from the tobacco barn and from the top of the hill. The men in the tobacco barn poured in a well directed volley, which dismounted many a Briton and drove the rest beyond the rivulet.

Tarleton now almost frantic, drew off his whole forces and having formed in the new, made a desperate charge against the Americans posted on the top of the hill. Here he was met by a small band of one hundred and fifty riflemen under Twiggs and Jackson of Georgia. These men fought with desperation and in the moment when about to be trampled down by the British horses, a company of reserves, under Colonel Richard Winn, came up and turned the tide of victory. Tarleton, seeing that he was beaten, fled.

Whilst the battle was raging at Blackstock's house, Clarke, Chandler and Hammond with one hundred men under their command, were ruining the British in the rear. The horses which the British had left behind when they made the charge had all been taken by Clarke and his party. When the British came back they found that the horses were gone. It was dark when the British began to retreat and all rushing to the rear, Clarke and his men turned loose all the horses except a few and set out for Sumter's camp.

In this battle the American loss was three killed and five wounded. Colonel Sumter was wounded in the breast early in the battle. The command of the troops and management of the battle devolved upon Twiggs and Jackson. The fight lasted near three hours after Sumter was wounded. The British left on the battle field between ninety and one hundred killed and near one hundred wounded.

The Americans having buried their three dead men and made provision for the comfort of the wounded British moved off in good order. The wounded Whigs were taken with them. Colonel Sumter was borne on a litter between two horses. After crossing the Tyger the troops were disbanded. The Georgians directed their course westward; the Carolinians went to their old camping grounds. One hundred men accompanied Sumter to North Carolina, Colonel Lacey of Chester returned to Liberty Hill camp at William Burris' Mill on Turkey Creek, York county. It is evident that the Americans gained a most signal victory at Blackstock. The forces were nearly equal in numbers; but Tarleton's forces were regulars, while Sumter's were mostly raw militia. The Americans did not pursue the flying British, because night had come on. Tarleton camped so soon as the remainder of his forces and those driven from the battle ground met.

Installment XXX

THE BATTLE OF COWPENS

Everything in this world is attended with uncertainty. When the British captured Savannah and Charleston and in a short time after literally demolished the army of General Gates at Camden, the people of Great Britain were jubilant. They thought the blow had been struck which would reduce the

American colonies into subjection to the British crown. The British officers in South Carolina thought they had nothing to do now, but by easy marches advance as far as Chesapeake. This done, Georgia, South Carolina, North Carolina and Virginia would be reduced to hopeless servitude to the majesty of Great Britain. The plan adopted by the British commander was to advance through the country, establish garrison's at convenient places, and thus keep in subjection the territory overrun. The military posts were designed to be so many places of rendezvous for the Tories and loyalists. His majesty's troops were expected to live on plunder.

This was not the dream of mere novices in the art of war. It was the device of officers of whom England is today justly proud. American liberty is enhanced in value, when we reflect that it was won by raw militia against officers trained in the best schools of Europe. Those who talk about Cornwallis, Tarleton and Rawdon as fools and cowards, suffer their judgment to be perverted to blind prejudice. No braver man ever drew a sword or commanded a military organization than he who fell on King's Mountain. No man understood better how to make a victory complete than Tarleton. To out-general Cornwallis or out fight Tarleton is the highest encomium that can be passed upon any officer. To thwart the purposes and disconcert the plans of these men as our fathers did, is sufficient to write their names on the highest niche of military fame. Those who say that the British officers were destitute of military skill and that the British soldiers they led were cowards, either have never studied the history of the Revolutionary war or have studied it to no purpose.

That Cornwallis might be enabled to execute with ease and promptness his plans for subjugating the whole of the southern colonies, and consequently all the American colonies, General Leslie was sent by General Clinton from New York with a corps of three thousand choice troops to the Chesapeake. Leslie set out from New York about the 10th of October and landed at Portsmouth, Va., about the middle of the same month. The object for which General Leslie was sent to Virginia, was to destroy all the public property belonging to the Americans and prevent General Washington from sending any forces to the assistance of the partisan leaders in the south.

These plans of the British officers were concocted immediately after the fall of Charleston and matured and attempted to be put in execution on the defeat of Gates at Camden. Cornwallis expected to advance to Charlotte where he would meet the brave Patrick Ferguson, and having established and fortified Charlotte in a way similar to Camden, he would then advance on to Portsmouth.

In the meantime the Whigs of Georgia and the two Carolinas were not idly pining over past misfortunes. Their defeats had only stimulated them to invincible energy. On the seventh of October - a few days after Cornwallis reached Charlotte - Patrick Ferguson and his whole army were surrounded on King's Mountain and literally annihilated. A chasm was made in the plans of the British chieftain which no strategy could span. The advance in the direction of Virginia was impossible under the existing circumstances. The region around Charlotte swarmed with Scotch-Irish Whigs. To remain in that locality was to jeopardize his whole command. Following the dictates of a wise policy, he retreated to Winnsboro and ordered General Leslie to leave Portsmouth and join him in South Carolina. This must have been sad news to Leslie. He had expected to hear of Cornwallis far on his way to Virginia when he landed at Portsmouth. Heretofore every victory had crowned every effort of the British and nothing but apparent defeat attended the undertaking of the Americans.

The country was not, as we have already seen, subdued. Partisan leaders had sprung up in all sections of the state. These were followed by men who were ready to suffer and die for their bleeding country. Marion and his men were lurking in the swamps of the Santee and Black rivers, ready whenever an opportunity presented itself to emerge from their watery hiding places and pour destruction and death into the ranks of the invading foe. Sumter and his illustrious coadjutors were in upper and western South Carolina, breaking up military posts and slaughtering the troops of the active and valiant Tarleton. Immediately before the battle of King's Mountain, it seemed as if the sun of American liberty had gone down to rise no more. It was only the darkness which precedes a rising sun.

On the Sabbath morning after Patrick Ferguson slept his last sleep on the rocky summit of King's Mountain, the sun rose as it had never been seen to rise before by the Americans. The tide of victory had turned. From this time onward it continued to flow in favor of the patriots, until it terminated in the imposing sight of General O'Hara surrendering the sword of Earl Cornwallis to General Lincoln at Yorktown.

Until General Leslie would arrive, Cornwallis was obliged to remain at Winnsboro. He did not, however, abandon his original plan to advance northward through North Carolina and Virginia. Soon after Leslie was called south from Virginia, the traitor, Arnold, was sent thither with a considerable force. He laid the country waste with fire and sword. He fought with the same mad desperation now for the British that he had once fought against them. Rather he now fought against liberty as recklessly as he had once fought valiantly for it.

A junction of the forces under Cornwallis and Arnold would have ruined the cause of American Liberty. With the forces of his command, it was all that Cornwallis could do to hold his own. He contemplated advancing into North Carolina, but not by the way of Charlotte. It was his intention to pass up Broad River and thus flank the Scotch-Irish of the "Hornet's Nest" region. This move he designed making so soon as he was joined by General Leslie and his forces.

On the thirteenth of December, General Leslie landed at Charleston. Here he found orders directing him to join Cornwallis with all possible speed with one thousand five hundred and thirty men. Cornwallis needed the whole of the forces under the command of General Leslie; but in order to protect Charleston it was necessary to leave one half at that point. This shows what a turn things had taken after the battle of King's Mountain. The British felt they were not safe behind their own fortifications. Several days were spent in procuring transportation wagons and horses.

On the nineteenth of December, Gen. Leslie set out to join Cornwallis by way of Camden. As early as the first of November, Cornwallis had begun to make preparations for his advance into North Carolina. Emissaries had been sent into various portions of the country to stir up the loyalists and ascertain the feeling of the inhabitants. The British were not easy. They could not feel that they were altogether safe. The emissaries could learn nothing of any importance favorable to the British and besides the country abounded with floating rumors of the hostile movements of the Americans. A report was brought to Cornwallis that the "mountain men" were collecting with the intention of making an attack upon Ninety-Six. The horrors of King's Mountain presented themselves to Earl Cornwallis and to prevent Ninety-Six from experiencing a similar fate with Ferguson and his men, Tarleton was sent out to look after these "mountain men." The rumor had no foundation but in the fears of those who first reported it and those who afterward circulated it.

Finding that the report of the advance of the "mountain men" had no foundation in fact, Tarleton a short time after the battle of Blackstock, moved down and camped on the east side of Broad River at what was then Brierly's Ferry. At Winnsboro, Cornwallis was making all preparations for the contemplated move into North Carolina. The country was scoured in search of horses to mount his soldiers and draw his baggage wagons. The sick who had been quartered in private families in the neighborhood were brought into camp, and the arms and ammunition got in readiness for a campaign.

Whilst the British general was thus actively engaged in preparing for the reduction of the country, the American officers were not idle. General Gates had collected the fragments of his army at Hillsborough, North Carolina. Here the troops had been reorganized. The Maryland and Delaware lines were consolidated and put under the command of Otho Holland Williams. The remains of those regiments, formerly commanded by Baylor, Bland and Moyland, together with some recruits were embodied into one regiment and put under the command of Lieutenant Colonel William Washington. About the same time, Daniel Morgan was made brigadier general and assigned to the southern army. Recruits from Virginia joined Gates about the same time. A division of North Carolina militia under Sumner and Davidson as well as a volunteer corps under Davie, had taken the field.

After the unfortunate battle of Camden, congress either having lost confidence in General Gates or having grown wise enough to correct a former error, determined to supply his place with a more efficient man. The honor of making the selection was awarded to the commander-in-chief. General Washington selected for his important field Nathaniel Greene, at that time quarter-master general. Gen. Greene was assigned to the command of the southern army on the thirtieth of October, 1780. He resigned the office of quarter-master general and set out at once for the south. General Gates had moved his headquarters from Hillsborough to Charlotte. General Greene arrived at Charlotte on the second of December and on the next day formally took command of the southern forces. It was only the frame work of an army consisting as it did of only four thousand five hundred troops, a large number of which were undisciplined militia. After having made the necessary arrangement for supplies, General Greene divided his army into two detachments. One was to take post on the right of Cornwallis and the other on the left - the detachment on the right to be commanded by Greene himself and to be stationed in Chesterfield county, on Hicks' Creek. This post was about seventy miles from Winnsboro, the headquarters of Cornwallis. The detachment on the left to be commanded by General Morgan was to be stationed in Spartanburg county, between the Pacolet and Broad rivers.

It would seem that neither the Americans nor the British had any correct idea of each others' intentions. General Greene probably did not know that Leslie had left Portsmouth; nor did Cornwallis know that Greene had been assigned to the command of the southern army. It would only be conjecture to say why General Greene divided his army into two detachments. One week after General Leslie landed at Charleston, Greene set out for Cheraw and Morgan for the region between the Pacolet and Broad Rivers.

General Morgan and Colonel Washington having but recently returned from a tour in the region around Camden, in which they captured a British post at Rugeley's Mill, making the commander, Colonel Rugeley and one hundred men prisoners, set out for the region beyond Broad River. On the evening of the twentieth and morning of the twenty-first of December, Morgan and Washington crossed Catawba River at Wright's Ferry, and joined Lacey at his camp on Turkey Creek in York county. Lacey and his men broke up camp and accompanied General Morgan. The American force now under the command of Morgan, consisted of four hundred continental infantry and about one hundred cavalry, together with about five hundred militia. Near the last of December, Morgan encamped in the neighborhood of Pacolet Springs, in Spartanburg county. From this point Washington with his cavalry was frequently sent out to scatter small parties of Tories and destroy the military depots of the British. These excursions of Washington alarmed Earl Cornwallis. The country was full of Tories and British soldiers who prowled through the country under the command of Bill Cunningham or his subalterns. These parties kept the Whig settlers in continual terror. To break up these gangs of highway robbers and bloody scouts was a part of Colonel Washington's duty. In some of his expeditions daring feats of individual courage were exhibited. One will suffice as a specimen of the whole.

On one occasion a son of "Green Erin" by the name of Sam Clowney came in contact with eight British soldiers, all lusty fellows, armed to the teeth. These Sam managed, by adroitness, to capture and march for eight miles into Morgan's camp. On presenting the result of his day's work, General Morgan asked with no little surprise, "How on earth Sam did you manage to capture eight men?" With that promptness for which the natives of the Emerald Isle are noted, he replied, "Faith may it please your honor, I surrounded them."

Determined to put a stop to Morgan's operations, Cornwallis sent out Tarleton with his famous legion. At this point commenced a movement thrillingly interesting from the beginning and triumphant in its end - the surrender of Cornwallis at Yorktown, on the nineteenth of October, 1781.

The plan of the campaign which was devised by Lieutenant Colonel Tarleton and submitted to Cornwallis and by him approved, was for Tarleton to push Morgan beyond the Yadkin and thus leave the country open for an entrance into North Carolina. So soon as Tarleton would move toward Morgan, the main army was to move from Winnsboro up the ridge which divides the waters of Catawba from those of Broad River. General Leslie, in order to deceive General Greene, was to move along the eastern side of the Catawba, keeping opposite Cornwallis. The point at which the three forces were to unite, was King's Mountain.

On Sabbath, the sixth of January, Lord Cornwallis with the main army set out from Winnsboro for King's Mountain. Little did he and his troops think of what sad misfortunes awaited them. That he might co-operate with Tarleton in driving away Morgan, he commenced his march before that officer crossed the Broad River. The understanding between Tarleton and Cornwallis was that the latter with the main army would be at Bullock's Creek Church, in York county, on Saturday night after he left Winnsboro. For some reason Cornwallis failed to meet his engagement and strange to say gave Tarleton no intimation of his delay on the way. Cornwallis stopped at Bull Run in Chester county, to wait for Leslie. Cornwallis approved of the plan in all its details as suggested by Tarleton, but strange as it may appear, neglected to carry it out. On the eleventh of January, Tarleton commenced his march up Broad River and, although the roads were very bad, pressed forward and crossed the river near the mouth of Turkey Creek on the fourteenth. The orders which he had received from Cornwallis were to "push Morgan to the utmost." These orders he determined to carry out to the letter.

On the next day he gained certain intelligence of the position of Morgan. On hearing of Tarleton's approach and his superior force, Morgan at first retreated. This was what Tarleton expected. His plan now was either to destroy Morgan, or drive him across Broad River, into the hands of Cornwallis, who he thought was at Bullock's Creek Church. The plan was good but failed in its execution. On the evening of the sixteenth, Tarleton reached Morgan's camp, but found no one there. Morgan had left it only a few hours before Tarleton arrived. Leaving his baggage at this point, Tarleton pushed forward with all possible speed, taking a circuitous route as if intending to flank Morgan. He marched all night. About midnight a rumor of the advance of some "mountain men" disturbed Tarleton's thoughts and he concluded that it was safest to push directly after Morgan and bring on an action before the junction with Morgan of the "mountain men" of whom he had heard and whom he dreaded. On he pushed, as if his very existence depended upon engaging Morgan at once. He scarcely expected that Morgan would dare to encounter him alone, hence he thought that all he had to do in order to capture Morgan and all his force, was to get up with them.

At eight o'clock on the morning of the seventeenth, Tarleton and his force came in sight of the American camp. Tarleton was disappointed. Instead of finding Morgan retreating in disorder, men were drawn up in battle array. Morgan was one of those men who always retreat reluctantly. On the evening before, he had determined in his mind to retreat no further. The place where Morgan was encamped was called the "Cowpens." A ridge crossed the road at right angles. In the rear of this ridge is another similar ridge, about four hundred yards distant. The location was by no means favorable for such a force as that commanded by Morgan. It was more favorable for Tarleton than for Morgan. Tarleton had a strong cavalry force, whilst Morgan had only eighty. There was nothing for Morgan's flanks to rest upon. Everything was favorable for Tarleton. All his troops were tried soldiers whilst the majority of Morgan's were militia. Military men, perhaps, would have advised Morgan not to risk a battle. One of the characteristics of Morgan was that he always depended upon his own judgment. Tarleton concluded that the only reason that Morgan had determined to risk a battle, was the fact that he was so closely pursued that he could not do otherwise than fight. Such, however, was not the case. Morgan had contemplated fighting at the Pacolet on the 15th, but retreated that he might gain some advantage.

When the British force came in sight, Morgan's men had breakfasted and were ready for the conflict. On the evening before, Morgan had ordered each rifleman to get twenty-four rounds of powder and ball prepared before he retired to rest. The order in which the troops should be arranged for battle was also written out and read to the officers on the evening before. The troops were marshaled in accordance with the following order: The Georgia and Carolina militia, in front. These were commanded by McDowell, Cunningham, Hammond and Donnelly. Immediately in the rear of the militia was Colonel Howard's command, which consisted of the continental infantry and two companies of Virginia militia. These last were commanded by Taite and Triplett. On the left of Howard, was Pickens command; on the right Triplett and Beaty. Colonel Washington with the cavalry was stationed in the rear. The horses belonging to the infantry were tied at a convenient distance in the rear of the whole.

Tarleton's vanguard advanced and deployed across the road, with a ravine between them and the American front line. The artillery was placed on the road a short distance in the rear of the advance guard. The cavalry was divided and stationed in the rear to the right and left of the road. In the rear and in a line parallel with the cavalry, was placed the seventy-first regiment, under Major McArthur as a reserve.

Before the battle commenced, Morgan spent a few moments in exhorting his men to do their duty and the victory was sure. About nine o'clock Tarleton, who was in the front line of the British, gave the order to advance. With a shout the column rushed forward, expecting the American militia to break and flee in confusion. In this they were disappointed. The militia stood firm and when the British came within range, discharged a well aimed volley which thinned the ranks of the enemy. The British pressed forward, shouting and firing incessantly. The militia fell back to the ranks of the line commanded by Pickens. The British now rushed forward with bayonets. The militia now fell back to the second line and those under McCall fled to the horses. This, however, produced no disturbance, for Morgan, thinking that the militia would give way, had declared it as a part of his plan that the militia were to fire and fall back. Tarleton, seeing the militia giving way, ordered a general charge. The Americans met him with a firmness which would have done credit to any troops. The contest was fearful and the result doubtful. Soon the line of the enemy began to bend. McArthur now brought up his reserves. This animated the yielding British and the contest was renewed. Never did men fight harder. Everything was done by both parties that could be done and the contest was in fearful doubts. McArthur attempted to gain Howard's flank. Howard ordered his first company to charge the British. The company, mistaking the command to charge for an order to fall back, the whole line now began to retreat in disorder. Morgan, with the greatest presence of mind, ordered it to fall back behind the cavalry and halt. This checked the retreat. Tarleton ordered another charge. When the British had approached within a short distance of Howard's men they were ordered to face about and fire. This they did and literally covered the ground with wounded and dead British. The living were brought to a halt. Howard seeing this, ordered his men to charge them with the bayonet. This decided the day in favor of the Americans. The British infantry were in the utmost confusion.

Some of Tarleton's cavalry had gained the rear and were slaughtering McCall's militia by the whole-sale. Colonel Washington saw the condition in which things were and dashed in upon the cavalry of the enemy and put them to flight. The British infantry and cavalry were now so mixed up that it was impossible to rally them. The few of the British who were not wounded or killed fled in every direction, each man for himself.

The history of the Revolutionary war contained no more wonderful battle than that of the Cowpens. The advantages at the outset were all on the side of the British and yet the gains in the end were all on the side of the Americans. The American loss was twelve killed and forty-eight wounded. The British loss, by their own account was one hundred killed and five hundred and twenty-three taken prisoners. The spoils which fell into the hands of the Americans were all the enemy's baggage, thirty-five baggage wagons, eight hundred horses, two standards, two pieces of artillery and eight hundred muskets. The victory was just as complete as any victory could be. Tarleton filled with sorrow, fled from the battlefield and never stopped until he crossed Broad River at Hamilton's Ford.

THE BATTLE OF COWPENS AND ITS RESULTS, INCIDENTS, ETC.

It is natural for us to dwell with special delight upon the worthy deeds of our ancestors. By an instinct which nothing but death can overcome, we cherish the spot which gave us birth. The exile from his native land revisits in dreams the play grounds of his childhood. In his lonely cell, thoughts fill his mind which may be expressed in this short sentence: "Take me home to die." If we may innocently love our native land with an intensity which no oppression can destroy, may we not also as intensely love those who gave us existence and bequeathed us to that native land?

The part which the south took in the Revolutionary war is not understood by the American people, at least it has never received that prominence which it justly deserves. The battles of Lexington, Saratoga and Bennington, together with an almost countless number of skirmishes which took place in the north, form the woof and warp of Revolutionary history; whilst the battles of King's Mountain and Cowpens are treated with silent neglect. British offi-cers did not think these battles small affairs, which might be forgotten in a few days. Lieutenant Colonel Tarleton, in speaking of the fall of Ferguson, deliber-ately declared that the discomfiture of the British at King's Mountain put a period to the first expedition of the British into North Carolina and the affair of the Cowpens overshadowed the commencement of the second with gloom. It is easy to see according to all human probabilities, what would have been the result had Ferguson been victorious at King's Mountain. Cornwallis would have formed a junction with General Leslie at Portsmouth, and in that event it would have been impossible for General Washington to have concentrated troops to resist either Cornwallis or Clinton. The British camp would have swarmed with loyalists, whilst the American army would have been annihilated by desertions. Had Tarleton been victorious at the Cowpens, General Greene would have been ruined. Cornwallis could have either cut him off and forced him to surrender or run him into the arms of the traitor, Arnold. The loss of either King's Mountain or Cowpens would have lost to the Americans, Georgia, the two Carolinas, and Virginia, and ultimately all of the thirteen colonies.

It must be remembered that the victories gained at King's Mountain and the Cowpens, forever broke the spirit of the Tories and loyalists from the Dan to the Savannah. As we will see in the sequel, this class of citizens lost all confidence in the king's troops to pro-tect them. These were no idle fears. It was a deliber-ate conclusion deduced from the facts. At King's Mountain the British lost absolutely everything and the Americans comparatively nothing. At the Cowpens, the British lost in killed and prisoners nearly as many men as the Americans had in the bat-tle. The news of these sad disasters spread amongst the loyalists from Cross Creek, North Carolina, to Augusta, Georgia. Dreadful was the consternation which it produced among the friends of King George. On the other hand, joy and gladness filled the hearts of the friends of liberty.

Perhaps most of those military chieftains who have learned all their theories of war second handed would be ready to censure both Campbell and Morgan. Ferguson was well posted on a craggy moun-tain. He was well provided with men and the muni-tions of war. The patriot band who attacked him were self-made soldiers. They knew little of the science of war as taught in the schools. The same remark will apply to the heroes of the Cowpens. Colonel Tarleton was certainly a brave man and a skillful officer. His men were well provided with everything that such a corps required.

General Daniel Morgan, the principal in com-mand at the battle of the Cowpens, was one of those men whose real character is likely to be misunder-stood. There are multitudes of the human family who have learned the art of selling themselves for more than they are really worth. In a social and moral point of view, they appear to be better than they really are. They put on airs and look wise and pretend to be good and wise and the multitude in process of time accord to them all that greatness and goodness which they claim. To this class of men General Morgan did not belong. He was a better man in every respect than he appeared to be. By birth he was a native of New Jersey. His ancestors came from Wales. In his veins no doubt there was some blood which the Caesars could not subdue. His parents were poor and unable to bequeath to their son anything but a life of toil. His education was neglected as was the case with many others in those days.

In 1751, when young Morgan was in his seventeenth year, he left the humble home of his parents and came to Frederick county, Virginia. He engaged with one of the wealthy planters of that region as a day laborer. Even at that early period in his life, he contemplated by industry and proper management, bettering his condition in life. The planter made him his wagoner. Morgan so increased his means that in the expedition which General Braddock led against the Indians and in which he was killed, he accompanied the army, driving a wagon of his own.

During this expedition of Braddock, Morgan incurred the displeasure of a British officer and was sentenced to receive five hundred lashes. After the punishment had been inflicted, it was discovered that Morgan was not guilty of the crime for which he had been so cruelly treated. At the time Morgan bore the indignity like a stoic, and in after life manifested no resentment toward British officers whom the fortunes of war placed in his hands. The whipping was performed by a bugler who discharged the duty with great reluctancy. In his excitement he made a miscount, inflicting only four hundred and ninety-nine lashes. In speaking of this, Morgan was accustomed ever afterward to say that "the British government owed him one lash yet."

Physically Morgan was a giant. He was not quarrelsome, but had not inclination to keep down disturbances. He was at one time a noted gambler and at the same time disposed to work all sorts of mischief on his associates. It so happened that Berryville, the town which he frequented was so noted for the fist and skull fights in which he and his associates were engaged, that it was known in the community by the name of Battletown. In these fights Morgan always came out best.

All this is calculated to give us an unfavorable opinion of the hero of the Cowpens. We must take into consideration the civilization of the times. One hundred years ago a frolic without a fight was no frolic at all. We must not conclude that a man who would fight any and everybody in the community who wanted to fight, had no influence. Such was not the case. Morgan possessed great influence in the neighborhood of Berryville and raised soon after the difficulties between the Americans and British commenced, a rifle company of near one hundred men, which had no equal in the American army.

It is not our purpose, however, to write a biography of General Morgan at present. The manner in which he arranged the forces under his command for battle at the Cowpens was, as a military man of no mean fame has said, "masterly."

A little incident which is related by himself as having taken place on the eve of battle, gives an insight into the moral character of Morgan. When he was an old man, broken down with rheumatism, he would often exclaim, when speaking of the past: "Ah! People said old Morgan never was afraid - old Morgan never prayed. They were mistaken. I trembled at Quebec, and in the gloom of morning when approaching the fort at Cape Diamond, I knelt down in the snow and prayed. Before the battle of the Cowpens I went out into the woods and having ascended a tree, poured out my soul to God, for protection." The men of those times were often much better at heart than they appeared to be. They had rough work to do, and He who manages everything had fitted them for their work.

One of the prominent actors in the battle of the Cowpens was Colonel William Augustine Washington. On that occasion, Colonel Washington was in command of the cavalry. These were less than eighty in number and were placed in the rear and composed the main guard. As we have already seen, at the moment the discerning eye of Washington saw the British cavalry charging in disorder upon McCall's militia, he dashed in upon them. This, together with a well directed fire by the militia under Howard and Pickens, struck terror among the troops of Tarleton. They commenced to flee in the utmost confusion. Tarleton did everything mortal man could do to restore order, but all in vain. His infantry threw down their guns and surrendered and his cavalry, deaf to the threats and encouragements of their officers, fled in confusion in every direction. The field was cleared of every Briton in a few minutes. Washington impetuously dashed forward far in advance of his men. Tarleton with a few officers, still lingered on the margin of the battlefield. A body of forty cavalry remained with Tarleton as a guard. "The rest unmindful" as

Tarleton says, "of their duty had left their commander unprotected." So soon as Tarleton saw Washington alone he ordered his body guard to wheel about and charge upon the single horseman. In a moment Washington was surrounded by British dragoons. A hand to hand fight began. A struggle for life ensued. One of Tarleton's aids aimed a blow with his sword at Washington. At this important juncture of affairs, an American sergeant dashed forward into the conflict and with a well guided blow, disabled the arm about to strike his commander. At the same moment, another British officer on the opposite side of Washington was aiming a blow at him with his glittering blade. A little bugler by the name of Ball, whose arm was too weak to wield a sword, came up at the moment when all depended on promptness of action and, with a pistol, wounded Washington's assailant. Tarleton and Washington were now alone, standing face to face. Tarleton discomfited, but still brave, made a thrust at the head of Washington. The blow was warded off and as the heavy saber of Washington glided down the sword of Tarleton, it glided down Tarleton. Some authorities say that some of the fingers of Tarleton were cut off. This statement is probably exaggerated.

After the battle of Cowpens, when the British army was on its way to Yorktown, Tarleton was entertained at the house of an American Whig. The ladies were loud and perhaps a little tantalizing in their praises of Col. Washington. Tarleton could not bear to hear any one speak favorably of the man who had driven him off the field. To mortify the feelings of the ladies and in this way get revenge, Tarleton remarked "that he had understood that Colonel Washington was a very illiterate man, who could scarcely write his name." Mrs. Jones, a daughter of Colonel Montfort of Halifax, North Carolina was present. So soon as Tarleton had finished his remark, Mrs. Jones replied with keen emphasis. "Ah! Colonel you ought to know better, for you bear on your person proof that he knows very well how to make his mark."

On another occasion Tarleton, inconsiderately, was speaking disrespectfully of Washington. With a kind of sarcastic sneer he said, "he would be glad to see that Colonel Washington about whom the Americans made so much ado." It so happened that Mrs. Ashe, another daughter of Colonel Montfort, was present. This Whig lady replied, "If you had taken time to look behind you at the battle of Cowpens, Colonel Tarleton, you could have enjoyed that pleasure." Colonel Tarleton lost all control of himself and laying his hand on his sword manifested a disposition to take revenge. General Leslie was present and checked the rage of Tarleton, saying at the same time to Mrs. Ashe, "say what you please Mrs. Ashe; Colonel Tarleton knows better than to insult a lady in my presence."

MORGAN'S RETREAT

The most celebrated retreat on record is that of the ten thousand Greeks who espoused the cause of Cyrus, the younger, in his expedition against his brother Artaxerxes. After the death of Cyrus, these ten thousand Greeks cut their way through an enemy's country and returned to their native land. So wonderful was this retreat that it is historically designated as the "Retreat of the ten thousand."

Great as was the bravery and skill exhibited by the Greeks, the retreat of General Morgan from the Cowpens and the subsequent retreat of General Greene through North Carolina and over the Dan, into Virginia is no less remarkable. Since "it is distance that lends enchantment to the view," we have no doubt but some day, in the future history of the world, the Morgan and Greene's retreat will eclipse that of Xenophon.

The battle of Cowpens was fought, as already stated, on the 17th of January, 1781. The conflict began about 9 o'clock in the morning. That same evening, Earl Cornwallis was informed of Tarleton's defeat. On the day after the battle of Cowpens, General Leslie formed a junction with Earl Cornwallis in York county, on the plantation of John Hillhouse, now owned in part by Samuel C. Youngblood. The British camp was in front of the residence of Mr. Youngblood. Colonel Tarleton encamped on Broad River near Hamilton's Ford. Tradition says that several of his soldiers who had been wounded at the Cowpens died at Hamilton's Ford and were buried on land now belonging to Junius W. Thompson. Not many years since, it is related that those cultivating these lands exhumed human bones, which in all probability were the remains of some soldiers who died from wounds inflicted by Morgan's men.

Long after the war was over and prosperity has effaced the devastation caused by the British army in its progress through the country, a pair of silver sleeve buttons, upon which were engraved the initials of a British officer's name, were found near Samuel C. Youngblood's. These relics of the times that "tried men's souls" are in the possession of some one in Chester. To the mind that is fond of reveling in the past, these things possess an interest, which can be better felt than described. A strange and indescribable feeling pervades the soul when we stand upon the ground where once camped a British army. Every movement made either by the army of the patriots or by their enemies is full of interest.

On the afternoon of the memorable day on which Morgan defeated Tarleton at the Cowpens, Morgan set out to cross Broad River. A small detachment was left under the command of Colonel Pickens to bury the dead of both armies and make provisions for the comfort of the wounded. On the evening after the battle, Morgan crossed Broad River above the South Carolina line and, by forced marches, on a route leading him over the spot where King's Mountain station on the Air Line Railroad is now located, he passed through the lower edge of Cleveland and Gaston counties and crossed the Catawba at the Island Ford. Here, through couriers, an arrangement had been made between General Greene and General Morgan for a conference. Morgan crossed the Catawba on the 29th of January. His march had been slow, on account of the number of prisoners and baggage captured from the British at the Cowpens.

So soon as Earl Cornwallis heard of Tarleton's defeat, with a heavy heart he began to make arrangements for his advance into North Carolina. During his stay at Winnsboro and on his march from Winnsboro to Turkey Creek, he had collected a large number of horses. These were gathered up by the Tories, who were generally experts in horse stealing. An organized band of these depredators infested the country. Their headquarters was on the western side of Broad River, in the present county of Newberry.

On the night after the battle of the Cowpens, General Leslie encamped on Sandy River, in Chester county. The next day Leslie marched his forces in the camp of Cornwallis. It had already been determined by Cornwallis to push forward and if possible prevent Morgan from crossing the Catawba. Arrangements were made to mount the soldiers and convert the whole British forces under his command into light infantry. It was the dead of winter and the roads were in a wretched condition. The country over which they had to pass was broken and roads had to be cut. The country was sparsely settled and consequently provisions scarce. Cornwallis, whilst encamped at Hillhouse's (now Youngblood's), began to grow disheartened and when he heard of Tarleton's defeat at the Cowpens his hopes of subduing the country almost failed. He met with few friends amongst the inhabitants and the Whigs would prowl around his camp, shoot his sentinels and, like Arabs, dash into the very midst of his camp and plunder his quarters.

The house in which Cornwallis had his headquarters stood east of the road, opposite the residence of Samuel C. Youngblood. On one occasion a courier rode into the camp and tied his horse to the cheek of the door, in which were Cornwallis and his aids. The redoubtable Jack McLain, seizing the opportunity, rushed up, untied the horse, and mounting him rode out of the British camp unhurt.

The 18th of January, 1781, was a busy day in the British camp on Turkey Creek. The united forces were, as we may say, re-organized and arranged for the capture, first of Morgan, then of Greene, and finally the complete subjugation of all North Carolina. It was the dream of a sick man. It was hope against hope. Generals, like private soldiers, often suffer their hopes and fears to control their judgment. The following is the order in which the troops were to march up Broad River. In front, marched the Yagers. These were a corps of infantry mounted on horses and armed with rifles. Their office was to scour the country in front of the main army and drive away the Whigs from the line of march. The Yagers were followed by a corps of road cutters. The duty of opening up a road for the wagons belonging to the army was assigned to these. By this corps the road leading from Winnsboro to Little Broad River, in Cleveland county, N.C., was opened. In some places it has been abandoned, but in the main it continues the same that it was ninety-five years ago. For a long time after the war it was called the King's Road; at a later period it was known as the Charleston Road. Both these appellations are at present nearly forgotten. The corps of road cutters were followed by two three-pounders. The next in order was the brigade guards; then the regiment of Bose; then followed the North Carolina Tories. As if to protect these loyal subjects of the king, but unpatriotic citizens, two six-pounders were ordered to follow in their rear. The two six-pounders were followed by Lieutenant Colonel Webster's brigade of cavalry. Next followed the wagons, which bore the baggage of Earl Cornwallis. Then the wagons in which were placed the baggage belonging to the field officers. In the rear of these were the ammunition wagons, hospital wagons and wagons belonging to the different regiments. Then followed the provision train and loose horses. One hundred men selected from Colonel Webster's brigade of cavalry, under the command of one captain and two subalterns, formed the rear guards.

At eight o'clock on the night of the 18th of January, 1781, Earl Cornwallis issued orders for the whole army to be ready to move off in the order already stated at eight o'clock on the next morning. We can only imagine the grand and imposing spectacle which the army of Cornwallis presented as it moved slowly along through the wilderness. No doubt John Hillhouse was glad when Cornwallis vacated his house and no doubt he and his few neighbors were in a deplorable condition. The British troops had been quartered on them for several days. A considerable field lying in the direction of Turkey Creek from Samuel C. Youngblood's residence, was cleared by the British soldiers in securing firewood.

The first day, the army made its way as far as Wolf's Creek. On the twentieth, the Yagers were detached and sent to Tarleton, who was still at Hamilton's Ford. On the same day, Tarleton, in obedience to the orders of Cornwallis, crossed Broad River for the purpose of gaining intelligence of the movements of Morgan and also rendering aid to his troops who had been scattered in the recent battle. It would seem from this move that the British were ignorant of Morgan's movement. Tarleton having learned that Morgan was not on the west side of Broad River, re-crossed the river at Smith's Ford.

On the night of the twentieth, Cornwallis camped on Buffalo Here he was joined by Tarleton and the resolution was formed to pursue Morgan. Up to this time the intention was to cut Morgan off. On the night of the twenty-third, following the trail of Morgan, the British reached Old Tryon Courthouse in the western corner of the present county of Gaston, about twenty miles from Lincolnton. The next day, hungry and footsore, they reached Ramsour's Mill, in the vicinity of Lincolnton. Cornwallis had heard of Ramsour's Mill before. The mention of the name awakened unpleasant recollections. There on the twentieth of June, 1780, the loyal North Carolinians, under the ill starred Colonel Moore, met with a sad and ruinous defeat.

At Ramsour's Mill they remained three days, collecting provisions and making arrangements for continuing the pursuit of Morgan. The weather was exceedingly bad, and the progress through the country very slow. Cornwallis had learned since he left Turkey Creek that it was impossible to effect anything, encumbered as he was with baggage. Determined to do everything and make any sacrifice that he might succeed in his undertaking, Cornwallis issued an order on the twenty-fifth for all superfluous baggage to be destroyed. All the wagons belonging to the army, except those loaded with salt, hospital stores, ammunition, and four empty wagons for the sick were committed to the flames. Officers as well as men were ordered to reduce their private baggage. That this order might be obeyed cheerfully by all the officers, Earl Cornwallis promptly reduced the quantity of his own baggage. It is difficult to say whether this was a wise or foolish act. It seems to have been the act of a man whose motto was success or ruin.

RETREAT OF GENERAL GREENE

We left Earl Cornwallis at Ramsour's Mill in Lincoln county, N.C., and General Morgan on the east side of the Catawba - nearly opposite the camp of the British chieftain.

On the evening after the battle of Cowpens, Morgan commenced his retreat, and on the morning of the next day at 8 o'clock, Cornwallis set out in pursuit. For ten days both armies toiled with all their energies. The Americans struggled that they might escape; and the British hastened the pursuit that the prisoners captured at Cowpens might be rescued, and their captors captured, or cut to pieces.

It was the dead of winter. There were few roads and the country through which the armies passed was hilly - in some places mountainous - and the weather very bad. The consequence was that the progress of both armies was slow. The distance traversed by each was nearly equal. On the 28th of January, Morgan crossed the Catawba at Island Ford. Two hours after his rear guard had reached the eastern bank, the van guard of the British, under Brigadier General O'Hara, appeared in sight. Morgan and his men were safe. The sun was setting. Dark and ominous clouds covered the face of the sky. The British general concluded to spend the night on the western bank of the river, cross early the next morning, rout the forces of Morgan and rescue Tarleton's men who had been taken prisoners. During the night the rain fell in torrents and by daylight the waters of the Catawba had interposed an insurmountable barrier between the pursued and the pursuer. Thus, for 48 hours the waters of the river continued to leap over their banks, holding the British earl completely in abeyance. The rains continued to fall and the British were thoroughly drenched. They were forced to fall back and kindle large fires in order to dry their wet baggage and powder. The headquarters of Cornwallis was at the house of Jacob Forney. The story of this man is too thrilling to be omitted.

Jacob Forney was a descendant of the French Huguenots. His father, after the revocation of the edict of Nantes, in 1685, fled from his native country and settled in Alsace on the Rhine. When his son Jacob was about four years old, the elder Forney died. At the age of fourteen, young Forney, now an orphan, left Alsace and went to Amsterdam. Here he heard glowing accounts of the New World. The tales which he heard of the sufferings of his fathers fired his soul with hatred for tyrants, and a love of liberty, both political and religious. In the first ship bound for America he took passage, and in due time landed on the shores of the New World and took up his temporary abode in Pennsylvania. A few years afterwards he returned to Germany in order to get possession of a small legacy which had fallen to him. His business arranged, young Forney set out again for America. The vessel on which he embarked had a number of emigrants from Berne in Switzerland. Amongst these was a beautiful girl by the name of Maria Berger. Between Jacob Forney and Maria Berger an acquaintance was formed. This acquaintance was, in due time, matured into love. On arriving in Pennsylvania, they were married and in 1754 came to Lincoln county, N.C.

Jacob Forney was in his day a pillar in his community. The Cherokee Indians feared him and his neighborhood depended upon him to defend them in every emergency. So frequently had he been shot at by the Indians and so often had his clothing been pierced by bullets without being wounded, that his neighbors really believed that he was bullet proof. On one occasion, it was reported that after coming out of a fight with the Indians, he unbuttoned the bosom of his coat and "near a peck of bullets fell out."

When Cornwallis was in pursuit of Morgan and found that he could not cross the Catawba, on account of its being swollen by the recent rains, he came back to Jacob Forney's. A Tory by the name of Deck informed the British earl of the condition of Jacob Forney. His house was about two miles from the main road and no doubt was the best one in the whole community at that time. Everything we may suppose was in abundance. The house consisted of two stories and a cellar. Cornwallis made the upper story his headquarters. Here he devised, during his three days' stay, his plans for future operations. Forney's hogs, cows, chickens, corn, fodder, and everything which either man or horse could eat, was appropriated without stint. This did not satisfy the invading foe. Deck had informed them that Forney had a large sum of money hidden somewhere on the premises. This was true at least in part. He had a sum of money which at that day and in that community was thought to be very large. The legacy which he had received in Germany had been saved. Some of the identical coin which he had brought with him to America, was still in his possession. Diligent search was made for this money. At last it, together with some jewelry, was found. Up to this time, Jacob Forney, making a virtue of necessity, had remained quiet in the cellar. He was now an old man and, being found unarmed, the British did not disturb him further than to drive him into the cellar. So soon however, as he learned that his money was found and hopelessly in the hands of the enemies of his country, he lost all control of himself and seizing his gun,

threatened to kill Cornwallis. This he would have done had it not been for the prudence of his wife. He had actually begun to ascend the stairs leading to the room occupied by Cornwallis. His wife pulled him down and through her persuasion he was induced to desist from his bold but dangerous undertaking.

Deck, the Tory who acted as guide and informer for the British earl, was a near neighbor to Forney. By some means it was found out as soon as the British left, the part Deck had acted. He and Forney had been on intimate terms, but Forney determined that he should be treated only as an enemy in the future. A messenger was sent by Forney to tell him that if he did not leave the country immediately he would shoot him on first sight. Deck knew that Forney meant all that he said. Still, for some reason he did not see fit to leave the neighborhood at once. It was ascertained that he was concealing himself in the woods. Forney armed himself and went in pursuit of his treacherous neighbor. One day he found him lying down fast asleep. He raised his gun and was about to fire. The thought occurred to him that he ought to awake him before killing him. This he accordingly did. So soon as Deck was aroused from his slumbers and perceived his perilous condition, he began to beg in the most suppliant manner, that his life might be spared, promising at the same time that he would, if spared, leave the country at once. Forney, although greatly incensed on account of the wrongs which he had been caused to suffer by Deck, spared his life and he left, never more to be heard of in the community. Jacob Forney lived to see his country free and died, loved and respected, in 1806, at the advanced age of eighty-five.

Immediately after the victory at the Cowpens, General Morgan sent a courier to General Greene, then encamped on Hicks' Creek, in the present county of Chesterfield, South Carolina. On the 28th of January, Greene, accompanied by one aid and two or three cavalrymen, set out to join Morgan. The army was left in command of General Huger of South Carolina and Colonel O.H. Williams of Maryland. On the way he learned that Cornwallis was in hot pursuit of Morgan. He at once dispatched to Huger and Williams to break up their camp and march with all possible speed to join Morgan at Charlotte or Salisbury. On the 31st of January, Greene reached Sherrard's Ford on the Catawba. The distance between Hicks' Creek and Sherrard's Ford is about one hundred and fifty miles. So soon as Greene arrived at the headquarters of Morgan, the two officers held a conference respecting the future movements of the army. What Morgan's plans were, we are unable to say certainly, but they were different from those proposed and put into execution by Gen. Greene. The result was, Morgan submitted under protest, that in no way would he be accountable for the final results of the plan proposed by his superior. To this Greene replied that he and not Morgan was accountable for whatever might be the consequences of the future movements of the army. It is very probable that Morgan never forgot this disagreement which took place between him and Greene. A short time before the battle of Guilford, he left the army and never again rejoined it. Greene, on the contrary, continued to cherish during life the highest regard for Morgan, both as a man and an officer. The probability is that Morgan proposed to file to the left and lead his troops to the mountain region of North Carolina. Greene, on the contrary, was anxious to unite his forces so that they could not be attacked and cut off in detachments. Another object he had in view was to protect Speedwell's Iron Works, on Troublesome Creek, North Carolina. After the destruction of Hill's Works on Allison Creek in York county, South Carolina, no other works of the kind of any consequence remained in the south.

If we are correct in this supposition, the superior generalship of Greene over that of Morgan is manifest. In no other way than that chosen by Greene could the American forces have been made effective. Had Morgan attempted to retreat beyond the mountains, the probability is that he would have lost all the prisoners he had captured at the Cowpens. This in itself would have been bad; but the depressing effect which such an event would have had upon the minds of the Whigs both in North and South Carolina, would have been a great deal worse. With great promptness, Greene made arrangements for the future movements of the army. Word was sent to Huger and Williams to lead the forces under their command to Guilford, and not to Salisbury or Charlotte as they had been previously instructed. The prisoners had been put in the charge of General Stevens to be conducted to Charlottesville, Virginia. Here again we have an example of the military power of General Greene. The time of the Virginia militia, which Stevens commanded, would soon expire. This made it eminently wise to select them as a guard to conduct the prisoners to a point at which they would be out of the reach of Cornwallis. The main body of the army under Morgan was ordered to advance in the direction of Guilford. The North Carolina militia under the command of General Davidson were stationed at the fords on the river to impede the progress of the British in crossing. This done, General Greene set out for Salisbury. Had this noble chieftain never done anything else, the planning of this retreat, in so short a time, would have placed him in the rank of the greatest military heroes of his day. It shows that his mind acted promptly and clearly.

Whilst the American general was devising plans by which he might unite his forces and protect his country, the British general was equally busy in devising schemes by which he might advance the interest of his royal master. The rains had ceased and the Catawba, which separated the two armies, was falling as rapidly as it had risen a few days before. On the evening of the last day of January, the very day that Greene reached the camp of Morgan, Earl Cornwallis ordered his troops to be ready to march at one o'clock the next morning. It was thought by the British earl that General Davidson with the Mecklenburg and Rowan militia was stationed at Beattie's Ford. Colonel Webster was ordered to take the thirty-third regiment, the second battalion of the seventy-first regiment, Hamilton's corps of loyalists and Yagers, the six-pounders, and all the wagons belonging to the army, and march directly to Beattie's Ford. He was ordered to fire his cannon and do everything in his power to draw the attention of the Americans to him. At one in the morning, Cornwallis with the main body of his forces set out for Cowan's or McCowan's Ford, six miles below Beattie's. This was a private ford, and Cornwallis supposed that the American officers would overlook it. The night was dark and the roads narrow and muddy. One of the three-pounders overset in a swamp. This produced in the darkness no small confusion. The line of march was broken, the men became scattered, and the gunners, in assisting to readjust the three-pounder that had overset, got separated from their own guns. Just as day began to break the British reached the river. Everything was in a state of confusion. The three-pounders were of no use, from the fact that the artillerymen were some at one place and others at another.

From the camp fires on the opposite side of the river, Cornwallis discovered that he had erred in supposing that the Americans would neglect to place a guard at McCowan's Ford. Determined to cross, Cornwallis ordered General O'Hara to form his guards into a column and march into the river. The Catawba was considerably swollen and at this ford more than a quarter of a mile wide. The bottom of the river was rocky and the ford angling across it. The guards under O'Hara were ordered not to fire until they reached the opposite bank. In the brave guards plunged. In quick succession they were followed by their fellow soldiers. The cold water reached to their waists. Infantry and cavalry moved along slowly but steadily. Davidson and his men were on the opposite side of the ford. So soon as the American sentinel discovered the approach of the British, he fired his gun. This aroused the camp of Davidson, which was distant some half a mile. The men in Davidson's command were concealed among the brushwood of the forest, opposite the ford. Captain, afterwards General, Joseph Graham commanded a company in General Davidson's corps of militia. These were the first to reach the bank of the river and open fire upon the enemy. The moment Captain Graham's men commenced firing upon the advancing British, the guide, who was a Tory, fled. This was attended with no little confusion, both to the British and the Americans. The British guards, under O'Hara, at this moment were near the middle of the stream. The ford, instead of passing directly across the river, turned at the point at which the British had arrived, considerably down the river. Colonel Hall, who was leading the British van, not knowing this and deserted by his Tory guide, led the troops straight across. This frustrated the plans of the Americans. They were forced to make a quick movement to the right and form in the new. The change was made as quickly as possible; but the troops under Davidson being militia, it was not effected until the van of the British under Colonel Hall had nearly reached the bank. In the crossing of the river, the British marched in platoons, that they might support each other against the current of the swollen waters.

Although the British were not prevented from crossing, still it cost them very considerably. Colonel Hall was killed just as he ascended the bank. The horse on which Cornwallis rode was shot while in the river and fell, plunging his rider in the stream, and died as soon as he had carried his master across the river. Three privates were killed and thirty-six wounded. The American loss was trifling in numbers but severe, from the fact that the brave and promising General Davidson was killed. He was shot by a Tory while changing the position of his troops. So soon as the main body of the British succeeded in crossing the river, the North Carolina militia, in obedience to the command of the officers, fled to the woods. The body of General Davidson was found after the enemy had passed on, by Capt. Wilson. It was stripped of every garment. Captain Wilson took it up before him on his horse and buried it in Hopewell graveyard. The congress of the United States voted a monument to this noble man; but no monument has been erected. His memory, however, is perpetuated by the college in Mecklenburg county, North Carolina, which bears his name. A county in the "Old North" state has also been honored with his name. And more than all this, his name will be cherished until men forget to love liberty.

THE RETREAT OF GENERAL GREENE - CONTINUED

General Greene hoped that the North Carolina militia would be able to detain the British at the Catawba long enough to allow Morgan to get his forces out of their reach. In this he was disappointed. All that the militia stationed at the fords of the Catawba could effect was to retard the progress of the British so that the main forces might gain time. Under the circumstances all was done that could be. Still, it amounted to nothing. The British crossed the river not without loss, but the American gain amounted to nothing.

So soon as the guards under O'Hara effected a crossing, the militia dispersed in every direction. The place some ten miles distant, called Terrant's Tavern, had been appointed as a place of rendezvous. This fact Cornwallis learned and sent Colonel Tarleton with the cavalry to attack them. It had been raining all day and the guns of the militia could not be fired. Tarleton came upon the militia at Terrant's Tavern in a defenseless condition, killed a few and put the whole to rout. The loss was not great, but it discouraged the militia. Had its powder not been wet, the result would have been, in all probability, very different.

The two divisions of the British army - the one under Webster which crossed the Catawba at Beattie's Ford and the other under Earl Cornwallis which crossed at McCowan's Ford - were again united on the second of February about five miles from the river on the road to Salisbury. From this time the race began. The freedom of the American colonies depended upon the skill, endurance and perseverance of the forces under General Greene. The destiny of the thirteen colonies was in their hands. Greene was ill-provided with means to do what he felt must be done or the cause of his country would be hopelessly ruined. Provisions were scarce, the men were ragged, many of them nearly naked and barefooted, and there was not a dollar in the money chest.

The only thing which was favorable to Greene and promised success to his undertaking was the fact that he was now in a community in which the British had few friends and the Americans many. In no place in America were there truer Whigs than in the region in which Greene had now entered and through which he proposed to lead his united forces. Colonel Tarleton called the region the "Hornet's Nest." The region around Charlotte, North Carolina has ever claimed to be, in a particular sense, the birthplace of American liberty. In North Carolina the first blood in defense of American liberty was shed; in Charleston, South

Carolina, the proposition was first made to sever, absolutely, the ties which bound the colonies to the mother country; but in Charlotte, North Carolina, the first Declaration of Independence was drawn up and signed.

It is interesting to inquire into the origin of this love of liberty which characterized the people of that region. Things insignificant in the eye of human wisdom often are the base upon which mighty events are built. The storm cloud which sweeps with fury over half a continent, filling the hearts of man and beast with terror, has its origin in tiny vapors which cannot be discerned by human eye. The events which terminate in the dethroning of kings and the elevating of beggars from the dust and investing them with the insignia of royalty, often escape the observation of the multitude. The men who by their swords win the victory rarely begin the strife. The Trojan war had its origin in a wedding feast. Years rolled away before the clash of arms began. The prime actor and apparent cause of that dreadful conflict spent his youthful days as a humble shepherd, with no higher ambition than to disperse prowling robbers who preyed upon the flocks of Mt. Ida. Admitting that the fatal apple, Paris, Helen and the Trojan war had no actual existence but were the creations of the fertile brain of Homer, still the names changed, the leading events narrated by Homer have transpired in many lands. If American liberty was born and cradled in the new world, it was conceived in the Old World. The first man in South Carolina who talked about severing, absolutely and forever, the ties which bound the American colonies to the British throne was an humble blacksmith.

In England at the time of the Restoration in 1660, there lived two brothers by the name of Johnson. These brothers became dissatisfied with the political condition of affairs in their native land and went to Holland. This was in 1662 or '63. In process of time, they came to America and one of them settled in the city of New York on or near the spot where Trinity Church now stands. On going to Holland they exchanged the English name, Johnson, for the Dutch, Yansen.

On coming to America, they retained for a time their Dutch name. All their land deeds were granted to Yansen, and not to Johnson. As, however, they were amongst an English speaking people, they very naturally concluded to surrender their Dutch name and assume their original name, Johnson. There was nothing villainous in this. It was only what any other man would have done, but it vitiated their title to their property, and that property which today is worth perhaps millions, was confiscated.

After this, some of the descendants of these brothers came to Charleston, South Carolina. one of them, William Johnson, was in Charleston in 1776, after the repeal of the stamp act. By trade he was a blacksmith and in 1766 was running a forge at which was made ship irons. The redress of grievances, which meant the repeal of the stamp act, satisfied Massachusetts; but nothing less than liberty would satisfy William Johnson. He conversed with the mechanics of Charleston and infused into them a love of liberty. Christopher Gadsden became their orator. In this way multitudes of South Carolinians, although they had been the pets of the English government, were prepared to resist its encroachments upon the rights of the sister colonies.

Long before this, the seeds of rebellion had been sown in Pennsylvania. The soil, at that time at least, was not adapted to its growth, and the good seed would not germinate. The forest had to be cleared and the soil broken before the germ of liberty could grow and bear fruit. Alexander Craighead, a native of Ireland, a descendant of ancestors originally from Scotland and consequently a Scotch-Irishman, was licensed to preach the gospel and ordained to the full work of the ministry by the presbytery of Donegal about the year 1736. He was a zealous man, full of energy; orthodox in his creed and in his preaching; pious in his deportment but unwilling to be bound by those conventional regulations which were common among his brethren and by them held to be as important as the word of God. He imbided the spirit of Whitfield and on account of his zeal for the salvation of perishing sinners, he was charged in 1740, by his presbytery, of irregularities. The majority of the members of the presbytery were against him, but such was his zeal and energy that even in the presbytery he made for himself at least ardent sympathizers. His case was taken before the synod of Philadelphia. Here, on account of the great revival which was progressing at that time, the case was lost sight of. For a long time his name was stricken from the roll of his presbytery, and consequently from the roll of the synod.

In 1751, in the month of August, the anti-Burger synod of Scotland received a petition from Alexander Craighead, "earnestly beseeching that the synod would appoint some ministers to labor in that part of America." At this time he was at Middle Octarara, in Pennsylvania. The question may be asked, why did he in conjunction with others, "earnestly beseech" the anti-Burger synod to come over and help him. The answer is this. Sometime previous to 1743, Alexander Craighead had published a pamphlet in which he gave utterance to sentiments far in advance of his age. The theme was civil and religious liberty. He acknowledged George the Second, the rightful sovereign of Great Britain and her colonies; but claimed that Jesus Christ is the King of Zion. In other words, he advocated the dismemberment of the church and state. This was a treasonable sentiment and so regarded by Thomas Cookson, a justice of the king of Lancaster county, Pennsylvania. The pamphlet was laid before the synod by Cookson. Either through fear or from principle, the synod disavowed the sentiments contained in the pamphlet and declared that they were "calculated to foment disloyal and rebellious practices and disseminate principles of disaffection." Cut off from his brethren and without sympathizers among the leaders, in both church and state, Alexander Craighead and many of the people wrote to the anti-Burger synod of Scotland for assistance.

In 1733, Ebenezer Erskine, William Wilson, Alexander Moncrief and James Fisher, on account of the heterodox doctrines which had crept into the church of Scotland, and on account of the unrighteous practice which prevailed in that church respecting the law of patronage, seceded from the established church of Scotland, and at Gairney bridge on the 5th of December, formed the Associate presbytery. Such was the origin of what is known as the Secession Church. In 1747, during the time that Alexander Craighead was under censure on account of his seditious pamphlet, as the synod styled it, a division took place in the Secession Church of Scotland. This division occurred in the following way. At the meeting of the Associate synod at Sterling in March, 1745, an overture was introduced with reference to the lawfulness of what was called the "Burgess Oath." In the Burgess oath these words occur, "I protest before God and your Lordships, that I profess and allow, with my heart, the true religion presently professed within this realm and authorized by the laws thereof; I shall abide threat and defend the same to my life's end."

One portion of the synod declared that they had seceded from the religion presently professed in this realm and could not take the Burgess oath. The other part thought differently, declaring that they had not seceded from the established church of Scotland, but from a "corrupt party in that church." The men in both parties were very similarly constituted. Right or wrong, they thought they were right and were willing to maintain and defend their opinions to their "life's end." The more rigid of the parties - the one which would not take the Burgess oath - was called anti-Burgers; the others Burgers. The sentiments of the anti-Burgers were in harmony with those held and promulgated by Alexander Craighead, hence he wrote to the anti-Burger synod in 1751 - beseeching them to send ministers of the gospel to Lancaster, Pennsylvania.

Although foreign to our present object, it will no doubt be interesting to many to know that to Alexander Craighead is due the credit of introducing the Associate church into America. In response to his petition, the anti-Burger synod ordered Mr. James Hume and John Jamieson to go to America as missionaries. Neither of these individuals saw fit to obey the order of synod. The anti-Burgers were intensely anxious to grant the request of Alexander Craighead and appointed Alexander Gellatly and Andrew Bunyan to the same field. Bunyan in effect refused to obey and was severely dealt with. His place was supplied by the appointment of Andrew Arnot. Gellatly and Arnot were the first ministers of the Associate or Secession church in America. They landed in 1753.

About the time that Gellatly and Arnot arrived in Pennsylvania, Alexander Craighead, to get rid of the odium in which he was held on account of his pamphlet, removed to Virginia. In July 1775, Braddock was defeated by the Indians and the whole frontier of the state of Virginia left exposed to the mercy of those infuriated savages. Terror reigned throughout the whole region in which Alexander Craighead was settled. Again he determined to change his place of abode. Crossing the Blue Ridge he descended into the peaceful territory now known as Mecklenburg county, North Carolina.

A number of years previous to this time, two streams of population had been pouring in this region. One stream came mainly from Lancaster, Chester, and Bucks counties, Pennsylvania. The other came directly from Ireland, through the port of Charleston, South Carolina. The two streams had a common origin. Both came bubbling up from the Scotch-Irish population of Ulster, Ireland.

In September, 1758, Alexander Craighead became the pastor of Rocky River congregation. Here was the first Presbyterian congregation in western North Carolina. The first Presbyterian minister in this region was Alexander Craighead. In this quiet territory he preached the pure gospel of the Saviour and indoctrinated his hearers in the principles of civil liberty. In a spiritual and civil point of view, the labors of this good man were greatly blessed. The churches which bear the respective names of Popular Tent, Rocky River, Centre, Hopewell, Providence, Sugar Creek and Steel Creek all sprang into existence as fruits of his labors. The land was fertile and the people being industrious and moral, soon accumulated an abundance of the necessaries of life.

In March, 1776, Alexander Craighead died and

was buried in Sugar Creek grave yard. No monument marks the spot where his ashes repose. Tradition says that when the coffin which contained his remains was taken to the graveyard, it was borne by four men on two sassafras handspikes. When the grave was filling up, these sassafras poles were thrust into the grave, one at the head and the other at the foot, as a temporary mark for the grave. These sassafras handspikes grew and continued, until recently, to mark the resting place of the ashes of this faithful minister of the gospel and staunch advocate of civil and religious liberty.

The signers of the Mecklenburg Declaration of Independence were all members of the congregations founded by Alexander Craighead.

When the body of John Knox was laid in the grave, the Regent, Morton, looked upon it and pronounced in an audible voice the well-known words, "There lies he who never feared the face of man." All Scotland had imbibed the spirit of the great reformer. When the British commander entered Mecklenburg county, he pronounced it a "hornet's nest." All that region had imbibed the spirit of Alexander Craighead. He was dead but he had left the impress of his mind upon the inhabitants of the whole county. The whole territory passed over by Greene in his retreat before the pursuing British earl had been brought under the influence of Craighead and his successors. Greene and his army were hailed as friends, while the British were regarded as the enemies of the country. Greene knew he was amongst friends, whilst Cornwallis soon found out that he was in the midst of bitter and unmitigating enemies of tyrants.

THE RETREAT OF GENERAL GREENE - CONTINUED

General Greene was not long in discovering the intentions of the British earl. He determined to disconcert all his plans and frustrate all his strategy. When Morgan left the Cowpens, the forces of Greene were so situated that they could not act with any concert. The main force was on Hicks' Creek, in Chesterfield county, and Colonel Lee with the main body of cavalry was sixty miles below Cheraw, acting in concert with Marion. The object which Cornwallis at first had in view was to rescue the prisoners captured by Morgan at the Cowpens. Failing in this, his next object was to overtake Morgan and destroy his division before it could be joined by Huger and Lee.

So soon as Green discovered the condition of things, he ordered Huger, Williams, and Lee to join Morgan, either at Charlotte or Salisbury. It was not long before it became evident that this could not be done. Guilford Court House was then appointed as the place at which the several detachments should unite. Apparently the existence of Greene's army depended upon this union. On the other hand, the success of the British depended upon keeping the several detachments separate. To form this junction required everything that is requisite to constitute a military chieftain of the highest rank.

Looking at the thing coolly and dispassionately, the chances were all against Greene and in favor of Cornwallis. Nothing but dire necessity could induce any officer to undertake what Greene undertook. He knew that he was dealing with a general of no ordinary skill and courage. He was fully persuaded that every wrong move on his part would be promptly improved by his enemy. As we have seen, Cornwallis, that he might succeed in his undertaking, had destroyed on the 25th of January, all his superfluous baggage.

Having completed the arrangements for the advance of Morgan's troops, General Greene set out from the Catawba for Salisbury. A few miles from Torrence's Tavern, he and Smith halted, that General Davidson and the militia might come up. Here, exposed to the rain and cold, Greene remained until midnight, when he was informed of Davidson's death and the rout of the militia at Torrence's Tavern. Had Tarleton only known where Greene was, with a few men he could have captured him and thus blasted all the plans of the southern army. So soon as Greene learned the actual condition of things with the North Carolina militia, he set out at once for Salisbury.

Here he arrived some time between midnight and day break. Cold and wet, hungry and benumbed, disappointed and distressed in spirit, he went to a tavern kept by Elizabeth Steele. Dr. William Read, a surgeon in the American army, was at this time quartered in Salisbury. General Greene immediately sent for him. Read arose from his bed, and having hastily dressed, went at once to meet Greene. When the men met, Read, with intense anxiety, inquired what was the matter. "Sir," said Greene, "I am here alone. I am worn out with fatigue. I am hungry and I am without a cent of money."

These words were heard by Mrs. Steele and it was not long until breakfast was brought into his room. While General Greene was eating his breakfast, his patriotic hostess entered the room with a small bag of specie in each hand. This money, the earnings of several years, was delivered to her guest. At first he refused to receive it, but Mrs. Steele forced it upon him, saying, "take it; you need it and I can get along without it."

In the room in which Greene was breakfasting, there hung a portrait of the king of England. Greene took it down and wrote upon the back these words: "O, George hide thy face and mourn;" and then hung the portrait up again with the face turned to the wall.

General Greene having learned immediately before his arrival at Salisbury that the British were pursuing Morgan, with all possible speed sent his aids and other attendants to bear dispatches to the different detachments of the southern army. Some were sent to assist Huger, Williams and Lee in joining Morgan, and others were sent to Morgan to inform him of the movements of the British.

The news of Davidson's death and the dispersion of the militia and the advance of the British was known in Salisbury by a certain class of citizens before Greene arrived. A plundering party, probably part British and part Tories, had that night, but a short time before General Greene's arrival, entered the town and plundered the houses of several of the citizens. Evidently it was not prudent for Greene to remain long in a place where he might be captured at any moment. Morgan's corps - at least a portion of it - soon passed through the town and Greene followed it. Many of the Whigs in the surrounding country abandoned their homes and, with their wives and children, followed Morgan. During the day and night of the second of February, Morgan crossed the Yadkin at Trading or Island Ford. The horses forded; the army baggage was transported in flats. Some of the wagons belonging to the country people, together with a number of citizens, were still on the west side of the Yadkin. For more than ten days it had been almost constantly raining. The streams were all flush and in a condition to be rendered impassable by even a moderate rain. When Morgan's forces left Salisbury, it was raining hard. Greene knew that the Yadkin would soon be brim full. Hence his push to cross. On the night of the second of February, Earl Cornwallis, with the royal army, camped in Salisbury. The headquarters of the British earl was in the house of Dr. Anthony Newman. This gentleman, although a genuine Whig, dispensed a generous hospitality to the invading foe. Here an incident occurred which will serve to illustrate the spirit of the times.

The two little sons of Dr. Newman were engaged in "playing war." Their forces were represented by grains of corn. Part of these corns were red - these representing the British; another part was white - these represented the Americans. The boys had their men and their officers. Prominent among the commanders were Colonel Washington and Colonel Tarleton. The battle the boys were at this time engaged in planning was that of the Cowpens. Having imbibed the spirit of their native land, they so marshaled their forces that the white grains of corn chased the red. Then the little fellows, with joyful shouts, would scream at the top of their voices: "Tarleton runs - hurrah for Washington." Tarleton, who was so unfortunate as to be present, bore this innocent, but cutting, language for a time with becoming dignity. It is the truth however, that hurts. The rash Englishman, no longer able to bear the insult, turned to Cornwallis and said; "Do you see those cursed little rebels?"

Cornwallis ordered General O'Hara to take his guards, the regiment of Bose and the cavalry and pursue hastily after Morgan. He had been informed by his scouts that Morgan had not yet crossed the Yadkin. The night was dark, the roads bad, and it was raining. The result was that O'Hara did not reach the Trading Ford until midnight and when he did arrive he found that Morgan's men, except a small detachment left to guard the wagons of the citizens who were following the army, were all over the river and the flats all on the east bank.

The American army moved on with all possible speed toward Guilford Court House. On the seventh of February, the whole American army, including Lee's cavalry, arrived at the point which had been designated for a junction. On the next day, the united forces were mustered and found to be two thousand and two hundred. Of these, five hundred were militia and two hundred and seventy were cavalry. All were in sad condition. Morgan's men had been moving constantly since the battle of the Cowpens. They, to avoid Cornwallis, had marched one hundred and fifty miles over bad roads, crossed by swollen streams, in twenty days. The forces under Huger had marched about one hundred miles. The distance traversed gives us no proper idea of the labor these men encountered. It was the dead of winter. The army wagons and army teams were wretched in the last degree. The men were all nearly naked; there were but few blankets in either Morgan's or Huger's corps, and no small number of the men were absolutely barefooted. The wonder is that these hungry, naked, and barefooted soldiers did not sink beneath the toils of the march and breathe out their lives by the way. The trials and difficulties of the American soldiers, while in winter quarters at Valley Forge, are constantly mentioned as an example of patriotic endurance. Greene's army was in a far worse condition and yet the men were forced to march night and day. The road over which they passed was covered with blood which ran from their bare feet.

Baffled again by an interposition of Divine Providence, Cornwallis called O'Hara from Trading

Ford to Salisbury. From documents found in possession of some of the militia who had fallen into his hands or been killed since crossing the Catawba, Cornwallis had learned, with very great accuracy, the plans of General Greene. But for the rains which made the Yadkin impassable, all Greene's plans would have been blasted. Unable to cross the Yadkin at Trading Ford and unwilling to remain inactive and let Greene escape quietly beyond his grasp, Cornwallis commenced his march on the west side of the river, determined to continue it until he would reach a point where the river could be forded. Even in this direction the way was not entirely open. The militia of the country had rallied and destroyed the bridge over Grant's creek. This amounted to only a temporary delay; for the bridge was soon repaired and the militia dispersed. The British army, without meeting any other important opposition, moved forward and crossed the Yadkin at the Shallow Fords, and passed into the Moravian settlement on the very day that the American forces reached Guilford Court House.

The two armies were now within twenty-five miles of each other. In respect to numbers, the British was about three hundred the larger and in every particular, except cavalry horses, better provided for. Cornwallis was on Greene's left, and equally as near the Shallow Fords of the Dan. Having failed to prevent the junction of the detachments, Cornwallis now determined on forcing the American general to fight. This he knew must be done before Greene crossed the Dan. Greene, on the other hand, determined, in view of the circumstances by which he was surrounded, to make a desperate effort to keep for the present out of the reach of Cornwallis.

Never during the whole war had the affairs of the south been in a more critical condition. If Greene was only across the Dan, he would be safe; but how was this to be accomplished? All the streams were swollen and Cornwallis was nearer than Greene to points where it was barely possible to ford the Dan. Cornwallis was as well prepared to pursue as Greene was to retreat. Under the circumstances, Greene dared not risk an engagement. Cornwallis knew this, and hence having failed in all his previous plans, he determined to bring on a general fight before Greene could reach the river and cross over into Virginia.

The country was filled with distress. Every one that could leave home, connected themselves with Greene's army. All the able bodied men and boys among the Whigs entered the army as militia soldiers. The old men and old women and little children only were left at home. This was the case only when the pecuniary circumstances of the family would not allow them to do otherwise. The country was left to the mercy of the Tories and the British. These, in small squads, scoured the country, devouring and destroying everything within their reach. To avoid their treacherous cruelty, old men were forced to conceal themselves in the thickets. The purpose of Cornwallis, when he left Winnsboro, was to supply his army from the country through which he passed. This purpose he literally carried out. No requisitions were made upon the British treasury for supplies. The campaign cost the English government nothing in money. It was a terrible tax upon the Whigs in the region through which the army passed.

THE RETREAT OF GENERAL GREENE - CONTINUED

At Guilford Court House, the forces under General Greene were re-organized. Rather, a council of war was held and arrangements made to hasten the retreat and avoid, if possible, a general engagement with the British. To cross the Dan at the Shallow Fords was regarded, on account of the recent rains, as barely within the range of possibilities. Cornwallis was equally as near these points as Greene, and calculated with certainty that Greene would direct his course to these crossings by the nearest route.

Lieutenant Colonel Carrington, quarter master general, suggested that the attempt should be made to cross the Dan at Irwin's Ferry. This point was seventy miles from Guilford Court House. The suggestion made by Colonel Carrington was regarded as eminently wise and consequently was adopted. To keep out of striking distance of Cornwallis required great military skill on the part of Greene, and promptness of action and much physical endurance on the part of the common soldiers. Having determined to cross the Dan at Irwin's Ferry, the next thing was to select a force which should protect the main body of the Americans whilst retreating and retard the progress of the pursuing British. For this purpose a force of seven hundred men was selected. This force consisted of the choice of the infantry under Colonel Howard, Colonel Washington's cavalry, Colonel Lee's legion, together with a few militia riflemen under Major Campbell.

The command of this corps was offered to General Morgan. For some reason Morgan refused to accept it, and at the same time resigned his command and retired from the army and never again joined it. The reason assigned by General Morgan for this strange conduct, at this critical moment in his country's history, was that he was so afflicted with rheumatism that he could no longer continue in service. There is no doubt of his being afflicted with rheumatism. The kind of life which he had led from boyhood was sufficient to impair his constitution and render him liable to an attack of rheumatism, at any time. During the whole winter of 1781 he was exposed to all kinds of weather and since he was subject to attacks of rheumatism, we may well suppose that he was actually suffering with that disease when Greene's army was at Guilford Court House. Still, this, after all, was not the only reason, nor was it the principal reason why Morgan retired from the army.

At Sherrill's Ford on the last day of January, Greene and Morgan disagreed with respect to the plan of the campaign. Sharp words passed between them and whilst it is certain that Greene forgot the whole affair and in the fullest sense forgave Morgan, such was not the case with Morgan. This is not by any means saying that Morgan was revengeful. Such was not the case, but the kind of warfare which General Greene was at that time conducting was not the kind in which General Morgan delighted. He had no taste for systematic retreats. His idea of war was, meet the foe on your ground if you can; if not, meet the foe anywhere.

General Morgan having retired from the service, the command of the select corps was given to Colonel Williams of Maryland. Colonel Carrington was sent forward to make arrangements for the army to cross the river. All the boats above and below Irwin's ferry were conducted to that point. On the tenth of February, General Greene set out for the Dan. The distance is about seventy miles, but the roads were almost impassable. Cornwallis had commenced his march on the previous day, not directly in the rear of Greene but on his left on a parallel road.

After Greene had left Guilford Court House, Colonel Williams on the same day, broke up his camp and filed to the left for the purpose of throwing his forces between those of Greene and Cornwallis. Evidently, the greater the distance which intervened between the two armies, the greater the probability that Greene would escape unharmed across the Dan. The main body of the American army pushed forward and, without being materially incommoded, crossed the Dan on the thirteenth. The safe retreat of Greene was mainly due to the skill with which Colonel Williams managed the movements of his corps. In this he was aided by the illustrious Colonel Lee and by Colonel Washington, of the cavalry, and by Major Campbell.

Leading to the Dan there were three roads nearly parallel to each other. Greene was marching on the lower one, Cornwallis on the upper one, and Williams on the middle one. Thus the forces of Williams were between Cornwallis and Greene. It was necessary that Williams provide that Cornwallis should not slip past him and get between him and Greene. Such an event would have proved fatal to both Williams and Greene. In order to retard as much as possible the progress of the British, the rear of Williams force and the van of the British were in sight of each other during the whole day. The British advance was commanded by O'Hara, an experienced and brave officer. The rear guard of Williams was commanded by the dashing Lee.

During the retreat from Guilford Court House to Irwin's Ferry on the Dan, neither the officers nor men in William's command had much time to eat or sleep. The only meal that they pretended to take was breakfast. At three in the morning the march commenced. A party was sent ahead to kindle fires, generally at some farm house where there was a probability of obtaining some corn meal and bacon, together with corn and fodder for the horses. When the men came up, a halt was ordered for one hour during which the horses were fed and the men baked their ash cakes and roasted their bacon on the coals. This was not all. So vigilant was the watch, that each man only got six hours sleep out of forty-eight. To prevent an attack at night, Williams took the precaution to camp as far as possible from the British. So soon as the men entered the camp, which was always late in the night, those not on patrol threw themselves down anywhere to sleep.

During the night of the twelfth or morning of the thirteenth, Cornwallis determined to change his course and fall into the middle road. This would make him directly rear of Williams. The move was made with skill and so secretly that it was not observed by Williams until effected. The front of his army was required to continue as before, whilst he with the main body pressed from the upper to the middle road.

On the morning of the thirteenth, Williams set out as usual at three o'clock. Parties were sent forward to kindle fires at which to prepare breakfast. The weather was cold and a drizzly rain was falling. The wood was wet and much difficulty was experienced in kindling the fires. Everything was arranged as usual. Lieutenant Carrington, who was with a patrolling party watching the movements of the enemy, reported from time to time that everything was as usual. Just as the cold and wet and hungry soldiers had got their ash cakes in the fire and their bacon on the glowing coals, a countryman rode into the camp. He had been sent by a sergeant of a patrol party. The man, on being conducted to headquarters, related that only a short time before the British had fallen into the road on which the Americans were, and that Cornwallis was only about four miles in the rear. The man rode a very small pony which was very much exhausted.

In order to ascertain the truth of this statement and allow the men time to eat their breakfast, Colonel Williams requested Lieutenant Colonel Lee to send back a detachment of cavalry. The countryman was ordered to accompany them as guide. A squad of cavalry was soon selected and captain Mark Armstrong placed in command of them. These had not left camp long before a messenger came from Lieutenant Carrington, with the news that the van of the British was moving slowly. This led Colonel Williams to suspect that some new movement was making in the British forces. To support Armstrong, Colonel Lee was sent back with another detachment. It was understood that the two detachments would unite and Lee take command of the whole. A single horseman was sent on at full speed to overtake Armstrong and inform him of what had been done and request him to move slowly until the detachment under Lee would overtake him. When Armstrong had gone about a mile he was overtaken by Lee, then the whole advanced two miles farther. No enemy was to be seen, and some began to suspect the veracity of the guide. Lee himself concluded that though he might be an honest man and a true patriot, he was in some way mistaken. It was concluded that Lee and the larger number of the detachment should return to the camp and finish their breakfast. Captain Armstrong and three cavalrymen were ordered to take the countryman as a guide and proceed to the spot where he said he had seen the British an hour before.

The countryman who had willingly accompanied the detachment up to this moment, now refused to go unless a good horse were given him. This fact led all to credit the statements which he had previously made. The bugler, a beardless youth by the name of Gillies, was placed on the pony of the countryman and sent back to camp and the countryman placed on the horse on which the bugler rode. This was agreeable to both. The little bugler mounted the pony and set out for the camp of Williams, and the countryman, mounted on the bugler's horse, set out to find the whereabouts of the British.

So soon as Armstrong left, Lee and his men rode into the woods so as to keep concealed from the enemy, should any be near. Armstrong had advanced but a short distance when the report of muskets announced the fact that the enemy were near by. The American videttes came dashing in at full speed, pursued by a detachment of British dragoons. Lee felt no anxiety for Armstrong and his companions, for he knew they were well mounted; but his anxiety for the little bugler, mounted on the countryman's pony, was great. Waiting until the British passed by, he fell into the road and dashed forward after them at full speed. Armstrong and his men dashed past the bugler, who was overtaken and barbarously put to death by the British, although he begged for quarters. This was done in the sight of Lee, who became furiously enraged when he saw the boy literally butchered when crying for mercy. The moment of vengeance did not linger long. The horses upon which the British rode were inferior and their riders were drunk. Exasperated by the cruelty practiced upon the helpless bugler, Lee, contrary to his usual practice, shouted to his men to show the enemy no quarters. In this affair the British had eighteen killed and several taken prisoners. Amongst the prisoners was Captain Miller. Lee charged Miller with the murder of the bugler and ordered him to be hanged on the spot, but the British van approaching, it was deferred for the time.

Having advanced a short distance, Lee handed Miller a pencil and a piece of paper and told him to note down any communication which he might desire to send his friends, telling him that he would hang him so soon as they reached the foot of the hill which they were then descending. Again the approach of the British van prevented Lee for executing his purpose. Captain Miller and the other prisoners were sent forward to Williams and by him sent to General Greene - afterwards exchanged. The American loss was nothing except the bugler.

Before the affair between Lee and Miller was concluded, Colonel Williams had his forces in motion. The road on which he was marching led to Dix's Ferry and the designated point of crossing was Irwin's Ferry. Thinking Greene, of whom he had heard nothing, was now out of reach of the enemy, he filed to the right for the purpose of falling into the Irwin's Ferry road. The officers having been informed of the movement, he hastened forward with all possible speed. Cornwallis was directly in the rear of the Americans and everything depended on promptness of action. Many of Lee's men had eaten nothing since the morning of the 12th. Having learned from his guides that there was a nearer road than that traveled by Williams, Lee determined to take it, so that he might gain time sufficient for his men to dispatch a hasty meal and feed their horses. Having arrived at the house of a well to do farmer, preparations were made for a substantial dinner. The horses were fed and the soldiers were preparing to repast. A few videttes were stationed in the rear; but no surprise was feared since the road which they had taken was a mere path.

Scarcely had the horses began to eat when the

videttes gave the alarm that the British van was approaching. The British were as much surprised as the Americans. They had no idea that the two armies were so near together. Lee saw at once that it was now either fight or fly. In his front was a swollen stream over which was a bridge. The infantry were ordered to rush to this bridge and hold it. Lee drew up his cavalry so as to cover a retreat. The British not expecting to overtake the Americans, were for the moment nonplused. Before they could advance they had to form. Whilst they were forming the Americans crossed the bridge and were soon out of danger. The nearer the approach to the Dan, the more energetic was the pursuit by Cornwallis. The night of the thirteenth was cold, dark, and rainy. Neither the darkness nor the cold nor the rain put a stop to the pursuer. On he pushed. His only hope was to capture Williams. This he new must be done either than night or the next day.

At eight o'clock in the night, the Americans beheld in front of them a number of camp fires. This filled the hearts of those brave men with sadness. They naturally concluded that General Greene and the main body of the southern army, unconscious of the proximity of the foe, were warming at these fires. Williams, like a brave man, began to prepare for the conflict. His plan was to throw his forces directly in front of the British and, by every means in his power, retard their progress till Greene should have time to get out of danger. Before the conflict between Williams and Cornwallis began, it was learned to the inexpressible joy of both officers and men that it was Greene's camp, but Greene and his men were not there. They had camped on the spot two night before and were gone. The fires had been kept burning by the Whigs in the neighborhood. Delivered from their fears, the Americans pressed forward. Cornwallis, finding that he could not grasp his prey that night, halted. So soon as the Americans discovered this, they encamped. Long before day both the Americans and the British were in motion. This day's work was to put an end, if they were successful, to the present toils of the former; and it was to crown with success or stamp with defeat, the plans of the latter. On both parties pushed, through mud, over hills and across valleys. Neither man nor horse was allowed time to eat or sleep.

At midday a courier - his horse covered with foam and the sweat streaming down his body - he himself covered with mud, but with a countenance bright with joy, met the forces of Williams. He bore a letter from General Greene to Colonel Williams, in which it was announced that the former with his forces had crossed the Dan on the thirteenth. No sooner was this news known than a glad shout was uttered which echoed from hill to hill. The British heard the shout and understood its meaning. At three o'clock in the afternoon, when fourteen miles from the river, Williams, leaving Lee in front of the enemy, filed off in the direction of Boyd's Ferry. Here he crossed the Dan before sunset. Later in the afternoon, Lee ordered his infantry to follow Williams, whilst he, with his cavalry, still remained in front of the enemy. At dark, Lee bade an adieu to O'Hara and set out for Irwin's Ferry. Here he crossed before nine o'clock. This for the time put an end to the toils of the southern army. The plans of Cornwallis were frustrated and his hopes blasted.

In reviewing this retreat, we are unable to determine who among the two thousand and three hundred men and officers is deserving of most praise. All acted their part well. The history of the world presents few if any cases in which men suffered so much and so cheerfully. Lee says of his men, "they were in good health and good spirits."

INCIDENTS OF GENERAL GREENE'S RETREAT

No sooner had Cornwallis learned with certainty that General Greene with his whole force and all his baggage was over the Dan than, with a heavy heart, he directed his course to Hillsboro, the capital at that time of North Carolina. All that mortals are capable of doing had been done by Cornwallis to thwart the purposes of the American general and yet he had failed, signally failed. That Greene's army might be destroyed, he had deliberately destroyed his baggage, marched his men night and day for near a month through mud, over swollen creeks and rivers, and in all sorts of weather. Bravely the British soldiers pursued the Americans amid teeming rains, drifting snows and pelting sleet. But all accomplished nothing. On the morning of the fifteenth of February, the British earl looked upon the Dan and saw the American army quietly encamped in Halifax county, Virginia. Cornwallis knew that Greene, for the present, was safe. Without giving his army but a single day to rest, he wheeled about and marched to Hillsboro.

Here, on the twentieth of February, he erected the royal standard, published a flaming proclamation, and invited the loyalists of the surrounding country to join him in his efforts to subdue the Whigs. This proclamation of Cornwallis is in some respects a most remarkable document. It scarcely contains a syllable of truth. The first sentence is a lie in that it was intended to deceive the unsuspecting loyalists. "Whereas" he starts, "it hath pleased the Divine Providence to prosper his

Majesty's arms in driving the rebel army out of this (North Carolina) province, and whereas it is his Majesty's most gracious wish to rescue his faithful and loyal subjects from the cruel tyranny under which they have groaned for many years." Neither of these statements contained in this proclamation was true and Cornwallis knew it. He knew that the British had suffered more by the escape of Greene across the Dan, than the Americans had; he also knew that his majesty was not desiring to rescue his subjects from cruel tyranny.

The truth is, Cornwallis never did approve of the course which the British government took toward her American colonies. In 1770, Lord Camden protested against taxing the American colonies. He was joined in that protest by four young peers, one of whom was Cornwallis. Chief Justice Mansfield said with a sneer, "Poor Camden could get only four boys to join him." As a statesman, Cornwallis was opposed to the American war, but as a solider he did everything in his power to advance the arms of the King of England to squash the rebellion.

In his proclamation, he invited the loyal North Carolinians to repair to his standard, "without loss of time, with their arms and ten days' provisions." Straws show which way the wind blows. In this proclamation, which begins with a boast that North Carolina is subjected, it is at the same time intimated that he who had conquered the province could neither arm nor feed his recruits. In the next sentence of this proclamation, it is admitted that there is still in North Carolina "the remains of rebellion" and the loyal people of the country are requested to combine with his majesty's army in attempting to suppress it.

"Like murder, the truth will out." So far from being able to provide for recruits, Cornwallis was unable to feed the soldiers then under his command. The supplies in the country around Hillsboro were soon exhausted, and although the British army remained there only ten days, so great was the scarcity of food that Stedman, one of the officers of the British army, was obliged to take a file of men and gather up supplies from the citizens of the place. This he did by going from house to house and taking whatever he could find in every family. This was no plundering party acting without, or contrary to, orders of the commanding officers; but a regularly constituted party of men acting in obedience to the directions of Cornwallis. Stedman gives as an excuse for such remarkable conduct, the pressing necessities of the British army. In other words, the army of Cornwallis was whilst at Hillsboro, reduced to such a strait that it was either take by force the bread out of the mouths of helpless women and children or starve.

The friends of the British from the adjacent country came into the camp of Cornwallis and with him and his officers talked over the condition of things in the country. Recent events had very materially cooled the ardor of the Tories and loyalists. The British had made great promises, but performed nothing. For this they were not censurable. Taking it for granted that all the promises that Cornwallis had been making to the loyalists of North Carolina since he arrived at Camden, South Carolina, in August of the preceding year, were made in good faith and that it was his honest purpose to fulfill them all, he was excusable for having up to this time done nothing, because the American army under Greene, Morgan, Lee, Williams, and other leaders would not permit him to assist his friends. His own preservation and that of the army under his command required all his time and attention.

The loyalists who visited Cornwallis all expressed themselves as desirous that peace be restored to the country and that the English government be established; but few if any at all of them were willing to join the standard of the king and assist in restoring the so much desired peace and in establishing the English government. The fact is manifest that the more sensible of the loyalists feared the Whigs and had lost all confidence in the British army. They say that Greene over the Dan was in a better condition than Cornwallis in Hillsboro. The Tories proper cared nothing for either party. All they had in view was plunder. To them war was better than peace, and anarchy better than any government. They hated law and order because they delighted in thieving. In addition to this notwithstanding the declaration of the British general about driving the American army out of the province of North Carolina, he had scarcely arrived at Hillsboro until the American cavalry were in sight of his camp, cutting off his foraging parties, interrupting his communications and in a variety of ways, keeping him in a state of continual solicitude.

This seems to be the proper place to mention the fact that before Cornwallis left Winnsboro, he ordered Colonel Balfour to send from Charleston, South Carolina, a detachment under convoy of a naval force to take possession of Wilmington, North Carolina. To this point it was contemplated to ship army stores. These supplies it was thought could be conveyed on the Cape Fear River to the army of Cornwallis. In obedience to his instructions, Balfour sent Major Craig with four companies of the eighty-second regiment and two hundred men. These with a supply of army stores came up the Cape Fear River as far as Wilmington. Craig fortified the place making it a military post, from which Cornwallis might obtain supplies for his army. The distance between Wilmington and Hillsboro, together with the presence of the American cavalry, rendered the supply from that quarter precarious.

The moment General Greene's army crossed the Dan, things began to present a different aspect. Every man was conscious of having done and suffered what the circumstances of his bleeding and downtrodden country required. The troubles of the past were narrated with real delight. The American soldiers never for a moment thought that they had been driven out of North Carolina. Reinforcements began to pour in from various sections of the country. Not in large numbers, but composed of good and true men. This was what General Greene desired. General Stevens, as we have seen, was sent with some militia, whose time of service was nearly expired, to conduct the prisoners captured by Morgan to Charlottesville, Virginia. This done, he led the militia to Pittsylvania Court House. Then their arms were deposited and the men disbanded.

From Pittsylvania Court House General Stevens repaired to the Scotch-Irish settlements of Augusta and Rockbridge counties, where he collected a considerable number of men. With these hardy sons of the mountains, he joined Greene in Halifax county, North Carolina. Greene was also at this time reinforced by two companies of Marylanders under Captain Oldham and by a body of militia under Andrew Pickens. Afterwards and before the battle of Guilford Court House, reinforcements from Virginia under General Lawson; from North Carolina, under Colonel Cleveland - one of the heroes of King's Mountain - and from Montgomery county, West Virginia, under Colonel Preston, came in.

Two things conspired together to prevent Gen. Greene from lying inactive for any considerable length of time. The restless nature of the troops which composed the body of his army made it necessary that they be constantly employed. The existence of his army depended on its being kept consistently in motion. Again, notwithstanding the fact that the loyalists were disheartened because of the neglect with which they had been treated by the British, still as Cornwallis with his army was in their midst offering them protections they could soon be induced to espouse heartily the cause of the enemy.

With a perfect knowledge of these facts, General Greene ordered Colonel Lee of the cavalry, together with Brigadier General Pickens who had recently joined the army with a corps of South Carolina militia and Captain Oldham with two companies of Marylanders,

to recross the Dan and gain the front of Cornwallis and keep as close to him as was compatible with their own safety.

On the morning of the eighteenth of February, Lee, Pickens and Oldham with the several commands, crossed the Dan, and set out in the direction of the enemies' camp. On the same evening they encamped on the road leading from the Haw River and the other in the direction of Hillsboro. General Greene, that he might more fully communicate his plans to Lee, Pickens, and Oldham, left his camp on the Dan and under an escort of Colonel Washington's cavalry, reached the camp of these officers late in the evening and spent the night with them.

Early on the morning of the nineteenth the scouts sent out in the direction of the Haw returned to camp. They had learned that on the day before their arrival, Colonel Tarleton, with a body of cavalry, infantry and artillery, had passed through the country. How many were in the body it was not learned, but the object of the British officer, it was ascertained, was to cross the Haw, collect a corps of loyalists, and act as an escort to them whilst on their way to Hillsboro. General Greene set out for his camp on the Dan, on the morning of the nineteenth and Lee, Pickens, and Oldham set out in search of Tarleton. The nineteenth and twentieth were spent in various marchings and counter-marchings for the purpose of gaining correct information respecting the number and movements of the enemy.

On the twenty-first the Americans crossed the Haw and learned as they had suspected that the loyalists between the Haw and Deep rivers were making rapid preparation to join Cornwallis at Hillsboro at an early day. From Ephraim Cooke, a sort of half way Tory, they ascertained that Tarleton's forces consisted of four hundred foot soldiers, two small brass field pieces and the large number of his own legion. From the same individual they learned that Tarleton was encamped only about three miles ahead. Cooke said Tarleton, thinking himself in no danger, had ordered all the horses to be unsaddled. The American officers at once determined, although their numbers were less than those of the British, to make an attack at once. They calculated from the reports which they had just heard that they would be able to surprise Tarleton. They formed themselves for the attack and dashed forward as stealthily as possible. On arriving in sight of the camp they discovered that the British were gone. A few cavalrymen dashed up to the farm house at which the British detachment had been recently camped. Two officers who had remained behind to settle their bill with the owner of the farm were captured. From these prisoners it was learned that Tarleton had gone to the plantation of Colonel William O'Neil.

This Colonel William O'Neil was professedly a Whig, but in reality an ignominious swindler. At the outbreaking of the war he was poor but before the war ended had grown rich. One of the ways by which he increased his wealth was to cause the rich in the community and all the sons of large and dependent families to be drafted for the army and then, for pay, furnish them with a substitute or permit them to remain at home to be in a short time drafted again. From those who were unable to pay him money to get off from going to the army, he would take horses and when he had collected a drove would send them off to be sold. He always managed to keep at a respectable distance from the enemy, and consequently was never in a battle. The unrighteous acts of this colonel, pretending to be acting in accordance with the commands of the American government, greatly incensed many of the citizens of the country between the Haw and Deep rivers. So great was their indignation towards the infamous O'Neil that they lost all affection for the American cause and determined to give their assistance to the British.

On learning that Tarleton was at O'Neil's, Lee, who was evidently the master spirit of the American detachment, determined to resort to stratagem in order to capture him. Between the cavalry of Lee's legion and that of Tarleton there was a striking resemblance. Persons not accustomed to scrutinize men closely would be likely to mistake the one for the other. The South Carolina militia, under Pickens, was so placed that they would be as much out of sight as possible and Lee announced to his men that his intention was to pass off for Colonel Tarleton, and his men were ordered to favor the stratagem. In front of the whole, at the distance of a few hundred yards was a small scouting party. The legion with Colonel Lee, accompanied by the two prisoners at its head, followed. The prisoners were ordered, on pain of death, to favor the deception.

In this order, they had not gone far when the van was met by a couple of young men mounted on splendid steeds. Joy beamed in their countenances. They were evidently young recruits and knew nothing of the wiles of war. The van of the Americans, feigning to be Tarleton's men, halted them and asked to whom they belonged. These unsuspecting young soldiers replied that they belonged to Colonel Pyle's command and had been sent out by their commander to find Colonel Tarleton's camp. In the simplicity of their hearts, the two young cavalrymen stated frankly all about the intentions of their commanding officers.

They were at once sent back to Colonel Lee, with an American solider, who was to give a correct account of all that had transpired. The two young loyalists saluted Colonel Lee as Colonel Tarleton and Lee returned the salutation. The adjutant of Lee's legion was sent to Pickens, requesting him to keep his riflemen concealed.

Just at this time Captain Graham had joined Lee and his forces were with Pickens. All was intense excitement. A body of unsuspecting loyalists were about to be caught in a trap. "Everything is fair in war" is a motto that will not bear to be closely examined. Lee, however, designed nothing more than to disarm Colonel Pyle and his men and send them back to their own firesides or give them a chance to come out and fight for their country against the British. The thing turned out far differently; but still Lee was not to be blamed.

One of the loyal young soldiers was sent forward to bear Colonel Tarleton's compliments to Col. Pyle and to ask him to so dispose of his troops on the side of the road that his weary forces could pass without inconvenience. Pyle promptly replied that he would be happy to comply with the request. Lee, the pretended Tarleton, accompanied by the other unwary horseman of Pyle, now advanced. Pyle had drawn up his men as requested, and was himself at the end of the column most distant from the approach of Lee and his men. As Lee rode along the road past Pyle's men he complimented them for their good looks and praised their horses. The poor dupes smiled most graciously. At last he reached the position occupied by Colonel Pyle and advanced towards him. Then all along their line the loyalists and Tories shouted "God save the King."

The understanding was that so soon as Lee would grasp the hand of Pyle, that the cavalry of Lee would close in upon the loyalists and demand an unconditional surrender. It so happened that at this moment the militia under Pickens and Graham were discovered by the loyalists on the left. They saw that they had been led into a trap, and commenced firing on the rear guard of the American cavalry, commanded by Capt. Eggleston. The fire was promptly returned by Eggleston, and soon became general. Pyle commanded 400 men, ninety of whom were in a few moments lying dead, and a large number of the remainder badly wounded. Pyle himself was severely wounded. In the confusion he fled to a pond of water near by and lay concealed beneath the water all except his nose and mouth until dark and then crawled out. Those of the loyalists not wounded fled in every direction. The Americans did not pursue them.

Such is war and such it ever will be. It is said that Colonel Pyle and his men had been carousing about in the community for several days, enjoying a kind of drunken holiday, before setting out to join Cornwallis. Lee taught both the loyalists and British a very salutary lesson. Pyle's defeat was a terrible episode on the proclamation of Cornwallis. It was now discovered that the rebels were not conquered. This event took place only five days after Cornwallis had proclaimed that it had pleased Divine Providence to drive the rebel army out of the province of North Carolina. Most probably the earl now thought that it had pleased Divine Providence to bring the rebel army back into the province of North Carolina.

Installment XXXVIII

GREENE'S RETURN TO NORTH CAROLINA - CORNWALLIS LEAVES HILLSBORO

When Lee unexpectedly met Colonel Pyle, it was late in the afternoon. The sun was setting when the affair closed. A consultation was held between Lee and Pickens and it was determined not to pursue Pyle's fugitives; but to advance in the direction of O'Neil's plantation, for the purpose of attacking Tarleton.

Pyle's Pond - the place at which Pyle's loyal force was nearly exterminated - is about midway between Hillsboro and Greensboro, on the west side of the Haw. Colonel O'Neil's plantation, at which Tarleton was encamped for the night, was about three miles distant from Pyle's Pond.

Lee and Pickens approached to within a mile of Tarleton's camp and learned that the British had partaken of a sumptuous supper, and were carelessly encamped and in a good condition in every way, as they thought to be surprised. The capture of Colonel Tarleton would have covered his captor with glory. No man was dreaded by the American soldiers of the south and especially by the militia, so much as Tarleton. This dread was not ill-founded. For in the kind of warfare in which they were engaged, Tarleton was far superior to Cornwallis. Notwithstanding the fact that Morgan defeated him at the Cowpens, his name created a kind of terror wherever it was mentioned in the American camp. He was cruel, but all war is cruel. Tarleton was brave and energetic, full of perseverance and no man could be more vigilant. It was creditable in the highest degree to Lee and Pickens and the men under them even to undertake to attack Tarleton. None but the bravest of the brave, with an equal number of men, would have dared such a thing.

The forces of Lee were arranged for the attack upon Tarleton at an early hour on the next morning. The horsemen lay down to rest with their bridles in their hands and the infantry with their guns primed and ready for action. Perhaps neither officers nor men, although tired, could sleep much. Who could sleep sweetly knowing that Tarleton and his fierce dragoons were only a mile distant.

During the early part of the night, Colonel Preston of Montgomery county, Virginia, with three hundred mounted volunteers came into Lee's camp. Many of the men under Preston were the hardy sons of the mountain region, whom the gallant Colonel William Campbell had led at King's Mountain. Campbell, leading a similar force, was in the vicinity and joined Lee a few days afterward. Campbell and Preston - neighbors and kinsmen - had hastened with a body of volunteers to aid General Greene. A very considerable number of the men in their commands were the men who fought so bravely at King's Mountain and won so glorious a victory over the gallant Colonel Ferguson. The infantry commanded by Pickens were, many of them, King's Mountain boys. "As iron sharpeneth iron," so the meeting of those who had gazed upon heaps of dead British and Tories on the morning after the battle of King's Mountain and seen the wagons of Ferguson drawn across his camp fires and burnt up, must have infused new energy in Lee and Pickens and the men in their several commands.

Shortly after midnight, the men in Lee's command were aroused and at 3 o'clock in the morning they set out for the camp of Tarleton. Before reaching the place, it was discovered that Tarleton had, during the night, broken up his camp and set out for Hillsboro. This news filled the mind of both men and officers in Lee's command with disappointment. All had confidently counted on a surprise and the chances were favorable for capturing Tarleton and his whole command.

Tarleton was also disappointed. Many of those belonging to Pyle's party, who escaped the sword of Lee's dragoons, fled to Tarleton's camp. Wounded and covered with blood they complained that they had been attacked by the British. So completely were they deceived by the appearance of Lee's legion that it was not until after they reached Tarleton's camp that they discovered that they had fallen into the hands of the Americans. The British were making preparations to avenge the blood of the loyalists under Colonel Pyle, who had been wounded and killed, when Tarleton received orders from Cornwallis to come back to his camp, which was at that time on the west bank of the Eno.

General Greene had crossed the Dan on the twenty-second and twenty-third, and was moving into North Carolina. So soon as Cornwallis learned this fact, he began to fear that his forces might be attacked in detachments and his whole army destroyed. To prevent this he ordered Tarleton back to camp. So intensely anxious was Cornwallis for the return of Tarleton, that he sent no less than three couriers at different intervals during the day with orders for his prompt return. It is probable that Tarleton would have measured swords with Lee had he been ordered to camp but a single time.

From O'Neil's, the Haw was distant about four miles. At this point the river was crossed on a ferry boat. One mile below there was another ferry. Seven miles below was the ford at which both the Americans and British had crossed on the preceding day. The American officers thought it probable that Tarleton would attempt to cross at one or both of the ferries. It was determined to pursue the trail of the enemy, thinking it possible to overtake his rear at the river. The morning was dark and time precious. In order that the troops might follow directly in the track of the enemy, Lee's legion kindled pine torches and led the way. Tarleton led his men first along the road leading to the nearest ferry, then passed to the right and fell into the road leading to the ford. When day broke, the Americans following directly in the enemy's trail, were within two miles of the ford. The cavalry accelerating their speed, pushed on to the river, leaving the infantry to follow. When they came in sight of the river, the rear guard of the British were descending the hill to the ford. The main body had just crossed, and taken a position to protect the rear.

Again for the third time in twenty-four hours, Tarleton had been nearly within the grasp of Lee and Pickens and each time escaped. Within sight of the escaping foe, a consultation was held by Lee and Pickens with regard to the propriety of marching rapidly up the Haw and crossing at the nearest ferry and then falling behind Tarleton with the view of crippling him. It was thought however, on more mature deliberation, that Cornwallis had in all probability learned what Lee and Pickens were doing and would send succor to Tarleton. Fearing that the pursuit might result in needless exposure, they desisted from pursuing the wary foe; and marching up the west bank of the Haw, encamped and refreshed their troops in the first settlement that was able to afford them supplies.

Tarleton reached the camp of Cornwallis, without having experienced any great loss, but he had failed completely to effect the purpose for which he had been sent out. The object which he had in view was to encourage the loyalists, between the Haw and Deep rivers, and act as a kind of escort to the loyal Pyle in his march to Hillsboro. Poor Pyle, as we have already seen, fell into the hands of Lee's legion and was, at a single blow, exterminated. Never was any body of men more unfortunate than that which was commanded by Pyle. Whatever interest in the British government the presence of Colonel Tarleton had inspired in the inhabitants of the country between the Haw and Deep rivers, the defeat of Pyle more than counteracted it. The hopes of the loyalists were ready to die. Cornwallis saw that something must be done. Under the circumstances, he concluded to march his whole force into the region lately abandoned by Tarleton. On the twenty-sixth of February, he left his camp on the Eno, and marching his troops through Hillsboro, encamped on Alamance Creek, on the twenty-seventh, in the neighborhood of what is called "Stinking Quarter."

On the twenty-second, as we have seen, General Greene commenced to cross the Dan and lead his troops back into North Carolina. The work was completed on the twenty-third. Two reasons induced General Greene to take this step - the preventing of Cornwallis from embodying the loyalists and Tories of the country and employing his own troops. It was then as it is now, and ever will be that no small number of the human family are ready to attach themselves to the side that seems to be in the ascendancy. "Like dumb driven cattle," they are wholly under the control of others. Both Cornwallis and Greene knew this. If Cornwallis remained in quiet possession of North Carolina, multitudes of passive creatures would flock to his standard; and whilst they would add nothing to the real strength of his army, they would prove a continual source of annoyance to the true Whigs of the country. General Greene knew that his appearance in the country would either induce some of these miserable creatures to espouse the American cause or it would fill them with astonishment and render them neutral. The character of many of Greene's forces also made a move necessary. With them arms was not a profession - it was a necessity. They had no love for lying up in camp and drilling. They had in obedience to the promptings of principle entered the army to fight. Not that they loved fighting, but they hated tyranny. When actively engaged they were contented; but when idle in camp they were restless and inclined to be insubordinate. Hence when General Greene gave the order to cross the Dan and return into North Carolina, joy beamed in every eye.

Greene, on entering North Carolina, directed his course towards the Haw, which he crossed near its source and camped between Troublesome Creek and Reedy Fork. So soon as it was ascertained that Cornwallis had quitted his position at Hillsboro, Greene placed between himself and Cornwallis, a corps similar to that which had been placed between them on the retreat. The command of this force was given to the vigilant Col. Williams. To this corps, as in the retreat, a number of able and experienced officers were attached. Amongst them were Lee, Campbell, Pickens, and Preston - men all as brave as Caesar and true as steel. This force hung around the British; at one time cutting off their supplies and capturing their foraging parties; at another time capturing their pickets and thwarting the progress of the main body.

For a period of more than ten days, both generals kept their armies in continual motion. Greene changed his camp every day. One day he was on one side of the Haw, on the next day on the other. Cornwallis was perplexed. He could obtain no certain information respecting Greene's plans. The loyalists and Tories were hopelessly discouraged. During the short stay of Cornwallis at Hillsboro and on the Eno, no less than seven companies of loyalists had been enrolled. These were disbanded and scattered to the winds when he left Hillsboro and retired beyond the Haw. On the contrary, small bodies of men and single individuals in the capacity of volunteers from the surrounding Whig settlement, were steadily increasing the strength of Greene's army. His men, although undergoing severe hardships and suffering great deprivations, were in good health and buoyant spirits.

Between the British and Williams' corps, frequent skirmishes took place. On the second of March a skirmish occurred between a part of Tarleton's legion and Colonel Preston's mountain men, in which the British lost thirty men. At Wetzell's Mill, on Reedy Fork, a thrilling incident occurred. Williams had taken his position near the camp of Cornwallis. Alamance Creek lay between them. Under cover of a thick fog, a strong detachment of British cavalry, supported by a body of infantry and a few pieces of field artillery, was sent to dislodge Williams. Concealed by the fog, the British gained a favorable position and it became necessary for the Americans to retreat. At first it was thought the British were advancing to attack Greene. A messenger was immediately dispatched to Greene's camp to inform him of the supposed intentions of the British and of the course proposed by Williams to baffle his undertaking. Colonels Campbell and Preston were stationed in a thick cluster of trees, near the ford of the creek, at Wetzell's Mill, to delay the passage of the enemy at that point.

Near the ford was a small log school house. In this house, Campbell placed twenty-five of the best riflemen in his command. So expert were these men with their rifles, that they were accustomed to amuse themselves, when in camp, by placing an apple on the end of a ramrod and whilst one held the ramrod in his hands, his comrades would shoot at the apple. Rarely was the apple missed. These twenty-five skilled marksmen were placed in the school house, with instructions to act as their good sense might direct. The British were on the opposite hill. So an officer approached them and after having given the soldiers some instructions which the marksmen in the school house could not hear, he turned away and dashed down the hill toward the ford in the direction of the school house. Without a moment's delay he plunged into the creek. The bottom of the ford was rough and he was obliged to move slowly. He rode a beautiful black horse which felt his way carefully through the stream. The eyes of twenty-five rifleman were upon him. He was in full view and within rifle shot. One after another of the twenty-five men in the school house took deliberate aim and fired, each expecting to see either the horse or rider fall into the stream. Steadily, as if nothing was transpiring, the officer moved on. Thirty-two balls from accurate rifles, aimed by skillful marksmen, were hurled at him as he rode calmly across the stream. Unharmed he reached the bank near the school house, drew up his bridle reins, and dashed down the creek to his own men, whom he immediately led against the Americans. The back-mountain men stood gazing upon each other in astonishment. They concluded that both the man and his horse were bullet proof. It was afterwards learned from British prisoners that the officer was Lieutenant Colonel Webster. He was not however bullet proof, for he fell a short time after at the battle of Guilford Court House. Notwithstanding the failure of the riflemen to kill Webster, the British detachment failed to entrap Williams.

BATTLE OF GUILFORD COURT HOUSE

Soon after the affair at Wetzell's Mill, Cornwallis finding that by his constant marching and countermarching, he was wearing out his army, exhausting his supplies, and still unable to bring Greene to a general engagement, determined to abate the struggle for a time for the purpose of giving his troops rest. To effect this object, he retired down Deep River to Bell's Mill, about fourteen miles south of the present Jamestown and about the same distance east of High Point. General Greene with the main body of the

Americans was northeast of Guilford Court House, at Speedwell's Iron Works on Troublesome Creek. The two armies were now about thirty miles apart. The movements of the British were closely watched by Williams. On the other hand, every movement of the Americans was closely observed by Tarleton.

The fight at Wetzell's Mill occurred on the sixth of March. Greene was anxiously awaiting the arrival of reinforcements. These reinforcements were beginning to come in from Virginia under General Lawson; and from North Carolina under Generals Butler and Eaton. Colonels Campbell, Preston and Lynch had previously joined Greene.

The American general now began to think that he was able to meet the British in a general engagement. From the twenty-third of February up to the present moment, a period of fifteen days, all had been excitement. A false move on the part of either Greene or Cornwallis would have been attended with disastrous consequences. During this period, the two forces were never more than thirty miles apart - seldom more than twenty, and often within striking distance. The vidette of corps of the two armies often met in bloody conflict, whilst the main forces were only permitted to be lookers on. Williams and Lee of the Americans were pitted against Tarleton and Webster of the British. Cornwallis was anxious to test the strength of the two armies and the valor of the troops by a general engagement. General Greene saw this and determined to ward off a general engagement until such time and place as was agreeable to his own judgment.

Reinforced as we have seen, Greene left his fortifications at Speedwell's Iron Works on the twelfth of March and encamped at Guilford Court House in battle array on the thirteenth. His determination now was to give the enemy battle. The infantry in Colonel Williams corps was called in, whilst Lieut. Col. Lee with his legion was left in the front of the enemy to watch his movements. Cornwallis was not slow in discovering the intentions of Greene. Since the eighteenth of January - near two months - he had been endeavoring to meet the Americans. Without a moment's delay he hastened to embrace the first opportunity. He left Bell's Mill and moved all his forces toward New Garden Meeting House. This place is south of Guilford Court House and distant four or five miles. On the evening of the fourteenth, under an escort consisting of Hamilton's Tory regiment, a detachment of one hundred and fifty infantry and twenty cavalry, the British general sent back his wagons and baggage, together with his sick and wounded, to Bell's Mill. The next morning at early dawn, he determined to advance

with his main body against Greene. His object was to free himself of every encumbrance. He was anxious to engage in the contest, but was by no means sanguine with regard to its results.

Cornwallis had confidently expected the larger number of inhabitants of the country to declare boldly for the British, when he led his army into the region surrounding Hillsboro. In this he was sadly mistaken. The incursions of Williams and Lee filled those of the inhabitants, who were inclined to favor the cause of the British, with sorrow and sadness. Every skirmish to their minds rendered the final results doubtful. The presence of Cornwallis was nothing. Before the timid loyalists and cowardly Tories could be induced to respond to his call for volunteers, he must strike a blow which would clearly vindicate his superiority to Greene. In others words, so long as Cornwallis permitted General Greene to command an army which menaced the camp of the British earl himself, the Tories and loyalists determined to remain as neutral as possible. In order to vindicate his claims as an officer and to assert the majesty of the English government, he promptly responded to the invitation to fight, given by Greene.

The British greatly exaggerated the number of Greene's men. British historians say that Greene's army had been so increased that it now amounted to between seven and ten thousand. This is a mistake; but it is not difficult to discover how the mistake was made. The British obtained this information mostly from prisoners who were not correctly informed with regard to the real strength of Greene's army. Another thing which the British either did not know or did not take into consideration in estimating the number of Greene's army caused them to exaggerate the number of the Americans. Shortly after Pyle's defeat, and on the arrival of Col. William Campbell, General Pickens and the corps of South Carolinians under his command were relieved and returned to the western part of South Carolina. No doubt, the British in estimating General Greene's force did not, as they did in their own case, deduct the sick and wounded.

The whole number of men in Greene's army, fit for active duty, was on the eve of the battle of Guilford Court House, four thousand, four hundred and four. On the day before the battle he was joined by forty horsemen, under the Marquis of Bretagne. This made the force four thousand, four hundred and forty-four. Of this number only one thousand, four hundred and ninety were regulars. These consisted of seven hundred and seventy-eight, led by General Huger; the remaining six hundred and thirty regulars were Williams' Maryland brigade, to which was attached one company from Delaware and eighty-two infantry, belonging to Lee's legion. There were two thousand, seven hundred and ninety-three Virginians. The cavalry consisted of two hundred and one. Eighty-six commanded by Colonel Washington; seventy-five by Lieut. Col. Lee and forty by the Marquis of Bretagne.

The exact number of men in the army of Cornwallis that we are aware of, is no where stated. It was in all probability not less than two thousand nor more than two thousand five hundred. So far as simple numbers are concerned, the army of Greene was fully twice as large as that of Cornwallis; but the latter had the decided advantage in that nearly or quite all his men were tried regulars led by experienced officers. Nearly every man in the British army was a solider by profession. He had been trained to arms. Less than two thousand of Greene's forces were regulars; and even these were not regulars in the same sense that the soldiers in the army of Cornwallis were regulars. More than one half of Greene's army was nothing but undrilled militia. No small amount of them had fled to Greene's army for protection. They were brave men and as true patriots as ever lived, but it was utterly impossible that they could be good soldiers.

To make a good soldier, more is necessary than either physical or moral courage. The first impulse of the new recruits, on going into battle, is to run. He may be conscious that the cause for which he is fighting is just and right, but the clash of the first onset is too much for his nerves. To stand firm and repel an advancing foe is a sore test for him who knows nothing of a battle but what he has learned from others. To advance upon an enemy is not so severe a test. In this case his own onward motion has the appearance of defeating the foe, and he continues to advance without having his nerves shocked.

Cornwallis knew the character of Greene's troops. He knew that only a few of them were regulars that could be relied upon in the moment of extreme danger. Anxious as he was to meet Greene, that he might dispel the gloom which hung over the cause of the British government in the south, he never would have ventured nearer Guilford Court House than Bell's Mill, had all Greene's forces been regulars. Taking all things into consideration, the forces of Cornwallis, although only one-half in number, were equal in a pitched battle to those of Greene.

On the night of the fourteenth, the two armies lay encamped within eight miles of each other. Both generals were preparing for battle. The most sublime spectacle which mortal eyes can behold in this world is a contest between two armies led by brave and experienced officers. High physical and moral courage, in conjunction with a long course of training and much experience, together with a sense of responsibility, may enable individuals to behold such a scene with composure, but not with indifference. There are some things which we never can gaze upon in the character of idle spectators. The empty traveler may laugh in the face of a highway robber, but he is forced to be solemn when he sees the mighty oak shattered into a thousand pieces by lightning.

Guilford Court House is situated about five miles northeast of the town of Greensboro, the capital of Guilford county. The village in which the court house was situated, was originally called Martinsburg, in honor of Alexander Martin. Both Martinsburg and the old court house have crumbled into ruin. It was situated on the State Road leading from Salisbury to Virginia, Salisbury being at that time the most important town in the western portion of North Carolina. The battleground was on a slope, near one-half mile in length and inclining southward in the direction of New Garden Meeting House, where it was known the British were. The slope terminated in a small valley through which flowed a small stream that empties into the Haw. On the west side of the road and between the stream in the valley and the top of the hill was a large field. On the east side of the road there were two small fields, with a wood two hundred yards wide between them.

On the fourteenth, Lieutenant Colonel Lee came into General Greene's camp at Guilford Court House. He was immediately sent to take a post within three or four miles of New Garden Meeting House, with instructions to watch the movements of the enemy. Lee sent Lieutenant Heard, with a detachment of cavalry still nearer the British camp instructing him to report every occurrence promptly. About 2 o'clock in the morning Heard sent a dispatch to Lee stating that a large body of the enemy's horse was advancing in the direction of New Garden. Lee at once forwarded this intelligence to General Greene. Lee instructed Heard to proceed with a few men toward the flank of the advancing cavalry, that he might be able to learn whether the main body of the British was advancing or not. Communication between Lee and Heard was kept up at intervals of every half hour. After a series of efforts, Heard reported that on account of the extent of the enemy's patrols, he was unable to gain the flank of the cavalry, but he was confident from the rumbling of wheels which he heard that the whole army of Cornwallis was in motion. Lee ordered his men to arms and at the same time directed them to eat their breakfast with dispatch.

General Greene having been informed of the supposed advance of Cornwallis, ordered Lee to advance against the cavalry of the enemy, drive in his patrols and learn certainly whether the enemy was advancing in force or not. It was now about four o'clock in the morning. Lee ordered his horsemen to mount. He at their head at once advance towards the enemy, directing the infantry to follow. The cavalry had not gone more than two miles when they met Lieutenant Heard and his detachment, retiring before the enemy's cavalry. The British horsemen were not pursuing Heard and his men hotly, but simply advancing leisurely. Lee not wishing to come in contact with the van of the British when their main forces were so near and he so distant from Gen. Greene and his own infantry, ordered his men to retire in troops. The rear which now became the front under Rudolph dashed off at full gallop. The squad under Rudolph was followed by that under Eggleston in the same manner.

Lieutenant Colonel Tarleton, who was as truthful as he was brave, was still liable to be grossly mistaken. Not discerning the movements of Lee, he supposed the Americans were panic stricken. Tarleton and his van dashed forward upon Mark Armstrong, who led Lee's front, but on account of the recent change in the movements of the legion was now in the rear. Although the squads under Rudolph and Eggleston were retiring at the gallop, Armstrong, for the want of room, was forced to retire at a walk. Tarleton not understanding why Armstrong retired so slowly, ordered his men to fire. Their pistols being emptied, Armstrong still remained as sullen as before. Tarleton now ordered a charge. On came the British cavalry. The front section had nearly reached Armstrong when Lee who had been attentively watching the movements of Tarleton, ordered his men to right-about and charge.

Both parties were in a long lane with high fences on each side of the road, the fences following the winding of the road. Lee chose this place as favorable to the American cavalry. The horses in Lee's legion were strong and in good condition, whilst those belonging to Tarleton were inferior and in bad condition. Lee felt confident that could his cavalry meet Tarleton's in the lane that he would be able to trample a large number to death. Only one squad of each legion met. So soon as Tarleton saw what Lee was doing, he ordered a retreat. In this skirmish Tarleton lost a number of both men and horses killed. The Americans lost nothing.

Lee now directed his course towards New Garden Meeting House. At this point he arrived just as the sun was rising. The van of the British infantry and Lee's cavalry reached New Garden Meeting House at the same moment. Both parties prepared to fight. Lee ordered the cavalry to retreat, and whilst the cavalry was retiring before the British, the infantry attached to Lee's legion, and the riflemen under Col. William Campbell rushed up and poured in a most destructive fire upon the enemy. For a few moments the conflict was sharp. Several were killed on both sides. Either in this skirmish or in the one which occurred a few hours previous, Colonel Tarleton was wounded by a ball in his right hand.

The conflict between Lee and the British infantry at New Garden Meeting House was heard by General Greene and he now began to make the final disposition of his troops for action. On the previous day he had sent his wagons and baggage to Speedwell's Iron Works on Troublesome Creek. This place Greene had fortified since he recrossed the Dan and consequently it afforded a safe retreat from Guilford Court House should he be unsuccessful in the approaching engagement. Greene was by no means sanguine with regard to the results of a general engagement. He was willing to risk it believing that should the Americans succeed, the British army under Cornwallis would be hopelessly ruined; and should the British succeed the Americans would only be crippled for a short time.

The road leading from Salisbury to Virginia, crossing the Dan at Boyd's Ferry, passed through Martinsburg to the right or east of the court house. The bearing of the road was about fifteen degrees east of north. The bearing of the stream which runs through the valley south and east of the village was about forty-five degrees east of north. From the court house to the point at which the road crossed the stream was about two miles. The first line of the Americans was placed across the road, a little more than a mile from the point where the road crossed the stream in the valley. This line was composed of North Carolina militia, commanded by Generals Butler and Eaton. It was a good position, the men being protected from the fire of the enemy by the fences which enclosed the fields and a grove of trees.

Captain Singleton, with two six-pounders, was placed in the road a few rods in front of the first line. The second line composed of Virginia militia under Stevens and Lawson, was placed across the road about three hundred yards in the rear of the first line. The division of Stevens was placed on the east of the road; that of Lawson on the west, the right flank of Stevens upon the left flank of Lawson. This line was protected by the woods which lay between the fields around the court house and those farther down on the slope near the valley.

About four hundred yards in the rear of the second line, near the court house in the field and on the west of the road was placed the third line. It consisted of about fourteen hundred and fifty Continental regulars embraced in four regiments. The two Virginia Continental regiments, under General Huger, were commanded by Colonel Greene and Lieutenant Colonel Hawes. The two Maryland regiments, under Colonel Williams, were commanded by Colonel Gunby and Lieutenant Colonel Ford. Colonel Greene's command was stationed near the court house and Lieutenant Colonel Ford on the extreme left. Lieutenant Colonel Washington with his cavalry, the company of Delawares under Captain Kirkwood and Colonel Lynch with a battalion of militia from Virginia were posted on the right. Lieutenant Colonel Lee with his legion and Colonel William Campbell with the "back mountain men" were placed on the left. Washington and Lee with the forces under them were instructed to watch the flanks. In the rear of the whole and near the court house, were parked two pieces of artillery, all that General Greene had except the two six-pounders, which were placed in front in charge of Captain Singleton. Such was the disposition which General Greene made of his forces in anticipation of meeting in a general engagement, the forces under Cornwallis.

The sun was just rising when the van of the British army reached New Garden Meeting House. Here as we have seen a sharp skirmish occurred between Campbell's riflemen and the British infantry. Lieutenant Colonel Lee perceiving that the enemy was advancing in force, called off his troops and retired from before the enemy to Greene's camp and took his place in battle order.

From the forks of the road where Lee and Campbell encountered the enemy, to Guilford Court House, the distance is between five and six miles. The British took the Salisbury Road and in solid column advanced to Guilford Court House. It was about noon when the van reached the valley south of Greene's lines. The army of Cornwallis marched in the following order: The cavalry under Colonel Tarleton and the light infantry under General O'Hara were in front. Then followed Colonel Webster's brigade and the regiment of Bose. In the rear of Bose was a brigade of guards. The artillery advanced with the division to which it belonged.

When the British van entered the valley and approached in the direction of the Americans, Captain Singleton opened upon it with his two six-pounders. Lieutenant McLeod of the royal artillery rushed forward with two pieces which he posted near where the road crosses the stream in the valley and commenced returning the fire. Neither Singleton nor McLeod effected anything of importance.

From the firing of Singleton, Cornwallis knew that Greene was near by, prepared for battle and waiting for his arrival. Cornwallis knew that Greene had double the number of men that he had and that Greene had leisurely chosen his ground and arranged his men for battle. Still he determined to fight. When Singleton commenced firing the main forces of the British were more than a mile in the rear, but in full view of the American lines. Their burnished arms gleamed in the sun light and the gay uniforms of the officers and men presented an imposing sight when contrasted with the tattered uniforms of the American officers and the dirty and ragged garments of the American soldiers.

Having determined to hazard a battle, Cornwallis made the following disposition of his forces: Major General Leslie with Fraser's Highland regiment, (the 71st) and the Hessian regiment under Colonel Bose, was ordered to file to the right and advance against the American left. Colonel Webster with the twenty-third and thirty-third regiments was instructed to file to the left and advance against the American right. Lieutenant Colonel Norton with the first battalion of guards was ordered to support General Leslie; and General O'Hara with the second battalion of guards and grenadiers was directed to support Colonel Webster. The royal artillery commanded by Lieutenant McLeod and supported by the light infantry of the guards and Yagers was ordered to advance directly up the road. Tarleton was ordered to keep his cavalry in reserve with instruction to act as circumstances might indicate.

During the time that the British were firing and until the first division had reached the edge of the slope on which the American forces were drawn up in battle array, Captain Singleton kept up a brisk cannonade. In about half an hour the British began to advance for battle. Singleton according to instructions retired to the rear near the court house, where the other two pieces of artillery were placed. Having crossed the stream and approached within a few hundred yards of the field, the British began to deploy, Leslie filing to the right and Webster to the left. The left flank of Leslie and the right flank of Webster rested on the road. Cornwallis had but one line. This being formed, the command was given to advance.

The left wing of Leslie and the right wing of Webster had to cross an open field to meet the first line of the Americans. The men commanded by both Leslie and Webster were experienced soldiers.

Without a wave the line moved forward, the supports in regular order taking their proper places.

The North Carolina militia commenced firing at random when the British were one hundred and fifty yards distant. At this distance no injury was inflicted upon the enemy. As they approached nearer, many of the Highlanders, who were in the British van were mowed down by Campbell's men. Still as if nothing was transpiring, Leslie and Webster and the men in their commands continued to advance without firing a gun. When the British came within about sixty yards of the first American line, they threw in a fire which did no damage. No one was killed and not a single man wounded. So soon as the British delivered their fire, they rushed forward with a shout, and to the utter dismay of every one, the North Carolina militia threw down their guns, stripped themselves of their knapsacks and canteens and ran through the woods in every direction. Their commanders, Butler and Eaton, Lieutenant Colonel Lee, Colonel William Davie - at that time commissary general - and a multitude of other officers of every grade, endeavored to stop the fugitives, but in vain. So great were their fears and so ungovernable was the panic that they would have died rather than gone back to meet the enemy.

The cowardly flight of the first line of the Americans, before the battle had begun, threw everything in confusion and disconcerted the plans of General Greene and his officers, Lee's legion and Colonel Campbell's "back mountain men" were left to sustain the whole weight of General Leslie's command. They were in danger of either being cut off or utterly demolished.

As an indication of what might have been the results, had the North Carolinians stood their ground and fought bravely it may be mentioned that Leslie was forced to order into line the support under Lieutenant Colonel Norton, before Lee and Campbell could be dislodged. In fact, so soon as the British came within range of the rifles of Campbell's men, these hardy sons of the mountains poured in such a constant and effectual fire that it was thought at one time the British right would not be able to reach the first line of the Americans.

The British left under Webster pressed forward and attacked the Virginians under Lawson. These stood their ground manfully. Lee and Campbell set upon by the whole of Leslie's division was forced to give way or be slaughtered to a man. The base flight of the North Carolinians left the way open for the advance of the royal artillery. On the flight of the first line of the Americans, a gap was formed between Leslie and Webster. This was soon closed by O'Hara filing to the right and resting his right wing upon General Leslie's left.

The whole British force except the cavalry, with determined courage and splendid discipline, now attacked the Virginians under Lawson and Stevens. The most of the men under Stevens were Scotch-Irish from Rockbridge and Augusta counties, Virginia. One company was principally members of the congregation of the Rev. James Waddell, the blind preacher whose melting eloquence is so graphically and tenderly described by Wirt in his British Spy.

To prevent any one in his brigade from leaving, Stevens had before the battle commenced, placed forty riflemen, twenty paces in the rear with strict orders to shoot any one of the brigade who should dare to leave his post. These brave Virginians to their lasting credit, stood like well tried veterans, although pressed by the whole British force. Colonels Washington and Lee kept the flanks secure. The contest was hard and the result doubtful. Balls were flying thick as hail, and men on both sides were falling thick and fast as leaves from a forest tree in an autumn morning after a biting frost.

Colonel Washington, in order to succor the hard pressed Lawson, sent Colonel Lynch to attack Webster's flank. Webster was already sorely pressed. O'Hara with the grenadiers and second battalion of guards were now ordered into line to assist Webster. The thirty-third regiment was turned upon Lynch, and Webster, with fixed bayonets, rushed forward against Lawson. Overpowered and unable, like most militia, to stand the sight of cold steel, Lawson's men, and soon those under Stevens, gave way and fell back to the line of the Continentals.

In the first conflict between Webster and the Virginians on the left, the infantry of Lee's legion and Campbell's "mountain men" struggled with unremitting ardor against Colonel Bose's Hessian regiment. Lee and Campbell's riflemen kept Norton and Bose so closely pressed that their forces could not be brought to bear upon the second line of the Americans.

The first and second lines of the Americans were broken, but General Greene still had hope that the day was not lost. Washington and Kirkwood were at their posts ready and anxious to render support to the Continentals under Huger and Williams. The Continental troops were not discouraged, but on the contrary were full of vigor and ready for the conflict. General Greene passed along the line and exhorted his troops to stand firm and do their duty like men.

The British seemed to be determined to conquer or die. Cornwallis did not stop for one moment to consolidate his forces. Webster, unsupported and with only a part of his command, advanced over the ground occupied by Stevens and Lawson at the outset to attack the American's third line. The ground over which Webster's command had to advance was uneven and hence part of his command fell behind. With more zeal than prudence, he rushed to within close fire of the Continentals. He came in contact with the first Maryland regiment commanded by Colonel Gunby and Lieutenant Colonel Howard. The forces of Webster had been weakened in their conflict with the Virginians and when they were set upon by Gunby, supported by Hawes' regiment of Virginians and Kirkwood's company of Delawares, they were obliged to give way. Webster led his troops back across a ravine and on a favorable eminence awaited the remainder of his command. Soon Lieutenant Colonel Stuart with the first battalion of guards followed by the remainder of Webster's command, swept across the field near the court house. Stuart discovered the second Maryland regiment, under Ford, on the left of the first under Gunby, and concealed from the first by a grove of trees, rushed forward to attack it. Ford's regiment was supported by Captain Finley with two six-pounders.

Colonel Williams being elated on account of the good conduct of his first regiment under Gunby, had no doubt but that the second would conduct itself as gallantly as the first had done. With this expectation he began to concentrate his forces for the purpose of utterly annihilating Stuart's command. To the astonishment of Williams, the regiment under Ford gave way at the first shock and fled, leaving the two six-pounders to the enemy. Stuart pushed forward in pursuit of Ford's regiment. Gunby being left unemployed by the departure of Webster over the ravine and seeing the flight of Ford and pursuit of Stuart, turned his regiment upon Stuart, when a desperate conflict ensued. Colonel Washington posted after the Virginians fell back on the wing of the Continentals, rushed forward to aid Gunby.

Never did men fight more bravely. Francisco, a brave Virginian with a broad sword, cut down in succession eleven of the enemy. One of the British guards thrust his bayonet through Francisco's leg and into his horse's side. The deadly weapon stuck fast. The leg of Francisco was pinned to the horse's side and the gun of the British soldier could not be used by its owner. Francisco and the guard united in drawing the bayonet from Francisco's leg, when the latter, quick as thought, grasped his broad sword, and with one blow, divided the poor fellow's head from the crown to his shoulders.

Stuart and his veterans could not withstand such desperate courage as the Americans exhibited. They soon began to give way. With sword in hand, Colonel Washington and his cavalry, followed by Howard and his infantry with fixed bayonets, charged into the very midst of the enemy. Captain Smith of the first Maryland regiment killed Stuart with his sword. The two six-pounders were retaken and multitudes of the enemy slaughtered. The probability is that the whole of Stuart's command would have been either killed or captured had not Cornwallis resorted to a most extraordinary measure. Seeing the imminent danger in which his troops were placed, he ordered Lieutenant McLeod to draw up the artillery and fire upon Washington and Howard with grapeshot. Every fire from McLeod's artillery endangered the British as much as the Americans. It was effectual and showed the ability of Cornwallis. Washington and Howard seeing a regiment of the enemy on the right and one on their left, retired leading their commands back to the line of the Continentals. After Washington and Howard fell back, Gen. O'Hara, although severely wounded, united the remnant of Stuart's guards with the seventy-first and twenty-third regiments. These were the regiments that Howard and Washington saw on their right and left.

Webster, seeing Stuart putting Ford's regiment to flight, advanced across the ravine and attacked Hawes' Virginia regiment, supported by Kirkwood's Delawares. O'Hara led the seventy-third and twenty-third regiments and the remnant of Stuart's guards back and closed up the interval between the British. The center was thus closed and the conflict was renewed with great vigor in this quarter.

On the enemy's right the contest had continued from the beginning with unabated energy. Lee and Campbell had kept Bose and Norton at a respectful distance from the American lines during the whole of the conflict. Each party kept constantly inclining towards the flanks of the main forces to which they belonged. When they approached the road, Norton leaving Colonel Bose to grapple with the infantry under Lee and Campbell, dashed off to join Fraser's regiment. So soon as Norton drew off his guards, Lee sent his cavalry, which he had been holding as a reserve, to join the flank of the Continental line.

Lee and Campbell now renewed the attack upon the regiment of Bose with great energy. The Hessians under Colonel Bose and Major DeBuy fought bravely, but they were forced to give way before Lee and Campbell and take refuge behind Norton's guards. Lee, leaving Campbell to continue the contest with Bose, hastened on to unite his infantry with his cavalry which he had sent to the left flank of the Continental line. On his way, Lee found Norton with his forces, upon the spot where Lawson's brigade had been posted when the battle began. Lee attacked Norton, drove him back and he and Campbell then cut their way through the British and joined the Continentals near the court house. Before Lee reached the court house, however, General Greene had determined to withdraw his troops.

His reasons for coming to this conclusion were the fact that he did not know what had become of Lee; the British were still in line; his ammunition was nearly exhausted, and it was his fixed determination never to risk a total overthrow. Another circumstance had much to do in causing General Greene to decide on withdrawing his forces. In the execution of all the plans that had been devised respecting the battle, much confusion had sprung up. From a multitude of causes General Greene did not know, and could not know, the real condition of either his own army or that of the enemy. Many of his troops had fought with unexampled courage and performed deeds of unparalleled valor. Others had behaved badly. The enemy had during the whole of the engagement fought as only brave men can fight. In no conflict either before or afterward did the British officers show more skill or the British soldiers better discipline or more courage. Under these circumstances General Greene thought it prudent to withdraw his troops before it might be too late.

Huger and Williams were ordered to draw off their respective commands. The command was executed with promptness and in good order the troops were led from the field of battle, leaving the artillery to the enemy. Colonel Greene with his Virginia regiment, was directed to take a position in the rear for the purpose of covering the retreat. Three miles from the battlefield, Greene halted for the purpose of giving the stragglers and fugitives time to come in. From this point he marched slowly to Speedwell's Iron Works on Troublesome Creek.

The battle of Guilford Court House was in many particulars a very important one. It commenced about one o'clock on the 15th of March, 1781, and lasted about two hours. The British held the battleground and claimed the victory, but it was a dear bought victory. In fact it was no victory at all and never was regarded by British statesmen as anything but a defeat. Fox declared in a speech made at the time that "another such victory will ruin the British army." The younger Pitt boldly declared that the further prosecution of the war by the British ministry against the Americans was "wicked, barbarous, unjust, and diabolical."

Cornwallis lost in killed and wounded, near if not altogether one-fourth of his men, besides about one hundred and fifty officers, many of whom were the best in his army. The rank and file of the British in killed and wounded amounted to more than 600. Colonel Stuart and Lieutenant O'Hara, the brother of General O'Hara, were killed, General O'Hara, Lieut. Colonel Webster, Captains Schultz, Mayard, Wilmouski and Ensign DeTrott were severely wounded, all of whom, except O'Hara, afterwards died as a result of wounds.

The American loss in killed and wounded was 421 and fourteen officers. Of these the Continentals lost, in killed and wounded, 312, the Virginia militia 100, and the North Carolina militia nine. Major Anderson of the Maryland line was killed and Generals Huger and Stevens wounded.

THE RETREAT OF CORNWALLIS

About the middle of the afternoon of the 15th of March, 1780, General Greene drew off his troops from the field at Guilford Court House. Neither Greene nor Cornwallis had a clear idea of the results of the battle. Greene retreated to Speedwell's Iron Works and made preparations for another conflict. Cornwallis was much too crippled to pursue him. For a period of two months, Cornwallis had been exerting all his energies and plying every strategy his fertile mind could devise, to bring on a general engagement with Greene. At last the long wished for moment arrived and the conflict came. While its management did honor to the military talents of the British general, its results paralyzed his arm and rendered the accomplishing of his ultimate purpose hopeless. Since leaving Turkey creek, in York county, on the 18th of January, he had lost one-half of his army and nearly all his baggage. Instead of making friends of the inhabitants of the country through which he passed, his operations had converted many of the loyalists into Whigs or caused them to assume a passive attitude.

The night after the battle of Guilford Court House was cold and rainy. The dead and wounded, both of the Americans and British, lay scattered promiscuously all over the field of conflict. The groans of the wounded rose above the noise of the falling rain. More than fifty of the wounded died during the night. The next morning was devoted to burying the dead and caring for the wounded. This duty devolved upon the British army. To the honor of Cornwallis, he devoted as much attention to the dead and wounded of the American army, as he did to those of the British.

So soon as the dead were buried and the wounded cared for, Cornwallis set out for New

Garden Meeting House. This was not the course a conquering general would have taken. Had Cornwallis really believed that "his Majesty's arms had been crowned with signal success," he would most certainly have followed General Greene. Instead of doing this, he led his depleted and dispirited army back to New Garden Meeting House. There he was joined by the baggage wagons which had been sent off, before the battle, to a place of safety. Notwithstanding his boastings of victory, Cornwallis was now actually retreating from Greene and in accordance with the principles of that philosophy which prompts the little boy to whistle when passing a grave yard, that he may frighten away the ghosts, the British general issued a proclamation in which he announced that a complete victory had been gained over the rebel forces on the 15th, at Guilford Court House.

On the 18th, leaving under a flag of truce seventy of his wounded, who were unable to be moved, and a few wounded Americans at New Garden, he set out for the Scotch settlement on the Cape Fear River, at what was then called Cross Creek - now Fayetteville. On its way to Cross Creek, the royal army encamped at Bell's Mill on Deep River. About the middle of the afternoon, Cornwallis and the van of the royal army reached the house of Mr. Bell. The British earl dismounted and entered the house. Having taken a general survey of everything in the house, he asked Mrs. Bell where her husband was.

"In Greene's camp" was the prompt reply. "Well, madam," continued Cornwallis, "I must make your house my headquarters for a few days and take your mill to grind corn for my soldiers."

"Sir, you have the power to do as you please, but permit me to ask, do you intend to burn my house and mill when you leave?"

"Why do you ask that question?"

"Answer me first and then I will tell you."

"No," said Cornwallis, "your house and mill shall not be burned. I will make your house my headquarters and your person and property shall be protected from insult and injury."

"Well, sir," said Mrs. Bell, "since you were so kind as to answer my question, I will answer yours. Had it been your intention to burn my mill and house after using them, I had determined to save you the trouble by burning them myself before you used them."

At this bold and fearless declaration, Cornwallis took no offense. As the different divisions came in, he gave instructions to each in a nervous manner, which attracted the attention of Mrs. Bell. He would sit down but remain only for a moment and then rising up excitedly, walk hastily across the house for a few times and then sit down again, and soon rise and walk across the house as before.

During the time that he was exhibiting so much nervousness, he told Mrs. Bell in a rather boasting tone that he had completely annihilated General Greene's army. "Never again," he said, "will Greene be able either to assist his friends or injure his enemies."

The evening was cold and Mrs. Bell had closed the door, Cornwallis went to the back door and having opened it, looked excitedly up the road for a few moments and commenced his tramp across the house. Mrs. Bell got up and quietly shut the door which the earl had left open. Again Cornwallis opened the door and gazed up the road and in a few moments began to walk across the house, leaving the door open as before. For a number of times Cornwallis opened the door and Mrs. Bell closed it. Finally, Cornwallis opened it and said in a commanding tone that the door must remain open. Mrs. Bell, not daunted by the commanding tones of a British general, remarked that it was cold and she could see no good reason for keeping the door open.

"Why," said Cornwallis, "I do not know what moment Greene, with his rebels, may attack me."

"I thought you said you had killed all the rebels in Greene's army."

"Well, madam, I never saw such fighting in my life and to tell you the truth, the rebels will not remain conquered."

There was a vast amount of truth in the last sentence. No sooner did Cornwallis leave Guilford Court House than Lee with his legion and Campbell with his riflemen were sent to pursue him. Greene himself with all his forces would have given him chase at once, had he not been compelled to wait at Speedwell's Iron Works for ammunition.

When Greene drew off his troops from the battlefield at Guilford Court House, he did not know how much injury he had done the enemy; neither did Cornwallis know how much he had suffered. In some communication that passed between the two generals shortly after the battle, something was said by Cornwallis about the four pieces of cannon which had fallen into the hands of the British. Greene replied that he had four more pieces that he would be very glad to let his majesty have on the same terms he had obtained the others.

At Bell's Mill Cornwallis remained two days, and then removed to Ramsey's Mill on Deep River near its mouth, in Chatham county. Lee and Campbell were close in his rear, inflicting injury upon him as opportunity was afforded. Cornwallis did not permit his troops to straggle off in detachments. Even the daring Tarleton acted with great caution. Cornwallis was now as anxious to avoid an engagement, as was Greene during his retreat from the Catawba to the Dan. The rear guard of the British, which was commanded by Tarleton, was constantly insulted by Lee and Campbell, but never dared to hazard even a skirmish. The fact is, Cornwallis did not know but Greene, with his whole forces, might at any moment come down upon him and ruin him before he could reach Cross Creek.

It was the purpose of Cornwallis on leaving New Garden to remain at either Bell's or Ramsey's Mill a considerable length of time in order that his wounded might recover. This he was not allowed to do. Lee and Campbell soon made their appearance and he was obliged to move.

To facilitate his retreat from Ramsey's Mill, Cornwallis commenced constructing soon after his arrival a bridge across Deep River. Greene, whose pursuit was greatly impeded by the almost absolute destitute condition of his commissary department, ordered Lee and Campbell to prevent if possible the completion of the bridge. In order to put this order into execution, Lee and Campbell crossed the river ten miles above Ramsey's Mill with the intention of dislodging the guard on the south side. This end of the bridge was guarded by two hundred men under the command of a major. The night was dark and the way difficult. Still the Americans under Lee and Campbell reached the spot in due time. Nothing, however, could be accomplished for during the night Cornwallis suspecting, no doubt, that an attempt would be made to destroy his bridge, had reinforced the guard and the American officer desisted from making an attack. On the same day Cornwallis crossed over the bridge and hastened as much as the feeble condition of his army would permit, his retreat to Cross Creek and then to Wilmington. Multitudes of his wounded died on the way. At Elizabethtown the gallant Webster died, and there he was buried with the honors of war.

On the twenty-eighth, Greene at the head of the American forces, reached Ramsey's Mill. Cornwallis had left two days before. Unable as was Cornwallis to make a hasty retreat, Greene was equally as unable to hasten the pursuit. He had accomplished his object and defeated the plans of the British general and now he determined to stop the pursuit and grant the weary troops time to rest. More than rest he could not give them. The country had been stripped of provisions. All the food that Greene's army could procure was corn meal and such beef as the country furnished. The beef was inferior in quality and stinted in quantity. Strange as it may seem both men and officers were in high spirits.

Viewing this whole affair from its commencement at Cowpens, on the 17th of January to the 28th of March, when Greene halted at Ramsey's Mill, master of all North Carolina, except the single town of Wilmington, it is one of the grandest achievements of the Revolutionary war. From the Cowpens to Irwin's Ferry on the Dan, in a direct line is near two hundred miles. For more than ten days in the dead of winter, without money, without tents, without blankets, without any food only as could be gathered on the march, General Greene retreated with an army of undisciplined militia, hotly pursued by the veterans of Europe, led by as able and skillful an officer as was in the British army, aided by Tarleton and Webster, as brave men as ever drew a sword. The battles of King's Mountain, the Cowpens, and Guilford Court House, inflicted a mortal wound upon the cause of Great Britain in America. After the battle of Guilford Court House, the sun of Liberty rose and shed its refulgent beams over the whole country. Seven months afterward, Cornwallis surrendered.

Installment XLI

THE SECOND BATTLE OF CAMDEN

At Ramsey's Mill on Deep River, General Greene consulted with the officers in his army with reference to the proper course to be pursued. Cornwallis was gone. Evidently the British, although boasting that they were victorious, were not disposed to meet Greene again. The majority of the officers in Greene's army advised that the pursuit of Cornwallis be continued, either by advancing directly to Wilmington or by placing the American forces between Wilmington and Virginia so as to be able to prevent the advance of Cornwallis in that direction.

Colonel Lee proposed that Cornwallis be left to act as he saw fit and that the American army be led back into South Carolina for the purpose of restoring the state to the American union. The debate was warm on both sides and many strong arguments were advanced by the advocates of each plan. The course proposed and advocated by Colonel Lee was finally adopted. The details of the scheme were that the main army under General Greene should march directly to Camden, South Carolina, while Colonel Lee with the light corps under his command should advance farther south and join General Marion, then on the Black River in Williamsburg county.

For the purpose of keeping the state of South

Carolina in subjection as well as for the purpose of supplying their own troops with food and clothing, the British had established a chain of forts extending from Camden to Ninety-Six. The plan proposed by Lee contemplated a simultaneous attack upon all of these forts. Since the defeat of Gates, on the 16th of August, 1780, the state of South Carolina had been under the heel of the British. After Cornwallis in pursuit of Gen. Greene had left the state, small partisan corps were raised which kept up the appearance of resistance. Marion, with a few followers, operated in the east and southwest section of the state. Such, however, was the character of the inhabitants of the country in which he operated that he was unable to effect anything decisive in its results.

In that portion of South Carolina, extending from Richmond to Robeson counties, North Carolina, to the Santee there were a multitude of Tories. In this section of the state there have ever been gangs of robbers. In the same region there were many good Whigs, who suffered as much for liberty as any other individuals in the Confederacy. All that Marion and the Whig settlers could do in the absence of the main army was to keep these Tories partially in subjection. To do this was not a bloodless task. For the sake of liberty many good men lost their lives.

Sumter having recovered, from the wound received at Blackstock, collected a chosen band and struck terror into the minds of the Tories in the center of the state. Colonels Harden and Baker kept up a spirited resistance in the region south of Charleston. The state was overrun, but not subdued. The Tories were reveling in lust and the Whigs were burning with rage. The more sensible of the loyalists were filled with bloody apprehensions. Such briefly was the condition of things in South Carolina during the winter of 1780-81.

At Ramsey's Mill, General Greene dismissed all his militia except a few North Carolinians. Arrangements were rapidly made for the return of the army into South Carolina. Greene sent a general outline of his proposed plan of operations to Sumter and Pickens. Both were ordered to collect all the men they could and prepare for active service. Sumter was ordered to join the main army at Camden and Pickens was instructed to make an attack upon Ninety-Six or to so environ it that reinforcements could not be sent from that place to Camden.

On the 6th of April, Colonel Lee with his legion and Captain Oldham's detachment of Marylanders set out to join Marion. After a successful march of eight days, Lee and Oldham reached Marion's hiding place in the swamps of Black River. On the 7th of April,

General Greene with the main army broke up camp at Ramsey's Mill. On the 19th they reached Camden. Lord Rawdon had commenced to fortify Camden. When Greene arrived in the vicinity of the town, he found it well fortified and Lord Rawdon in command of nine hundred effective men. General Greene, after the detachment under Lee and Oldham had been sent off, had only fifteen hundred men. With this force he was unable to carry the place by storm, nor was he able to besiege it with any hopes of success.

The town of Camden is situated in Kershaw county on the left bank of the Wateree River, and about one-half mile distant. It is elevated above the level of the river about seventy-five feet. Between the river and the town, flows Belton's Branch on the east and on the south flows Pinetree Creek. Belton's Branch flows into Pinetree Creek, south of the town, a short distance from where Pinetree Creek empties into the river. On the west, south and east the town is surrounded by water and on the north the tributaries of Belton's Branch and little Pinetree Creek nearly meet. Camden is the oldest inland town in the state of South Carolina. Here, in 1750, some Quakers from Ireland settled. Robert Milhouse and Samuel Wylie erected mills on Pinetree Creek and for many years the place was called Pinetree. About 1760, Colonel Joseph Kershaw, having for some years been successfully engaged in merchandising, laid out the place in regular lots and streets, and in honor of Lord Camden gave it its present name. Its first charter was granted in 1769. North of Camden and about one mile distant, is a considerable elevation called Hobkirk's Hill. Descending the southern slope of this elevation, General Greene encamped on the 19th of April at Logtown within one-half mile of the British entrenchments.

Lord Rawdon had been informed of the approach of General Greene. He was astonished, having heard that General Greene was ruined. Such, however, was the strength of his position and so strongly was he fortified that the approach of Greene's army gave him very little uneasiness. General Greene, after reconnoitering and finding that he could effect nothing with his present force, either by siege or storm, fell back to Hobkirk's Hill with the intention of awaiting the arrival of Sumter.

Previous to the arrival of Greene, Rawdon had sent out Colonel Watson, with four or five hundred men, to watch the movements of Marion. On the 21st, General Greene heard that Colonel Watson was marching, with all possible dispatch up the Santee in order to join Rawdon at Camden. Greene at once concluded that it was incumbent on him to prevent the junction of Rawdon and Watson. To effect this it was deemed advisable to intercept Watson at a considerable distance from Camden. General Greene with a sufficient number of men, set out forthwith to accomplish this design. He crossed Sand Hill Creek, and on the 22nd encamped east of Camden on the road leading to Charleston. Finding that the artillery could not be transported across the swamps, it was sent back under Colonel Carrington in the direction of Lynch's Creek. Here, it was thought, it would be safe from the enemy. General Greene soon learned that he had been falsely informed respecting the movements of Colonel Watson. This being the case he returned to Hobkirk's Hill on the 23rd. Colonel Carrington and the artillery arrived on the morning of the 24th.

Although General Greene had no apprehension that Lord Rawdon would attack him, nor did he design making any aggressions on the enemy until after the arrival of Sumter, still his army was encamped in order for battle. The Waxhaw Road, the road leading through the Waxhaw settlement to Salisbury, passed directly over Hobkirk's Hill. On the west of the road, was encamped Huger's Virginia brigade; on the east of the road was Colonel Williams' Maryland brigade. The light troops under Kirkwood formed a picket line in front. In the rear was placed Colonel Washington's cavalry and the North Carolina militia. In the rear of Williams and between the two lines was the reserves under Greene himself. On the left or east of the American camp, less than a mile distant, was little Pinetree Creek; on the right or west, was the Wateree River less than two miles distant. The position was favorable for resisting an attack. The American army was encamped in a line extending across the neck of land which lies between the Wateree River and Little Pinetree Creek.

On the 23rd, Captain McKay, the commandant of Fort Watson, at Wright's Bluff on the Santee, in Clarendon county, was forced to surrender to Lee and Marion. A number of the prisoners captured had at one time been in the American army. In order that they might escape the doom which awaits the deserter, they stated that having fallen in the hands of the enemy, they joined the British army that they might have a better opportunity of again entering the service of their country. Among this class of prisoners was a drummer by the name of Jones, a native of Maryland. Jones, together with the prisoners who had once been American soldiers, were sent to General Greene. They arrived at the American camps sometime during the 24th. Sometime during the same night, Jones deserted and made good his escape to the enemy. From him Lord Rawdon learned the condition of things in the American camp. He learned that Fort Watson had capitulated, that Greene was daily expecting strong reinforcements under Sumter and that he was without supplies. He was also told that Colonel Carrington was absent with the artillery from Greene's camp. Carrington had returned to camp when Jones left, but unknown to the latter.

In view of all the circumstances by which he was surrounded, Lord Rawdon concluded that something must be done to sustain the sinking cause of the British. Of Cornwallis he knew nothing and he saw that unless some stop was put to the progress of the American partisan leaders, he would soon be cut off from Ninety-Six and Charleston, and be forced for the want of supplies to surrender. On the morning of the 25th he armed every man who was able to carry a gun. Even the musicians and drummers were ordered into ranks. His fortifications and baggage were committed to the care of the sick and Tories who had congregated in the town.

About two o'clock in the morning, Rawdon with all his available force marched out of town for the purpose of attacking the Americans. Every move was made with the utmost silence. Taking the road leading to Pinetree Creek, he filed to the left leading his forces close to the stream. The whole region north and northeast of Camden was at that time a dense forest. Such was the order preserved by the British forces that the Americans did not discover their approach until a portion of them had gone beyond the pickets and were opposite the Americans' left flank. The picket line, commanded by Captain Benson of Maryland and Captain Morgan of Virginia, supported by the remains of the Delaware regiment under Kirkwood, did not discover the advance of the enemy until they had arrived within less than five hundred yards of the American camp. Had it not been for the peculiar nature of the ground the Americans would have been completely surprised.

Colonel Carrington had brought in with him an abundant supply of provisions and rations had been issued to the soldiers but a short time before the British made their appearance. Gen. Greene and his suite were leisurely eating their breakfast under the shade of the trees near Martin's Spring, a short distance east of the road. Some of the soldiers were cooking, others were washing their clothes and many of them were lying idle about camp. The horses were unsaddled and nothing was in readiness for battle except that the several divisions of the army were properly located.

The first intimation that General Greene received of the advancing of the British was announced by the firing of the British van, into the American picket line. The Americans laid aside everything and prepared for battle. The baggage was ordered to Rugeley's, some eight or nine miles in the rear.

The American army was soon ready to meet the enemy and notwithstanding the unexpectedness of the attack, General Greene felt confident that he would gain a complete victory. Such being his calculations he ordered Colonel Washington to turn the enemy's right and charge upon them in the rear.

In the meantime, the pickets fought bravely, disputing every inch of ground until Rawdon advanced with his whole force, and Kirkwood was forced to fall back into line. The brigade on the American right commanded by General Huger was led by Lieutenant Colonel Richard Campbell and Capt. Hawes. That on the left commanded by Colonel Otho H. Williams was led by Colonel Gunby and Lieutenant Colonels Howard and Ford. The artillery was placed under Colonel Harrison and so situated as to command the road. The North Carolina militia, about two hundred and fifty, who were stationed in the rear under Colonel Washington, were commanded by Colonel Reade.

The King's American Volunteer regiment formed the British right; the Sixty-third regiment was on the left and the New York volunteers composed the center. The British right was supported by Robertson's corps and on the left by the Irish volunteers. As the enemy's forces advanced, presenting a narrow front, Campbell and Ford were ordered to turn his flanks, while Gunby with the Maryland regiment was directed to attack his center. Lord Rawdon on discovering Greene's plans strengthened his position by ordering the Irish volunteers into line and thus extending his front.

The battle commenced on the British left and extended to the right, General Greene aided by Huger, Campbell and Hawes led the two Virginia regiments. The Virginians stood firm and even drove the enemy back, whilst Colonel Washington with his cavalry was carrying every thing before him on the British right. Colonel Harrison in the center, was thinning the ranks of the British with the artillery. At this juncture of affairs, Gunby's Maryland regiment rushed forward with fixed bayonets. The British began to falter and Col. Hawes was ordered to charge the New York volunteers. To all human appearances victory was about to declare in favor of the Americans. Just at this important moment, Captain William Beatty who commanded the right battalion of Gunby's veteran regiment was killed, and his command paused and soon the whole regiment gave way. Colonels Williams,

Gunby and Ford all endeavored to stop it, but failed. In the attempt, Ford was mortally wounded and carried to the rear. Gunby finding that he could not restore the regiment to order on the field ordered it to fall back to the rear and then form. This order proved most ruinous. As the American regiment fell back, the British rushed forward with a shout and soon the whole American army began to retreat.

Colonel Washington at this moment was in the rear of the British striking terror in every direction. When the retreat commenced he had no less than two hundred prisoners. When he learned that General Greene was retreating he paroled the British officers he had captured and taking with him fifty prisoners, cut his way to Greene with the loss of only three men.

So soon as General Greene saw that it was necessary to withdraw his troops, Hawes was ordered to cover the broken line. The British pursued and kept up, at intervals, the action until about four o'clock. The Americans had crossed Sanders' Creek four miles from the battle ground. At this point Colonel Washington with his cavalry and the North Carolina militia turned upon the pursuing foe. He charged with characteristic fury the New York volunteers, killing nine and scattering the whole. Here the British drew off and the fight ended. The Americans encamped for the night two miles north of Sanders' Creek, and the British returned to Camden. The dead were left on the battlefield.

The loss in killed, wounded, and missing was nearly equal on both sides. The American loss was two hundred and sixty; that of the British two hundred and fifty-eight. Very few on either side were killed. The British loss in killed was thirty-eight; that of the Americans only eighteen, but two of these were Colonel Ford and Captain Beatty, both gallant officers.

Never was any officer more disappointed than was General Greene in the results of this battle. From the firing of the first gun by the pickets, which announced the approach of the enemy, he calculated with certainty on a glorious victory. Evidently the pivot upon which the results of the battle turned was Gunby's regiment. Had it stood firm, it is highly probable that the victory in favor of Greene would have been complete. The moment it faltered, the scales began to turn and so soon as it began to fall back in disorder, the day was lost to Greene. The conduct of Gunby's regiment on this occasion was very remarkable. It was regarded as the choice regiment in the southern army. At the Cowpens and at Guilford Court House, it had fought bravely. At Hobkirk's Hill, there was some defect about the manner in which the regiment was led into battle. About this matter Greene was displeased with Gunby and Gunby was displeased with Greene. What was the exact character of the difference of opinion between these two officers we can not now learn.

Without censuring, we may be permitted to say that General Greene, under the circumstances attempted too much at once. That the victory might be complete, he so led his troops into battle that a simultaneous attack would be made upon the whole front and rear of the British. This was an admirable arrangement to secure a complete victory, had it been infallibly certain that none of his troops would give way. Greene's forces, if not surprised, were led into battle before they were properly arranged, and the wonder is that they fought as well as they did. As it turned out, the British, although claiming a victory, were terribly crippled. By their own account more than one-fourth of Lord Rawdon's men were rendered unfit for service. One British officer was killed and eleven captured and paroled.

Installment XLII

MARION AND HIS MEN - CAPTURE OF FORT WATSON

Shortly after the defeat of General Gates at Camden, General Marion began to operate independently in the southeastern section of the state of South Carolina. For some time Lieutenant Col. Lee and he were together, but on the removal of General Greene's forces from Hicks' Creek near Cheraw, Marion was left alone. Sometimes his forces numbered several hundred; at other times they amounted to no more than a score.

The headquarters of Marion and his men was Snow's Island. The place is in Williamsburg county, a short distance below the confluence of Lynch's Creek and the Great Pee Dee. On the north, east, and south, Snow's Island is flowed round by the Pee Dee; whilst on the west it is bounded by Clark's Creek and impassable swamps. The island itself is a high river swamp and at the time of the Revolution was covered with canes. From north to south it is about three miles long, and from east to west it is about two miles broad. Nature fortified it and rendered it admirably adapted to the purposes for which Marion and his men selected it. From this stronghold the gallant partisan often lead his few but faithful followers against the Tories and British.

In the exploits of Marion and his men there is more of romance than in the deeds of any other partisan corps that was in existence during the Revolutionary war. The military record of no officer is better than that of Francis Marion. He never was surprised; he never made a serious blunder and he never was driven from the field of conflict. He fought according to no military rules. Wherever he found his foe he dashed in upon him, fought until his ammunition was exhausted, and then retired. No officer, it is but just to remark, was ever more faithfully and energetically aided by his subalterns than was Marion. Among these may be mentioned as worthy of honorable distinction, Peter Horry, the James brothers, Henry Mouzon, John McCauley, William McCottry, Gavin Witherspoon, Joseph Scott, John Baxter, John Swinton and John Erwin. These are not all. The Postells, the Bacots and many other have carved their names on the tablets of the nation's memory.

Major Horry led a brigade of cavalry. All the implements of offense and defense in this brigade were of the most primitive character. The saws were taken from the mills and being placed in the hands of ordinary blacksmiths, were converted into swords. From the middle of November 1780, to the middle of April, 1781, Marion and his men kept the British and Tories in and around Georgetown in a state of constant alarm. No great and decisive battles were fought; but at Georgetown, at Socastee Swamp, at White's Bridge, at Wiboo Swamp, at Mount Hope, at Black River Bridge, at Samplit Bridge, and at various other localities, battles were fought by Marion or his subalterns which had a favorable effect upon the American cause. In all of these battles, small as they were, the American cause gained something; while in all of them the British and Tory loss was very considerable.

On the fourteenth of April, 1781, Lieutenant Colonel Lee joined General Marion in one of the many swamps of Black River, in Williamsburg county. The plans of General Greene were unfolded to Marion by Lee and without a moments delay these two officers agreed upon a scheme for immediate operations. It was at once determined to make an attack upon Fort Watson. This place was garrisoned by about one hundred and twenty men, two-thirds of whom were regulars; the other third was loyalists. Lieutenant McKay, a young man, but brave and energetic officer, was in command of the fort.

Fort Watson was in Sumter county, on the left bank of the Santee River. From Kingstree, the county seat of Williamsburg, it is distant nearly west about thirty-five miles and south of Sumterville about thirty miles. The spot upon which the fort was erected was a mound nearly fifty feet high. Here it was thought the Indians had in times past deposited their dead. The garrison was supplied with water from Scott's Lake.

Fort Watson could not be regarded, in the modern sense of the word, a strong place. It was a simple stockade with no cannon. It was notwithstanding an important place. It was a link in the chain of fortifications which the British had established through the country and along the rivers, for the purpose of keeping open their communications with Charleston. The fall of Fort Watson would necessitate the evacuation of Camden. Determined if possible to reduce it, Marion and Lee set out on the morning of the 15th of April for the locality.

Colonel Watson, in honor of whom the fort had been named, was at that time on Catfish Creek, near the site of the present town of Marion. Captain Gavin Witherspoon, with a small body of men was left to watch Watson's movements. On the evening of the fifteenth, Marion and Lee reached the neighborhood of Fort Watson and on the morning of the 16th their forces were stationed preparatory to regular siege. Marion sent in a flag demanding an unconditional surrender of the fort. This McKay promptly refused.

The supply of water was soon cut off, but McKay soon sunk a well within the stockade, to a depth below the level of the lake and then cut a ditch from the lake to the well. The supply of water was cut off for only three days. This perplexed both Marion and Lee. They had thought that so soon as the supply of water was cut off, McKay would surrender. Time was precious. They did not know at what moment Colonel Watson, who was in command of about five hundred infantry, might come to the relief of the fort. This being the condition of things, Marion and Lee were greatly perplexed. So great was the elevation of the stockade above the level of the surrounding country, that without cannon, no injury could be done to the garrison.

In Marion's command there was an individual by the name of Hezekiah Maham. He was a native of St. Stephen's parish and was lieutenant colonel of an independent corps of cavalry. This individual suggested a novel but practical plan by which to reduce the fort. He suggested the idea of erecting near the fort an oblong pen so high that it would overlook the fort. The plan was at once adopted. Individuals were mounted on horses and sent in all directions through the surrounding country for the purpose of procuring axes. So soon as a sufficient number of axes were secured, all hands were taken to the woods. Some were put to felling trees and cutting logs of the proper length; while others were directed to carry the logs to the proper place. The garrison saw all this going on but were unable for the want of artillery to prevent its progress.

On the night of the 22nd, Maham's tower, as it was called, was finished. Near the top and about the height of the stockade was placed a floor of logs. In front was a kind of breast work. In this high pen near its top and overlooking Fort Watson, a chosen band of riflemen was placed so soon as the work of erection was completed.

The night of the 22nd was cloudy and dark. Silently but rapidly the work of erecting Maham's tower advanced. Just at the dawn of day the riflemen placed in the top of the pen began to fire upon the garrison below them. At the same moment detachments from the forces of Marion and Lee rushed up the mound and began a vigorous attack upon the abattis, which protected the ditch that supplied the garrison with water. McKay now seeing that resistance would result in complete slaughter, hung out a white flag. The garrison capitulated, the Americans having lost two killed and six wounded. The British lost everything. Only a few were killed but the whole garrison, officers and men were taken prisoners and all the supplies fell into the hands of the needy Americans.

The success of Marion and Lee at Fort Watson was justly ascribed to "Maham's tower." This tower has been styled "one of those ingenious devices which are perhaps more readily found by a primitive than an educated people." This may be true; still the erection of this tower made the name of Maham illustrious in South Carolina during the remainder of the war, and it will perpetuate his memory for many generations yet to come.

It is but just to remark, that the suggestion was not original with Maham. In February, 1781, General Sumter made an attack upon Fort Granby near Columbia. The besiegers labored under the same disadvantages that Marion and Lee had to contend with at Fort Watson. Colonel Thomas Taylor, a citizen of Columbia and an unfaltering Whig devised a structure of this kind. The only difference in the two structures was that Taylor used fence rails and Maham used logs internotched so that they were steady and strong. So far as we know, whatever merit is due the device it should be given to Colonel Taylor. Maham is justly due the credit of having greatly improved it.

THE BATTLE OF ORANGEBURG - SURRENDER OF FORT MOTTE

That we may have a correct idea of the movements of the contending parties in the state of South Carolina, immediately after the second battle of Camden - or as it is sometimes called, and appropriately too, the battle of Hobkirk's Hill - we must watch the plans of General Greene and Lord Rawdon. It is scarcely possible to conceive of a man more crushed for the moment than was Greene on account of the results of the battle of Hobkirk's Hill. He calculated with certainty on a victory, and instead of this he met with defeat. It is true like most of the victories gained by the British during the Revolutionary war, it advantaged them nothing. Still Greene was not successful, and he was prepared neither in mind nor body to sustain a defeat. Sad and gloomy on the morning after the battle he moved his troops to Rugeley's Mill.

Sumter had been ordered to join him but for some reason, which it was not easy to explain satisfactorily, this officer had failed to obey. Truth demands that we say that Sumter had been interfering with the recruiting officers of Marion, and that he had paid no sort of attention to the orders of General Greene; but continued to act as he had been doing for a long time, independently. This was a source of great mortification to General Greene. Strange as it may sound to those who are accustomed to hear nothing but praise spoken of the heroes of the Revolutionary war, it is still true that General Greene was for the time completely nonplused by the turn which things took in the battle of Hobkirk's Hill.

On the morning of the 26th, he ordered Lieutenant Colonel Lee to return immediately to his camp and then in a short time revoked this order and sent Captain Finley with a small detachment and one six-pounder to assist Marion and Lee in their struggle with Colonel Watson.

As Lieutenant Colonel Lee had proposed and advocated the plan of leaving Cornwallis and advancing into South Carolina, it is almost certain that General Greene after the battle of Hobkirk's Hill, began to doubt the wisdom of the move and in his mind to censure Lee. Sure he censured and perhaps justly, the conduct of General Sumter. It is possible that Sumter had intercepted some of Rawdon's dispatches which that officer had sent to some of his posts, and from the information thus obtained, Sumter was induced to act as his own judgment indicated. Be this as it may, Sumter did not obey Greene's orders to join him at Camden, and was tacitly censured by Greene, Lee, and Marion.

General Greene soon rose above his misfortune. Lee and Marion were instructed to prevent if possible the junction of Rawdon and Watson. In order to cut off all supplies from Camden from the west, General Greene crossed the Wateree River and stationed himself in the neighborhood of Camden Ferry. It was now evident that Watson could not reach Camden in this direction. Lee and Marion were watching Watson, who was now in Orangeburg county, near the confluence of the Wateree and Congaree. It was doubtful where he would cross the river. Marion and Lee were endeavoring to overtake him and bring him to battle; but in spite of Marion and Lee, Watson on the 6th of May crossed the Congaree and on the next day crossed the Wateree and on the same day entered Camden.

General Greene learned in a short time after the arrival of Watson, that the junction between him and Rawdon was formed. He wisely concluded that Rawdon would begin immediately to advance upon the American army. This connection being fixed in his mind and not desiring to bring on a general engagement, General Greene retired to a ridge on Sawney Creek, near the dividing line between the counties of Kershaw and Fairfield. The forces of Greene and Rawdon each numbered about twelve hundred men. On the 8th, the day after the arrival of Colonel Watson, Rawdon crossed the Wateree at the point where the bridge now spans the river and immediately directed his course towards Greene's camp. General Greene now retired to Colonel's Creek, in Fairfield county, a short distance from the present site of Longtown.

Lord Rawdon becoming satisfied that he would not be able to dislodge General Greene and being startled by the intelligence that the American army was rapidly increasing in strength, returned to Camden and began at once to make preparation for evacuating the post. So alarmed was he for the safety for his various military posts, that he posted a messenger to Cruger, ordering that official to abandon Ninety-Six and retire to Augusta. At the same time, Maxwell who commanded the garrison at Fort Granby, a short distance below the present city of Columbia was ordered to retire to Orangeburg. All of the messengers sent by Rawdon were captured and the orders they bore never reached the persons for whom they were designed.

On the 10th of May, Lord Rawdon led his forces out of Camden. Before leaving the town, he burned the mills, jail and a number of private residences. All his supplies, except so much as he could conveniently take with him were burned. In his train followed five hundred Negroes, who had flocked to his camp from the surrounding country. The most noted royalists in the adjacent country left their farms and followed the British army. The scales they saw had begun to change. Heretofore the poor Whigs from all sections of the state had been dragged to Camden and tortured. Some were hanged like dogs, multitudes were starved to death or suffered to die of sheer neglect, and all were grossly insulted. During all this time, the Tories and loyalists in and around Camden had been feasting on the luscious dainties of the earth, and supinely reclining beneath the folds of the British flag. When Lord Rawdon marched his forces out of the town, a cold tremor ran through the bodies of every Tory and loyalist in the region. The day of rejoicing was done and phantoms of future misery frightened them.

In the meantime, the partisan leaders, Marion, Lee, Sumter, and Horry were not idle. General Sumter, possibly on receiving the orders of General Greene at Camden, but for some reason which as said before cannot now be satisfactorily accounted for, turned aside and laid siege to Fort Granby.

The British post was located on the right bank of the Congaree River, about two and one-half miles below the site now occupied by the city of Columbia. At an early day some one came to this point from Pine Tree, (afterwards Camden) and erected a store house for the purpose of trading with those boating produce down the river to the lower country. This attracted other settlers and the result was that a small village sprung up, which has long since ceased to exist. In the neighborhood were several individuals by the name of Friday. They were of German descent and managed their affairs with thrift. Unfortunately for themselves and for their country all of them, except two brothers, were loyalists. One of these Friday brothers lived at Fort Granby. He owned a mill and the ferry by which the river at that point was crossed belonged to him and bore his name. The only individual residing at that time within the present limit of the city of Columbia, was Colonel Thomas Taylor. He and General Sumter were warm friends and had been together since shortly after the fall of Charleston, on the 12th of May, 1780.

In February, 1781, Sumter made an attack upon the British stationed at Fort Granby, but with no decided results. Again he and Taylor began to besiege the place shortly before Rawdon evacuated Camden. When Rawdon learned that Sumter had laid siege to Fort Granby, he ordered the garrison at Orangeburg to retire. Sumter on learning this, left Colonel Taylor to continue the siege of Fort Granby and hastened to Orangeburg, that he might attack the garrison before it would leave.

On the 11th, the day after Rawdon evacuated Camden, Sumter appeared before the fortifications at Orangeburg. The garrison consisted of eighty-two men, twelve of whom were British regulars - the remainder Tory militia. After Sumter had fired two volleys into the garrison, the officer in command made an unconditional surrender of the fort, men and stores. The casualties, though not stated were it may be supposed very trifling. The British and Tories were completely demoralized. Sumter paroled the prisoners and set out to return to Fort Granby.

On the 12th, the day after the British post at Orangeburg fell into the hands of Sumter, Fort Motte was taken by Marion and Lee. Fort Motte was located on the right bank of the Congaree River a short distance west of the point where the South Carolina railroad crosses the stream. By the Congaree River and Buckhead Creek, a small tract of land is nearly surrounded by water and may be with propriety called a peninsula. On the peninsula once resided Jacob Motte, and here at the time of the Revolutionary war, resided his accomplished and patriotic widow. The dwelling of Mrs. Rebecca Motte occupied the center of the British fortification. Around the house a deep ditch was dug and on the river margin of the ditch a high parapet was erected. Mrs. Motte and her family were driven from the house and forced to shelter themselves in an old house a short distance north from the dwelling.

A glance at the map of this state will serve to convince any one that Fort Motte was of vital importance to the British army. It was the principal deport for all the supplies designed for both Camden and Ninety-Six. The garrison was commanded by Captain McPherson.

So soon as Marion and Lee discovered that Colonel Watson had frustrated their attempts to prevent him from joining Lord Rawdon, they directed their attention to Fort Motte. The siege was begun in earnest and carried on with unceasing vigor. The usual force stationed at Fort Motte was one hundred and fifty; but only a few hours before the approach of Marion and Lee, their force had been increased by the arrival of a large number of cavalry. Lieut. Col. Lee with his division of the American forces took post on the hill on which stood the house occupied by Mrs. Motte and family. General Marion took post on the eastern slope of the hill on which stood the fort. Near Marion's quarters a mound was raised and upon it was placed the six-pounder under the management of Captain Finley. The six-pounder was favorably placed to rake the northern face of the enemy's breastworks. Between the headquarters of Lee and the eminence occupied by the fort, was a vale. Such was the nature of the valley that it was safe for the Americans to approach within four hundred yards of the garrison. At this point Marion broke ground. The work was pressed forward without cessation. Negroes were brought in from the surrounding country and put to work. The soldiers were divided so that each relay was required to work four hours and rest four. Parallel after parallel was completed and on the tenth, Marion and Lee determined to summon McPherson to surrender. The demand was made but the gallant McPherson refused to comply.

McPherson had no artillery and his only hope was that he would in due time receive succor from Rawdon. On the afternoon of the same day, the American officers received the intelligence that Rawdon had evacuated Camden and during the night the rumor was confirmed by the arrival of a courier from General Greene. Time now became precious. The work was pressed forward with double vigor. The forces of Marion and Lee could not withstand those under Rawdon.

On the night of the 11th, the camp fires of Rawdon were seen gleaming from the Santee hills. These fires filled the minds of the men in the fort with joy, whilst they were anything but pleasant to Marion and Lee. These officers were convinced that they could batter down the enemy's work; but to effect this would require more time than they had at their disposal. It was correctly judged that burning the house of Mrs. Motte would force the garrison to surrender at once. The ditch cut by the Americans was now within bow-shot of the house. Lieutenant Colonel Lee suggested that the house be set on fire by hurling ignited arrows on the roof. Marion accepted the suggestion and determined to reduce the proposed plan to practice.

Individuals were charged with the duty of preparing the bows and arrows; but neither Marion nor Lee were willing to burn the house without first mentioning their design to Mrs. Motte. They naturally supposed that she would object to having her splendid new mansion reduced to ashes. Colonel Lee, who was at that time enjoying the hospitality of Mrs. Motte, was charged with the delicate duty of communicating the fact to her and also explaining to her that nothing but pressing necessity could have induced the American officers to resort to such a measure. So soon as Colonel Lee communicated the plans of himself and General Marion to Mrs. Motte, she not only assented but heartily approved of it, and proposed to furnish Lee with a fine bow and bundle of arrows which she had received from the East Indies. The self-sacrificing spirit of this patriotic woman greatly relieved the minds of both Marion and Lee.

The way being open now for burning the house and the material all prepared, it was determined to summon McPherson again to surrender. Dr. Irvine, surgeon of Lee's cavalry was sent with a flag to state the true condition of things, and that an immediate surrender of the fort would save the spilling of much blood. McPherson still refused to surrender.

At 12 o'clock, when the shingles on the house had been thoroughly dried by the rays of the sun, a bow and a number of arrows were placed in the hands of Nathan Savage, a private in Marion's brigade. Soon the shingles were seen to be on fire, and rapidly the flames began to spread over the roof. It was a moment of intense anxiety to the American forces and of fearful consternation to the British forces in the fort. McPherson ordered some of his men to knock off the shingles and put out the fire. This had no sooner commenced than Marion opened his battery upon those thus engaged and drove them from the upper part of the house. Captain McPherson now made a virtue of necessity and hung out a white flag. The Americans ceased firing and the flames were extinguished. At one o'clock the garrison surrendered. The prisoners were paroled and sent off to Lord Rawdon.

During the siege the British did not lose a single man. The brave Sergeant McDonald and Lieutenant Cruger of Marion's brigade were killed during the siege of Fort Motte.

After the garrison had surrendered and the prisoners were paroled, Mrs. Motte invited both the American and the British officers to partake of a sumptuous dinner, which she had prepared. All were treated alike. No one could discover any difference which this noble woman made between her conquering friends and vanquished foes. She was kind to her friends and generous to her enemies. By her kindness she banished from the mind of McPherson the gloom which succeeds discomfiture.

Installment XLIV

SURRENDER OF FORT GRANBY

The attentive student of history cannot but be struck with the precarious nature of every human state, condition or circumstance. "All is well that ends well," and present indications are deceptions. He must be stupid indeed, who does not discover in the terminus to which transpiring events are tending the hand of an all powerful providence.

From the fall of Charleston, in May 1780, to the latter part of April, 1781, South Carolina lay prostrated beneath the heel of the British. It is true there were small and insignificant partisan corps operating in various sections of the state. These corps were composed of as self-sacrificing patriots as ever lived and they were led by as brave officers as ever drew a sword; but such were the circumstances by which they were surrounded that they could effect little more than check the ravages of the enemy. The British thought and said the state was subdued. The great mass of people in several sections of the state had given up in hopeless despair. The wonder is not that so many despaired, but that any retained hope that the American cause would ultimately prevail. The moment, however, that General Greene entered the state, the condition of things seems to have assumed a new aspect. The report had been extensively circulated that Cornwallis had annihilated Greene's army. The people generally did not understand the movements of the American general, and as men usually suffer their hopes and fears to control their judgment, the people concluded that Cornwallis had driven Greene out of the state. The return of Greene corrected this false notion and infused hope into many sad hearts.

The battle of Hobkirk's Hill, the first fought by Greene after this return, was a failure, Rawdon gained a victory. He lost more than one-fourth of his army and the single announcement that General Greene had met the British at Camden, inspired the Whigs at every section of the state with a fresh spirit of resistance. In the course of a fortnight, Camden, Fort Watson, Orangeburg and Fort Motte were in possession of the Americans. This was not all. The British officers no longer confident of success were despondent and instead of believing that the state was conquered, were intensely anxious for the safety of the British troops stationed in the state.

Sumter, as we have already seen, had left Taylor at Fort Granby to prosecute the siege whilst he would hasten to Orangeburg. This post fell into the hands of the Americans on the 14th of May - four days after Sumter commenced its investment. Sumter immediately began his return to Fort Granby. Lieutenant Colonel Lee, however, set out for the same point so soon as Fort Motte surrendered. The distance from Orangeburg to Fort Granby is in a direct line about forty miles; from Fort Motte to Granby is about twenty-five miles.

On the afternoon of the 12th, Fort Motte surrendered and during the early part of the night of the 14th, Colonel Lee with the infantry attached to his legion and Captain Finley, with the six-pounder which General Greene had sent to Marion and Lee, appeared before Fort Granby. Lee began to lay siege to the place with his usual energy. Within a little more than a quarter of a mile of the fort, they commenced the work of erecting a battery. The morning of the 15th was cloudy. A dense fog had settled on the face of the country and before the enemy had discovered that the Americans had commenced any new plans for their overthrow, Lee had his six-pounder mounted and was ready to open fire upon the garrison.

For several reasons, Colonel Lee was anxious to bring the matter to a final issue as soon as possible. Lord Rawdon with his forces began to cross the Santee at Nelson's Ferry on the 13th. On the afternoon of the next day, all the British forces under Rawdon had been transported across the river. The first object the British general desired to accomplish was to relieve the garrison at Fort Motte. In order to effect this, he set out on the night of the 14th from Nelson's Ferry, on the road leading from Nelson's Ferry, on the Santee, to McCord's Ferry on the Congaree. Lee was well informed with regard to the movements of Rawdon, and was aware that Fort Granby must be taken within a few days or the siege abandoned.

The character of the commander of the garrison induced Lee to act with promptness or even with apparent rashness. Major Maxwell who was in command of Fort Granby was a loyalist - a refugee from Maryland. He had entered the royal army not from any love which he cherished toward the house of Hanover; neither did the desire to be ranked among the military heroes of his age urge him to enter the camp. In one word, he had none of the characteristics of a military chieftain. He was morbidly fond of money and notoriously cowardly. He had converted Fort Granby into a depot, in which he stored away the valuables which he wrested from the inhabitants of the surrounding country. Colonel Lee knew that Major Maxwell would readily surrender the garrison together with all the military accoutrements provided he would be permitted to reclaim the spoils of his plundering expeditions.

In the fort there were about three hundred and fifty men. By far the larger amount of this number were Tories and loyalists. The remainder were Hessian cavalry. Determined to give Maxwell no time to think, Colonel Lee ordered Captain Finley to open upon the fort with his six-pounder so soon as the fog cleared away. The moment that the six-pounder was fired, the American infantry advanced and opened fire upon the enemy's picket. So unexpected to the enemy was this movement on the part of the Americans that the pickets of the former were cut off from the fort. The garrison was thrown into the utmost confusion. The commander having no military experience and having no taste for anything but money-making, was completely nonplused. Lee soon discovering the confusion into which the garrison had been thrown by his unexpected attack, sent Captain Eggleston with a summon to Maxwell to surrender.

Although Maxwell felt no doubt that he and his garrison were wholly at the mercy of the American commander, still he did not forget to lay plans for the retaining of the plunder which he had stored away in the fort.

So soon as Eggleston set out under a truce flag to summon Maxwell, the Americans ceased firing. At this juncture of affairs, the British pickets that had been cut off from the fort by the American infantry attempted to make their way into the fort. This was promptly prevented by a rapid movement of the American cavalry. Colonel Lee sent an officer to Captain Eggleston for the purpose of informing him of what had been done by the enemy's pickets and requiring Eggleston to inform Maxwell that such a move would not be permitted with impunity. Maxwell immediately upon hearing the remonstrance of Colonel Lee, ordered the pickets back to the position occupied by them when the Americans ceased firing.

Major Maxwell readily agreed to surrender the garrison as prisoners of war, together with the military store, provided each individual in the fort should be permitted to retain his private property of every description, not subject to search. Eggleston discovered at once that the object which Maxwell had in view by this provision was to save the valuables which he had stored away in the fort for his own advantage. Eggleston knowing that Colonel Lee ever made it a point to restore to its rightful owner all private property which he might find in the hands of the enemy, was at a loss how to act, although he had been empowered to bring the negotiations to a final conclusion.

Capt. Eggleston, hesitating to terminate the negotiations for the surrender without first informing Colonel Lee of the proviso inserted by Maxwell, made by letter a statement of the conditions upon which Maxwell would surrender to Colonel Lee. Maxwell also requested of Lee that two covered wagons be granted him, individually, for the purpose of conveying his private baggage. Maxwell further requested that these wagons not be subject to search. Lee in reply instructed Captain Eggleston to grant the request of Maxwell, with the exception that the horses fit for service belonging to the Hessian cavalry be retained. Maxwell was willing to accede to this, but so soon as the Hessians learned that their horses were to be taken from them, their officers went in a body to Captain Eggleston and declared that they would not submit to this article of capitulation.

Captain Eggleston promptly informed Colonel Lee with regard to the declaration of the Hessians. It so happened at this moment that a courier arrived from Captain Armstrong, who had been sent out with a detachment of cavalry to watch the movements of Rawdon. From this courier it was learned that Rawdon was advancing in the direction of Fort Motte. In view of this fact, Lee thought it best not to demand too much or delay too long, lest he would be obliged to retire on account of the near approach of Rawdon. The Hessians in view of the circumstances were allowed to retain their horses. The articles of capitulation were now signed and at noon on the 15th of May, 1781, Captain Rudolph fixed the American flag on one of the bastions of Fort Granby. The garrison no doubt well satisfied that they were relieved from the dangers and privations of a long siege and permitted to retain their private property marched, under escort, for the camp of Rawdon.

Conspicuous among the departing throng was Major Maxwell's two covered wagons, known to be loaded with private property which he had taken from the citizens of the country. Two pieces of artillery, a large amount of salt, distilled liquors, and ammunition, constituted a part of the spoils which fell into the hands of the victors. Not a single man was killed on either side and only three rounds fired by the Americans. Everything gained by the patriots was a clear gain.

So soon as the garrison were paroled and sent off to Rawdon, Colonel Lee sent an officer of his command, with the glad tidings to Gen. Greene. Although Lee did not know it, General Greene had advance to within a short distance of Friday's Ferry on the Congaree. The army under General Greene continued its march until it came to what was then known as Ancrum's plantation, near Friday's Ferry, and camped. General Greene crossed the river and visited Fort Granby, now in possession of Lee's command. Joy and gladness pervaded every breast.

Sometime during the night of the 15th, a courier from Armstrong announced that Rawdon had retired in the direction of Monck's Corner, and early on the morning of the 16th, another courier arrived bringing the cheering intelligence that General Sumter had on the 14th captured the garrison at Orangeburg.

This within less than a month after General Greene led the American army into South Carolina, every British post in the interior of the state except Ninety-Six had been seized. When the announcement was made that Sumter had captured Orangeburg, a glad shout was raised by the soldiers in Greene's army.

Alas! All human joy is short lived. Sumter on his way from Orangeburg to Fort Granby, learned that Colonel Lee had anticipated him and forced the garrison at Fort Granby to surrender. This was sad news to

Sumter. He had confidently expected to have the honor of sending a summon to Major Maxwell. In anticipating, he was enjoying the pleasure of dictating terms of capitulation to that avaricious loyalist. The success of Lee blighted all his hopes. He was mortified that Lee had granted Maxwell so favorable terms of surrender. He was more than mortified and on the moment, anger so far got the better of his judgment, that he wrote General Greene an insulting letter and enclosed his commission as brigadier general.

Although for some reason which probably will never be fully known, Greene had been displeased with Sumter on account of the course which the latter had recently been pursuing; still Greene had great confidence in the patriotism, courage and military talents of Sumter and consequently returned the commission on the next day after its reception. The return of Sumter's commission was accompanied with a letter from General Greene to Sumter. Instead of censuring Sumter, Greene gave utterance to the high esteem in which he was held. Here the difficulty ended, at least publicly. The friends of Lee and Sumter still remembered it, and on future occasions censures were passed by the admirers of the disaffected chieftains, whose origin can be traced to the affair at Fort Granby. That no wrong impression be made, it should be distinctly understood that Sumter was not angry because Fort Granby was captured, but because General Lee and not Brigadier General Sumter had taken it.

The terms of surrender granted Maxwell by Lee do appear to be remarkably easy, but Lee did not at the time know that Rawdon, instead of pursuing the Americans, had gone to Monck's Corner that he might be out of danger. There is scarcely a shadow of a doubt but that Maxwell could have been forced in a few days to make an unconditional surrender. In his haste Sumter charged Lee with taking advantage of his absence and snatching from him a victory for which he had been struggling for near three months. There is no evidence, however, that Lee knew anything about the movements of Sumter.

Installment XLV

THE CAPTURE OF FORT BALFOUR

After the fall of Fort Granby, the American officers promptly continued the plan of operation which had been previously adopted. Marion was already before Georgetown, having gone to that point immediately on the surrender of Fort Motte. Lord Rawdon had returned to Eutaw, and was making arrangements to proceed to Monck's Corner and establish at that point a recruiting camp. Generals Marion and Sumter were ordered to remain in the lower section of the state to watch the movements of Lord Rawdon. Lieutenant Colonel Lee was directed to advance at once against Augusta; whilst Gen. Greene with the main body of the American army was to advance against Ninety-Six. Such is a brief outline of the position and plans of the Whigs after the capture of Fort Granby.

In order that we may have a correct notion of the operations of the Whigs, in future, it will be necessary that we direct our attention to several moves which transpired previous to the capture of Fort Granby. For some cause not now well understood, the militia from Georgia, South Carolina, and from the counties of Rowan and Mecklenburg, North Carolina, in the command of Colonel Andrew Pickens, were dissatisfied respecting the affair which took place at Wetzell's Mill in March previous to the battle of Guilford Court House. It so happened that Governor Rutledge was at that time in General Greene's camp. To avoid a difficulty and also to gratify these militia corps, they were detached under the command of Colonel Pickens and sent back into South Carolina with instructions to operate in the Ninety-Six district.

When General Greene determined, while in camp at Deep River, to pursue Cornwallis no longer, but to lead the American army under his command into South Carolina for the purpose of wresting, if possible, the state out of the grasp of the enemy, he detached Majors Samuel Hammond and James Jackson from the army and sent them into the regions of South Carolina and Georgia, bordering on the Savannah.

Colonel Pickens, rewarded by congress for his bravery and skill at the battle of Cowpens, with a brigadier general's commission was instructed to invest Ninety-Six, if he thought it advisable. At all events he was to use his utmost exertion to prevent reinforcements from being sent from Ninety-Six to Camden. Hammond and Jackson having disclosed Greene's plans to Pickens, were to cross the Savannah and encourage the Whigs in Georgia to collect their forces and render what assistance was in their power to General Greene. Clark, McCall, and Williams listened attentively to the plans of General Greene, and most heartily cooperated with Hammond and Jackson in proceeding to put the proposed plans into execution. McCall died a short time after of smallpox, and Clarke on account of the same disease was for some time prevented from taking the field.

Previous to this period active operations - on a small scale, it is admitted - had been in progress.

About the time that General Greene left Deep River, Colonel William Hardin, who since the fall of Charleston, had been operating in conjunction with General Marion, set out with a detachment of seventy-six men - the greater number of whom were inhabitants of Beaufort and Barnwell - for the region of country lying between Savannah and Augusta. The main object which Colonel Hardin had in view by this move, was to check the ravages of the Tories and encourage the Whig inhabitants of this section of the country. Colonel Baker and Major Cooper with a few Georgians, who had taken refuge in the camp of Marion, formed an efficient portion of Hardin's command.

Leaving the swamps of Black River, Hardin with his small but patriotic band set out for the point of their destination. Before them the Tories fled in dismay. Their march through the country was hailed with joy by the Whigs. By trustworthy friends they were correctly informed of the operations of the Tories and British.

The principal point to which their attention was first directed was Pocotaligo, at that time a village of three hundred inhabitants, situated in Beaufort county, on Pocotaligo River and about midway between the Salkehatchie and Tulifinny. Here on the morning of the 16th of April, 1716, the Yemassee Indians, encouraged by the Spaniards, began the first and in some respects the most dreadful massacre the early settlers of South Carolina experienced. Now in April 1781, Pocotaligo was garrisoned by a rabble band of Tories and British. A fort bearing the name of Balfour had been erected and at the time was commanded by Colonel Lechmere.

On their way to Fort Balfour, Col. Hardin and his little band crossed the Edisto at Giveham's Ferry. They were informed that a body of Tories, under Captain Barton, was collected at Red Hill. This Tory band was giving the adjacent country no small amount of trouble by its plundering expeditions. Colonel Hardin detached Major Cooper of Georgia with a few men and sent him out to break up the encampment at Red Hill, while Hardin and the main body continued to advance in the direction of Pocotaligo. Cooper came upon Barton and his Tory gang as an eagle descends in a swoop upon its unsuspecting prey. The result was that Cooper and his little detachment with the loss of a single man almost annihilated the Tories. Only a few were permitted to escape. The greater part were either killed or captured. While Colonel Hardin was advancing, he was attacked by a squad of British cavalry, commanded by Colonel Renwick. The Americans were passing over a causeway when Renwick and his party began the attack. Although disadvantageously situated,

Colonel Hardin so maneuvered that after a brisk skirmish for only a few moments, the British retired taking with them one man killed and eight wounded. The Americans suffered no loss in killed and only a few were wounded.

On reaching, on the 12th of April, the vicinity of Fort Balfour, Colonel Hardin sent forward Captain Tarleton Brown, a native of Barnwell county, with a detachment of thirteen men to reconnoiter and if possible entice the garrison from the fort. When Captain Brown arrived near the fort he discovered a number of men running in the direction of the fort from a house about four hundred yards distant. He saw at once that these individuals had been surprised. A dash was made upon them and the whole party captured. Among the party was Colonel Renwick, who had attacked Colonel Hardin while passing over the causeway. Also Colonels Lechmere and Kelsal. From these prisoners it was learned that they had left the fort in command of Major DeVeaux, the brother-in-law of Lechmere, and gone to this farm house, which was used for a hospital, for the purpose of visiting their sick and wounded.

Fort Balfour was garrisoned by one hundred and ten men, well armed. The garrison was well supplied with everything necessary to stand a long siege. Besides, it was furnished with cannon and an abundance of small arms and ammunition. Colonel Hardin had no notion that he was able with his eighty men, poorly provided with the equipments of war, to reduce the fort. All he contemplated being able to accomplish under the circumstances was to keep the garrison within the fort and thus prevent its depredating on the surrounding country. On coming up and finding that Captain Brown had captured the officers of the fort, he was encouraged to make the attempt. Without waiting a moment's time, he scattered his men through the woods so as to make as great a show as possible. DeVeaux was panic stricken. He had no means of forming even a conjecture as to the strength of the Americans.

Hardin made it a point to place the captured officers of the fort so that they were in full view of the garrison. This had the effect to throw Major DeVeaux into a very uncomfortable state of mind. Hardin had no cannon but he so maneuvered his troops that DeVeaux could not discover the fact. When Colonel Hardin got everything in proper condition, he sent in a flag to Major DeVeaux, demanding an immediate and unconditional surrender of the fort and garrison. Only a few moments were spent in discussing the terms of capitulation. It was agreed that the fort, with all its contents, should be surrendered without reserve into the hands of the Americans, and that the garrison should deliver themselves up as prisoners on parole. The work was soon consummated. The garrison soon marched out of the fort, tied their horses to the abattis and laid down their arms. Colonel Hardin with his men rode between the garrison and the fort, and took possession of the arms and horses; when to the dismay of the British, it was found that one hundred and ten men, strongly fortified and furnished with artillery had surrendered to a body of eighty cavalry, without cannon or any other means by which to lay siege to the place or in any way injure it.

In the fort the Whigs found a large number of their personal friends and neighbors. Some were confined, whilst others had been forced to enter the ranks of the enemy. These were released and they immediately entered Colonel Hardin's command. The effect upon the southwestern section of the state was similar to that experienced by the southeastern section on the capture of Fort Motte. The cloud of gloom which had so long been hanging over this section of the state began to move away and the cheering rays of hope began to beam upon the country.

Installment XLVI

SIEGE AND CAPTURE OF AUGUSTA

The siege and capture of Augusta properly belongs to the history of the battles of Georgia, but like Guilford Court House, it cannot be dissevered from the history of South Carolina. It is a link in that chain of events which led to American independence and is a part and parcel of the history of both South Carolina and Georgia.

Augusta is one of the oldest towns in the state of Georgia. It was founded in 1735, under the direction of that great and good man, General James Edward Oglethorpe. It was fortified at an early period and had attained a position of great importance on account of its Indian trade, long before the Whigs of America attempted to throw off the yoke of the mother country. In no section of the United States did the Whigs and Tories bear toward each other such bitter hatred, and in no section did they inflict upon each other such deeds of horrid cruelty. Augusta was alternately in the possession of the Americans and the British. Each retained it so long as they could and each gave it up only after a death struggle. Many and desperate were the conflicts which took place in and around Augusta. Men fought as men rarely fight and endured as men seldom endure. Passion and patriotism were arrayed against passion and loyalty, and bitter and unyielding hatred was confronted by a spirit of revenge.

After the surrender of Fort Galphin on the 21st of May, 1781, Lieutenant Colonel Lee with that promptness for which he was noted began to make preparations to carry out the instructions of General Greene. After only a few hours' rest, a detachment under Major Eggleston, Captains Armstrong and O'Neale was ordered to cross the Savannah below Augusta and join General Pickens and Colonel Clarke on the west of the town.

Eggleston was directed to summon Colonel Brown, the commander of Fort Cornwallis, to surrender so soon as he joined Pickens and Clarke. Everything was done with dispatch. Brown was waited upon by an officer bearing a white flag and summoned to surrender; but that officer thinking that the summons came from Colonel Clarke, whom he bitterly hated and dreadfully feared, refused to surrender and even treated the American flag with contempt.

On the same evening Lieutenant Colonel Lee with all his forces crossed the Savannah and joined Pickens, Clarke and Eggleston. The American officers were rendered frantic with rage on account of the contemptuous manner in which their flag had been treated. They decided to have no more friendly communications with the British colonel. A plan by which Augusta might be forced, was in a moment suggested by Lee and readily assented to by all the other officers. The plan was this: Fort Grierson was first to be reduced, and then out of all danger of being molested by this place, the whole force of the Americans was to be brought to bear upon Fort Cornwallis.

At Augusta the course of the Savannah River is nearly east. Fort Cornwallis was located near the center of the town. The plain on which the town is situated is intersected by a small rivulet which empties into the river a short distance north of the town. The margin of this rivulet was a swamp. On the northwestern border of this swamp, was erected Fort Grierson. It was perhaps a mile from Fort Cornwallis. In comparison with Cornwallis, Grierson was a weak place. The garrison consisted mainly of Tories and loyalists from the surrounding country.

It was planned by Lieutenant Colonel Lee that Fort Grierson should be assaulted on both sides and in front at the same time. The troops under Clarke and Pickens were to attack the northwest; Eaton's command together with some Georgia militia, under Major Jackson were to march round and to attack the northeast side, whilst Lieutenant Colonel Lee with the infantry attached to his legion took position south of Fort Grierson and between the two forts - Grierson and Cornwallis. The cavalry under Eggleston were stationed in a skirt of woods south of Lieutenant Colonel Lee. Such was the position occupied by the American forces, that the garrison of Fort Grierson could not escape to Fort Cornwallis nor could Colonel Brown, the commander of Fort Cornwallis, render aid to Grierson, the commander of the fort which bore his name.

When Colonel William Brown discovered the movements of the American forces, he advanced with two field pieces, with the determination, apparently to save Fort Grierson. Soon, however, he discovered that he was about to be attacked in the front by the infantry under Lee, and in the rear by the cavalry under Eggleston. In view of this fact he wisely concluded to leave Fort Grierson to its fate and immediately took shelter behind the wall of Fort Cornwallis.

The resistance made by the garrison in Fort Grierson was short and feeble. The Americans had a few men wounded and Major Eaton killed. A few of the garrison escaped to the river and by creeping along the side of the bank, succeeded in reaching Fort Cornwallis. With the exception of these the garrison officers and men fell into the hands of the Americans. Colonel Grierson was taken prisoner but was shot immediately afterward. This act was not approved of by the American officers. So incensed was General Pickens at the act, that he offered a large reward for the discovery of the man who killed Grierson; but no one was willing to give the desired information. It was made public afterwards that Colonel Grierson was shot by Captain Samuel (some authorities say James) Alexander. Both Grierson and Brown were bitterly hated.

In both British forts, there were a number of Whig prisoners. Some of these were old men and boys unfit for military duty. Whenever either garrison was attacked by American partisan corps, it was the practice of the commanding officer to place these old men and boys in front of their men, so as to protect them from the fire of the Americans. In this way it often happened that sons were firing at their fathers and fathers at their sons. The father of captain Alexander was in Fort Grierson at the time it was taken by the Whigs. The old man had been exposed to the fire of his own friends. For this Captain Alexander is said to have shot Colonel Grierson. In fact, it was with great difficulty that the American officers restrained the troops under their command from killing all the prisoners. Many were killed. Colonel Brown had perpetrated many cruel deeds and the Whigs, especially those of the surrounding country, were determined on being revenged. The army stores together with all the arms and ammunition contained in Fort Grierson, fell into the possession of the Whigs. The spoils captured in Grierson enabled the American officers to proceed at once to laying siege to Fort Cornwallis.

On the bank of the river between Fort Grierson and Fort Cornwallis there stood a large brick house. This house was the property of a loyalist who had joined Colonel Brown. Colonel Lee with his forces took post at this house; Pickens with his militia were placed in a skirt of woods southwest of the fort. Between the river and the fort a body of men consisting of several small commands under Clarke, Rudolph, Oldham, Handy, Hammond and others was posted. At this point Colonel Lee who was the ruling spirit among the besiegers, determined to begin the work. There were only two pieces of artillery in the American camp - one an old iron piece that Colonel Clarke had picked up and a small brass six-pounder commanded by Captain Finley. With these it was determined to battle down Fort Cornwallis and force Colonel Brown to surrender.

Every individual in the American camp was in good spirits and not only willing but anxious to do his part. All the tools captured at Forts Balfour, Galphin and Grierson, together with many collected from the farms in the neighborhood, were put into the hands of the soldiers and in a short time the two pieces of artillery were mounted upon batteries.

The garrison in Fort Cornwallis was not idle. Colonel Brown had collected from the adjacent country, previous to the commencement of the siege, not less than two hundred Negroes. With these and details made from the garrison he strengthened his works and prepared to die like a brave man. Bags of sand were heaped upon the ramparts and both his riflemen and artillery kept up a constant fire.

Such was the nature of the ground that the Americans could not bring their two pieces of cannon to bear with effect upon the enemy's works. To remedy this defeat it was proposed to erect a Maham tower. That its erection might be concealed from the enemy, the rear of an old house was chosen as its site.

In the meantime Colonel Brown seeing that he had a determined and skillful foe to meet, adopted the resolution to frustrate the approach of the Americans by making sallies upon the besiegers. Accordingly at midnight on the 28th of May, a strong force rushed out of the fort and made a desperate attack upon the American works near the river. The American guard was driven off and the trenches cleared. At this critical juncture of affairs, Captains Handy and Oldham with their companies came to the support of their comrades. A furious conflict ensued, but finally the British gave way and retired to their fort. On the next night another sally was made against the same quarter, but the American officers were prepared for it and the conflict was neither so long nor so serious.

In order that he might be ready to repel any assaulting force which might be sent from the fort, Colonel Lee assigned on the 29th the duty of watching the night movements of the enemy, exclusively to the infantry attached to his own legion. No sooner had the sallying party began its second attack upon the entrenchers, than Captain Rudolph rushed upon it with the bayonets and drove it with considerable loss back to Fort Cornwallis.

The Maham tower was completed on the last day of May. The logs were all internotched and the framework raised to a level with the enemy's parapets. The interior was filled with stones, brick, wood and earth so as to give it solidity. On this tower, the six-pounder commanded by Captain Finley and a small piece brought from Fort Grierson were mounted on the 2nd of June and declared to be in readiness to open on the enemy's works.

Whilst the Americans were erecting their tower, the garrison were making strenuous efforts for its defense. On an angle of Fort Cornwallis, opposite the Maham tower, a platform was constructed and upon this two of the heaviest guns were placed. Before the Maham tower was completed these two guns began to open upon those engaged in its construction.

About noon on the 2nd of June, Captain Finley had, with his six-pounders, dismounted the enemy's two guns and done considerable damage to the interior of the fort. At the same time the only other piece of ordnance which the Americans possessed was so situated on their right as to enfilade the fort. At every fire, Captain Martin, who commanded this gun, raked the platform. Unfortunately, Captain Martin and several of his men were killed by the enemy's riflemen, but still the old iron cannon was not suffered to cease firing. General Pickens rushed up a body of men to its support.

During the afternoon of the 2nd, the six-pounders place on the Maham tower and the old iron piece placed on the enemy's left kept up a continual firing. The works of the enemy were fast giving way before their well directed aim. Colonel Brown was now driven to the last extremity. He saw that he would not remain long within his stronghold, unless speedy deliverance was brought him. Cut off from all communication with the British posts in the neighboring country, his only hope was to effect by strategy what he was unable to accomplish by force.

Between the British post and the Maham tower erected by the Americans there were several old houses. The American officers had permitted these houses to remain, thinking that they would be of advantage in the final assault. Colonel Brown thought the burning of the houses nearest the tower would in all probability set the Maham tower on fire. Of this thing he was convinced so long as the Maham tower stood intact, the British garrison was not safe. In other words, he was convinced that he must either destroy the Maham tower or surrender at an early day. To effect the destruction of this tower, he sent at midnight on the 3rd, a Scotchman, under cloak of a deserter, into the American works.

This pretend deserter was a shrewd man and sergeant of an artillery company. He pretended that for some cruelty shown him by Colonel Brown, he had deserted. By his crafty conversation, he at once insinuated himself into the good graces of Lieutenant Colonel Lee. This wily Scotchman pointed out the mode by which the fort might be reduced. This plan was to throw hot balls into the portion of the fort where was stored away the powder. To aid in carrying out this, as Lee first thought, admirable plan the pretended deserter was sent in care of Colonel Lee's adjutant to Maham's tower as an assistant to Captain Finley. This was just what the deserter desired. The real object of his mission was to burn or otherwise destroy the tower. Fortunately Lee on farther reflection sent for the deserter and had him put under guard to await future developments.

About daybreak on the morning of the 5th, a party sallied out from the fort and set several of the houses between the fort and tower on fire. No effort was made by the Americans to extinguish the flames. Nine o'clock on the 5th of June was designated by the American officers to make an assault upon the fort. The house nearest the fort was selected by Lee and Pickens as a proper place in which to station a number of marksmen. A small detachment was sent to this house during the night of the 4th to ascertain how many riflemen could be employed with advantage in the house. This they did and reported to General Pickens. The number was selected and ordered to take possession of the house at daylight on the coming morning. All things were now in readiness for the final assault.

At three o'clock in the morning the Americans were aroused by a violent explosion. The earth shook and heavy timbers were heard falling all over the field. The house chosen for the riflemen was blown up. Colonel Brown for several days had been piercing the space between his fort and the house chosen by Lee and Pickens for their riflemen with a sap. From what he could see he concluded that the Americans would occupy the house with a body of men, and thinking that the detachment which had gone to examine it during the night were still in it, he blew it up, supposing that their destruction would cool the ardor of their companions. He was in too great a hurry. No one was in the house. Had he delayed for only a few hours, he would have inflicted a severe blow upon the besiegers.

To avoid the destruction which Lee and Pickens saw would follow an assault, these officers on the 31st of May summoned Colonel Brown to surrender. To this summons Colonel Brown replied: "It is my duty and inclination to defend this place to the last extremity." On the 3rd of June he was again summoned. To this second summons he replied in the identical language which he used in replying to the first. On the 4th, Lee and Pickens sent a request to Colonel Brown, desiring him to send the American prisoners in his possession out of the fort, to be regarded, they say, "yours or ours as the siege may terminate." With this humane request Colonel Brown refused to comply.

On the morning of the 5th, Brown sent an officer with a flag to the headquarters of the American officers. This officer bore from Colonel Brown a proposal to surrender. In his letter he stated by way, no doubt, of palliation of his former haughty air, that the American officers had proposed no definite conditions of surrender. He now proposed to surrender upon the same conditions which had been granted to the troops and garrison in Charleston.

To this communication Lee and Pickens replied that "Although we should be justified by the military law of both armies to demand unconditional submission, our sympathy for the unfortunate and gallant of our profession has induced us to grant the honorable terms which we herewith transmit." The terms of surrender transmitted were briefly that the fort, just as it was, be surrendered to the Americans and that the garrison, men and officers be paroled and sent under a sufficient guard to Savannah.

At 8 o'clock on the morning of the 5th of June, 1781, Colonel Brown surrendered and at 12 o'clock the garrison marched out of Fort Cornwallis, laid down their arms and Captain Rudolph with a detachment of the light infantry of Lee's legion, took possession.

In the siege of Augusta the American loss was sixteen killed and thirty-five wounded, seven of whom afterwards died. The British lost in killed fifty-two, in prisoners, including the wounded, three hundred and thirty-four.

We can not but admire the bravery of Colonel Brown, while we censure his cruelty. It was discovered by the Americans on entering the fort that the garrison had been sorely pressed. To protect themselves from the murderous fire of the besiegers they had dug vaults in which to conceal themselves. At the close of the war, or in July 1872, Brown left Savannah and went to St. Augustine. In 1809 he received from the British government a grant of six thousand acres of land in the island of St. Vincent. In connection with this grant, he became involved in a difficulty with the officers of the English government. The result was that the notorious Colonel Thomas Brown of Augusta, Georgia, was in 1812 tried for forgery in the city of London and found guilty.

BATTLE OF KING'S MOUNTAIN

COMPACT AND COMPREHENSIVE ACCOUNT OF MOST IMPORTANT EVENT OF THE WAR FOR AMERICAN INDEPENDENCE

REV. DR. LATHAN'S CENTENNIAL HISTORY

"Oh, heaven," they said, "our bleeding country save
Is there no hand on high to shield the brave:
What though destruction sweep these lovely plains!
Rise fellow men! Our country yet remains:
By that dread name we wave the sword on high,
And swear for her to live; for her die."

CAMPBELL'S PLEASURE OF HOPE

The year seventeen hundred and eighty was the darkest period of the Revolutionary struggle. From the mountains to the seaboard, a gloom rested upon the whole country. For five years the colonies, against fearful odds, had been battling for freedom. The country was overrun, its treasury was empty, and its soldiers were hungry and naked. From the hills of Massachusetts to the savannas of Georgia, the darkness that could be both seen and felt, enveloped the land. This was especially the case in South Carolina and Georgia. From the repulse of Sir Peter Parker, on the 28th of June, 1776, until the autumn of 1779, South Carolina, although in open and determined rebellion against the mother country, enjoyed comparative peace. Supplies of arms and munitions of war, together with food and clothing for the army, were landed by different nations of Europe at Charleston. From this point, these army stores, together with rice and other products of the fields of South Carolina, were transported, by wagon trains, as far north as New Jersey. During this period, South Carolina grew and flourished, notwithstanding the existence of war.

In the autumn of 1778, the scene began to change. Col. Campbell was sent from New York, by Sir Henry Clinton, to reduce Savannah, the capital of Georgia. On the 29th of December, Gen. Howe was forced to capitulate. Georgia fell into the hands of the enemy, and South Carolina now became a border state, exposed to the active military operations of the enemy. A bloody struggle was made, near a year afterward, for the recovery of Savannah, but it proved unsuccessful. It soon became evident that the British were determined to capture Charleston. Prevost, in May, 1779, had attempted to take the city by siege, but his plans were frustrated by the adroitness of Gov. Rutledge and the military prowess of General Moultrie.

On the 26th of December, 1779, Sir Henry Clinton, with the larger part of his army, sailed from New York for the south. In January of the following year, he landed on the coast of Georgia. He had but one object in view, and that was to crush the rebellion in all the southern colonies. His purpose was to begin at the southern extremity and go northward, leaving the country in his rear in complete and absolute, if not willing, submission to the British government. The first thing to be done to effect his purpose was the reduction of Charleston. On the 10th of February, he set out from Savannah to accomplish the cherished purpose of his heart. He was successful. Whether all was done that could have been done to save the city, or not, we shall not here inquire. Perhaps it would have been wise, under the circumstances, not to have attempted its defense. The attempt, however, was made. Sir Henry Clinton commenced and carried on the siege with as much respect to the rules of military science, as if he had been conducting the siege of an old walled town. Reduced almost to starvation, and poorly provided for every way to stand a siege, the defenders of the city, after a close siege of nearly eight weeks, capitulated on the 12th of May, 1780. The terms of the surrender were hard, and the conduct of the British commander afterward was calculated to cast a gloom over the patriots. The civil government of Britain was established in the city, and plans were laid for establishing it over the whole state. Everything was done that could be done to encourage the Tories and loyalists and dishearten the patriots.

Early in June, Clinton and the fleet sailed for New York, leaving Lord Cornwallis to complete the establishing of civil government in the state. He commenced his march northward. Parties were sent out in all directions to disperse the patriots and gather up the Tories and loyalists with which to swell his ranks. This was not enough. He determined to force those who, from the results of the war, were resting quietly at home, to take up arms against their friends and against the cause which they loved. Lord Cornwallis soon found that the country still remained, and there were many who had sworn for it to live and for it to die. In South Carolina, there was not then a regularly organized American army. There were small parties of men, in almost every section of the state, who disputed every inch of ground with Cornwallis. Still he pushed on. Tories and loyalists flocked to his standard, and many who, heretofore, had been regarded as good Whigs, sought British protection. The country was full of Tories and British. Property was destroyed, old men and children were abused and cursed, and women insulted. Many, in despondency, gave up the cause as hopeless. Calamity after calamity fell upon the afflicted country. On the 16th of August, General Gates, the hero of Saratoga, was defeated and his army routed near Camden. Two days after, the brave Sumter was surprised at Fishing Creek by Tarleton and his command scattered.

Such was the general condition of things in South Carolina and Georgia. Many brave men had hidden themselves beyond the mountains that, like Alfred of old, they might emerge from these mountain vastnesses and rout the invading foe. These voluntary exiles received a welcome from the patriots of Watauga and Nollichucky. There they met Isaac Shelby and John Sevier. Amongst those refugees was Colonel Clarke of Georgia, with about one hundred of his overpowered, but not subdued, men. These refugees told the tales of suffering which they had seen in the states of Georgia and South Carolina. Their stories aroused the patriotism and stirred the spirits of the hardy pioneers of the forest.

After the defeat of Gates at Camden, Cornwallis, as had been done by his predecessor, Clinton, proceeded at once to establish civil government in the upper section of the state. Tarleton and Ferguson were ordered to scour the state. The object was to beat up the Tories and loyalists and disperse the Whigs. Ferguson, with about 1,000 loyalists and one hundred and ten regulars, had been in the Ninety-Six district for some time, and portions of his command had been, on several occasions, badly cut up by the Whigs. Patrick Ferguson was a major in the British army, and brigadier general of the Royal Militia of South Carolina. The second officer in his command was Capt. DePeyster, a loyalist. The Whig colonels, McDowell, Sevier, Shelby, Clarke and Williams, were known to frequent this section of the state. The fact that small detachments of Tories had been attacked and routed by the bold partisans, greatly incensed the British officer. Meetings of the Tories and loyalists were held throughout the Ninety-Six district. Those who claimed to be Tories or loyalists, were threatened with severe punishment if they did not take up arms and assist his majesty's troops in putting down the rebellion. Ferguson now found that the rebellion which Clinton and his successor, Cornwallis, thought was crushed out, was stalking over the land like a giant. Whigs, Tories and loyalists, found that each party was in earnest, and a desperate effort must be made, or all would be lost.

On the 18th of August - the day on which Sumter was surprised by Tarleton at Fishing Creek - Colonel McDowell was encamped at Smith's Ford on Broad River. He had learned that a party of Tories, near five hundred in number, were encamped at Musgrove's Mill, on the south side of the Enoree River. Colonels Williams, Shelby and Clarke, were detached for the purpose of surprising them. It was a dangerous undertaking, for Ferguson was encamped, with his whole force, midway between McDowell and the Tories. At sun set, the party moved, and by taking a right hand road, passed Ferguson's camp in safety. The Tories were commanded by Col. Innis and Major Frazer. Shelby, Williams, and Clarke arrived at the Tory camp just at day light. The attack was made, and although the Tories had been reinforced by six hundred regulars under Innis, a complete victory was gained. Flushed with victory, the conquerors determined to make an attack upon Ninety-Six. Just at this moment a courier arrived, bringing the sad news that General Gates had been defeated on the 16th at Camden. They were urged by McDowell to make no delay, lest they should be captured by Ferguson. They had more than two hundred prisoners. The men were tired, and so were their horses. The prisoners were divided out amongst the men, giving every three men two prisoners. After they were completely out of the reach of Ferguson, Shelby went home, leaving Clarke and Williams in charge of the prisoners. Col. Clarke having accompanied Col. Williams for a short distance after the departure of Shelby, took his command and returned home, leaving Col. Williams in charge of the prisoners, by whom they were taken to Hillsborough, North Carolina. Governor Rutledge of South Carolina, who, at this time, was in Hillsborough, seeing Williams in charge of so many prisoners and supposing that he had been the principal actor in the affair, immediately gave him a brigadier general's commission as a reward for his supposed brave and heroic exploit.

McDowell, so soon as he heard that Gates was defeated, broke up his camp at Smith's Ford and marched for the mountains. His command was scattered. Some of his men went home, whilst others accompanied their commander beyond the mountains. Ferguson was left in full possession of the field. The Whigs were plundered of their property and driven from their homes. Many of them were forced to hide out in unfrequented spots, whilst not a few were caught and cruelly murdered. The brave and enterprising British officer pushed his way as far as Gilbert Town, near the present site of Rutherford, North Carolina. South Carolina was now under the paw of the British lion. Some crouched and begged for quarter; but there were a few noble spirits - enough to save the country - who had sworn for their country to live, and for her to die. Ferguson was not ignorant of this fact. He knew the history of those men who were beyond the mountains. He knew that their ancestors, for more than two hundred years, had been fighting for freedom, and he saw that the wilds of America had strengthened the love of liberty in their children. He knew that they were Scotch-Irish and Huguenots by descent. He knew that they could be crushed into the earth, that they could be torn limb from limb, that they could be buried beneath the earth, but he feared their very dust.

He had his spies in the mountain country, and from them he had learned what was going on in the valleys of Nollichucky and Watauga. These spies often brought him the startling news that their fellows were caught and hanged, while others were tarred and suffered to return as a taunt to their champion leader. Ferguson raged. He cursed the rebels for their daring, and he cursed the Tories and loyalists for their want of courage.

While Colonel Ferguson lay at Gilbert Town, he paroled Samuel Phillips, a patriot, whom he held as a prisoner, and sent him with a threatening message to the back mountain men. The purport of this message was, that if the patriots of Watauga and Nollichucky did not lay down their arms and submit to the King of England, he would come over the mountain and hang the last one of them. This was not a mere boast. He contemplated doing what he said. Ferguson was no idle boaster. No sooner had Samuel Phillips delivered his message, than the horrors of past generations loomed up before the eyes of the patriots of Watauga and Nollichucky. The blood of John Sevier and Isaac Shelby was stirred. Sevier was eloquent under the impulse of a holy resentment, and the brow of Shelby was knit with indignation, and his whole countenance indicated stern defiance. These noble men at once concluded that they would thwart Ferguson in his bloody purpose, and if there was any hanging to be done, they would do it.

The plan for raising a sufficient number of men to accomplish their purpose was soon devised. To Sevier was assigned the duty of communicating with McDowell and the other officers who were then in voluntary exile beyond the mountains. Shelby assumed, as his part of the work, the writing of a letter to Col. William Campbell of Washington county, Virginia. The letter was written. The threat of Ferguson was stated, and the plan for his destruction revealed. In his letter Campbell was earnestly requested to co-operate. This letter was placed in the hands of Moses Shelby, a brother of Isaac, and duly delivered. Colonel Campbell declined to render his assistance, stating that his intentions were to assist in preventing Cornwallis from reaching Virginia. This message was returned by Moses Shelby. Colonel Shelby immediately wrote another letter to Col. Campbell, in which he urged him, more strongly, to lend his assistance. Although Campbell was as firm and unyielding as a mountain, still he was not blind to reason or deaf to the call of duty. He sent Shelby word that he would come and bring his whole command. This was more than was expected. The place of general rendezvous was Sycamore Shoals on the Watauga; the time, the twenty-fifth of September.

At the appointed time, the entire inhabitants of the back mountain region assembled at Sycamore Shoals, and Campbell, with his Virginians, was there. Everybody was in earnest. There were no gay uniforms; no costly plumes; no long trains of baggage wagons; no ambulances; no surgeon; no chaplain. Officers and men were clad in suits made by their wives, mothers, and sisters, and each man intended for the expedition was armed with a faithful Deckhard rifle. (1)

All assembled; but all dare not leave the settlement. The Cherokee Indians were on the borders, watching for an opportunity to descend with the torch and tomahawk upon the neighborhood. On the morning of the 26th of September, preparations were made for the advance. To victory or to death, was the feeling of every breast. They were rough men externally, but they had brave and tender hearts. Charles McDowell moved amongst the multitude with all the grace and ease of nobility. John Sevier was full of impulse and an energy which never tired. Isaac Shelby had little to say. His knit brow meant speedy action.

William Campbell showed, by his stern dignity, that he was born to be free. The officers proposed, before they set out, that the company be called together and the divine blessing be asked. A prayer, solemn and appropriate, being offered up, the party designed for the expedition mounted their horses, and the rest returned to their homes. With anxious hearts did these wait until the result was heard.

The troops left Sycamore Shoal on the twenty-sixth. They were all mounted and unencumbered by baggage of any kind whatever. They expected to support themselves, on the way, by their rifles, or by forcing the Tories to feed them and their horses. The force consisted of one thousand and forty men, as follows: From Burke and Rutherford counties, North Carolina, Colonel McDowell, 160 men. From Washington county, North Carolina, (now Tennessee) Col. Jon Sevier, 240 men. From Sullivan county, North Carolina, (now Tennessee) Col. Isaac Shelby, 240 men. From Washington county, Virginia, Col. William Campbell, 400 men.

The Sycamore Shoal is near the head of the Watauga. From this point, they pursued nearly an eastern direction, across the Yellow Mountain; afterward their course was nearly south. The first night they spent at Matthew Tolbot's mill. The second day, two of their men deserted and went ahead to the enemy. On the 30th of September they reached the foot of the mountain on the east side. Here they were joined by three hundred and fifty men from Wilkes and Surry counties, under the command of Colonel Benjamin Cleveland and Major Joseph Winston. Cleveland and Winston were keeping themselves concealed that they might join in with any party going against the enemy. The first of October - the second day after the junction with Cleveland - was so wet that it was thought advisable not to move. Ferguson was thought to be at Gilbert Town, and as the guns in those days were all flint and steel locks, it was indiscreet to approach an enemy with wet guns.

Up to this time there was no commanding officer. Shelby perceived that there was a great defect in their organization and during the rain called a council of the officers. They were now in Colonel Charles McDowell's region, and advancing against an enemy with which he had lately been contending. He was, moreover, the senior officer, and it was natural that he would be expected to take the command of the whole. No one doubted Charles McDowell's patriotism or bravery; but it was thought that he was not the man to command a partisan corps on an enterprise like that in which they were at that time engaged. Shelby proposed William Campbell as commander-in-chief for the present, and that a messenger be sent to head-quarters, wherever that might be, for a commanding officer, who should take charge of the whole corps. This proposition was readily assented to by all and Col. Chas. McDowell volunteered to go to headquarters after a general officer, and his brother, Joseph McDowell, took command of his men until he would return.

Here, for a time, let us leave these patriotic mountain men, until we can bring up the other forces who were prominent actors in the battle of King's Mountain. After Sumter's defeat at Fishing Creek, on the 18th of August, he and Colonel Edward Lacy, with a small portion of Sumter's command, passed over into Mecklenburg, North Carolina. They camped on Clem's Branch. Lacy was sent by Sumter into York and Chester counties, to gather up the Irish of that region, who were known to be true Whigs, and also to collect all that he could of Sumter's army that was scattered at Fishing Creek.

After Lacy's return to Sumter's encampment on Clem's Branch, Colonel James Williams, who, as we have seen, was made a brigadier general by Governor Rutledge shortly after the battle of Musgrove's Mill, arrived in camp, and having shown his commission, claimed the authority to take command of all the South Carolina troops in that section. On the 8th of September, Williams had been ordered, or rather "requested", by Abner Nash, governor of North Carolina, "to go into Caswell county and such other counties as he might think proper, and raise a body of volunteer horsemen, not to exceed one hundred." With these and a few other troops, Williams came to Sumter's camp on Clem's Branch. The South Carolina soldiers of Sumter's command positively refused to submit to Williams as a general. They preferred Sumter. The main objection that the soldiers had against Williams was that, having at one time been the commissary of Sumter's command, he had acted in some way or other so as to gain the ill will and even the hatred of many of the men. What the facts in the case were, it is impossible, at this late date, to learn with sufficient accuracy to warrant us in saying who was to blame, Williams or the men. No doubt, both were, to some extent, in the fault. Be this as it may, a difficulty sprung up between Sumter and Williams, and but for the presence of the enemy, it might have ended in something serious.

Whilst the difficulty was pending, it was learned that Rawdon and Tarleton, with a large force, were making preparations for attacking them. It was concluded by both parties, that they would cross the Catawba River at Bigger's Ferry (now Wright's).

Having crossed the river, a council of officers was called to settle the difficulty. Col. William Hill, who was wounded at the battle of Hanging Rock, was made chairman of the council. Whilst the council was discussing the matter, Rawdon and Tarleton appeared on the opposite bank of the river, and commenced firing at them across the river. It was evident that the enemy would not allow them time to look into the matter, and their existence depended upon perfect harmony among themselves. It was agreed to refer the whole matter, with all the facts in the case, to Governor Rutledge, then at Hillsborough, North Carolina. In the meantime, however, Sumter was to retire from the army until the decision of Rutledge was heard. Williams would remain in command of his North Carolina troops, and Colonels Hill and Lacy would take command of the South Carolina troops.

Colonels Winn, Middleton, Thomas, and Hampton were sent as commissioners to Governor Rutledge; and Lacy and Hill, in the hope of forming a junction with General William Davidson, led the army up the Catawba, and crossed at Tuckaseege Ford. Governor Nash of North Carolina, had instructed Colonel Williams (then general) to proceed in any direction and operate against the enemy. His instructions were very general, leaving the whole matter to the discretion of Williams himself. While the army, consisting of about four hundred and fifty men, then under the command of Hill, Lacy and Williams, were on the east side of the Catawba River, in the neighborhood of Tuckaseege Ford, Williams' scouts brought the information that a body of back-mountain men were already on the east side of the mountain, on their way to fight Ferguson. They immediately crossed the Catawba at Beattie's Ford, with the intention of going in pursuit of Ferguson. Here they were joined by Majors Graham and Hambright, with about seventy-five men, and not long afterwards by Colonels Hammond and Roebuck, and Majors Chronicle and Hawthorne, with about sixty men.

Williams had his scouts out watching Ferguson. He was the more prompt in doing this, from the fact that his home was on Little River, in what is now Laurens county. This territory was embraced in Ferguson's field of operations. A consultation was held by Williams, Hill, Lacy, Roebuck, Graham, Hammond, Hambright, Brannon, Hawthorne and Chronicle, as to what should be done. It was at once determined that a messenger should be sent to communicate with the back-mountain men, to inform them with regard to Ferguson's movements and his place of encampment, and to make arrangements for the co-operation of the two forces. Colonel Edward

Lacy, whose home was a few miles northwest of the present town of Chester, and who owned a large amount of the lands on which the town of Chester is built, was chosen as the messenger. It was a good choice. Lacy was recklessly brave, and although a rough man, still, a man of good address. He was a sterling Whig. It turned out that the two camps were, at that time, sixty miles apart; but Lacy never stopped a moment until, late at night, he reached the camp of Campbell. This was on the night of the 4th of October. Lacy was seized by the patrolling party and, without ceremony, blindfolded. He asked to be taken, without delay, to the commander's quarters. He was at first regarded as a spy, and had he not been a true Whig, and shown it by every word and action, he would have paid the penalty in a few minutes.

That day, Campbell and his mountain men had reached Gilbert Town, and finding Ferguson had decamped, and learning that he was gone to Ninety-Six, which had lately been repaired and reinforced, a council of war had been held but a short time before Lacy arrived, and it was concluded to abandon the chase. Lacy then informed them that Ferguson was in the neighborhood of Cherokee Ford - that he was not aiming to reach Ninety-Six; but his point of destination was Charlotte, North Carolina. They were urged to annul the previous resolution of the night, and meet the troops under Williams, Hill and other leaders, at a place called the Cowpens, on the 6th. This was done, and after Lacy had fed his horse, eaten a supper of what the partisan camp could afford, and enjoyed a few hours' sleep on the ground, he was up and away to join his command, which was now on its way to the Cowpens.

Let us leave the two armies and trace the movements of Colonel Ferguson. On the 4th of October - the day that Campbell and his men arrived at Gilbert Town - Ferguson had broken up his camp. The two deserters from Campbell's command had informed him of what was going on. He knew the men he had to deal with. He had met some of them before. Wisely, he concluded that his safety depended on getting out of their way. It would not be true to say that Colonel Ferguson was frightened, for no braver man ever lived or fought or died on a battlefield; but he most assuredly felt that he was in a critical situation. Cornwallis had already perceived the danger with which Ferguson was surrounded, and had ordered him to join him at Charlotte. Ferguson now saw that it would require all his skill to reach that point. On breaking up his camp at Gilbert Town, he sent two Tories - Abe Collins and Peter Quinn - to Cornwallis at Charlotte, to inform that officer of his

critical situation and to request aid. The messengers were hindered on the way by the presence of the Whigs in the neighborhood, and did not reach Charlotte until the 7th; consequently, the aid was not received. Ferguson, on leaving Gilbert Town, made the impression that he was going to Ninety-Six, and when Campbell and his party arrived at Gilbert Town, they were told that Ferguson was distant fifty or sixty miles. This was a feint. On the fourth of October, Ferguson camped at the Cowpens, about twenty miles from Gilbert Town. On the 5th, he crossed Broad River at Tate's Ferry, near where the Air Line railroad now crosses Broad River, and spent the night about a mile above the ferry. On the 6th, he pushed on up the ridge road between King's Creek and Buffalo Creek, until he came to the fork near Whitaker Station, on the Air Line railroad. There he took the right prong, leading across King's Creek, through a pass in the mountain, and on in the direction of Yorkville. Here, a short distance after crossing King's Creek, on the right of the road, about two hundred and fifty yards from the pass in the mountain, on an eminence which he claimed, in honor of his majesty, to have called King's Mountain (2), and which still retains the name, he encamped, determined to remain until his reinforcements from Cornwallis would arrive.

From Gilbert Town to King's Mountain, he evidently was retreating. He felt that he had a terrible foe to deal with. He begged, he entreated the Tories and loyalists to turn out and render him assistance. Finding that gentle measures accomplished nothing he threatened to hang them if they did not shoulder their muskets and march against the rebels. His threats were as unavailing as his entreaties. On arriving at King's Mountain, he granted some of the royalists and Tories permission to go into the surrounding country for the purpose of beating up recruits.

The inhabitants of the region surrounding King's Mountain were, with a few exceptions, Tories. These recruiting officers of Ferguson went to plundering their Whig neighbors. Instead of hunting up recruits for the King's army, they went to robbing the gardens and killing the hogs of the Whigs in the community. Here, strongly posted on King's Mountain, let us, for a short time, leave Colonel Ferguson.

Before sunrise on the morning of the 6th of October, the forces under Colonel Campbell were ordered to march. The immediate point of destination was the Cowpens. The whole of the night previous had been spent in selecting from his entire force, which now numbered about three thousand, the best men, the best horses and the best guns. The number selected was nine hundred and ten. These were ordered to advance rapidly in pursuit of the foe, whilst the remainder were to follow leisurely. Before sun-down, they reached the Cowpens. There they found Col. Hambright and Major Chronicle, with sixty North Carolinians from Tryon county, and Col. James Williams with near two thousand South Carolinians. From these, nine hundred and thirty-three were selected to join the nine hundred and ten under Campbell, in pursuit of Col. Ferguson. (3) Many of the officers were without commands, occupying simply the position of men in ranks. It was raining and dark, but all were enthusiastic. They had set out to find Ferguson, and find him they would. An hour was given the troops to rest, during which time two beeves were killed; but the time was so short that some of the men did not get a mouthful prepared. There were several bands of Tories in the neighborhood, whom they could have easily captured, but they were in search of Ferguson, and they let the Tories alone, although it was known that these Tories were to join Ferguson the next day. By eight o'clock every man was in the saddle and on the trail of Ferguson. It rained all night, and was dark. The guide got lost for a time. The men, in order to keep their guns dry, wrapped them up with their overcoats and blankets when they had them, and with their hunting shirts when these were wanting. On the morning of the 4th, just before sun-rise, they reached Broad River, about a mile and a half below Cherokee Ford, expecting to find Ferguson on the east bank. They crossed the river and marched up its bank, and soon came to Ferguson's camp of the night of the 5th. Here a halt was made, and those who had anything to eat, ate it, and those who had nothing did without. The delay was only for a moment. Although hungry, wet and tired, they pushed on with as much zeal as if the search had just commenced. Ferguson's trail was fresh, and they knew that they would soon see who would do the hanging! For a distance of twelve miles, they saw no one but their own party, and learned nothing of Ferguson's whereabouts. When they had gone about twelve miles, after crossing Broad River, the advance party met some persons coming from Ferguson's camp. At the same time, a boy about fourteen years old, by the name of John Fonderin, was found in an old field. The boy said his brother was in Ferguson's camp. The story of the men and boy agreed, and from them it was learned that Ferguson's camp was only three miles distant. The location was accurately describe by these men and young Fonderin, and the intentions of Ferguson learned. A dispatch which he had sent to Cornwallis for aid, was afterward intercepted. From this his force was learned, and also what he thought about being able to defend himself. In that dispatch he boastingly, or rather profanely, we should say, declared that such was the nature of the place he had chosen for a camp, "that all the rebels out of hell could not drive him from it." This dispatch, with the exception of the statement of the number of Ferguson's force, was read aloud to the men. The officers held a consultation on horseback, and concluded upon the mode of attack.

It was agreed that since Campbell had come the greatest distance, and had brought the largest number of men, that he should be the commander in chief. It was now past 12 o'clock. The rain had ceased, the clouds had passed away, and the sun was shining brightly. The pursuers of Ferguson had followed his trail from 8 o'clock on the previous night, and now they were within four miles of his camp. The order was given "to tie up overcoats and blankets, throw priming out of pans, pick touch holes, prime anew, examine bullets, and see that everything is in readiness for battle." They were now within sight of the object for which some of them had been in search for nearly two weeks. They were fully aware of the kind of foe they had to encounter - a brave man and a cool officer. They had to face British regulars, who would rush upon them with bayonet; and Tories who knew it was victory or death. On they went, determined to be free or die. They ascended an eminence on the western side of the mountain, and Ferguson's camp was in full view. They dismounted and tied their horses and prepared for the conflict. The mode of attack determined upon was to surround the mountain and pour in a deadly fire upon the enemy from all sides at the same time.

King's Mountain, upon which Colonel Ferguson was encamped, is a spur of the Blue Ridge. It is a narrow, oval shaped knoll, having the direction of the Blue Ridge, and terminates abruptly at its northern extremity. It is covered with a kind of slate stone. The ridge, which is about one hundred and twenty feet above the ravines by which it is surrounded, and about a mile long, is not more than thirty yards wide, and the sides, especially on the north, are precipitous. It is situated in York county, South Carolina, about a mile and a half from the North Carolina line. Many of the men in Colonel Williams' command were Whigs from the surrounding country. They had left their hiding places when, in the language of an old Revolutionary war song, "Old Williams came from Hillsborough, they flocked to him amain." These men understood the nature of the ground accurately. They had hunted deer on the same place frequently. In view of this fact, the guides for the other troops were chosen from Williams' men.

When the exact location of Ferguson's camp was learned, the army of pursuers marched in four columns. Col. Campbell's regiment, with part of Cleveland's regiment, commanded by Major Winston formed the right center. Col. Shelby's regiment, the left center. Col. Sevier's regiment composed the right wing; and the troops under Col. Williams and the remainder of Col. Cleveland's regiment, commanded by himself, formed the left wing.

On arriving in full view of the enemy, and having tied their horses and leaving a small guard to watch them, the troops commanded by Shelby, Sevier, McDowell, Campbell and Winston, were ordered to file to the right and pass round the enemy's camp on the mountain. Those under Cleveland, Chronicle, Hambright and Williams, were to file to the left and pass round. Both parties were to continue their march, without firing, until they met. Then the enemy's camp would be completely surrounded. The order was then to face toward the enemy, raise the Indian war whoop, and rush forward upon the foe.

It was near 3 o'clock on the afternoon of the 7th of October, 1780. The destiny of American liberty was in the hands of a few undisciplined militia. It never was in better hands than when it was entrusted to those brave men who fought and bled and died and won the victory over Colonel Ferguson on King's Mountain. The order is given to march. On they go, with the steadiness of veterans. Every order is executed with as much promptness as if they had been trained regulars.

The British commenced to fire upon Shelby's men as the right wing passed round the mountain. McDowell returned the fire, and the action became general. The keen crack of the deadly Deckhard rifle, and the Indian war whoop, heard all round the enemy's camp, announced that every man was in his place. Ferguson ordered his regulars to charge upon the right wing of the Whigs. This drove McDowell, Shelby and Campbell back; but at this very moment Chronicle, Hambright, Cleveland, and Williams had ascended the opposite extremity of the mountain and driven the British Tories behind their wagons. Ferguson was here himself. His men were falling on all sides. He immediately sent for DePeyster, who had led the charge against McDowell, Shelby, and Campbell. As DePeyster passed back along the ridge, the South Carolinians, under Williams, poured in a deadly fire upon him. His ranks were soon thinned and the regulars thrown into confusion. They, however, immediately rallied and made a dreadful push against Chronicle and Cleveland, driving them down the mountain. Here Chronicle was killed. The charge

of the British upon the left of the Whigs was mistaken by the right under Shelby, McDowell and Campbell, for a retreat, and the shout was raised, "Huzzah, boys, they are retreating. Come on." On, on the left wing of the Whigs, in solid phalanx, rushed upon the enemy. Ferguson was forced to meet the right wing. The left wing, as the right wing before had done, mistook the charge of the British for a retreat, faced about and rushed upon, as they thought, the retreating foe. Thus each charge of the enemy was mistaken by the Whigs on the opposite side for a retreat, Ferguson galloped back and forth along his lines, encouraging his men with entreaties and with curses. In spite of all his skill and the desperate courage of his men, his ground was taken from him and he was forced to occupy a small portion of the ridge near the northern extremity. He ordered his cavalry to mount; but this proved unavailing. The men were shot down as soon as they mounted. He prepared for a last and desperate charge. The Tories were ordered to sharpen the handles of their butcher knives and fasten them in the muzzles of their shotguns and, with the British regulars, charge upon the rebels. This also was of no avail. The Whigs were all around them, and confusion was in the British camp. DePeyster hoisted a white flag. Ferguson pulled it down. DePeyster raised it at the other extremity of the British camp. Ferguson saw it and darted at a full gallop and, with his sword, cut it down, swearing that he would never surrender to militia. He had been wounded in the hand, but in this wounded hand he bore a silver whistle, whose shrill sound inspired courage in the already vanquished. A ball from some unknown rifle threw the hero from his charger, and DePeyster again hoisted the white flag.

The Tories and British ceased firing, but the Whigs, either not understanding the import of a white flag, or knowing that it had been hoisted twice before and was pulled down, continued to fire. The officers ordered their men to cease firing; but the blood of the Whigs was warm and fire they would. Col. Shelby then ordered the British to lay down their arms, and the men would understand this as a sign that they surrendered. This was done, and the British were ordered to leave their guns, most of which were loaded, and march to another place. The Whigs then marched up and took possession of the enemy's camp.

The victory was complete. Neither man nor horse escaped. The whole force of the British amounted to eleven hundred and twenty-five men, of which number eleven hundred and five fell into the hands of the Whigs. Twenty were out on a plundering expedition. Of the eleven hundred and five taken by the Whigs, five hundred and five were either dead or so badly wounded as not to be able to be moved. The Whig loss was twenty-eight killed and sixty wounded. Everything pertaining to the camp of Ferguson fell into the hands of the Whigs. Besides his provisions and camp equipage, the Whigs got a number of splendid horses and fifteen stand of arms and a supply of powder and bullets. When the patriots saw what they had achieved, they raised a shout which was heard for "seven miles on the plain."

The Whigs slept on the battle-field the night after the fight. The next morning the dead were hurriedly buried, the wounded Whigs cared for, the enemy's wagons burned and the patriots departed. Lacy and Hill marched down into York county and encamped on Bullock's Creek. Campbell and the North Carolinians took the prisoners and hastened to get beyond the mountains. As they had more prisoners than men, and as it was important to save the captured guns, the flints were all removed and the prisoners made to carry them.

At Bickerstaff's old field, a court marital was held in order to decide what should be done with the Tories. Thirty were condemned to be hanged; but all but nine of the most notorious were pardoned.

No victory ever was more complete than that of King's Mountain, and none was more timely for the interest of America. The British, Tories and loyalists, in every section of the country, were panic stricken, and the Whigs encouraged. Cornwallis took fright and left Charlotte, abandoning his contemplated march into Virginia.

As a revolutionary relic worthy of preservation, we append the following rather rough piece of poetry, which was called "The Battle of King's Mountain." We suppose the author's name is unknown to any one. Rough as it is, it is still worthy of being preserved.

———————————

Old Williams from Hillsborough came;
To him the South Carolinians flocked amain.
We marched to Cowpens; Campbell was there.
Shelby, Cleveland and Colonel Sevier;
Men of renown, sir, like lions so bold.
Like lions undaunted ne'er to be controlled.
We set out on our march that very same night;
Sometimes we were wrong, sometimes we were
   right;
Our hearts being run in true liberty's mold,
We valued not hunger, wet, weary nor cold.
On the top of King's Mountain, the old rogue we
   found,
And like brave heroes his camp did surround;
Like lightning the flashes, like thunder the noise,
Our rifles struck the poor Tories with sudden sur-
   prise.
Old Williams and twenty-five more,
When the battle was over, lay rolled in their gore,
With sorrow their bodies were enterred in the clay,
Hoping to heaven their souls took their way.
This being ended, we shouted amain,
Our voices were heard seven miles on the plain;
Liberty shall stand - the Tories shall fall;
Here is the end of my song, so God bless you all.

———————————

1. In its day, the Deckhard rifle was as famous as is the Enfield rifle of the present time. It was made in Lancaster county, Pa., and bore the name of its maker. The barrel was three feet and six inches long, and carried a ball which weighed about one-fourth of an ounce. The gun usually weighed about seven pounds, was trained with great care, and in the hands of a frontiersman, was a deadly weapon.

2. Notwithstanding this declaration of Colonel Ferguson, it is probable that King's Mountain was so called from a man by the name of King, who lived in the neighborhood. From the same individual, it is probable that King's Creek derived its name.

3. It is not very easy to determine, with any degree of certainty, the exact number of Americans actually engaged at the battle of King's Mountain. The western army, that is, that portion of the forces, commanded by Campbell, Shelby, Sevier and Cleveland, numbered, on the 5th of October, about three thousand. Of this number, nine hundred and ten, both Campbell and Shelby say, were selected to pursue Ferguson. The South Carolinians, which according to Col. Hill amounted to near two thousand, were made up of individuals who had joined the army in its march from Bigger's Ferry, in York county, to the Cowpens in Spartanburg. Before King's Mountain was reached, a very large number of the men had fallen behind. Some of the companies had lost their way, and it is almost certain that not more than one thousand men were in the fight. In fact, one account puts the number at about seven hundred. This, we think, too small. It is a fact that the men were coming in during the whole of the fight. Countrymen having learned what was going on, mounted their horses, bare-backed, and some of them took their horses from the plow, and without taking time to lay off the harness, mounted and rushed to the scene of action, having no arms but their squirrel guns. The number of men selected for the enterprise was much greater than the number engaged in the battle, and many were in it, who had not been selected. They had come of their own accord and fought in true partisan style.

SIEGE OF NINETY-SIX

The village of Cambridge was situated in the southeast corner of the present county of Abbeville. In a direct line it was about twenty miles nearly due east from the site of Abbeville Court House; six miles west of the Saluda River, and about one half mile north of the line which divides the counties of Abbeville and Edgefield. A short time prior to the Revolutionary war, the name "Cambridge" had been exchanged for that of Ninety-Six. Tradition has preserved two reasons for this change of name. The one is that Cambridge was ninety-six miles distant from Port Prince George. The other is that at one time after the Indians had planned a massacre of the frontier settlers, an Indian girl mounted a horse and rode, in one day and part of a night, ninety-six miles to give the white settlers warning of the impending danger. The point at which she communicated to the whites the contemplated outbreak of the Indians was Cambridge. From this circumstance, says one tradition, the name of Cambridge was exchanged for that of Ninety-Six.

At an early period in the settlement of the up-country, Cambridge or Ninety-Six became a place of importance second to none other in the state of South Carolina. To protect the frontier settlers against the attacks of the Indians the place was fortified. From time to time as necessity demanded, these fortifications were improved.

When the difficulties between the colonies and mother country began to assume a threatening aspect, Ninety-Six became the scene of bloody conflicts between Whigs and loyalists. The region around Ninety-Six was the most populous and perhaps it may be said the most wealthy section in the up-country previous to the Revolution. It had been the abode of wild Indians, who made anything else than agreeable neighbors to the Europeans residing in the interior of the state.

A special effort was made to induce white settlers to take possession of this region of country. Grants of one and two hundred acres of land, on terms the most favorable, were made to any one who would occupy them. The region was represented as one of fabulous fertility. The result was that both the ambitious and the needy were attracted to the new country. Population of all kinds flowed in from various quarters. Ruffians of the vilest sort and bands of lazy free booters flocked into the region. The frequent outbreaks of the Indians gave these outlaws the semblance of a pretext for making attacks upon the property of their industrious neighbors. House breaking and horse and cattle stealing became common occurrences. The law was powerless and every one went to bed at night with the dread on his mind that before morning his property would be raided upon by these desperadoes.

To meet the exigencies of the case, the more respectable of the community organized themselves for the purpose of mutual protection. Without the ordinary forms of law, these organized bands proceeded to inflict summary punishment upon all offenders who came into their hands. That which was at first organized with the design of promoting only the public good was soon abused. Individuals undertook under the cloak of correcting a public wrong, to punish private injuries. The good of the whole was forgotten in punishing individual wrongs. The result was that those who had no connection with the lawless raiders who infested the region were often seized and punished to appease the hatred of some private individual. Neighbors soon began to cherish towards each other bitter animosities and the whole country was thrown into a state of anarchy and confusion.

In 1766, Governor Montague and the council sent a man by the name of Scovile to adjust the difficulties which existed between the settlers. Scovile proved to be an unprincipled villain and instead of establishing peace, came very near bringing on a civil war.

In 1769, a court of justice was established at Ninety-Six. The seeds of hatred and strife had, however, been sown broadcast, and had germinated and were flourishing with a growth too vigorous to be checked by the forms of law. Regulator and Scovilite continued until 1775, when the former was exchanged for that of Whig and the latter for that of Tory or loyalist.

For a period of twenty years, multitudes on each side had been nursing their wrath. Each party charged the other with opprobrious epithet of coward; but truth demands that we say that neither deserved the title. They were brave - in many instances cruelly so. Every circumstance, both in the settlement of the region and on the intercourse of the settlers with each other, conspired to make the war in that community fierce. The main object the British had in garrisoning Ninety-Six was to keep up their intercourse with the Indians. The power of the savages had been broken, but their fierce spirits had not been subdued. The British fed the flames of revenge which still blazed in the bosoms of these grossly wronged, but desperately cruel, sons of the forest. The fortifications of Ninety-Six were erected in the forks of the two roads, One of these roads led from Charleston by the way of Saxegotha to Ninety-Six. The other road led from Augusta, Ga., to Ninety-Six. A short distance north of the fortification was the town. On the west of the fortification was a small stream by which the garrison was furnished with water. On the west bank of this stream on a slight eminence was a stockade, and on the east bank of this stream was the jail, which was also fortified and garrisoned. On the northeast of the village was erected a star-shaped redoubt. This was the principal place of defense. It consisted of a stronghold, built with sixteen salient and an equal number of re-entrant angles. Around this was dug a deep circular ditch, traces of which are still to be seen. The whole was strengthened by a fraise and abattis. The entire village was enclosed by a line of stockades and covered communications extended from the star redoubt to the several stockades. As the garrison was supplied with water from the rivulet on the west, this point was protected by the stockade on the eminence west of the village and by the garrison stationed in the jail, which occupied the site between the rivulet and the village.

The garrison at Ninety-Six was commanded by Col. John Cruger, a man of good family, a native of New York City, a brave soldier, and a very superior officer. His command consisted of five hundred and fifty men. Of these two hundred were New Jersey volunteers and one hundred and fifty were a detachment from Delancey's loyal battalion of New York. The remainder were Tories from the neighborhood commanded by Colonel King. It will be seen that in the conflict which we are about to describe, American was pitted against American and neighbor against neighbor.

So soon after the capture of Fort Granby as Lieutenant Colonel Carrington had completed his arrangements for transporting the baggage of the American army and the stores which had been secured at the several forts recently captured, General Greene broke up his camp at Friday's Ferry on the Congaree, and set out by the most direct route for Ninety-Six. The distance between Friday's Ferry and Ninety-Six is about sixty miles.

On the 22nd of May - the day after the surrender of Fort Galphin - General Greene arrived in the immediate vicinity of the only remaining British post in South Carolina, in the interior of the state. By the prudence, skill and indomitable courage of the subaltern officers and troops belonging to General Greene's army, the British strongholds and provision depots had melted away like morning clouds. Ninety-Six would have been abandoned had not all the communications between it and the other British posts been so completely cut off by the Americans.

General Greene could not but feel intensely anxious with regard to the success of his undertaking. His individual successes heretofore in the south, had consisted rather in baffling the undertakings and disconcerting the plans of the enemy, than in positive victories. As yet no British officer had been forced to surrender to him in person. At Guilford Court House and Hobkirk's Hill, his victory consisted in depriving his enemy of a grand triumph. It must be confessed that from the moment of his arrival at Ninety-Six, General Greene was not very sanguine of success. He found the place in a good condition both to resist an assault and to stand a siege. Colonel Cruger had not been idle. Aided by Lieutenant Haldane, a skillful engineer belonging to the corps attached to Cornwallis' command, he continued day and night to strengthen his work. General Greene determined to undertake the reduction of this post by regular siege. His force consisted of less than one thousand Continental soldiers and a varying number of undrilled militia. These latter troops in some kinds of warfare did wonders; but in a regular siege or pitched battle they were not of much avail. These troops were stationed in four camps, about a half mile distant from four sides of the enemy's work. Such was the position of the American encampments, that the enemy, as well as the spring from which they received supplies of water, were entirely enclosed.

Thaddeus Kosciusko, the celebrated Polander was with General Greene as chief of his engineers. On the evening of the 22nd of May, ground was broken a short distance north of the star redoubt. Colonel Cruger was not slow in discovering the designs of the American generals. With a promptness and energy which showed that he was a superior officer, he began to make preparations to repel the approach of the Americans. He possessed but three pieces of cannon. These he mounted on wheels and placed upon a platform constructed for the purpose. His parapets were manned with infantry whose accuracy with their deadly rifle seldom missed the object of their aim. Under cover of the artillery and riflemen, a sallying party under Lieutenant Roney, supported by Major Greene, rushed out of the enemy's ditches upon the besiegers. In a moment the guards were either bayoneted or driven away; the lately begun works of the Americans were destroyed and their entrenching tools carried off. The gallant Roney was mortally wounded. This was all the loss the enemy sustained. So vigorously and so promptly did the sallying party act, that although General Greene sent a reinforcement to succor Kosciusko, the work was completed before the detachment arrived. Under the direction of Kosciusko, ground was again broken on the night of the 23rd. This time, the besiegers commenced operations at a point more distant and under cover of a ravine.

A grave mistake seems to have been made at the very outset. The garrison were supplied with water by the spring. This was guarded by a stockade fort and the fortified jail. It would seem that the first effort should have been made to deprive the garrison of the use of the spring. Instead of this being attempted, the approaches by parallel was begun on the opposite side of the enemy's works, thus leaving them undisturbed possession of the spring and rivulet. The pick axe and spade were plied day after day by the Americans, but the work advanced slowly. The brave Kosciusko was censured on account of his slowness and General Greene was blamed for submitting to his engineer so entirely.

On the forenoon of the 8th of June, Colonel Lee with his legion arrived at Ninety-Six and General Pickens followed in a few days. Lee and Pickens were directed to operate against the stockade fort which in part guarded the spring. Lee pushed forward the work assigned him with great dispatch. On the second day after his arrival he had completed his ditch to the point designed for the erection of a battery. On the same day the battery was erected, a six-pounder was placed in position and Lieut. Finn put in command of it.

Cruger was now pushed both on the right and left. He began to feel that his situation was perilous. His only hope was in receiving succor from Rawdon. With this officer he was, however, wholly unable to communicate. When Kosciusko had completed his second parallels, General Greene directed Colonel Otho Holland Williams, adjutant general, to summon Colonel Cruger to surrender. Cruger replied verbally, through his adjutant, that he was determined to hold the place to the last extremity and that he held in perfect disregard both the threats and promises of the American General.

At this stage of the siege, sallying parties were sent out by the enemy to thwart the progress of the American works. The conflicts with these sallying parties were fierce and bloody. It was no child's play. Brave men rendered desperate by their surroundings, were met by brave men in whose bosoms the fires of hatred had been covered for years. In no instance were these sallying parties of the British successful. Failure did not, however, dishearten them; but only render them more desperate. The hopes of the American general and American soldiers were growing brighter and brighter each hour, while on the other hand dark and gloomy forebodings filled the mind of the brave Cruger. Evidently the crisis was fast approaching. It was only a matter of time if things continued as they were, then the last garrison in the interior of South Carolina would be forced to surrender.

In war as in everything else, appearances are often deceptions. The best laid plans pushed with the most consummate skill often are blighted in the moment of their final accomplishment. On the 11th of June, General Greene received a dispatch from General Sumter containing the startling intelligence of the landing at Charleston on the 3rd of portions of three regiments, a detachment of the guards and a considerable number of volunteers, all under the command of Colonel Gould. These forces were designed for Cornwallis, but that officer in order that South Carolina might be retained in possession of his majesty assigned them to the succor of Rawdon.

So soon as the Irish troops landed, Rawdon, who was in camp at Monck's Corner, repaired to Charleston to make preparation for the relief of Ninety-Six. Previous to this time he had not heard of the fall of Augusta, nor of the investment of Ninety-Six. His fears, however, for both these posts were great; but with the force then at his command, beset as he was by Sumter and Marion, he was unable to render Cruger and Brown any assistance. On the 7th of June, Rawdon set out from Charleston for Ninety-six. Soon after leaving Charleston, the troops led by Rawdon at Monck's Corner joined those led by Gould. The whole consisted of seventeen hundred infantry and one hundred and fifty cavalry. On the way a few others joined him, so that on arriving at Orangeburg, his command amounted to more than two thousand. Rawdon soon heard of the fall of Augusta and the siege of Ninety-Six.

On hearing of the advance of Rawdon, the first thing that suggested itself to the mind of General Greene was to meet and disperse the force advancing to relieve Cruger, and then return and force Cruger to surrender. To effect this design, Marion, who was in the low country, was ordered to place himself in front of Rawdon. General Sumter was ordered to collect all the forces on the Congaree and join General Greene at some point between that river and Ninety-Six. General Pickens together with all the cavalry under Col. Washington were sent to join Sumter. Although the plan of first beating Rawdon was undertaken, it was soon discovered that it could not be put into execution. The concentration of the forces under Sumter was necessarily too slow and the movements of Rawdon too rapid to put into execution such a plan.

It was determined next by General Greene to raise the siege and lead his forces into some safe retreat. To this both the officers and men in the American camp objected. Some were anxious to wipe out old stains; others were desirous to give an exhibition of their skill and prowess; whilst many rendered reckless by cruelties and suffering inflicted by the enemy, were longing for an opportunity to satiate their vengeance. It was manifest to all that the post must be taken by assault or abandoned. Rawdon was moving forward to its relief with all possible dispatch.

In the meantime neither party had slackened its labors. The work of the besiegers was pressed forward whilst the besieged labored night and day in strengthening their fortifications. The American marksmen often drove the artillerists from their guns. It was attempted to burn the houses of the villages with arrows, as was done at Fort Motte; but Cruger promptly had the houses stripped of their roofs. Major Greene, who commanded with distinguished ability the star redoubt, on seeing the American third parallel and the erection of a Maham tower, covered his parapet with sand bags, leaving an aperture between the bags for the use of his riflemen. It now became evident to all that an error had been made in not directing the main force to the reduction of the stockades that guarded the spring.

In order to cut the enemy off from their supply of water, Col. Lee proposed to General Greene the propriety of attempting to set the stockade fort on fire. On the 12th whilst a dark and portentous cloud was rising in the west, Lee asked General Greene permission to make the attempt to set the stockade fort on fire. The request was granted and a sergeant and nine infantry belonging to Lee's legion, were immediately selected for the perilous undertaking. This intrepid little band was furnished with combustible material and directed to advance to the stockade fort by the most concealed route. At the same time the batteries in every quarter opened a terrific fire upon the enemy designing to produce the impression that a general assault was about to be made upon the star redoubt. The gallant sergeant and his faithful little band made their way amid the raging of the storm and the thunder of the cannon until they had reached the stockade fort and were in the act of applying the fire. At this critical moment they were discovered and the sergeant and five of his men were instantly killed. The other four escaped unhurt, notwithstanding many muskets were fired at them as they ran across the field back to their command.

On the 17th, the fire of the Americans was very destructive. The enemy were forced to withdraw their forces stationed between the spring and the stockade fort. The garrison soon began to suffer greatly on account of being deprived of the use of the spring. The females in the British camp, sheltering themselves beneath the respect due to their sex, undertook to supply the garrison with water. Unable to supply the demand, the soldiers, it was discovered, dressed themselves in female attire and went to the spring. This being discovered, the order was given to fire upon every one going to the spring, no matter whether male or female.

Although Rawdon had been advancing rapidly since the 7th to relieve Cruger, the latter was in total ignorance of the fact. In the neighborhood, only a few miles distant from Ninety-Six, resided a young woman who had lately married a British officer in Ninety-Six. The young lady was the daughter of a patriot, and she had a brother who had heartily espoused the cause of the Whigs. This woman the British bribed to communicate to the commander of Ninety-Six the fact that succor would soon arrive. Rawdon was at Orangeburg when he sent his emissary to contract with this woman. She communicated the facts in the case to a young loyalist in the community. Dressed in citizen's clothes, this loyalist appeared on the afternoon of the 13th, riding along the American lines, south of the village, talking carelessly to the soldiers. No notice was taken of him, as the country people were accustomed to visit the American camp daily. So soon as he reached the road leading to the village, he straightened himself in the saddle and putting spurs to his horse, dashed through the American line into the village. The sentinels and guards nearest him fired upon him but he escaped unhurt. When out of danger he took a letter from his person and triumphantly waved it back at the Americans. The garrison received him with shouts of joy The gate was opened for his admission and he was conducted to headquarters with loud and prolonged huzzahs. Cruger already brave, was on the reception of the intelligence that Rawdon was advancing to his aid, rendered confident.

Both the besieged and besiegers began to press matters with great vigor. Each knew that the contest must come to a close within a few days. On the left the third parallel was completed, also two trenches and a mine which reached within a few feet of the enemy's ditch. On the right the trenches were within twenty yards of the enemy's works. The garrison was nearly cut off from the spring and rivulet and suffering had already begun. Rawdon had by inclining to the right, passed Sumter, and such was the rapidity with which the British general marched, that Sumter could never gain his front. The only American party which harassed Rawdon on his march, was Colonel Middleton, with three hundred cavalry and mounted militia. Colonel Middleton had been sent from the Congaree to hang upon the rear of the enemy, capture stragglers and particularly to cut off the foraging parties of Rawdon. This partisan corps after giving the enemy considerable trouble, was unfortunately led into a well planned ambush and charged upon by Major Coffin at the head of the body of the royal cavalry. Middleton and his party were so completely scattered that they never made their appearance again.

The Americans were of the opinion that thirty hours would be sufficient to reduce, without assault, the garrison at Ninety-Six; but they dared not wait so long a time, lest the arrival of Rawdon would expose them to total overthrow. In view of the circumstances it was determined to attack the place by general assault.

Mid-day on the 18th of June, was appointed as the moment when at a given signal, the forces would advance to the assault. Long poles with iron hooks were prepared with which to pull down the sand bags on the enemy's fortifications, and material was collected for the purpose of filling up the ditches. Lieutenant Colonel Campbell of the First Virginia regiment, with a detachment from the Maryland and Virginia brigades, was directed to lead the attack on the left; Lieutenant Colonel Lee with his legion of infantry and Kirkwood's Delaware regiment, were charged with the attack on the right. Lieutenants Duval of Maryland and Seldon of Virginia led the forlorn hope on the left; Captain Rudolph of Lee's legion, that on the right.

The signal for attack was to be given from the center battery. At eleven o'clock the third parallel was manned and the sharpshooters took their position in the Maham tower. On the firing of the first cannon, which was the signal for the assailants to prepare for action, the American columns entered the trenches. The men were full of enthusiasm. At the hour of twelve, the second cannon was fired and simultaneously and in good order the assailing columns under Lee and Campbell, advanced. Cruger, if not expecting the assault, was fully prepared for it. The parapets gleamed with pikes and bayonets and through the apertures between the sand bags, the riflemen of Major Greene mowed down the ranks of the assailants. On an intermediate battery, Cruger had placed his three pieces of cannon. These, as circumstances seemed to demand, he sometimes directed upon the column led by Campbell sometimes on that led by Lee. Cruger's mind was cool and prompt, and his men well trained and desperately brave. The cannon was used with telling effect upon the Americans. Colonel Campbell and his brave Marylanders and Virginians pressed forward amidst showers of leaden hail. No one flinched. With the hooks, the soldiers were dragging the sand bags on the enemy's parapets

into the ditch below. The moment was near at hand when Campbell would ascend the parapet and terminate the contest in a hand to hand conflict. Major Greene, who commanded the star redoubt, discovered the progress which the Americans were making and fearing the results of a hand to hand fight between the garrison and assailants on the parapets, determined to try the bayonet in his ditch as well as on his parapet. At a sally port he sent out with small detachments, Captain French of Delancey's corps, and Capt. Campbell of New Jersey. Taking opposite directions in the ditch, Campbell soon encountered Duval, French and Seldon. The conflict was dreadful. The Americans had to encounter the enemy on the parapet and those in the ditch. They stood their ground and fought gallantly until both Duval and Seldon were wounded. Then the forlorn hope was with great loss, forced to retire to the American trenches. Only a few survived. The most were left in the enemy's ditch.

The assailing columns led by Lieutenant Colonel Lee was more successful. Captain Rudolph gained the ditch which surrounded the stockade fort, and being followed by the main fort when the garrison fled to the main works. Lee was about to make an assault upon the jail and then to assist in reducing the star redoubt. General Greene seeing the slaughter which had taken place in the ditch in front of the star redoubt, and unwilling to sacrifice any more of his troops, ordered Lee to hold the stockade and attempt nothing more. The assailing column led by Campbell lay in the trenches and that led by Lee remained in the stockade until dark when both were withdrawn.

General Greene now determined to retreat to avoid Rawdon. On the evening of the day after the assault, the siege was raised and General Greene led his forces across the Saluda and retreated rapidly in the direction of the Enoree.

The siege of Ninety-Six lasted from the twenty-second of May until the eighteenth of June. The American loss during the siege was Captain Mark Armstrong, shot through the head on the day of the assault and one hundred and eighty-five men in killed, wounded, and missing. The garrison lost eighty-five. It is remarkable that only one officer on each side was killed.

The failure to capture Ninety-Six was very mortifying to both the officers and men in the army. Whether all was done and done in the right way and at the right time that could have been done to capture the place, cannot at this late date be ascertained satisfactorily. At the time Kosciusko was censured on account of his slowness, and some thought General Greene should have exercised more of his own judgment with regard to the manner of conducting the siege. Charity bids us say that all acted their part well from patriotic motives.

ABANDONMENT OF NINETY-SIX

The failure of General Greene to capture the British post of Ninety-Six disconcerted somewhat the plans of both the Americans and the British. Previous to the assault upon the enemy's works Greene had sent his sick and inefficient men off in the direction of Charlotte, N.C. After raising the siege he, with the whole of his forces, followed by as rapid marches as the circumstances would allow.

Lord Rawdon reached Ninety-Six on the morning of the 21st. Both he and Cruger were delighted. Under circumstances the most trying, the latter had defended himself and surrounded by difficulties which only a brave man, the leader of veteran troops could overcome, Rawdon had come to Cruger's relief. In fourteen days, Rawdon had marched his men in the heat of summer from Charleston to Ninety-Six, a distance of near two hundred miles.

No small number of his troops were Irish volunteers, who had landed at Charleston on the 3rd of June. Deceived by the false reports which they had heard at home, of the success which had attended his majesty's forces in crushing the rebellion of the colonies, these troops had come over to possess the subjugated country. Each one thought that on arriving at Charleston, all he would have to do in order to become the owner of a large landed estate was to make his selection and have his land marked out by metes and bounds. Three days after landing they discovered, no doubt to their sorrow, that before they could settle down in the country as landlords, they must first conquer the present inhabitants.

Although Lord Rawdon had by rapid marches reached the vicinity of Ninety-Six soon enough to drive away General Greene and save the garrison, he was not disposed to give himself or troops up to supineness. On the very evening after reaching Ninety-Six, he selected his best men and horses and set out in pursuit of General Greene. The sick and broken down men and horses were left with Cruger. He crossed the Saluda and pushed on to the Enoree. Here his van encountered the American rear, under Colonel Washington and Lieutenant Colonel Lee. General Greene with the main forces had crossed the Enoree and Tyger and perhaps Broad River and consequently was now out of danger.

Lord Rawdon discovering very soon the superiority of the American cavalry to that of his van, concluded to abandon the pursuit of the Americans and return to Ninety-Six. Rawdon seems to have come to the conclusion that General Greene had determined to leave the state of South Carolina and go either to North Carolina or Virginia. Laboring under this mistake, the British general concluded to circumscribe the field of his operations to the tract of country included between the Edisto, Congaree and Santee Rivers. Within this tract of country he contemplated establishing in the most eligible position a military post from which he might lead out his forces and act as his surroundings might indicate. On returning to Ninety-Six he promptly set about making preparations for the abandonment of that post. Many circumstances indicated this as a proper course to be pursued. Even had it been true as Rawdon no doubt thought, that Greene and his army was forced to leave the state of South Carolina to the mercy of the British, still Ninety-Six was too far in the interior of the country and too much exposed to attacks from the various partisan corps which were known still to exist, to warrant its retention. This was not all. The various other posts in the up country had been captured and their garrisons made prisoners. Under such circumstances, the maintenance of a garrison at Ninety-Six would have been attended with great difficulties.

The plan chosen by Rawdon for the abandonment of the post and the future disposition of the troops was that Rawdon, with a portion of the whole forces then at Ninety-Six was to proceed directly to Friday's Ferry on the Congaree, whilst Cruger, with the remainder in charge of the baggage, loyalists and sick, was to incline to the right and advance to Orangeburg. At Friday's Ferry and Orangeburg, cantonments were to be established. Colonel Stewart was ordered from Charleston to form with the troops under his command, a junction with Rawdon at Friday's Ferry.

Before, however, the troops moved from Ninety-Six, Lord Rawdon discovered that his conclusions with respect to the intentions of General Greene were incorrect. On leaving the Enoree he was followed by Lieutenant Colonel Lee's corps. General Greene from the moment he raised the siege at Ninety-Six, contemplated regulating his future movements by those of his enemy. His purpose was to keep at a safe distance from his foe, and yet near enough to improve any advantage which might be presented.

Previous to advancing upon Ninety-Six, General Greene had sent his hospital stores and heavy baggage to Winnsboro. So soon as the intentions of Rawdon were discovered, General Greene ordered his stores at Winnsboro to be removed to Camden. Lieutenant Colonel Lee was ordered to watch the movements of the enemy and communicate all intelligence gained to General Greene. Sumter and Marion were apprised of the movements of the enemy and also of the aims and intentions of the American general.

It was at this time that an event transpired, which has furnished a theme for the poet or novelist and a fit subject for the painter. When General Greene had written a letter to General Sumter, containing an outline of his plans and orders, he found it difficult to find a person who was willing to convey the letter to General Sumter. The advance of Lord Rawdon into the up country, had encouraged the Tories and loyalists to take a bold stand. The country through which the bearer of the letter would necessarily have to pass, in some places swarmed with gangs of horse thieves and unprincipled Tories. No one was willing to volunteer to bear the letter to its destination. At this critical juncture of affairs, a young girl of scarcely eighteen years of age, the daughter of a German planter of Fairfield county, offered her services for the perilous task. Her name, which has become historical, was Emily Geiger. General Greene readily accepted the offer.

The maid was mounted upon a fleet horse and the letter placed by General Greene in her hands. Fearing lest some mishap might befall the heroic girl, General Greene took the precaution to communicate to her the contents of the letter. Without molestation she passed through the country, crossed the Wateree River at the ferry below Camden, and was nearing Sumter's camp. In one of those low bottoms in which that region of country abounds, she was on the second day of her journey, halted by a small scouting party of Tories. In accordance with the principle laid down by the Scotch poet that the "real hardened wicked are to a few restricted," the Tory scouts individually forbore to search Emily, in order to discover whether or not she was the bearer of any contraband documents. She was taken to a house in the neighborhood and a woman sent for to make the search. Emily was shut up in a room above, there to remain until the individual designed to search her person should arrive. During this interval, Emily deliberately and wisely chewed up and swallowed the letter placed in her charge. When her person was searched, it was found that there was nothing about her that was suspicious or that furnished a reasonable cause for her longer delay. Mortified that they had acted so harshly, the gallant Tories apologized to the fair maiden and permitted her, without further delay, to pursue her journey.

She reached Sumter's camp; and since she had eaten up the letter, promptly delivered the message from General Greene to General Sumter. Emily Geiger afterwards married a gentleman by the name of Thurwits and settled in Lexington county.

RETREAT OF GENERAL GREENE AND FIGHT AT QUINBY BRIDGE

From Ninety-Six, General Greene led his forces in the direction of Charlotte, North Carolina, as far as the cross roads, a short distance east of the site of the present town of Chester. Here he learned with certainty the movements of Rawdon and Cruger. The former designed passing from Ninety-Six, in a direct course to Fort Granby; the latter to Orangeburg. Lieutenant Colonel Lee pressed Rawdon both on his rear and flanks. From the cross roads, General Greene took the road passed over by Cornwallis, early in January of the same year. Passing through Winnsboro, General Greene then led his forces to Fort Granby. Cruger, watched closely by General Pickens, was advancing toward Orangeburg. Rawdon, annoyed by Lee and not feeling safe at Fort Granby, had retired to Orangeburg before the arrival of General Greene.

It is manifest that the siege of Ninety-Six had disconcerted the plans of the British, whilst the failure to capture the place had thwarted for the moment, the purposes of the American general. Rawdon had ordered Lieutenant Colonel Stewart with a considerable force to join him on the Congaree, Stewart set out from Charleston, but he had not proceeded far when the commander of the post ordered him back. General Greene ordered General Marion to retard as much as possible the advance of Stewart and then to join Colonel Lee. Stewart was again ordered to join Rawdon. His advance was slow. This rendered the advance of Marion slow. The result was that both Lee and Rawdon were disappointed on arriving at Friday's Ferry. Here Lee expected to meet Sumter and Marion, and Rawdon expected to be joined by Stewart.

Rawdon reached Friday's Ferry on the Congaree, on the first of July and camped. Lieutenant Colonel Lee having a perfect knowledge of the country and knowing that Rawdon was dependent on the surrounding country for supplies, began promptly to make preparations to cut off all foraging parties of the enemy. Lee was on the left bank of the Congaree, whilst Rawdon was on the right. In order to gain the enemy's front it was necessary that Lee should cross the river. This was done with dispatch and a reconnoitering party of thirty cavalry under Eggleston and a similar party under Armstrong were sent to the southern portion of Lexington county, for the purpose of striking any foraging parties Rawdon might sent out.

At an early hour the next morning a foraging party, consisting of between fifty and sixty cavalry and a number of wagons were discovered approaching a farm house. Eggleston permitted the party to advance to within striking distance and then dashing in upon it with spirit, captured the wagons and forty-five of the cavalry. In this affair the Americans did not lose a single man.

Rawdon left Friday's Ferry and advanced slowly towards Orangeburg. On the road to Orangeburg he was joined by Stewart.

General Greene, who was encamped near the confluence of the Broad and Saluda Rivers, when Rawdon precipitately retired from Friday's Ferry, followed by rapid marches, thus preventing Rawdon from entrenching himself. The American forces now increased by the commands of Marion and Sumter, numbering in all about two thousand, encamped five miles from Orangeburg.

Cruger had not yet reached Orangeburg, and General Greene for the moment was unable to decide what course to pursue. Rawdon's forces, although augmented by the corps of Stewart, was inferior to that of Greene, but was favorably situated and protected by the buildings of the town. On account of the difficulty in crossing the Edisto, an attempt to intercept Cruger and cut him and his loyalists off before uniting with Rawdon would be, thought Greene, attended with great risk. In view of all the circumstances General Greene thought it prudent not to hazard an assault but to retreat to the High Hills of the Santee.

The American army remained in the vicinity of Orangeburg only a few days; but during that time the men experienced great suffering from lack of food. The supply was limited and to most of the troops the quality was very unpalatable. For bread they had rice in limited supplies. To the Maryland and Virginia troops, who had been accustomed all their lives to bread made from wheat flour or corn meal, rice was very unpalatable. In addition to this the supply of rice was inadequate to the demand. Fortunately the swamps, lagoons and rivers furnished an abundance of frogs and alligators. The troops subsisted mainly on frogs. The cravings of appetite overcame all aversion to these creatures and both officers and men sought them with avidity. The weather was oppressively hot and the troops began to sicken. General Greene, that

he might give his army a short period of repose, left Orangeburg on the 13th of July and reached the High Hills of Santee on perhaps the 16th.

Before leaving Orangeburg, General Greene ordered Sumter, Marion and Lee, with the troops in their several commands, to advance in the direction of Charleston for the purpose of breaking up the British posts at Dorchester and Monck's Corner. These officers were also charged with the duty of cutting off all communications between Rawdon and Balfour, the commander of Charleston. These objects accomplished, they were to join Greene on the Santee Hills. The commands of the partisan leaders, Marion and Sumter, were made up of small companies of state troops led by Taylor, Maham, the two Hamptons, Lacey, and Horry. Leaving Orangeburg, these gallant officers each led his command into the particular section of country assigned him by General Lee. They soon swept the whole region between Orangeburg and the capital of the state.

Colonel Wade Hampton dashed in upon a party of British cavalry and loyal refugees, within five miles of the city of Charleston. The garrison was thrown into the utmost confusion. The drums were beat, the bells rung, alarm guns fired, and the whole available force of the city hurriedly collected, and together with the garrison drawn up to meet the Whigs. Hampton having captured between forty and fifty prisoners, exhibited them to the view of the sentinels on the more advanced redoubts and retired at his leisure. Colonel Hampton also burned four vessels bearing supplies for the British army.

Colonel Lee took the British post at Dorchester, scoured the whole surrounding country, capturing a large number of wagons and wagon horses, conveying provisions from Charleston to Rawdon.

Whilst Sumter and Hampton were operating in front of Charleston and Lee in the neighborhood of Dorchester, Marion and Maham, having crossed the Cooper River near its head and Wadboo Creek, were operating in the neighborhood of Biggin Church.

At Monck's Corner about one mile distant, Lieutenant Colonel Coates was stationed. His command consisted of the Nineteenth regiment. The American officers were exceedingly anxious to overthrow Colonel Coates and his regiment. For this purpose Lee and Sumter having effected their plans in the sections to which they had been ordered, led their troops to join Marion in the region of Monck's Corner. On the assembling of the forces, the first object to be accomplished was to destroy the bridge over Cooper river. The cavalry of Coates advanced with the determination to prevent the destruction of the bridge. Here a severe skirmish took place in which the Americans were successful. Coates drew out all his forces to protect his cavalry and Sumter supposing that Coates was advancing to bring on a general engagement, retired to a more favorable position. Coates had no such design. Waiting until the day had passed away; then under cover of the night, he collected the greater part of his stores into Biggin Church and setting fire to the whole, quietly but rapidly withdrew his forces in the direction of Wadboo and Quinby.

The flame which illumined the surrounding country, revealed to the American officers the plans of the enemy. Without a moment's delay, the Americans began the pursuit. Lee and Hampton led the van. On crossing the Wadboo, they discovered that the infantry and cavalry of the enemy had separated. The cavalry had directed its course to the right, keeping close to the Cooper River, while the infantry had pursued a more easterly route.

Colonel Hampton set out in full pursuit of the cavalry, whilst Lee followed the infantry. The enemy's cavalry advanced so rapidly that before Hampton could overtake them, they had crossed the bridge and were out of reach.

Hampton returned to assist Lee whom he found near Quinby's Bridge about eighteen miles from Monck's Corner. Here a severe skirmish took place. A short distance north of the bridge a detachment of the cavalry of Lee and Marion came upon a detachment of one hundred men belonging to the lately arrived Irish regiments. The American detachment under Marion and Eggleston made a famous charge upon the enemy. Without making the slightest resistance the Irish recruits surrendered. No alarm gun was fired; no effort was made either to retreat or defend themselves; although within a mile of the main force of Colonel Coates he heard nothing of it.

The greater portion of the enemy's force had already crossed Quinby Bridge. Colonel Coates with a howitzer was on the opposite side, waiting until his rear would pass over, when the bridge would be demolished. Already the planks were loosened from the sleepers. Ignorant of the location of the bridge and the proximity of the enemy, a detachment of Lee's legion of cavalry under Armstrong came dashing up. Both parties were taken by surprise. Neither suspected the other to be within striking distance. Armstrong reported the condition of things to Lee, neglecting to mention the fact that Quinby Bridge interposed between him and Colonel Coates. Lee hastily and imprudently ordered, in an angry tone, Armstrong to strike the enemy boldly without a

moment's delay. Armstrong obeyed promptly, leading his detachment hurriedly over the partially demolished bridge in the face of Colonel Coates' howitzer. Rendered furious by the angry commands of Lee, Armstrong madly rushed in upon the British, drove the artillerists from the howitzer and swept everything right and left before him. Lieutenant Carrington followed Armstrong. Captain O'Neal at the head of the third section attempted to follow Carrington, but by this time the loose planks had by the rapid motion of the horses been thrown from the sleepers causing a chasm in the bridge. O'Neal could not urge his horses to leap the chasm. At this moment Maham, at the head of a detachment of Marion's cavalry came up and passed O'Neal. Maham's horse was shot down. Captain McCauley, who was leading Maham's front section, leaped the chasm in the bridge and joined in the fierce hand to hand conflict with the enemy.

The British by this time began to collect in force and the American detachments which had crossed the bridge were sorely pressed, whilst those on the opposite side of the creek could render them no assistance. Colonel Lee, assisted by Maham and Dr. Irving, exerted himself in attempting to repair the bridge but without success. Armstrong, Carrington, and McCauley soon found themselves alone. Of the few soldiers who had been able to cross the bridge, but a single one remained. Coates and a few followers under cover of a wagon fought desperately. His infantry were fast coming to his support.

In this perilous condition of affairs, Armstrong, Carrington and McCauley, determined to save themselves by flight. Through the confused squads of British forming on the causeway in front of the bridge, these gallant soldiers dashed. So soon as they could, they fled to the left and concealed themselves in the woods.

Coates now left without a foe, soon advanced to the bridge and with the howitzer which still remained he soon drove away Lee, and having completed the destruction of the bridge, retired with the howitzer to Shubrick's plantation and took post behind the houses. The creek was narrow but deep and such was the swampy nature of the banks that it could not at that place be crossed except on the bridge.

The Americans determined to fight, readily made a circuitous march and having crossed the creek came up with Coates late in the afternoon. Here the fight was renewed. Colonels Lacey, Polk, Middleton and Taylor of Sumter's command closed in upon the enemy. Marion's shattered command was divided into two divisions and a fight resembling in many respects that of King's Mountain was begun with spirit and waged with determination. Coates had the advantage of position and whilst he had but one piece of artillery, the Americans had none.

The Americans were now within striking distance of Charleston. Lest they should be overpowered and cut to pieces by succor sent to Coates from that post, it was deemed proper to retire. At dark the thinned divisions of the partisan chiefs were led from the field of conflict. Armstrong, who with Carrington and McCauley had again joined their commands, was sent to the field of conflict at Quinby's Bridge to bring off the dead and wounded. The dead were placed on the pommels of the saddles before the men and thus carried off. The wounded were conveyed away in the easiest manner possible. Out of reach of the enemy, one grave was dug and the dead place in it and covered.

The affair at Quinby's Bridge was one of the most spirited fights that occurred during the Revolutionary war. The loss of the Americans in killed, wounded and prisoners is not accurately given. In proportion to the number of men engaged, it was very great, mostly in killed and wounded as few prisoners were taken. The British lost in the several engagements, in prisoners alone near two hundred men and nine officers. A large amount of valuable stores, wagons and horses fell into the hands of the Americans. Besides these the Americans captured the paymaster's money chest which contained seven hundred and twenty guineas. This money General Sumter ordered to be divided amongst the soldiers.

Of the troops engaged at Quinby's Bridge and Shubrick's farm, the majority were South Carolinians. On the 20th of August, the day after the battle, the troops reached Nelson's Ferry. Here they rested for a day and night and then by easy marches proceeded to join General Greene on the High Hills of Santee.

INSTALLMENT L

GENERAL GREENE AT THE HIGH HILLS OF THE SANTEE

From Orangeburg, as we have seen, General Greene retired with the larger portion of his army to the High Hills of the Santee. After the battle of Quinby Bridge, the partisan leaders - Lee, Sumter, Marion and others - repaired to the camp of Greene.

The principal object Greene had in view in selecting this locality for his camp, was to discipline his troops and receive reinforcements from North Carolina and Virginia. The locality was also chosen with special reference to the health of his army. For a period of near seven months, the army of Greene had

been doing hard service on what may, with the utmost regard to truth, be called rations of the most ordinary kind. Many of the soldiers were sick. This is not a matter to be wondered at; but it is a matter of wonder that they whole of Greene's army had not fallen down dead. They had marched - some of them - from near the center of South Carolina, across the whole of North Carolina into Virginia, pursued by two of the most dashing officers in the British army. From the Dan they had marched to Camden, South Carolina; from that point they marched to Ninety-Six; from Ninety-Six they retreated across the state as far as Chester. From that point they went to Orangeburg; and some of them as far as the city of Charleston. During all this time they were pressed by hunger and privations of every kind and pursued or watched by veteran foes. The hardships which these men had endured and the privations which they had experienced are almost incredible. During this time they had fought many battles and won several grand victories. They had broken the power of the British and humbled the Tories.

The British had not been reposing, during this time, on beds of down and feasting on the luxuries of the earth. From the day that Greene pitched his camp on Hobkirk's Hill, the living of the British army became precarious. They depended on supplies sent them from Charleston by wagon trains. These the patrolling parties of Greene, led by Lee, Sumter and the invincible Marion and other partisan leaders of little less note seldom failed to capture.

After the battle of Quinby Bridge, the British made Orangeburg their headquarters. Here they felt that the condition of things had changed. Their commissary stores had been exhausted and they were forced to live almost entirely on beef which they procured at the risk of their lives from the surrounding country. Greene was master of the position. He had virtually rescued the state from the British. The Tories and loyalists were heart broken.

The High Hills of the Santee are in Sumter county, east of the Wateree River about five miles. These hills extend in a northeastern direction, nearly parallel with the Wateree River for a distance of between fifteen and twenty miles. The climate compared with that of the more southern sections of the state is delightful and healthy. In this favored region the sick in Greene's army rapidly recovered their health and the tired and broken down regained their strength.

There is an item of historic interest connected with these Santee Hills, which we must not omit. When Chas. Edward, the grandson of James II was defeated at the battle of Culloden, his followers were placed in a most critical condition. Some of them had voluntarily joined the Young Pretender. Others although convinced of the fruitlessness of the attempt to reinstate a Stewart upon the throne of Great Britain, had under the promptings of national pride - although contrary to their judgment and interest - supported the claims of the Pretender. Multitudes of the Scotch, who had either taken up arms in support of the claims of Charles Edward or otherwise supported his cause were apprehended. Old men trembling with the infirmities of years, were executed. The heart of George the III at last sickened, and he granted his once rebel, but now vanquished subjects a conditional pardon. The conditions were that they take the oath of allegiance - and emigrate to the plantations. These Highlanders - at least many of them - preferring banishment to either death or the humiliating condition to which they had been reduced in their native land, accepted the offer of the king. To a part of those pardoned Highlanders the region of country around the High Hills of the Santee was granted. Reaching the coast of North Carolina they were driven by contrary winds into Cape Fear. Following the course of the river they in process of time occupied a large tract of country of which Cross Creek, afterwards Cambleton and now Fayetteville was the center. The lands reserved for these exiled Scots was afterwards granted to some Virginians and by them settled. Prominent among these settlers, may be mentioned General Thomas Sumter, and General Richard Richardson. The first settlers in the region bore the names of Chellet, Furman, Mathers, and Nettlers. Richard Richardson was a surveyor, a profession at that day held in high repute. By him the lands were located and some of them are still in the possession of his descendants.

Whilst General Greene lay on the High Hills of the Santee, his militia were thoroughly drilled. During the first years of the war there were a very considerable number of persons in every section of the state who as far as it was possible remained neutral. They were neither British nor Tory. From the beginning of the contest they had entertained no hope that the colonies would succeed in throwing off the British yoke. The history of past rebellions against the English government made them timid. When, however, these individuals saw that Cornwallis and Tarleton were gone and Rawdon, Cruger, and Balfour were unable to keep General Greene in check they came out to espouse the cause of the Whigs. These recruits, whilst they increased the number of men in Greene's army, did not render it more efficient because they were undrilled. For the short time that Greene remained on the High Hills of Santee, these new recruits were drilled that they might be ready to meet the enemy.

The successes of the southern army had already attracted the attention of the government and that the last blow might be struck and the arm of the enemy completely paralyzed, reinforcements were ordered to be sent to General Greene. Baron Steuben with a body of men, was assigned to the southern army. The order was countermanded and the baron did not arrive. A considerable force was sent from North Carolina. These joined General Greene in his camp on the High Hills of Santee.

Whilst Gen. Greene was preparing for a general engagement, the partisan leaders of the south, with their well tried corps, were harassing the enemy in every section of the state. Sumter and Pickens were operating against the Tories in the up-country, whilst Marion, Taylor and Maham were sweeping over the region between Orangeburg and Charleston. The British were reduced to so perilous a condition that they lived at the risk of their lives. The British soldiers were obedient to their officers, but all hope of subjugating the state had died in their breasts, and no small number of them were devising plans by which they might desert the standard of George the Third and join the Americans. No doubt some of these were influenced by no other motive than that which impels men to espouse the cause which appears to be most popular. Others were impelled to desert the British standard because they believed the war was waged to establish tyranny. The British officers were careful to prevent all desertions and no less careful to conceal them from the world, when they could not prevent them.

Installment LI

BATTLE OF EUTAW SPRINGS

During the short period that the southern army under General Greene lay encamped on the High Hills of the Santee, a plan was devised to wrest Wilmington, North Carolina, from the hands of the British. Major Craig with a garrison of about three hundred men held this place in subjection and by his influence and exertion kept the people of North Carolina rent with internal feuds. In order to effect the object in view it was necessary that every movement on the part of the Americans be conducted with great secrecy. The army of General Greene had, whilst contending with the greatest difficulties, forced the British to give up their occupancy of all South Carolina and Georgia except the cities of Charleston and Savannah and their suburbs. Virginia was overpowered and the efforts of North Carolina in behalf of freedom, to a great extent were nullified by her own factions.

In order to sustain Virginia whilst sorely pressed by the enemy, General Greene wisely concluded that it was necessary to deliver North Carolina from the grasp of the foe and restore harmony and sentiment among her own people. This could not be done so long as Major Craig remained in quite possession of the city of Wilmington. That his plans might be concealed and his movements misunderstood, Gen. Greene ordered Col. Lee, with his own legion together with Kirkwood's Delaware troops and Handy's Marylanders to be ready to begin the execution of the proposed plan of capturing Wilmington. That the movement might be completely concealed from the enemy, Colonel Washington was directed to lead his cavalry across the Wateree River, whilst Marion with his militia, was detached and sent to the region of country skirting upon the Combahee.

Colonel Lee detached Captain Rudolph with a few men for the purpose of proceeding to the neighborhood of Wilmington that the strength of Major Craig's defenses might be accurately learned and also to ascertain whether it was probable that the American army could cross the Cape Fear River. Rudolph promptly and successfully executed the task assigned. He learned that a large number of Craig's men were sick and that he was unable to man his works properly. He also learned that small boats could be secured in sufficient numbers to transport the American infantry and that the horses could swim the river.

Arrangements were made for the advance of Lee's legion upon Wilmington. The route he was to take and the day for his departure were settled. The declared purpose of the expedition was to succor a convoy which was reported to be on its way from Virginia. In the meantime, General Greene received a dispatch from General Washington, informing him that it was probable that the French West India fleet would land somewhere on the coast of South Carolina at no distant period in the future. The particular point at which the French fleet would attempt to land was not known. Washington instructed Greene to make every preparation in his power so as to be ready to co-operate with the French, no matter where they might land. This induced General Greene to change, to some extent, his plans of operation and abandon for a time an attack upon Wilmington.

During the period that the army under General Greene lay encamped on the High Hills of the Santee,

the British forces lay at Orangeburg. Lord Rawdon having been driven by a few undisciplined militia from post to post, and forced to confine himself within narrow bounds, left the army in command of Lieutenant Colonel Stewart and sailed for Europe. To the camp of Stewart flocked the loyalists and Tories from every quarter of the state. Whilst these swelled his numbers, they added very little to his effective force.

A little more than a month had passed since General Greene had arrived at the High Hills of the Santee. The weather was still excessively hot; but during the short period of repose the sick and wounded in the American army had been greatly benefited by the pure water and pleasant climate of the hills. On the 21st of August, General Greene broke up his camp on the Santee and set out in search of his enemy. He led his forces across the Wateree River at Camden. From this point he advanced to the Congaree, which he crossed a short distance below the present city of Columbia. At this point General Greene was reinforced by a body of militia under Pickens and a small body of infantry under Colonel Henderson. This last was a corps of state troops recently raised. The Congaree crossed, General Greene determined to advance upon his enemy. Lee with his legion and Henderson with his new body of state troops were detached to form the van; whilst the whole force followed within supporting distance.

When Stewart learned that Greene was advancing, apparently to attack him, he retired from Orangeburg to the Eutaw Spring, on the Santee. Here he was joined by a convoy with supplies from Charleston. Stewart was aware that the cause of the British in South Carolina was in a critical condition, but the nearer he approached Charleston the less were his apprehensions of danger.

Eutaw Springs is in Charleston county in St. John's Berkely parish. From the foot of a slight elevation the water gushes out in a bold stream and after flowing near one hundred yards, it descends into a subterraneous passage, and again at a distance of about two hundred yards it rushes out and forms Eutaw Creek; and at a distance of about two miles empties into the Santee at Nelson's Ferry. The stream notwithstanding its extreme shortness, is of sufficient volume to drive a large flouring mill, but it has not fall. So nearly is the spring on a level with the Santee that during a freshet the waters of the river flow back as far as the spring.

General Greene, on crossing the Congaree, proceeded by slow marches in pursuit of Stewart. At Orangeburg, Marion, who was in the region of country watered by the Edisto, rendering assistance to

Colonel Hardin, who was about to be entrapped by Major Fraser, was ordered to join General Greene in the neighborhood of Eutaw Spring. On the 5th of September, Marion having made a forced night march reached the plantation of Henry Laurens a few miles from the enemy's camp. On he evening of the 8th, Greene and the main force reached Burdell's plantation several miles from Eutaw Spring. Here he encamped for the night.

Colonel Stewart seems to have been totally ignorant of the proximity of the American army. During the night of the 7th, two North Carolina conscripts belonging to Sumner's command deserted and gave Colonel Stewart the first intimation that General Greene was advancing to give him battle. During the day Stewart's scouts had been up the Congaree Road but for some reason had failed to discover the American army. This led the British colonel to conclude that the North Carolina deserters were spies. Giving little credence to the information received from the deserters, Stewart as usual sent out, on the morning of the 8th, an unarmed force to dig potatoes. Captain Coffin by whom Stewart had lately been reinforced was sent out with a small body of cavalry to make observation and if necessary to recall the potato diggers.

Just as day began to break on the morning of the 8th, the American army under General Greene was put in motion. The whole force amounted to two thousand and three hundred men. Of this number, about sixteen hundred including the cavalry, artillery and foot were regulars; the remainder were militia, a few of whom had some experience. The rest had never been in a battle. The whole force moved forward in two columns. Each of these columns was composed of the troops designed to form the lines of battle.

The front line was composed of four battalions of militia. Two of the battalions consisted of North Carolinians and the other two of South Carolinians. The North Carolina battalions were commanded by Colonel Malmedy. One of the South Carolina battalions was commanded by Pickens - the other by Marion. The whole front line was commanded by Marion. Three greatly reduced brigades of Continental troops constituted the second line. One of the brigades was from North Carolina, another from Virginia and the remaining one from Maryland. The North Carolina brigade was divided into three battalions and placed on the right. Majors Blount and Armstrong and Lieutenant Colonel Ashe, each commanded a battalion - the whole commanded by Gen. Sumner. The Virginia brigade commanded by Lieutenant Colonel Richard Campbell was posted in the center. This was divided into two battalions, the commanders which were respectively Major Snead and Captain Edmund. The Maryland brigade commanded by Colonel Otho H. Williams, deputy adjutant general, was posted on the right of the second line. The Maryland brigade was divided into two battalions, the commanders of which were Lieutenant Colonel Howard and Major Hardman. The right wing was covered by Lee's legion, commanded by himself. The state troops, the several divisions of which were commanded respectively by Colonels Hampton, Middleton and Polk - the whole commanded by Colonel Henderson - covered the left wing. The reserve was composed of Colonel Washington's cavalry and the Delaware troops under Captain Kirkwood. Captain Gaines, with two three-pounders, moved forward with the second line. Lee's legion led by himself and the state troops, commanded by Henderson, advanced in front of the whole. Such is a brief outline of the order in which the American army, under General Greene, moved forward on the morning of the 8th of September, 1781.

Colonel Stewart with about two thousand soldiers lay at Eutaw Spring. His line extended from Eutaw Creek, north of the Charleston Road, across the road, for a considerable distance. The line passed in front of the residence of William Sinkler.

At eight o'clock, Lee and Henderson came in contact with Captain Coffin and his "potato diggers." Captain Coffin seems to have been ignorant of the advance of the American army. Captain Armstrong was leading Lee's reconnoitering party. So soon as Coffin discovered Armstrong, he dashed forward and made a spirited attack upon him. Armstrong fell back upon Lee. The legion and state troops were soon arranged to receive the attack. Lee, supposing that Stewart was apprised of the nearness of the American army, dispatched a courier to General Greene to inform him of what was taking place. The American van was now near four miles from Eutaw Spring. Coffin boldly attacked Lee and Henderson and was as boldly met by these officers. Major Eggleston made a quick movement and gained Coffin's rear. Pressed both in front and rear, Coffin was soon forced to yield. A large number of his infantry was killed and forty, including their captain, were taken prisoners. Coffin's cavalry so soon as they discovered Eggleston in their rear, put spurs to their horses and fled in confusion. The unarmed party which had been sent out to dig potatoes fled back to camp so soon as the firing commenced and thus escaped.

The American van under Lee and Henderson, encouraged by the results of this skirmish, pressed forward with vigor. About a mile from the camp of Stewart, they were met by another detachment of the enemy, which had been sent to aid Coffin. Both Americans and British seemed to have been surprised by this occurrence. Stewart now for the first time seems to have been convinced that General Greene with his whole army was approaching. The British fell back a short distance and the main body of the Americans soon arrived on the ground.

Both armies began now to prepare for battle in earnest. Stewart drew up his forces in battle array and General Greene steadily advanced. Stewart formed but one line. The thirty-third regiment called the Irish Buffs commanded by Captain Coffin was posted on the right; Colonel Cruger with the remains of several corps was stationed in the center; the 63rd and 64th regiments of regulars were posted on the left. Major Majoribanks with a battalion composed of grenadiers and light infantry was posted on Eutaw Creek. The enemy's artillery was distributed along the line - part on the Charleston Road and part on the road leading through the enemy's left wing to Roach's plantation. In his rear Stewart had stationed two separate bodies of infantry and cavalry to be called into action as necessity might demand.

The American front line closely followed by the second artillery pressed forward. At a few minutes past nine, the musketry and artillery began a spirited fire upon the British line. The British replied promptly. From flank to flank the Americans poured in a constant fire and from flank to flank the British gallantly responded. The conflict was fearful. The Whig militia stood their ground like veterans. Stewart brought his line into action. His artillery played incessantly upon the advancing column of militia. Steadily they moved forward amid a shower of cannon and musket balls. The infantry of Lee's legion was fiercely met by the 63rd, whilst Malmedy and his corps was furiously assailed by the 64th. The North Carolinians gave way and the enemy's left pressed forward. The state troops under Henderson were now furiously set upon by the flank battalions under Majoribanks and by the Irish Buffs. Just at this critical moment one of the field pieces of the British was disabled and both of the three-pounders of Gaines were silenced. Left unsupported by artillery, the state troops still continued to fight like tried veterans. Not until they had fired seventeen rounds did they give way, and then only because overwhelmed by superior numbers.

To fill the gap made by the giving way of the militia, General Greene ordered up the second line, under General Sumner. Stewart at the same moment brought into action his infantry reserves. These fresh troops fought each other with desperate fury for a short time. Unfortunately, Colonel Henderson was disabled by a wound. This produced a moments confusion in the American ranks. Hampton, Polk and Middleton discovering the critical condition of affairs, exerted themselves and soon restored order.

The brigade which Sumner commanded, being composed mainly of raw recruits, gave way and fled in confusion. The British rushed forward and were soon in as great disorder in pursuit as the militia were in flight. General Greene ordered Williams "to sweep the field with bayonets." The Virginians under Campbell and the Marylanders under Williams rushed forward determined to change the aspect of affairs or die in the attempt. At the distance of forty paces from the enemy, these veterans discharged their muskets and with trailed arms and a deafening shout, the whole second line of the Americans rushed to the charge. The confusion of the British, already great on account of the eagerness with which they pursued the fleeing militia, was now rendered doubly great by the furious charge to which they were subjected. So soon as the smoke was blown away and the confusion of the British was discovered, Captain Rudolph of Lee's legion wheeled his cavalry in upon them and swept everything before him. The Marylanders under Howard and the Irish Buffs were fighting hand to hand. In a number of instances the combatants stood transfixed with each other's bayonet. The British right and center gave way and the Americans raised the shout of victory.

During the charge of the American's second line, Majoribanks who was posted along the banks of Eutaw Creek kept pouring in a deadly fire into the American flank. Colonels Washington and Hampton were ordered to dislodge him. The position held by Majoribanks was not capable of being approached by cavalry, except by a small tract between him and the creek. Washington divided his cavalry into sections and attempted to gain the rear of Majoribanks. The creek was on one side and a dense thicket on the other. Washington had advanced but a short distance on this narrow path when a volley of musketry, fired by men concealed behind the thicket, proved fatal to numbers of those brave men, who had fought so many hard battles. Col. Washington's horse was shot dead and he himself bayoneted, and but for the interposition of a British officer would have been killed in a moment. The ground was literally covered with dead men and horses. One-half of Washington's cavalry was either killed or wounded and every officer except two.

Hampton, who had not joined Washington when the latter attempted to gain Majoribanks' rear, now gathered up the scattered remains of the cavalry. In the meantime, Kirkwood with his Delawares attacked Majoribanks. The whole British line now began to give way. Majoribanks attempted to cover the retreat. Everything seemed favorable to the Americans. The British were retreating in confusion. Some were running down the Charleston Road, depending for safety only in the speed with which they fled from the field of conflict. The enemy's tents stood just in the rear of the line of battle. In their flight they passed through their own camp, destroying as far as time would permit their stores. In the British army there was nothing but confusion. The veterans were slowly retreating whilst the loyalists, who had sought protection in the camp of Stewart, panic stricken lest they might fall into the hands of the Americans, mounting a horse wherever they could find one, fled in terror, many of them to Charleston.

At the forks of the road was a large brick house with a number of servants' houses together with other outbuildings and a garden. Stewart had erected some defenses at this point. Majoribanks made a halt behind the garden, and Major Sheridan with a number of New York volunteers, fled into the brick house. Stewart himself was down the Charleston Road, rallying his fleeing soldiers.

In the pursuit the Americans passed directly through the enemy's camp. The commissaries had not been able to destroy all the stores. The prize was too tempting for the majority of the American soldiers. Hungry and nearly naked as most of them were, they began to appropriate without stint the good things in the tents of the British. The pursuit partially ceased, and the pursuers began to eat and drink until some were stupid from eating to excess and others reeling with drunkenness. All was confusion. The men ceased to respect or obey their officers. Majoribanks began to fire from behind the garden upon the Americans now prowling about in the British camp, and Coffin who had taken position in a thicket now moved upon them and poured in a destructive fire. Sheridan kept up a constant fire from the windows of the house. Some of the Americans took shelter in the British tents, whilst others attempted to shield themselves from the fire of the enemy by getting behind the tents.

With anguish of heart, we may suppose, General Greene saw the condition of his troops. Those in the British camp were, many of them, so inflamed with drink that they would obey no command. That he might save the imprudent from utter destruction, he dispatched a courier to Colonel Lee, ordering him with his legion to fall upon Coffin. Lee was gone in pursuit of the British. Maj. Eggleston of Lee's command, with

a small party of cavalry, undertook to execute the order, but was repulsed by Coffin. Colonel Hampton came to the assistance of Eggleston. Coffin in turn was repulsed and driven from the field of conflict. Unfortunately, the command of Hampton unexpectedly came within range of Majoribanks' muskets, and was in a moment almost exterminated.

Whilst the conflict was raging on the right and left, Sheridan with a few swivels which he had with him in the brick house, was pouring destruction upon the Americans in all quarters. All the field pieces of the British had been captured by the Americans and brought to bear upon the brick house, but so near had they been placed to the house that the artillerists were soon all killed or driven from the guns. After Majoribanks had scattered Hampton's command, he advanced to the brick house and dragged the captured guns under the windows of the house. One of these guns was re-captured and retained as a trophy of the fierce conflict.

The fight had now continued near four hours. In every quarter success was beginning to declare against the Americans. Colonel Howard having commenced at attack upon Majoribanks was wounded. The troops under his command fell back and Majoribanks remained master of the situation. Stewart was returning up the Charleston Road to renew the battle. General Greene determined to draw off his troops. This was all he could attempt and it was doubtful whether he could accomplish this. His cavalry was scattered in every direction; his battalions were broken and his artillery all either disabled or in the hands of the enemy. Colonel Hampton was left near the enemy's camp, with a strong guard, and the rest of the troops were led to Burdell's plantation seven miles from the scene of the conflict.

Stewart was too badly crippled to even attempt pursuit. Both sides claimed the victory. The loss on both sides, considering the number of men engaged, was very great. The American loss was, in killed, wounded and missing, six hundred and twelve. Of this number there were twenty-two officers killed and thirty-nine wounded. The British loss was six hundred and ninety-three - five hundred of whom were taken prisoners.

INCIDENTS OF THE BATTLE OF EUTAW SPRING

The day on which was fought the battle of Eutaw Spring was intensely hot. Both armies suffered for the want of water. Many of the Americans were almost naked and entirely barefooted. The water of Eutaw Spring was reddened with the blood of the wounded, who crept there to quench their thirst. There is a tradition that for some time after the battle the volume of water which bursts from this fountain was considerably diminished. This decrease in the amount of water was attributed to the blood which was mingled with the water. How much credence is to be given to this tradition we will not undertake to say. All that we aver is that we have seen individuals who declared that for some time after the battle the Eutaw "went nearly dry."

Both parties claimed a victory at Eutaw. The American general received a vote of thanks from the congress of the United States for the "most signal victory" which he had gained. A British standard was also presented to General Greene, as "an honorable testimony of his merits." In addition to this General Greene was presented with a "golden medal emblematical of the battle and victory." General Greene was instructed to present the thanks of congress to his aids-de-camps, Hynre, Pierce, Pendleton and Shubrick. Pierce who bore General Greene's dispatches giving an account of the victory to congress, was presented with a sword.

On one side of the "golden" medal presented to General Greene is the profile of a man - designed for the general himself, no doubt. Around the profile are the words: "Nathanieli Greene egregio duci comitia Americana" - The American Congress to the distinguished leader, Nathaniel Greene." On the other side of the medal is the Goddess of Victory gracefully gliding down upon the earth. In her right hand is a wreath with which to crown the victor; in her left hand a quiver. Gently she descends and places her left foot upon a broken shield. The head of the goddess is encircled with the words, "Salus Regionum Australium" - "The Safety of the Southern region." Underneath her feet are the words, "Hostibus ad Eutaw Debellatis, VIII Sept. MDCCLXXXI" - The enemy conquered at Eutaw on the 8th of Sept. 1781.

The congress of the United States passed a vote of thanks to the several divisions of troops which composed the army of General Greene.

From all this we would be led to believe the Americans had in reality gained "a most signal victory." The British on the other hand claim a victory and rest their claim upon two facts. They were able to hold the brick house and palisade garden during the whole of the contest and in the end force the Americans to abandon the conflict. The truth is neither party gained at the time a signal victory. The ranks of both armies were fearfully thinned. In no battle during the whole Revolutionary war did the Americans lose so many officers. Colonels Washington, Howard and Henderson were wounded and Col. Richard Campbell was killed. Of the six colonels only two - Williams and Lee - were unhurt. The whole number of American officers killed was seventy-two; the number of wounded thirty-nine. This in itself was a severe blow upon the American army.

The troops on both sides fought bravely. The British admit that the bayonet which heretofore had been so much dreaded by the Americans, had lost all its power to produce terror in them and had become in their hands a most deadly weapon. With this weapon in the hands of the Virginians and Marylanders, General Greene drove the British regulars from the battlefield. Evidently the Americans were eminently successful until the hungry and thirsty soldiers entered the British camp. Here they began to plunder and were soon incapacitated for anything.

An amusing scene took place in front of the brick house. So great was the rush of the British to enter the brick house and so closely were they pursued by the Americans that the more advanced of the latter reached the door before the hindmost of the former. The British were in haste to enter the house and the Americans were in haste to reach the place before the door could be shut. Lieutenant Manning and a few daring followers reached the door almost as soon as Major Sheridan and his men. One of Manning's men actually made his way partly into the house. Sheridan began to push him out and Manning at the same time push him in. Finally Sheridan succeeded. The door was immediately closed and barred. Many of the British were left out.

Among those was a brother of the somewhat remarkable Colonel Isaac Barre. The brother of this Irish colonel held a captain's commission. Lieutenant Manning finding that he could not force the house turned his attention to the unfortunate British who were too late to enter. So soon as Captain Barre found that he could neither enter the brick house nor escape, he began with a glibness of tongue for which the Irish are noted and with a solemnity in harmony with his circumstances to recite his titles. "I am" said he, "Sir Henry Barre, deputy adjutant general of the British army; captain of the 52nd regiment, secretary of the commandant at Charleston....." "And my prisoner," interrupted Manning. "You are the very man I have been looking for. Come with me and I will take good care of you."

It soon became necessary for Manning and his followers to retire from this dangerous position. In order to effect this, he so arranged his own men and the prisoners that both were alike exposed to the fire from the brick house.

The British loss was fearful. Colonel Stewart was wounded and Majoribanks was thrown into a fever, of which he died in a few days. Numbers of the Irish Buffs deserted and joined the Americans shortly after the battle.

The loyalists in the British army fought better at Eutaw Springs than the regulars. The loyalists regarded it as victory or death. The aspect of things had become general that the British could not subjugate the colonies and the result was that numbers of individuals who heretofore had been neutral or even Tories, now readily joined General Greene.

There were several individuals who won for themselves the title of Revolutionary soldiers by being at Eutaw on the 8th of September, 1781. Before this they had been tender hearted loyalists or plundering Tories. Their infamy is forgotten by the world and never was known by their descendants. Among the British who deserted shortly after the battle of Eutaw Spring was a man by the name of Keenan. After the war, James Keenan settled in York county on the water of Dutchman creek. His grave is some three miles northwest of Ebenezer on the plantation of John Barron, Sr.

Installment LIII

HILL'S IRON WORKS

In the northeastern section of York county on the road leading from Yorkville to Charlotte, about eleven miles from the former place is what is now called the "Clay Hill neighborhood." The limit of this region like all others of a similar character are marked out neither by metes nor bounds. It has no fixed "butts and bindings" but extends so far in all directions as is agreeable to the desires and inclinations of the inhabitants.

Through this region there flows a bold stream which for more than a century has borne the name of Allison Creek. This stream rises near Bethany Church at the foot of Henry's Knob and empties into Catawba River a short distance above Thorn's Ferry. This Clay Hill region was once a part of that extensive region known all over the upper section of South Carolina by the name of Bethel.

It is impossible at this late date to fix with absolute certainty, the exact period when this section of country was settled by white men. It is highly probable that at a very early period, Indian traders took up their abode among the red men of the forest. It seems that at several points on the Catawba River the traders had settled as early as the year 1736. The most of these Indian traders were Scotchmen. It is highly probable that the Bethel region was settled by white men as early as 1740. The tide of immigration from Pennsylvania and Virginia continued to flow gently into this region for a number of years. In 1755, the defeat of Braddock forced multitudes to leave Pennsylvania and Virginia and seek a quiet home in the south. These immigrants were nearly all Scotch-Irish. A few were of the old Puritan stock. Bethel Church was organized by the Rev. William Richardson in 1764.

There is abundance of evidence that this region of country which we now call Clay Hill was settled long before the Revolutionary war, and that the people had accumulated at least some wealth and provided themselves with many of the comforts of life. Among the early settlers of this Clay Hill region was Colonel William Hill, the grand father of General D. H. Hill.

The region of country north of Allison Creek abounds in iron ore. At an early period, Colonel William Hill established a furnace on Allison Creek at the point at which now is located Miller's Mill. A co-partnership in this furnace existed between Colonel Hill and Isaac Hayne. During the Revolutionary war, the furnace was where Duff's Mill now is. At these iron works were cast cannon and balls with which in part to supply the southern division of the American army. Not only so, but the farmers for a considerable distance in every direction around these works, were supplied by them with iron for agricultural purposes.

After the fall of Charleston on the 12th of May 1780, the British army under Cornwallis, Rawdon, Tarleton and others advanced into the interior of the state and established its headquarters at Camden. This emboldened the Tories and loyalists of the state. The Whigs were in an unorganized condition and destitute of every means of defense. They had no fire arms except their squirrel guns; and powder and lead we may well suppose, were extremely scarce. In this critical condition of things, the men abandoned their homes, leaving their domestic affairs in charge of their wives and children. The Tories prowled through the country like so many hungry wolves devouring and destroying every thing in their reach. Generally speaking the Tories were unprincipled wretches, who neither feared God nor regarded man.

In this Bethel region on Rocky Allison a few miles southwest of Hill's Iron Works was established a kind of store house in which was deposited salt and many other articles for the support of the Whig families. This store house was a large stone and brick building. Its site was on the plantation now owned by Mrs. Eva

274

Gillespie, midway between the Wright's Ferry and Thorn's Ferry roads. For small quantities of salt the Whig women were accustomed to ride on horseback from the neighborhood of Winnsboro, in Fairfield county to this place. Colonel Watson was in charge of this store house. It is more than probable that it was not often full of supplies.

We may as well notice that after the Revolutionary war, the brick of which this store house was in part constructed, were moved out on the Charlotte Road, about six miles from Yorkville and used in constructing what was once known as the "Red House." This house was recently torn down by the present owner, Mr. Lee Williams, and these old bricks are again to be worked up in another house on the site of the old "Red House."

One object of the British and Tories had in scouring the country was to destroy such institutions as Hill's Iron Works and Watson's Store House. Many things prevented the completion of this design, longer than might be supposed. The British were in a strange and at the same time a hostile country. It was not safe for the friends of King George to make distant excursions into the interior. The distance from Camden was considerable and the country was inhabited by Whigs, bold and defiant.

Some time in the summer or early fall of 1780, a party of Tories and British was organized for the special purpose of burning Hill's Iron Works. Who was the commander of this party, when it was organized, or on what particular day or month it perpetrated the deed, are facts which we are unable so far to ferret out. The impression is on our mind that Captain William McGill said that Hill's Iron Works were burned but a short time before the battle of King's Mountain was fought. At present we must be satisfied to know that Hill's Iron Works were burned, and burned by the British and Tories.

This was regarded by the whole surrounding region as a sore calamity. As an evidence of this, it is related that some time during the year 1781, the people in a portion of Rutherford county, N.C. were assembled together, when one John Miller, an Irishman by birth, a Whig by every instinct of his nature and an elder in the Presbyterian church, was called upon to lead the assembly in prayer. Tradition has preserved the words of the prayer. They are as follows: "Good Lord, our God that art in heaven, we have great reason to thank thee for the favors we have received at thy hands - the many battles we have won. There is a great and glorious battle of King's Mountain, where we killed the great General Ferguson and took his whole army; and the great battles at Ramsour's and

at Williamson's; and the ever memorable battle of the Coopens (Cowpens) where we made the proud Gen. Tarleton run down the road helter-skelter; and good Lord if thee had na suffered the cruel Tories to burn Billy Hill's iron works, we would na have asked any mair favors at thy hands. Amen."

Whether good old John Miller ever offered up this prayer or not, we dare not assert. All that we say is that tradition has preserved it and that the last sentence shows the estimate which was put upon Hill's Iron Works.

On their way to the iron works, the British and Tories - at least a part of them - passed by the place where John Barron, Jr. now lives. James Simril at that time lived in the field only a few hundred yards from the present site of John Barron's house. This James Simril was a lover of fine stock and somewhat addicted to horse racing. He had on his plantation race paths, traces of which are to be seen today. The stables and barn of Simril were burned by the British and Tories but it does not appear that any of the horses were burned. Some time after the Revolutionary war, another James Simril, or perhaps the same, had his barn, stable and four horses burned up. This latter was the work of a private enemy. These two events are often confounded.

Leaving James Simril's, the next deed which the burning party executed was the scalping of John Forbes. Mr. Forbes was a true Whig and lived at that time on Rocky Allison, near where Spratt Wright now lives. It seems that there were two Forbes brothers, both living in the same locality. When the British and Tories approached their dwelling both ran in the direction of Catawba river. By some means one of the brothers made good his escape. It is said that on arriving at Charlotte he was wholly unable to tell where or how he crossed the river. Unfortunately, the other brother was captured after running only a short distance and being scalped, was left as was supposed dead or dying. In this condition he lay unconscious for several days. By accident, a young girl by the name of Prudy Hall, in looking for the cows, passed by the spot and discovered him. His head was awfully mangled and alive with maggots. He was removed and finally recovered, and lived to be an old man. The bones which were cut off his head are still preserved by his descendants.

The burning party were now within two miles of the iron works. They had captured a man by the name of Henderson, and forced him to conduct them to the ford of the creek below the iron works.

Colonel Hill was in the army. His sons were at home. The two oldest - Robert and Andrew - had received some intimation that the British and Tories were coming. They had prepared a small cannon and having mounted it upon a stump, stood with match in hand waiting until the party would come in sight. The hill on which they had their cannon mounted over-looked the whole adjacent country to the south - the direction in which the boys supposed the party would come. To their utter astonishment, before they were aware of it, a party of British came upon them from the east. Their cannon was pointing in the wrong direction. Without inflicting any injury upon the brave but out-generaled boys, their cannon was taken from them and carried to the foot of the hill and thrown into the creek.

Here it lay for years. The din of war had died away and the country was enjoying peace and prosperity. The little cannon was forgotten. One day Mr. Garvin, the miller, was engaged in fishing. His seine became entangled. In order to extricate it he was obliged to thrust his hand into the water. He found to his astonishment that his seine had become entangled on a piece of iron. The iron was raised to the surface of the water and, behold, it was a veritable cannon. For a number of years after its discovery this little cannon was used by the boys in the neighborhood to shoot big guns on Christmas and the Fourth of July. Finally by overcharging it, it was bursted. Fragments of it are still to be seen. One piece is in the possession or was some time ago, of Mr. A. A. Barron of Clay Hill.

The iron works were burned and the British and Tories departed. Poor Henderson who had been forced to act as their guide, was stripped of his clothes, tied to a tree and whipped. He was left tied. In this act there was something inhumanly cruel.

After the war, the iron works were rebuilt, but did not prove remunerative. General Hampton - the grandfather of Governor Hampton - rendered considerable pecuniary assistance to the parties; but the debt kept increasing and finally General Hampton took the Negroes belonging to the firm in payment of his claim. Some idea of the sum due General Hampton can be formed from the fact that it took near one hundred Negroes to liquidate it.

The iron ore found in this region is said to be in great abundance and for some purposes, of very superior quality.

We omitted to mention in its proper place that previous to the arrival of the British all the cannon balls had been hauled down to the creek and thrown in. These balls have, so far as we know, never been found.

A TRIP TO CHARLESTON IN THE OLDEN TIME

Previous to the Revolutionary war and for a number of years afterward, the people of the back country did most of their trading in the city of Charleston. To this point they wagoned their tobacco, indigo and whatever else of agricultural products they had to dispose of. To Charleston they drove any live stock they might have to sell. From most northern sections of the state a trip to Charleston was no little undertaking. It consumed about a month. Generally, several neighbors joined in getting up the team, wagons and produce. Seventy or eighty years ago, a man who owned a wagon and team was regarded as being rich. It was only a few neighborhoods that were able to afford such a man.

Tobacco was generally packed away in large hogsheads. When the time for transporting it to Charleston arrived, the hogshead itself was converted into a wheel. This was done by surrounding the hogshead with something which resembled the felloe of a modern wagon wheel. With large wooden pins this hoop felloe, or whatever it may be called, was secured to the hogshead; one of these hoops being attached to each end so high as to raise the hogshead itself off the ground. In each end of the hogshead a wooden gudgeon was fastened. To the gudgeons were attached something that might be called shafts. The whole when complete constituted a cart of the most primitive kind.

In vehicles of this kind did the first settlers of this country transport their produce from all sections of the state to Charleston. A trip to Charleston in those days was attended with as much romance as is a trip to Europe at the present time. It was an onerous undertaking; still it was full of excitement. To go to Charleston in the manner above described was the highest ambition to which the boys of the country aspired. A long life time was too short to tell all that they saw and heard during such a trip. Really there was crowded into the space of a month - the time during which one of these trips was made - a vast amount of human life in all its different aspects.

Rarely did a single individual undertake a trip to Charleston alone. Generally a small caravan was formed before leaving home. On the way the number was increased so that often the road for a considerable distance was crammed with primitive carts. Every company made it a point to have a supply of "the good greature." At every watering place the "little brown jug" was brought out and its contents tasted by the whole crowd. The caravan consisted of wagons of all shapes and descriptions, together with a number of cows and calves and mountain steers. The cows were milked night and morning, just as if at home and the traders lived very much as they did when on their farms. They were in no great hurry. They took the world easy and rarely deserted a fellow trader in distress. If the wagon of one of the party broke down, the whole company called a halt and went to work to repair the injury. They shared to the fullest extent each others' and sorrows. Around the camp fire at night, they cracked jokes, discussed questions of grave importance, both in church and state or worked pranks on each other. Not unfrequently their fun would end in earnest and a hearty laugh was often followed by a hard fight. That was, however, in the days before big knives and pocket pistols had been introduced, and a fight only resulted in black eyes and sore ribs. Neither did they allow their anger to burn continually. A fight generally was an end to all strife.

A man who would have gone to court in those early days of our republic with an assault and battery case would have been regarded by every one in the community as a consummate coward and a sneaking puppy. We, in this age of advanced civilization and refined customs, may be shocked at the barbarous manner in which the first settlers of our country adjusted their petty grievances, but it may be questioned whether the ends of justice are better secured now than then. A fight cost the community nothing and a good sound thrashing proved more effective in reforming the disturbers of the public peace than either the county jail or state penitentiary of the present day do.

We will undertake to defend neither the fighting mode of adjusting private difficulties nor the trial justice mode. Both indicate a bad state of morals. In those primitive times in the wilds of North America, every man constituted himself a judge, lawyer and jury and settled his own difficulties without troubling his neighbors. There may have been more fighting in those days than now, but there is more quarreling and lawing now than then.

On one of those Charleston trips, it was generally understood that some trick was to be worked on every one that was met. Sometimes in working these tricks the moral law was not observed very strictly. The following incidents will give the reader some knowledge of the character of the pranks that these primitive traders were accustomed to play.

Sometime after the close of the Revolutionary war, four individuals from York county set out for Charleston with a drove of cattle. Amongst the crowd was one by the name of Ezekiel Price. They passed down what was then called the "Bratton Road" in the direction of Chesterville. The road leading from the western portion of Chester county to White's Mill in the eastern portion of the county and this road united at that time about a mile above Chester Court House.

On reaching the point at which the two roads intersect, a gentleman was seen approaching them from the direction of Catawba River. He rode a fine horse and was provided with saddle bags. Everything indicated that the man was not in his own neighborhood. On approaching within speaking distance he inquired of the four cattle drivers if they could tell him the road to Augusta. Three of them said that they could not. Price, however, said "That, sir, is the road that goes to Augusta," pointing in the same direction from which the traveler was coming.

No doubt Price only designed playing a trick on the traveler. Whether he knew the road that led to Augusta or not he certainly knew that the road he pointed out to the stranger did not lead to Augusta. His object probably was to induce the traveler to turn back. Be this as it may, the traveler, without saying a word, rode on. In a short time, Price and his companions reached the place where now is the town of Chester. At the corner once occupied by George Kennedy, there was a "public house" as a hotel in those days was called. Price had forgotten all about directing the stranger as to the road to Augusta. He was, it happened, in the rear of the cattle, whilst his three companions were, one in front, one on each wing. Just as Price made the turn to go down the hill, the stranger stepped out of the door of the hotel and confronting Price, asked him in a cool and deliberate tone if he was the man who directed him the road to Augusta. Price without suspecting anything said he was. Without uttering another word the traveler grasped Price by the throat and first jerking him forward and then pushing him backward, threw him on the ground. Without letting go his grasp upon his throat he placed his knees upon his breast and violently choked hum until poor Price was black in the face and his tongue protruded from his mouth, when the traveler stooped down and bit off the top of it. This done he rose saying, "Now tell another man a lie." Price was unable to proceed; but was forced to remain under such medical treatment as could at that day be obtained, until his three companions drove their cattle to Charleston, disposed of them and returned.

The incident which we are about to relate will give us some idea of the fighting proclivities of at least some of the first settlers of this country. In York county, in the region bordering on King's Mountain there lived a numerous people by the name of Henry. Amongst the Henrys was one who was known by the name of "Big Jim." At a very early period in the history of the country, Big Jim Henry had made a trip to Charleston. On his return some short distance above Yorkville, he met a wagon. The driver was a large man but advanced in years. Neither Henry nor he knew each other. On meeting him, Henry accosted him in the following style: "I have been to Charleston and am nearly home again and have not had a fight yet. Get down sir; I am determined to have a fight before I go home." To this the bantered man replied: "I am too old to fight; you must let me off." About this time the son of the old man came up and without any other provocation than what had passed, declared his willingness to fight Henry. Both stripped and at it they went with as much energy as if they had been enemies for years.

It will no doubt gratify the reader to know that Big Jim Henry got not only a fight but a sound thrashing. Who the young man was, Big Jim Henry never knew; but the thrashing he never forgot.

At present when it is reported that two men have fought, we conclude that they were either drunk or one had cheated the other. In fact, a modern fight is a poor concern. It usually occurs at a place where the parties are sure to be separated about the time they strike the first blow. Then they foam at the mouth and rant. This was not the way those old fellows fought. They felt their manhood and they had an ambition to try the powers of any one who claimed to be a bully.

We are not to suppose that because they did not like to go to Charleston and return without a fight, that they were savages. Fighting is a barbarous custom, but every age has its relics of barbarism. Refined vices are the worst vices in the world. However hateful fighting may be, it is not a refined vice.

THE END

SECTION THREE

LATHAN FAMILY HISTORY

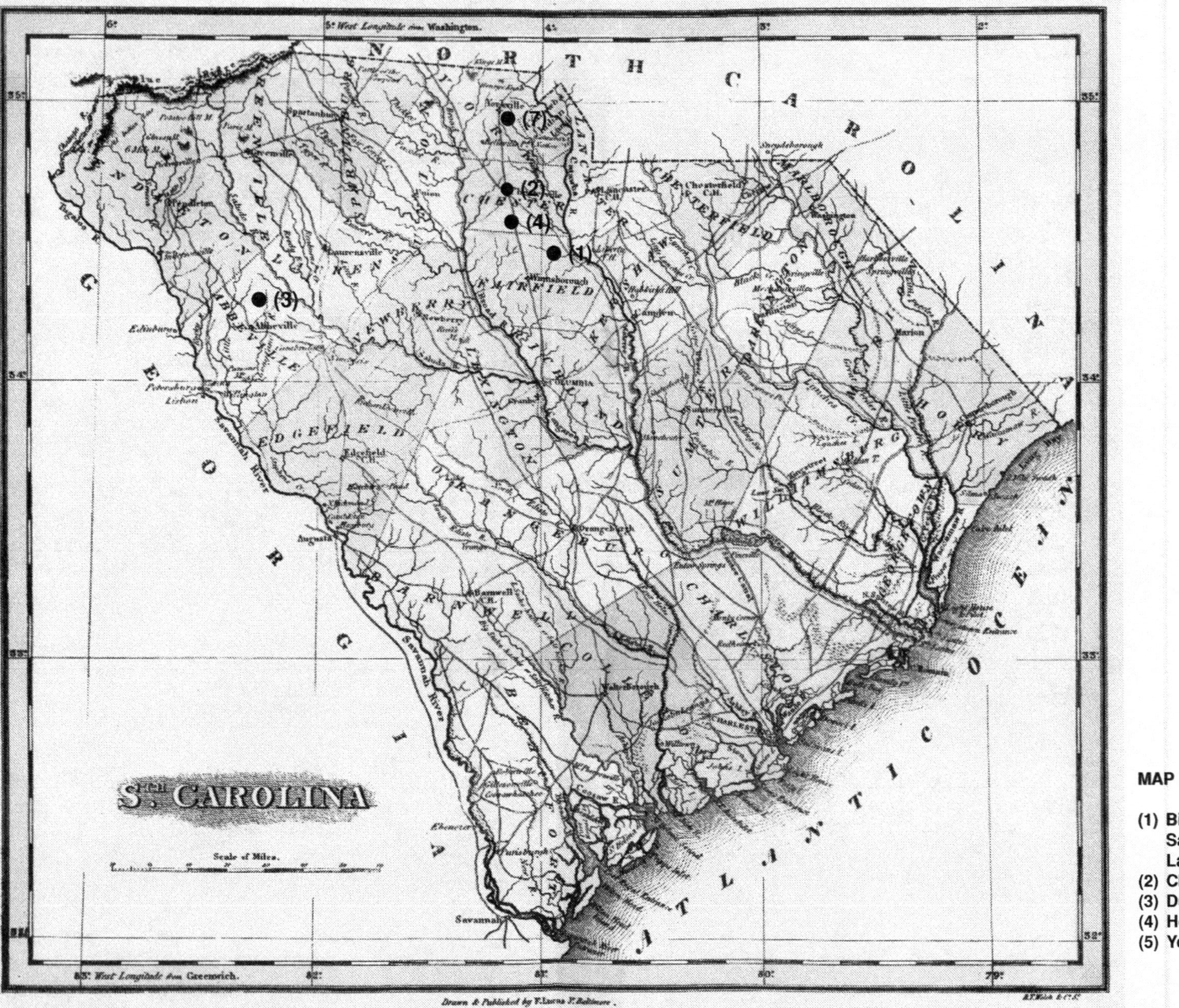

MAP LEGEND

(1) Big Wateree Creek
    Samuel M. Lathan Plantation
    Lathan Family Private Cemetery
(2) Chesterville
(3) Due West
(4) Hopewell Cemetery
(5) Yorkville

The Lathan Family

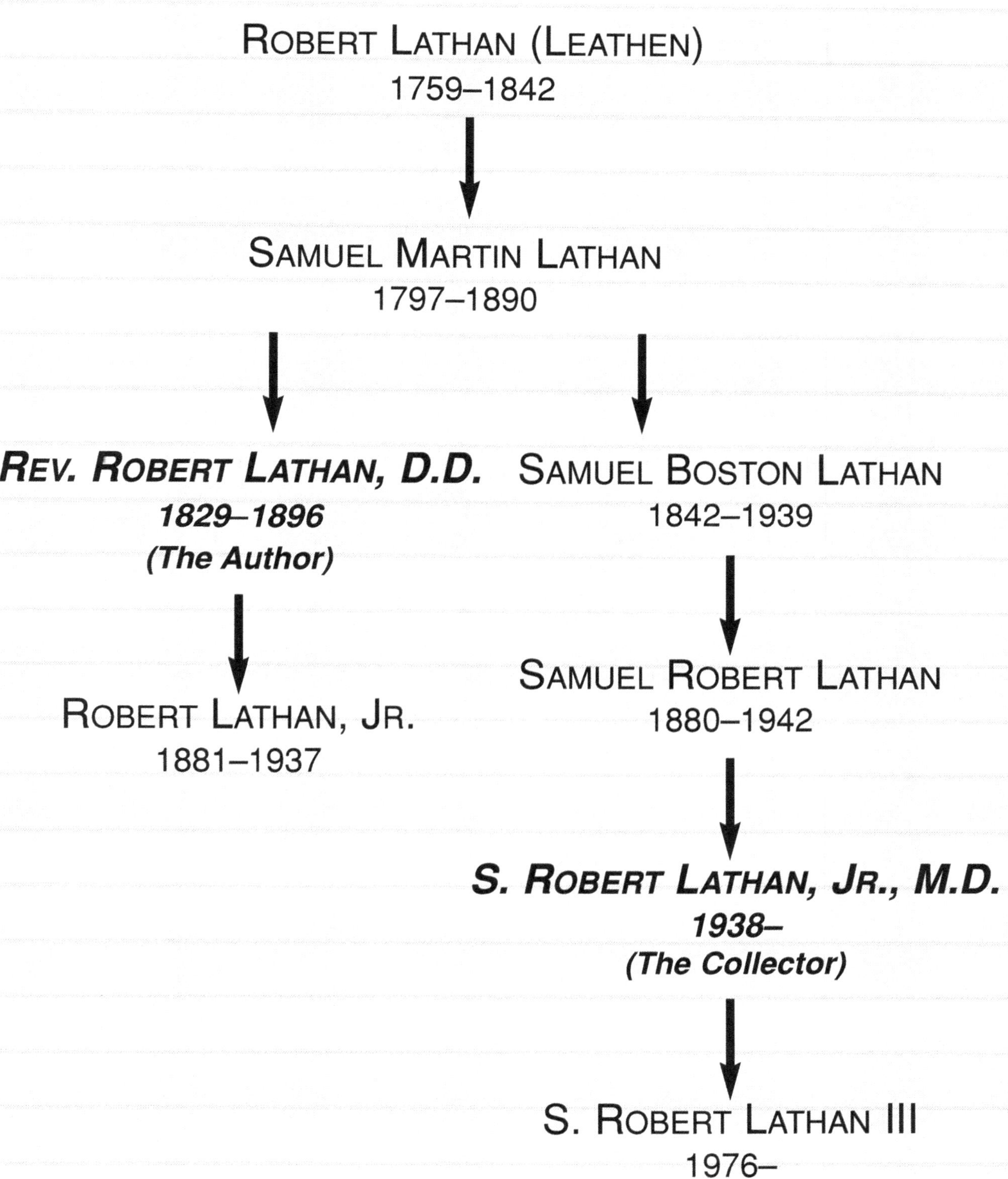

ROBERT LATHAN (LEATHEN)
1759-1842

"From the crowning of James First, 1605, until the enthronement of William Prince of Orange, 1688, a great many people from the north of Scotland took refuge in North Ireland. Among these were the Lathans, then spelled Leathen."

Robert Lathan was born in 1759 in Ballymena, County Antrim, one of the sons of James and Peggy Waugh Lathan. Shortly after the Treaty of Peace between the United States and Great Britain, three of the Lathan brothers emigrated from Ireland to the United States. William settled in Lancaster, South Carolina. David settled in Genesee County, New York, and Robert along with his wife, Nancy Agnes Martin, and five children, arrived in Charleston in 1788.

A year after arriving in Charleston the family moved to Lancaster County and then later settled in Fairfield County in the Wateree Section near what is now known as White Oak. Land deed records show that in 1796 he purchased acreage in the county for the sum of fifty pounds sterling. In 1812 he petitioned for and received citizenship in the United States. Five of their children attained maturity, Sarah, John, William, Nancy and Samuel. He later sold 188 acres to each son.

After his wife died in 1840, Robert moved to Tennessee to live with his daughter. He was buried there in Salem Cemetery, Tipton County, 1842.

SAMUEL MARTIN LATHAN
1797-1890

The son of Robert Lathan, was born October 22, 1797, in Fairfield County. He was married in 1829 to Martha Patterson. He owned and farmed a plantation in Blackstock near White Oak, SC on the Big Wateree Creek, which flows into the Catawba River. One hundred eighty-eight acres of the plantation was purchased by him from his father in 1819 for $500.00 Later he purchased adjacent acreage from his brothers. During the War Between the States, Union Army General William T. Sherman's army passed by his plantation on their march from Savannah to Columbia and further north.

Samuel and Nancy had eleven children. One of the sons, Robert, a minister and an educator is the author of the chronicles on the *History of South Carolina*. Another son, Samuel Boston was a Confederate infantryman and the grandfather of Dr. S. Robert Lathan, Jr., the person who collected, assembled and distributed these chronicles.

Samuel died September 1, 1890 in Blackstock and is buried in Hopewell Cemetery in Chester County.

**REVEREND ROBERT LATHAN, D.D.
1829-1896**

The oldest son of Samuel Martin Lathan was born December 27, 1829 in Blackstock, Fairfield County. His parents of Scotch-Irish heritage were farmers who encouraged the education of their children. In the home was a large "collection of useful and instructive books," creating the foundation for a thorough education.

At age nineteen he attended a school taught by Rev. James Gilland, a Presbyterian minister, as preparation for college. In 1953 he entered the sophomore class at Erskine College, graduating with high honors in 1855. He continued to study for the ministry under Rev. R. W. Brice, pastor of Hopewell ARP Church in Chester County, also supporting himself by teaching school. Later he returned to Due West and graduated from Erskine Theological Seminary in 1858.

From 1859-1884 Rev. Lathan lived in Yorkville, as pastor of the ARP churches there and in Tirzah, South Carolina. He was married in 1859 to Frances Eleanor Barron, the daughter of Dr. A. I. Barron, of Yorkville. They had three sons and four daughters.

Rev. Lathan also taught school in York for twenty years and was county commissioner of education for ten years where he organized and implemented with little means available a highly regarded public school system. He was a noted historian and read the Old Testament from the original in Hebrew and the New Testament from Greek and Latin. He wrote several historical sketches and is best known for his *History of the Associate Reformed Presbyterian Synod* in 1882 and also a *History of South Carolina* from early settlements through the Revolution. In 1881, he received the degree of Doctor of Divinity, conferred upon him at Westminster College in Pennsylvania.

In connection with his work as a minister and educator, Rev. Lathan was for years a contributor to the *Yorkville Enquirer* writing a weekly column entitled "Reading for the Sabbath."

In 1884 he moved to Erskine to accept a professorship in the Seminary and taught there for ten years. He left Erskine in 1894 and preached in Abbeville County, SC for two years until his death on June 15, 1896.

Rev. Lathan was inducted posthumously into the Academic Hall of Fame at Erskine College, Due West, SC in April 2002.

He is buried in Rose Hill Cemetery, York, SC.

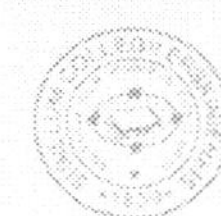

Erskine College

*cordially invites you to attend the
Board of Counselors Spring banquet and
Academic Hall of Fame Induction honoring:*

*John G. Brawley, Jr.
Terry M. Hommel
Robert Lathan
James Parthemos
James H. Young*

*This banquet is also in honor of
scholarship donors and major contributors.*

*Please join us in Moffatt Dining Hall
Friday, April 5, 2002 at 7 p.m.*

*R.S.V.P. by March 29, 2002 to (864) 379-6502 or
Erskine College, P.O. Box 605, Due West, SC 29639*

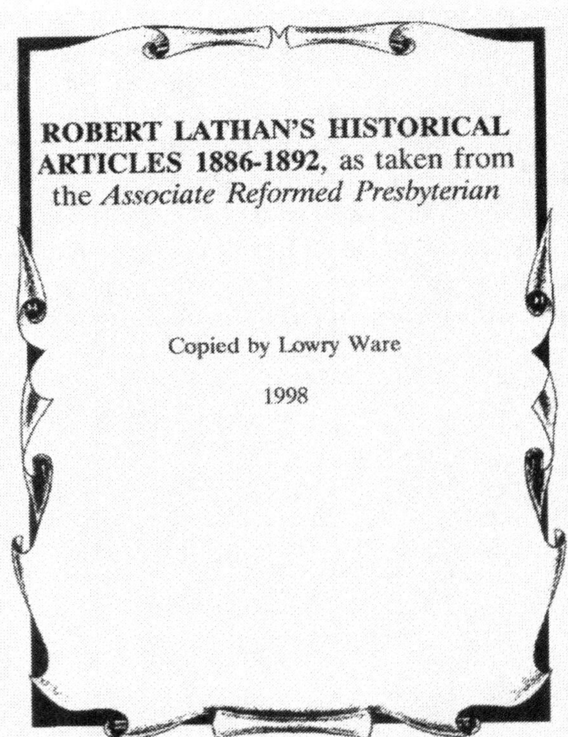

INTRODUCTION

Robert Lathan (1829-1896) was an educator, a minister, and a theological seminary professor, but he was best known as the leading historian of the Associate Reformed Presbyterian church. His *History of the Associate Reformed Synod of the South* was printed in 1882, and it earned him the D. D. degree from Westminster College in Pennsylvania. Lathan sometimes called himself an "scribbler," and he contributed dozens of articles to newspapers, primarily to the *Yorkville Enquirer* and the *Associate Reformed Presbyterian.* For the former, his most ambitious series was a full length history of South Carolina.

His historical articles were based in part in two sources which no longer survive. In 1892, fire destroyed the old main building at Erskine College with a library of books and booklets which could not be replaced. Lathan's chief reliance, however, was on his own personal library which contained up to 3,000 volumes and manuscripts. Ten years after Lathan's death, his library, which had passed to his son-in-law, Rev. T.B. Stewart, was also lost to fire.

Lathan sometimes alluded to persons whom he chose not to name, such as on pages 35-36 where he writes of some Rocky Creek Covenanters who "sold their slaves, pocketed the money and followed the rest of the covenanters to the free States. With the money which they received by the sale of their slaves, they bought land, built houses, educated their children, erected churches and constructed *underground railroads.*" To give their names, he said, would only serve "to mortify their innocent off-spring" and might prove "injurious to a common Christianity." Even more intriguing was his reference on page 78 to a "monster," a wealthy planter on Big Wateree Creek in Fairfield District who used his slaves and servants to steal from his neighbors and drive them to move to the West. He explained, "I need not mention the name of this monster. He amassed, for his day, a vast fortune."

Lowry Ware

HISTORY

OF THE

Associate Reformed Synod

OF THE

SOUTH,

TO WHICH IS PREFIXED

A History of the Associate Presbyterian

AND

Reformed Presbyterian Churches.

BY

REV. ROBERT LATHAN, D. D.

HARRISBURG, PA.:
PUBLISHED FOR THE AUTHOR.
1882

PREFACE

THE ASSOCIATE REFORMED CHURCH has had an organic existence for one hundred years. Still its origin and history are scarcely known to any outside of its pale, and but poorly known to many inside. The reason of this is obvious. No continuous history of the denomination has ever been given to the world. Sketches of detached portions have, on various occasions, been published, but the Church as a whole has no written history. The synod of the South has been singularly neglected, in that no one has either had the time, or the means, or the inclination to trace its use and progress. The following is an effort to supply a long-felt want. The attempt has been made to trace the history of the Associate Reformed Church from its rise in the first Secession, in 1788, under the Erskines, down to the present time. The facts have been gleaned from every source accessible. Neither expense nor labor have been regarded. The principal authorities consulted and drawn upon are McKerrow's History of the Secession, Gibb's Display, Head's History of the Presbyterian Church of Ireland, Hetherington's History of the Church of Scotland, Struthers History of Scotland, Woodrow's History of the Sufferings of the Church of Scotland, Hetherington's History of the Westminster Assembly, Bailor's Letter and Journal, Crookshank's Works, besides a number of minor works.

In that part which refers more immediately to the history of the formation of the Associate Reformed Church, and especially to the history of the Synod of the South, the principal authorities are the original documents. The minutes of the Associate Presbytery of Pennsylvania, the minutes of the Associate Reformed Synod, the minutes of the General Synod, the minutes of the Synod of the South, have been relied upon for facts. In addition to these, research was had to old, musty pamphlets which had long since found a resting place in garrets and waste-boxes.

An effort was made, with what success we cannot say, to render each part complete in itself, and at the same time to preserve the unity of the parts. This involved a considerable amount of repetition.

To a number of individuals, the author desires to return his sincere thanks for favors. To Drs. John Forsyth, Joseph T. Cooper and Thomas Sproul, he is under many obligations: but especially he is under obligations to Dr. James B. Scouller, of Newville, Pa. From Dr. James Boyce, of Due West, S.C., he received much valuable aid and encouragement. It would be an act of lasting ingratitude were he not to mention his indebtedness to Dr. R.A. Ross, his co-Presbyter, who, hour after hour, sat patiently hearing the manuscript read.

Whether this work is a success or failure, the author cannot tell. The reader must judge. Its preparation has been a work of great labor, but of intense delight. Should it prove worthy of publish support, it will be followed by another volume, containing a history of each of the congregations in the Associate Reformed Synod, and a biographical sketch of all its ministers, both living and dead.

R.L.

Yorkville, S.C.

PREFACE

To the reader we have but little to say in the way of preface. Difficult as has been the work of gathering the materials for this brief history and these short biographical sketches, it has been, to the author, one of intense delight. He is convinced that there are multitudes of individuals in every section of the United States, who feel an interest in HOPEWELL. If the author has, in even a small degree, contributed to deepen that interest, he feels rewarded for his labor.

THE AUTHOR.

FOREWORD

Dr. Lathan's "A Historical sketch of Union A.R.P. Church, Chester County, S.C. is perhaps as much a history of this region with its Revolutionary War battles, its churches, and the various branches of Presbyterianism as it is a history of this particular church, its ministers, and its members.

It was written and published in 1888 but not widely distributed. A great deal of genealogical information is contained herein which should be of assistance to those seeking ancestors who had roots in the Chester, Kershaw, Lancaster, and York Counties of South Carolina.

Dr. Lathan, born of Scotch-Irish parents, was a teacher, school administrator, minister, professor in Erskine Theological Seminary, and a talented writer as well. He was born in Fairfield County December 27, 1829 and died June 15, 1896 in Abbeville County. In 1859 he married Fannie Barron of Yorkville and to them were born seven children, one of whom was Dr. Robert Lathan, Jr. who became editor of the Charleston News and Courier and in 1924 was awarded the Pulizer Prize for his enditorial entitled "The Plight of the South."

ROBERT LATHAN, JR.
1881-1937

The son of Rev. Robert Lathan, D.D., was born May 5, 1881, in York, South Carolina. He was educated in public and private schools and attended Erskine College. He started his career as a schoolteacher, but in 1900, joined the editorial staff of *The State* in Columbia, South Carolina as secretary to N.G. Gonzales, founder and editor of *The State.* In 1906 he came to the *Charleston News and Courier* as state news editor and at age twenty-nine, in less than four years, rose to the rank of Editor. He married Bessie Agnes Early.

In 1924 he was awarded the Pulitzer Prize for his editorial, "The Plight of the South." For three years he was President of the South Carolina Press Association. In 1927 Mr. Lathan moved to Asheville, North Carolina to be the editor of *The Citizen.*

He was well known throughout the South and the nation as an outstanding editor. He was considered an eloquent public speaker and an active civic leader in both Carolinas. In 1927 he was selected to participate with other editors in a European tour by the Carnegie Endowment for international peace.

He died suddenly of a cerebral hemorrhage at age fifty-six in Asheville in 1937. He is buried in Darlington, SC.

In 1979 the South Carolina Press Association named him to the Press Hall of Fame.

The Plight of the South By Dr. Robert Lathan, Jr.
Pulitzer Prize Winning Editorial
Published in *News and Courier,* Charleston, SC
November 5, 1924

This article is being written on election day but before the result of the voting can possibly be known.

No matter. The suggestions it contains will still be pertinent whatever the story told by the first page this morning. It makes very little difference what any of us think about the outcome of yesterday's balloting. It makes a considerable difference whether or not the people of the South realize the precarious situation which this section has come to occupy politically.

As yet we doubt if very many of them do realize this: and yet it is, we think, the outstanding political development of the time so far as we are concerned. Look at the facts. They are not pleasant to contemplate but they cannot be ignored longer. We are in a sad fix politically in this part of the country and if we are to find a remedy for our troubles we must first of all determine what they are. That will take considerable discussion and all we can hope to do now is to help start the ball of this discussion rolling. If that can be accomplished we may achieve the new program and the new leadership which we so much need.

For at the root of the South's present plight lies the fact that it has today virtually no national program and virtually no national leadership. Is it strange that it should be treated by the rest of the country as such a negligible factor? What is it contributing today in the way of political thought? What political leaders has it who possess weight or authority beyond their own States? What constructive policies are its people ready to fight for with the brains and zeal that made them a power in the old days?

The plight of the South in these respects would be perilous at any time. In a period when political currents are deeper and swifter that ever before, with more violent whirlpools, more dangerous rocks and shoals, ours is truly a perilous position. Changes which used to be decades in the making now sweep over us almost before we know they are in contemplation. It is true everywhere. In all the countries of Europe the pendulum is swinging, now far to the left, now far to the right. Center parties have lost their power. They are in a very bad way. And the South has belonged to the school politically which sought as a rule the middle of the road, eschewing ultra-conservatism on the one hand and radicalism on the other. With Labor organized and militant, with radicalism organized and in deadly earnest, with conservatism organized and drawing the lines sharply, what is the South to do, what course shall she take, where do her interests lie, what is due to happen to her?

These are questions which already begin to press for answer. Who is to speak for the South? How many of her citizens are prepared to help formulate her replies?

SAMUEL BOSTON LATHAN
1842 – 1939

The son of Samuel Martin Lathan, was born May 2, 1842 in Blackstock, SC, Fairfield County. He was the younger brother of author Robert Lathan. The Civil War stopped his plans to study law. He served four years in the Confederate Army with the Seventeenth South Carolina Infantry Regiment, Compay D. After initial duty off the coast of South Carolina, the regiment was sent to Virginia in May, 1862. He fought at Malvern Hill, Rappahannock River, and Second Manassas.

In the Maryland Campaign, he was wounded on September 14, 1862, during the Battle of South Mountain (Boonsboro), which preceded the Battle of Antietam (Sharpsburg). After release from a Baltimore prison, he rejoined his regiment in Wilmington, NC, in January, 1863, and marched to Charleston, SC. Later the regiment fought in Mississippi, Georgia, South Carolina, North Carolina, and Virginia. Finally he surrendered as a part of General Joseph E. Johnston's army in North Carolina on April 29, 1865, and then walked home to Chester.

Following The War, he taught school, served as principal of the Vineville, Georgia schools and after seven years returned to Chester in 1872 at age thirty. He began his business career as a bookkeeper and later worked as a cotton factor. He was married to Susan Amanda Meek on October 22, 1874. She was born in 1845 in Louisville, Mississippi, and later moved to York, SC. Following her father's death, the Lathans lived on Saluda Street and had four children:

Leila Hope Lathan, James Martin Lathan, Susan Meek Lathan, and Samuel Robert Lathan.

Dr. Lathan was awarded an honorary Doctor of Literature by Erskine College in 1934 for his scholarship and educaional interests. His nickname was "Boss" and he was known as Chester's "Grand Old Man." He was Chester's last surviving Condfederate Veteran and the oldest Royal Arch Mason in South Carolina. A recognized authority on the history of upper South Carolina, he wrote many historical "sketches" for the local newspaper. He also taught Sunday School for sixty four years and served in the Chester ARP Church as a deacon for four years and as ruling elder for fifty-six years.

Mrs. Lathan died at age seventy-nine in 1924. Dr. Lathan died at his home, two months short of ninety-seven years, on March 8, 1939. He is buried in Evergreen Cemetery, Chester, SC.

SAMUEL ROBERT LATHAN
(1880-1942)

The son of Samuel Boston Lathan, was born October 10, 1880 in Chester, SC. He graduated from Chester High School in 1897, and from Erskine College in 1902. He worked for a short time with the A. M. Aiken Cotton and Brokerage Company and then entered business with Frank K. Spratt. Later he formed a partnership with his brother, James M. Lathan, under the firm name of the Lathan Grocery Company, which grew to be one of the most outstanding wholesale grocery concerns in upper South Carolina. Bob represented the firm as traveling salesman. After more than thirty years in business, the brothers retired in 1937.

He was a life long member of the Chester ARP Church and served on the Board of Deacons for ten years. He was a Mason, a Shriner, and a member of the Lions Club.

On July 15,1929, he was married to Caroline (Callie) Mims Purvis, of Timmonsville, SC. She was a sister of Mrs. Nell Davidson of Chester and of Melvin Purvis, the famous FBI agent who captured the gangster, John Dillinger. She graduated from Columbia College where she was Vice-president of the literary society, president of the Athletic Association, captain of the basketball team, Secretary of the Student Council, member of May Court, and Editor-in-Chief of the annual.

After graduating from college, she taught in the Chester schools for many years. She was a member and past president of the Up-To-Date Book Club, past president and charter member of the Chester Assembly, member and past president of the Violet Sunshine Club, member of the Chester County Historical Society, and a member of the Chester ARP Church.

This popular couple, Bob and Cal, took an active part in the social and civic affairs of the community in the 1930's. Following a lengthy illness, Mr. Lathan died in Chester on July 3, 1942. Mrs. Lathan died October 21, 1981 in Atlanta, GA. Both are buried in Evergreen Cemetery in Chester.

Mrs. Samuel Robert Lathan (Cal)

SAMUEL ROBERT LATHAN, JR., M.D.
1938 –

The son of Samuel Robert Lathan and Callie Mims Purvis Lathan was born April 28, 1938 in Charlotte, North Carolina. In 1959 he graduated cum laude and Phi Beta Kappa from Davidson College where he was a member of the Kappa Alpha Order and managing editor of *The Davidsonian.*

He received his M.D. degree from the Johns Hopkins University School of Medicine in 1963 and was a member of the Pithotomy Club at Hopkins. He spent an elective quarter in Pathology in 1961 at Guy's Hospital in London. His post-graduate training consisted of an internship at Duke Hospital and a fellowship in Cardiopulmonary Diseases and a residency in Internal Medicine at Grady Memorial Hospital, Atlanta, Georgia.

From 1967-69 he was Chief of Professional Services at the US Air Force Hospital, Perrin AFB, Texas. Since 1969, Dr. Lathan has been in the private practice of Internal Medicine and Cardiopulmonary Diseases in Atlanta and is on the active medical staff of Piedmont Hospital and Shepherd Center. He also serves as Clinical Assistant Professor of Medicine at Emory University School of Medicine.

Dr. Lathan is board certified in Internal Medicine and a Fellow of the American College of Physicians and the American College of Chest Physicians. For five years he served as Editor of *Atlanta Medicine* and has published numerous scientific papers. He won the Montague Boyd Award for medical writing at Piedmont Hospital in 1998 and again in 1999. Presently he is co-chairman of the Atlanta Coalition against Tobacco and served as medical director of the Main Press Center for the Atlanta Committee for the Olympic Games. As an avid long distance runner, he completed a total of 28 marathons (including eight Boston Marathons) and 22 ultra-marathon races.

On March 19, 1966, he was married in Atlanta to Mary Amelia (Millie) Hudson. Millie graduated from Wellesley College and also earned a Masters Degree in Education from Harvard University and later a Masters Degree in Art History from Emory University. Millie is an antique dealer and is Chairman of the Board of Trustees of the Cashiers (NC) Historical Society. The Lathan have three children: Caroline, Stewart, and Rob.

Millie and Bob Lathan

Caroline Mims Lathan was born June 26, 1967 and graduated from the Westminster Schools in Atlanta in 1985 and from Brown University in 1989, magna cum laude, with Honors in Visual Arts. Caroline later obtained her Masters Degree in Fine Art from Maine College of Art. She was married September 25, 1993 to Van Richard Stiefel in Cashiers. Van is a graduate of Yale University in Music and is an accomplished classical guitarist. He has recently earned a Ph.D. in Music Composition from Princeton University. A son, Samuel Clark Stiefel, was born February 8, 2002. Caroline has had numerous art exhibitions in Atlanta and is presently an art teacher and printmaker.

Marion Stewart Lathan was born November 8, 1969 in Atlanta and graduated from the Westminster Schools where she was President of the Senior Class. In 1992 she graduated from Davidson College with a degree in Art History. At Davidson she was an Executive Board member of Rusk House and sweetheart of Sigma Alpha Epsilon. After working for the Atlanta Committee for the Olympic Games, she served as Associate Director of Development for the Lovett School in Atlanta, and presently is Vice President of Institutional Advancement at the Atlanta

College of Art. She was married to Carrick Mollenkamp on October 13, 2001. Carrick is a reporter for the *Wall Street Journal* and was nominated previously for a Pulitzer Prize for his book *The People Versus Big Tobacco.*

Samuel Robert Lathan, III was born August 10, 1975 in Atlanta. He graduated from the Westminster Schools in 1994 where he was Secretary of the Senior Class, and an outstanding varsity swimmer and football player, winning the Mac Shreve Award in football his senior year. He graduated from the University of North Carolina, Chapel Hill in 1998, where he was a member of the Phi Delta Theta Fraternity. He is presently employed in New York City in advertising and is also involved in stand-up comedy and improv activities.

Rob Lathan, Stewart Lathan Mollenkamp,
and Caroline Lathan Stiefel